HANDBOOK OF DOMESTIC VIOLENCE INTERVENTION STRATEGIES

HANDBOOK OF DOMESTIC VIOLENCE INTERVENTION STRATEGIES

Policies, Programs, and Legal Remedies

Edited by
Albert R. Roberts

UNIVERSITY PRESS

2002

OXFORD
UNIVERSITY PRESS

Oxford New York

Athens   Auckland   Bangkok   Bogotá   Buenos Aires   Cape Town
Chennai   Dar es Salaam   Delhi   Florence   Hong Kong   Istanbul   Karachi
Kolkata   Kuala Lumpur   Madrid   Melbourne   Mexico City   Mumbai   Nairobi
Paris   São Paulo   Shanghai   Singapore   Taipei   Tokyo   Toronto   Warsaw

and associated companies in
Berlin   Ibadan

Library of Congress Cataloging-in-Publication Data
Handbook of domestic violence intervention strategies : policies, programs, and
legal remedies / edited by Albert R. Roberts.
     p.   cm.
Includes bibliographical references and index.
ISBN 978-0-19-515170-1
     1. Family violence—United States.   2. Conjugal violence—United States.
3. Abused women—Services for—United States.   I. Roberts, Albert R.
HV6626.2 .H36   2002
362.82'927'0973—dc21   2001036813

9 8 7 6
Printed in the United States of America
on acid-free paper

Foreword

There is a social consensus that violence against women is no longer to be tolerated. Government action now is viewed as appropriate to stop violence against women by their family members. In addition, service methods have evolved in light of experiences at battered women's shelters and in community organizations.

The most effective way to build on the legal system improvements is to enhance the cooperation among all helping professionals. Experience thirty years ago showed that counseling or psychotherapy alone did not end the risk of harm to women who live with abusive partners. Civil and criminal justice remedies were insufficient to enable women to marshal their personal and financial resources to achieve safety and independence. All the professionals to whom battered women turned for help had to change their perceptions and responses and work together to provide resources and offer alternatives.

The chapters in this handbook provide state-of-the-art theory, research, and protocols for effective responses to domestic violence by lawyers, lay advocates, social workers, nurses, psychologists, psychiatrists, primary care physicians, emergency medical personnel, police, probation officers, prosecutors, parole officers, and judges. Using this information, we can continue making progress toward the goal of reducing all forms of violence against women.

Since my admission to the New York Bar in 1971 until I became a New York City Family Court Judge in 1986, I was an attorney in a free, federal legal services project. I represented thousands of women who suffered from violence and threats by their spouses or partners. From 1986 to the present, I have presided in thousands of cases in which women sought court orders of protection. Current laws, and police, prosecutor and judicial response to domestic violence give victims legal remedies and protection not available in 1971. These advances must be built upon so that the incidence and prevalence of violence against women decrease further.

The current effort to protect battered wives emerged in the early 1970s, when the women's movement turned its attention to the crime of rape. In the course of operating rape crisis telephone services, the women found that the calls came primarily from women who were being beaten by their husbands or companions.

Domestic violence also became a focus of advocacy by government-funded, free community legal services offices. They responded to the needs of their clients. In more than 80 percent of their divorce cases, the clients were women battered by their husbands.

From these two, unrelated organizations came movements in every state to expand police authority to arrest wife beaters, to promote prosecution and crime victim services, and to create civil-legal remedies for battered women. This campaign achieved substantial successes in legislative and policy reforms. It generated public sympathy for battered wives and reaction against domestic violence, also.

There are several, technical reasons for these successes. Ostensibly, wife beating was included in the definition of the crime of assault before the reform efforts began. "Consent" was never an issue in the crime of assault by contrast to the crime of rape, in which lack of consent to sexual contact is an essential element. Victims of domestic violence, unlike those of rape, have physical injuries to "corroborate" their claim of assault. Thus, domestic-violence law reforms did not require fundamental changes in criminal laws.

The legislative response to domestic violence, however, included creation of new, civil-legal remedies for battered women. "Orders of protection" are available in nearly every state. They may contain provisions directing abusive spouses to cease beating and threatening their spouses and children, to remove themselves from family homes, and to stay away from their spouses or companions and children. Child custody may be awarded to victims, and visitation by offenders may be prohibited or limited to supervised settings. This relief is available on an immediate, temporary basis prior to the time set for a full hearing, and before notice is given to the accused. Most state statutes authorize the police to arrest spouses alleged to have violated these civil orders on the same basis that persons alleged to have committed crimes may be arrested.

In spite of these successes, women's accusations are often denied the credibility accorded to men's denials of wrongdoing. The sexist attitudes visible in the rape laws continue, in a subtler fashion, to affect the criminal justice response to domestic violence. Battered women, therefore, need social workers, psychologists, nurses, physicians, and lawyers who can help them marshal resources and who can explain the problems they will encounter as they try to free themselves from violent relationships.

In this volume, twenty-seven experts examine the latest theories and practices for services to abused women and accountability for abusive men. The *Handbook of Domestic Violence Intervention Strategies* is a well-written, inclusive, scholarly, and practical source book. It is one of the few books that synthesizes clinical practice, legal remedies, and public policy.

The book begins with Professor Albert R. Roberts's chapter providing an overview of the family violence field and a preview of the chapters to follow. Professor Roberts shatters the most common myths about battered women and domestic violence. He describes the latest research findings, social action, public policy, and counseling strategies.

The contributors to this outstanding handbook examine current issues and changes in the past fifteen years regarding laws and legal remedies, governmental policies, clinical approaches, and services for battered women and their children. They provide a wealth of practical information for attorneys, domestic violence advocates, judges, forensic social workers, court personnel, and trainers working to reduce violence against women.

October 15, 2001   Marjory D. Fields
Justice of the New York State Supreme Court
County of New York

Preface

In this new millennium, the pendulum has finally swung in the direction of full federal and state funding for victims and survivors of domestic violence. Public attitudes of attorneys, judges, legislators, mental health counselors, nurses, physicians, psychologists, and social workers recognize the pervasive nature of domestic violence. Although professionals continue to search for solutions to the horrendous problem of domestic violence, and there are no easy answers, this handbook documents the latest and most promising intervention strategies.

There are two primary goals of this volume. The first is to offer the reader the latest and most advanced legal and criminal justice practices, risk assessment and advocacy practices, program developments, social services, and mental health treatment responses to domestic violence survivors and their children. The second is to offer the reader case illustrations and case applications and detailed information on how to advocate for and intervene on behalf of battered women.

This handbook offers an examination of the most promising and effective policies, programs, intervention strategies, and legal remedies for dealing with domestic violence. Several important policy reforms, risk assessment protocols, and program developments have taken place during the 1990s and 2000. At the beginning of the 21st century in October 2000, President Bill Clinton signed the second Violence Against Women legislation into law.

This was a major boon to the growing domestic violence and victim assistance industry with $3.3 billion allocated for the years 2000–2005 for domestic violence services and advocacy activities, and police and court training and program enhancements. Thus, we have witnessed increased federal funding for research, criminal justice training, social services, and demonstration projects through the Violence Against Women Act I (VAWA, 1994) and VAWA II (2000). A number of recent research studies have identified risk factors, protective factors, early warning signs for domestic violence, and programs to reach the most vulnerable and hidden victims of domestic violence.

This handbook highlights the most promising innovations, policy and legislative changes, and expansion in the delivery of social services and health care, as well as technologically advanced 24-hour criminal justice responses, including:

1. Increased training seminars and workshops for judges, prosecutors, police, domestic violence advocates, crisis counselors, and health care advocates;
2. A five-level typology of the duration and severity of woman battering among 501 battered women. This includes the identification of psycho-social diagnostic indicators necessary to prevent an escalation of life-threatening battering injuries;
3. An analysis of the characteristics of battered women who have killed their abusive partners, compared with those battered women who did not kill their ex-partners;
4. The emergence of integrated domestic violence courts and how they work;
5. Specialized educational and mental health programs for children who witness domestic violence and are at risk of acute crisis episodes or traumatization;
6. The use of electronic technology to protect battered women, and to better monitor the batterers' compliance with restraining orders;
7. Adult abuse protocols and brief treatment at outpatient mental health clinics, community health clinics, hospital emergency rooms and trauma centers, and other departments in hospitals;
8. Findings of the first state-by-state national survey of domestic violence coalitions;
9. Research throughout Canada documenting the effectiveness of support groups in helping battered women to permanently leave their abusive partners;
10. The differential impact and effectiveness of batterers' treatment programs;
11. Overcoming the special needs and problems of Asian, Latina, lesbian, or elderly battered women.

Domestic violence, also known as intimate partner violence, family violence, women abuse, and spouse abuse, is prevalent throughout the United

States and Canada. The National Family Violence Survey (NFVS) of 1985 and the National Violence against Women Survey of 1995–96 both documented the high prevalence estimates of intimate partner perpetrated violence. American estimates of the prevalence of women battering range from 6 to 8.7 million annually. The epidemiological, sociological, health care, and criminal justice utilization research provide compelling evidence of the medical, mental health, and occupational (i.e., lost productivity and absenteeism), and criminal justice system costs emanating from domestic violence incidents. It has also been clear that the consequences of domestic assaults and abusive acts range from cuts and bruises to life-threatening beatings to homicides. On October 12, 2001, the Division of Violence Prevention and the National Center for Injury Prevention and Control of the Centers for Disease Control (CDC) released its report entitled *Surveillance of Homicide among Intimate Partners—United States, 1981–1998*. This report provided summary statistics on intimate partner homicides, specifically with regard to women in the United States who were homicide victims. According to this report, approximately one in three murders (300,522) were intimate partner homicides.

To anyone trained in the fields of law, criminal justice, counseling, psychology, and social work, the study of domestic violence is certainly a challenging and most worthy endeavor. Each year in the United States and Canada, several million women are physically injured, sustain permanent injuries and losses to one of their senses, or are killed by their abusive partners. We receive almost daily reminders in the media of the magnitude of intimate partner violence throughout North America. This is the first multidisciplinary handbook to view domestic violence as a criminal justice, public health, and social work problem. The framework of this handbook calls for a coordinated and systematic approach to finding solutions on all levels—individual, group, family, community, and society—by legal and criminal justice, public health and mental health, and social work professionals working together to implement the latest policies and practices. The crime of domestic violence, and strategies to lessen and eventually eliminate it from the United States and Canada, are the focus of this handbook.

Much has been accomplished in the past 30 years since the point of departure—when the first shelter for battered women and their children was opened in London, England. Within a few years of 1975 emergency shelters for battered women were opened in different parts of the United States such as the one in New York City; St. Paul, Minnesota; and Fresno, California. In 1978–79, the editor conducted the first national survey of the organizational structure and functions of 89 shelters for battered women throughout the United States.

By 1984–85, major initiatives were begun toward improving the police and courts responses to battered women. Researchers and legislators became aware of the effectiveness of arresting the batterer in order to deter an escalation of the battering episodes. Landmark victim assistance and victim services legislation passed both houses of the U.S. Congress in 1984, and the Victims of Crime Act (VOCA) was signed into law by President Ronald Reagan. During fiscal year 1985, the amount of $68.3 million was made available to support state victim compensation programs as well as grants for victim service and witness assistance programs. In applying for these new federal funds, each state was required to certify that it was giving priority to providing funding for local victim assistance programs that focused on aiding victims of sexual assault, spouse abuse, or child abuse. In 1990, the editor's national organizational survey of 184 victim service and witness assistance programs was published in book form, and titled *Helping Crime Victims*.

Emergency shelters expanded considerably in the late 1980s and 1990s, and by the year 2000 there were over 2,000 shelters nationwide. The most recent emerging and incremental developments are job training programs, and transitional and long-term congregate housing opportunities for battered women leaving emergency shelters in large and small cities. As a direct result of the Violence Against Women Act II (VAWA, 2000) programs were expanded nationwide with emphasis on enhancing the role of the courts in combating violence against women through training, education, and technical assistance for judges and court personnel, and technological improvements in the courts; reauthorization and enhancement of services; and Training for Officers and Prosecutors (STOP) grants. These grants increase funds to police and prosecutors for victim service collaborations, to state domestic violence and sexual assault coalitions; and for dating violence prevention programs. Other grant programs under Title II of VAWA II strengthen services to victims of violence and include legal assistance to victims of domestic violence and sexual assault, expanded shelter for battered women and their children, transitional housing assistance for victims of domestic violence, continuation funding for the National Domestic Violence Hotline, federal victims counselors grants programs, as well as enhancing protections for older and disabled women from domestic violence and sexual assault. Finally, Title III of VAWA II focuses on limiting the impact of domestic violence on children. This includes supervised visitation and safe visitation exchange of children of battered women, child abuse victims, or child sexual assault victims; reauthorization of the victims of child abuse programs, which includes the funding of special advocate programs, and the judicial personnel training program, and prosecutor grants for closed circuit televised testimony of children; and the study of parental kidnapping laws.

The leading experts in the United States and Canada present their comprehensive intervention models and legal remedies and as with any newly developed model program they continue to evolve and improve. It is my earnest anticipation that the readers of this handbook will benefit from our experiences (case studies and research findings), risk assessment and intervention guidelines, and program development blueprints as we all strive to ultimately eliminate the tragedy and pervasiveness of domestic violence assaults and domestic violence homicides.

Albert R. Roberts, Ph.D., Professor
Department of Criminal Justice
Faculty of Arts and Sciences
Livingston College Campus
Rutgers, the State University of New Jersey
Piscataway, N.J.

Acknowledgments

It was not possible to compile a comprehensive handbook without a team of 27 brilliant chapter authors. First and foremost, I am grateful to each chapter author for writing original, up-to-date, practical, and empirically based chapters. Without their significant contributions, this handbook would not have been possible. In terms of my own research projects, which constitute chapters 3, 4, and 5, Gloria Bonilla-Santiago, Patricia Brownell, and Pamela Valentine each provided valuable technical and editorial assistance that strengthened the research. In addition, Karel Kurst-Swanger deserves major credit for her collaboration with me on chapters 6 and 7. I am thankful to Elaine P. Congress, Beverly Schenkman Roberts, Michael J. Smith, Pamela Valentine (particularly for chapter 4), and Joan Zorza. This group of reviewers labored diligently with painstaking care for detail and made very helpful editorial suggestions.

Special gratitude is extended to my former research assistants/interviewers who contributed to the research project on the duration and severity of intimate partner violence in which I was principal investigator: Roger Borichewski, Shari Botwin, Sonia Bouradimos, Sgt. Mark Boyer, Lt. James Brady, Kathleen Burkhard, Glenna Campbell, Lisa Cassa, Sgt. Patricia Cassidy, Melanie Cobb, Patricia Dahl, Beth Feder, Wanda Garcia, Donna Gilchrist, Karen Larsen, Yun Lee, Tamara Maher, Megan McChesney, Heidi V. O'Donnell, Patrice Paldino, Joann Paone, Gina Pisano Robertiello, Joann Gonsalez, Jeannine Reiss, Dawn Renn, Dante Sanchez, Jeannine Saracino,

Joella Sperber, Melinda Strangeway, Lisa Trembly, and Jill Sabowski. I was also fortunate to have had three research professors in the late 1960s and early 1970s, Paul Ephross, the late Peter P. Lejins, and the late Daniel Thursz, whose advice and insights led to my first book *Sheltering Battered Women: A National Study and Service Guide* (1981) on family violence. The foundation practice knowledge and research skills eloquently transmitted by my doctoral mentors in criminology, criminal justice, and social work have served as an inspiration to me in my teaching and research career.

I express my appreciation to Dr. Arnold Hyndman, Professor and Dean of Livingston College, for his strong encouragement and support of my recent family violence research endeavors, to Joan Bossert, Editorial Director at Oxford University Press, for her intellectual stimulation and editorial support, and to Irene Bertoni of Oxford University Press for valuable technical assistance. Finally, my heartfelt gratitude goes to Beverly, my loving wife of 30 years, for being a sounding board and editor extraordinaire on this handbook as well as my previous 23 books.

Contents

Part II: Criminal Justice and Legal System Responses

Part III: Health Care, Addictions, and Mental Health Treatment

Contributors

Editor

Albert R. Roberts, Ph.D., B.C.E.T.S., D.A.C.F.E., is Professor of Criminal Justice and Social Work in the Faculty of Arts and Sciences, Livingston College Campus at Rutgers, the State University of New Jersey in Piscataway. Dr. Roberts received an M.A. degree (major in Sociology; minor in Counseling) from the Graduate Faculty of Long Island University in 1967, and a D.S.W. in 1978 (which became a Ph.D. in 1981) from the School of Social Work and Community Planning at the University of Maryland in Baltimore. Dr. Roberts is the founding editor-in-chief of the *Brief Treatment and Crisis Intervention* journal (Oxford University Press). He is an editorial advisor to Oxford's Professional Book Division in New York City and currently serves on the editorial boards of five professional journals.

Dr. Roberts is a member of The Board of Scientific and Professional Advisors and a Board Certified Expert in Traumatic Stress for The American Academy of Experts in Traumatic Stress. He is also a Diplomate of the American College of Forensic Examiners. Dr. Roberts is the founding and current editor of the thirty-six-volume Springer Series on Social Work (1980 to present). He is the author, co-author, or editor of approximately 150 scholarly publications, including numerous peer-reviewed journal articles and book chapters, and 24 books. His recent or forthcoming books and articles include: "A Century of Forensic Social Work: Bridging the Past to the Present" (with Patricia Brownell) in *Social Work*, July 1999; *Ending the Terror: Dating and Marital Violence* (co-authored with Beverly J. Roberts, Oxford, 2003), *Social Workers' Desk Reference* (co-edited with Gilbert J. Greene, Oxford, 2002), *Crisis Intervention Handbook: Assessment, Treatment and Research, 2nd edition* (2000, Oxford), and *Battered Women and Their Families: Intervention Strategies and Treatment Approaches*, 2nd edition (1998). Dr. Roberts recent projects include directing the new 21-credit *Certificate Program in Victim Advocacy, Crisis Management, and Criminal Justice* at Livingston College of Rutgers University; training crisis intervention workers and clinical supervisors in crisis assessment and crisis intervention strategies; training police officers and administrators in domestic violence policies and crisis intervention; and revision of his *Critical Issues in Crime and Justice* text. He is a lifetime member of the Academy of Criminal Justice Sciences (ACJS), has been a member of the National Association of Social Workers (NASW) since 1974, and has been listed in *Who's Who in America* since 1992. Dr. Roberts is the faculty sponsor to Rutgers's Sigma Alpha Kappa chapter of the Alpha Phi Sigma National Criminal Justice Honor Society (1991 to present).

Chapter Authors

Amy P. Barasch, J.D., Associate, Lanser & Kubitschek; New York, New York

Mary Boes, MSW, DSW, Associate Professor, Department of Social Work, University of Northern Iowa, Cedar Falls

Mary P. Brewster, Ph.D., Associate Professor and Graduate Coordinator, Department of Criminal Justice, West Chester University, West Chester, Pennsylvania

Patricia Brownell, Ph.D., CSW, Assistant Professor, Fordham University, Graduate School of Social Service, Lincoln Center Campus, New York, New York

Sophia F. Dziegielewski, Ph.D., LCSW, Professor, School of Social Work and Public Affairs Doctoral Program, College of Health and Public Affairs, University of Central Florida, Orlando

Bea Hanson, MSW, Vice President, Domestic Violence Programs, Safe Horizon, Inc., New York, New York; Adjunct Professor, Hunter College School of Social Work, City University of New York

Thomas L. Jackson, Ph.D., Clinical Psychologist and Training Consultant, Fayetteville, Arkansas

Susan Keilitz, J.D., Training Consultant, Domestic Violence Courts, Sherwood Associates; former Director of Research, National Center on State Courts, Williamsburg, VA

Karel Kurst-Swanger, Ph.D., Assistant Professor, Public Justice Department, State University of New York at Oswego, Oswego

Mo-Yee Lee, Ph.D., Associate Professor, College of Social Work, The Ohio State University, Columbus

Peter Lehmann, Ph.D., LMSW-ACP, Associate Professor and Director, BSW Program, School of Social Work, The University of Texas at Arlington

Victoria L. Lutz, J.D., Executive Director, Pace Women's Justice Center; Adjunct Professor of Law, Pace University Law School, White Plains, New York

Virginia McDermott, RN, BA, Medical Surgical Nurse, Allen Memorial Hospital, Waterloo, Iowa

Linda G. Mills, J.D., MSW, Ph.D., Professor of Social Work, Ehrenkranz School of Social Work, New York University; Affiliated Professor of Law, New York Law School

Patricia A. Petretic-Jackson, Ph.D., Associate Professor of Clinical Psychology and Director, Psychological Clinic, Department of Psychology, University of Arkansas,Fayetteville

Carrie Petrucci, MSW, Ph.D. Candidate, Department of Social Welfare, School of Public Policy and Social Research, University of California at Los Angeles

Stephanie Rabenstein, MSW, Madame Vanier Children's Services, London, Ontario

Janice L. Ricks, MSW, Director of Day Habilitation, Albuquerque, New Mexico

Beverly Schenkman Roberts, M.Ed., Director and Health Advocate, Medical Mainstreaming for the Developmentally Disabled, Arc of New Jersey, North Brunswick

Michael A. Rothery, Ph.D., Professor, Faculty of Social Work, University of Calgary, Calgary, Alberta Canada

Gloria Bonilla-Santiago, Ph.D., Director and Professor, Center for Strategic Urban Community Leadership at Rutgers, The State University of New Jersey-Camden Campus, Camden, New Jersey

Evan Stark, MSW, Ph.D., Associate Professor, Graduate Department of Public Administration; Director, Graduate Program in Public Health, Rutgers, The State University of New Jersey and the University of Medicine and Dentistry of New Jersey, University Heights, Newark

Leslie M. Tutty, Ph.D., Professor, Faculty of Social Work, University of Calgary, Calgary, Alberta Canada

Carol (Jan) Vaughn, MSW, Social Worker, Winter Park, Florida

Tricia H. Witte, Ph.D. Candidate, Department of Psychology, University of Arkansas

Theresa M. Zubretsky, MSW, Director, The Safety Zone, Troy, New York

Part I

INTRODUCTION, PUBLIC POLICY, RESEARCH, AND SOCIAL ACTION

Myths, Facts, and Realities Regarding Battered Women and Their Children: An Overview

ALBERT R. ROBERTS

Denise, a 21-year-old senior at New York University, talked about her 2½-year relationship with her boyfriend, Rosario. They were both students at NYU, and they started living together just 6 months after they began dating. Although Denise said that she was madly in love with Rosario, she also had the feeling that he was cheating on her. Denise and Rosario had arguments about Denise's parents, who had made it quite clear to Denise that they thought Rosario was a "psycho." Although Rosario had hit her several times before, he always apologized and brought her flowers, and Denise wanted to believe that it would never happen again. Denise discussed the violent incident that caused her to end the relationship:

> We were driving back from the shopping mall in my parents' car. On the way back, my parents called on my cell phone to make sure I was okay and they wanted to say "hi." My parents and Rosario do not get along, so I usually just don't mention his name if they call. Well, they started lecturing me about how I should be studying on a Sunday afternoon instead of going shopping, and Rosario got mad because he thinks that they are way too strict on me. So then Rosario took the phone, and he and my father got into an argument, and my father's calling him a "son of a bitch" and my boyfriend is calling my mother a "bitch." I was caught in the middle. Then Rosario started going off about how I could never see my parents again, and I have to choose him over them. I thought I wanted to stay with him at the time, so I promised that I loved him and would never

talk to my parents again. Later, he wanted me to prove my love by break-ing the windows of my parents' car because then my parents would have to pay to replace them. I refused to do that, so he busted all of the car windows with a baseball bat. I was begging him not to damage my car, and as we argued, he hit me with the bat over my head, and I passed out and had a concussion. (Author's files)

Susan, aged 19 and a student at Boston University, broke up with Martin following a 9-month dating relationship.

Martin verbally abused and threatened me when he said "If you ever date or have sex with someone else, I will injure you real bad." One afternoon the second week after I started my summer job, Martin picked me up at work. He said: "I noticed you smiled and waved good-bye to your co-worker. I know you probably fucked him at lunch, and you are going to give me AIDS." I knew Martin had a real jealous streak, but I was shocked by his statement. We had just left the parking lot, and Martin then locked the doors of the car and smacked me in the face twice, and punched me in the arm and chest several times. Soon after getting to my off-campus apart-ment, I cleaned up my bloody mouth and lips and called the police to file for a temporary restraining order. I tried to break up with him, but it didn't end until about 2 months later. He stalked me and made threatening phone calls, between 15 and 30 calls per day. First, I changed my phone number to an unlisted phone number. Somehow he managed to get the new unlisted phone number. He continued to stalk me and seemed to be watching me a lot because each time I would go to the food store or a restaurant, he would come up behind me and start threatening me. I had to transfer to another university in a different state to finally get away from him. (Author's files)

Rachel, aged 34, described her abusive partner's self-destructive patterns and his death threats against her which finally led to her decision to end the relationship:

He had been doing drugs, and he started getting paranoid and accused me of making signals out to someone in the hall—and there was no one out there. He asked me to go downstairs to get something and he locked him-self in the room, and I knew that he was upset and I heard the click of a gun being dry fired, and I could hear him spinning the barrel and I started getting scared. Finally I convinced him to open the door. He acted like he was gonna shoot himself. I begged him not to. The kids were down the hall [sleeping]. I got angry with him and said, "Go ahead, do it"; then I said, "Give it to me—I'll do it." He gave me the gun. I put it down and went downstairs. He came after me and held the gun to my head and said, "If I can't have you, no one can!" He cocked it [the gun]. We were there for a long time. I was crying and told him I never cheated on him, and finally through talking, I convinced him not to do it. For a long time I thought I was gonna die that night. (Roberts, 1996)

These case illustrations are typical of the different severity levels and duration of domestic violence cases. Denise, Susan, and Rachel were victims of battering by either a boyfriend or a husband. The four brief case summaries illustrate that dating and marital abuse can range from one violent incident to a chronic pattern that is endured for many years. While victims may be assaulted from one to hundreds of times by their abusive partners, and their injuries or trauma may sometimes be permanent, these cases indicate that the physical abuse can be stopped.

The prevalence of woman abuse in intimate relationships provides challenges and opportunities for implementing new and responsive legislation, funding appropriations, legal remedies, law enforcement policies, and the full spectrum of mental health, substance abuse, shelter and transitional housing, and social services. The next section of this chapter provides up-to-date information on domestic violence myths and facts. The third section provides a brief historical background on domestic violence policies and programs, with particular emphasis on shelters, police- and court-based domestic violence programs, and social services. The chapter closes with a discussion of important current legislation—the Violence Against Women Act (VAWA) 2000—which has transformed and bolstered the movement to prevent and eliminate woman battering as a major public health and criminal justice problem.

CORRECTING THE COMMON MYTHS

A number of myths and stereotypes hinder both an accurate knowledge of the nature, extent, diversity, and intensity of woman battering and effective intervention. Enormous progress has been made in the past few years in regard to major policy reforms and program development. Recent legislation, increased federal and state funding, more sensitive police and court responses, and community-wide case management approaches offer much promise to lessening the battering of women in the United States. But for agency policies and program developments to be implemented effectively, our attention needs to be directed toward the facts and realities of domestic violence against women rather than the myths. This book was written to debunk the traditional myths and replace them with new knowledge and strategies for research, social action, public policy, legal remedies, and intervention.

The overriding objective of fact statements is to end the prejudice and emotional fervor of societal myths and replace them with accurate information based on systematic research. Unfortunately, myths maintain and reinforce faulty and incorrect assumptions about woman battering, as well as distorting public attitudes and promoting misunderstanding of the issues. To help develop realistic intervention strategies, legal remedies, and responsive legislation, I delineate the main myths regarding woman battering and correct them with real cases and facts. Academic scholars, educators, domestic violence advocates, criminologists, social workers, psychologists, and family violence researchers are committed to correcting myths with scientific facts, research findings, and realistic solutions to eliminating domestic violence.

Myth 1 Woman battering is a problem only in the lower socioeconomic class.

Facts and Reality Woman battering takes place in all social classes, religions, races, and ethnic groups. Although violence against women seems to be more visible in the lower class because it is more frequently reported to the police and hospital emergency rooms in inner-city neighborhoods, it is increasingly being recognized as a pervasive problem in middle- and upper-class homes as well. There is a large and hidden group of battered women living in highly affluent suburbs throughout the United States. Because the battering incidents in wealthy households are usually intermittent, sometimes even skipping a year, and the women may live on 2- or 3-acre estates, the neighbors rarely hear the violence. Women in these tormenting, volatile, and unpredictable marriages become traumatically bonded to their abusive partners. Unfortunately, these women rarely report the abusive incidents to the police, and when they need medical treatment, they see the family physician and explain that they are accident-prone.

Case Illustration Arlene is a 39-year-old alumna of Radcliffe College. She was a debutante and grew up in Westchester County, New York. Her mother was a socialite, and her father was a chief executive officer of a Fortune 100 company. She married immediately after graduating from college without having ever had a job. She married Steven, vice president of a family-managed Fortune 500 company. The first battering incident occurred on Arlene's honeymoon in Hawaii, and she felt that she deserved it because she woke Steven up by accident when she went to the bathroom at 9:00 A.M. She has been intermittently abused once every 6 to 14 months for the past 17 years. She claims that there have been a lot of good times, and she and Steven take big vacations twice a year. She also feels that he is very good to their three children. She said that she had to go to the hospital only twice, and there were only scars, no permanent injuries. She plans to stay in the relationship for the sake of her children and because she enjoys her social prominence, which she feels would be compromised with a divorce because there would be such a bitter legal battle (Author's files).

What do the following six men have in common besides their six-figure annual incomes? A San Diego (California) municipal court judge, medical doctor, and attorney; and a New York City former Supreme Court judge, medical doctor, and attorney. All six of these prominent men with aspiring careers have a history as perpetrators of domestic violence against their intimate partners.

Other examples of wealthy batterers and their partners include attorney Joel Steinberg, who psychologically tortured and abused his intimate partner, Hedda Nussbaum (a children's book editor at Random House), for many years and murdered their daughter Lisa Steinberg; and homicide victim and former model Nicole Brown Simpson, whose violent death received intensive media scrutiny during 1994 and 1995 because of police reports that she had been beaten several times by her ex-husband, former football legend O. J. Simpson. Several years ago, headlines in the *New York Times* and *Washington Post* revealed that John Fedders, former head of the Securities and Exchange Commission, battered his wife for many years before she filed for divorce. Also, in her book, Georgette Mosbacher, former wife of the CEO of Fabergé, describes the years of battering she endured while married.

Although woman battering occurs in all socioeconomic classes, it is reported to be more prevalent in the lowest economic groups. According to a special report of the Bureau of Justice Statistics (Rennison & Welchans, 2000) on intimate partner violence, women living in low-income households defined as having annual household incomes under $7,500 were almost seven times more likely to be victimized by their partners than women with annual household incomes of $75,000 and over (20% versus 3% per 1,000). The U.S. Department of the Justice's National Crime Victimization Survey Report for 1993 to 1998 indicates that women with a family income under $7,500 were approximately five times more likely to be a victim of a violent incident perpetrated by an "intimate" than were women with a family income of $50,000 to $74,000 (Rennison & Welchans, 2000).

Myth 2 Woman battering is not a significant problem because most incidents are in the form of a slap or a push that do not cause serious medical injury.

Facts and Reality Woman battering is a very serious problem that places victims at risk of medical injuries as well as homicide. The lifetime prevalence of intimate partner battering reported by studies of hospital emergency rooms ranges between 11% and 54% (Dearwater et al., 1998). According to the National Violence Against Women survey, 41.5% of the women in the survey sustained injuries as a result of being attacked. The injuries included cuts and bruises, broken bones and internal injuries, knife wounds, gunshot wounds, and being knocked unconscious (Tjaden & Thoennes, 2000). One study found that one in three battered women (35%) had suffered a head injury from an assault (Monahan & O'Leary, 1999).

Many cases of domestic violence have lethal consequences. According to the Federal Bureau of Investigation (FBI) Uniform Crime Reports, 32% of the 3,419 women killed throughout the United States in 1998 were murdered by an intimate partner—a husband, former husband, current boyfriend, or former boyfriend. Recently, a growing number of states have passed legislation authorizing domestic violence fatality reviews, the goal being to develop a database and profiles so that law enforcement and public health officials will be in a better position to predict potentially deadly cases of domestic violence and institute safety plans to prevent homicides of battered women, as well as murder-suicides. In 2000, five states—Florida, Iowa, Minnesota, Tennessee, and Washington—passed legislative measures to either create or institutionalize trained interdisciplinary teams to perform fatality reviews of domestic violence–related deaths. Legislation in Kentucky permits the county domestic violence coordinating councils to create their own domestic violence fatality review teams.

Case Illustration Delores, age 42, described her injuries from years of battering: "Two broken ribs, scars on my elbows and thighs, bruises on my back and neck. Broke my bridge in five places. All of my top teeth are loose. My glasses were broken." In addition, "He threatened to kill me. If he was drunk enough, I thought he would. He always said, 'If I ever catch you with another man, I'll kill you' and 'If you leave me, I'll blow your brains out (author's files).'"

The following random selection of woman battering cases from my research files illustrates the nature and types of medical injuries sustained by battered women:

Case 1: I needed medical assistance for a broken arm, but I refused to tell the doctor the source of my injury. My husband was in the emergency room with me (fear of retaliation, and worse injuries).

Case 2: I never received medical attention. As a result of the abuse, I had black eyes, bruises, a concussion, and bleeding from scrapes.

Case 3: I was taken to the hospital after my husband pushed me down a flight of stairs. I had a broken leg and severe back pain after that incident.

Case 4: I was badly beaten when I was pregnant, and I needed medical attention. Hemorrhaging began, and I was afraid to return to the hospital. The doctor told me that it was possible the baby won't survive the abuse.

Case 5: I never needed medical help. My abuser choked me and then just walked out.

Case 6: I needed to go to the hospital for severe burns all over my body, but I was afraid to leave the house.

Case 7: I needed to go to a doctor because I was bleeding from my ear, and Pedro had broken my jaw.

Case 8: I fought back, and slashed my abuser with a box cutter. We were both arrested.

Case 9: Theodore used a razor on me and cut up my face. I needed 113 stitches to my face and neck, plus I had numerous wounds on my breasts that needed stitches.

Myth 3 The police never arrest the batterer because they view domestic violence calls as a private matter.

Facts and Reality As of 2001, all 50 states had implemented warrantless arrest policies. In recent years there have also been sweeping changes in terms of mandated domestic violence police training, specialized police domestic violence units, collaborative community police and prosecutor response teams, enhanced technology, and collaboration between victim advocates and police to enhance victim safety and offender accountability. For complete information on police responsiveness and program developments, see chapter 6, on police responses to domestic violence, and chapter 17, on police-based crisis intervention programs in Arizona, Texas, and New Jersey. Before 1985, police often did not want to arrest the batterer when they were called to the scene in a domestic violence case. However, the decision in *Thurman v. The City of Torrington* (1985) served notice to police departments across the country to treat domestic violence reports as they would any other crime in which the perpetrator and victim do not know each other.

In this Torrington, Connecticut, case, Tracey Thurman had repeatedly begged the police for protection from her former husband, Charles "Buck" Thurman. In one instance, the police were called to Tracey Thurman's residence because her former husband was beating and stabbing her just outside her home. When the police officer finally arrived (his arrival was delayed for approximately 20 minutes while he went to the station to "relieve himself"), he asked Buck for the knife but did not handcuff or attempt to arrest him. Buck then continued to brutalize Tracey, kicking and stomping on her and causing serious injuries, including partial paralysis. Tracey won her lawsuit against the Torrington police department for its negligence in not arresting Buck and for violating her constitutional rights to equal protection. Tracey Thurman was awarded $2.3 million in compensatory damages, which was later reduced to $1.9 million. Because of this large settlement, this case is credited as being the catalyst for the development of mandatory arrest laws in a growing number of states.

As discussed in chapter 6, by 1999, a total of 21 states had enacted mandatory arrest policies for the perpetrators of domestic violence, although in several of the states arrest is mandatory only when the batterer violates a restraining order. In addition, chapter 6 discusses changes in state statutes expanding the police's arrest powers. Specifically, arrest is recommended when there is probable cause—reasonable grounds such as a visible injury.

New York's Family Protection and Domestic Violence Intervention Act of 1994 requires police to make arrests in cases in which there is reasonable cause to believe that a felony or misdemeanor was committed by one family or household member against another or if an order of protection was violated. As of 1994, arrest is mandatory in New Jersey if a woman suffers an injury or complains of injury. In addition, weapons are seized whether or not the batterer has a gun permit and needs his weapon because he is a police officer or correctional officer. New Jersey law states that arrest is mandatory for violating a restraining order if it involves a new act of domestic violence.

Case Illustration I had black eyes from his hitting and punching me. I called 911, and the police came, and I said to arrest him. He told them I was nuts because I was on pills from the doctor. The house was a mess, and I had the baby. The police officer believed me, and they arrested him. One officer asked me if I had anywhere to go, so I said I was from New Jersey and my mother was there. He advised me to go back to New Jersey with the money I had. The police said otherwise it would happen again. So I called my mother, bought a ticket, and left the next morning. He [the batterer] called and told me to drop the charges while I was packing to leave. I told him no (Roberts, 1996).

Myth 4 Temporary restraining orders and protective orders rarely are effective in stopping the battering.

Facts and Reality In recent years, family, criminal, and specialized domestic violence courts have instituted major institutional reforms, including technology enhancement, automated case tracking systems, more victim protection of their confidentiality rights (e.g., new address, new unlisted phone), and offender accountability. The research has begun to demonstrate that thousands of women are being helped and having their legal rights protected by court orders. Recently, courts have revised their policies on child custody visitation rights when domestic violence is an issue, as demonstrated in chapter 7. The newest innovations are around-the-clock methods of issuing temporary restraining orders and providing pro bono attorney 24 hours a day, 7 days a week (see chapter 9). In addition, approximately, 60 law schools throughout the United States have student domestic violence law clinics and seminars. Women who cannot afford an attorney now have an additional alternative besides a legal aid attorney in specially trained law students. For further details on the latest program developments, see chapters 7 and 9.

Myth 5 All batterers are psychotic, and no treatment can change their violent habits.

Case Illustration Ralph was 28 years old when he was referred to the 6-month family service batterers counseling program in Indianapolis. He was one of the 30 batterers with whom the author conducted voluntary in-depth interviews. This case illustrates intense work-related stress, negative self-talk, and unrealistic expectations of one's wife as precursors to intimate partner violence. It also illustrates some of the benefits of group counseling.

> In the words of Ralph: It's a dangerous job. The stress was that I had to get something better than carpentry, even though I loved building furniture. Then, I got a better job, a line man for the power company, but it was very dangerous. Guys have gotten their arms blown up, and you wear rubber gloves and sleeves. I felt I could really do it if I tried hard enough. They have electric utility poles 120 feet up in the air. I needed the higher salary to pay for Julie's college tuition. Unfortunately, I would come home tired after work. Julie would want to go out almost every night, especially during senior year. She would go bowling herself. One night I went out to look for her. I found her in a car making it with another guy in the bowling alley parking lot. She got out of the car when she saw me, and the guy took off. I took her home. I couldn't sleep, so I woke up and started choking her. I almost killed her. I felt real bad afterward.
>
> In group counseling, I've learned that I was trying to control her life. It upset me when she flirted with other guys. I kept giving myself the wrong messages that once she graduated with her accounting degree and got a big job, she would leave me. I kept telling myself that she didn't love me and that's why she refused to stay home with me at night. Actually, she was just blowing off steam and would never go out if she was working on a school assignment or studying for a test. I guess I'm insecure because she eventually graduated college, and I never went to college. All through our 3-year marriage I was afraid that she would leave me. (Author's files)

Joann and Paul were in their early 30s and living in a five-bedroom Colonial (which cost $500,000) when the abuse started. Joann called this home her dream house in the suburbs. In addition, both Joann and Paul leased relatively new cars and had recently joined the local country club. Joann and Paul had dated for 6 years before they got married. She supported him through his last 2 years of dental school. During the time they were dating, Paul would spend what little money he had on gifts of flowers and perfume for Joann. The physical abuse started after they had been married for almost 5 years. Joann made a lot of money as a television writer and was able to give Paul the money he needed to become a partner in a thriving dental practice. They also had two children, aged 1 and 2, when Paul's temper tantrums and abuse started.

> It was the week after New Year's, and he came home from work drunk. I tried to keep his dinner warm until 10:00 P.M. when he got home. Paul started screaming and yelling and threw the food on the floor. He then knocked me down on the slate floor and started choking me. During this time he is yelling at me that I am a bad Catholic because the house is

sloppy, and dinner was burnt. He beat me about eight times during the next 6 months until I finally left him, and got a permanent order of protection from the court. I learned at an early age in my church that when you get married, you are married forever. If you make a mistake like overcooking dinner, you try to do better. If your husband makes a mistake and gets drunk, you forgive him and make up. It was June, and I was having nightmares almost every night. My 2-year-old son was acting out and throwing toys at me and the other kids in playgroup. The last straw was on a Sunday afternoon in early June, and it was pouring buckets of rain outside. I had made egg salad for lunch, and Paul had a tantrum in front of our babies. He spread the egg salad on the wall and then ripped the phone cord out of the wall and started punching me and pulling my hair out. He was an officer in the army reserves and had been in the Persian Gulf War. He told me that the military had taught him how to torture and kill the enemy, and I was the enemy sometimes because I was a terrible cook and forgot to take the garbage out to the garage. He was yelling that he was going to remove all of my teeth and was dragging me by my hair into the master bathroom. Somehow I had a burst of adrenaline and was able to get loose and hit Paul in the head with the bathroom scale and kick him in the balls and run outside to a neighbor's house and call the police. My head needed 14 stitches in the hospital emergency room, and my hair still has not grown back in the place where he yanked it out. To this day, Paul does not understand why I divorced him, obtained full custody of our two kids, and moved away. (Author's files)

Facts and Reality The majority of men who assault women can be helped. Three main types of intervention are available for men who assault their intimate partners: arrest, psychoeducational groups, and court-mandated group counseling. There is a dearth of longitudinal outcome studies on the effectiveness of batterers' treatment programs, but a number of program evaluations indicate that this approach is successful in reducing recidivism. A review article evaluating the effectiveness of different types of batterers' intervention programs indicated that a large proportion of abusive partners stopped their physical abuse after completion of such a program; positive outcomes ranged from 53% to 85% (Edleson, 1996). A New York study sponsored by Victim Services demonstrated that participants in a 6-month batterers' counseling program (26 weekly sessions) had significantly lower recidivism rates at both 6 and 12 months after sentencing (court-mandated counseling as part of probation) when compared with participants in 8-week batterers' counseling programs or community service, fines, or traditional probation supervision (Davis, Taylor, & Maxwell, 2000). The most frequently used treatment approaches are cognitive-behavioral approaches anger management techniques, communication and empathy skills, and the psychoeducational approach. Earlier studies have shown that mandatory arrest has worked for some types of batterers but not others. In their study of 1,200 cases in Milwaukee, Sherman and associates (1992) found that arrest seemed to result in an escalation of battering among unemployed minorities, whereas arrest had a deterrent effect among abusers who were employed, white, and married at the time of the study. See chapter 6 for a detailed discussion of the recent studies of the deterrent effect of arrest of different subgroups of batterers.

The Duluth, Minnesota, Domestic Abuse Intervention Project (DAIP) conducted a 12-month follow-up study in which battered women were asked their opinion of the intervention that the project had used in an effort to make the batterer change his violent habits. Of the women studied, 60% said they felt there was improvement when the batterer took part in education and group counseling, whereas 80% stated that the improvement had resulted from a combination of involvement by the police and the courts, group counseling, and the shelter (Pence & Paymar, 1993).

Myth 6 Although many battered women suffer severe beatings for years, only a handful experience symptoms of posttraumatic stress disorder (PTSD).

Facts and Reality Tina, age 25, recounted her suicide attempt and intrusive thoughts about the traumatic abusive incidents:

I tried to kill myself because of depression over life in general. I was fed up—sick and tired of being beaten and miserable and taken advantage of. I kept having recurring nightmares about the battering and death threats. Thoughts of the beatings kept popping into my mind almost every morning. . . . My body took the drugs. I couldn't OD [overdose]. I tried to hang myself in my backyard, but someone pulled into my driveway and rescued me. I found recently I have a lot to live for. (Roberts, 1996)

Three clinical studies of battered women living in shelters or women attending community-based self-help groups found PTSD rates ranging from 45% to 84% (Astin, Lawrence, Pincus, & Foy, 1990; Houskamp & Foy, 1991; Kemp, Rawlings, & Green, 1991). These studies revealed a significant association between the extent and intensity of battering experiences and the severity of PTSD symptoms. See chapter 13 for a detailed discussion of assessment scales, PTSD symptoms, and mental health interventions with battered women.

Chapter 11 provides a detailed discussion of the admissibility of expert testimony on battered woman syndrome and PTSD to support self-defense claims made by battered women charged with killing their abusers. In some cases the expert testimony and the distortions of it by the press can lead to a more severe sentence (e.g., 15 to 20 years or a life sentence).

Myth 7 Battered women who remain in a violent relationship do so because they are masochistic.

Facts and Reality Most battered women who remain in an abusive relationship do so for the following reasons:

Economic need (e.g., financial dependency)

Intermittent reinforcement and traumatic bonding (e.g., the development of strong emotional attachments between intimate partners when the abusive partner is intermittently kind, loving, and apologetic for past violent episodes and promises that it will never happen again, interspersed with beatings and degrading insults)

Learned helplessness (e.g., when someone learns from repeated, unpleasant, and painful experiences that he or she is unable to control the aversive environment or escape, that person will gradually lose the motivation to change the situation)

The fear that the abuser will hunt down the victim and kill her if she leaves

Fear that leaving the relationship and moving to a new location will be a disruption for the children, and she can lose custody permanently

See chapter 2 for a detailed discussion of the theories and causal explanations of woman battering, with case applications of each theory.

Myth 8 Children who have witnessed repeated acts of violence by their father against their mother do not need to participate in a specialized counseling program.

Case Illustration We had been arguing; I can't remember what about. He became violent and ripped the phone wire off because I tried to call the police. He tied me up with the wire and burned me with an iron. He ran outside and ripped some kind of plug from my car so that it wouldn't work. Both my children were there. My daughter was 6, and she was screaming. My son was 5, and he just stayed away and hid under his bed.

Facts and Reality Research indicates that in the United States between 3.3 million and 10 million children are exposed to domestic violence annually. Several studies have consistently demonstrated the long-lasting harm to children resulting from exposure to violence between their parents. These children exhibit a range of adjustment and anxiety disorders, cognitive and emotional impairments, difficulty in school, social deficits, and aggressive and acting-out disorders. Boys who have witnessed their mother being assaulted by a father or stepfather have a greater likelihood of becoming an abuser when they become adults, and girls have a greater likelihood of becoming a victim of domestic violence when they reach adulthood (Fantuzzo et al., 1997; Carlson, 1984, 1996; Behrman, 1999).

A report from the American Bar Association (1994) entitled *The Impact of Domestic Violence on the Children* urges lawyers and judges to more actively protect children from the devastating impact (both physical and psychological) of domestic violence. The report provides the following revealing statistics about children and youth who have witnessed domestic violence: Seventy-five percent of the boys who were present when their mothers were beaten were later identified as having demonstrable behavior problems; between 20% and 40% of chronically violent teens lived in homes in which their mother was beaten; 63% of males in the 11-to-20 age-group who are incarcerated on homicide charges had killed the man who battered their mother.

Jaffe, Wolfe, and Wilson (1990) found that although group counseling was helpful for children with mild to moderate behavior problems, more extensive individual counseling was required for children who witnessed on going and severe violent episodes. Jaffe and associates reported on a 4-year study of 371 children who had lived in violent homes. They found that group counseling had helped the children "improve their self-concept, understand that violence in the home was not their fault, become more aware of protection planning, and learn new ways of resolving conflict without resorting to violence" (p. 90).

See chapter 16 for a detailed discussion of crisis assessment and intervention, shelter-based programs, and group therapy for children of battered women, as well as a review of the evaluations and outcome studies of these programs.

Myth 9 There are no marginalized and "throwaway battered women"—no women with serious mental health disorders, AIDS, PTSD, polydrug abuse, and/or developmental disabilities.

Facts and Reality Many thousands of battered women in the United States and Canada suffer from psychiatric conditions, substance abuse, physical handicaps, developmental disabilities, and life-threatening medical conditions such as AIDS and cancer. For years, these most vulnerable battered women have largely been neglected by domestic violence programs, the health care system, and the criminal justice agencies. More recently, several model programs have been developed to provide them with legal advocacy and legal representation, medical and/or mental health treatment, financial assistance, addictions treatment, and a continuum of community support services. For further details, see chapters 9, 14, and 15.

Myth 10 Alcohol abuse and/or alcoholism causes men to assault their partners.

Facts and Reality Although research indicates that there seems to be a higher rate of domestic violence among heavy drinkers than among nondrinkers, the majority of batterers are not alcoholics, and the overwhelming majority of men classified as high-level or binge drinkers do not abuse their partners (Straus & Gelles, 1990).

In many cases, alcohol is used as an excuse for battering, not a cause. Disinhibition theory suggests that the physiological effects of heavy drinking include a state of lowered inhibitions or control over the drinker's behavior. Marlatt and Rohsenow (1980) found that the most significant determinant of behavior right after drinking is not the physiological effect of the alcohol itself but the expectations that individuals place on the drinking experience. Removing the alcohol does not cure the abusive personality. See chapter 15 for a discussion of the need for two independent forms of treatment for chemically dependent battered women.

Myth 11 It is extremely rare for a battered woman to be homeless.

Facts and Reality A survey of the large cities by the U.S. Conference of Mayors found that domestic violence was the primary cause of homelessness among women. Statewide surveys of women in homeless shelters in Massachusetts, Michigan, Minnesota, and Virginia indicated that 24% to 56% of the women were homeless, at least in part, due to domestic violence.

Myth 12 Elder abuse is neither prevalent nor dangerous.

Case Illustration In chapter 23, P. Brownell describes the case of Mr. and Mrs. M., both of whom are 90 years old. Mr. M., now retired, was a manual laborer and is in good health. Mrs. M. has a heart condition and is physically frail and emotionally depressed. Both refuse home care beyond the 28 hours per week of home health care funded by Medicare, in spite of the around-the-clock needs of Mrs. M., which Mr. M. provides. One afternoon Mr. M. gets drunk and beats up Mrs. M. in the front yard, where the neighbors can witness it. An ambulance is called, and Mrs. M. is hospitalized. She claims not to remember the battering incident and refuses to prosecute her husband.

Facts and Reality As described in chapter 25, research data indicate a 3 to 12 per 1,000 prevalence rate of elder abuse among adults who are 60 years of age and older. According to the 1990 report of the House of Representatives Select Committee on Aging, *Elder Abuse: A Decade of Shame and Inaction*, more than 1.5 million older persons may be victims of abuse by their aging spouses as well as their adult children. This figure is only an estimate because there is no accurate reporting system for elder abuse incidents. Given the hidden nature of elder abuse and the increased longevity of vulnerable elderly persons, we can expect a sharp increase in elder abuse. This projection is based on the anticipated increase to 25.1 million Americans at least 75 years of age and over, and 6 million Americans who will be 85 years of age or older by 2025. See chapter 23 for a discussion of battered and neglected elderly women, social service plans and police complaint reports as a source of early case findings, the need for statutory or mandatory reporting of elder abuse and financial exploitation (as is done in child abuse cases), and a model case-management strategy.

HISTORICAL BACKGROUND

Women have been battered by their partners for centuries. Indeed, in most societies, brutal whippings and beatings seem to have been the most salient way of keeping spouses from leaving their husbands. The Chicago Protective Agency for Women and Children was established in 1885. According to feminist historian Elizabeth Pleck (1987), this organization—which provided legal aid, court advocacy, and personal assistance—was the most important agency effort of the nineteenth century to help women who were victims of physical abuse. An abused woman could receive up to 4 weeks of shelter at the refuge run by the Women's Club of Chicago; in addition, battered women were able to receive an equitable amount of property in divorce settlements. The agency also helped abused women secure legal separations and divorces after proving extreme cruelty and/or drunkenness on the part of their husbands.

Between 1915 and 1920, another 25 cities followed Chicago's lead in establishing protective agencies for women, but only a few of these programs lasted beyond the 1940s. The new Women's Bureaus were a separate unit of the police department and were responsible for helping runaway girls, prostitutes, abused women, and abused children. Although the police social workers in these units did not supply legal aid, they did provide counseling, court advocacy, and job placement and arranged for temporary housing for abused women and transient youths. The largest numbers of police social workers in Women's Bureaus were in Chicago, Cleveland, Baltimore, Detroit, Pittsburgh, Los Angeles, Minneapolis, New York City, Portland, Seattle, St. Louis, St. Paul, and Washington, D.C. (Roberts, 1990). However, by the 1940s most of the police Women's bureaus had been eliminated by a new police chief, city manager, or mayor. In a few police departments the bureaus were changed to crime prevention bureaus, and a male police administrator replaced the woman director. Following the downfall of the police social work movement, it was rare for any help to be offered to battered women until new efforts grew out of the contemporary women's rights movement, which began in the 1970s.

By the late 1970s, emergency shelters, 24-hour hotlines, and a network of volunteer host homes were developed to aid battered women throughout the United States, Canada, and Great Britain. The first shelter, Chiswick Women's Aid, was opened in London in 1972 by Erin Pizzey, whose efforts to provide emergency housing for abused women and their children inspired others throughout the Western world to do the same. By 1977, a total of 89 shelters for battered women had been opened throughout the United States, and that year the shelters' 24-hour hotlines received over 110,000 calls from battered women.

The major self-reported strengths of emergency services were shelter, 24-hour hotlines, peer counseling, court advocacy, legal aid, and the commitment of staff and volunteers (many of whom worked 50 to 60 hours per week, including evenings and weekends). The main problems were overcrowding in the shelters, lack of stable funding, rapid turnover of full-time staff and attrition of volunteers, lack of cooperation by local police and the courts, and poor interagency relations and linkages (Roberts, 1981).

In the mid-1990s, the pendulum swung from an earlier emphasis on providing emergency shelter and collecting data on the number of women who were victimized to an emphasis on implementing legal remedies, proarrest policies, case management services, and treatment programs for battered women. Beginning in 2000, a new emphasis was taking hold, namely, the expansion of coordinated specialized police and prosecutor domestic violence programs, integrated case management and technology solutions via domestic violence courts, and support groups, transitional housing, and electronic technology to aid battered women and their children.

By 1990, there were more than 1,250 battered women's shelters throughout the United States and Canada (Roberts, 1990). In addition, crisis-oriented services for battered women are provided at thousands of local hospital emergency rooms, hospital-based trauma centers, emergency psychiatric services, suicide prevention centers, community mental health center crisis units, and pastoral counseling services (Roberts, 1995). By the year 2000, the number of shelters for battered women and their children had increased to over 2,000 throughout the United States (see chapter 17 for a detailed discussion of 24-hour crisis hotlines and emergency shelters for battered women and their children).

A number of states have enacted special legislation that provides funding for hotlines and shelters for victims of domestic violence. Every state and major metropolitan area in the country now has crisis-intervention services for battered women and their children. Although the primary goal of these services is to ensure the women's safety, many shelters have evolved into much more than just a place for safe lodging. Crisis intervention for battered women generally includes a 24-hour hotline, a safe and secure emergency shelter (the average length of stay is 3 to 4 weeks), an underground network of volunteer homes and shelters, and welfare and court advocacy by student interns and other volunteers (Roberts, 1984, 2000). Many shelters also offer peer counseling, support groups, information on women's legal rights, and referral to social service agencies.

In some communities, emergency services for battered women have expanded to include parenting education workshops, assistance in finding housing, employment counseling and job placement for the women, and group counseling for the batterers. In the all-too-often neglected area of assessment and treatment for the children of battered women, a small but growing number of shelters provide group counseling, play therapy, art therapy, or referral to mental health centers.

Planned social change and a sharp reduction in a serious social problem such as woman battering usually take place after (1) legislators, human service administrators, prosecutors, and judges become aware that the problem affects a large number of people (more than 1 million) and is life-threatening; and (2) collective action is taken by large organizations, interest groups, and statewide coalitions to alleviate the problem.

In this book, the contributors document the extensive efforts, demonstration projects, research, and recent legislation on behalf of battered women. We know that legislation aimed at resolving a social problem has the most potential for success if a major appropriation is attached to compliance with the legislation. For example, to receive federal funds from the Juvenile Justice and Delinquency Prevention Act of 1974, each state had to develop and implement a plan to deinstitutionalize all status offenders and neglected and abused youths from juvenile institutions and adult jails. A number of states complied with the mandate and monitored adult jails for many years afterward to make sure that juvenile status offenders were not confined with adult offenders.

Funding for domestic violence programs and services has utilized an incremental approach to building support year after year to ultimate passage of the Violence Against Women Act (VAWA) of 1994. This legislation included a $1.2 billion appropriation for fiscal years 1995–2000 (1) to improve the criminal justice response to violent crimes against women; (2) to expand services and community support for domestic violence victims; (3) to improve safety for women in public transit and public parks and assistance to victims of sexual assault; and (4) to provide support for a variety of educational, health, and database services (e.g., educating youth about domestic violence, developing national projections of injuries caused by domestic violence and recommended health care strategies, and improving the incorporation of data regarding stalking and domestic violence into local, state, and national crime information systems).

Although considerable progress has been made in funding domestic violence programs in the past 8 years, much remains to be done. There is still disproportionately less funding for victim assistance programs than for programs and institutions for convicted felons. For example, the Violent Crime Control and Law Enforcement Act of 1994 authorized nearly $9.9 billion for prisons and an additional $1.7 billion for alternative detention programs, whereas the VAWA of the 1994 crime bill authorized a total of only $1.2 billion over 5 years for criminal justice programs and social services to aid battered women and victims of sexual assault. However, the federal government did increase funding substantially with Congress's reauthorization of the VAWA in October 2000 and the authorization of $3.3 billion over 5 years for a continuum of community services to aid survivors of domestic violence, sexual assault, and stalking.

On the positive side, VAWA 2000 has created new targeted programs (e.g., grants to encourage arrests, judicial training, legal assistance for victims, transitional housing after short-term emergency shelter, emergency shelters and crisis intervention services in rural communities, and rape prevention and education programs) and significantly increased funding authorization levels for domestic violence and sexual assault intervention programs, with demonstrated results.

Federal grants for law enforcement agencies and prosecutors' offices to develop timely criminal justice system responses, domestic violence training for police and prosecutors, and integrated criminal justice programs with the community network of domestic violence services are known as Services and Training for Officers and Prosecutors (STOP) grants. Within the VAWA 2000 legislation, the STOP program encourages community-wide collaboration between specialized police-based domestic violence units, the city and county prosecutors' offices, victim-witness and victim service units, and battered women's shelters.

One of the primary limitations of VAWA 2000, which domestic violence advocates are addressing, is its decreased funding for the formula STOP grants as a result of Congress's decision to fund new specialized domestic violence and sexual assault programs and rapidly increase services to targeted underserved populations. In anticipation of further decreases in the 2002 fiscal year federal budget, domestic violence coalitions recently began campaigning for and advocating full funding of VAWA, including separate appropriations for STOP grants, which have been the cornerstone of VAWA from the beginning in 1994.

Later chapters will provide detailed discussions of innovative national and local police- and court-based programs, emergency shelters, crisis hotlines, and extensive networks of support groups, as well as national and statewide coalitions and how these criminal justice practitioners, social service providers, and advocacy groups were instrumental in improving responses to battered women. Chapter 19 provides information on the effectiveness of support groups for battered women. Starting in 1984 with the passage of the Victims of Crime Act (VOCA), the federal government has allocated millions of dollars through state and local agencies to support prosecutor-based victim-witness assistance for all victims of violent crimes, sexual assault demonstration projects, battered women's shelters, and court-based victim assistance. The VAWA, which was signed into law by President Clinton on September 13, 1994, provided an appropriation of $1.2 billion to improve and expand crisis services, criminal justice agency responses, housing, and community support programs for victims of domestic violence and sexual assault. Finally, a significant federal funding increase took place in October

2000 with the reauthorization of VAWA 2000, which provides an additional $3.3 billion funding over 5 years to aid battered women and their children.

The next chapter provides a detailed discussion of domestic violence theories and then applies each theory to a case illustration. Chapter 3 presents illustrations of critical incidents during childhood and adolescence, incidents that triggered victims' worst battering episodes, terroristic and death threats, the nature and extent of injuries, and suicide attempts among a representative sample of 105 imprisoned homicidal battered women and a matched community sample of 105 battered women.

REFERENCES

American Bar Association. (1994). *The impact of domestic violence on children*. Chicago: Author.

Astin, M. C., Lawrence, K., Pincus, G., & Foy, D. (1990, October). *Moderator variables for PTSD among battered women*. Paper presented at the convention of the International Society for Traumatic Stress Studies, New Orleans, LA.

Bachman, R. (1994). *Violence against women: A national crime victimization survey report*. Washington, DC: U.S. Department of Justice, Bureau of Justice Statistics.

Bureau of Justice Statistics (BJS). (1994). *Criminal victimization in the United States, 1992*. Washington, DC: U.S. Department of Justice, Bureau of Justice Statistics.

Davis, R. C., Taylor, B. G., & Maxwell, C. D. (2000, January). *Does batterer treatment reduce recidivism? A randomized experiment in Brooklyn*. New York: Victim Services. Unpublished report.

Edleson, J. L. (1996). Controversy and change in batterers' programs. In J. L. Edleson & Z. Eisikovits (Eds.) *Future interventions with battered women* (pp. 154–169). Thousand Oaks, CA: Sage.

Houskamp, B. M., and Foy, D. W. (1991). The assessment of post-traumatic stress disorder in battered women. *Journal of Interpersonal Violence, 6*, 367–375.

Jaffe, P. G., Wolfe, D. A., & Wilson, S. K. (1990). *Children of battered women*. Newbury Park, CA: Sage.

Kemp, A., Rawlings, E. I., & Green, B. L. (1991). Post-traumatic stress disorder (PTSD) in battered women: A shelter sample. *Journal of Traumatic Stress, 4*, 137–148.

Klingbeil, K., & Boyd, V. (1984). Detection and assessment of battered women in the emergency room. In A. R. Roberts (Ed.), *Battered women and their families: Intervention strategies and treatment programs* (pp. 7–32). New York: Springer.

Marlatt, G. A., & Rohsenow, D. J. (1980). Cognitive processes in alcohol use: Expectancy and the balanced placebo design. In Nancy K. Mello (Ed.), *Advances in substance abuse behavioral and biological research* (pp. 159–199). Greenwich, CT: JAI.

McLeer, S. V., & Anwar, R. (1989). A study of battered women presenting in an emergency department. *American Journal of Public Health, 79*, 65–66.

Monahan, K., & O'Leary, K. D. (1999). Head injury and battered women: An initial inquiry. *Health and Social Work, 24*, 269–278.

National Crime Surveys. (1981). *National sample, 1973–1979*. Ann

Arbor, MI: Inter-University Consortium on Political and Social Research, University of Michigan.

Pence, E., & Paymar, M. (1993). *Education groups for men who batter: The Duluth model*. New York: Springer.

Pleck, E. (1987). *Domestic tyranny*. New York: Oxford University Press.

Roberts, A. R. (1981). *Sheltering battered women*. New York: Springer.

Roberts, A. R. (1984). *Battered women and their families: Intervention strategies and treatment programs*. New York: Springer.

Roberts, A. R. (Ed.). (1990). *Crisis intervention handbook: Assessment, treatment and research*. Belmont, CA: Wadsworth.

Roberts, A. R. (1995). *Crisis intervention and time-limited cognitive treatment*. Thousand Oaks, CA: Sage.

Roberts, A. R. (2000). An overview of crisis theory and crisis intervention. In A. R. Roberts (Ed.), *Crisis intervention handbook: Assessment, treatment and research* (2nd ed., pp. 3–30). New York: Oxford University Press.

Sherman, L. W. (1992). *Policing domestic violence: Experiments and dilemmas*. New York: Free Press.

Straus, M., & Gelles, R. (1990). *Physical violence in American families*. New Brunswick, NJ: Transaction.

Tjaden, P., & Thoennes, N. (2000). *Extent, nature, and consequences of intimate partner violence*. Washington, DC: U.S. Department of Justice, U.S. Government Printing Office.

2

Domestic Violence Theories, Research, and Practice Implications

MARY P. BREWSTER

Violence against women has received unprecedented attention during the past decade. The first piece of federal legislation addressing intimate violence, the Violence Against Women Act (VAWA), was passed by Congress in 1994 and brought greater legal protection for abused women and stiffer penalties for batterers. Congress also increased funding for domestic violence research and for programs to protect women from domestic violence perpetrators. Media coverage of the VAWA has also increased public awareness of the issue of domestic violence.

Despite the increased acknowledgment of battering, ambiguity and contradiction abound with respect to definitions of domestic violence, statistics regarding the prevalence and incidence of the problem, explanations of domestic abuse, and research findings on battering. This chapter addresses each of these areas and discusses implications for programs and policies.[1]

DEFINITIONS OF DOMESTIC VIOLENCE

Definitions of domestic violence vary. Two areas of disagreement are described by Garner and Fagan (1997): "the nature of the acts that constitute 'violence' and the types of relationships that qualify as 'domestic'" (p. 54). Some definitions have been limited to acts that intend to cause physical harm to another (e.g., murder, rape, assault), while others have also included threats of physical harm and intimidation. Still others have expanded the

23

definition to include other acts of psychological or emotional aggression. In terms of the relationship necessary to constitute "domestic" violence, some definitions have been limited to male-on-female violence, and others have included female-on-male violence and violence among partners of the same gender. Some have considered domestic violence to include only that between married partners, although most recent definitions have included present and former marital and dating partners. The broadest definitions have included physical assault, threats, emotional abuse, verbal abuse, harassment, and humiliation by current or former intimate partners (see, e.g., Crowell & Burgess, 1996).

EXTENT OF THE PROBLEM OF DOMESTIC VIOLENCE

A number of researchers have attempted to measure the incidence and prevalence of domestic violence. Estimates have varied based on the definition of domestic violence and the methodological approach taken to measure such incidents. Attempts to measure the prevalence of domestic violence have included the National Family Violence Survey (Straus & Gelles, 1986), the National Crime Victimization Survey (NCVS; see Rennison & Welchans, 2000), and the National Violence Against Women Survey (Tjaden & Thoennes, 2000).

One popular measure of domestic violence, the Conflict Tactics Scale (CTS), was administered to a national sample of intact couples in the National Family Violence Surveys in 1975 and 1985. The CTS is a self-report instrument intended to measure various ways in which couples handle situations of disagreement. "Conflict tactics" include discussion, verbal and nonverbal hostility, and physical violence. The instrument includes specific items asking respondents the frequency with which various acts of physical violence (e.g., pushing, shoving, shooting, stabbing) had occurred within their current relationship. Sexual assault and stalking are not measured through this instrument. The National Family Violence Surveys have resulted in an annual estimate of one in six couples experiencing intimate partner violence (Straus & Gelles, 1986). Similarly, Schafer and Caetano (1998) used the CTS to survey a national sample of 1,635 couples. Their estimates of rates of intimate partner violence ranged from 7.84% to 21.48%. The lower estimate was based on violent incidents that both partners agreed had taken place. The higher estimate was based on violent incidents reported by at least one of the partners. Another telephone survey of a random sample of women in Georgia revealed a 6% rate of intimate partner violence during the past year and a 30% rate of women reporting having experienced intimate partner violence at any time during their past (Buehler, Dixon, & Toomey, 1998).

The NCVS definition of intimate partner violence includes murder, rape, sexual assault, robbery, aggravated assault, and simple assault committed by an intimate partner. The partner may be of the same or opposite sex (Rennison & Welchans, 2000). Data from this survey suggest that over 1 million violent offenses were committed by intimates or former intimates in 1998 (Rennison & Welchans, 2000). Most (about 85%) of the intimate partner violence involved a female victim. Over one fifth of violent crimes against women between 1993 and 1998 were committed by current or former intimate partners (Rennison & Welchans, 2000).

Perhaps the most accurate source of data regarding intimate partner violence to date is the National Violence Against Women Survey conducted by the National Institute of Justice and the Centers for Disease Control and Prevention. This telephone survey of a nationally representative sample of 16,000 men and women revealed a greater prevalence of intimate partner violence than earlier estimates. Based on the results of this survey, it has been estimated that about 1.5 million women and 830,000 men are victims of intimate violence each year in the United States. About 1.5% of the women surveyed reported having been physically assaulted and/or raped by a current or former intimate partner within the past year. About one quarter had been assaulted or raped by an intimate partner within their lifetime (Tjaden & Thoennes, 2000). In addition to measuring experiences of physical violence by intimate partners, the survey included questions pertaining to stalking. The results revealed that 1 percent of women were stalked during the year prior to the survey, and 8 percent of women had been stalked during their lives.

Between 1993 and 1998, the rates of lethal and nonlethal intimate violence have decreased (Rennison & Welchans, 2000). Some have attributed this decrease to the passage of the VAWA in 1994. Despite sources that report a decline in the number of female victims of intimate partner violence in recent years, the prevalence of domestic violence remains astoundingly high (Tjaden & Thoennes, 2000).

THEORIES OF BATTERING

Numerous and varied theories have been applied to battering. Generally, these fall into one of three categories: psychological, sociological, and feminist perspectives. Some of these theories address why men batter, others attempt to explain why women stay in abusive relationships, and some try to explain both phenomena.

Psychological Theories

A number of theorists and researchers have considered various psychological factors and their relation to battering. Psychological theories and perspectives of domestic violence have inferred that battering is the result of childhood experiences (e.g., being abused as child); personality traits (e.g., high need for power); personality disturbances (e.g., borderline personality disorder); head injury; psychopathology (e.g., antisocial personality disorder); or other psychological disorders or problems such as posttraumatic stress disorder, head injury, poor impulse control, poor self-esteem, or substance abuse (see, e.g., Dutton, 1994, 1995; Dutton & Starzomski, 1993; Hart, Dutton, & Newlove, 1993; Hamberger & Hastings, 1986, 1988; Hotaling, Straus, & Lincoln, 1989; Kantor & Straus, 1987; Rosenbaum et al., 1994; Simoneti, 2000).

Dutton and Starzomski (1993) studied borderline personality and anger among a group of 120 batterers. They found that men's scores on instruments used to measure borderline personality and anger were strongly correlated with their partner's or former partners' reports of psychological abuse and mildly correlated with physical abuse. In another study, diagnostic assessment of 840 men was conducted just prior to their participation in one of four batterer programs (Gondolf, 1999b). The findings indicated that about two fifths of the men exhibited narcissistic or antisocial personalities. These rates, however, represent much less pathology than earlier research findings had suggested.

Other researchers and writers have focused on domestic violence perpetrators' feelings of low personal control or desire to maintain or regain control as causes of battering (Campbell, 1993; Dutton, 1988; Stets, 1988, 1992). This theory is supported by evidence that battering worsens in situations of separation and divorce (Reiss & Roth, 1993), as illustrated by the experiences of Susan, a 39-year-old victim of domestic violence and stalking:

> As soon as I told him I was leaving, he totally lost it. He told me he'd kill me before he'd ever let me move out. And he practically did. I was a wreck when I finally managed to get separated from him. Then the stalking began. . . . Constant threatening phone calls, showing up at my door, showing up at my office—the separation made him worse, not better. (Author's files)

Sociological Theories

Sociological theories that have attempted to explain domestic violence include family systems theory, social learning theory, resource theory, and exchange theory. Proponents of the family systems model of intimate partner violence propose that all family members play a role in the "construction and maintenance of a system of violence and that violent behavior is transmitted from generation to generation" (O'Leary, 1993, p. 484 in Chornesky, 2000). According to this model, a battered partner remains in the abusive situation because of the system's resistance to change and need to maintain balance (Chornesky, 2000). The couple involved in domestic violence is caught in a cycle of violence. The following account by Mary, a 28-year-old battered woman, provides an example of how this cycle comes about:

> I can barely remember how it all started . . . and how it became sort of normal to us. He was soooo nice to me when we started dating. And he was so into me—he was very attentive, almost obsessed. The first time he hit me was after we became engaged. He was mad that I talked to some guy at a club we went to. It wasn't like I was interested in the guy—I didn't even know his name. It was completely innocent small talk. But it really set my husband—fiancé at the time—off at the time. He didn't hit me at the club. He took my arm and sort of forced me out of the club to the car. He gave me the silent treatment on the way home. As soon as we got to the apartment, though, he flipped out—yelling and screaming. And then when he hit me, I was shocked! I attributed it to the fact that he had been drinking, it wasn't really his fault. I *was* talking to the guy at the club. But I was also upset that he would hit me. He apologized after-ward—profusely! Said he'd never do it again. Never say never. After a while, it just became a pattern with us. (Author's files)

Another sociological theory that has been applied to battering is social learning theory, which is based on the premise that people learn behavior through watching others and modeling their behavior. If reinforcement oc-curs (i.e., the results of the behavior are positive), the behavior will continue. Based on this theory, those who observe violent behavior may imitate it in their own relationships. If the behavior results in desired effects (i.e., submis-sion by partner) without negative consequences (e.g., no legal action), it is likely to be repeated. The impact of social learning is highlighted by Tara, a 31-year-old victim of battering:

> His father had a history of hitting his wife. I'm sure that's where he picked up the behavior. His mother stayed with his father no matter how bad it got. It's like his parents were teaching him that beating your wife is a good way to get her to do whatever you want. His father never suffered any negative consequences as a result. His wife never left. What did he have to lose? He had complete control over his wife, and she did nothing to stop him. (Author's files)

Several scholars have written about the intergenerational transmission of family violence based on social learning theory. Research has suggested that those who witnessed marital violence in their families of origin are more likely to experience intimate partner violence themselves. Doumas and col-leagues, for example, found that males exposed to violence in their families of origin were more likely to become perpetrators of domestic violence, whereas females who observed violence in their families of origin were likely to be subjected to their partners' aggression (Doumas, Margolin, & John, 1994). Violence in one's family of origin has consistently been correlated with battering perpetration and victimization (Crowell & Burgess, 1996; Hotaling & Sugarman, 1986). Carol, a 35-year-old victim of domestic assault, describes how she followed in her mother's footsteps:

> It's strange how it worked out. My mother was abused by my father . . . physically and mentally. I hated him. I certainly never thought I would fall in love with someone who would do the same things to me. I literally turned into my mother. It makes me sick to think of how I let that happen to me. (Author's files)

Related to social learning theory is the subculture of violence theory, which holds that domestic abuse occurs more often in certain subcultures than in others. According to this theory, battering occurs in lower-class families more often than in middle-class families because violence is a more acceptable way to settle conflict in the lower-class subculture. Members of the lower class learn these norms within their subculture.

Resource theory and exchange theory are two other fairly popular sociological explanations of domestic violence. Resource theory is based on the assumption that force or the threat of force is inherent in all social systems. Those with greater resources (e.g., income, property, social contacts, prestige) have greater force or decision-making power. Men typically have the advantage of greater financial resources, resulting in their female partners being more vulnerable. On the other hand, those with few personal, economic, or social resources may resort to violence as a way to dominate or control others (Gelles, 1993). The first violent incident can permanently change the power dynamics in a relationship. Egalitarian relationships, on the other hand, are least likely to be characterized by violence. These ideas are related to feminist theory (described later). The following passage describes the experiences of 46-year-old Lori:

> Whenever he felt that I was likely to leave him, the beatings got worse. It was like he was threatened by potentially losing his power over me. He always had to be in complete control of me, us, our relationship. I had virtually no say in anything. When I dared to show any initiative, he felt threatened by it. This was especially true when I started a new job and tried to save some money so that I could move out and get away from him. When I finally left, he went nuts. He followed me everywhere, called me constantly, and assaulted me one day when I pulled into my driveway after work. (Author's files)

Exchange theory, on the other hand, draws on behavioral psychology and is based on costs and benefits (Homans, 1961). This theory, developed by sociologist George Homans, was intended to apply to all social interaction and can easily be applied to domestic violence situations. As in any exchange relationship, partners in an intimate relationship provide each other with services and/or benefits. Each partner continues to provide the other with desired affection, money, love, sex, and so forth, as long as the partner reciprocates with something that is as desirable (e.g., appreciation, praise, love). Over time, one partner may use force to get what he wants from the other. If he suffers no legal or other negative consequences, the violent partner perceives violence as a beneficial and effective tactic to get whatever he desires from his partner (Gelles, 1983). The partner not only has avoided punishment for his actions but also may be rewarded for his behavior through his partner's compliance. Similarly, abused women may comply with their partners' desires to avoid being beaten. According to exchange theory, behavior can be molded through rewards and punishments by others. Battered women may seek to avoid punishment (i.e., violence) by complying or staying in an abusive relationship to avoid possible death as threatened by her partner. If kindness is shown by her typically abusive partner, this, too, reinforces her behavior. The rare display of kindness becomes a valuable reinforcer to the abused woman, and she may be compliant in the hope of gaining that reward. Lynn, 36 years old, describes how her behavior was altered through her interactions with her boyfriend:

> Our relationship was fine at the beginning. We were both very much in love with one another. I respected him, and I thought he respected me. Sometimes, when I was short on cash, he'd help me pay my rent. I really appreciated his help. He seemed to like helping me. I tried to show him how much I loved and appreciated him in other ways. It really did seem like an ideal relationship at the beginning. Several months into the relationship, after I got pregnant and moved in with him, he hit me. I was shocked. He apologized for it, and for a very short time he was even nicer than he was before. I figured that he had just had a very stressful week at work or something, so I forgave him for it. When he did it again, I didn't know what to do. I couldn't afford to move out on my own, plus I was pregnant. I was very dependent on him. I started to really watch the way I behaved around him. I was real careful not to say anything that would set him off. I would compliment him, even if I didn't mean it. I'd have sex with him even though I didn't want to. Anything to avoid having him beat me. And when he was actually nice to me, that was a real bonus. After a while, I would do just about anything to get him to say something nice to me . . . to treat me the way he did before I got pregnant. (Author's files)

According to exchange theory, actors will behave in certain ways in anticipation of gaining desirable outcomes and avoiding undesirable outcomes. If an individual expects that violence will result in positive outcomes and will be unlikely to result in negative consequences, he will be more likely to use violence. For example, in a study of 1,965 eighth- and ninth-grade students, youths who had more positive outcome expectations and fewer negative outcome expectations of violence were more likely to have perpetrated violence on their partners (Foshee, Bauman, & Linder, 1999).

Feminist Theory

Feminist theory as applied to battering emphasizes the role of violence in maintaining control over a female intimate partner. This "violence" includes "physical violence, emotional abuse, sexual violence, social isolation, and withholding of financial resources" to "undermine a woman's autonomy and limit her power in the relationship" (Chalk & King, 1998, p. 37). Feminist theory also posits that the social structure supports social inequities that lead to the perpetuation of male dominance. This theory attempts "to explain partner abuse on the basis of traditional gender-role expectations and the historical imbalance of power between women and men in a patriarchal society" (Chornesky, 2000, p. 487). Because of this basis, Chornesky (2000) calls the feminist perspective a "sociological-structural" approach to understanding domestic violence. According to this perspective, the male perpetrator is to blame for the violence, and women are unlikely to leave because they "lack economic and political power." The influence of patriarchal ideas is evident in 26-year-old Cheryl's story of life with her husband:

> He would say that I was his wife and so I couldn't leave, couldn't go places where and when I wanted to go. Since I married him, I had to be there for him. He decided where we'd go, who we'd hang out with, what I wore, what we bought. The fact that I worked part-time didn't matter. He took my paycheck and paid the bills, wouldn't give me a dime to spend on myself. He thought he owned me . . . I guess he did own me. (Author's files)

Many theorists have considered the role of the power differential in the patriarchal structure as a factor that encourages and enables domestic violence. However, control plays a large role on its own in the "generation of violence," as suggested by Johnson and Ferraro (2000). Power and control are important factors in understanding intimate partner violence regardless of the patriarchal structure of society. For example, violence may be used as a form of control within same-sex intimate relationships.

THEORIES OF WHY WOMEN STAY IN DOMESTIC VIOLENCE SITUATIONS

While some theories attempt to explain the batterer's behavior, others have focused on the behavior of the victim. The question of why women stay in abusive relationships—a response that seems illogical—has been posed by many researchers. Psychological theories that have tried to explain why women remain in abusive relationships have suggested that any of several factors may be responsible, including self-blame, denial, loyalty to the sanctity of marriage, and feeling responsible for helping the batterer (see, e.g., Ferraro & Johnson, 1983; Follingstad, Neckerman, & Vormbrock, 1988; Gondolf & Fisher, 1988). Six of the theories used to explain this seemingly irrational behavior are described here: the cycle of violence, learned helplessness, the battered woman syndrome, the Stockholm syndrome, traumatic bonding theory, and psychological entrapment theory.

1 . **Cycle of Violence**

According to Lenore Walker's cycle of violence model, there are three critical phases in the cycle or pattern of abuse: the tension-building phase, the acute battering incident phase, and the honeymoon phase (Walker, 1979). During the tension-building phase, there may be minor physical battering and verbal abuse. The woman often attempts to "placate" her partner, though rarely successfully. This phase is followed by the acute battering phase, during which the man's physical violence escalates and the woman is unable to placate him. Following this extremely violent phase comes the honeymoon phase, during which the man shows remorse toward the victim, attempts to convince his partner of his love for her, and promises that he will not hurt her again. Often he will give her gifts and pay a great deal of attention to her and her needs. The woman is convinced that the man she "sees" during this phase is the one she loves, and she typically remains in the relationship. She convinces herself that the honeymoon phase can last. And the cycle continues. Cloe, a 40-year-old battered woman, describes the cycle of violence in which she was caught:

> I could tell when he was gonna hurt me. At first, it was mostly verbal. He would say things just to hurt me . . . with no basis. It's like he wanted me to feel bad. He would nitpick . . . there was something wrong with my cooking, the laundry wasn't finished, I had left the car door unlocked . . . stupid things, really. So I would try to cook better or finish the laundry before he got home. But nothing was good enough. He *wanted* to be angry at me. Then something stupid would set him off. It could be some guy looking at me at the mall. He'd say I must have looked at the guy first. Or one time he was mad because a bill had slipped behind the breadbox in the kitchen. I didn't know it was there, so it wasn't paid. When we got a late notice, he flipped out and blamed me. That time, he gave me a black eye. I missed work for a few days. . . . But every time he'd hit me, he'd be real apologetic afterward. Apologetic and loving. It's like all the things that attracted me to him in the first place came flooding back. He was thoughtful and kind, affectionate, loving . . . the man I fell in love with. I know I must seem like an idiot for falling for this over and over again, but he had me convinced each time that there was a chance he would really stop . . . that it was really the last time he'd hit me. (Author's files)

2 . **Learned Helplessness**

The theory of learned helplessness was based on research initially conducted with dogs. Martin Seligman, a psychologist, placed dogs in cages and administered random shocks to them. Like most domestic violence, the shocks were not based on the dogs' behavior in any way. The dogs tried to escape from the cages and tried to avoid the shocks, but nothing worked. Eventually, they stopped trying, since their attempts were repeatedly unsuccessful. Even when the researchers tried to teach the dogs to escape, the dogs were hesitant. It wasn't until repeated efforts were made by the researchers (e.g., dragging the dogs to their escape) that the dogs finally learned to escape to avoid the shocks. One important aspect of this theory is that even when it was apparent that the dogs could escape, they did not do so because of the learned helplessness. They had reached a point where they perceived that nothing they did would help them to alleviate the shocks. Similarly, outsiders often fail to understand why abused women do not simply leave their relationships. The battered woman's perception of her own control over her situation has a great deal to do with it. Even if she were able to escape, if she *believes* that she cannot leave or cannot survive on her own, she will not leave (Walker, 1978, 1979, 1989). Learned helplessness is apparent in the experiences of 34-year-old Mary:

> I've tried to figure out why it took me 9 years to leave him. He treated me like crap. I wanted to leave so many times. Early on, I almost did. But at some point, I sort of just gave up. He had beaten me down physically and emotionally. . . . I just couldn't even try to stop him or get away from him anymore. I know it sounds crazy, but I felt like I had to stay . . . there was no way out. (Author's files)

3. Battered Woman Syndrome

Related to learned helplessness and the cycle of violence is the concept of the battered woman syndrome. Lenore Walker (1979) theorized that some women remained in physically, sexually, or psychologically abusive relationships because of extreme fear and the belief that there is no escape. The victim also feels as though she has no choice but to remain with her abusive partner. This syndrome develops over time, as the cycle of violence occurs and the woman loses hope and feels unable to deal effectively with her situation. An example of "battered woman syndrome" was clear in an interview with 40-year-old Denise, who was battered for over 10 years:

> It was damned if you do, damned if you don't. I knew he'd hurt me if I stayed, but I felt as though I couldn't leave because he would probably do much worse to me . . . even kill me. I tried to do things so that he wouldn't hurt me, but nothing I did made much of a difference. If he was gonna beat me, he was gonna beat me. Finally, I just stopped trying. I realized that I had no control over the situation. I couldn't stop the beatings from happening. It would happen and then it was over. Then it would happen again. I just stayed and took it for 10½ years. (Author's files)

4 - ## Stockholm Syndrome

Another theory of why women remain in relationships with their batterers is based on the Stockholm syndrome or hostage syndrome. Theorists have argued that battered women are analogous to hostages because of the physical and psychological threats made by the perpetrator. Such women feel as though there is no way out of this situation in which their intimate partners are in complete control. However, the battered woman experiences occasional kindness and support from her partner and, as a result of her isolation from outsiders, develops a bond with her captor (Graham & Rawlings, 1991). Her survival depends on her partner, as evidenced by the story of 36-year-old Shannon:

> He was very controlling, but I knew he loved me. At first, I was flattered by his obsessiveness. He wanted to be with me all the time. But eventually it became him completely controlling my life. He wouldn't let me get a job. I wasn't allowed to go out during the day while he was at work. He did the banking and all the errands. I was allowed to go once in a while. I was prohibited from using the phone unless I was supervised by him. I was lucky if he'd let me call for pizza. I never saw my friends. My family lives on the West Coast, so they weren't around either. Whenever my mother called, he said I wasn't home. I was sitting right there, but he wouldn't let me speak to her. She finally hardly ever even tried to call anymore. I couldn't really blame her. So he was all I had. . . . And he decided when we'd eat, what we'd eat, how much I would get to eat. . . . But he was my life, he was all I had. Somehow I managed to overlook the beatings and the verbal abuse. I never stopped loving him no matter what he did. I lived for those rare occasions when he treated me okay. (Author's files)

5. ## Traumatic Bonding Theory

Some theorists have blamed domestic violence on intimate emotional bonding and unhealthy attachment (Bowlby, 1988; Dutton & Painter, 1993). Bowlby (1988) posits that sometimes partners have strong, but unhealthy, attachments to one another based on anxiousness and fear of abandonment. Each partner creates ways to control the other or to avoid being abandoned. In some cases, this includes violence. In addition, there is some evidence that women who had unhealthy attachments to their parents when they were younger (as a result of abuse or neglect) are more likely to develop unhealthy attachment styles as adults. Women who have secure attachment styles are less likely than those with anxious attachment styles to perpetrate or experience emotional abuse (O'Hearn & Davis, 1997). Holtzworth-Munroe, Stuart, and Hutchinson (1997) found that physically abusive male partners were more likely than nonviolent men to have unhealthy attachment styles.

Traumatic bonding between partners may explain why abused women stay with, or return to, their abusive partners. Dutton and Painter (1993) argue that abusive relationships have the characteristics necessary for traumatic bonding—strong emotional ties and intermittent abuse. After being physically or emotionally assaulted, the victim is in need of affection and is open to the claims of remorse and love made by her partner. The intermittent abuse resulted in vulnerability and the victim's need for positive treatment by her partner. The kindness shown by her partner following an incident of abuse, however, reinforces her emotional bond to him. Jana, 44 years old, describes her unhealthy bond to her ex-husband:

> I really did love him. And I believe that he loved me even though he'd hit me a lot. I was very attached to him. When I look back on it, I know it wasn't a healthy relationship. But after he'd beat the crap out of me, I was so desperate for love that I willingly believed his remorse and promises not to do it again. And, for a short time, we'd be back to being a normal, fairly loving couple. But the good times between the beatings got shorter and shorter, and the beatings got worse and worse. (Author's files)

6.
Psychological Entrapment Theory

The theory of psychological entrapment implies that a woman is unable to exit an abusive relationship because she has invested time, energy, and emotion toward achieving the goal of a nonviolent intimate relationship. Although the abuse continues, the woman may feel as though she has too much invested to give up. Morgan, 44 years old, provides the following example of psychological entrapment:

> I had spent most of my adult life with him. How could I just leave it all behind? Granted, things weren't pretty. But I had put so much into that relationship. I desperately wanted it to work out. (Author's files)

MULTIFACTOR ECOLOGICAL PERSPECTIVE

While a number of theorists have attempted to explain why men batter and why battered women remain in an abusive relationship, no single-factor theory has effectively explained the phenomenon. For this reason, an integrated, "multifactor model" may be the best approach to understanding the complexities of domestic violence (see, e.g., Crowell & Burgess, 1996; Heise, 1998). This popular approach, called the *ecological perspective*, draws upon a number of earlier theories described previously. It grew out of Carel Germain and Alex Gitterman's Life Model, a social work perspective that views "human needs and problems [as] generated by the transactions between people and their environments" (Germain & Gitterman, 1980, p. 1). It "recognizes that people's actions are determined by a variety of factors located within themselves, in their families of origin and procreation, in the social structure, and in the larger sociocultural environment" (Carlson, 1997, p. 292). Theorists who advocate this approach believe that abusive situations may be the result of the interaction among personal, situational, social, political, and cultural factors (see, e.g., Heise, 1998; Perilla, 1999).

Lori Heise (1998) argues that the results of the extant research on domestic violence support an ecological model composed of four levels: personal history, the microsystem, the exosystem, and the macrosystem. A number of researchers have attempted to identify individual-level, or personal, factors that distinguish batterers from nonbatterers, and battered women from non-abused women. In reviewing the research, Heise identifies three consistent risk factors: having witnessed marital violence as a child, having been physically or sexually abused as a child, and growing up without a consistent father figure. For example, violence in one's family of origin and childhood sexual abuse have both been found to be significantly correlated with domestic violence during one's lifetime (Cohen et al., 2000; Kantor & Jasinski, 1998). In a study of 47 batterers receiving treatment, Simoneti (2000) found that a history of childhood abuse was related to dissociative experiences, which in turn were related to domestic violence perpetration. Additionally, violence committed by those experiencing dissociative symptoms was more frequent and severe.

The microsystem is made up of the situational factors surrounding the abuse. Situational risk factors that have emerged in the research include male dominance in decision making in the relationship, male economic control in the relationship, marital conflict, and alcohol use. For example, in a longitudinal study of newlywed couples in Buffalo, New York, researchers found that alcohol was correlated with, and predictive of, the frequency of intimate partner violence (Leonard, 1999). The relationship between drinking and aggression was strongest for those couples who reported high levels of verbal aggression in conflict situations. According to Chornesky (2000), drugs and alcohol are disinhibitors in cases in which men are enraged, and their use may result in violence toward their partners (see also Brookoff, O'Brien, Cook, Thompson, & Williams, 1997).

Exosystem factors are factors within the formal and informal social structures and institutions that impact the situation. In her review of the literature, Heise identifies unemployment/low socioeconomic status (SES), social isolation, and "delinquent peer association" as factors that have been correlated with domestic violence. For example, a telephone survey of a random sample of 3,130 women in Georgia indicated that low SES increases the risk of intimate partner violence. Those in the lowest income bracket (under $20,000) were nine times more likely to have experienced intimate partner violence than those in the highest income category (over $50,000; Buehler, Dixon, & Toomey, 1998). Social isolation, or having limited contact with family and friends, has also been correlated with domestic abuse. Delinquent peer associations, or attachment to others who legitimize violence against women, is another consistent predictor of battering (see Heise, 1998).

The macrosystem, according to Heise (1998), is the "broad set of cultural values and beliefs that permeate and inform the other three layers of the social ecology." Important macrosystem factors include a definition of manhood that includes dominance and aggression, "adherence to" traditional gender roles, "sense of male entitlement/ownership over women," approval of "physical punishment of women," and cultural support for the use of violence in settling interpersonal conflicts.

Although Heise identifies the key risk factors most consistently found in the domestic violence research, the interplay among these factors is believed to be complex. Not every adult male who was abused as a child becomes an abusive partner, and not every batterer was abused as a child. Not all low-income families experience domestic violence, and middle- and upper-class families are not exempt from this problem. The complex interaction among factors in the ecological model is more valuable in trying to explain domestic violence than any single factor in isolation.

The value of the ecological approach to understanding domestic violence lies in its recognition that many factors contribute in varying degrees to domestic violence, and that the interaction between factors is of even greater importance. The ecological model has important implications in terms of treatment programs for batterers and victims. A simplistic program will not solve the problem; rather, a multipronged approach addressing the various "levels" of the ecological model is called for.

EMPIRICAL RESEARCH RESULTS ON DOMESTIC VIOLENCE

In addition to the research related to the prevalence of domestic violence and the theories of abuse described previously (i.e., risk factors), research on domestic violence has also focused on other areas, including the consequences or effects of domestic violence, the effectiveness of treatment programs for batterers and victims, and the nature of stalking by intimate partners.

Effects of Battering

Battering results in both short- and long-term effects—including physical, psychological, financial, and social difficulties—for victims, their children, and other associates. Typical psychological effects include "posttraumatic stress disorder, depression, and lowered self-esteem" (Johnson & Ferraro, 2000, p. 957). Particular attention has been paid to posttraumatic stress disorder (PTSD) among battered women. Symptoms of PTSD include "persistent intrusive and distressing recollections of the traumatic event in dreams or flashbacks," "persistent avoidance of stimuli associated with the trauma," and "persistent symptoms of increased arousal" (Baldinger & Nelson, 1995, p. 56). While the prevalence has varied from one study to the next, the prevalence of PTSD among abused women is substantial (typically over 45%, sometimes as high as 84%). The samples on which these estimates are based, however, consisted of women from shelters, mental health clinics, and hospitals (see, e.g., Astin, Ogland-Hand, & Coleman, 1995; Saunders, 1994.) Lower rates may exist among women who have not yet sought help from such agencies. The effects of domestic assault on 38-year-old Joann are typical of many battered women:

> It's terrifying. I haven't had contact with him in over a year, yet I still have trouble sleeping and I still have anxiety attacks. Some nights I dream that I'm still married to him and he's hitting me and I wake up sweating. . . . I'm soaked . . . and terrified. I also have had problems with my boyfriend sometimes. . . . My boyfriend jokingly went to throw something at me in the kitchen the other day, and I lifted my hands up in front of my face and just froze. It was just a crumpled piece of paper, and he didn't even throw it. He just acted like he was going to. But I responded like I did when [my ex-husband] would throw something at me or hit me. (Author's files)

One research study involving interviews with a national sample of over 10,000 people revealed that women who are battered have a lessened sense of personal control as a result (Umberson, Anderson, Glick, & Shapiro, 1998). In another study of women using domestic violence shelters, McNamara and Brooker (2000) found that battering resulted in a wide range of impairments to victims, especially in terms of relationship disability and life restrictions.

Several researchers have examined the effects of battering on the abused woman's parenting style. The results of this body of research are inconclusive. Some findings indicate that battered women report being less nurturing and less effective as parents than nonabused women, while other research results suggest that battered women perform as well as nonbattered women as mothers (Levendosky, 2000). In interviews with battered women, Levendosky found that most women believed that the abuse had had an effect on their parenting. Women in the sample reported both negative impacts (e.g., inability to set limits, impatience, anger) and positive impacts (e.g., greater empathy, increased protectiveness) of their victimization on their parenting. The following account illustrates how Ann, 39 years old, improved her parenting approach:

> In some ways, this whole situation has made me a better parent. The meaner he became, the closer I was to my children. They were protective of me, and I was definitely more protective of them. I tried to make the

good times—when he wasn't hurting us—mean a lot. I tried to spend quality time with them as much as possible. We would sit and watch videos together or play board games. I guess sometimes I'm not strict enough with them. [Their father] yelled and screamed enough to last a lifetime. I sort of felt like I should try not to yell to make up for it. (Author's files)

A great deal of research has examined the impact of exposure to domestic violence on children. Research findings reveal consequences such as acting out aggressively, anxiety, sleep disorders, guilt, low self-esteem, and withdrawal (see, e.g., Carlson, 1996; Hughes, 1988; Jaffe, Wolfe, & Wilson, 1990).

Treatment Programs for Victims and Batterers

Crisis theory (Burgess & Holmstrom, 1978) offers an important perspective on domestic abuse and appropriate intervention programs. According to this theory, an event may occur that is beyond a person's normal coping abilities. An example might be an incident of physical violence committed by one's intimate partner, resulting in extreme psychological distress. The individual will try to deal with the distress through adaptive or maladaptive coping strategies (e.g., substance abuse). Generally, this "coping" will occur within 6 weeks of the crisis (Resick & Nishith, 1997). Interventions with victims of domestic violence should initially focus on the crisis at hand, so that the victim is assisted in developing adaptive, or healthy, coping strategies. Crises, or the failure to cope, may be viewed as the result of a combination of overwhelming events and internal responses (Roberts, 1990). Crisis intervention, then, should approach both the management of the external events or situation and the individual's ability to cope with it. Dwyer and colleagues identify several ways in which battered women may access crisis intervention, including "hotline programs, police crisis team programs, and hospital emergency room programs" (Dwyer, Smokowski, Bricout, & Wodarski, 1996, p. 77). They also stress the importance of special training of those who will deal with battered women so that their approach is sensitive, immediate, and effective.

One model of crisis intervention that is well suited to dealing with domestic violence situations is the seven-step model developed by Albert Roberts (2000). This model recommends taking the following steps, which are believed to be effective in helping individuals in crisis:

1. Plan and conduct a thorough assessment (including lethality, dangerousness to self or others, and immediate psychosocial needs).
2. Make psychological contact, establish rapport, and rapidly establish the relationship (conveying genuine respect for the client, acceptance, reassurance, and a nonjudgmental attitude).

3. Examine the dimensions of the problem in order to define it (including the last straw or precipitating event).
4. Encourage an exploration of feelings and emotions.
5. Generate, explore, and assess past coping attempts.
6. Restore cognitive functioning through implementation of action plan.
7. Follow up and leave the door open for booster sessions 3 and/or 6 months later. (pp. 15–16)

In applying Roberts's model to victims of domestic violence, crisis intervenors must first determine whether the victim is in imminent danger, as is often the case among battered women who seek outside help. Roberts (2000) provides an example of a case in which the daughter of a battered woman calls a domestic violence hotline to report violence perpetrated on her mother by her mother's live-in boyfriend:

> An emergency call was received at 8:00 one morning from Jasmine, the 15-year-old daughter of Serita, who begged the crisis worker to help her mom, frantically explaining, "My mom's live-in boyfriend is going to kill her." The crisis worker reported that the daughter described previous incidents of violence perpetrated by the boyfriend. Jasmine described a serious argument that had erupted at 6:00 that morning, with loud yelling from the boyfriend, who threatened to kill Serita with the gun he had recently obtained, while pointing it directly at her. (p. 26)

Knowing that Jasmine's mother, Serita, was in imminent danger, the crisis hotline worker developed rapport with the girl and gathered additional information about the situation and her mother's whereabouts. The crisis intervenor was able to contact Jasmine's mother at a neighbor's apartment and assist Jasmine and her mother in coordinating an immediate response to the situation. The crisis worker arranged transportation for the mother and daughter to Georgia, where they were able to stay with Serita's sister until Section 8 housing arrangements were made. The case example illustrates how crisis intervention may take several hours to stabilize a situation.

Beyond assisting victims of battering in escaping immediate danger, crisis workers should also provide help to the victim in terms of exploring the roots of the crisis and developing adaptive coping skills for the future. Roberts's model advocates focusing on the client's strengths as a positive way of developing new coping techniques. This strength-based model of "crisis intervention utilizes empowerment, resilience, healing and wholeness, collaboration, and suspension of disbelief" (Roberts & Roberts, 2000, p. 184).

The theories and research results reviewed earlier have provided the basis for many interventions designed to help battered women. Some of these programs are designed for battered women, while others attempt to alter the behavior of the perpetrators. Others have integrated services for both perpetrators and victims.

There is a growing awareness among therapists who work with battered women and their abusers that it is not sufficient to rely exclusively on one theoretical orientation. An openness to a range of explanations for understanding violence in relationships and the use of multiple lenses to examine the phenomenon are valuable and congruent with feminist principles and concerns for justice and safety. (Chornesky, 2000, p. 499)

The research just described that highlights the effects of battering on women and their children clearly makes the case for a comprehensive response to domestic violence. Such a response should include crisis intervention (including shelter and other protective services), as well as transitional programs and long-term treatment (e.g., housing assistance, vocational training, child care, transportation, psychological counseling for women and children, drug and alcohol treatment). The understanding that batterers' and victims' behavior is the result of individual characteristics, family background, social structural factors, and societal cultural factors calls for interventions that take a multipronged approach (see Carlson, 1984). The extensive and varied effects of battering on women and children underscore the need for a coordinated system that includes legal, mental health, physical health, and financial (housing, education, vocational training, child care, etc.) services.

One example of such a comprehensive program is the House of Ruth, which opened in 1977 as a shelter for battered women in Baltimore. The program has evolved over the years and now includes "emergency and transitional shelter, community outreach, counseling and legal assistance to battered women and their children, peer support, an abuser intervention program, a hotline, community education, and advocacy" (Campbell, Dienemann, Kub, Wurmser, & Loy, 1999, p. 1144). This type of program attempts to meet the needs of battered women, batterers, and their children, with the hope that the combined impact of these services will provide a greater chance of reducing the domestic abuse problem than any single service in isolation.

Not all programs for battered women are as clear in their approach as the House of Ruth. In a national survey designed to assess the types of treatment strategies and practice models used in battered women's shelters, Roberts and Burman (1998) found that most of the 87 program directors surveyed were unable to answer a question requesting such information. Of those who did respond, the most frequently cited technique was to review options with the victim and refer her to a support group ($n = 28$). Other approaches were "explore and validate feelings" ($n = 19$), "assess immediate needs of clients" ($n = 15$), "work with client to plan and formulate goals" ($n = 14$), and "short-term crisis intervention" ($n = 12$). The least common responses were "active listening" ($n = 9$), "problem-solving method" ($n = 8$), and "referral to community resources and private practitioner" ($n = 8$) (Roberts & Burman, 1998, pp. 9–10). Roberts and Burman suggest a combination of "crisis intervention [as described earlier] and cognitively oriented problem solving" (p. 5). They suggest that crisis intervention will assist in reestablishing equilibrium, while cognitively oriented problem solving will "reinforce the prolonged acquisition and internalization of survival and actualization skills" (Roberts & Burman, 1998, pp. 20–21).

Although numerous programs for battered women exist, few have been evaluated, and those evaluations that *have* been conducted have generally been weak methodologically. Evaluations that have been carried out to assess the effectiveness of treatment programs for battered women have typically relied on small samples, lacked a control group, and been based on a weak overall research design. In addition, findings from these program evaluations have revealed mixed results (Abel, 2000). In a review of evaluations of psychosocial interventions with battered women, Abel described the research designs and outcomes for assessments of shelter services, group intervention, shelter-based advocacy services, support groups, and brief counseling. While some evaluations emphasized positive results, Abel argued that the weak methodological designs reduced confidence in the results. Abel noted that group work was the most common approach in the battered women's programs that had been evaluated. The programs included in her review had various theoretical bases, and some evidence suggested that a combination of grief resolution and feminist counseling might provide effective treatment to battered women.

Numerous programs also exist to prevent recidivism among batterers. Some programs are court-mandated, whereas others are voluntary. Existing programs vary in approach, although many involve group treatment focusing on anger management. In group treatment, men typically share their experiences with one another; these programs often also include role-playing and instruction regarding anger management, conflict resolution, and the development of other interpersonal skills (see, e.g., Decker, 1999; Pence & Paymar, 1993). Some programs for batterers offer limited services and rely on making referrals for offender problems such as substance abuse or mental health issues. Others are more comprehensive and include individual and group counseling, substance abuse treatment, mental health treatment, and services for battered women (see Gondolf, 2000a).

As is the case with victim treatment programs, few batterer treatment programs have been thoroughly evaluated, and the evaluations that have been conducted reveal mixed results. One recent large-scale study of 840 batterers who underwent batterer treatment in one of four cities revealed that nearly half of the men who do reassault their partners do so within a relatively short period (i.e., 3 months). The research results also indicated that batterers who received court-ordered treatment had lower recidivism rates than voluntary participants and program dropouts (Gondolf, 1997, 1999a). In a separate study, Gondolf (2000c) found that court review (i.e., monitoring) improves the rate of completion in batterer programs.

In one study, 443 men who had participated in batterer treatment programs were asked how they avoided reassaulting their partners (Gondolf, 2000b). Most (53%) reported using "interruption methods" such as leaving the room, taking a "time-out," or stopping to think before acting. Fewer batterers relied on discussion (19%) or "respect of women" (5%) to avoid using violence against their partners.

Stalking by Intimate Partners

In recent years, definitions of domestic violence have often incorporated stalking behaviors such as following and harassing former intimate partners (e.g., Tjaden & Thoennes, 2000). In addition to the estimates of the prevalence and incidence of stalking based on the National Violence Against Women Survey, a growing body of research has explored the nature of stalking victimization and offending (see, e.g., Fremouw, Westrup, & Pennypacker, 1997; Hall, 1997; Meloy, 1998; Pathe & Mullen, 1997). Stalking can be defined as repeated harassment, following, and/or threats that are committed with the intent of causing the victim emotional distress, fear of bodily harm, and/or actual bodily harm. This author (Brewster, 1998) conducted in-depth semistructured interviews with a convenience sample of 187 female victims of stalking by former intimate partners. Content analysis of the interview transcripts revealed a great deal about women's domestic violence and stalking experiences. Nearly two thirds of the women had been physically abused during their prior relationship with their stalker. Following their escape from the relationship, the victims reported various disturbing behaviors such as phone calls (90% of respondents), watching (79% of respondents), and following (68% of respondents) (Brewster, 1998). Nearly three quarters of the women reported that their stalkers had made threats of violence against them, and 46% reported actual physical assaults during the stalking. Trish, a 40-year-old stalking victim, described her stalker's fairly typical behaviors:

> I went to my grandmom's and lived with her for a while. He would be parked outside of her house and be calling me up at work and threatening to kill me. "You can't leave me. I won't let you leave me. I'll kill you." And then I got my own apartment and the same thing—he'd be parked outside or follow me around. One time my friend and I were on our way to my mother's house, and he was trying to run me off the road. I had to finally get a restraining order. (Author's files)

Most legal and extralegal approaches taken by the stalking victims to discourage their stalkers were reportedly ineffective. Stephanie, aged 23, describes her frustrations with trying to deter her stalker:

> I tried everything, but nothing worked. I couldn't get rid of him. He wouldn't leave me alone. I called the police, but they said they couldn't do anything unless they caught him trespassing or something. I tried to get a restraining order but couldn't because he hadn't assaulted me yet. I called

the DA's office, and they didn't even return my calls. I changed my phone number, and he started calling me at work instead. It was crazy. I had to physically move, change jobs, start a new life to get rid of the guy. (Author's files)

Victims reported numerous and serious psychological, physical, financial, and quality-of-life consequences of the stalking. Some of these were described by 33-year-old Sarah:

What effect did the stalking have on me?! Let's see . . . where should I begin? Stress . . . lots of stress. I feel nauseous just thinking about him. I still am startled when the phone rings. I constantly look over my shoulder. I had to get a PO box so that he couldn't steal my mail anymore. I have more deadbolts on my door than someone living in North Philly. I never go out alone after dark anymore. My friends have to pick me up at my house, otherwise I won't go anywhere. Talk about a crimp in your social life. I also lost my job because he kept showing up and was so disruptive. I ended up taking a lower-paying job. I could go on and on, if you'd like. (Author's files)

IMPLICATIONS FOR THE FUTURE

The recognition that multiple factors contribute to the problem of domestic violence has led to arguments for a multipronged approach in dealing with the problem. For example, Hage (2000) argues for prevention programs to stop violence before it ever occurs, early intervention for those at risk, treatment for perpetrators and victims, and institutional, community, and governmental programs and policies that "promote healthy relationships." Programs should emphasize treating the batterer, empowering the victim to consider choices, and treating children to minimize passing on violent tendencies to the next generation. As these programs continue to develop, evaluation plans should be put into place to assess their effectiveness in empowering women and preventing battering. The challenge for researchers will be to identify which programs, parts of programs, and/or combinations of services provide the most effective approaches for dealing with victims, batterers, and their children.

In addition to comprehensive treatment services for battered women, legislation that assists victims to survive outside of an abusive relationship should help them overcome some of the traditional obstacles. For example, the VAWA provided greater legal protection for women. Another piece of legislation that has assisted battered women is the Family Violence Option (FVO), which Congress added "to the 1996 welfare reform legislation. The FVO allows the states to exempt violence victims temporarily from federal work requirements while they receive services to eliminate violence in their lives" (Raphael, 1999, p. 449). Raphael argues that while the FVO is a good idea, ongoing monitoring and evaluation are needed to determine its effectiveness.

In light of the theories and research presented here, much can be done to address the problem of intimate partner violence. A combination of educational prevention programs, crisis intervention approaches, long-term treatment for victims and batterers, and institutional changes that both reduce intimate partner violence and empower victims to overcome abusive relationships is an appropriate, multifaceted approach to helping battered women.

NOTE

1. Despite the fact that men may be victims of domestic violence, this chapter will focus predominantly on women because they are typically the victims in these situations.

REFERENCES

Abel, E. M. (2000). Psychosocial treatments for battered women: A review of empirical research. *Research on Social Work Practice, 10,* 55–77.

Astin, M. C., Ogland-Hand, S. M., & Coleman, E. M. (1995). Posttraumatic stress disorder and childhood abuse in battered women: Comparisons with maritally distressed women. *Journal of Consulting and Clinical Psychology, 63,* 308–312.

Baldinger, B. G., & Nelson, D. T. (1995, February). Crime victims and psychological injuries. *Trial,* 56–64.

Bowlby, J. (1988). *A secure base: Parent-child attachment and healthy human development.* New York: Basic Books.

Brewster, M. (1998). *An exploration of the experiences and needs of former intimate stalking victims.* Final report submitted to the National Institute of Justice.

Brookoff, D., O'Brien, K. K., Cook, C. S., Thompson, T. D., & Williams, C. (1997). Characteristics of participants in domestic violence: Assessment at the scene of domestic assault. *Journal of the American Medical Association, 277,* 1369–1373.

Buehler, J., Dixon, B., & Toomey, K. (1998). Lifetime and annual incidence of intimate partner violence and resulting injuries—Georgia, 1995. *MMWR: Morbidity and Mortality Weekly Report, 47,* 849–853.

Burgess, A. W., & Holmstrom, L. L. (1978). Recovery from rape and prior life stress. *Research in Nursing and Health, 1,* 165–174.

Campbell, A. (1993). *Men, women, and aggression.* New York: Basic Books.

Campbell, J. C., Dienemann, J., Kub, J., Wurmser, T., & Loy, E. (1999). Collaboration as a partnership. *Violence Against Women, 5,* 1140–1157.

Carlson, B. (1984). Causes and maintenance of domestic violence. *Social Service Review, 58,* 569–587.

Carlson, B. (1996). Children of battered women: Research, programs, and services. In A. Roberts (Ed.), *Helping battered women* (pp. 172–187). New York: Oxford University Press.

Carlson, B. (1997). A stress and coping approach to intervention with abused women. *Family Relations, 46,* 291–298.

Chalk, R., & King, P. A. (1998). *Violence in families: Assessing prevention and treatment programs.* Washington, DC: National Academy Press.

Chornesky, A. (2000). The dynamics of battering revisited. *Affilia: Journal of Women and Social Work, 15,* 480–501.

Cohen, M., Deamant, C., Barkan, S., Richardson, J., Young, M., Holman, S., Anastos, K., Cohen, J., & Melnick, S. (2000). Domestic violence and childhood sexual abuse in HIV-infected women and women at risk for HIV. *American Journal of Public Health, 90,* 560–565.

Crowell, N. A., & Burgess, A. W. (1996). *Understanding violence against women.* Washington, DC: National Academy Press.

Decker, D. (1999). *Stopping the violence: A group model to change men's abusive attitudes and behaviors.* New York: Haworth.

Doumas, D., Margolin, G., & John, R. S. (1994). The intergenerational transmission of aggression across three generations. *Journal of Family Violence, 9,* 157–175.

Dutton, D. G. (1988). *The domestic assault of women: Psychological and criminal justice perspectives.* Boston: Allyn and Bacon.

Dutton, D. G. (1994). The origin and structure of the abusive personality. *Journal of Personality Disorders, 8,* 181–191.

Dutton, D. G. (1995). Trauma symptoms and PTSD-like profiles in perpetrators of intimate abuse. *Journal of Traumatic Stress, 8,* 299–316.

Dutton, D. G. & Painter, S. (1993). Battered woman syndrome: Effects of severity and intermittency of abuse. *American Journal of Orthopsychiatry, 63,* 614–627.

Dutton, D. G., & Starzomski, A. J. (1993). Borderline personality in perpetrators of psychological and physical abuse. *Violence and Victims, 8,* 327–337.

Dwyer, D. C., Smokowski, P. R., Bricout, J. C., & Wodarski, J. S. (1996). Domestic violence and woman battering: Theories and practice implications. In A. Roberts (Ed.), *Helping battered women* (pp. 67–82). New York: Oxford University Press.

Ferraro, K., & Johnson, J. (1983). How women experience battering: The process of victimization. *Social Problems, 30,* 325–339.

Follingstad, D., Neckerman, A., & Vormbrock, J. (1988). Reactions to victimization and coping strategies of battered women. *Clinical Psychology Review, 8,* 873–890.

Foshee, V. A., Bauman, K. E., & Linder, G. F. (1999). Family violence and the perpetration of adolescent dating violence: Examining social learning and social control processes. *Journal of Marriage and the Family, 61,* 331–342.

Fremouw, W. J., Westrup, D., & Pennypacker, J. (1997). Stalking on campus: The prevalence and strategies for coping with stalking. *Journal of Forensic Sciences, 42,* 664–667.

Garner, J., & Fagan, J. (1997). Victims of domestic violence. In R. C. Davis, A. J. Lurigio, & W. G. Skogan (Eds.), *Victims of crime* (2nd ed., pp. 53–85). Thousand Oaks, CA: Sage.

Gelles, R. J. (1983). An exchange/social control theory. In D. Finkelhor, R. J. Gelles, G. T. Hotaling, & M. A. Straus (Eds.), *The dark side of families: Current family violence research* (pp. 151–165). Beverly Hills, CA: Sage.

Gelles, R. J. (1993). Through a sociological lens: Social structure and family violence. In R. J. Gelles & D. R. Loseke (Eds.), *Current controversies on family violence* (pp. 53–85). Newbury Park, CA: Sage.

Germain, C. B., & Gitterman, A. (1980). *The life model of social work practice.* New York: Columbia University Press.

Gondolf, E. W. (1997). Patterns of reassault in batterer programs. *Violence and Victims, 12,* 373–387.

Gondolf, E. W. (1999a). A comparison of reassault rates in four batterer programs: Do court referral, program length and services matter? *Journal of Interpersonal Violence, 14,* 41–61.

Gondolf, E. W. (1999b). MCMI-III results for batterer program participants in four cities: Less "pathological" than expected. *Journal of Family Violence, 14,* 1–17.

Gondolf, E. W. (2000a). The cost of batterer programs. *Journal of Interpersonal Violence, 15,* 566–586.

Gondolf, E. W. (2000b). How batterer program participants avoid reassault. *Violence Against Women, 6,* 1204–1223.

Gondolf, E. W. (2000c). Mandatory court review and batterer program compliance. *Journal of Interpersonal Violence, 15,* 428–437.

Gondolf, E. W., & Fisher, E. R. (1988). *Battered women as survivors: Alternatives to treating learned helplessness.* Lexington, MA: Lexington Books.

Graham, D., & Rawlings, E. (1991). Bonding with abusive dating partners: Dynamics of Stockholm syndrome. In B. Levy (Ed.), *Dating violence: Young women in danger* (pp. 119–135). Seattle, WA: Seal Press.

Hage, S. M. (2000). The role of counseling psychology in preventing male violence against female intimates. *Counseling Psychologist, 28,* 797–828.

Hall, D. (1997). *Outside looking in: Stalkers and their victims.* Ann Arbor: University Microfilms International.

Hamberger, L. K., & Hastings, J. E. (1986). Personality correlates of men who abuse their partners. *Journal of Family Violence, 1,* 323–346.

Hamberger, L. K., & Hastings, J. E. (1988). Characteristics of abusive men suggestive of personality disorders. *Hospital and Community Psychiatry, 39,* 763–770.

Hart, S. D., Dutton, D. G., & Newlove, T. (1993). The prevalence of personality disorder among wife assaulters. *Journal of Personality Disorders, 7,* 328–340.

Heise, L. L. (1998). Violence against women: An integrated, ecological framework. *Violence Against Women, 4,* 262–290.

Holtzworth-Munroe, A., Stuart, G. L., & Hutchinson, G. (1997). Violent versus nonviolent husbands: Differences in attachment patterns, dependency, and jealousy. *Journal of Family Psychology, 11,* 314–331.

Homans, G. (1961). *Social behavior: Its elementary forms.* New York: Harcourt Brace.

Hotaling, G. T., Straus, M. A., & Lincoln, A. (1989). Intrafamily violence and crime and violence outside the family. In L. Ohlin & M. Tonry (Eds.), *Family violence* (pp. 315–376). Chicago: University of Chicago Press.

Hotaling, G. T., & Sugarman, D. B. (1986). An analysis of risk markers in husband to wife violence. *Violence and Victims, 1,* 101–124.

Hughes, H. M. (1988). Psychological and behavioral correlates of family violence in child witnesses and victims. *American Journal of Orthopsychiatry, 58,* 77–90.

Jaffe, P., Wolfe, D. A., & Wilson, S. (1990). *Children of battered women.* Newbury Park, CA: Sage.

Johnson, M. P., & Ferraro, K. J. (2000). Research on domestic violence in the

1990s: Making distinctions. *Journal of Marriage and the Family, 62,* 948–963.

Kantor, G. K., & Jasinski, J. L. (1998). Dynamics and risk factors in partner violence. In J. L. Jasinski & L. M Williams (Eds.), *Partner violence: A comprehensive review of 20 years of research* (pp. 1–43). Thousand Oaks, CA: Sage.

Kantor, G. K., & Straus, M. A. (1987). The "drunken bum" theory of wife beating. *Social Problems, 34,* 213–230.

Leonard, K. E. (1999). Alcohol use and husband marital aggression among newlyweds. In X. B. Arriaga & S. Oskamp (Eds.), *Violence in intimate relationships* (pp. 113–135). Thousand Oaks, CA: Sage.

Levendosky, A. A. (2000). Mothers' perceptions of the impact of woman abuse on their parenting. *Violence Against Women, 6,* 247–271.

Lore, R. K., & Schultz, L. A. (1993). Control of human aggression. *American Psychologist, 48,* 16–26.

McNamara, J. R., & Brooker, D. J. (2000). The Abuse Disability Questionnaire. *Journal of Interpersonal Violence, 15,* 170–183.

Meloy, J. R. (1998). *The psychology of stalking: Clinical and forensic perspectives.* New York: Academic Press.

O'Hearn, R. E., & Davis, K. E. (1997). Women's experiences of giving and receiving emotional abuse: An attachment perspective. *Journal of Interpersonal Violence, 12,* 375–391.

O'Leary, K. D. (1988). Physical aggression between spouses: A social learning theory perspective. In V. B. Hasselt, R. L. Morrison, A. S. Bellack, & R. J. McMahon (Eds.), *Handbook of family violence* (pp. 11–55). New York: Plenum.

Pathe, M., & Mullen, P. E. (1997). The impact of stalkers on their victims.

British Journal of Psychiatry, 170, 12–17.

Pence, E., & Paymar, M. (1993). *Education groups for men who batter: The Duluth Model.* New York: Springer.

Perilla, J. L. (1999). Domestic violence as a human rights issue: The case of immigrant Latinos. *Hispanic Journal of Behavioral Sciences, 21,* 107–133.

Raphael, J. (1999). The Family Violence Option: An early assessment. *Violence Against Women, 5,* 449–466.

Reiss, A. J., & Roth, J. A. (1993). *Understanding and preventing violence.* Washington, DC: National Academy Press.

Rennison, C. M., & Welchans, S. A. (2000). *Intimate partner violence.* Washington, DC: Bureau of Justice Statistics.

Resick, P. A., & Nishith, P. (1997). Sexual assault. In R. C. Davis, A. J. Lurigio, & W. G. Skogan (Eds.), *Victims of crime* (2nd ed., pp. 27–52). Thousand Oaks, CA: Sage.

Roberts, A. R. (Ed.). (1990). *Crisis intervention handbook.* Belmont, CA: Wadsworth.

Roberts, A. R. (2000). An overview of crisis theory and crisis intervention. In A. R. Roberts (Ed.), *Crisis intervention handbook: Assessment, treatment, and research* (pp. 3–30). New York: Oxford University Press.

Roberts, A. R., & Burman, S. (1998). Applying crisis intervention and problem-solving therapy to battered women: A national survey and case illustration. In A. R. Roberts & S. Burman (Eds.), *Battered women and their families* (2nd ed., pp. 3–28). New York: Springer.

Roberts, A. R., & Roberts, B. S. (2000). A comprehensive model for crisis intervention with battered women and their children. In A. R. Roberts (Ed.), *Crisis intervention handbook: Assessment, treatment, and research* (pp. 117–208). New York: Oxford University Press.

Rosenbaum, A., Hoge, S., Adelman, S. Warnken, W., Fletcher, K., & Kane, R. (1994). Head injury in partner-abusive men. *Journal of Consulting and Clinical Psychology, 62,* 1187–1193.

Saunders, D. (1994). Posttraumatic stress symptom profiles of battered women: A comparison of survivors in two settings. *Violence and Victims, 9,* 31–44.

Schafer, J., & Caetano, R. (1998). Rates of intimate partner violence in the United States. *American Journal of Public Health, 88,* 1702–1704.

Simoneti, S. (2000). Dissociative experiences in partner-assaultive men. *Journal of Interpersonal Violence, 15,* 1262–1283.

Stets, J. E. (1988). *Domestic violence and control.* New York: Springer-Verlag.

Stets, J. E. (1992). Interactive processing in dating aggression: A national study. *Journal of Marriage and the Family, 54,* 165–177.

Straus, M. A., & Gelles, R. J. (1986). Societal change and change in family violence from 1975–1985 as revealed by two national studies. *Journal of Marriage and the Family, 48,* 465–479.

Tjaden, P., & Thoennes, N. (2000). *Extent, nature, and consequences of intimate partner violence: Research report.* Washington, DC: National Institute of Justice and the Centers for Disease Control and Prevention.

Umberson, D., Anderson, K., Glick, J., & Shapiro, A. (1998). Domestic violence, personal control, and gender. *Journal of Marriage and the Family, 60 (2),* 442–452.

Walker, L. (1978). Battered women and learned helplessness. *Victimology, 2,* 525–534.

Walker, L. (1979). *The battered woman.* New York: Harper and Row.

Walker, L. (1989). *Terrifying love: Why battered women kill and how society responds.* New York: HarperCollins.

3

Comparative Analysis of Battered Women in the Community With Battered Women in Prison for Killing Their Intimate Partners

ALBERT R. ROBERTS

Prevalence estimates of the extent of domestic violence in the United States during the past decade indicate that between 2 million and 8 million women are beaten in their homes each year (Biden, 1993; Roberts, 1998; Roberts & Roberts, 1990; Sugg & Inui, 1992; Tjaden & Thoennes, 2000). The battering of an intimate partner is much more widespread and prevalent than society and the general public realizes. Woman battering, also known as domestic violence, is finally being recognized as one of the greatest social and public health problems of our times, and this recognition is increasing year by year as the number of injuries and the death toll continue to climb. Several studies have found that 22% to 35% of emergency room visits were made because of symptoms or injuries related to physical abuse (Hasselt, Morrison, Bellack, & Hersen, 1988; Randall, 1990; Tjaden & Thoennes, 2000). According to the findings of the National Violence Against Women Survey, approximately 2 million women are battered annually in the United States and sustain injuries severe enough to warrant medical attention. Unfortunately, only an estimated 550,000 will receive any type of medical treatment annually (Tjaden & Thoennes, 2000). The habitual nature, escalation, self-destructive precursors, and lethality of woman battering are only beginning to be assessed.

Violent crimes against women, particularly assaults by husbands, ex-husbands, or boyfriends, are often brutal, degrading, and debilitating. The subject of woman battering has received widespread attention from the print and television media, with such statements as the following, which appeared in *Time*: "Women are at more risk of being killed by their male partners than by any other kind of assault" (July 4, 1994, p. 21).

This chapter compares two types of battered women. The first sample consists of 105 women offenders who were incarcerated for killing their husbands or boyfriends in New Jersey. This group of formerly battered women is compared with a sample of 105 nonviolent battered women who were living in towns and cities in New Jersey at the time of their in-depth interviews. One of the most intriguing types of women are those who were formerly battered and have killed their intimate abusive partners. Criminologists are keenly interested in whether certain types of personality characteristics, demographic or psychosocial factors, and/or behavior patterns are likely to precipitate homicidal acts among chronically battered women. This study compared 105 incarcerated battered women with a matched sample of 105 battered women living in the community on 200 variables and identified 8 likely factors in the profile of homicidal battered women. The two most important precipitants seemed to be recurring nightmares and flashbacks, and a specific death threat by the batterer in which he vividly described the details of how he would kill the woman (i.e., the day, location, and method of her murder). Many of the women offenders' self-reports showed that they believed their only choice was to kill the batterer or be killed by him.

PREVIOUS RESEARCH ON BATTERED WOMEN WHO KILL

The percentage of battered women who kill their batterers is quite small. Although national estimates indicate that between 2 million and 8 million women are battered each year by their partners, approximately 750 battered women kill their abusers each year (Roberts, 1996, 1998).

This chapter looks at whether clues or predictive variables can be found in a retrospective sample of battered women who kill and those who do not. Unfortunately, hardly any data exist that compare battered women who killed their partners with those who did not. Most earlier studies of battered women relied on data from a cross section of the general population (Straus & Gelles, 1990; Straus, Gelles, & Steinmetz, 1980); police or court records (Hirschel, Hutchison, Dean, & Mills, 1992; Pence, 1983; Roberts, 1988; Sherman, 1992; Sherman & Berk, 1984); and shelter-based studies (Cascardi & O'Leary, 1992; Gondolf & Fischer, 1988, 1991; Roberts & Roberts, 1990). These studies focused on currently battered or formerly battered women who often were separated or divorced from their mates. Finally, two studies compared battered women in general with a small sample of battered women who killed their partners (Browne, 1984; Walker, 1984).

Psychologist Angela Browne's (1984) exploratory study compared 42 battered women who had killed their partners with 42 battered women who had not killed or attempted to kill their mates. The comparison group was a subset of battered women drawn from Lenore Walker's (1984) earlier study. The variables that were more likely to predict battered women who would kill were the following: Women who would kill had suffered more severe injuries; their batterers used drugs and were intoxicated more frequently; their partners had threatened or made sexual assaults; the women had threatened suicide; and the women's partners had threatened to kill them.

Table 3.1 examines the similarities and differences in the major findings from Browne's and Walker's research. In Browne's (1984) study the battered women who had killed indicated that their batterer was often intoxicated (80%), frequently forced them to have sexual intercourse (75%), and forced them to engage in sodomy and bestiality (62%). Similarly, Walker's (1984) homicide group reported that the batterers were frequently intoxicated (88%) and had threatened to kill the battered woman or her close relatives (57%). The primary difference between Browne's and Walker's findings was that twice as many batterers in Browne's study had been forced to engage in sodomy, bestiality, and other degrading sex acts (62% of Browne's homicide group vs. 31% of Walker's homicide group). Surprisingly, Browne's nonhomicide group was very similar to Walker's homicide group in regard to suicide threats and attempts (31% of Browne's nonhomicide group vs. 34% of Walker's homicide group). In addition, the percentage of men who threatened to kill a spouse or her close relatives was very similar in Browne's nonhomicide group (59%) and Walker's homicide group (57%).

According to Walker's (1984) study of 50 battered women who killed in self-defense, all had resorted to violence as a last-ditch effort to protect themselves from further physical abuse and emotional harm. In her book, Walker (1989) reviewed 150 murder trials and concluded that all the battered

Table 3.1.   Comparison of Two Previous Studies on Battered Women Who Kill

	Browne's Homicide Group %	Browne's Nonhomicide Group %	Walker's Homicide Group %	Walker's Nonhomicide Group %
Batterer was frequently intoxicated	80	40	88	67
Partner forced victim to have sexual intercourse	75	59	—	5
Partner forced insertion of objects in victim's vagina, anal sex, oral sex, and/or sex with animals	62	37	31	41
Victim threatened to commit suicide	49	31	34	—
Batterer threatened to kill spouse or her close relative	83	59	5	—
Victim was frequently intoxicated	—	—	48	20

women for whom she testified had "killed as a last resort. They killed to save their own lives, and often the lives of their children" (p. 7).

Most of the 50 women in Walker's 1984 study killed their mates with guns that belonged to the men. These battered women reported that no one took them seriously, and so in order to survive "they alone had to protect themselves against brutal attacks, and . . . they knew by observable changes in the man's physical or mental state that this time he really would kill them" (p. 40). Almost all the 50 abusive men were fascinated with weapons, especially guns. In fact, 38, or 76% of the battered women who used a gun to kill an abuser "used the same weapon with which he had previously threatened her" (p. 42). Walker also listed three additional factors that indicated a high risk of homicide: the batterer's excessive jealousy, the victim's social isolation from family members and friends, and frequent alcohol intoxication and drug use.

When battered women who have killed their abusers are brought to trial, the prosecuting attorney typically files charges of murder or manslaughter, and the defense attorney presents a case of self-defense. During the trial, the prosecutor usually asks, "Why didn't the woman leave him if she was really being abused?" Such a question implies either that the woman was not really beaten or, if she were, that she could have just walked away and put an end to the violence. To an increasing extent, however, a woman who has ended a violent relationship is likely to be stalked and threatened with murder by her former partner, or the batterer frequently threatens the woman with a slow, torturous death if she should attempt to leave.

In answering the question of why victims did not just leave their abusers, defense attorneys have increasingly presented evidence of the battered woman syndrome, which is considered a subcategory of posttraumatic stress disorder (PTSD) in the fourth edition of the *Diagnostic and Statistical Manual of Mental Disorders* (1994). Walker was the first researcher to use the term *battered woman syndrome* and to document its incidence among more than 400 abused women in her Colorado study (1984).

People who experience severe trauma (e.g., Vietnam War veterans) or who suffer from repeated and unpredictable brutality (e.g., battered women) may develop psychological symptoms that persist long after the original trauma has subsided. Ongoing trauma, such as battering, may lead the victim to develop coping mechanisms that make her unable to predict the result of her actions, and so she acts in a way that offers her the greatest safety (Walker, 1989, 1993).

The psychologist Martin Seligman developed the theoretical concept of learned helplessness, which Walker (1984) applied to battered women to explain why they do not flee from a violent relationship. In Walker's (1989) view, *learned helplessness* "means that a woman can learn she is unable to predict the effect her behavior will have. People suffering from learned helplessness are more likely to choose behavioral responses that will have the highest predictability of an effect within the known, or familiar situation; they avoid responses—like escape, for instance—that launch them into the unknown" (pp. 50–51).

My own study builds on the earlier two studies by Browne (1984, 1987) and that by Walker (1984), by examining the extent to which forced sexual acts, threats by the batterer to kill his spouse or her close relatives, alcohol and drug abuse, and/or suicide attempts were reported by the battered women in my 1992 New Jersey study. In addition, this chapter extends the findings of earlier research by using more than 200 variables, most of which were not used previously.

METHODOLOGY

This research was designed to ascertain whether there were differences between a group of battered women who were incarcerated for killing their abusive partners and a random community sample of battered women. My six trained interviewers and I conducted in-depth interviews (lasting approximately 1 to 3 hours) with currently and formerly battered women. To ensure the confidentiality of the information, those women who volunteered for the study signed the consent form given to them by the superintendent's administrative assistant or the interviewer; neither the project director nor the trained student interviewer knew the subjects' last names.

The sample for my study came from three sources. The prison sample was drawn from the Edna Mahon Correctional Institution for Women in Clinton, New Jersey (105 women), and the community sample was drawn from two suburban New Jersey police departments (50 women) and two battered women's shelters in New Jersey (55 women). The women in the prison sample had been found guilty of killing their partners; the overwhelming majority had been convicted of second-degree murder or manslaughter. They were serving sentences ranging from 3 years to life, with an average time served before parole of 9 years.

The second part of the data collection involved finding a comparison group of battered women in the community through a convenience sample. Battered women who were similar in age, race, and occupational background were randomly selected from two large suburban police departments and two battered women's shelters. The data were analyzed on demographic characteristics, battering history, educational and occupational background, stressful life events, nature and extent of criminal violence, physical and mental health problems, illnesses requiring medical treatment, use of psychotropic and/or illegal drugs, types and utilization of social services and agencies, coping skills, and anticipated life goals 3 and 5 years hence.

I carefully worded the questions and pretested them with a focus group of 18 formerly battered women at the women's prison. As a result of the pretest, I revised the 39-page interview schedule of questions to maximize the number of answerable questions.

The limitations of this study were as follows:

1. This prison sample is not representative of all battered women who have killed their batterers, since it does not include those women who were acquitted; who pleaded guilty to a reduced charge and were given probation, a suspended sentence, or a short prison sentence; or who entered a plea of insanity or diminished capacity and were committed to a psychiatric institution.
2. Both the prison and community samples are biased, since they are representative of just the state of New Jersey. However, unlike social problems such as drug abuse and crime, woman battering does not seem to vary from one state or jurisdiction to the next.
3. Since this study relied on the memory of the battered women and the most common source of self-report data is filtered or faulty memory recall, I cannot claim 100% accuracy. But no interview or questionnaire study that relies on an individual person's ability to recall past events can claim complete accuracy, particularly with some hidden independent variables (e.g., what event precipitated the first battering incident).

RESULTS

Prison Versus Community Samples

I began my analysis with a description of the similarities and differences between the prison sample and the community sample of battered women. Although the two samples shared some characteristics, they also showed marked differences. Table 3.2 illustrates the similarities and differences in background variables (e.g., educational level, income, and marital status). Table 3.3 indicates the similarities and differences related to whether a weapon was used, the severity of injuries from the worst battering incident, and whether the partner had made death threats. Comparisons were also made on the women's coping methods and skills, such as seeking emergency medical treatment, reporting the violence to the police, and/or being intoxicated or using drugs.

No significant difference was found in the percentage of the women who had been abused by an intoxicated or drug-abusing partner (imprisoned battered women, 22, or 21.0%; community sample, 25, or 23.8%) or who had never completed a vocational training course (prison sample, 62.9%; community sample, 62.9%). Other similarities between the two groups included suffering depressive and anxiety episodes, experiencing one or more severe battering episodes (prison sample, 43.8%; community sample, 40.0%), and reporting the battering to the police (prison sample, 55.2%; community sample, 62.8%).

Table 3.2.   Demographics and Background Variables

Variable	Prison Sample N	Prison Sample %	Community Sample N	Community Sample %
Education				
Never graduated from high school	61	59.2	15	14.6
High school graduate	42	40.8	88	85.4
Vocational training				
None	66	62.9	66	62.9
Completed vocational training	39	37.1	39	37.1
Family income in 1990				
Under $10,000	55	54.0	20	19.2
$10,001–$25,000	24	23.4	43	41.4
$25,001–$40,000	12	11.3	23	22.2
$40,001 and above	14	13.3	19	18.2
Sources of income*				
Public assistance	50	47.6	21	20.2
Food stamps	36	34.3	16	15.4
Unemployment compensation	1	1.0	10	9.6
Child support	8	7.6	9	8.7
Wages or salary	62	59.0	82	78.1
Marital status				
Cohabiting	59	56.2	32	30.5
Currently or previously married	46	43.8	73	69.5

*A number of the battered women had two or more sources of public welfare from which they received assistance (e.g., public assistance or monthly welfare checks, and food stamps).

Contrary to the earlier findings by Browne and Walker, my study found almost no differences between the two groups with regard to terroristic and death threats by the batterer against the battered woman, although the community sample had a slightly higher response to this question (prison sample, 69, or 65.7%; community sample, 70, or 66.7%). In addition, the majority of women in both groups were repeatedly forced to have sexual intercourse with their abusive partner (prison sample, 64.2%; community sample, 60.2%).

Several differences between the two samples are apparent. The battered women who killed their partners were much more likely than those in the community sample to have dropped out of high school, to have been poor and on public assistance, and to have never married their abusive partners. Although the majority of both groups were from the lower socioeconomic class, almost half the prison sample (47.6%), in comparison with one fifth (20.2%) of the community sample, had been on public assistance at the time of their worst battering incident. Although very few of the women in either group had a college degree (prison sample, 1%; community sample, 5%), the prison sample differed significantly in the number of high school drop-

Table 3.3.   Family Violence Incidents and Positive and Negative Coping Methods

Variable	Prison Sample		Community Sample	
	N	%	N	%
First incident of family violence				
Abused by intoxicated or drug-abusing partner	22	21.0	25	23.8
Abused by nonintoxicated partner	83	79.0	80	76.2
Worst incident of family violence				
Severely battered (e.g., broken bones, concussion)	46	43.8	42	40.0
Pushing, slapping, or punching, resulting in bruises or scrapes	59	56.2	63	60.0
Weapon used				
Yes	42	40.0	16	15.2
Police response				
Reported violence to police	58	55.2	66	62.8
Police helpful	35	33.3	63	60.0
Emergency medical response				
Received treatment	58	60.4	48	47.5
Substance abuse				
Drug use	60	62.5	50	49.5
Drunkenness	63	67.7	71	68.3
Death threats				
Threatened to kill victim	69	65.7	70	66.7
Threatened to kill children	19	18.0	24	22.8
Threatened to kill relative	17	16.1	33	31.4

outs (59.2% of the women in prison sample never graduated from high school, compared with 14.6% of the community sample). Most of the battered women who killed had never been married and had lived with the abusive partners for a number of years, compared with less than one third of the community sample (prison sample, 59, or 56.2%; community sample, 32, or 30.5%).

Critical Incidents During Childhood and Adolescence

Two major findings of my study were related to critical incidents during the women's childhood and adolescence. First, the overwhelming majority of battered women who killed their partners reported having been sexually assaulted and physically abused two or more times during childhood and adolescence, and they were considerably more likely to have had an alcoholic mother or father who was violent toward them in the aftermath of a drunken episode. In contrast, very few of the battered women in the community sample had been sexually assaulted during childhood or adolescence. Second, most of the battered women in the community sample had experienced nonviolent stressors such as divorce, death of a loved one, or moving to a new city because of their father's changing jobs.

Critical Incidents: Selected Illustrations From the Battered Women Who Kill

Tina and Gladys both experienced a horrendous series of violent, traumatic, and degrading incidents during their childhood and early adolescence: They were beaten, raped, sodomized, and humiliated by sexual assaults by their fathers, relatives, or neighbors.

Tina is 25 and has one daughter. She recounted several terrible events during her childhood that she will never forget:

> I was 9. I was raped and sodomized by a teenager from the neighborhood. I knew him. He was about 16. I kept it in for 16 years. I kept a lot in. I'm just learning now to talk about it. . . . My father tried to kill me when I was 13. He was drunk. It was about 3:00 A.M. He came home drunk. I was sound asleep, and I woke up to him strangling me. My mother was on top of his back trying to pull him off of me. There was no reason for it. He was drunk. . . . I was raped and sodomized by my ex-fiancé when I was age 17. I was tied up to a chair and raped. I was beat up. My face looked like the elephant man by the time he was done with me. It happened more than once.

Because Gladys's parents were very poor, she and her five sisters were placed in foster homes when Gladys was 7 years old. When she was 15, she and her older sister went to Philadelphia to live with an aunt. Gladys was pregnant at the time. Her father had died the year before, so her mother also moved to Philadelphia to live with them. Gladys was gang-raped when she was 13 and was raped again at age 15 and again at age 16:

> I was raped, actually a few times. I went to a dance hall when I was 13. I was just standing there, and this boy came over and he wasn't really a stranger. I seen him around before. I knew him from high school. He asked me if I wanted something to drink. I said OK, and he brought me a glass of orange soda. Then we were talking, and I started feeling kinda weird. He asked me if I wanted a ride home, and I said OK. All I remember after that is getting into the car and then being in a dark house, hearing a lot of men's voices and my body being used. . . . When I was 15, I was drugged up again and raped by a stranger.

Critical Incidents: Selected Illustrations From the Nonhomicidal Battered Women in the Community

Typical of the battered women who did not kill their abusive partners, Amy and Consuela recalled several critical childhood incidents that were neither violent nor degrading. Amy, aged 19, remembered two incidents regarding moving and a broken romance:

> My second move was hard for me. I had to make new friends. I was a little fat kid, and everyone picked on me. I didn't like where I moved at first, but then I adjusted. . . . I was going with Eric for 7 months, and my best friend Brenda went out with him on the day I broke up with him. Me and her don't talk any more.

Consuela, aged 26, is a high school graduate who grew up in central New Jersey. She worked for several years at Saks Fifth Avenue, putting price tags on clothes, checking inventory, and loading trucks. Consuela remembered two incidents regarding minor surgery and her parents' divorce:

> When I was 9, I had to have surgery for a tumor, or I think it was a cyst in my back. It was very painful. I was in the hospital for 2 weeks. . . . When I was 15, my parents divorced. My father moved back to Puerto Rico, and I didn't get to see him very often.

Triggering Events: Drunkenness, Drug Abuse, and Extreme Jealousy

My study revealed three major findings: First, almost two thirds of the battered women who killed their partners had had very little education (never graduated from high school), were in cohabitating relationships, had received emergency medical treatment because of the seriousness of their injuries, and had a history of being sexually assaulted by men other than their abusive partners.

Second, the prison sample seemed to be in imminent danger from specific terroristic and death threats from their batterers, threats that included how and when he was going to kill them. Third, most of the battered women who killed their partners first attempted suicide by overdosing on drugs as a self-destructive method of coping. When their "cry-for-help" suicide attempts failed to end the battering, they decided that the only escape was to kill the batterer before he killed them.

Triggering Events: Selected Illustrations From the Homicidal Battered Women

When the battered women shared their recollections of the events that seemed to trigger the abuse, it became apparent that the barterer was drunk, "stoned," "smashed," or doing drugs. In addition, the batterer seemed to be extremely jealous and to fear losing his girlfriend or spouse. Both Rachel and Janet observed that their abusive partner's alcohol or drug abuse frequently precipitated the violent battering incidents and that the battering quickly intensified because of the abuser's jealousy and fears that his wife or girl-friend might leave him for another man.

Rachel is a 30-year-old married woman with three children and had been a bookkeeper at an auto parts store. According to her, the incidents precipitating the abuse were as follows:

> What triggered him was drug use. He would get paranoid and accuse me of things, of having a boyfriend. We started arguing, he put a gun to my head and said if he couldn't have me, then no one could. Some fights I would fight back. He never hit me. I got bruises from him holding me down, but he never hit me. The mental abuse was the worst part of it.

Janet is a 29-year-old widow with two children who had worked part-time as a secretary for a social work agency. She described her abuse as follows:

> The third time I went out with him, I was slapped, but I can't remember. We were outside the Quick-Check. I was 23, and he was 24. I always think it was never his fault. I blame myself. He had an alcohol problem, and it happened after he was drinking. He always made me think it was my fault. I did something to make it happen. I'd look at someone, or the dinner burned, or I talked to a guy. I couldn't look at a man while I was talking. It would happen over anything.

Triggering Events: Selected Illustrations From Battered Women in the Community

There seemed to be four types of events that precipitated the worst battering incidents: the batterer's drunkenness, extreme jealousy, intense need to isolate his victim socially, and dependency. Kathy, aged 31, is a cashier at a local supermarket. She described the events that led to her being abused:

> I was living with George for a year; I moved into his apartment; he threw me out 8 months ago; he was seeing someone else; he beat me up and told me to get out; he was accusing me of cheating on him, and he was the one seeing someone else.

Lynn is 21, a full-time student, and a part-time waitress. For her, the events causing the abuse were as follows:

> He was always very jealous of me. The first incident of abuse was when he became jealous over something stupid and we began arguing. He slapped my face. Then every time he became jealous, he would cause an argument, and he would end up hitting and slapping me. He became jealous of all men—he was jealous if I even looked at another man. He even became jealous if I spent time at my older brother's house or at my friend's house. He stopped me from spending time with all my friends. He then started to argue about every stupid little thing. . . . Every time he provoked

an argument, I noticed his "special mood" he had before beating me. After every time he beat me, he became "the perfect gentlemen" and would apologize and buy me roses and presents and promise he would never hit me again.

Donna, aged 21, is a cashier at a toy store. She recollected the events that precipitated the abuse from her boyfriend:

Last year the abuse got real bad. I was 9 months pregnant, and we were constantly arguing. We went to my brother's house, who he hates, to pick up a pair of vice grips, and he started beating me for going there. He would beat me for going or being with any of my family or friends.

Imminent Danger: Terroristic and Death Threats

The overwhelming majority of the battered women who killed received death threats in which the batterer specified the method, time, and location of their demise. For example, Mary, aged 23, received death threats that resulted in nightmares and flashbacks. When she was working, she alternated between painting houses and doing maintenance work. When not employed, she received unemployment compensation, and when that ran out, she received welfare and food stamps. Her recollections of death threats are as follows:

December 6, 1991, he tried to kill me. I was late coming home from work, and he called me a liar, this, that, and the other thing. He was drunk and drugged out. I was living at a friend's house having dinner, and he pounded on the door. I came outside to see what he wanted, and he came after me and told me he was going to kill me, and when I saw the knife, I ran. He was coming right at me, and he chased me down the street. My friends had already called the cops, and the cops came and he took off. . . . I seen him one day and took off. I tried to talk to him to ask him why he wanted to kill me. He calls me all the time and leaves messages that he's gonna do this to me or that to me. I asked him why, and all he had to say was that I better drop the charges or I was gonna end up a dead man.

Mary answered yes to the question "Did your partner ever threaten to kill you?" Her response to the follow-up question—"Can you recall some of the words he used?"—supplies some insight into the specificity of method and magnitude of the death threat:

I remember exactly what he said: "Do you remember the guy from *Goodfellas* [the movie], the crazy one? Well, I'm worse than that." He said he was gonna shoot me in the head and hang me on the tree on Cranbury

Street so all my friends can see, and he said he was going to pistol-whip my roommates. I feel bad because I live there, and their lives are in danger because of me.

Delores, aged 42, told us:

He threatened to kill me. If he was drunk enough, I thought he would. Especially if I was with another man. He always said, "If I ever catch you with another man, I'll kill you" and "If you leave me, I'll blow your brains out."

She described her injuries from years of battering:

Two broken ribs, scars on my elbows and thighs, bruises on my back and neck. Broke my bridge in five places. All of my top teeth are loose. My hearing aids and glasses were broken.

Suicide Attempts

In contrast with the community sample of battered women in my study, many of the battered women in the prison sample had a history of alcoholism and or drug abuse. Those who attempted suicide frequently did so by overdosing on drugs. Theresa, Tina, and Martha tried to escape the cycle of violence by attempting suicide.

Theresa, aged 33, is an X-ray technician who is married by common law and has two children. She tried to commit suicide twice by cutting her wrists and also by overdosing on drugs. Her girlfriend found her both times and bandaged her up because she was afraid to go to the hospital. Theresa reported that she took Valium, heroin, cocaine, reefers, and crack.

Tina, aged 25, talked about her suicide attempt:

I tried to kill myself because of depression over life in general. I was fed up—sick and tired of being beaten and miserable and taken advantage of. My body took the drugs. I couldn't OD. I tried to hang myself in my backyard, but someone pulled into my driveway. I found recently I have a lot to live for.

Martha, aged 48, is a business consultant. She recounted her suicide attempt as follows:

In 1988, I already had five children and let all my stress be buried. I realized I was married to an alcoholic and wife beater. I took a lot of pills because no one wanted to help me. My husband found me. They pumped my stomach. I was in the hospital for about 5 days. After that, a multitude of promises such as no more drinking, but I realized that wouldn't be the case and said I'd never let this happen to myself again.

CONCLUSION

As stated earlier, the purpose of this study was to examine the similarities and differences between a group of battered women who had killed their partners and a community group of battered women who had not killed their partners. The findings highlight several key points. The majority of battered women who killed their abusive partners were much more likely than the nonhomicide group to have dropped out of high school, to have erratic work histories of several unskilled jobs (e.g., part-time painter or cleaning lady), to be cohabiting with their partners, to misuse drugs, to have attempted suicide by overdosing on drugs, to have received emergency medical treatment for battering-related injuries, and to have had access to the batterers' guns. In contrast with the homicide group, the battered women in the community sample were much less likely to be alcoholics or drug addicts, have experienced alcohol-related blackouts and/or seizures, have received psychiatric treatment, have attempted suicide, and/or have access to a gun. In conclusion, the major findings support the idea that once a battered woman fears she cannot escape successfully because of receiving a death threat and has failed in her attempt to "drown her sorrows" in alcohol or drugs or to commit suicide, she is at higher risk of killing her batterer.

REFERENCES

American Psychiatric Association. (1994). *Diagnostic and statistical manual of mental disorders* (4th ed.). Washington, DC: Author.

Biden, J. R. (1993, June). Domestic violence: A crime, not a quarrel. *Trial,* 56–60.

Browne, A. (1984, July). *Assault and homicide at home: When battered women kill.* Paper presented at the Second National Conference for Family Violence Researchers, Durham, NH.

Browne, A. (1987). *When battered women kill.* New York: Free Press.

Cascardi, M., & O'Leary, K. D. (1992). Depressive symptomatology, self-esteem, and self-blame in battered women. *Journal of Family Violence, 7,* 249–259.

Gondolf, E. W., & Fisher, E. B. (1988). *Battered women as survivors: An alternative to treating learned helplessness.* Lexington, MA: Lexington Books.

Gondolf, E. W., & Fisher, E. B. (1991). Wife beating. In R. T. Ammerman & M. Hersen (Eds.), *Case studies in family violence* (pp. 273–292). New York: Plenum.

Hasselt, V. N., Morrison, R. L., Bellack, A. S., & Hersen, M. (Eds.). (1988). *Handbook of family violence.* New York: Plenum.

Hirschel, J. D., Hutchison, I. W., Dean, C. W., & Mills, A. (1992). Review essay on the law enforcement response to spouse abuse: Past, present and future. *Justice Quarterly, 9,* 247–283.

Pence, E. (1983). The Duluth Domestic Abuse Intervention Project. *Hamline Law Review, 6,* 247–275.

Randall, T. (1990). Domestic violence intervention calls for more than treating injuries. *Journal of the American Medical Association, 264,* 939–940.

Roberts, A. R. (1981). *Sheltering battered women: A national survey and service guide.* New York: Springer.

Roberts, A. R. (1988). Substance abuse among men who batter their mates: The dangerous mix. *Journal of Substance Abuse Treatment, 5,* 83–87.

Roberts, A. R. (Ed.). (1996). *Helping battered women: New perspectives and remedies.* New York: Oxford University Press.

Roberts, A. R. (Ed.). (1998). *Battered women and their families: Intervention strategies and treatment approaches.* (2nd ed.). New York: Springer.

Roberts, A. R., & Roberts, B. J. (1990). A model for crisis intervention with battered women and their children. In A. R. Roberts (Ed.), *Crisis intervention handbook: Assessment, treatment and research* (pp. 105–123). Belmont, CA: Wadsworth.

Sherman, L. W. (1992). *Policing domestic violence: experiments and dilemmas.* New York: Free Press.

Sherman, L. W., & Berk, R. A. (1984). The specific deterrent effects of arrest for domestic assault. *American Sociological Review, 49,* 267–272.

Straus, M., & Gelles, R. (1990). *Physical violence in American families.* New Brunswick, NJ: Transaction.

Straus, M., Gelles, R., & Steinmetz, S. (1980). *Behind closed doors: Violence in the American family.* Garden City, NY: Doubleday/Anchor.

Sugg, N. K., & Inui, T. (1992). Primary care physicians' response to domestic violence: Opening Pandora's box. *Journal of the American Medical Association, 267,* 3157–3160.

Tjaden, P., & Thoennes, N. (2000). *Extent, nature, and consequences of intimate partner violence: Research report.* Jointly sponsored by the National Institute of Justice and the Centers for Disease Control and Prevention under NIJ Grant no. 93-IJ-CX-0012. Washington, DC: U.S. Department of Justice Office of Justice Programs.

Trafford, A. (1991, February 26). Why battered women kill: Self-defense, not revenge, is often the motive. *The Washington Post,* p. 11.

Walker, L. E. (1984). *The battered women syndrome.* New York: Springer.

Walker, L. E. (1989). *Terrifying love.* New York: Harper.

Walker, L. E. (1993). Battered women as defendants. In N. Z. Hilton (Ed.), *Legal responses to wife assault* (pp. 233–257). Newbury Park, CA: Sage.

4

Duration and Severity of Woman Battering

A Conceptual Model/Continuum

ALBERT R. ROBERTS

This study provided the data to develop a new five-level classificatory schema or continuum of the duration and chronicity of woman battering based on interviews with 501 battered women. Having no preconceived ideas of what this typology would actually look like, we were able to examine women's experiences and develop a framework based on the common themes presented by their interviews. Our goal is to describe different types of battering relationships with a greater level of detail to enhance our understanding of the variety of ways in which battering relationships occur and endure.

The subjects included 501 battered women and were comprised of four subsamples from a state women's prison; from two shelters for battered women; from three suburban police departments; and from a modified snowball sample. A snowball sample is a nonprobability method of sampling used when a population or group is very difficult to find by random sampling, and where members of the subsample recommend one another to the interviewer. Each interviewer and subject is asked whether they know of a person that fits the proposed characteristics of the potential sample. If they know such a person, then they are asked to furnish the first name and phone number of a potential interviewee who may be a neighbor, friend, relative, or former acquaintance. Snowball sampling is the best way to locate hidden groups such as drug abusers, incest survivors, and wealthy battered women who usually have no contacts with formal agencies and social institutions (e.g. hospital, police department, or prosecutor's office). A 39-page standardized interview schedule was prepared by Roberts, pretested, and modified. The findings indicated a significant correlation between a low level of education, a chronic pattern of battering, and post-traumatic stress disorder (PTSD), as well as explicit death threats, and battered women who kill in self-defense. Continua can provide a useful assessment measure for identifying and determining lethality risk factors among battered women. The main advantage of the continuum presented in this chapter is that it provides clinicians and forensic specialists with diagnostic indicators so that they can intervene before violence escalates in hopes of preventing permanent injuries and death among battered women in imminent danger.

SCOPE OF THE PROBLEM

Violence among current and former intimate partners is pervasive in American society. Every year an estimated 8.7 million women are abused by their partners (Roberts, 1998). Two national studies have provided methodologically rigorous national estimates of the prevalence of woman battering. Tjaden and Thoennes's (2000) National Violence Against Women Survey was based on a national representative sample of 8,000 women and 8,000 men 18 years of age and older. The report based on this study indicated that almost 25% of the women surveyed and 7.6% of the men stated in telephone interviews that they had been raped and/or physically battered by a spouse, cohabiting partner, or date during their lifetime; 1.5% of the women surveyed indicated that they had been physically abused or raped by an intimate partner during the previous 12-month period. A study by Straus and Gelles (1991) was based on a national representative sample of 5,349 couples and 3,334 children. Based on self-reports, Straus and Gelles estimated that approximately 16% of American couples had encountered family violence incidents such as punching, kicking, and assaults with a heavy object or a weapon. This estimate results in approximately 8.7 million battered women annually, based on the U.S. population of couples. However, these estimates are likely to be gross underestimates because of underreporting. The large number of assaults has led to many head, face, neck, arm, leg, back, and torso injuries, permanent scars, miscarriages, infants born with birth defects, and dead battered women. Each year for the past 20 years, approximately 1.5 to 2 million women have needed emergency medical attention as a result of domestic violence (Roberts, 1998; Straus, 1986). Annual estimates indicate that approximately 2,000 battered women are killed by their abusive partners, and the majority of these homicides take place after the victim has tried to leave, separate from, or divorce the batterer. In addition, 750 chronically battered women have killed their mates each year as a result of explicit terroristic or death threats, PTSD, and/or recurring nightmares or intrusive thoughts of their own death at the hands of the batterer (Roberts, 1998).

The aftermath of domestic violence assaults has a destructive impact on the battered woman and her children. Stark and Flitcraft (1988) have indicated that the battered woman syndrome results in subsequent high rates of medical problems, mental disorders, miscarriages, abortions, alcohol and drug abuse, rape, and suicide attempts. Carlson (1996) estimated that each year more than 10 million children witness woman battering in the privacy of their own homes. The impact of growing up in a violent home often results in an intergenerational cycle of violence.

Although most researchers and practitioners would agree that family violence occurs frequently, very few authorities mention the dearth of qualitative studies on battered women. For too long, researchers have examined woman battering as a lower-class and/or pathological phenomenon. There is no single characteristic that determines a woman's potential for leaving her batterer (Roberts, 1996). Rather, a cluster of personal and situational characteristics taken together can provide significant predictors of whether a battered woman will stay in the relationship. The literature has neglected to measure these ecological factors and both the length of battering relationships and the chronicity of battering histories. After thoroughly reviewing the professional journal articles on woman battering, I realized that a new study was needed on specific types of battered women based on the duration and intensity of battering, the lethality of the worst battering incident, emergency room visits, police responses, depression or anxiety disorders, sleep disturbances, alcohol or drug use by the victim, and coping methods. To fill this lacuna, I assembled a database on psychosocial variables, duration of battering, and levels of violence against battered women. The qualitative data are integrated within this chapter.

PURPOSE AND FOCUS OF THE CHAPTER

The purpose of this chapter is to examine a new classificatory schema or continuum of the duration and chronicity of woman battering. Typologies and continua can provide a useful tool for identifying and assessing lethality risk among battered women. The primary advantage of continua and other assessment schemata is that they provide clinicians with diagnostic indicators to help them intervene before violence escalates and, if possible, prevent permanent injuries and death.

The duration of woman battering ranges from short-term (e.g., one to three incidents over a 6-month period) to chronic (e.g., 20 years); severity ranges from less severe violence such as a push, slap, or punch to the very severe acts such as choking, blows to the head, specific death threats, and attempted murder. This chapter documents the duration, severity, and lethality of woman battering within each of five levels, based on the words and experiences of the interviewees. Some of the victims had observed their mothers being battered on and off for many years. In general, these women blamed themselves and accepted the violence by their partners as part of marriage or a cohabiting relationship. In some cases, a woman refused to stay with a partner who was assaulting her and was able to end the relationship shortly after the violence began.

It is important to examine the differences between women who are assaulted once or twice and those who are chronically abused for many years. This chapter considers the complex nature of battered women's self-reports.

METHODOLOGY

The study sample came from four sources:

1. Battered women who have killed their partners were found at a large state women's prison in the northeastern part of the United States ($n = 105$).
2. Three suburban New Jersey police departments ($n = 105$).
3. Two battered women's shelters in New Jersey ($n = 105$).
4. A convenience subsample of 186 formerly abused women was drawn by inviting 30 graduate students in two sections of my MSW family violence course and 15 criminal justice honor students to locate and interview one to three friends, neighbors, or relatives who have been battered during the past 4 years. This type of convenience subsample is also known as a *modified snowball sample.*

The final sample of 501 battered women consisting of the four waves of subsamples comes very close to the authors' plan of sampling battered women from different educational levels, income levels, and racial backgrounds. The results of this exploratory and qualitative study indicate that the duration and severity of battering vary at different levels of chronicity.

The four subsamples of battered women all came from New Jersey. Thus, the findings are not generalizable to all battered women. Although the study sample was carefully selected, there is always some small amount of sampling error.

All the interviewers were college seniors or graduate students. They received 30 hours of training on interviewing skills—including role-playing and practice interviews—and qualitative research on woman battering. The woman-battering questionnaire, which consisted of a 39-page standardized interview schedule to guide the interviews, was prepared, pretested, and modified.

The first 210 interviews were conducted by Roberts and seven student interviewers. In general, the depth and patterns of information collected in these interviews seemed to be of high quality. The second phase, consisting of approximately 300 additional interviews, was based on a police department sample, a shelter sample, and a modified snowball sample of formerly abused women conducted by my graduate students. These interviews also included detailed information and in-depth responses.

FINDINGS

In this study, the 501 battered women had three experiences in common: They had endured one or more incidents of physical battering by their partners; they experienced jealous rages, insults, and emotional abuse; and over one fifth received terroristic and/or death threats from their abusive partner. Some of the women were hit a few times and left the batterer permanently. Others were assaulted intermittently over a period of several months to 2 years before leaving the batterer and filing for divorce. The majority of the women endured chronic abuse for many years before permanently ending their relationships. The extent and degree of chronicity of battering are plotted on a continuum of woman battering among the 501 cases.

Table 4.1 describes a woman-battering continuum based on five levels. The definition of each level is selective and limited to the data obtained from this New Jersey statewide sample of battered women in prison, shelters, police departments, and the community.

Level 1+, short-term victims: The level and duration of abuse experienced by short-term battered women was determined from interviews with 94 battered women who reported experiencing one to three misdemeanor abusive incidents by their boyfriends or partners. Most of the victims were high school or college students in a steady dating relationship. The overwhelming majority of the women were not living with their abusers. The abusive acts could usually be classified in the mild to moderate range of severity (e.g., pushing, slapping, and punching with no broken bones or permanent injuries). Most of these women were between 16 and 25 years of age and ended the relationship with the help of a parent or an older brother. Short-term victims generally call the police or their parents and ask for help. Most of the women in this level were middle-class.

Level 2+, intermediate: The level and duration of battering in this category ranged from 3 to 15 incidents over a period of several months to 2 years. The 104 battered women in this category were usually living with the abuser in either a cohabiting or a marital relationship. None of the women in this level had children. The women ended the relationship with the help of the police, a family member, or a friend after a severe battering incident. Many of the women had sustained serious injuries such as a broken jaw, a deep cut requiring stitches, broken ribs, and/or a concussion. These women often obtained a restraining order and

Table 4.1a. Duration and Severity Level of Woman-Battering Continuum

1+	2+	3+	4+	5+
Short-Term (n = 94)	Intermediate (n = 104)	Intermittent Long-Term (n = 38)	Chronic and Predictable (n = 160)	Homicidal (n = 105)
Less than 1 year (dating relationship); mild to moderate intensity	Several months to 2 years (cohabiting or married); moderate to severe injuries	Severe and intense violent episode without warning; long periods without violence, then another violent episode; married with children	Severe repetitive incidents; frequent, predictable pattern; violence often precipitated by alcohol or polydrug abuse; married with children	Violence escalates to murder/manslaughter precipitated by explicit death threats and life-threatening injuries (cohabiting or married)
1–3 incidents	3–15 incidents	4–30 incidents	Usually several hundred violent acts per woman	Numerous violent and severe acts per woman

Table 4.1b. Psycho-social Variables and the 5-Level Woman-Battering Continuum

1+	2+	3+	4+	5+
Short-Term (n = 94)	Intermediate (n = 104)	Intermittent Long-Term (n = 38)	Chronic and Predictable (n = 160)	Homicidal (n = 105)
Usually middle-class and steady dating relationship (severity, e.g., push, shove, and sometimes severe beating; woman leaves after first or second physically abusive act; caring support system, e.g., parents or police)	Usually middle-class and recently married or living together (severity, e.g., punch, kick, chokehold, or severe beating; woman leaves due to bruises or injury; caring support system, e.g., new boyfriend or parents)	Usually upper-middle or upper social class, staying together for children or status/prestige of wealthy husband (woman stays until children grow up and leave home; no alternative support system)	Usually lower socioeconomic or middle-class, often devout Catholic with school-age children at home (abuse continues until husband is arrested, is hospitalized, or dies; husband is blue-collar, skilled or semiskilled)	Usually lower socioeconomic class, high long-term unemployment, limited education (majority of battered women dropped out of high school; woman usually suffers from PTSD and BWS)

moved to a safer residence. Most of the women in this level were middle-class.

Level 3+, intermittent/long-term: The intensity of each incident was usually severe, and the duration of battering was 5 to 40 years. Most women in this category were economically and socially dependent on their husbands. In addition, they were often religious and for that reason would not seek a divorce. They were nurturing and caring mothers who wanted to keep their families together for the sake of the children. A woman in this group may have experienced no physical violence for several months, and then because of pressures (e.g., at his job), the husband vented his anger and frustration by beating her. Most of these 38 women were middle- or upper-class, and they rarely went to the hospital. When they went to their family physicians for treatment, they usually offered an excuse for the causation of the injury (e.g., being accident-prone).

Level 4+, chronic and severe with a regular pattern: The duration of battering for this group was 5 to 35 years, with the intensity of the violence increasing over the years. The 160 battered women in this category all reported a discernible pattern of abuse during the recent past (e.g., every weekend, every other weekend, every Friday night). Many of the batterers (68%) had serious drinking problems, including binge drinking drunkenness, and blackouts. However, about three-fourths of them battered their partners when they were sober. After many years, especially after the children are grown and out of the house, the battering became more extreme and more predictable and included the use of weapons, forced sex, and generalized death threats. The injuries for these victims were extensive and included sprains, fractures, broken bones, cuts, and head injuries that required treatment in a hospital emergency room.

Level 4.5, subset of chronic with a discernible pattern: mutual combat: Twenty-four of the 160 level 4 cases fit the mutual combat category. This category sometimes leads to dual arrests; at other times, the police arrest the partner who appears to have the lesser injuries. The level of violence against the women in this group was sometimes severe, and the duration of battering in this category lasted from 1 to 25 years. The study identified two types of mutual combat. In the first, the man initiated a violent act such as punching the woman, and she retaliated (e.g., slapping or punching him back). He then retaliated more violently by beating her severely. In the second type of mutual combat, the woman was the primary physical aggressor and used a weapon (typically a knife) to assault the man. The 10 battered women in this category had either a chronic alcohol or drug problem or a history of violent aggressive acts in adolescence (e.g., cutting another girl, boy, or adult with a knife). In 14 of the 24 cases, both the abusive male and the female had drug problems. Generally, there were severe injuries to one or both parties. Many of the women in this level were lower-class, and many of these couples separated after a few years.

Level 5+, homicidal: The duration of the battering relationship in this category was generally 8 years or longer, although the range was 2 to 35
years. The majority of these women were usually in a common-law relationship (cohabiting for 7 years or longer) or a marital relationship, or
were recently divorced. The majority (59.2%) of these women lacked a
high school education and the skills to earn a decent income on their
_own (Roberts, 1996). Almost half (47.6%) of the homicidal battered
women had been on public assistance for many years during the battering episodes.

The violence against the 105 women in this category began at level 2 and
usually escalated to either level 4 or level 5 for several years, after which
the death threats became more explicit and lethal. In a number of cases,
the victim had finally left the abuser and obtained a restraining order,
which he violated. Most of the women in this category suffered from
PTSD, and some had attempted suicide. The most significant finding
related to the homicidal battered woman is that the overwhelming majority (65.7%) received specific death threats in which the batterers
specified the method, time, and/or location of their demise. (Roberts,
1996, p. 41)

Short-Term Abuse

Most of the victims who were abused for several months were in a steady
dating relationship, as illustrated in the cases of Angela and Patti. Victims
in relatively short-term abusive relationships are often helped by parents or
the police.

Angela was an 18-year-old high school senior, from a middle-class family,
when her boyfriend started abusing her. Her career goal was to go to college
and graduate school and become a psychologist. The abuse started after she
and her boyfriend had been going steady for 3 months. Her boyfriend was
very controlling; during the 6 months of abuse before Angela broke up with
him, most of the abuse consisted of his pushing, shoving, and slapping her
and forcing her to have sexual intercourse. She became pregnant, and when
she told her boyfriend, he punched her in the stomach so hard that she lost
the baby. The next week he was very apologetic and tried to force her to
have oral sex. She was upset about the miscarriage: "I tried to leave and
started screaming at him. He hit me in the back with a golf club until my
spine went into a spasm and I passed out." She was taken to the hospital,
and her parents refused to let her see him again.

Patti is a 23-year-old white college graduate who currently lives with her
parents. She is a successful manager at a local restaurant in North Jersey,
supervising a staff of 18 people and earning an annual salary of $48,000.
During Patti's senior year at the University of Virginia, she was dating one
of the star football players. Although they had sexual intercourse about 15
times, he never physically forced her to be intimate. Patti indicated that they

would always have sex on Saturday night after a fraternity party because, in her words, "I would be drinking and feel kind of weak. He would make me feel guilty by repeating again and again everybody's doing it in the bedrooms, until I agreed."

Patti was abused twice. The first incident occurred right after he caught her "flirting with another football player at a fraternity party" in December. The boyfriend shoved her several times and smacked her once. The second and last incident occurred in July 1994, after Patti had graduated from college and moved back home to New Jersey. She was visiting her boyfriend in Virginia when they got into an argument because she "egged him on" by telling him that she "was dating a former boyfriend in New Jersey. First he started yelling at her, saying, "You can't be trusted, you are always whoring around in New Jersey." He then began throwing his shoes and a book at her. After about 20 minutes of arguing, he hit Patti several times in her face with an open hand.

Patti's injuries included swollen lips, cuts from the boyfriend's college ring on her face, and some black and blue marks. She did not go to the hospital because many of the hospital staff were big football fans." Reflecting on this abuse, which happened 2 years ago, Patti states, "I wish I would have stood up to him and verbalized my feelings, instead of not saying anything until I got back to New Jersey."

Patti telephoned her boyfriend 3 days after the second battering incident. She told him that if he ever came near her house, she would have him arrested.

Intermediate Abuse

Most of the 104 battered women at the intermediate level were battered for less than 2 years. There were no warning signs prior to each abusive incident, and there was no pattern with regard to the intervals between each incident. The overwhelming majority of the women in this category were college educated and deeply in love with their partners. Most of these victims left the batterer right after the abuse escalated to one final violent attack. As illustrated in the case of Josephine, when her husband broke her jaw, she realized that her life was in danger and that he did not love her anymore.

Josephine came from a family that enjoyed spending a lot of time together and found it important to remain close. She attended college and then graduate school, where she received her master's degree in counseling. While she was in graduate school, she got engaged. The night of her engagement was the first time her fiancé abused her, but she ignored the abuse and blamed it on her own provocation and figured it would not occur again. However, after they married, the abuse escalated. She frequently received bruises all over her body and also was verbally abused. Although at the time Josephine was learning about woman battering in graduate school, she chose to ignore the abuse and deny it was actually happening to her. It was not until a year later, after her husband broke her jaw, that she decided to leave him and get help. She never received emergency treatment for her jaw, but she called Women's Space (an emergency shelter for battered women) and also went to a private counselor. She lived at Women's Space for approximately 3 months, and her sessions with the private counselor finished in December 1994. Josephine admits that she denied the abuse because she wanted her marriage to work. She still has problems with her jaw because of not receiving emergency care. Nevertheless, she feels she has gotten her life back together. She began a new relationship and was married in January 1996 after receiving premarital counseling with her fiancé. She believes that many problems could have been avoided if she and her first husband had received similar counseling.

Josephine described her worst battering incident:

> This incident occurred going into our first-year anniversary. The worst incident happened in our new house in Alice Court. We were driving home from a bar, we were both drinking, but I wasn't really drunk. I think he was upset with me because I was tired and wanted to leave. So we left, and he invited some people over. We were talking on the way home, it was a neutral conversation, nothing provoking. We pulled into the garage, and I don't know what it was, but he got very mad and grabbed me. This was the only time before we got married, but once we married in September it started happening more often. Especially around that Christmas.
>
> At the time I thought it was only a rare beating, but when I think back it happened on an almost daily basis. I have learned that things that he did to me were abusive, but I didn't know they were at the time. I remembered going to lunch once, and we were talking, and I said something to him joking around, and he kicked me under the table. I was in tears, and he never apologized. I got a bruise, and I knew it was crazy the way he was acting, but I didn't think of it at the time as abuse. He always did something like that if he didn't like what I would say; it was his way of controlling me. When there were beatings, they weren't long. There was no pattern. He would basically start yelling about anything he was mad at. The first incident occurred 11 months into the relationship; we were engaged at the time. I knew he had a bad temper. He was very cold and had no empathy. I didn't understand how someone who said they loved me so much could be so cruel.

Intermittent/Long-Term Abuse

The battered women in this category were usually married and had several children. Most neighbors and the community rarely knew about the violent abuse these women endured over the years. The assaults came without warning and could rarely be prevented. Since most of the batterers were successful wage earners, charming from time to time, and kind to their children, the battered women became traumatically bonded to them. These women were highly dependent, very materialistic and status seeking, and/or totally focused on caring for their children and keeping the family together despite the costs to their own self-esteem and mental health.

Arlene is a 39-year-old woman with three children. She was a debutante from a wealthy New York family and earned her bachelor's degree from Radcliffe College. She married immediately after graduating from college without having had a job. Arlene's mother was a socialite, and her father was a chief executive officer of a Fortune 100 company. Arlene was aware that for 27 years her father had intermittently abused her mother. Her mother was never hospitalized but occasionally was treated by the family physician. Arlene thought her mother deserved to be abused because she had done something wrong. The first incident of Arlene's own battering occurred on her honeymoon, and she felt that she deserved it. She has been intermittently abused for the past 17 years. In describing the violent episodes, she described periods of traumatic violence and periods of calm. Sometimes 6 to 9 months would go by between incidents. During those periods she wanted to believe that the abuse would never happen again. She does not think her husband will kill her because he has only put her in the hospital twice. She plans to remain in the relationship for the sake of her children and because she enjoys her social prominence, which she feels would be compromised by a divorce because there would be such a bitter legal battle.

Chronic and Severe Abuse
With a Regular Pattern

The women in this category have been abused for years. The abuse escalated until it was either a weekly occurrence or occurred several days a week. These women were highly dependent, both emotionally and economically, on the batterer. They had low self-esteem and often had an alcohol or drug problem. In many cases, the abuse ended only after the victim experienced some type of "jolt" that caused her to leave the relationship, such as receiving severe injuries, hearing about other battered women who were killed, or the husband being hospitalized for alcoholism or polydrug abuse.

Naomi is a 34-year-old single parent who was chronically abused by her husband for 7 years. She is a high school graduate and has worked for the same company for the past 14 years as a customer service representative. Her father was an abuser. She described her injuries as follows:

Broken nose, he's tried to choke me so many times I feel that when I get older I will have cancer of the throat. I have bruises all over my body. I have a bad back, and on three different occasions my eye has been swollen from his punches. He likes to punch me in the mouth. He does it without warning. The last time he strangled me in the kitchen, I faked passing out, and he left. He might have killed me if I didn't fake passing out..

Naomi finally left her husband after attending a support group for battered women. In her own words: "I sat there and listened to their stories. It made me feel helpless because some women were battered for 25 years. I felt I was taking on their problems instead of helping myself. I decided I had to leave him. I went to the court and got a restraining order."

Mutual Combat and Dual Arrest
Subcategory of Chronic Battering

Many of the women involved in mutual combat exhibited violent behavior during adolescence. These women often grew up in low-income single-parent families with a parent or siblings who had criminal histories. Their proneness to violence was influenced by the extreme stress of being a teen mom, being unemployed and on welfare, and/or growing up in a drug subculture. Almost half of these 24 violent women had a criminal record for drug dealing and prostitution. The women reported that they often got involved in drugs to help their abusive partners.

The case illustration of Lenore reveals the negative influence of a violent environment and neighborhood. Lenore grew up fast and learned about violence and death at age 13. The critical incident during early adolescence that had a major impact on her life was the death of her father, for whom she cared deeply. Lenore described this loss and her long-delayed grief, repressed anger and rage, teen pregnancy at 16, and violence. "My father was stabbed."

Many of the women in the mutual combat category exhibited violence and acting-out behavior in adolescence. In the words of Lenore:

> My father was stabbed when I was 13. He was being robbed. My pop was my pride and joy. I come from a family of 10, and I'm the second oldest. I had a lot of responsibility. I'm my father's only child, so I grieved alone—he did everything for me, and when he was gone, I really missed him. I had to grow up real fast and alone because I was so close to him. But no one should have helped me then. I had to deal with it myself after all the pain's inside so no one can make it feel better. When I lost my dad, I became cold to the world and never cried about it. All the anger built up inside me, and once I heard these girls coming into my ex-boyfriend's apartment, and the first one that came inside I stabbed the shit out of her. I stabbed her 14 times. But no one found out it was me. I kept it to myself like I do everything else in life. People on the streets, they all know me as a bad ass. I couldn't cry when my dad died; I would have let everyone down.

Lenore further described her lost adolescent years and her reaction to the stress of being a teen mom:

> At age 16 I moved out on my own, the judge granted me stay, and I got my first job at 17. I graduated from high school with a big stomach and

come September I had my first child. I missed out on high school and all the partying because I had to work and take care of children. All the other kids were partying, and I was changing diapers, that was the worst thing for me in my teen years. I regret it, but I had to do what I had to do just to survive. You know where I'm coming from. My whole life was sacrifices. Well, honey, let me tell you something, I'm making up for it all now. I go out and make that son-of-a-bitch watch the kids; after all, they are his too. I love my kids, but sometimes you get to feeling like there's something missing in your life—well, I'm going after that something. That causes a lot of battles between me and him because he thinks I should stay home with the kids while he goes out and parties. He gotta get a grip on things, I ain't no one's fool.

For the past 10 years, Lenore and her husband were involved in mutual combat. She described her recollection of the violent incidents and the events that seemed to precipitate the violence: "He'd bring drugs in the house and tell me that he was the king, and I better suck his big black dick, swallow him. I'd say no way, he'd say my clothes will be off in 10 seconds. He'd . drop his pants, and I'd pull my knife, then he would start punching me. . . . he knows I would then cut him." Lenore described the last battering incident as the worst: "I think he had the same injuries. I filled out the papers and got a restraining order." Lenore's future goals related to woman battering are as follows: "I don't think I am ever gonna get away from him; 3 years from now I'll still be fighting for my life. In 10 years I will still be fighting, if I'm not dead by then. I mean he'll never let me alone. He'll haunt me for the rest of my life."

Homicidal Battered Women

The battered women who kill a violent partner in self-defense usually have a low level of education and have witnessed their mother being battered throughout their childhood. The intergenerational cycle of violence continues, since these women often cohabit or marry young to escape from a dysfunctional and abusive home. They often are teen mothers with alcohol and substance abuse problems.

When Maribell (a pseudonym) was growing up, her parents were always fighting. As she recalled:

My mother and father fighting. Always big fights and the police or ambulance would come. A few times a month over just normal things. Usually the neighbors called the police. It was usually physical and verbal. I tried to forget most of it, so I can't remember one particular incident. We never talked about it.

Maribell got married at 18 and left home. Her husband had an alcohol and drug problem, and the abuse got worse after she became pregnant. She mentioned some events that led to incidents of abuse: "The dinner burnt, or I talked to a guy. I couldn't look at a man while I was talking. It would happen over anything.

Maribell gave a detailed account of the worst incident of abuse:

I had two black eyes, he hit or punched me. We were in the bathroom at his mother's. I was pregnant, and I ran down the street barefoot and called the police, and they came an hour later. He insulted me and called me names. I was stupid or a bad mother. His mother did nothing. In Oakland, California, Friday night, that's why it took the police so long. The cop looked at me, and I told him what happened. My husband left. I didn't sign a formal complaint. The last time before I left I called 911, and the police came, and I said arrest him. He told them I was nuts 'cause I was on pills from the doctor. The house was a mess, I had the baby. The police believed me, and they arrested him. One officer asked me if I had any-where to go, so I said I was from New Jersey. He advised me to go back to New Jersey with the money I had. He said it would happen again. So I called my mother and told her. My daughter was 6 months old. My girl-friend brought me to the bank to get the money, and I bought a ticket and left the next morning. He called and told me to drop the charges while I was packing to leave. I told him no. He said I love you. He kept calling, and finally I stopped answering. I moved in with my mom. Her boss at Ancora opened Volunteers of America on the grounds of where we lived, and I got my job with them. He came back to New Jersey after 10 months.

I had another baby during this time. He moved into my mother's house and he got a job. I told him to move out 'cause the arguments started again. He was physically abusive when my mom wasn't around. He stayed and didn't move. He was still drinking, and we were fighting.

I don't remember the exact details of the incident. A guy came over to visit my brother, and Ron called me to the door and said, someone is here to see you, and the guy said he was looking for my brother. The guy left, and we started arguing and fighting over it. He was drinking that day. Verbal argument to begin with. I can't remember if it got physical, I guess it did. I told him to get out, and he wouldn't. Somehow or another I picked up a knife, and he kept coming toward me, and I hit him with the knife. I remember doing it once, but the police report said three times. I thought it was his shoulder, but it was further down. A kitchen knife. He fell to the floor, and there was blood all over. I tried to stop the bleeding, and he was talking to me. So then I grabbed the phone, and I couldn't dial. I ran to a neighbor to get help, and they called the police. The police came, and we waited for an ambulance. Then they arrested me. He went to the hospi-tal, and I went to the police station and gave a statement and tried to protect him. I don't know why. I knew when he got out I'd be in worse trouble than I was at the police station, can't remember what I told them. Throw out the plea bargain, that's what they kept telling me. My state-ment, for 2 years I tried to remember it and I can't.

Charged me with murder one and weapons charge (knife).

Dropped all of it and charged me with aggravated manslaughter. I took a plea bargain for 20 years flat sentence. They offered me 30 with 10 stip while I was on bail. My lawyer told me to take the 20 flat. Served 2 years already. June 1994. First parole hearing.

He died that day.

The police came immediately. The one police officer was nice 'cause they knew us, my mother. The person I gave the statement to wasn't very nice.

CONCLUSION

It is important for health care and mental health professionals and criminal justice practitioners to document the duration and intensity of battering histories among clients in order to provide the best possible care and effective intervention strategies. The prediction of both the duration and the severity of woman battering is one of the most complex issues in forensics and the social sciences. Nevertheless, the courts, mental health centers, family counseling centers, intensive outpatient clinics, day treatment and residential programs, public mental hospitals, and private psychiatric facilities rely on clinicians to advise judges in civil commitment and criminal court cases. This chapter provides a new framework or continuum for evaluating battered women and improving risk assessments of dangerousness. The authors' findings regarding the duration and chronicity of battering can be used to facilitate court decisions on whether battered women are at low, moderate, or high risk of continued battering and/or homicide.

All assessment continua or typologies should start with an evaluation of the harm and injury of the victim, the duration and chronicity of violent events, and the likelihood that the victim will escape and end the battering cycle. The continuum conceptualized in this chapter provides a classificatory schema by which forensic specialists and clinicians can make reasonably clear predictions of lethality and the likelihood of repeated violence. The short-term and intermediate levels from the continuum seem to be amenable to crisis intervention, brief psychotherapy, support groups, restraining orders, and a relatively brief period of recovery. The prognosis for the chronic/ long-term category, whether with an intermittent or a weekly pattern of battering, is much more negative. The chronic recidivist cases are frequently put into a life-threatening situation. However, when there are specific death threats and a loaded handgun in the house, the short-term and intermediate battering cases can also escalate to a life-and-death situation. In chronic cases, the human suffering, degradation, and emotional and physical pain sometimes end in permanent injuries to the victim or the death of the batterer or the battered woman. At other times, the chronically battered woman temporarily escapes to a shelter, a relative's home, or the police precinct. In many of the latter cases, the victim returns to the batterer or is dragged back to the violent home. Finally, a small but growing number of chronically battered women leave the batterer and stay free of violence because they are empowered through a support group, counseling, or other forms of therapeutic intervention (see chapter 18 for a detailed discussion of the importance of support groups in breaking free and staying free of a violent relationship).

REFERENCES

Astin, M. C., Lawrence, K. J., & Foy, D. W. (1993). Risk and resiliency factors among battered women. *Violence and Victims, 8,* 17–28.

Browne, A. (1987). *When battered women kill.* New York: Free Press.

Carlson, B. E. (1996). Children of battered women: Research, programs and services. In A. R. Roberts (Ed.), *Helping battered women: New Perspectives and remedies* (pp. 172–187). New York: Oxford University Press.

Cascardi, M., O'Leary, D., Schlee, A., & Lawrence, E. (1993). *Prevalence and correlates of PTSD in abused women.* Paper presented at the 27th annual conference of the Association for the Advancement of Behavior Therapy, Atlanta, GA.

Federal Bureau of Investigation. (1992). *Crime in the U.S.: 1991.* Washington, DC: U.S. Government Printing Office.

Roberts, A. R. (1996). *Helping battered women: New perspectives and remedies.* New York: Oxford University Press.

Roberts, A. R. (1998). *Battered women and their families: Intervention strategies and treatment approaches* (2nd ed.). New York: Springer.

Stark, E., & Flitcraft, A. (1988). Violence among intimates: An epidemiological review. In V. B. Van Hasselt, R. L. Morrison, A. S. Bellack, & M. Hersen (Eds.), *Handbook of family violence* (pp. 293–317). New York: Plenum.

Straus, M. A. (1986). Medical care costs of intrafamily assault and homicide. *Bulletin of New York Academy of Medicine, 6,* 556–561.

Straus, M. A., & Gelles, R. J. (1991). How violent are American families: Estimates from the National Family Violence Resurvey and other studies. In M. Straus & R. Gelles (Eds.), *Physical violence in American families: Risk factors and adaptations in 8,145 families* (pp. 95–112). New Brunswick, NJ: Transaction.

Tjaden, P., & Thoennes, N. (2000). *Extent, nature, and consequences of intimate partner violence: Findings from the National Violence Against Women Survey.* Washington, DC: National Institute of Justice, U.S. Department of Justice.

Walker, L. A. (1984). *Battered women syndrome.* New York: Springer.

5

National Organizational Survey of Domestic Violence Coalitions

PATRICIA BROWNELL
ALBERT R. ROBERTS

The women's movement has reached full maturity. As a direct result of increased societal awareness through public education and media attention, and the statewide and national coalitions' legislative successes, the prevalence of woman battering has begun to decline in recent years. Women's organizations and coalitions took the lead starting in the late 1970s in facilitating the expansion of shelters, support groups, community education, and other services to battered women. This chapter provides data on the first national survey of the specific role, activities, and achievements of domestic violence coalitions. Each year millions of dollars are allocated by the federal government and disbursed to each of the 50 states to facilitate the expansion of programs and services for battered women and their children. Our summary will inform the reader about the budgets and specific funded activities for the 39 responding statewide domestic violence coalitions, ranging from police training to lobbying and legislative advocacy, to a statewide database and court monitoring of restraining orders, to training thousands of state child welfare workers, to pro bono civil and criminal legal representation of battered women and sexual assault victims.

In addition, by the early 1990s, prominent professional associations made a commitment to developing model domestic violence codes, judicial education and court reforms, and policy research and development. Specifically, the National Council on Juvenile and Family Court Judges Association, the National Center on State Courts, and the American Bar Association, Criminal Justice Section, have made important strides on behalf of victims of domestic violence in the legal, judicial, and legislative arenas. For detailed information on legal remedies and specialized domestic violence courts and on child custody legislative reforms, see chapters 7, 8, and 9.

Coalitions focus on organizing and empowering functional statewide and local communities. The primary focus of these coalitions is advocacy for social justice, including policy changes that "promote acceptance and inclusion of their chosen issue" (Weil & Gamble, 2002). Domestic violence coalitions and functional communities—which grew out of a grassroots movement to build political power and influence for economically marginalized and vulnerable battered women—respect the inherent dignity of the individual battered woman and focus on advancing legislative, distributive, and social justice (Weil & Gamble, 2002). Three major functional communities, also known as national, state, and local advocacy organizations, are the following:

1. The National Coalition Against Domestic Violence (NCADV) and the 50 state domestic violence coalitions lobby and advocate for improved social services and legal rights for battered women and their children. The NCADV is an organization of domestic violence advocates, self-identified battered women, professional social workers, nurses, and attorneys, as well as service providers and lobbyists.
2. The Arc (formerly the Association for Retarded Citizens) advocates for the rights of children and adults with developmental disabilities. Its members include individuals who have a relative with mental retardation or other developmental disability, as well as health and disability advocates, service providers, and other concerned professionals.
3. The National Alliance of the Mentally Ill (NAMI) advocates for improved mental health services for children and adults diagnosed with a serious mental illness. Its members are professionals or parents of the mentally ill.

Feminist organizing through coalition building has been instrumental in the passage of the Violence Against Women Act (VAWA) and other domestic violence legislation, the development of domestic violence service delivery systems, community education, and state legal codes to protect battered women and their children.

Legislative and planned change advocacy consists of defining specific rights and service needs of vulnerable groups, publicizing one's mission and goals, and building spheres of influence by negotiating, lobbying, educating legislators, cooperating, and compromising. A recent example of coalition building occurred when several influential and concerned women's advocacy coalitions, namely, the NCADV, the National Network to End Domestic Violence, and the National Coalition Against Sexual Assault, mobilized and worked with the International Association of Chiefs of Police and the National District Attorney's Association to lobby for full funding of the STOP program of VAWA 2000.

STATE DV COALITIONS AND VAWA FUNDING NEGLECT DOMESTIC VIOLENCE LEGAL AND SOCIAL WORK EDUCATION

State domestic violence coalitions and the Violence Against Women Office (which provides VAWA grants) have failed to recognize and fund domestic violence internships and courses, and have failed to collaborate with university-based education programs. As a result, each year over 100,000 new attorneys and social workers will not have the educational preparation and skills to advocate for battered women. The American Bar Association Task Force Report titled, *Narrowing the Gap: Statement of Fundamental Lawyering Skills and Professional Values* (The MacCrate Report) aptly criticized traditional law school education. Noteworthy was documentation that hardly any attention is given to teaching the psychological components of lawyering including danger assessment skills, interviewing and empathy skills, and the impact of PTSD (Personal Communication, Joan Meier, November 18, 2001). Multidisciplinary legal education can provide students with an opportunity to integrate psychology and social work knowledge and skills into domestic violence legal interventions. A small number of innovative law schools and schools of social work offer students multidisciplinary opportunities to take team taught courses from domestic violence legal experts, forensic social workers, and psychologists. Fordham University at Lincoln Center (Graduate School of Social Services and the Law School), George Washington University Law School Domestic Violence Clinics, and the Pace University Women's Law Center are leading the way with promising practicums and seminars. See Chapters 7–9 in this volume for further details.

During the past decade, we have witnessed a strong response from individuals and society to prevent and eventually end gender violence. Roche and Sadoski's (1996) large national survey of 622 battered women's shelters (adapted from Roberts's Ph.D. dissertation, Rutgers University) indicated that both social action and direct practice activities of the shelters had been implemented fairly consistently throughout the United States. Roche and Sadoski documented the patience, optimism, and significant incremental social changes through battered women's coalitions and shelters, describing the dual social change missions of shelters and the battered women's movement: (1) improving and expanding direct services such as 24-hour crisis hotlines, crisis counseling, emergency shelter and food, legal advocacy, expert testimony in court cases, and support groups; and (2) advocating for societal changes, including changing cultural beliefs and values that foster violence against women, changing institutional and community decisions that support individual men's use of coercive and abusive tactics against women, building a political movement of women, and increasing the collective power of women. The following is an overview of the movement's history:

HISTORY OF DOMESTIC VIOLENCE COALITIONS

The local, state, and national domestic violence coalitions grew out of the women's movement that began in the 1960s. The following is an overview of the movement's history.

Point of Departure: Early Coalition Building

The history of the women's movement in the United States is one of exclusion and the fight for inclusion. The suffrage movement culminated in the Nineteenth Amendment to the U.S. Constitution, which gave women the right to vote. However, women did not attain full gender equality in the home or the workplace. By 1961, pressure from women's organizations resulted in the establishment of the Commission on the Status of Women by President John F. Kennedy, who appointed Eleanor Roosevelt as leader of the first White House Conference on the Status of Women. A 1963 report of the commission stated that despite the right to vote, women continued to experience discrimination (http://nownyc.org.past.hml).

In June 1966, delegates to the Third National Conference of Commissions on the Status of Women were precluded by the rules of the conference established by the Johnson administration from passing resolutions recommending that the Equal Employment Opportunity Commission (EEOC) enforce its mandate, codified in law, to end gender discrimination. Delegates reacted by forming the National Organization of Women (NOW), which held its first organizing conference in October 1966 in Washington, DC (http://nownyc.org/past.hml).

Task forces were established by the NOW leadership to address barriers to women's equality in education, employment, law, media images, poverty, and politics. While NOW members joined leaders from other feminist organizations to found the National Women's Political Caucus, a nonpartisan coalition of women in politics, local grassroots groups were forming to respond to identified problems of women in the community related to inequality in the workplace and in the home (Schechter, 1982).

These problems were identified as interrelated: Many women were subjected to abuse by male partners but were unable to leave abusive households and support their children and themselves on their own because of discrimination in the workplace, including low wages, lack of child care, and inadequate time and leave policies. Other barriers included laws that favored the male as head of household, male-dominated local law enforcement departments that ignored misdemeanor- and felony-level offenses perpetrated against women by their male partners, lack of services that supported women with or without children in leaving abusive households, and community sentiment that viewed wife battering as a private affair.

The barriers identified by both NOW and local grassroots organizations that prevented women from achieving full gender equality were based on legal statutes as well as social convention. As a result, local groups advocating for changes on the community level on behalf of women began to form first local, then state, coalitions. At the same time, NOW and other organized groups on a national level began to form political associations to promote the election of women and male sympathizers into public office, as well as changes in legislation at all levels of government to end discrimination against women.

The movement for social change toward gender equality necessitated the formation of local and state-based organizations. NOW's founders collaborated with existing local and state coalitions to establish state chapters. While many state-based women's coalitions were founded to advocate for more funding for services and changes in local and state laws, NOW chapters focused on building political support for candidate election as a strategy for accomplishing these objectives.

The founding chapter of NOW and one of the strongest chapters is in New York City. The Michigan chapter of NOW and NYC NOW are two of the organization's strongest chapters. Many of the organization's founding members of NOW, including Betty Friedan, Catherine Conroy, and Marjory D. Fields, were from New York, and the New York City chapter includes a legal defense component that continues to actively seek to change laws and policies in the judicial arena and law enforcement practice. By the second half of the 1970s, Michigan NOW members had sponsored and helped develop shelters for battered women in Ann Arbor, Kalamazoo, Muskegon, Saginaw, St. Joseph, Traverse City, and Ypsilanti. Several of the early accomplishments of the national coalition were public education about violence against women; monitoring and influencing state and federal legislation related to domestic violence; technical assistance in developing state and regional coalitions; increasing access and building a national network of shelters for battered women fleeing their state or city (underground railroad); developing and securing funding for resources for all member organizations; providing guidelines and consultant services in budgeting, grants management, computerized record-keeping and fiscal management systems; and program-based monitoring and evaluations.

Best-selling books can raise public awareness of the critical need for services and legal remedies to protect battered women and their children. Two important books, published in 1976 and 1977, focused on the epidemic number of assaults by men against their spouses. The earlier book, *Battered Wives*, was written by Del Martin, a California domestic violence advocate. The second book, *Battered Women: A Psycho-Sociological Study of Domestic Violence*, was compiled and edited by Maria Roy, the first director of Abused Women's Aid in Crisis (AWAIC), a crisis hotline and counseling center to aid battered women in Manhattan.

New Shelters for Battered Women

"Nowhere to go" became the rallying call for the battered women's shelter movement that gained momentum in the 1970s (Schechter, 1982). The first shelters specifically designed for battered women were established in 1974 (Koss et al., 1994; Pleck, 1987; Roberts, 1981). They provided emergency short-term shelter, food, and clothing for women and their children fleeing battering situations (Roberts, 1981). While the early shelters provided refuge and protection for individual women, they quickly became part of the battered women's movement and adopted social change objectives, including coalition building within the battered women's shelter movement; educating communities, along with health and law enforcement professionals, about wife battering; and advocating with local and state elected officials about the need for legislative changes and funding.

Comprehensive Employment and Training Act: Funding of Paraprofessionals in Battered Women's Shelters

Several sources of government funding emerged to supplement private funding for the early battered women's shelters. These included the Comprehensive Employment and Training Act (CETA) of 1977, Title XX of the Social Security Act (SSA), and Emergency Assistance to Families (EAF; Title IV of the SSA), which became an optional funding source for domestic violence shelters to indigent women and children at state discretion in 1978.

Among the most important sources of government funding was CETA (Roberts, 1981, 1998). While CETA was legislated as an antipoverty program to provide entry-level employment for minorities and women at the margins of the workforce, it became a significant source of funding for battered women's shelter staff in the 1970s and early 1980s. The elimination of CETA and the legislation of Title XX into a state block grant program during the Reagan administration severely curtailed federal support for battered women's shelters during this time. EAF, a means-tested funding stream that could be used at state option for domestic violence shelters, was folded into the Temporary Assistance for Needy Families (TANF) block grant in 1996. The effect of the changes in government-sponsored programs on battered women's shelter funding has not been fully studied to date.

National Coalitions Against Domestic Violence: Summary of History

National Coalition Against Domestic Violence

The NCADV was formed in 1978 as an alliance of state coalitions and shelters and consists of a representative from each state (Roche & Sadoski, 1996). The impetus for development of the national organization of the NCADV was the U.S. Commission on Civil Rights hearing on battered women in Washington, D.C., which was attended by over 100 battered women from across the country (http://www.ncadv.org).

However, key events like the International Women's Year conference in Houston, Texas, in November 1977, which brought together grassroots womens' groups from all over the country, laid the foundation for the NCADV. On the government side, the Civil Rights Commission can be credited with helping to legitimize the battered women's movement within government by providing space to begin a national organization, legitimating the needs of battered women, and brokering contacts between advocates and federal agencies (Schechter, 1982).

NCADV's mission includes coalition building on the local, state, and national levels; its board of directors represents local and state coalitions, as well as diverse groups of women affected by domestic violence. The coalition not only serves as a national information and referral center but also has an active public policy office that lobbies Congress, monitors state and federal legislative developments, and advises grassroots organizations on legislative developments (http://www.ncadv.org).

Battered women have served as active members and spokeswomen within the NCADV. As Barbara Hart, one of the founding members, stated in her address celebrating the founding of the coalition, "I am also a battered woman" (Hart, 2001). The national coalition successfully lobbied for passage of federal legislation that supported the battered women's shelter movement, as well as significant omnibus legislation intended to attack the problem of domestic violence on many fronts, like the VAWA of 1994 and 2000.

National Network to End Domestic Violence

The National Network to End Domestic Violence (NNEDV), established in 1990, is another membership and advocacy organization of state domestic violence coalitions. It began as a small working group of state domestic violence coalitions and national domestic violence advocates. As of 2001, it provided services to over 2,500 local member programs. Like its sister organization the NCADV, the NNEDV provides assistance with coalition building and advocacy to strengthen the responsiveness of federal public policies that concern battered women and their children. The NNEDV developed domestic violence policy that was instrumental in the drafting of the VAWA 1994. The national network has been successful in having the federal funding appropriation for domestic violence coalitions and programs raised from $20 million to almost $90 million between 1995 and 2000. The network views itself as the voice of domestic violence advocates before Congress, the executive branch, state legislative bodies and committees, and the courts. Fund-raising for domestic violence shelters and services has become especially critical since the elimination or curtailment of key federal funding sources such as CETA and Title XX of the Social Security Act. Lynn Rosenfeld, executive director of the NNEDV, persuasively states: "Without a public policy voice through our network of advocacy organizations, the urgent human needs of battered women survivors are ignored."

Violence Against Women Act

The VAWA of 1994 was a milestone in federal legislation that provided a broad range of protections for battered women from diverse backgrounds, ranging from nondocumented women to elder abuse victims (Brownell & Congress, 1998). It allocated supplementary funding for shelter and legal and counseling services, established policy guidelines for state law enforcement and legal representation, and strengthened constitutional protections for battered women, including victims of elder abuse and mistreatment. A revised legislative act, known as VAWA II, was signed into law by President Clinton in October 2000, and the funding level was raised to $3.3 billion. For further information on this act, see chapter 1 in this volume.

Victims of Crimes Act

Another legislative victory was the Victims of Crime Act (VOCA) of 1984, which provides support for victims of domestic violence by authorizing annual grants to states to assist and compensate victims. This act also allocates funding for battered women's shelters and law enforcement–based crisis intervention. Prior to VOCA, victims who could not afford to pay their own mental health counseling and legal fees had no other recourse (Koss et al., 1994).

NATIONAL SURVEY OF 39 STATEWIDE DOMESTIC VIOLENCE COALITIONS TO ELIMINATE OR END WOMEN BATTERING

During a working conference in Washington, D.C., sponsored by the NNEDV in April 2001, a questionnaire survey was distributed to representatives from all 50 state domestic violence coalitions. The survey sought to obtain information on a broad range of issues, objectives, public policy and legislative advocacy agendas, organizational structure, board membership, self-reported major achievement of each coalition (during the past 2 years), caucuses and task forces representative of underserved battered women, decision making, staffing patterns, training and public education, and annual operating budgets from coalition members.

Methodology and Sample

A national organizational study of the 50 statewide domestic violence coalitions was conducted to determine policy and advocacy priorities, major accomplishments, funding sources and priorities, staffing patterns, boards of directors, types of decision making, operating budgets, and training priorities, and the number and types of program members in each state. The study sample was derived from the 50 state domestic violence coalitions that are members of the NNEDV (Roberts, 2001). A three-page questionnaire was developed by Sarah J. Lewis (Columbia University School of Social Work) and Albert R. Roberts. It was then pretested with Barbara Hart (Battered Women's Justice Project and the PCADV) and Lynn Rosenfeld (NNEDV). As a result of the pretest, the questionnaire was revised and distributed by Lynn Rosenfeld at the Washington, D.C., meeting of the NNEDV. Thirty-nine coalition directors or staff designees completed and returned the survey questionnaire, a 78% response rate. The responding state coalitions represent a cross section of coalitions throughout the United States. The rest of this chapter summarizes the self-reports of the respondents.

Findings of the National Study

Types of Statewide Domestic Violence Coalitions

Respondents identified their coalitions as representing one of two types. The first constitutes the important work of state domestic violence coalitions ($n = 27$), task forces, and advocates nationwide, and the second consists of state coalitions and advocates whose focus is on advocating for both domestic violence and sexual assault survivors ($n = 12$).

Types of Service Programs Represented on State Coalitions

A number of both residential and nonresidential direct service programs are represented on state domestic violence coalitions. Of the 37 respondents to the question about the total number of direct service provider members of each statewide coalition, survey respondents reported an average of 28 residential program members and 18 nonresidential service program members. There was variation in the type and number of local agency/program members from one state coalition to the next. For example, the Hawaii coalition indicated that it has 7 residential shelters and 12 nonresidential programs for battered women. The South Carolina coalition responded that it has 14 domestic violence residential programs and 18 nonresidential sexual assault intervention programs.

Self-Reported Accomplishments Identified by Coalition Survey Respondents

Coalitions responding to the survey identified a number of specific accomplishments over the past 2 years ($n = 33$). Starting with the primary goal of ensuring that women affected by domestic violence achieve safety and a life free of abuse, achievements included successful legislative advocacy, improving the responsiveness of health and legal systems to domestic violence victims, developing and enhancing domestic violence programs, designing and implementing training and public relations and information campaigns, and improving internal functioning. These achievements are described in detail in the following.

Moved Toward Reaching of Overarching Goal

- Seemed to help women threatened with domestic violence stay alive

Successfully Advocated for Legal and Legislative Changes, Including Funding

- Successfully advocated for passage of staff funding bill
- Successfully advocated for increase in state general revenue funds for domestic violence services by $18 million, bringing the total to $21.9 million
- Organized grassroots public relations to help with the reauthorization of the Violence Against Women Act (VAWA 2000)
- Successfully advocated for the passage of state legislation
- Increased state funding for domestic violence programs by $2.5 million
- Successfully advocated for statewide legislative changes
- Obtained state funding for programs
- Supported court cases at the appellate and supreme court level that culminated in decisions advantageous to battered women
- Increased sustainability of funding for adult abuse advocates, child abuse advocates, and family violence victim advocates
- Coordinated a unified coalition membership coordinated stance during a government restructuring that resulted in legislation to create an interagency task force on domestic violence and sexual assault

Implemented Training Programs

- Established a TANF-funded project in collaboration with a state social service department that resulted in the training of thousands of workers
- Developed an antiracism training program
- Trained every person in the department of social services
- Created resource and training institutes
- Conducted welfare training
- Standardized training for domestic violence staff
- Established a full-fledged training institute for staff of domestic violence programs to positively influence the quality of services to all battered women in New Jersey

Improved Responsiveness of Health System to Domestic Violence

- Established a health initiative, the Family Violence Prevention Fund, for which advocates and medical facilities staff teamed up to develop protocols for identifying and assisting victims of domestic violence in 22 health care facilities

Improved Access to Legal Services and Responsiveness of Criminal Justice System

- Established a pro bono information and referral line staffed by volunteer attorneys twice a month and provided other pro bono work for victims of domestic violence and sexual assault
- Engaged in court monitoring

Expanded and Improved Programs and Services for Domestic Violence Victims

- Developed a uniform set of standards for programs
- Created a statewide database that contains unique client identifiers and tracks them through multiple incidents with perpetrators
- Engaged in program development
- Prioritized support for a domestic violence shelter
- Expanded programming with more staff and technical assistance
- Provided services to local domestic violence agencies
- Developed a Web-based data collection system on service provision for domestic violence, sexual assault, and stalking victims
- Developed the Workplace, a résumé service in New Mexico
- Initiated groundbreaking work on behalf of women of color, children, older battered women, and immigrant women

- increased membership of domestic violence and sexual assault programs, with support from law enforcement (police, legal aides, and prosecutors)
- Developed special projects for victims statewide, including health insurance, civil legal representation, and advocacy on behalf of rural women

Promoted Public Relations and Information Campaigns

- Sponsored a domestic violence and sexual assault conference in 2000
- Designed and publicized all program materials needed for distribution to victims and community residents at no cost to the community or state
- Successfully advocated for the governor to proclaim domestic violence as public enemy number one in Maine
- Conducted community surveys to determine levels of awareness and response from criminal justice systems to social service agencies
- Implemented an effective public awareness campaign that included production of a reporters' handbook to help journalists more effectively cover domestic violence; initiated domestic violence awareness month campaign using television, radio, print, billboards, and bus advertisements; initiated a sports campaign using amateur and professional athletes to promote nonviolence in relationships

Improved Organizational Functioning and Structure

- Dramatically increased provision of member services as a result of organizational growth
- Completed a structural reorganization
- Improved collaboration among state coalition member agencies
- Developed committees to address issues and policies affecting women of color and established a certification process for domestic violence advocates

Operating Issues

Year of Incorporation

Thirty-six of the respondents indicated the year in which their coalitions were established. The average year of incorporation was 1982.

Operating Budgets Based on Income Sources/ Funding Sources

The average operating budget reported for the statewide coalition respondents to the survey ($n = 39$) was $1,457,595. Average reported revenues in the form of membership dues totaled $50,673. Direct state funds averaged $290,316; direct federal funds averaged $775,618.

Other sources of funding included the following: fund-raising events; Americorps Program; private and foundation grants; federal pass-through funds; state pass-through funds; Nine West lawsuit; Federal Rural Domestic Violence Grant; Federal Arrest Grant; Victims of Crime Act Grants; fees from training and conferences; Main Share; investment interest; contractor fee for service; corporate sponsorships; annual dinner; planning meeting; in-kind contributions; resource sales; miscellaneous; VAW Net; Department of Transportation (DOT), subcontract on a "rural grant"; domestic violence and sexual assault STOP funds; Department of Public Welfare; Blue Cross/ Blue Shield administration; Department of Health and Human Services Hotline Operations; and individual member contributions.

Full- and Part-time Staff Employment by Statewide Coalitions

The average number of full time equivalent (FTE) staff members employed by statewide coalitions ($n = 39$) is a little over 18 (18.4). The average number of reported part-time staff is 2.2.

Staff Management Structures Utilized by Statewide Coalitions

Most statewide coalition survey respondents (34) reported using the executive director type of management structure. Other types of staff management structures used by respondents included codirectors (3), team coordinators, administrators with an executive committee, and coordinator. None reported utilizing a collective staff management structure.

Use of Contract Services or Consultants

Of the responding coalitions ($n = 39$), most (34, or 87%) reported regular use of contract services or consultants. Only five (13%) did not. Coalitions reported using contract services or consultants primarily for technology (23) or training (19). Other reported uses included accounting (15), lobbying (11), publications and public relations (6), planning (6), grant writing (5), and administrative or management functions (4). Other functions mentioned by respondents included special projects, hotline activities, graphic art, legal services, personnel issues, writing and editing training materials, facilitating a support group at a women's prison, audits, site visits, facilitating board meetings and peer reviews, managing and assisting with special and grant-funded projects, evaluation, and organizational restructuring/long-range planning.

Presence of a State-Appointed Domestic Violence Coordinating Council, Task Force, or Similar Body

The majority (28, or 69%) of statewide coalitions ($n = 39$) reported having a state-appointed domestic violence coordinating council, task force, or similar body. Of the other respondents, 10 (28%) did not have a state-appointed coordinating council, and 1 (0.5%) did not report.

Operation of a Statewide Hotline

Of responding statewide coalitions ($n = 39$), the majority (24, or 60%) reported not operating and maintaining a statewide hotline, and 15 (40%) reported operating such a hotline.

Operation of a Statewide Computer Network

Most statewide coalitions (28 out of 39 respondents, or 70%) responded that they did not operate and maintain a statewide computer system, while 12 coalitions (30%) stated that they do.

Organizational Structures and Issues

Number of Voting Seats

The average number of voting seats for responding coalitions ($n = 36$) was 23. For example, New Hampshire has between 12 and 18 voting seats, and Louisiana has 19 voting seats, with each participating battered victim receiving one third of a vote.

Methods by Which Coalition Boards of Directors Are Constituted

The survey identified four different methods by which coalition boards are constituted. Among the respondents to this question ($n = 38$), directors are elected or appointed from member programs or individual coalition members in 11 (29% coalition boards); all member programs have a board seat in 18 (47%); directors are elected or appointed from member programs only in 6 (16%); and directors are elected or appointed from members and nonmembers in 6 (16%). The Delaware coalition responded that its board consists of all members, member programs, and nonmembers. The Pennsylvania coalition consists of all member programs, the executive director, and three caucuses with two votes each. In the Iowa coalition, all "active" member programs get a vote. Jane Doe coalition responded that members receive 18 votes and the community receives 7 votes. The Louisiana coalition board of directors consists of an executive committee, president, vice president, and secretary, as well as a director from each task force.

Number of Annual Meetings of Boards of Directors Representing Coalition Members

According to survey respondents ($n = 37$), boards of directors meet on average seven times during the year.

Decision-Making Processes Governing Coalition Boards of Directors

Decision-making processes reported by respondents for governing the boards of directors can be grouped in three categories. Of the responding coalitions ($n = 36$), 22 (61%) report using simple majority rule; 12 (33%) use consensus; and 2 (0.5%) use supermajority rule. As examples, North Carolina and North Dakota reported that they utilize a modified consensus process, and Rhode Island reported using a simple majority rule except for funding issues and membership.

Types of Standing Committees of the Statewide Coalition Boards of Directors

There were six main standing committees of boards of directors as reported by responding coalitions ($n = 39$). These include finance (25), personnel (21), membership (21), legislative (16), executive (15), and bylaw/strategy planning (13). Other reported standing committees include nominating (9), fundraising (7), and policy (7). Five coalitions reported certification, contracts and development, and training standing committees; and four reported resource development, ad hoc, and steering committees. Two coalitions reported coordinating committees, diversity committees, public awareness, special events, and standards review as standing committees. A number of other standing committees were utilized by a single coalition. These include administrators' working group, advocacy, appropriations, batterer intervention program, clergy, client concerns, conflict resolution, domestic violence shelter directors, effective communications, fund distribution, governmental affairs, grants, health care, human resources, internal communications, leadership, operations, peer review, program development, publication, quality assurance, research and education, rural outreach, services, silent witnesses, standards, survivors' advisory, treatment providers, welfare and poverty, and white women working against racism.

Use of Caucuses or Task Forces to Represent Underserved Constituencies

Of the responding statewide coalitions ($n = 39$), the majority (28, or 72%) reported using caucuses or task forces to represent underserved constituencies. Eleven coalitions (28%) responded that they did not have caucuses or task forces, and 1 coalition surveyed did not respond. Rural caucuses were reported by 5 coalitions; survivors' advisory, battered and formerly battered women, women of color, and lesbian caucuses were reported by 3; multicultural awareness by 2; and safe home and shelter, children, educators, white allies, Native American forum, Sisters Overcoming Abusive Relationships (SOAR), and housing and economic justice were each reported by a single coalition. Of identified task forces, 13 coalitions identified women of color; 10 identified Lesbian and Gay Battered Women's Task Force (LGBT) and allies; 8 identified formerly battered and battered women; 4 identified sources to rural women; 2 identified multicultural and nonresidential; and 1 each identified sources to Latina, and African-American women, legal advisory services, teen dating violence prevention, batterer intervention, social justice, sexual assault services, battered lesbian, and formerly battered women of color. Most respondents (15) reported not having a board vote for caucuses, 11 responded that they do have a board vote, 1 responded that it has a mechanism for caucuses that have one board vote, and the other coalitions did not include a response.

Mechanisms for Emergency Decision Making

Of the responding statewide coalitions ($n = 39$), the majority (36, or 93%) stated that the executive committee of the board of directors is authorized to make emergency decisions between regularly scheduled meetings of the full board. No authorization for making emergency decisions between regularly scheduled board meetings was reported by 2 (0.5%) respondents, and 1 coalition did not respond.

Future Directions

Looking to the future, statewide coalition respondents were asked to identify their priorities in the current fiscal year related to public policy ($n = 33$). Seeking legislative changes was cited most frequently as a priority, reflecting the advocacy and empowerment orientation of battered women's coalitions (Busch & Valentine, 2001; Saunders, 1995). Promoting and establishing programs and services for battered women and their children demonstrated the commitment of battered women advocates to protect and serve the children whose mothers are domestic violence victims (Hughes & Marshall, 1995). Strengthening the internal structures of coalitions and fund-raising were also cited as key priorities, reflecting the respondents' understanding of the importance and complexity of coalition building and strengthening (Mizrahi & Rosenthal, 2001). Their specific responses are given below.

Seek Legislative Changes

- Support gun confiscation with restraining orders and protective orders
- Advocate for state legislative changes to achieve congruency with VAWA II
- Work with the state to provide privilege to domestic violence advocates
- Advocate with the state on an implementation plan for VAWA and VOCA funding
- Seek general funding for local programs
- Seek amendment to the stalking statute
- Seek changes to state custody laws to make it easier for battered women to obtain custody of children
- Engage in legislative advocacy to maintain the family violence option in the reauthorization of the Personal Responsibility and Work Opportunity Reconciliation Act of 1996 (PL. 104-193), which sunsets in 2002
- Provide legislative education to governor and related state legislation
- Seek expansion of protective orders to include dating violence
- Advocate for welfare reform
- Seek protective order revisions
- Advocate for firearms-related legislation
- Focus on confidentiality issues
- Advocate for expansion of legal definition of the family
- Seek implementation of current laws
- Obtain certification of batterers' programs
- Seek changes to the Wisconsin focus on implementation of the TANF program
- Seek changes in parental notification laws
- Advocate for mandatory HIV testing for convicted sexual assault felons
- Cosponsor legislation to secure $25 million of state general funding for domestic violence programs and services
- Advocate for a domestic violence omnibus bill
- Seek revision of the primary aggressor language in warrantless arrest laws
- Search out and advocate against legislative bills that adversely affect domestic violence victims and services
- Seek implementation of legislation on terminating parental rights registry

Promote and Establish Programs and Services for Children and Families

- Promote health services for children and domestic violence victims
- Maintain integrity of services related to substance abuse services
- Develop model protocols for child welfare workers on handling domestic violence cases

- Expand housing services for children
- Advocate for mandatory training of child protective services workers on domestic violence
- Advocate for establishment of visitation centers
- Seek to maintain the integrity of specific services for battered women and their children
- Address conflict between child abuse and domestic violence issues
- Promote civil justice issues, especially those related to child custody
- Advocate for mandatory domestic violence curriculum in schools

Strengthen Organizational Capacity and Effectiveness of Coalitions

- Develop the coalition's newly created policy committee, including setting a policy agenda and providing training for committee members on the legislative process
- Initiate multicultural outreach
- Identify underserved populations and collaborate with them to determine what assistance they need
- Continue review of bail conditions and policy
- Become more inclusive of native communities with planning and financial opportunities
- Continue interagency subcabinet liaison work with the state government

Expand Funding for Services

- Seek funding for shelter and legal services
- Seek increased funding for domestic violence and sex abuse programs
- Establish and seek funding for forensic nurse examiner programs
- Seek funding to continue Employees Against Domestic Violence initiative

CONCLUSION

The movement to end sexual assault and domestic violence against women has come a long way during the last quarter of the 20th century. The grassroots activism and advocacy of state and national domestic violence organizations built strong momentum and public awareness since the beginning in 1978 and 1979. With the passage of VAWA II in October 2000, there has been a rapid and sustained proliferation of state legislation, model domestic violence and family violence codes, specialized domestic violence courts, and police-based and social service programs and services for battered women and their children. The subsequent chapters provide in-depth information on these trends, new legislation, legal remedies, and program developments throughout the United States.

REFERENCES

Brownell, P., & Congress, E. P. (1998). Application of the culturagram to assess and empower culturally and ethnically diverse battered women. In A. R. Roberts (Ed.), *Battered women and their families* (2nd ed., pp. 387–404). New York: Springer.

Busch, N. B., & Valentine, D. (2000). Empowerment practice: A focus on battered women. *Affilia, 15*, 1, 82–95.

Del Martin. (1976). *Battered wives.* San Francisco: Volcano Press.

Hart, B. (2001). *Presentation.*

Hughes, H. M., & Marshall, M. (1995). Advocacy for children of battered women. In E. Peled, P. G. Jaffe, & J. L. Edleson (Eds.), *Ending the cycle of violence: Community responses to children of battered women* (pp. 121–144). Thousand Oaks, CA: Sage.

Koss, M. P., Goodman, L. A., Browne, A., Fitzgerald, L. F., Keita, G. P., & Russo, N. F. (1994). *No safe haven: Male violence against women at home, at work, and in the community.* Washington, D.C.: American Psychological Society.

Mizrahi, T., & Rosenthal, B. B. (2001). Complexities of coalition building: Leaders' successes, strategies, struggles, and solutions. *Social Work, 46*, 1, 63–78.

National Coalition Against Domestic Violence (NCADV). (2001). Legislative update March 5, 2001 107th Congress, federal agencies and international organizations work on domestic violence. http://www.ncadv.org/publicpolicy/legupdate.htm.

NCADV (2001). The public policy office of NCADV. http://ncadv.org/publicpolicy/policyhome.htm.

NCADV (2001). Violence against women appropriation fact sheet.

http://www.acadv.org/publicpolicy/approp2002.htm.

National Organization for Women (NOW) (2001). NOW's Past. http://nownyc.org/past.htm.

Pleck, E. (1987). *Domestic tyranny: The making of American social policy against family violence from colonial times to the present.* New York: Oxford University Press.

Roberts, A. R. (1981). *Sheltering battered women: A national study and service guide.* New York: Springer.

Roberts, A. R. (1998). The organizational structure and function of shelters for battered women and their children: A national survey. In A. R. Roberts (Ed.), *Battered women and their families: Intervention strategies and treatment programs* (2nd ed., pp. 58–75). New York: Springer.

Roberts, A. R. (2001). National network to end domestic violence: State coalition organizational profiles. Unpublished study findings.

Roche, S. E., & Sadoski, P. J. (1996). Social action for battered women. In A. R. Roberts (Ed.), *Helping battered women: New perspectives and remedies* (pp. 13–30). New York: Oxford University Press.

Roy, M. (Ed.). (1977). *Battered women: A psycho-social study of domestic violence.* New York: Van Nostrand Reinhold.

Saunders, D. G. (1995). Domestic violence: Legal issues. In R. L. Edwards (Ed.), *Encyclopedia of social work, 19th edition* (pp. 789–795). Washington, DC: NASA Press.

Schechter, S. (1982). *Women and male violence: The visions and struggles of the battered women's movement.* Boston: South End Press.

Weil, M. O., & Gamble, D. N. (2002). Community practice models for the 21st century. In A. R. Roberts & G. Greene (Eds.), *Social workers' desk reference.* New York: Oxford University Press.

Part II
CRIMINAL JUSTICE AND LEGAL SYSTEM RESPONSES

6

Police Responses to Battered Women

Past, Present, and Future

ALBERT R. ROBERTS
KAREL KURST-SWANGER

It was 1400 hours on September 6, 2010. Two police officers were dispatched on a report of a domestic violence complaint. Upon arriving at the scene, the officers spoke to the victim, Wilma R. She stated that her boyfriend, Louis, had been drinking the night before and became involved in an argument with her that ended with his punching her in the face and strangling her. The officers observed that Wilma had a cut on her upper lip and swelling in the area between her nose and mouth.

When the police officers questioned Louis, he said he never touched Wilma. He insisted that the bruises on her face resulted from her being clumsy and falling down the steps while carrying the laundry. He said she was making up the story of being beaten because she was angry at him for staying out late with his buddies the previous night.

To determine whether or not Louis had strangled his girlfriend, the police officers went to the car and brought in the compact portable laser unit. By aiming the laser at Wilma's neck, the first officer immediately obtained laser fingerprints, which he compared with Louis's. The results showed an identical match. While the first officer was matching the fingerprints, the second officer went to the car and turned on the Mobile Data Terminal (MDT) computer to run a criminal history on Louis. In less than 30 seconds, Louis's history appeared on the screen: two prior convictions for simple assault against a former girlfriend and resisting arrest. The incidents had occurred

3 years earlier in another state. In addition, Louis's record showed two arrests during the past 3 years for driving while intoxicated.

The officers' next step was to obtain a temporary restraining order (TRO) to prevent Louis from having any further contact with Wilma. They obtained the TRO by entering a summary of their findings at the scene on their portable computer and using the cellular phone to inform the judge that they were sending the report to her courtroom from their car fax. At the courthouse, the court clerk took the report from the fax machine and brought it to Judge Catherine Sloan for her signature. The court clerk then faxed the TRO back to the police car. The entire approval process took only 15 minutes.

Next the police transported Louis to the county jail, where the nurse-practitioner implanted a subdural electronic sensor in Louis's wrist. The police also gave a sensing receiver to Wilma to wear externally, on a chain around her neck. The computer at the police headquarters will monitor these sensors, as it has done with the 300 other domestic abuse cases reported to the police department during the past 12 months. The officers told Louis that if he comes within 500 meters of Wilma, the sensing device will immediately alert the police officers that he has violated the TRO, and he will be sent to jail.

In the future, technology and a commitment to ending family violence will merge to provide a response to domestic violence that ensures the safety of the victim and the accountability of the offender. We envision a future in which the police consistently regard instances of battering as serious criminal offenses in need of state intervention. This will require a commitment to continued research, policy development, and an investment in technological advancement. This chapter will explore the role of the police response in domestic violence by examining historical perspectives, present practices, and future opportunities.

HISTORICAL PERSPECTIVES

Although domestic violence has been recognized as a pervasive social problem fairly recently, its cultural bases are deeply embedded in Western history and culture. Even a cursory review of that history reveals the extent to which law and society have traditionally served to implicitly support and perpetuate the subordination of women to their husbands. In some parts of Latin America and Asia, especially in the upper classes, killing a wife for an indiscretion has usually been acceptable, although the same privilege generally is not extended to women as perpetrators. Various cultures and societies have permitted or tacitly encouraged some degree of family violence as a means to maintain that subordination. Demographic analyses of domestic violence offenses reported to the police confirm the observation that domestic violence is most frequently perpetrated by males against their female partners and that males constitute only a small fraction of the total number of victims in domestic violence cases.

As Murray Straus and Richard Gelles (1990) have noted, domestic violence is intrinsically linked to the maintenance of power and dominance within the family unit. Family violence and spousal assaults are facilitated when there are few effective formal and informal social control mechanisms, thereby allowing the rewards of maintaining power through violence to outweigh the costs of such violence. From this observation, we can infer that cultures that define violence within the family unit as unacceptable behavior and emphatically communicate an attitude of disapproval by applying potent social sanctions (e.g., ostracizing or publicly humiliating the perpetrator) have lower rates of domestic violence than do societies that ignore the issue or tacitly approve of intrafamily violence. Similarly, the availability of formal mechanisms for social control (e.g., the legal processes of arrest and punishment) also impacts the incidence of domestic violence. Straus and Gelles (1990) concluded that people use violence against members of their families "because they can" (p. 18).

History reveals that, until fairly recently, men were legally permitted to employ relatively unrestrained physical force against their wives and children to maintain family discipline. Social norms regarding family violence were mirrored by police practice. Buzawa and Buzawa (1990) note a variety of factors such as the occupational code of the police, structural impediments to police action, organizational disincentives, and past training practices that provide little motivation for the police to intervene in domestic violence cases. The classic police response to domestic violence involved a "do-nothing" approach or temporarily separating the parties until the abuser cooled off. Police were frequently accused of taking the side of male batterers and subscribing to the view that "a man's home is his castle." Furthermore, court staff tended to minimize the danger that battered women encountered and discouraged them from filing criminal or civil complaints. Consequently, these approaches have done little to reduce calls for service, and in some instances, violence between intimate partners escalated into more brutal attacks and even homicide.

During the 1960s, several discrete trends evolved in policing, law, and politics, and these ultimately converged in the 1970s and 1980s to set the stage for our current concerns and the attention paid to domestic violence issues. The confluence of these trends and pressures created a unique and powerful synergy, forcing American police agencies and lawmakers to reexamine their policies and practices and to adopt the strategies that prevail today.

Bridging the Past to the Present: Bolstering Incremental Change

During the past decade, domestic violence has increasingly been defined as a serious crime (i.e., a felony rather than a misdemeanor) by a growing number of state criminal codes and family court statutes. In fact, because of the prevalence and life-threatening nature of woman battering, all 50 states have passed civil and/or criminal statutes to protect battered women. In some areas, as many as 75% of all police calls involve domestic conflict and/or violence.

Society at large has finally recognized that beating women (wives, cohabitants, or companions) is a crime and a major social problem. This recognition grew out of four noteworthy activities. First, the women's movement was instrumental in drawing public attention to the plight of abused women. Second, two national prevalence studies on the extent of domestic violence in the United States were conducted, and the results confirmed our worst fears: Domestic violence occurs with great frequency and should be given top public policy priority (Straus & Gelles, 1990; Straus, Steinmetz, & Gelles, 1980). Third, a proliferation of research on battered women, culminating in numerous books and news articles, brought scholars, professionals, and the public closer to the issue (Fleming, 1976; Roberts, 1984; Roy, 1982; Walker, 1979, 1984). Finally, recent litigation and legal reforms have prompted institutional change (Hart, 1992).

As a result of such social changes, police departments have literally endured a metamorphosis in their customary practices, norms, and formal policies regarding domestic violence. Many police departments now have policies and procedures that specify how dispatchers, patrol officers, and investigators should handle domestic violence cases. Many departments coordinate their law enforcement roles with local victim service providers and the courts. Departments nationwide have embraced mandatory and pro-arrest policies as an important intervention strategy and have begun the process of retraining seasoned police officers.

However, the road toward implementing effective policies for batterers has been bumpy and uneven, and research studies on the short-term deterrent effects of arresting batterers are inconclusive. Nevertheless, Americans have come a long way from the time when the use of violence by men to control their partners was condoned. Mandatory and warrantless arrest laws are just one part of the improved police response to victims of battering. In addition, the police in highly populated cities and counties throughout the nation now provide immediate protection to battered women.

Social and political pressures for change, in conjunction with the passage of civil and criminal statutes to protect battered women in all 50 states, · have considerably altered the way that police officers and agencies currently respond to domestic violence. Police executives and public policy makers, as well as individual police officers, have become more sensitive to the issues involved as they have faced the burden of making appropriate choices from a range of competing alternative strategies. Because defining and practicing an appropriate police response to domestic violence entails consideration of a broad array of practical, legal, political, and social variables, supervisors, trainers, and street officers confront a difficult task. Despite a host of opinions, policies, agendas, and programs aimed at redressing the social problem and providing relief to victims, there currently appears to be little consensus regarding precisely what constitutes the most desirable and effective response to domestic violence. It may be that since no single response has proved successful, a multilevel approach should be implemented, but only after more effective policy research has been completed.

PRESENT POLICE RESPONSES
TO DOMESTIC VIOLENCE

Here we review several current strategies employed by police to intervene in cases of domestic violence. First we explore specialized police training and discuss how important training of both rookies and seasoned officers is to the effectiveness of any police response. Second, we review some of the recent research on the effectiveness of the police response when arrest policies are enacted. Third, we investigate proarrest and mandatory arrest policies as one of the most important strategic forces to reduce incidents of battering. Fourth, we discuss the benefits of specialized units or task forces within police departments as a tool to improve the investigation and prosecution of domestic offenses. We also examine the present and future role of technology, coupled with appropriate police responses, to ensure victim safety and offender accountability. Finally we provide examples of model police departments and explore the importance of the police as a partner with broader, community-wide efforts to reduce domestic assaults.

Specialized Police Training

Police academy and in-service training are an important part of teaching police their roles and responsibilities. The amount and duration of domestic violence training influence whether or not new police officers will take seriously their potential role in protecting battered women.

Between 1985 and 2000, many police departments mandated that training sessions on family violence should be part of their police academy curricula. These specialized training sessions have been implemented much more frequently in large city or county police training academies than in small towns. In addition, many police departments now require all officers to arrest a domestic violence suspect when the victim exhibits signs of bodily injury, when a weapon is involved in the commission of a domestic violence act, or when there is probable cause to believe that the named accuser has violated the terms of a restraining order or other no-contact court order.

Dr. Roberts, one of the authors of this chapter, conducted a national survey on domestic violence training and police responses to battered women. The survey was sent to 60 police chiefs and their staffs in metropolitan areas in every region of the United States. The study's findings indicated a wide variation in the amount of time devoted to specialized domestic violence training for new recruits, ranging from 3 to 40 hours at the police academies located in the largest cities, such as Baltimore, Boston, Indianapolis, Kansas City, Las Vegas, Memphis, Milwaukee, San Diego, Seattle, and Tucson. In this survey, most small-town police departments provided no specific training on domestic violence or victim rights. In some of these smaller towns and municipalities, state police or troopers are often called in to intervene in domestic violence cases.

State troopers are responsible for protecting residents in many rural areas that have no local police department or when the nearest law enforcement agency is the county sheriff's office. The majority of state police are trained to respond sensitively and compassionately to battered women. In general, state police academies provide comprehensive training to all state troopers on such policies and procedures, as well as on changes in the state criminal code, motor vehicle violations, investigative techniques, victims' rights legislation, and domestic violence.

Variation in police training is due to a number of factors, including state legislative statutes, variation in how training requirements are crafted, and differences in state versus county local control over police policies. For example, a study conducted by Miller (1998) found that state legislators have enacted laws that require police academies to include domestic violence in 30 states and the District of Columbia; however, in-service training was required by only 7 states.

Beginning in fiscal year 1991, the federal Office for Victims of Crime (OVC) of the U.S. Department of Justice began funding and providing technical assistance to state police training academies. The purpose of these federal grants has been to develop and implement training programs for state and local law enforcement administrators and officers on current policies and procedures for responding to family violence incidents. Currently the OVC continues to provide funding to federal, state, and local police departments for training regarding victim issues. For example, in fiscal year 2000 it funded the Federal Law Enforcement Training Center to provide training to federal law enforcement officers, representing 70 federal agencies, in basic and advanced victimology curricula.

The Violence Against Women Act (VAWA) of 1994 authorizes Services and Training for Officers and Prosecuters (STOP) grants, with required matching state funds, that provide money for training of law enforcement personnel. The Urban Institute conducted an evaluation of STOP grants and found that states were using their grants to improve training in a number of ways: expanding training requirements to be effective statewide; developing or updating training curricula; training process servers on issues related to domestic violence; developing multidisciplinary training for law enforcement, prosecutors, judges, and victim services; and creating specialized seminars, in-service courses, and "roll-call" packages. More information on model STOP grant programs in different regions of the United States is presented later in this chapter.

Training for police on domestic violence issues includes a wide array of topics such as dynamics of violent families and impacts on victims, understanding batterers' use of violence to maintain control over their victims, dispatcher protocol, securing the crime scene, assessment of victim safety, identifying and interviewing victims and witnesses, and the collection of forensic evidence. Since many state legislatures have moved to include pro-arrest and/or mandatory policies in the cases of domestic violence, training often focuses on the appropriate implementation of state law.

The VAWA has also provided funding in 2000 to the Federal Law Enforcement Training Center to implement its newly developed domestic violence train-the-trainer program for law enforcement officials in rural communities. This training, centered on domestic violence issues present in rural communities, provides officers with instruction on training curricula, copies of training materials, and videos for use in their own jurisdictions.

Contemporary police training has evolved to include topics and issues not typically considered in traditional police training. For example, the New Haven Police Department's Child Development–Community Policing Program is a promising example of multidisciplinary training aimed at increasing the competence of police officer in their interactions with children and families. The training—administered by the Yale Child Study Center and the New Haven Department of Police Service—is centered on reorienting police officers to approach their work from a mental health perspective and to learn to work in partnership with local social service providers. Both new and veteran police officers have the opportunity to complete a 10-week course on child development and community policing. Case conferences, consultation services, and child development fellowships for police supervisors are unique features of this police–mental health collaboration (New Haven Police Department, 2001).

Similarly, the International Association of Chiefs of Police, based on recommendations from the Summit on Family Violence, has included the following training recommendations for police departments. Training should be multidisciplinary, including professionals such as law enforcement, fire department, EMT workers, religious leaders, teachers and other school personnel, child care workers, health care workers, substance abuse providers, child welfare and public assistance workers, prosecutors, and judges. Training should be tailored to meet the specific needs of the local community and should include preservice, in-service, and continuing education curricula. The summit work groups also stressed the importance of establishing and maintaining multidisciplinary policy initiatives and suggested that agencies should pool resources to collaborate for effective intervention strategies (International Association of Chiefs of Police, 2001).

Research on the Deterrent Effects of Arrest

Several studies have been completed on the effect of arrest on subsequent intimate partner violence and on reducing the number of repeat calls for domestic violence. The first study, known as the Minneapolis experiment, found that arrest was more effective than to separate the parties or mediation in deterring subsequent battering.

The Minneapolis Domestic Violence Experiment (1981–1982), conducted by Sherman and Berk (1984), was the first research study to test the short-term deterrent effect of arrest in domestic violence cases with heterosexual, married, and cohabitating couples. In selected police precincts, domestic violence incidents were randomly assigned to one of three police methods of responding: (1) providing advice and informal mediation, (2) separating the couple by ordering the offender to leave the premises for 8 hours to cool off, and (3) arresting the alleged offender and detaining him overnight in the local jail.

A total of 330 eligible cases were tracked for 6 months. Repeat incidents of domestic violence were measured through official police department records to determine whether there had been additional domestic violence calls to the same address, and follow-up interviews with the victim were conducted every 2 weeks. The findings indicate that arrest in and of itself was almost twice as effective as other interventions in reducing battering. The violence was repeated in only 13% of the arrest cases, compared with a 19% failure rate among cases assigned to informal mediation and a 24% failure rate for the cases assigned to "cool off" for 8 hours.

The experiment encountered several methodological problems, however, including a small sample size, a disproportionate number of cases to which the same few officers responded, and inadequate standardization and controls over the treatments actually delivered by the officers. Despite these flaws, the Minneapolis experiment received widespread national recognition and had a significant impact on arrest policies nationwide. Between 1984 and 1987, police chiefs in thousands of police departments read the favorable reports in newspaper articles and a report by the National Institute of Justice (NIJ), which praised the study and stated that arrest was the best deterrent for spouse abuse.

Between 1984 and 1986, in the aftermath of the Minneapolis study, the percentage of large city police departments with preferred or proarrest "policies increased from 10% to 46%" (Walker, 1992, p. 321). By 1989, a total of 13 states had enacted mandatory arrest policies for domestic violence perpetrators. In some of these states, arrest is mandatory in misdemeanor- and felony-level domestic charges, as well as for violation of a restraining order. However, in 2 states (Delaware and North Carolina) arrest is mandatory only when the abuser violates a restraining order (Buzawa & Buzawa, 1990, p. 6).

To determine the validity of the Minneapolis experiment, the NIJ funded six replications in Atlanta, Georgia; Omaha, Nebraska; Charlotte, North

Carolina; Colorado Springs, Colorado; Dade County, Florida; and Milwaukee, Wisconsin. Similar to the Minneapolis experiment, the six later studies examined whether arrest was the most effective police response in preventing batterers from committing future acts of abuse.

In contrast with the Minneapolis experiment, three of the six replications found arrest to be a less effective deterrent than other police responses, for three main reasons: First, the majority of the batterers in these studies had prior criminal records (50% in Milwaukee, 65% in Omaha, and 69% in Charlotte), and thus arrest was neither innovative nor unexpected. Second, violence was a common and chronic problem among these study samples rather than a first-time occurrence. Therefore, it is unrealistic to expect a short arrest to have much impact on a long-term, chronically violent relationship. Third, there was wide variation among the studies in the amount of time the arrested.batterers were in custody. For example, in the Milwaukee study, the average time in custody for a "short arrest" was 2.8 hours, and for a full arrest, 11.1 hours; in Charlotte, the average time in custody was 15.75 hours (Dunford, 1990; Sherman et al., 1992). In contrast, for the Minneapolis study, the time in custody ranged from approximately 24 hours to 1 week (168 hours). Finally, arrest alone without graduated sanctions of incarceration and fines does not serve as a strong deterrent among persons with previous arrest histories.

Lawrence Sherman and his associates found that arrest did not have a deterrent effect among a particular subgroup of abusers in Milwaukee. The most unique finding of the study just cited is that even though arrest seemed to lead to repeated violence among unemployed batterers, it may prevent subsequent violence by abusers who are employed, married, and white (Sherman et al., 1992). Because of the large sample size, 1,200 cases eligible for randomization, the researchers were able to compare many subclassifications and matched pairs. The other replications were not able to subclassify as many variables as was done in the Milwaukee study.

Proarrest and Mandatory Arrest Policies or State Statutes

Regardless of the inconclusiveness of research findings, all states have passed legislation permitting the officer to make warrantless arrests when there is probable cause to believe a domestic crime has occurred (Miller, 1998). In the past, police officers could not make arrests on misdemeanor-level crimes unless they witnessed the assault or had a court-issued warrant for arrest of the subject. Therefore, this practice required a victim to go to great lengths to file a warrant for the abuser's arrest and limited the ability of the police to intervene in a formal way at the scene. Today, proarrest and mandatory arrest provisions have been embedded into every state's statutes, clarifying and expanding the arrest powers of the police.

A mandatory policy directs the police to a specific action and limits discretion. For example, a policy may dictate that a police officer "shall" arrest any person for committing a domestic assault when there is probable cause, whereas, presumptive policies (which also favors arrest) strongly suggest arrest (Buzawa & Buzawa, 1990). In the case of proarrest policies, a statute might say that arrest shall be the "preferred" or "presumptive" response in a case of domestic assault.

Policy changes such as the introduction of proarrest policies are the result of several social factors. Beginning in the early 1970s, the women's movement demanded that the public take notice of the plight of battered women and the blatant disregard of their needs by the police and the courts. The National Coalition Against Domestic Violence and statewide coalitions and advocacy groups were instrumental in drawing attention to the systemic problems associated with the "do-nothing" approach to battering.

Second, the Minneapolis domestic violence experiment on the deterrent effects of arrest (Sherman & Berk, 1984) showcased the possibilities of a concerted effort by the police in deterring battering. This study, followed by the final report of the U.S. Attorney General's Task Force on Family Violence (1984), citing the Minneapolis experiment, documented the prevalence and intense dangers of battering episodes. The report concluded that domestic violence is a major crime problem and that criminal justice agencies should handle it as such.

Finally, civil liability suits filed against police departments and prosecutors for their failure to provide for the equal protection of women resulted in the reexamination of both formal and informal policies related to domestic violence. Network television and newspaper coverage of the court decisions was instrumental in garnering public support for change. One case, *Thurman v. City of Torrington*, is most noteworthy.

In this case, Tracey Thurman of Torrington, Connecticut (*Thurman v. City of Torrington*, 595 F. Supp. 1531 [1984]), who had been beaten repeatedly by her husband, sued the Torrington Police Department. The basis for her lawsuit was the failure of the department to protect her, even though she had continually requested police protection over an 8-month period. And even though Ms. Thurman had obtained a court order barring her violent spouse from assaulting her again, it took the police 25 minutes to arrive on the scene of the most violent battering. After reaching the Thurman home, the arresting officer delayed arresting Mr. Thurman—who held a bloody knife—for several minutes. This gave Mr. Thurman plenty of time to repeatedly kick his wife in the head, face, and neck while she lay helpless on the ground. As a result, Ms. Thurman suffered life-threatening injuries, including multiple stab wounds to the chest, neck, and face; fractured cervical vertebrae and damage to her spinal cord; partial paralysis below the neck; lacerations to the cheeks and mouth; loss of blood; shock; scarring; severe pain; and mental anguish.

Tracey Thurman's award was unprecedented: $2.3 million in compensatory damages against 24 police officers. The jury found that the Torrington, Connecticut, police had deprived Ms. Thurman of her constitutional right to equal protection under the law (Fourteenth Amendment to the Constitution). The jury further concluded that the Torrington police officers were guilty of gross negligence in failing to protect Tracey Thurman and her son, Charles Jr., from the violent acts of Charles Thurman Sr.

In the wake of the court decision in the *Thurman* case and other similar cases, police departments throughout the country began implementing proarrest policies and increased training on domestic violence. The new policies were intended to serve two purposes: to change the behavior of both abusers and the police. These policies have also intentionally limited a victim's input into the decision to arrest, thereby freeing her from the responsibility of being the one to send her partner to jail. Criminalizing domestic abuse therefore provides an opportunity to make abusers accountable for their actions, sending a message that domestic violence is not a matter of male privilege but a crime against the state.

All states have passed laws expanding the police's arrest powers in cases of domestic assault (Mills, 1999). Specifically, these recent statutes require or suggest arrest when there is a positive determination of probable cause (i.e., the existence of a visible injury and/or the passage of only a small amount of time between the commission of the assault and the arrival of the police). Police departments are also legally required to arrest batterers who have violated protective orders granted by the courts. As of 1992, protective orders were available to abused women in 50 states and the District of Columbia. In more and more jurisdictions, women in abusive relationships have obtained protective orders against their abusers from their local courts to prevent them from coming to their residence. Police are called upon to enforce the protective order and to arrest the abuser if he violates any stipulations in the court order.

There is great variation among state statutes regarding the police response to domestic violence. State statutes set the boundaries on which police discretion is granted or limited. State policies generally specify the circumstances in which an arrest can, should or must be made or when arrest is the preferred course of action. Criteria used to determine when arrest is preferred or mandatory include stipulations such as the time period between when a crime occurred and when it was reported, evidence of noticeable injuries, and circumstances in which a dual arrest is or is not appropriate. Currently, at least 21 states and the District of Columbia have mandatory arrest statutes, and 2 of these limit mandatory arrest to felony crimes only. Eight states maintain a proarrest policy. In addition, 35 states and the District of Columbia require police officers to complete domestic violence incident reports and to provide documentation on why an arrest was not made (Miller, 1998).

Several issues, however, limit the effectiveness of such policies. First, in some jurisdictions, unmarried couples, especially if of the same sex are not included in the proarrest policy for domestic violence. This certainly limits the police, since it is generally recognized that the police receive proportionately more domestic violence calls from cohabitating women than married women. Second, several studies have indicated that 40% to 60% of batterers flee the residence before the police arrive on the scene. Third, some policies address only felony-level assaults, eliminating the vast majority of domestic battering from the purview of the law. Finally, although policies have been put into place, some argue that the police have been slow to embrace them. For example, Ferraro (1989) found that it took almost 4 years for the Phoenix Police Department to implement policy after the enactment of the law. Mignon and Holmes (1995) found that mandatory arrest policies have in fact led to increased arrests, especially in cases in which a protective order is in force. They found arrest was more likely when a victim's injuries were more serious and when a witness was present during the assault. Police compliance with new policies will be a gradual process.

These polices have promoted vast change in institutional responses to the problem of intimate partner abuse from a police perspective. Yet, some scholars argue we should approach policy changes with caution. Critics contend that further research into such policies indicates that the results found in the Minneapolis experiment have not been uniformly replicated in other cities. As noted in the previous section, Sherman and Berk (1984) conclude that arrest is most effective when the batterer is married and employed; for unemployed abusers, arrest is actually likely to increase future violence.

Second, since such policies eliminate victim choice, these strategies have flooded the courts with cases in which there are "uncooperative" victims. Although prosecutors are routinely challenged by uncooperative victims and witnesses, the latter generally make up only a small portion of the caseload. However, in domestic violence cases, the majority of victims are "uncooperative" (Davis & Smith, 1995), placing an added burden on prosecutors. Buzawa and Buzawa (1990) note that a lack of prosecutorial support from victims results in low conviction rates.

Third, some scholars argue that mandatory arrest policies deter victims from reporting incidents in the first place. Future research needs to cross classify women who attempt to leave permanently with those who do not after the police are called. Mills (1999) argues that mandatory interventions mirror the battering relationship itself, reinforcing a patriarchal system in which women have little power. She argues that these policies, although intended to help women, have in fact continued to oppress them.

Additionally, Rosenbaum (1998) raises some interesting questions that are worthy of further investigation. His research, conducted in California, found that mandatory interventions produced less violence against the family member on whose behalf the arrest was made but at the same time increased the level of violence perpetrated on other members of the family. He has coined this the *substitution effect theory*. His conclusions raise important questions on implications for the safety and well-being of other family members, particularly children.

Despite the potential limitations inherent in instituting proarrest and mandatory policies, considerable progress has been made in the past decade. The "do-nothing" approach of the past is no longer an acceptable strategy in domestic violence cases. The implementation of multi-level policy over time and further research will be our guide to future effective policy reform.

Specialized Domestic Violence Units

In addition to changes in arrest policies and customary practices in domestic cases, many police departments have created specialized domestic violence units to follow up on all domestic complaints. Specialized units have the ability to further investigate domestic crimes, make appropriate referrals and arrests, and ensure victim safety, long after the patrol officer has left the scene. In some cases, unit members serve as the first responders to domestic calls for service. Units are generally staffed with police investigators or detectives and are often linked with specialized units in a prosecutor's office. They offer an opportunity for personnel to develop specialized knowledge and expertise regarding the investigation and prosecution of domestic crimes. In theory, units create the infrastructure necessary for aggressive, proactive responses to domestic violence rather than the traditional reactive policing approach.

These units also provide an opportunity to link police services with shelter, victim-witness, and batterer programing. Multidisciplinary approaches, ones that integrate both legal and social service interventions, are likely to be the most effective in terms of protecting victim safety and ensuring offender accountability. The police departments described in the following sections are illustrative of the modern police response to domestic violence.

Ann Arbor Police Department

The Domestic Violence Enforcement Team in Ann Arbor, Michigan, in partnership with the local battered women's advocacy program, provides an example of innovative police practice regarding domestic violence. The team was strategically placed in a building adjacent to the SAFE House in an effort to break down the barriers between the police and victim advocacy services and to improve the outcomes for victims. The police unit is able to track the status of cases, cutting through bureaucratic red tape, expediting the serving of bench warrants, and so forth. Police attend every defendant arraignment and are able to take all domestic cases seriously. Police link with SAFE House staff after an arrest has been made, bringing immediate in-person services to the victim (Littel et al., 1998).

Austin Police Department

The Austin/Travis County Family Violence Protection Team in Travis County, Texas, is another example of a collaborative community response to family violence that provides multiple services in one location. Leading the community in a zero-tolerance policy toward family violence, the team— consisting of members of the Austin Police Department, the Travis County Sheriff's Office, SafePlace (formerly the Center for Battered Women and Rape Crisis Center), Legal Aid of Central Texas, the Women's Advocacy Project (attorneys), and the Travis County Attorney's Office—collaborates to investigate, prosecute, and provide legal and social services for victims.

Investigations center around cases of assault, kidnapping, stalking, and protective order violations. Legal services streamline the process for obtaining emergency or long-term protective orders. The majority of cases are processed by the county attorney's office, and felonies are handled by the district attorney's office. Victim services are provided by victim service counselors from SafePlace, the Austin Police Department, and the Travis County Sheriff's Department. The Austin Child Guidance Center is also available to provide free counseling for children. The team has been in operation since 1997, funded by the Violence Against Women Grants Office (Austin City Connection, 2000).

Longview Police Department

The Domestic Violence Impact Unit in Longview, Washington, consists of a sergeant, officers, civilian investigator, legal coordinator, crime analyst, and administrative specialist. The unit works to coordinate law enforcement, prosecution, probation, and victim services in domestic violence cases, as well as providing education and training to police officers, advocates, prosecutors, probation officers, and other community and criminal justice partners. An automated case management system assists the team in tracking of offenders and their activities as they are processed through the system.

Not unlike the departments highlighted here, specialized units provide police departments with the opportunity to thoroughly investigate misdemeanor-level domestic crimes, a function that in the past has been lost to other felony crimes. Following up on high-risk cases is critical to breaking the cycle of violence before it escalates to the felony level. Creating dialogue between police units, victims' programs, and victims promotes the protection of victims and the opportunity to prevent future acts of violence.

Police departments frequently organize their functions through the creation of specialized departments or units. Division of labor into smaller subunits has been an effective tool for contemporary police departments to manage the variety of tasks required of them. For example, police departments may have investigative units or squads that deal with narcotics, sex crimes, juvenile crimes, fraud, special weapons, arson, and so forth. Generally organized around specific crime types, specialized units have afforded police departments the opportunity to attend to the specific dynamics of particular crimes.

Although there are inherent challenges in the specialization of police functions, Peak (1998) identifies several advantages to such an approach. Specialized units place the responsibility for certain tasks with specific individuals, ensuring that the work is completed. This is especially true in the case of domestic violence. Historically, police investigators only followed up on domestic cases that involved felony-level assaults and/or homicides. Therefore, the majority of battering incidents were addressed only by patrol officers at the scene, with only the most severe cases of abuse transferred to an investigative bureau. Specialized units also provide for the development of expertise and training that ultimately lead to increased efficiency, effectiveness, and staff cohesion and improved morale.

Although the potential is great for specialized units, Krumholz (2001) argues that there may be a disjuncture between the image of the Domestic Violence Unit and the reality that some units merely serve a symbolic role. Her research with 169 police departments in Massachusetts revealed a number of concerns. First, only 8% of the police departments with Domestic Violence Units reported being supported from a line item in the department's budget, and 11% received partial funding by line item. The majority of departments acknowledge they were funded solely by grants, which raises serious questions about the stability of such units after the grant period has ended. Krumholz also found that police departments with Domestic Violence Units required, on average, only 2 more hours of training per year than departments without such units. Additionally, she found that the average unit was staffed by two full-time officers and that the majority of units operated only during normal business hours.

Further research is needed before we can fully understand the impact of specialized units in the creation of a local community environment where victims can be protected and abusers can be held accountable. Since many police departments find that the majority of their calls for service involve domestic incidents, specialized units may provide the most prudent organizational strategy to taking domestic assault seriously.

The Role of Technology in a Coordinated Community Response

Technology has already begun to revolutionize the police industry. Advanced photographic techniques, computers, DNA profiling, innovations in fingerprinting and forensic techniques, automated crime analysis, computer-aided investigations and dispatch, case management systems, simulated training tools, nonlethal weapons, and surveillance technologies are but a few of the many examples of innovative crime-fighting tools. As police departments become more familiar with such technologies and more skilled in using them, and as communities agree to invest more resources in this area, police departments are likely to apply such advancements to combat domestic violence in a broad way.

We have already begun to see the potential for using technology to protect battered women from their abusive partners and deter violent batterers from repeating their abusive acts. Cellular phones, electronic monitoring systems, and on-line police services are just a few of the applications of modern technology to policing domestic violence.

Cellular Phones

A national campaign to donate cellular phones for victims of domestic violence is currently under way. Sponsored by the Wireless Foundation, a philanthrophic organization dedicated to utilizing wireless communication for the public good, the Call to Protect program to date has received 30,606 donated cellular phones to provide links to emergency services for victims and their advocates. This national donate-a-phone campaign has been established by the Cellular Telecommunications Industry Association (CTIA) and is implemented by the Wireless Foundation. CTIA member carriers, Motorola and Brightpoint, Inc. distribution management partner, in partnership with the National Coalition Against Domestic Violence (NCADV), provide free wireless phones and airtime.

The phones are preprogrammed to notify authorities at the push of a button. Victim advocates have also received donated phones and airtime. This national initiative has involved numerous organizations, clubs, and companies in the fight against domestic violence. Additionally, the Wireless Foundation coordinates the Communities on Phone Patrol (COPP) program, in partnership with Ericsson and CTIA companies to provide free wireless phones and airtime to volunteer neighborhood watch patrols. On average 52,000 crimes and emergencies are reported each month in the United States by neighborhood watch groups using wireless phones (Wireless Foundation, WF, 2001).

Electronic Monitoring

Recent developments in electronic monitors, computerized tracking of offenders and victims, and video surveillance have greatly bolstered crime investigations and crime prevention efforts. The goal is to lessen and eventually eliminate violent crime by controlling the physical environment. In most severe cases, the formerly battered woman agrees to maintain an active restraining order, agrees to testify in court and cooperate with any criminal proceedings against the alleged batterer, has a telephone in her residence, and believes that she is in extreme danger of aggravated assault or attempted murder by the defendant. In these cases, a home electronic monitor (e.g., panic alarm or pendant), also known as the abused woman's *active emergency response pendant,* can deter the batterer from violating his restraining order.

Private security companies have recently begun donating and marketing electronic security devices called *panic alarms* to battered women. The main purpose of these portable alarms, which have a range of about 200 feet from the victim's home, is to provide a battered woman with an immediate and direct link to her local police in an emergency with just the press of a button. In some jurisdictions in Colorado and New Hampshire, the electronic pendant alarms are coupled with electronic monitoring of batterers through the Juris Monitor ankle bracelet, manufactured by B.I., Inc. If the batterer comes close to the victim's home, the ankle bracelet sounds a loud alarm in the home and immediately alerts the police. ADT Security has set up electronic pendants for battered women in 30 counties and cities throughout the United States. The women are carefully selected for each program by a screening committee composed of community leaders, including a prosecutor or deputy prosecutor, a supervisor from the local battered women's shelter, and a police administrator. In all cases, the victim has an active restraining order against the batterer and is willing to fully cooperate with the prosecutor's office. One major drawback of these alarms is that the unit will not work if the telephone line is cut or is not working.

Several companies—including T.L.P. Technologies, Transcience, and B.I., Inc.—are currently developing electronic monitors. The alarm system developed by T.L.P. Technologies works even when the phone lines are down and when there is no electric power. In the victim's home, police install the system, which includes a radio transmitter with a battery backup, an antenna, and a remote panic or motion-detector device. T.L.P.'s Visibility Plus Radio Data Alarm System integrates both the alarm system and computer-generated data immediately into the police radio channel instead of using a private security company as an intermediary. This system has been used with hundreds of battered women in both Nassau County and Suffolk County, New York.

The most promising device that pinpoints the location of the victim—whether she is at home, at work, or at the supermarket—was developed by Geo Satellite Positioning Equipment. This advanced technology works by means of a satellite that sends a special signal from a receiver on the ground to the local police computer screen. A street map comes on the screen and sends a burst of data over the network, including the alarm number and the longitude and latitude of the victim's location within 5 to 10 feet.

Because of the growing awareness of the acute injuries sustained by battered women throughout the Untied States, as well as the millions of dollars spent on health and mental health care for victims of domestic violence, we predict that the electronic monitoring programs will be expanded to thousands of battered women in every state by the year 2010. Unfortunately, as has been the case with other new legislation, a "high-profile" crisis situation needs to occur before Congress enacts new legislation.

On-Line Police Information

Police departments nationwide are beginning to use the World Wide Web as a tool to communicate with the community regarding crime issues. Through Web pages, police departments have created a vehicle in which information about domestic violence issues can be disseminated to the public at large. Police department Web pages can provide community members with critical information regarding the dynamics of domestic violence, what to do if you are a victim, and where to access community resources.

For example, the police department in Madison, Wisconsin, has a Web page dedicated to domestic violence information. Created by Detective Cindy Murphy, the page provides links to topics such as safety issues to consider when leaving an abusive relationship, personal safety plan, state laws regarding domestic violence, the cycle of domestic violence, myths and facts about domestic violence, domestic abuse risk assessment, how to obtain a restraining order, and referral to resources and programs available in the Madison area (Madison Police Department, 2000).

Both short-term emergency support and long-term security services are critically needed by battered women and their children. It seems important that emergency services, including the use of electronic pendants and/or cellular phones, be initiated for the thousands of battered women in imminent danger of suffering repeated assaults or being murdered by their former abusive partners. Funding for the new technology should come from both corporate sponsors and government agencies. But, first, research needs to be carried out to determine which emergency electronic systems are most effective in protecting battered women. Also, under what conditions does the electronic technology fail to ensure a battered woman's safety? *Before new electronic technology is purchased by battered women's shelters and law enforcement agencies, it is critical that comprehensive evaluations and outcome studies be planned and carried out.*

Community-Wide Intervention Programs

Some cities and communities have developed citywide and community-wide task forces to provide a well-coordinated response to family violence from the police, the courts, victim-witness assistance, and social service agencies. Many of these task forces have followed the model of the programs developed during the 1980s in such areas as Baltimore County, Maryland; Quincy, Massachusetts; Duluth and Minneapolis, Minnesota; Boulder and

Denver, Colorado; Memphis, Tennessee; Milwaukee, Wisconsin; Lincoln, Nebraska; and Seattle, Washington. The model police programs described in this chapter all stress the importance of linking police services with local community efforts.

The era of community and problem-oriented policing has unleashed a paradigm shift in many police departments across the country. Departments have come to recognize the role of engaging the broader community in solving and preventing crime-related problems. Victim assistance programs, health care workers, schools, child welfare agencies, prosecutors, judges, and others have come together, in conjunction with changes in state law, to initiate prevention and intervention programs.

For coordination among battered women's shelters, police, prosecutors, victim-witness assistance programs, and batterers' counseling programs to be effective, certain policies and practices are required. Agencies must have a mutual respect for the individual role of each agency, especially when those roles are in conflict with each other. Coordinated community responses should involve as many of the local "system" players as possible, with support and guidance from local business, religious leaders, public policy makers, and so forth. In addition, the voices of survivors should be central to any community-wide response.

At the same time, community education is an equally important component to reducing the incidence of domestic violence. Coordinated community-wide coalitions and task forces have the opportunity to educate community members about abuse and where to get help early in the process. For example, programs in local middle and high schools can educate young people about battering in dating relationships. Because violence often begins early in dating relationships, educating young people regarding the dynamics of abusive relationships provides a critical dimension in prevention.

Although the police play a substantial role in domestic violence cases, it is fair to say that police departments alone cannot reduce incidents of battering. Community efforts that encourage a multidisciplinary approach to violence reduction are likely to be most effective. Schools, businesses, victim assistance programs, offender treatment programs, and religious organizations all play a critical role in reducing violence in the home. Prevention and early intervention are probably key to interrupting the "cycle of violence."

MODEL POLICE DEPARTMENTS

The VAWA of 1994 strengthened federal law against domestic violence, sexual assault, and stalking and provided $3.3 billion in grant programs over 5 years to assist states and local communities in fighting violence against women. For fiscal year 2001, Congress authorized approximately $677 million toward such programs, although only $468 million was finally appropriated.

One of the largest grant programs under VAWA is the STOP program, which awards funding to every state and territory in the nation to combat violence against women. This program—whose primary goal is to improve law enforcement, prosecution, and victim services—has been authorized at an annual amount of $185 million for fiscal years 2001–2005. The STOP grant funding, along with other state and federal funding initiatives, have made it possible for local police departments to develop innovative practices.

In addition to the STOP funding, many police departments have utilized funding through the Violent Crime Control and Law Enforcement Act of 1994. This act created the Office of Community Oriented Policing Services (COPS) of the U.S. Department of Justice and has placed over $6.3 billion in almost 12,000 agencies nationwide. Many police departments have applied for COPS dollars to improve their response to domestic violence.

These grant programs provide the critical resources necessary to initiate new responses to domestic violence. Although it is too early to evaluate the overall effectiveness of such police initiatives, and it is unclear how police departments will fund such programs after the STOP and COPS grants are no longer available, police departments have had an opportunity to test out innovative practices. As a component of STOP funding, the VAWA grant office engaged in a study to identify and develop a comprehensive package of best practices for law enforcement and prosecutors. Although police departments vary in the strategies they use to respond to battering, the fundamental elements of any law enforcement response should be promoting the safety of women and their families; providing assistance to regain control and autonomy in the women's lives; and holding officers accountable (Littel et al., 1998). The following police departments have been cited as models of how specific best-practice protocols can be achieved in the field (Littel et al., 1998).

Duluth Police Department

The police department in Duluth, Minnesota, is an active partner in a community-wide strategy to develop a comprehensive, victim-sensitive law enforcement response to issues of domestic violence. The department participates in a program of ongoing evaluation through the Domestic Abuse Intervention Project (DAIP), a not-for-profit organization charged with monitoring the response to domestic violence by all agencies within the city's criminal justice system. It also serves on the DAIP's Emergency Response Team, which convenes members to solve system problems involving high-risk cases.

A key element of the police department's model response to domestic violence is a system of evidence collection and report writing, coordinated with the city attorney's office, to improve the rate of successful prosecutions. The department contributes information to the Domestic Abuse Information

Network (DAIN) by including data from incident and arrest reports, investigative reports, warrant requests, and 911 watch reports to provide information to other agencies in the project. The department, committed to responding to every report of domestic violence, uses a computer-aided dispatching system to provide patrol officers with critical information regarding orders of protection and previous calls for service. Officers have been trained to provide victim-sensitive support and to identify high-risk cases. A mandatory arrest policy coordinated with immediate victim services has been central to the success of the law enforcement response. After careful review of different arrest policies in Duluth, the DAIP concluded that a mandatory policy produced the most consistent race-neutral arrest results. Officers refer victims to the Women's Coalition and other victim services. Once the abuser has been booked, the jail staff contacts the on-call advocate at the Women's Coalition, who sends an advocate to the victim within a few hours of the arrest. These advocates provide crisis counseling, referrals, and information about the criminal justice system. They also complete a danger assessment that is used by the courts in decisions about sentencing and release.

Appleton Police Department

In Appleton, Wisconsin, the police department demonstrates its commitment to combating domestic violence by applying the fundamental elements of community-based policing to its response. Guided by a proarrest policy, the officers are strongly encouraged to arrest the party considered to be the primary aggressor, and in cases in which an arrest is not made, the officer must document the reasons for this action. Victims are encouraged to complete a Domestic Violence Victim Worksheet, providing an opportunity to document details of the incident, and are offered the services of Habor House (the local shelter) at the scene. Advocates from Habor House will respond to the scene if the victim wishes.

A unique feature of the department's response is the institutionalization of officer follow-up to the home, even when an arrest cannot be made. Officers remind abusers of the potential for arrest, emphasizing the seriousness of their behavior. The department has found that officer follow-up visits are most successful if conducted 24 to 48 hours after the initial incident. The Appleton Habitual Offender Program includes targeting the most serious domestic violence offenders and notifying the patrol of their high-risk status. Calls involving these offenders can then be "fast-tracked" into the criminal justice system.

Seattle Police Department

In Seattle, Washington, the Domestic Violence Unit of the Seattle Police Department operates a specialized unit dedicated to investigating and prosecuting both misdemeanor and felony domestic crimes. Staffed by eight sworn police officers and two Domestic Violence Court order process servers, the unit investigates an average of 80 cases per month and obtains felony arrests in over 45% of its cases.

Guided by a mandatory arrest policy, officers are required to submit a written report of each incident, regardless of arrest status. If no arrest is warranted, the officers must document the justification. Required only to arrest the primary aggressor, officers must conduct a thorough investigation at the scene, collect appropriate evidence, take photos of injuries, and document all statements made by the victim, offender, and witnesses. The Domestic Violence Unit conducts ongoing training to patrol staff regarding their role as first responders to incidents of domestic violence.

The Domestic Violence Unit coordinates with the Victim Assistance Office (also located in the police department), the city attorney's Domestic Violence Unit, as well as local shelters and community-based services. The department's commitment to combating domestic violence is evidence by the assignment of two detectives who work exclusively on misdemeanor cases. Interrupting violence early in the battering process is critical in the prevention of felony-level assaults.

Nashville Metropolitan Police Department

The Family Violence Division of the Nashville Metropolitan Police Department in Nashville, Tennessee, focuses on measures to stop stalking behavior. Staffed by 29 civilian employees and sworn officers, as well as many volunteers from the local domestic violence shelter, the division combines attention to victim safety with an aggressive investigative approach to apprehend stalking suspects. Technology, infused with the staff members' commitment to investigate such crimes, is central to the division's "counterstalking" tactics. The Division employs a six-phase Domestic Violence Counter-Stalking Plan, which uses technology to increase victim safety, deter pretrial and posttrial stalking behavior, prove offender violations, and gather evidence for trial. The division uses self-contained phone traps, cellular phones, VCR kits, GPS Tracking Systems, silent hostage alarms, and phone bugs to capture incriminating evidence against the stalker and to promote victim safety.

Colorado Springs Police Department

The Domestic Violence Enhanced Response Team (DVERT) of the Colorado Springs Police Department in Colorado Springs, Colorado, combines the philosophies of community policing and problem-oriented policing to its model of effective intervention in domestic violence. The DVERT, consisting of a multidisciplinary staff of 16, responds to cases in which there is a high risk for lethality. The team receives referrals from advocates, prosecutors, judges, and citizens. It reviews referrals on a weekly basis and determines if a case meets the criteria for lethality. Criteria used to determine lethality include perpetrator's previous history of domestic abuse, incidents of stalking, threats made to kill, perpetrator's access to weapons, a recent loss (such as a separation or divorce), and numerous prior police interventions. Once a case is determined to warrant the attention of the DVERT, the team immediately follows up. Departmental communication regarding the perpetrator is improved by adding a "hazard alert" label on the victim's and perpetrator's addresses, alerting members of the police department to the potential for lethality. When patrol officers are dispatched to an address with a hazard alert, three members of the DVERT (consisting of a police officer/detective, deputy district attorney, and victim advocate) also arrive on the scene to assist the victim and the patrol officer.

The DVERT provides the local community with the benefits of swift and dedicated attention to domestic violence. Team members receive specialized training across disciplines and promote community dialogue on domestic violence issues.

As evidenced by the model programs described here, initiative coupled with creativity and community partnership can ensure a police response that attends to the needs of victims and the accountability of offenders. Innovative police practice, with attention to the development of protocols, implementation of state mandates, and coordination with prosecutors and victim service programs, is likely to prevail as the preferred police response to domestic violence.

CONCLUSION: THE FUTURE

The complex constellation of social, legal, and political issues surrounding the police response to domestic violence is among the most enduring and contentious problems in the recent history of criminal justice theory and practice. The current salience of domestic violence as an issue of national concern for criminal justice theoreticians and practitioners is well illustrated by the degree of attention this subject has recently received in many spheres and by the body of research it has generated. Particularly in the past decade, efforts to define and institutionalize appropriate roles and responsibilities for police in responding to domestic violence have led to considerable academic research, have generated a significant body of statutory and case law, and have been the subject of an uncommon degree of public and political discourse.

Although substantial progress has been made in strengthening domestic violence laws and improving police training and responses, much remains to be done. Police departments must recognize and acknowledge that some police officers and civilian staff commit domestic violence against their intimate partners. In response to a growing recognition of this issue, the International Association of Chiefs of Police has issued a model policy for police officer domestic violence. The policy adopts a preventive approach by advocating for the education of officers early in their careers and early intervention into incidents to reduce the victimization of their partners and improve the chances of career stability.

Second, although criminal justice policies can play a critical role in changing the social paradigm regarding how families and intimate partners should treat each other, the police and the courts cannot carry the burden alone. Responsive communities must work toward an integrated response from the police, the courts, health care providers, and social service agencies and focus on innovative prevention strategies. In addition, we must not forget that intimate partner abuse is one of many forms of violence found in American families and is often a co-occurring factor in child abuse, sibling abuse, parental abuse, elder abuse, and so forth. We should attempt to explore coordinated community responses that do not continue to fragment systems and family services.

Third, we should continue to make the needs of survivors of domestic violence and their families a priority. We must work to remove disparities and barriers to services for special populations of survivors such as families who live in rural communities, minority women, gay and lesbian men and women, children, and the elderly. At the same time, we should invest resources into identifying promising approaches to abuser treatment. The cycle of violence, including intergenerational transmission, will only be interrupted if all members of the family can access the services they desire.

Additionally, we should examine and evaluate current programs against the predictions of future funding availability. As the salience of domestic violence diminishes, we are likely to see funding streams decline. How will the infrastructure of police and community programming be maintained? Finally, we should begin to examine and evaluate current technologies to provide better protection for victims and improved enforcement capabilities for the police.

REFERENCES

Austin City Connection. (2000). *Austin Police Department: Family violence protection team.* Available on-line: www.ci.austin.tx.us/police/afvpt.

Buzawa, E. S., & Buzawa, C. G. (1990). *Domestic violence: The criminal justice response.* Newbury Park, CA: Sage.

Davis, R. C., & Smith, B. (1995). Domestic violence reforms: Empty promises or fulfilled expectations? *Crime and Delinquency, 41,* 4, 541–552.

Dunford, F. W. (1990). The role of arrest in domestic assault: The Omaha Police Experiment. *Criminology, 28,* 183–206.

Ferraro, K. J. (1989). Policing women battering. *Social Problems, 36,* 61–74.

Fleming, J. B. (1976). *Stopping wife abuse.* Garden City, NY: Doubleday.

Hart, B. J. (1992). State codes on domestic violence: Analysis, commentary and recommendation. *Juvenile and Family Court Journal, 43,* 3–73.

Hirschel, J. D., Hutchison, I. W., Dean, C. W., & Mills, A. (1992). Review essay on the law enforcement response to spouse abuse: Past, present and future. *Justice Quarterly, 9,* 247–283.

International Association of Chiefs of Police. (2001). *Family Violence Summit recommendations.* Available on-line: www.theiacp.org/pubinfo/Research/FamVio.

Krumholz, S. T. (2001, June). *Domestic violence units: Effective management or political expedience?* Paper presented at the annual meeting of the Academy of Criminal Justice Sciences, Washington, DC.

Littel, K., Malefyt, M. B., Walker, A., Tucker, D. D., & Buel, S. M. (1998, February). *Assessing justice system response to violence against women: A tool for law enforcement, prosecution and the courts to use in developing effective responses.* Violence Against Women Online Resources. Department of Justice, Office of Justice Programs. Available on-line: www.vaw.umn.edu.

Madison Police Department. (2000). *Domestic violence information.* Available on-line: www.ci.madison.wi.us/police/domestic.

Mignon, S. I., & Holmes, W. M. (1995). Police response to mandatory arrest laws. *Crime and Delinquency, 41,* 430–442.

Miller, N. (1997). *Domestic violence legislation affecting police and prosecutor responsibilities in the United States: Inferences from a 50-state review of state statutory codes.* Paper presented at the Fifth International Family Violence Conference, University of New Hampshire, June 30, 1997. Available on-line: www.ilj.org/dv/dvvaw.

Mills, L. (1999). Killing her softly: Intimate abuse and the violence of state intervention. *Harvard Law Review, 113,* 550–613.

New Haven Police Department. (2001). *Child development–community policing program.* Available on-line: www.cityofnewhaven.com/police/cdcp.

Peak, K. J. (1998). *Justice administration: Police, courts, and corrections management* (2nd ed.). Upper Saddle River, NJ: Prentice Hall.

Pence, E. (1983). The Duluth Domestic Abuse Intervention Project. *Hamline Law Review, 6,* 247–275.

Roberts, A. R. (1981). *Sheltering battered women: A national study and service guide.* New York: Springer.

Roberts, A. R. (1984). Police intervention. In A. R. Roberts (Ed.), *Battered women and their families: Intervention strategies and treatment programs* (pp. 116–128). New York: Springer.

Roberts, A. R. (1990). *Helping crime victims.* Newbury Park, CA: Sage.

Rosenbaum, M. D. (1998). To break the shell without scrambling the egg: An empirical analysis of the impact of intervention into violent families. *Stanford Law and Policy Review, 9,* 409–432.

Roy, M. (1982). *The abusive partner.* New York: Van Nostrand.

Sherman, L. W. (1991). From initial deterrence to long-term escalation: Short custody arrest for poverty ghetto domestic violence. *Criminology, 29,* 821–850.

Sherman, L. W., & Berk, R. A. (1984). The specific deterrent effects of arrest for domestic assault. *American Sociological Review, 49,* 261–272.

Sherman, L. W., Schmidt, J., Rogan, D., Smith, D. S., Gartin, P., Cohn, E., Collins, D., & Bacich, A. (1992). The variable effects of arrest on criminal careers: The Milwaukee Domestic Violence Experiment. *Journal of*

Criminal Law and Criminology, 83, 137–169.

Straus, M., Steinmetz, S., & Gelles, R. (1980). *Behind closed doors.* Garden City, NY: Doubleday.

Thurman v. City of Torrington, 595 F. Supp. 1521 (D. Conn. 1984).

U.S. Attorney General's Task Force on Family Violence. (1984, September). *Final report.* Washington, DC: Department of Justice.

Walker, L. E. (1979). *The battered woman.* New York: Harper and Row.

Walker, L. E. (1984). *The battered woman syndrome.* New York: Springer.

Walker, L. E. (1992). Battered woman syndrome and self-defense. *Notre Dame Journal of Law, Ethics and Public Policy, 6,* 321–334.

Wireless Foundation. (2001). *Donate a wireless phone and save lives.* Available on-line: www.wireless foundation.org or www.donate aphone.com.

7

Court Responses to Battered Women and Their Children

ALBERT R. ROBERTS
KAREL KURST-SWANGER

We have come a long way during the past two decades as responsive prosecutors, judges, and legislators have begun to recognize family violence as a serious crime. All 50 states have passed civil and/or criminal statutes to protect battered women, and prosecutors' offices are beginning to implement efficient systems of screening and prosecuting cases. Police and courts, in a small yet growing number of jurisdictions, have set up an around-the-clock method of issuing temporary restraining orders and providing advocacy as cases move through court. Although court-mandated batterer treatment programs have been developed on a limited basis, more are needed. Further research into the effectiveness of different treatment modalities with battered women and their abusive partners is needed as well.

Historically, domestic violence has been handled by the courts in a fragmented fashion. Although court jurisdiction varies from state to state, typically a woman who was married to or had children in common with her abuser had to utilize the civil court system or divorce court, whereas a woman who has been battered by a partner to whom she was not married, or with whom she had no children in common, usually sought assistance from the family or criminal courts. Just as the police have been reluctant to intervene in cases of domestic abuse, family and criminal courts have been plagued by the same lack of knowledge about the dynamics of domestic violence. Civil courts provided a forum in which family problems could be addressed; however, they lacked the statutory power to truly sanction abusers. Criminal courts have historically been unresponsive to the needs of battered women, not taking cases of domestic violence seriously in comparison with other "real" crimes the court was responsible for processing. Battered women were often left feeling frustrated, unheard, and unprotected.

However, institutional reforms regarding domestic violence have led to sweeping changes in statutes and court responses to domestic violence. Recognizing the role of system fragmentation, many jurisdictions have moved to a more integrated court response. Courts have been challenged by an inability to identify and successfully track cases and court orders, and the court's tradition of responding with neutrality has limited interaction with community resources as a partner in intervention (Keilitz, Guerrero, Jones, & Rubio, 2000). Since the 1990s, the courts have begun to examine and reinvent court processes to improve victim protection and offender accountability. States continue to revise and improve legislation to enable the courts to respond appropriately to cases of domestic violence. Here we discuss recent trends in domestic violence legislation, protective orders, legal services provided by law students, prosecutor policies, sentencing options, and issues of child custody and visitation.

STATE DOMESTIC VIOLENCE LEGISLATION

States continue to revise and update their statutes to improve their ability to respond to issues of family violence. In 1994, the Model Code on Domestic and Family Violence was issued by the National Council of Juvenile and Family Court Judges. The Model Code provides communities with a comprehensive example of how best to address family violence issues from a public policy perspective. Since the development of the Model Code, the Family Violence Department at the National Council of Juvenile and Family Court Judges, with financial support from the Conrad N. Hilton Foundation, has continued to track the progress of state legislatures in developing appropriate family violence legislation and provide annual documentation of individual state efforts.

Since 1996, states have enacted significant legislation in a variety of contexts. Some states have updated and revised existing statutes, while others have created new legislation to address family violence issues. The following describes some of the legislative trends noted by the Family Violence Department of the National Council of Juvenile and Family Court Judges during the years 1996–1999.

Confidentiality of Identifying Information

Many states have enacted laws to prohibit the disclosure of identifying information in cases where there is reason to believe such information would endanger the safety of the victim(s). Some states have focused on protecting identifying information in dependency, neglect, and/or support proceedings, while others have addressed identifying information in protective orders. For example, Alabama and Tennessee enacted legislation in 1999 that created privileged communication between victims and victim service providers. Florida and California enacted legislation in 1998 that created address confidentiality programs, allowing program participants the ability to vote by absentee ballot. In 1997, Nevada amended a confidentiality statute by allowing a victim of domestic violence to file with the secretary of state to establish a fictitious address. Georgia made it a crime to reveal the location of a domestic violence shelter.

Weapons Restrictions

Many states have revised their statutes restricting access to firearms and other weapons by known batterers. For example, the West Virginia legislature amended a statute to require police officers to seize all weapons involved in acts of family violence and weapons that are in plain view or discovered during consensual searches. In Connecticut, the legislature amended a statute permitting police officers to seize firearms in cases in which an arrest will be made. Other states, such as Arizona, have addressed the issue of prohibiting the possession or purchase of a firearm during the period in which a protective order is in force. Others, including New York, have increased penalties for offenders who possess weapons when stalking.

Insurance Discrimination

Most states have now addressed discrimination against victims of domestic abuse in insurance. States have prohibited insurers from denying coverage, refusing to pay claims, or increasing premiums because a person is a victim or a potential victim of family violence. In 1996, Delaware broadened the restriction to include homeowner's and motor vehicle insurance, while Florida extended it to include health maintenance organizations.

Child Protection

Several states have addressed the issue of children witnessing domestic violence through the enactment of criminal penalties and/or enhancing the authority of child welfare policies. The Utah State Legislature created the domestic violence crime if the child can see or hear the act of domestic violence, and Delaware included witnessing violence by a child less than 18 years of age as a form of endangering the welfare of a child. These policies have been enacted in response to a growing body of evidence that clearly identifies the adverse effects of domestic violence on children. However, as the Family Violence Department of the National Council of Juvenile and Family Court

Judges appropriately notes, such policies raise important questions about the ultimate consequences such policies have unintended consequences. In this case there are questions regarding the impact of such policies on children and battered victims. Will these policies, which are meant to protect children, end up harming them?

States have also considered the impact of domestic abuse on children in determining custody and visitation policies. As of 2001, 47 states and the District of Columbia made domestic violence a factor in decisions about child custody and visitation, and several states have limited the use of mediation in cases in which domestic violence is a factor. (We will discuss child custody in greater depth later in this chapter.)

In addition to the trends already noted, states have addressed a wide range of issues in their recent policy adoptions, including creating funding streams to support legal aid services to represent victims of domestic violence; permitting or mandating courts to require attendance at batterer treatment or intervention programs; requiring domestic violence background checks for people applying to become adoptive or foster parents; expanding victim compensation funding; requiring abusers to pay restitution for the costs of medical and psychological treatment and/or reimbursing domestic violence programs for their services; requiring training for various professionals; prohibiting employers from discriminating against victims; and establishing policies that provide for bail or release conditions.

COURT ORDERS

Temporary restraining orders (TROs) became one of the most frequently used legal options for battered women during the 1980s. Although TROs are known by different names across the country, they are most commonly referred to as *protective orders, orders of protection, restraining orders,* or *temporary injunctions.* Civil protective orders are intended to put an immediate stop to violence by restricting an abuser's behavior. Protective orders dictate that an individual refrain from harassment, abuse, molestation, and/or contact with certain family members. The court usually forbids the alleged abuser from making contact with the victim, and in some cases, the order specifies the distance that the abuser must maintain from the person who requested the order.

Orders are generally granted by civil court judges; however, some jurisdictions have enacted legislation giving similar power to criminal court judges. States have statutes that govern the procedural and eligibility requirements to obtain protective orders, the length of time orders are in effect, and the consequences for when orders are violated (Davis & Smith, 1995). For example, 43 states have passed legislation making the violation of court order a separate criminal offense (Miller, 1998).

Protective orders require a lower standard of proof than criminal proceedings and can be issued relatively quickly. Temporary orders can be issued ex parte, which means that only one party needs to be present. Permanent orders require a hearing process in which court documentation is required and both parties are present. Depending on the state law, the court order may mandate that the abusive spouse move out of the house, refrain from threats of abuse or further physical abuse, pay support for the victim and minor children, and/or participate in a counseling program aimed at ending the violence or chemical dependency (both the batterer and the victim may be required to enter counseling).

How effective are protective court orders? Research on this topic yields mixed results. Previous studies have indicated that protective orders have not consistently deterred abusive behavior (Grau, Fagan, & Wexler, 1984; Harrell, Smith, & Newmark, 1993; Horton, Simonidis, & Simonidis, 1987), and one study (Berk, Berk, Loseke, & Rauma, 1983) found a positive relationship between obtaining a court order and subsequent incidents of abuse. A study conducted by the National Center for State Courts examined the civil protection order process in three jurisdictions and revealed that civil protective orders were valuable in helping victims regain a sense of well-being and were helpful in deterring the majority of batterers from repeated incidents of physical and psychological abuse. The study found that many of the women who sought protective orders had experienced severe abuse, and the majority of abusive partners had criminal records. In many cases, only temporary orders were necessary to stop abusive behavior, since many of the study participants did not return for permanent orders because the abusive behavior had stopped. The study concluded that a number of court-based initiatives are still warranted. First, although a full array of victim services was available, the majority of victims did not access local services; therefore, the courts need to improve linkages with local resources. Second, the police need to do more to assist prosecutors and help victims access the civil protection order process. Additional training for law enforcement officials is warranted to enhance their understanding of the dynamics of domestic violence, arrest policies, and enforcement procedures. Also, courts need to revise protective orders to include all possible forms of relief available to victims (Keilitz, Hannaford, & Efkeman, 1997).

More recently, Carlson, Harris, and Holden (1999) found evidence of a significant decline in the probability of abuse following the issuance of a protective order. Weisz, Tolman, and Bennett (1998), in an ecological study of services provided to 392 battered women, found that women receiving services from a battered women's program who had at least one protective order were more likely to have a completed court case, and their partners were more likely to have more police interventions. The authors note that it is difficult to ascertain whether the increase in police interventions and subsequent arrests was due to additional acts of violence or an increased feeling of empowerment that led these women to call the police for further assistance.

The most serious drawback of orders of protection is that they are extremely difficult to enforce. Because the police cannot be available 24 hours a day, 7 days a week, the courts and police must rely on the victim to call them if the batterer violates the court order. If the batterer violates any of the conditions of the protection order, he will be in contempt of court or guilty of a separate criminal charge for violation of the order. Most states have statutes that make the violation of a court order a separate criminal offense, but even in those states that rely on criminal contempt charges, a misdemeanor-level penalty is the likely remedy (Miller, 1998).

The enactment of the Violence Against Women Act (VAWA) of 1994 has attempted to redress some of the problems inherent in protective orders. The full faith and credit provision of the VAWA requires nationwide recognition and enforcement of civil and criminal protection orders. This section requires states, Indian tribes, and U.S. territories to honor "valid" protection orders issued by other states, tribes, and territories and to treat such orders as if they were their own (18 U.S.C. Sec. 2265). The law covers protective orders that have been granted in civil and/or criminal cases, whether they are temporary or permanent. States have followed the lead of Section 2265 by enacting state statutes further clarifying state policy regarding foreign protection orders. For example, by 1999 a total of 32 states had enacted laws to provide full faith and credit for valid orders of protection from other locations (National Council of Juvenile and Family Court Judges, 1999).

Although Section 2265 was intended to further protect women from their abusive partners, Judge Susan B. Carbon, Judge Peter Macdonald, and Seema Zeya (1999) point out the troubling aspects of the new federal law. They argued that it does not clarify procedures for enforcing orders across jurisdictional lines. One debate centers on whether or not the law covers custody and support orders, referring states to review their state Uniform Child Custody Jurisdiction Act (UCCJA) or Uniform Child Custody Jurisdiction and Enforcement Act (UCCJEA). In 2001 a total of 26 states and D.C. enacted the UCCJEA to better protect victims of domestic violence and their children (Joan Zorza, Personal Communication, Dec. 3, 2001). Second, the law does not prescribe specific enforcement procedures, thereby not clearly setting guidelines on how the service of such orders is to be delivered. For example, in some jurisdictions, victims are charged filing fees and costs related to providing the service. Judge Carbon and associates also note that the Protection Order File of the National Crime Information Center (NCIC) is currently not operating at full capacity, since some states do not have a registry that would allow law enforcement officers the opportunity to verify the existence of court orders. A nationally based, up-to-date database is required before law enforcement is able to verify all orders of protection. As of 1999, a total of 23 states were participating in the NCIC Protection Order File registry (Carbon et al., 1999).

There is wide variation, from one state code to another, in the penalties for violating a restraining order. States have begun to revise their statutes to enhance the criminal penalties for violations of protective orders. For example, in 1997, Indiana and South Dakota enhanced their penal codes to address sanctions for violations of protection orders. In 1998, Pennsylvania and Kentucky amended their penal codes to include protective orders as an aggravating circumstance in sentencing for murder, when at the time of the killing a defendant was subject to a court order relating to the protection of the victim.

Additionally, it is important for police officers, court personnel, and victim service providers to be knowledgeable about state law and process issues of protective orders. For example, Paula Rugowsky, director of Safe Horizons, a victim service agency in New York City, provides comprehensive training for professionals regarding protective orders. Training includes topics such as where a victim can get a protective order, implementing state mandatory arrest laws, what to do when there are dual complaints, and how family court and criminal court process protective·orders.

LAW STUDENTS PROVIDING LEGAL SERVICES TO BATTERED WOMEN

Many attorneys are interested in representing only clients with substantial financial resources, but many battered women cannot afford to hire an attorney. Therefore, because of the scarcity of legal services available to battered women, several law schools have established clinical practicum programs on battered women's rights. Many law students have the opportunity to help poor battered women, who often are single parents and sometimes are homeless. Battered women need legal services to assist them in receiving protective orders, custody orders, divorce and separation agreements, and so forth. Sometimes they need the assistance of a criminal attorney.

The advantages of such programs are enormous. Although law students lack experience, their energy and commitment are easily translated into excellent legal service for victims. Since clinics focus on teaching students legal skills, the law school helps to set standards for legal practice regarding cases of domestic violence when they run clinics; these standards are passed on to the students for their professional practice. Students generally receive specialized training related to domestic violence issues. Caseloads usually are low, providing student volunteers the opportunity to give their full attention to their clients.

Law clinics are organized in a variety of ways. Since most law schools offer some type of law clinic program as part of the overall curriculum, some programs allow students to earn credit for work in the clinic. Some law schools have specialized clinics for domestic violence, others have a domestic component to a more general law practice, and others are attached to a prosecutor's office. A few clinics specialize in providing criminal defense services to battered women (Littel, Malefyt, Walker, Tucker, & Buel, 1998).

Three law schools that have led the way with this type of program are George Washington University Law School's Domestic Violence Litigation Clinic, the Legal Aid Bureau at Harvard Law School, and the City University of New York's Law School at Queens College. However, today, many law schools offer such innovative programming. Examples of promising law school programs include the following:

Fordham University School of Law: The Battered Women's Advocacy Project places students who may represent battered women in civil proceedings, accompany women to court, assist them with other legal proceedings, and help to ensure their safety.

Northeastern University School of Law: The Domestic Violence Advocacy Project places students in the Boston Medical Center Research and Advocacy Project. Students work with battered women seeking emergency medical treatment and provide them with immediate legal assistance.

University of Minnesota Law School: The Domestic Abuse Prosecution Clinic places students with a prosecutor's office to assist in the prosecution of misdemeanor and felony cases in the Minneapolis area. The Gender and the Law Clinic allows students to provide assistance to victims in obtaining protection.

University of Missouri School of Law: The Family Violence Program, funded by the VAWA, provides students the opportunity to represent battered women in rural counties. The clinic serves a 14-county region, receiving referrals from courts, shelters, and the police.

George Washington University Law School: Domestic Violence Clinics allows students to represent abuse survivors in protection order and related litigation. Students in the Domestic Violence Emergency Department (DVED) Clinic respond to abuse victims in local hospitals and psychiatric units, providing counseling, safety planning, and legal and nonlegal options and resources. Both clinics have pioneered interdisciplinary teaching, providing students with co-teaching and supervision by a social worker along with a clinical law professor. Clients are offered psychological counseling as well as legal assistance.

CRIMINAL COURT RESPONSES

A change in the police response to domestic violence has also created change in how prosecutors and judges handle cases. Prosecutors and judges have sustained the same scrutiny as the police in regards to their past practices in domestic violence cases. Historically, criminal courts have required victims of domestic violence to sign formal complaints against abusers, obligating victims themselves to bring forward criminal charges. Therefore, victims of domestic violence, unlike victims of many other types of crimes, had the added burden of being responsible for having the defendant charged with a criminal complaint. The signing of a formal complaint could then lead to a warrant for an arrest or the issuance of an appearance ticket for the abuser. Consequently, the prosecution rates of domestic violence cases have been rather low. Prosecutors have failed to file charges, courts have failed to convict offenders, or judges have failed to sentence offenders in an equitable way. Victims, frustrated by the system and fearing retribution from the offender, have been reluctant partners with the courts.

However, since all states have now created statutes allowing the police to make warrantless arrests, police are now arresting offenders and bringing them directly to the court, with or without the consent of the victim. Mandatory and proarrest policies, coupled with state statutes enhancing the criminal sanctions for incidents of battering, have changed the complexity of the criminal court's role in domestic cases.

It is now very clear that prosecutors also have the potential to break the cycle of violence. Most victim advocates believe that more domestic violence cases should be actively prosecuted, particularly those acts involving alleged abusers with prior criminal histories. Responsive prosecutors have been instituting promising strategies and policies in regards to family violence, which have improved the different stages of the prosecution process. Prosecutors must delicately balance the goal of conviction with the goal of guarding victim safety. Today, prosecutors have embraced "no-drop" policies or "mandatory prosecution" policies in regards to domestic abuse cases. To prevent batterers from intimidating victims and pressuring them to drop charges or restraining orders, a growing number of prosecutors sign complaints themselves or file charges based on the arresting officer's signed complaint. When prosecutors take official responsibility by signing and filing charges themselves, they are sending the important message that domestic violence is a serious crime against the state, not a personal matter. Several prosecutors (e.g., in Madison, Wisconsin, and South Bend, Indiana) do not allow the battered woman to drop charges except under extraordinary circumstances.

There is some evidence to suggest that prosecutorial "no-drop" policies have in fact increased the number of cases processed through the criminal courts. For example, in San Diego and Washington, D.C., prosecutors have experienced a substantial increase in caseload and convictions after "no-drop" policies have been instituted. Additionally, San Diego has seen a substantial decline in the number of domestic violence–related homicides, from 30 in 1985 to 7 in 1994 (Epstein, 1999).

In some jurisdictions, specialized domestic violence courts have been created to enhance the management of such cases. In other jurisdictions, prosecutors have partnered with police departments and victim service programs to enhance their ability to protect victims and make offenders accountable. Changes in prosecutor policies have reflected a paradigm shift to viewing domestic violence as a crime against the state.

The VAWA of 1994 has been instrumental in providing funding for prosecutors and courts to revolutionize how they handle domestic violence cases. As discussed in an earlier chapter, Services and Training for Officers and Prosecuters (STOP) grants have been awarded to prosecutors' offices to improve their response to domestic violence. Littel and associates (1998) note that appropriate prosecutor responses include the following: assisting the victim with safety planning; coordinating with local victim advocates to communicate effectively with victims throughout the entire criminal justice process; advising victims regarding the collection of evidence, protective orders, calling the police if an order is violated, and so forth; using vertical prosecution models whenever possible; recognizing the work of victim advocates, who have the dual role of advocating for the victim and effecting systemic change; and establishing clear guidelines for deciding not to prosecute a case. Promising approaches include the following examples of prosecutor programs.

Cook County State's Attorney's Office, Domestic Violence Division

The Targeted Abuser Call (TAC) team, located in Chicago, is a specially trained prosecution-based collaborative unit. Composed of two felony-level prosecutors, one victim-witness specialist, two investigators, an administrative assistant, one private advocate from the Hull House Domestic Violence Court Advocacy Project, and a civil legal service attorney from Lifespan, the team employs a vertical prosecution approach to domestic violence cases. The TAC team focuses on high-risk misdemeanor cases of abuse, guarding victim safety and ensuring offender accountability. Its philosophy emphasizes providing victim services to build trust, enhance victim safety, and supply victims with appropriate referrals. Shortly after receiving a report of a domestic incident, TAC team investigators arrive on the scene to further interview the victim, collect evidence, take photographs, and search for additional witnesses. The team's ability to respond to misdemeanor-level incidents has been a critical change in the handling of domestic violence cases in the Cook County area.

Prosecuting Attorney's Office, City of Dover Police Department

In Dover, New Hampshire, the prosecutor's office has collaborated with the city police department to aggressively prosecute stalkers. The prosecutor's office is located in the police department, enabling the prosecutor to be involved in cases early on. Vertical prosecution, early intervention, and a good working relationship with victims are key components to the prosecutor's strategy. Victims are assisted with protective orders, safety plans, and information regarding the court process. This approach has also embraced the use of technology to improve victim safety outcomes. Dover prosecutors often recommend using the Juris Monitor system to monitor the behavior of stalkers after they have been released from custody on bail or probation. Prosecutors also provide victims with cell phones, donated by Cellular One, programmed to dial immediately to 911. Prosecutors also give pendant Alert Link alarms, donated by Elderwatch, to stalking victims. Elderwatch is a program that helps keep the elderly safe and is available in many local communities.

Office of the Los Angeles City Attorney

Los Angeles, California, uses an aggressive approach in prosecuting misdemeanor domestic violence cases. The Domestic Violence Unit vertically prosecutes all cases involving defendants with prior convictions, serious injuries, stalking, and child abuse, as well as cases with difficult issues of proof. Each branch has domestic violence prosecutors assigned to it to ensure consistency in prosecution across the city. Victim advocates provide critical victim services, and the unit's 24-hour telephone-answering service provides immediate referrals to victims for services. In addition, the city attorney's office participates in the legislative process and community partnerships.

Family Violence and Sexual Assault Unit

In Philadelphia County, Philadelphia, Pennsylvania, has created a specialized prosecution unit staffed by prosecutors, victim advocates, law clerks, detectives, police officers, support staff, volunteers, and law and undergraduate students. The unit prosecutes all felony and misdemeanor cases of domestic violence, child maltreatment, felony sexual assault cases, and elder abuse. The unit also is responsible for prosecuting violations of protection orders. Housing all in the unit has diminished barriers between professionals, enhancing victim participation and protection and ultimately leading to more successful dispositions. Investigators are able to respond to post-arrest investigations, evidence gathering, and locating of witnesses to strengthen the prosecution of cases. Victim advocates are able to provide victims with information regarding the court process, court accompaniment, and referrals to other services. The unit has also been successful in collaborating with local agencies to form a multidisciplinary approach to domestic violence.

SENTENCING OPTIONS

Once a domestic violence offender has been convicted of a criminal charge, courts generally have a wide range of sentencing options. Depending on the crime committed and the state statute, courts may sentence offenders to pay

restitution and/or fines, serve a jail or prison sentence, serve a term of probation, be placed on electronic monitoring, and/or be placed in a specialized
treatment program. Two of the most commonly used sentencing strategies
are probation and mandated treatment programs, with mandated treatment
often required as a condition of probation.

Probation

County and city probation departments can play an important role in optimizing the delivery of services to batterers and their victims. Probation officers can provide early identification of serious cases through their role in
conducting presentence investigations (PSI). Probation departments are routinely required to conduct PSIs for the court to assist judges in determining
appropriate sanctions for offenders. PSIs generally include a background investigation into the offender's psychosocial history, including past criminal
behavior, family life, school history, and medical problems. Probation officers also may gather information from victims through a victim impact statement and may monitor restitution orders as a part of the offender's sentence.

An offender may also be sentenced to a term of probation, a community-
based corrections alternative that allows offenders to serve their sentences
while under supervision. This court-ordered sanction requires offenders to
abide by a contract outlining the conditions of the term of probation. Probationers who violate the terms of their probation may be returned to court.
Typical general conditions state that probationers must obey all laws, maintain employment, remain within the jurisdiction of the court, possess no
firearms, and pay restitution and/or court fines. Specific conditions might
include treatment at a court-mandated batterer's treatment program or substance abuse treatment, submission to random drug testing, completion of a
General Education Degree (GED) course and/or test, or adherence to a cur-
few. Batterers on probation are also likely to have a protective order in force,
which, if violated, could lead to probation revocation.

As part of a community-wide intervention into domestic violence, many
probation departments have begun to develop specialized units to provide ·
supervision to offenders convicted of domestic crimes. Effective probation
practice is critical to the continuum of intervention in domestic violence and
has required probation departments to examine their paradigms regarding
the unique features of domestic violence. The following two examples illustrate how probation departments can infuse the goals of domestic violence
intervention with probation practice.

The New York State Probation Domestic Violence
Intervention Project

Funded by the U.S. Office of Justice Programs, the New York State Division
of Probation and Correctional Alternatives, the Office for the Prevention of

Domestic Violence, and the New York State Coalition Against Domestic Violence have collaborated to assist probation departments in developing local policies and protocols and ensuring that local probation departments work with local victim service programs and other criminal justice agencies to provide a consistent response to domestic violence.

To date, all but one probation department in the state has appointed staff members as probation domestic violence liaisons (PDVLS), who serve as the local resource person regarding domestic violence issues. In 2000, liaisons from around the state gathered to review a draft model of a PSI package developed by the project to assist probation officers in dealing with offender accountability while maintaining victim safety. Probation officers work to reinforce offenders' sole responsibility for their abusive behavior and is addressed with the probationer through accountability strategies, not necessarily through offender competency development, which is the typical probation philosophy.

Family Assault Supervision Team

The Family Assault Supervision Team (FAST) in Baltimore, Maryland, is a specialized form of intensive probation supervision for offenders of domestic crimes. Since 1974, FAST agents have accepted probation cases mandated by the circuit and district courts to provide intensive probation supervision. Each FAST unit includes a victim advocate who assists victims with their specialized needs by accompanying them to criminal court and/or protective order hearings, providing counseling, making shelter referrals, and so forth. Victims are notified about the offenders' conditions of probation and other pertinent information. Offender accountability and safeguarding victim safety are central components of the unit's philosophy.

Additionally, the unit has created a domestic violence manual that outlines significant policies and procedures for domestic violence probation supervision. The unit also provides training on domestic violence to other probation agents and other agencies in the community.

Batterers' Treatment Programs

Another sentencing alternative, although often ordered as a condition of probation, is court-mandated batterers' treatment. Treatment programs designed specifically to treat violent partners have become a popular intervention nationwide. Services may involve individual and/or group therapy sessions. Clinical interventions focus on alleviating the psychological and emotional factors that contribute to abuse, while at the same time educating the offender. Programs often offer a blend of psychoeducational programming that aims to break the abuser of his male privilege belief system, provide accountability for behavior, and/or teach anger management techniques. According to Jennings (1990), therapy should encourage the abuser to take responsibility for his behavior, assist him in developing a repertoire of peaceful alternatives, and help him to develop empathy and sensitivity.

Treatment issues cover a wide range of dimensions. Studies that compare abusers and nonabusers suggest that abusers employ a significantly lower level of moral reasoning (Buttell, 1999); have negative and unstable self-concepts (Ragg, 1999); differ in the cognitive domains of memory, learning, and executive and verbal functioning (Cohen, Rosenbaum, & Kane, 1999); and may have specific personality characteristics associated with abusiveness that are formed in early childhood (Dutton, Starzomski, & Ryan, 1996). Because substance abuse is also an issue for many men who batter, batterers' treatment programs must link with appropriate levels of substance abuse treatment (e.g., inpatient, outpatient, assisted living).

Given the wide range of treatment issues, it is likely that no single program model can be effective in treating all types of abusive individuals. A variety of behavioral health services are warranted to meet the needs of abusers in any given community. Substance abuse treatment, psychotropic medication, conflict resolution training, anger management programs, and psychoeducational groups all have a role in meeting the specific treatment demands of offenders.

Batterers' treatment programs show promise, yet research has yielded mixed results. Babcock and Steiner (1990) conducted a study comparing men who were court-mandated into a batterers' program with men who were incarcerated. They found that men who completed the domestic violence group treatment had fewer domestic violence reoffenses at the time of follow-up, while the men who had been incarcerated had a greater number. Feder and Forde (2000) conducted an experiment in Broward County, Florida, with 404 men convicted of misdemeanor violence. They found no difference in attitudes, beliefs, and behaviors regarding domestic violence between the men who received treatment and those who received probation only. Yet Gondolf (1997), in a 3-year study of over 800 men from four batterer programs in Pittsburgh, Houston, Dallas, and Denver, found that over two thirds of the men did not reassault their female partners for at least 1 year after entering the treatment program.

Dutton (1997) argues that violence can be reduced by batterers' treatment programs, with the exception of men who have been diagnosed with severe personality disorders. Gondolf (1997) found that men who abused alcohol after the completion of a treatment program were the most likely to reassault.

States have begun to address treatment programs through legislation. In 1997, seven states enacted legislation to permit or mandate courts to require participation in such programs. States, however, are also concerned about the standards of such programs. In 1997, four states enacted laws requiring the certification of programs within the context of individual state standards. In 1999, the State of Washington required treatment programs to include education regarding the effects of domestic violence on children for those offenders and victims with children (National Council of Juvenile and Family Court Judges, 1997, 1999).

Although sentencing options have begun to be crafted to address the unique features of domestic violence crimes, not all communities have specialized treatment programs available, and most probation officers carry caseloads well beyond the recommended limit. Without the appropriate level of staffing and monitoring, many offenders are able to slide through the system unnoticed.

DOMESTIC VIOLENCE
AND CHILD CUSTODY

Child custody and visitation are emotionally charged issues. In all custody disputes, child well-being must be balanced against the rights of parents. Even in families where violence has not been an issue prior to separation or divorce, a pattern of vicious parental behavior may surface as a result of custodial disputes. Turkat (1999) suggests an untested theory that a pattern of malicious behavior develops with some individuals when faced with this issue; his term *divorce-related malicious parent syndrome* is based on anecdotal material and describes behavior in which parents with no psychiatric history develop problematic malicious behavior with their spouse, with potentially detrimental consequences for their children.

Given the formidable task of family court judges in making fair and reasonable child custody and visitation determinations, the additional dynamic of domestic violence makes child custody resolution particularly difficult. Ample evidence of the detrimental effects of domestic violence on children exists, raising important questions about the appropriateness of various custodial arrangements. Doyne and associates (1999) note the dilemma judges face in making decisions. On one hand, courts can be presented with overwhelming evidence of the impact on children of living with an abusive parent. On the other hand, children may maintain a close bond with the abusing parent, whether that bond is genuine or the result of trauma or fear. Decisions may also be complicated by child welfare professionals who argue that the child is not safe with either parent because of the complex nature of interpersonal violence. Regardless of the family situation, there is generally no clear-cut or easy answer to such judicial quandaries.

However, family courts have begun to recognize the critical role they may play in the continuum of domestic violence intervention. All but 3 states revised their statutes to include domestic violence as a factor in child custody and visitation decisions. The Model Code on Domestic and Family Violence, issued by the National Council of Juvenile and Family Court Judges (1994) states that "it is detrimental to the child and not in the best interest of the child to be placed in sole custody, joint legal custody, or joint physical custody with the perpetrator of family violence" (p. 33). Many states have moved to include a rebuttable presumption that is it not in the best interest of the child to be placed in sole or joint custody with an abusive parent. In 1999, North Dakota amended legislation requiring courts to take into account any protective orders when considering the restriction or exclusion of custody or visitation right or duty. Arkansas amended legislation removing the absence or relocation of a parent due to domestic violence from the factors that weigh against a parent in determining custody or visitation (National Council of Juvenile and Family Court Judges, 1999).

States have also had to examine their policies on mediation, custody evaluations, and use of guardians ad litem. Since custody and visitation mediation have been common practice in most jurisdictions, many domestic violence advocates have raised important questions about the appropriateness of such a strategy when domestic violence is a factor (Keilitz et al., 1997). Mediation, in theory, supposes both parties share equal power in a relationship and require only the negotiation skills of a neutral third party. However, Keilitz and associates (1997) note that in the case of a battering relationship, the balance of power is so inequitable that even trained mediators cannot equalize the playing field. Considering the fact that the period of legal separation from an abusive spouse may in fact be the most dangerous time, the mediation process often can offer little assurance of safety for the victim. Also, the poor quality of mediation in many communities, indicated by deficient screening and training of mediators and lack of appropriate mediation resources, can create a potentially dangerous situation.

Therefore, courts must seriously consider cases of domestic violence and craft mediation programs that can better meet the needs of victims. For example, Keilitz and associates (1997) note that both the Model Code on Domestic and Family Violence (National Council of Juvenile and Family Court Judges) and a report from the Domestic Abuse and Mediation Project of the Main Court Mediation Service identify the following requirements for the mediation processes: All cases must be screened for domestic violence; participation in mediation must be voluntary, with the victim fully understanding what the process entails and what other options she may have; mediators must be well trained in the dynamics of domestic violence and be qualified to conduct and terminate mediation when necessary; and victims must have the right to bring an attorney, advocate, or other support person to the mediation sessions.

In addition to using mediation in making child custody and visitation decisions, many courts order custody evaluations and/or the appointment of guardians ad litem to gather information to help resolve custodial disputes. Keilitz and associates (1997) stress that courts should be especially cautious in using custody evaluations and guardians ad litem. They should carefully screen cases and ensure that the individuals involved in conducting evaluations or serving as guardians ad litem are properly qualified and trained in domestic violence.

The Model Code on Domestic and Family Violence recommends the following provisions relating to visitation when domestic violence is a factor:

- Children should be exchanged in a protected setting.
- Supervised visitation should be conducted with an identified individual, agency, or specialized visitation center.
- Specific conditions of the supervised visitation should be clearly spelled out if family or household members are supervising the visit.
- Any fees for supervised visitation should be paid by the abusive parent.
- Visitation should require a prohibition against the use of alcohol or other substances during visitation and for the 24-hour period before visitation.
- One condition of visitation should be completion of batterers' treatment and/or substance abuse treatment. (Keilitz et al., 1997, p. 47)

CONCLUSION

Although innovative court responses to domestic violence have flourished, embracing multidisciplinary approaches to reducing incidents of abuse, continued attention to systemic issues is warranted. Navigating the court system is generally a time-consuming and overwhelming ordeal for the victim of any violent crime. But for a woman who has been a victim of physical abuse, degradation, and terroristic threats by a spouse or boyfriend, "the thought of going to court may be so intimidating that no effort is made to get legal protection" (Roberts, 1981, p. 97). The court system is still plagued with many problems in its handling of family violence cases, including the following:

- Judges, trial court administrators, case managers, and intake officers who tend to minimize the dangers that abused women encounter and discourage them from following through with criminal or civil complaints
- Overloaded dockets and overworked judges in large cities that result in the court's inability to schedule a hearing and trial date in a timely manner
- A lack of specialized training on family violence for court and probation personnel
- Abused women who fail to call the police or go to court because they believe the criminal justice system will not be able to protect them
- A lack of counseling programs to which the court can refer both the batterer and the victim

More needs to be done to ensure that the legal rights of battered women are fully protected. Courts must remain sensitive to the unique dynamics of domestic violence. Every court clerk, case manager, legal advocate, probation officer, and judge in state and county courts throughout the United States should receive specialized training in handling battered women and their abusive partners. All courts need systematic guidelines, simplified mandatory forms, and step-by-step instructions for processing court orders. Police officers and court clerks should have a brochure available to disseminate to all victims of domestic violence to provide information on the battered woman's legal rights and options, instructions on how to obtain a court order or restraining order, and a list of local community resources.

Victim advocates, the police, child welfare workers, probation officers, and the courts should continue the dialogue on the availability of a continuum of interventions and the development of appropriate protocols for handling cases where domestic violence is a factor. Scholars and practitioners need to continue to come together to plan appropriate courses of research and to examine the unintended consequences of certain public policy choices.

REFERENCES

Berk, R. A., Berk, S., Loseke, D., & Rauma, D. (1983). Mutual combat and other family violence myths. In D. Finkelhor, R. J. Gelles, G. T. Hotaling, & M. A. Straus (Eds.), *The dark side of families: Current family violence research* (pp. 197–212). Beverly Hills, CA: Sage.

Buttell, F. P. (1999). Level of moral reasoning among African-American and Caucasian domestic violence offenders prior to targeted professional intervention. *Journal of Offender Rehabilitation, 30*(1/2), 95–106.

Buzawa, E. S., & Buzawa, C. G. (1990). *Domestic violence: The criminal justice response*. Newbury Park, CA: Sage.

Carbon, S. B., Macdonald, P., & Zeya, S. (1999). Enforcing domestic violence protection orders throughout the country: New frontiers of protection for victims of domestic violence. *Juvenile and Family Court Journal, 50*(3), 39–54.

Carlson, M. J., Harris, S. D., & Holden, G. W. (1999). Protective orders and domestic violence: Risk factors for re-abuse. *Journal of Family Violence, 4*, 205–226.

Cohen, R. A., Rosenbaum, A., & Kane, R. L. (1999). Neuropsychological correlates of domestic violence. *Violence and Victims, 14*, 397–411.

Davis, R. C., & Smith, B. (1995). Domestic violence reforms: Empty promises or fulfilled expectations? *Crime and Delinquency, 41*, 541–552.

Doyne, S. E., Bowermaster, J. M., Meloy, J. R., Dutton, D., Jaffe, P., Temko, S., & Mones, P. (1999). Custody disputes involving domestic violence: Making children's needs a priority. *Juvenile and Family Court Journal, 50*(2), 1–12.

Dutton, D. G. (1997). *The batterer: A psychological profile*. New York: HarperCollins.

Dutton, D. G., Starzomski, A., & Ryan, L. (1996). Antecedents of abusive personality and abusive behavior in wife assaulters. *Journal of Family Violence, 11*, 113–132.

Epstein, D. (1999). Effective intervention in domestic violence cases: Rethinking the roles of prosecutors, judges, and the court system. *Yale Journal of Law and Feminism, 11*, 3.

Feder, L., & Forde, D. R. (2000). *Test of the efficacy of court-mandated counseling for domestic violence offenders: The Broward Experiment.* Washington, DC: National Institute of Justice, U.S. Department of Justice.

Finn, P., & Colson, S. (1990). *Civil protection orders: Legislation, current court practice, and enforcement.* Washington, DC: U.S. Department of Justice.

Gondolf, E. W. (1997). *Results of a multi-site evaluation of batterer intervention systems.* Available online: www.iup.edu/maati/publications/execsum.html.

Gondolf, E. W., & Fisher, E. (1991). Wife battering. In R. T. Ammerman & M. Hersen (Eds.), *Case studies in family violence* (pp. 273–292). New York: Plenum.

Grau, J., Fagan, J., & Wexler, S. (1984). Restraining orders for battered women: Issues of access and advocacy. *Women and Politics, 4,* 13–28.

Harrell, A., Smith, B., & Newmark, L. (1993). *Court processing and the effects of restraining orders for domestic violence victims.* Final report to the State Justice Institute. Washington, DC: Urban Institute.

Hart, B. J. (1992). State codes on domestic violence. *Juvenile and Family Court Journal, 43,* 3–44.

Hirschel, J. D., Hutchison, I. W., Dean, C. W., & Mills, A. (1992). Review essay on the law enforcement response to spouse abuse: Past, present and future. *Justice Quarterly, 9,* 247–283.

Horton, A. L., Simonidis, K. M., & Simonidis, L. L. (1987). Legal remedies for spousal abuse: Victim characteristics, expectations and satisfaction. *Journal of Family Violence, 2,* 265–279.

Jennings, J. (1990). Preventing relapse versus "stopping" domestic violence: Do we expect too much too soon from battering men? *Journal of Family Violence, 5,* 43–60.

Keilitz, S., Davis, C., Flango, C. R., Garcia, V., Jones, A. M., Peterson, M., & Spinozza, D. M. (1997). *Domestic violence and child custody disputes: A resource handbook for judges and court managers.* National Center for State Courts.

Keilitz, S., Guerrero, R., Jones, A. M., & Rubio, D. M. (2000). *Specialization of domestic violence case management in the courts: A national survey.* National Center for State Courts, publication number R-202.

Keilitz, S., Hannaford, P. L., & Efkeman, H. S. (1997). *Civil protection orders: The benefits and limitations for victims of domestic violence.* National Center for State Courts Research Report, publication number R-202.

Littel, K., Malefyt, M. B., Walker, A., Tucker, D. D., & Buel, S. M. (1998). *Assessing justice system responses to violence against women: A tool for law enforcement, prosecution and the courts to use in developing effective responses.* Violence Against Women Online Resources, Department of Justice, Office of Justice Programs. Available on-line: www.vaw.umn.edu.

Miller, N. (1998). *Domestic violence legislation affecting police and prosecutor responsibilities in the United States: Inference from a 50-state review of state statutory codes.* Paper presented at the Fifth International Family Violence Conference, University of New Hampshire, June 30, 1997. Available on-line: www.ilj.org/dv/dvvaw.

National Council of Juvenile and Family Court Judges. (1994). *The model code on domestic and family violence.* Reno, NV: Author.

National Council of Juvenile and Family Court Judges. (1996–1999). *Family violence legislative update.*

Pence, E. (1983). The Duluth Domestic Abuse Intervention Project. *Hamline Law Review, 6,* 247–275.

Ragg, D. M. (1999). Dimensions of self-concept as predictors of men who assault their female partners. *Journal of Family Violence, 14,* 315–329.

Roberts, A. R. (1981). *Sheltering battered women: A national study and service guide.* New York: Springer.

Roberts, A. R. (1990). *Helping crime victims.* Newbury Park, CA: Sage.

Schmidt, J., & Steary, E. H. (1989). Prosecutorial discretion in filing charges in domestic violence cases. *Criminology, 27,* 487–510.

Turkat, I. D. (1999). Divorce-related malicious parent syndrome. *Journal of Family Violence, 14,* 95–97.

Weisz, A. N., Tolman, R. M., & Bennett, L. (1998). Ecological study of nonresidential services for battered women within a comprehensive community protocol for domestic violence. *Journal of Family Violence, 13,* 395–415.

8

Improving Judicial System Responses to Domestic Violence

The Promises and Risks of Integrated Case Management and Technology Solutions

SUSAN KEILITZ

By virtue of their wide-ranging jurisdiction over individuals and families, courts play a pivotal role in addressing domestic violence in our communities. This chapter explores this role and the various approaches courts are using to provide more comprehensive and effective remedies to domestic violence victims and their children. The chapter focuses on two key areas targeted by court initiatives: (1) case management principles and practices that promote greater safety, freedom, and confidence in the system for domestic violence survivors; and (2) technological applications that hold promise for improving both justice system practice and the well-being of the individuals the systems are designed to serve. The discussion includes descriptions of a few examples of these case management methods and technology applications.

THE COURT'S ROLE IN ADDRESSING DOMESTIC VIOLENCE

Imagine this simple scenario. Marsha calls 911 because her husband, Jack, has just punched her in the mouth and is shouting profanities at her while their 3-year old son, Jack Jr., is cowering behind the couch in terror and tears. Two police officers arrive at the home, arrest Jack, and take him to the county jail. They advise Marsha to go to the courthouse the following morning to file a petition for a protection order. Marsha takes their advice. After filling out several forms and waiting for 4 hours, she obtains a temporary order of protection that tells Jack to stay away from her and their son and orders him to appear at a hearing on a full order of protection in 2 weeks. Later that day, Jack is served with the protection order in jail and released. He goes to a friend's house, where he calls Marsha to try to persuade her to drop the protection order and let him come home.

Now imagine just a few of the various ways this story could proceed:

1. Marsha relents and does not return to court for a full protection order, the district attorney dismisses the charges against Jack, and the system never hears from Marsha or Jack again. This actually does occur in a small proportion of cases. (Keilitz, Hannaford, & Efkeman, 1997)

2. Marsha does not relent and returns to court for a full order of protection that includes custody of Jack Jr. and child support, exclusive possession of the home, and use of the family car. Jack also is ordered to participate in a batterer intervention program. The district attorney dismisses the charges against Jack. After a few months, Marsha and Jack reconcile, and she asks the court to drop the order. Marsha does not need the help of the justice system again.

3. Marsha does not relent and returns to court for a full order of protection that includes custody of Jack Jr. and child support, exclusive possession of the home, and use of the family car, but Jack is not ordered to batterer intervention. The district attorney dismisses the charges against Jack. Marsha and Jack eventually divorce, and she is granted custody of Jack Jr. Jack continues to harass her when he exercises his visitation rights with Jack Jr. Marsha finally moves to another state to avoid the harassment because the judge refuses to limit Jack's visitation. Jack files a motion against Marsha for leaving the state and obtains full custody of Jack Jr.

4. Marsha relents and does not return to court, the district attorney dismisses the charges against Jack, Jack continues to abuse Marsha and to terrorize Jack Jr., Marsha goes back to court for another temporary protection order, Jack talks her out of this one, too, but the person who helped her complete the petition and affidavit for the temporary order is concerned about the effects of Jack's behavior on Jack Jr., so she calls child protective services, which opens an investigation of Marsha and Jack.

5. Marsha does not relent, the district attorney proceeds with the case against Jack, and Jack pleads guilty and is ordered to participate in a batterer intervention program as a term of probation. Jack misses several classes, but the court does not revoke his probation. Jack assaults Marsha again, the district attorney prosecutes again, but now the court has a strict enforcement policy. The first time Jack does not appear at the batterer intervention program, a warrant is issued for his arrest. He receives a warning and notice that the next time he misses a class he will go to jail. Jack completes the program.

All these scenarios are played out every day in courts across the country. These examples do not include the horrific, and still too common, cases in which the victim tried to find safety for herself and her children through the justice system but the system totally failed her. These stories also all began in the criminal justice system. While criminal dockets are filled with domestic violence cases, a higher proportion of domestic violence victims seek redress solely in the civil system through protection orders (Fritzler & Simon, 2000; Harrell & Smith, 1996; Harrell, Smith, & Newmark, 1993; Keilitz, Hannaford, et al., 1997).

Victims of domestic violence may petition the court through a civil process to obtain a protection order, or protection orders may be issued in connection with the criminal prosecution of the defendant. The names and types of protection orders and procedures for obtaining an order vary and may include emergency orders, temporary orders, and final or permanent orders. Orders issued through a civil process are a critical tool for assisting domestic violence survivors seeking to end the abuse. Civil protection orders can be obtained relatively quickly and can afford a wide range of relief needed to achieve distance, protection, and independence from the abuser. Protection orders also provide an alternative to the criminal justice system, which can have negative consequences for the survivor and her children, including, for example, loss of support for the family, increased pressure on the victim to minimize the abuse, and increased feelings of guilt for bringing the justice system to bear on the batterer.

Protection orders are valuable and effective, however, only if they are enforced consistently and universally by law enforcement, prosecution, and courts wherever survivors are. Studies of the effectiveness of protection orders have indicated that from one third to one half of them are violated in some way (Harrell & Smith, 1996; Klein, 1996). Although enforcement of protection orders at the point of violation is a major responsibility of law enforcement, courts also have a significant role to play. Courts must establish regular review mechanisms to monitor compliance with orders that do not rely solely on the ability or willingness of the survivor to report violations. Enforcement also must extend beyond the borders of the jurisdiction that issues the order. Without an enforcement network that ensures their protection from the batterer's abusive behavior, domestic violence survivors cannot realize the benefits that protection orders are intended to provide.

To promote an effective enforcement system, the Violence Against Women Act (VAWA) of 1994 and the VAWA amendments of 2000 require state and tribal law enforcement and courts to recognize qualified protection orders issued by other jurisdictions and apply the same sanctions as they would for violations of their own protection orders. How to ensure that protection orders are quickly entered into data systems that are readily accessible by authorities everywhere the survivor might go is a growing issue for law enforcement and courts across the country (Carbon, MacDonald, & Zeya, 1999).

Many other cases involving domestic violence come to the court's attention through family law matters (Keilitz, Davis, et al., 1997). Custody and visitation disputes are some of the most common situations in which domestic violence exerts its negative impact. Various studies indicate that domestic violence is an issue in at least one quarter of contested custody and visitation cases (Chandler, 1990; Keilitz, Davis, et al., 1997). The detrimental effects of domestic violence on victims and children are now well known (Field, 1996; Jaffe, 1995; Jaffe, Wolfe, & Wilson 1990; Pagelow, 1990). It is also clear that the period of separation from an abuser is the most perilous time for victims (Jaffe, 1995; National Council of Juvenile and Family Court Judges, 1994; Zorza, 1992). When a domestic violence survivor files a custody or visitation claim, her action can cause an already dangerous situation to escalate. An abuser may retaliate with his own custody action, harass the survivor, maintain control over her, or wear down her resolve to leave the relationship. He also may file motions to increase costs and remain in a position of power over her.

By identifying cases in which domestic violence is occurring and addressing the issue, the court can help the victim protect herself through safety planning and referral to support services. The court also can ensure that the victim is not compelled to participate in court proceedings or mediation sessions that place her in further danger or compromise her access to justice. Judges can issue orders early in the case to blunt attempts by the abuser to manipulate both the victim and the judicial process. Courts also can ensure that custody determinations protect children's physical and emotional safety and ensure that orders specify visitation rights, times, and circumstances, as well as other terms needed to protect victims and children from abuse (Goelman & Valente, 1997; Goelman, Lehrman, & Valente, 1996; Lemon, Jaffe, & Ganley, 1995).

Courts have long played a major role in addressing child abuse and neglect, and the adjudication of dependency cases is governed by a large body of federal and state law. Researchers and practitioners also have made it clear that child abuse and neglect often occur in families where domestic violence exists (Appel & Holden, 1998; Edleson, 1999a, 1999b; Field, 1996; Osofsky, 1999; Schechter & Edleson, 1994). Yet despite this well-known overlap, few courts have proactively coordinated court procedures, programs, or resources to handle cases that involve both child welfare issues and domestic violence issues.

A relatively new development for courts is to collaborate with domestic violence service providers and child welfare systems to address both problems in ways that are most helpful and least harmful to families. For example, a consortium of private foundations and federal agencies is supporting demonstrations of such collaborations in six jurisdictions across the country (National Council of Juvenile and Family Court Judges, 2001). Other states and communities, including, for example, Colorado, Massachusetts, New Hampshire, Oregon, and Montgomery County, Ohio, have developed programs and processes to improve the system response (Schechter & Edleson, 1999).

These collaborations are controversial. Strong advocacy positions of child welfare agencies and domestic violence service providers often clash despite a commonly held interest in making families safe and strong. For good reason, as discussed in more detail in the next section, victim advocates are concerned that protections and services for their clients will be compromised by court processes that may lead to child abuse and neglect proceedings through a powerful, well-entrenched, and more adequately funded child welfare system. Child welfare advocates, on the other hand, must hold the interests of the child above all else. How courts will be able to balance and protect the rights and interests of children and domestic violence survivors may become one of the key challenges in improving their response to domestic violence.

As these examples of domestic violence issues addressed by courts demonstrate, courts play a critical and complex role in the justice system response to domestic violence. In exercising their jurisdiction in criminal, civil, and family matters, courts and judges intervene on numerous levels in the lives of those who perpetrate and those who are victimized by domestic violence. The court can use its unique authority to proscribe violent and abusive behavior, to monitor and enforce its orders, to harness the collective resources of its various jurisdictions, and to engage the community in coordinated initiatives to reduce domestic violence and bring peace and justice to its survivors (Epstein, 1999a).

The response a domestic violence victim receives from court staff and the judge can profoundly influence whether she stays involved in the system or gives up on trying to help herself. Examples of common barriers to the justice system are procedures that are unnecessarily complicated, lack of privacy while completing forms or talking with staff, staff whose demeanor ignores the trauma a petitioner may be experiencing, lack of security in waiting areas, lack of child care services, lack of effective methods of serving process on defendants, and lack of consistent procedures to monitor and enforce court orders (Epstein, 1999a; Keilitz, Hannaford, et al., 1997; Levey, Steketee, & Keilitz, 2001).

The judge's role is particularly critical in this dynamic. Judges must understand the effects that abuse can have on victims' ability to effectively express their needs or describe events. On the other hand, they need to recognize the manipulative behaviors of batterers, who often have learned to use the system to maintain control over the survivor who is trying to leave the relationship (Hart, 1995; Ptacek, 1999). This knowledge and sensitivity are essential if one is to fairly and effectively adjudicate criminal cases, protection order petitions, and child custody and visitation disputes (Epstein, 1999a; Fritzler & Simon, 2000). Judges hearing these cases have a continuing responsibility to use their authority to promote the integrity and fairness of the process and to proactively monitor compliance with orders issued by their court (Karan, Keilitz, & Denaro, 1999). These responsibilities can pose dilemmas for judges who acquire and apply knowledge about the intricacies

of domestic violence because they can risk appearing to have lost their neutrality (Epstein, 1999a). This is just one of the challenges courts face when
they implement new ways of managing, adjudicating, and monitoring domestic violence cases.

COURT CASE MANAGEMENT INITIATIVES
TO ADDRESS DOMESTIC VIOLENCE

Despite the far-reaching roles and responsibilities of courts and judges,
courts have been the last component of the justice system to engage in institutional reform to improve the system's impact on domestic violence (Buzawa & Buzawa, 1996; Epstein, 1999). Law enforcement and prosecution
have made dramatic advances and systemic changes since the early 1970s
(Epstein, 1999a; Little, Malefyt, Walker, Tucker, & Buel, 1998), largely in
response to legal action and political pressure from domestic violence survivors and their advocates (Schechter, 1982). With a few exceptions, courts
began focusing attention on domestic violence cases in the early 1990s (for
early recommendations regarding improving court practices in family violence cases, see Herrell & Hofford, 1990).

Some of the factors contributing to this delay relate to the breadth of the
courts' responsibilities in addressing society's problems. Drug crime has for
several years demanded court attention and resources, for example. Specialized courts for adjudicating drug-related offenses and monitoring defendants
have proliferated over the past decade and now are a widely used case management tool (Hora, Schma, & Rosenthal, 1999; National Association of
Drug Court Professionals, 1997). Another major area of court reform efforts
has been in juvenile and family cases. Juvenile courts have existed in various
forms for a century, and the juvenile justice system has continually been in
the public eye and the subject of legislative action. During the past three
decades, many jurisdictions have instituted a unified family court or adopted
a one-family/one-judge approach to more effectively manage the increasingly
complex and overlapping juvenile and family caseloads (Babb, 1998; Dunford-
Jackson, Frederick, Hart, & Hofford, 1998; Flango, Flango, & Rubin, 1999).

Although courts have directed their resources to address these pervasive
problems, they traditionally have preferred to respond to issues brought to
them as a neutral arbiter of others' disputes. The position of neutrality is
fundamental to the character and purpose of courts, and this traditional
ideal has impeded efforts to engage with one part of the community or one
side of an issue (Rottman, Efkeman, & Casey, 1998). Within the past few
years, however, the therapeutic justice movement (Fritzler & Simon, 2000;
Rottman & Casey, 1999; Simon, 1995; Wexler & Winick, 1996; Winick,
2000) and the promotion of community-focused courts (Sviridoff, Rottman,
Ostrom, & Curtis, 1997) have challenged this view of the court's role in

society. A significant advance was demonstrated recently when the Conference of Chief Justices, a body composed of the chief justice of each state court of last resort, adopted a resolution supporting the development of problem-solving courts (Conference of Chief Justices, 2000).

Finally, courts have focused their attention on domestic violence cases because they constitute a significant and growing portion of their caseloads. Ten-year trend data from the Court Statistics Project of the National Center for State Courts indicate that domestic violence filings in state courts increased 178% from 1989 to 1998 (Ostrom & Kauder, 1999). This trend is in sharp contrast to a report from the Bureau of Justice Statistics in May 2000 that indicated the rate of intimate partner violence fell by 21% from 1993 to 1998 (Bureau of Justice Statistics, 2000). One factor that has contributed to the rise in domestic violence court caseloads is the availability since 1994 of civil protection orders in all the states and the District of Columbia. Another reason for the higher numbers is the increased ability of court data systems to identify domestic violence cases in their domestic relations and criminal caseloads. Forty states were able to report domestic violence data for the years 1996–1998, and several jurisdictions, including Delaware and Brooklyn, have been able to determine that domestic violence cases make up one third of misdemeanor caseloads.

A key development in state courts in the past 5 years has been the institution of specialized structures, processes, and practices to address the distinct nature of domestic violence cases and the need for special attention to them. A recent national survey estimated that over 300 courts now are specializing in least one component of the criminal or civil process for domestic violence cases (Keilitz, Guerrero, Jones, & Rubio, 2000). These approaches have collectively come to be called *domestic violence courts*, but there is great variation among them. Unlike drug courts or juvenile courts, domestic violence courts are not a commonly understood court classification.

While specialization of domestic violence case management holds great potential to address domestic violence effectively, practitioners and advocates have expressed concern that specialization may compromise victim safety, access to justice, fairness, or batterer accountability for the sake of innovation (Epstein, 1999a). For example, specialized judges can lose their neutrality, or the appearance of neutrality, by becoming more educated about the effects of domestic violence and collaborating with the advocacy community. Their effectiveness thus may become compromised. On the other hand, a specialized bench may have reluctant members who do not have the interest or inclination to acquire the knowledge and skills required to be effective in these cases. Judges also can lose their effectiveness from the experience of hearing difficult and emotionally charged cases every day.

Another concern about implementing specialized calendars and judges is that specialized prosecution units also should be in place to achieve maximum efficiency in the court. The pursuit of efficiency, however, can lead to assembly line justice in which one size is made to fit all. Batterers can escape appropriate sanctions through plea bargains or diversion to ineffective and unproven treatment programs (Hanna, 1998). The survivor can be coerced to participate in the defendant's prosecution through threats of sanctions against her (Hanna, 1996). Prosecutors can ignore or act in opposition to the survivor's concerns about safety or status in her community (Crenshaw, 1991; Epstein, 1999b; Richie, 1996).

Perhaps the most chilling effect of specialized or integrated domestic violence case management is the information-sharing function designed to promote more consistent and complete relief for victims. Domestic violence cases can become entangled with child abuse and neglect issues, often because the batterer also is abusing children in the home or the children are suffering from the effects of the violence against their mother. In systems that screen cases and share information, mothers who seek relief from the court run the risk of becoming the target of dependency proceedings and losing custody of their children (Epstein, 1999a; Miccio, 1999; Schechter & Edleson, 1999). Fear of losing her children can be a major deterrent to a victim accessing the system to obtain relief from the violence perpetrated by the children's father.

The significant potential benefits of specialized processes and courts for families, batterer accountability, the community, and the justice system have outweighed these concerns. The major benefits of domestic violence courts cited by justice system practitioners, victim advocates, and researchers (Fritzler & Simon, 2000; Karan et al., 1999; Keilitz et al., 2000; Tsai, 2000; Winick, 2000) include the following:

- Enhanced coordination of cases and consistent orders in different cases involving the same parties
- More comprehensive relief for survivors at an earlier stage of the judicial process
- Advocacy services that encourage survivors to establish abuse-free lives
- Greater understanding by judges of the dynamics and effects of domestic violence on victims and their children
- More consistent procedures, treatment of litigants, rulings, and orders
- Increased batterer accountability
- Improved batterer compliance with orders
- Greater confidence in the community that the justice system is responding effectively to domestic violence
- Greater system accountability

The components and resources that courts have employed to achieve these benefits are described briefly in the following paragraphs.

Case coordination mechanisms and data systems are critical for identifying, linking, and tracking cases that involve the same parties or other members of their families. These cases could include civil protection orders, misdemeanor and felony prosecutions, divorce, child custody and support, and dependency and juvenile delinquency. Data relating to case histories and disposition could reside in several different court data systems and numerous other data systems maintained by law enforcement, prosecution, child protective services, and other agencies involved in the case. Information sharing among the various agencies, courts, judges, victim advocates, and prosecutors handling these cases can prevent judges from issuing conflicting orders that can put the victim and her children in danger or confuse the parties about their obligations or restrictions on their actions.

Specialized intake units orient victims to court procedures and assist them in understanding their potential role in the civil and criminal process, promote survivors' access to services and remedies they might otherwise not know about or pursue, and refer them to court-related or community-based assistance programs. Courts that integrate intake for civil, family, and criminal cases can offer one-stop shopping for these services to victims involved in more than one type of case (Fritzler & Simon, 2000). Intervention early in the case can help level the field for survivors, many of whom are economically disadvantaged and held hostage by their abusers' purse strings and tenacity (Epstein, 1999a; Mahoney, 1994). For survivors with children, the establishment and enforcement of child support orders, preferably through the federal Title IV-D agency, can be crucial to their ability to successfully leave abusive partners (Klein & Orloff, 1995; Menard & Turetsky, 1999). Survivors who have these support mechanisms are more likely to trust the system and to risk the dangers that often ensue from participating in the prosecution process or following through to obtain a final civil protection order (Sullivan, Tan, Basta, Rumptz, & Davidson, 1992). Specialized intake units also can facilitate the coordination of case management by linking, even if it is through a manual system, the present cases to any related case currently pending or subsequently filed.

Specialized calendars for various domestic violence matters have special benefits, including ex parte protection order petitions, hearings on final protection orders, preliminary hearings and trials in criminal cases, and compliance calendars in both civil and criminal matters. A central location for hearing domestic violence cases eases access to the judicial process and reduces confusion about where proceedings take place. Specialized calendars promote the use of uniform procedures by judges and court staff, which is an important element of procedural justice (Paternoster, Brame, Bachman, & Sherman, 1997; Tyler, 1997; Warren, 2000). Specialized calendars also facilitate case management for prosecutors and defense counsel and the provision of services to survivors. Counsel can handle higher caseloads and accommodate the court's scheduling more easily if all the cases are heard in one or more specialized courtrooms. Proceedings are more efficient, so litigants and counsel can spend less time in court. Service providers can more easily staff the courtroom and increase opportunities to support and address the needs of survivors.

The designation of specialized judges to hear domestic violence cases exclusively or as their primary assignment can dramatically affect court practice and exert control over defendants. Specialized judges have an opportunity to develop expertise in domestic violence issues, including an understanding of the dynamics of domestic violence, knowledge of legal remedies for victims, and familiarity with services available through government sources and in the community (Epstein, 1999b; Tsai, 2000; Winick, 2000). They also can improve their skills in adjudicating cases where one or both parties do not have counsel (Levey et al., 2001). This set of competencies promotes better decision making and more consistent and fair processes for victims and batterers. Victims who have full access to the judicial process are more likely to avail themselves of its protections. Batterers who are accorded all the protections of due process and given adequate information about their options, including services, are more likely to perceive the process as fair and therefore are more likely to comply with court orders (Paternoster et al., 1997). Specialized judges also are better able to monitor the behavior of abusers and their compliance with court orders, including the terms of protection orders and orders to batterer intervention programs. Greater judicial oversight of perpetrator behavior and imposition of significant sanctions for violations of court orders should be the hallmark of a domestic violence court (Keilitz et al., 2000).

Consistent and regular mechanisms for monitoring and enforcing batterer compliance with court orders are fundamental to effective justice system intervention in domestic violence cases (Healey, Smith, & O'Sullivan, 1998). These mechanisms ideally should include judicial review calendars held on specified days. Calendars set in this manner facilitate the ability of treatment providers to file or present reports on a routine basis and for prosecutors to be present to file charges for violations of orders (Keilitz et al. 2000). Regularly scheduled calendars and specialized assignment of judges promote the highest level of consistency in monitoring and enforcement and thus are most conducive to effective judicial oversight of batterer behavior (Karan et al., 1999).

Few courts have all or even most of these components, and there is great variation in the extent to which courts are implementing these processes, structures, and practices (Keilitz et al., 2000). Moreover, only a few studies are now reporting positive effects of specialized procedures and courts (Levey et al., 2001; San Diego Superior Court, 2000). Researchers have not systematically tested whether these benefits for survivors, their families, and the community are being achieved.

For example, in many courts, screening and case coordination are not standard operations. Many courts do not use available information systems for case screening and tracking or to inform decisions critical to victim safety, such as protection order provisions, safety planning, and bail arrangements. Most courts do not have systematic mechanisms for monitoring batterer compliance. Judicial training is severely lacking in most courts, even in those where judges have exclusive assignments to domestic violence calendars. Finally, few courts provide the full array of services needed to assist survivors, such as access to legal assistance for civil matters and economic support. This situation should be changing, however, as more courts apply for funding under the VAWA grant programs that previously were not readily accessible to them.

PROFILES OF TWO INTEGRATED DOMESTIC VIOLENCE COURTS

A growing number of courts are reorganizing their structure and changing their jurisdiction to better integrate management and adjudication of criminal cases and protection orders (Fritzler & Simon, 2000; Keilitz et al., 2000; Tsai, 2000). This section describes two of these courts, the Eleventh Judicial Circuit in Miami, Florida, also known as Dade County, and the District of Columbia Superior Court. Dade County was one of the first courts to integrate criminal cases with protection orders, and the District of Columbia patterned its court to a great extent on the Dade County model. Both courts were designed and implemented in a collaborative process involving the broad range of system components and community service providers and interest groups. In both courts, judges are assigned exclusively to hear domestic violence cases, but assignment to particular cases varies between the two courts. In Dade County, the judge who hears the protection order petition will not hear the related criminal case, whereas in the District of Columbia the same judge may hear both matters. Both courts have an intake process, but the management of intake varies considerably. Dade County employs case managers for each case, which is not a feature of the District of Columbia Domestic Violence Court. Other differences and similarities are described in the following.

The Dade County Domestic Violence Court

Dade County was in the vanguard of courts that recognized the need to coordinate court and community resources to address domestic violence more comprehensively and more effectively (Dakis, 1995). The court has evolved since its inception in 1992, but it has maintained its focus on the four goals that guided its design and implementation: (1) to stop the violence, (2) to protect the victim and the children, (3) to hold the offender accountable, and (4) to make treatment available as needed (Merryman, 1995). The Dade County Domestic Violence Court also was one of the first courts to articulate the goal of achieving therapeutic jurisprudence through meaningful intervention of the criminal justice system and the provision of resources to the family affected by domestic violence (Merryman, 1995).

The Dade County Domestic Violence Court was developed by a broad coalition of justice system professionals (judges, court clerks, prosecutors, public defenders, corrections officers, and law enforcement officers) and domestic violence advocates. The presiding judge demonstrated strong leadership to promote the work of the coalition and appointed the director of family court operations to provide direction, focus, and coordination to the coalition. With this high level of support, the coalition developed a plan for the domestic violence court in 4 months.

The court adjudicates criminal misdemeanors, protection orders, and violations of protection orders. Judges are assigned exclusively to the court and may hear all three types of cases. Each judge is assisted in the court process by a case manager, a judicial assistant who is an attorney, and other support staff. The case managers perform the important function of coordinating with social services and other agencies that may be involved with the parties in the domestic violence case. They also address issues of child support, visitation, and paternity. These support staff are part of the Domestic Violence Court Coordination Unit.

The second component of the domestic violence court is the Domestic Violence Intake Unit, whose design was visionary in 1992. The unit operates a 24-hour hotline, offers services in the courthouse and three satellite offices, and provides services when the court is not open. Most courts today do not provide this range of access to services. As in many other court intake units, these intake staff members provide assistance to clients in completing the forms necessary to file a protection order petition, coordinate the provision of comprehensive services for survivors, assist survivors in safety planning, and help clients prepare for hearings on permanent protection orders by explaining the process and advising the client on what documents and other items to bring to the hearing.

A critical element of the Dade County Domestic Violence Court is the attention it pays to batterer accountability. The court operates a daily judicial review calendar that monitors defendants' compliance with court-ordered batterer intervention, substance abuse treatment, and other terms of court orders. It also was one of the first courts to institute standards for batterer intervention programs. All providers must follow the Duluth model, require participation in at least 26 weekly sessions, provide information to the survivor about the defendant's participation in the program, and inform the court regularly about the defendants' status in the program. The judicial review calendar provides a structured forum for treatment providers to report to the court on the defendant's compliance with the court's orders. Attendance records are available to the court, and the judge can impose immediate sanctions for noncompliance. Many defendants walk into the courtroom armed with excuses, but they face a judge who has the information she needs to send the defendant to jail. For defendants who do not appear in court for the judicial review calendar, the judge issues an arrest warrant.

The Dade County Domestic Violence Court has served as a model for many courts across the country planning a specialized domestic court. Judges and court staff have been generous with their time in hosting visitors and reaching out to the court community through publications, public appearances, participation on national advisory panels, and education programs (see, e.g., Flango et al., 1999; Karan et al., 1999; Keilitz et al., 1997;). The court also continues its close relationship with the community and its justice system partners and continues to implement innovations to improve its processes and services for domestic violence survivors and their families.

The District of Columbia Domestic Violence Unit

The District of Columbia Superior Court's Domestic Violence Unit (DVU) opened its doors in November 1996. The DVU expanded the Dade County model to become one of the first, and one of the few, domestic violence courts that integrate case management and adjudication for civil, criminal, and related family cases. The DVU has jurisdiction for all divorce, custody, paternity, and child support cases involving parties to intrafamily domestic violence criminal and protection order cases. Four adjacent courtrooms and four judges are dedicated to hearing these cases.

The DVU is part of the District of Columbia's Domestic Violence Project, which is a collaborative initiative of several government, university, and community agencies, departments, and service providers. This initiative has made great strides in improving the District of Columbia's ability to address domestic violence. The system the project implemented, while not perfect, replaces a highly fragmented and dysfunctional set of services and processes for domestic violence victims (Keilitz, Hannaford, et al., 1997; Levey et al., 2001).

In the DVU, a dedicated clerk's office coordinates case processing by finding any related cases pending in other divisions of the court. Attorney negotiators triage protection order cases to reduce the issues the judges must decide in hearings. The role of the attorney negotiators does not include mediating issues between the parties to encourage victims to withdraw particular requests for relief in exchange for a consent to the order by the respondent.

The District of Columbia has a centralized intake unit, the Domestic Violence Intake Center (DVIC). The DVIC provides assistance to all petitioners for protection orders and victims referred by the police or the U.S. Attorney's

Office, which prosecutes domestic violence cases in the District of Columbia. The DVIC is staffed by intake counselors, victim advocates, attorneys from the Office of Corporation Counsel, representatives from the U.S. Attorney's Office, and other individuals who help victims to prepare their court documents to obtain temporary and final protection orders, as well as child support orders under the federal Title IV-D program. Attorneys from the Office of Corporation Counsel represent a small proportion of DVIC clients in hearings on final orders of protection and all clients in child support actions.

The DVIC is located in the courthouse, which is an important convenience for domestic violence victims seeking its services. However, the DVIC is managed by a consortium of a public agency (the Office of Corporation Counsel), a university program (the Emergency Domestic Relations Project at the Georgetown University Law Center and a victim advocacy organization (the District of Columbia Coalition Against Domestic Violence), which is a relatively rare management arrangement (Keilitz et al., 2000). While this model has the potential to better address the wide range of victims' needs, it has created some operational and practical challenges (Levey et al., 2001), including lack of clarity and consistency in training, procedures, and, most important, mission. The DVIC is working to overcome these challenges, but other jurisdictions should be advised to avoid them from the outset (Levey et al., 2001).

Two features of the District of Columbia's Domestic Violence Project are particularly positive for addressing domestic violence. First, the linkage to the Title IV-D child support program assists survivors in becoming independent from the abusing parent of their children. Although civil protection orders can require the respondent to pay child support, this relief is available only for the duration of the protection order. In most jurisdictions protection orders expire in 1 year or less. Obtaining a permanent child support order that a government attorney enforces is a much more complete remedy and help for the domestic violence survivor.

The second benefit of the District of Columbia's court model is the inclusion of jurisdiction for family law matters filed in the Superior Court. A few jurisdictions link pending family matters with domestic violence cases by transferring the domestic violence case to the judge hearing the family law case (Flango et al., 1999; Keilitz, Davis, et al., 1997). In the District of Columbia model, the cases flow in the opposite direction. To the extent feasible, the court consolidates the family matter with the domestic violence case. This approach facilitates judicial decision making that maintains a focus on the domestic violence issues in the case, rather than the domestic violence having a secondary influence on case outcomes. This context provides fewer opportunities for the batterer to stymie the survivor's efforts to leave the relationship and to use the family law process to further harass or exert power over the victim.

TECHNOLOGY APPLICATIONS TO
ADDRESS DOMESTIC VIOLENCE

Across the country today, state and local court systems are exploring ways that technology can improve court processes, save time and money, and ensure that the court system functions fairly and efficiently for the public. For over a decade, establishing and maintaining public trust and confidence in the courts has been high on the agenda for court leaders (Warren, 2000). Along with theories and movements such as procedural justice and therapeutic jurisprudence, technology plays an important role in achieving this goal.

Domestic violence also has been a key agenda item for the leadership of the courts (Karan et al., 1999). As the experiences of the Brooklyn and Bronx Domestic Violence Courts demonstrate, the implementation of specialized court processes for domestic violence cases has been accompanied by the application of technology to improve access to justice for domestic violence victims; fair outcomes in criminal, family, and protection order cases; and public trust and confidence that the courts will hold batterers accountable for their behavior and work to ensure survivor safety.

Other forces have propelled courts into using technology solutions to address issues raised by domestic violence caseloads. For example, various U.S. Department of Justice programs have supported the development and implementation of technology to address domestic violence, including the Bureau of Justice Assistance Byrne grants and the Bureau of Justice Statistics program to improve criminal history information systems (National Criminal History Improvement Program). More recently, the VAWA has supported technology projects through grants administered by the Violence Against Women Office. Two of these innovations are the Grants to Encourage Arrest and Enforcement of Protection Orders program and the STOP Violence Against Women grant program (STOP stands for "Services and Training for Officers and Prosecutors"). These programs have supported a variety of technology applications for courts, including protection order databases, case management systems, on-line systems for creating protection orders, and electronic filing of protection orders (Burt et al., 2000).

One area that technology is particularly poised to address is the enforcement of protection orders. Both within states and across state and tribal boundaries, the enforcement of protection orders is a major challenge for courts and law enforcement. Differences in state laws governing protection orders, including eligibility requirements, allowable duration of orders, and penalties for violations, are significant barriers to enforcement. The lack of resources (staff, time, technology) to ensure the accuracy of orders, consistency of data, and integrity of the enforcement process has stood in the way of achieving safety for domestic violence survivors and their children.

Although 46 states and the District of Columbia have implemented or are implementing a protection order registry, there is great variance in the types of data captured; methods for gathering, entering, and verifying the data; how long data are kept; coverage of the state; responsibility for management; and many other aspects of the form, content, and function of the registries. Finally, data systems created to store protection orders often are incompatible with other systems within the same agency or local or state jurisdiction or with other states and the FBI's National Crime Information Center.

A variety of systems and methods are used for capturing, storing, accessing, and transferring protection order data. Each of these approaches comes with a set of advantages and drawbacks. For example, most states have developed protection order registries. However, most registries include only a summary of the information from the actual order, and many contain only the order that is currently in effect. Many registries are "add-ons" to other existing data systems, such as a wants and warrants file, and cannot accommodate historical or other information that might be helpful for enforcement and future protection order proceedings. Another drawback is that many registries contain information entered locally or centrally from paper orders. The information in these registries is subject to data entry errors and missing orders. The differences between the two types of data systems can be significant in regard to cross-jurisdictional enforcement of orders.

One technology approach that has the potential to overcome many of the drawbacks in enforcing protection orders both within and across jurisdictions is the development of Web-based statewide protection order databases (Emmons, Keilitz, Southworth, & Trukenbrod, 2001). Databases have several advantages over registries. They may contain the full text of the order. In addition, because they may be purely electronic, databases allow orders to be viewed on a computer screen or printed. A database also may contain the entire record of the case, including all petitions, affidavits, notices, and orders issued in the case. This feature facilitates improved decision making in enforcement proceedings or subsequent family or protection order matters. Accessibility over the Internet to the full text of the order allows law enforcement officers and judges in other jurisdictions access to orders at all times. Law enforcement is most often called upon to enforce orders after the court has closed. Internet access to databases allows officers in the field to clearly determine whether the behavior of the restrained person has violated the order, no matter when it occurs.

Although a Web-based database has the advantage of providing instant access to orders, which more closed systems such as local area networks and wide area networks cannot do, the use of the Internet increases the risk that individuals who should not have access to the orders will be able to view them and obtain information that could cause harm to the survivor. Web-based databases should be designed to include digital certificates of authenticity, user passwords, firewalls, and other data security measures.

Electronic filing of court documents is another technology that is rapidly being explored and adopted in courts (McMillan, Walker, & Webster, 1998). An example of the use of electronic filing in domestic violence cases is a system piloted by the Missouri Office of State Court Administration in one county for filing protection orders from three local domestic violence shelters. With this pilot project funded by the VAWA STOP grant program, Missouri became the first state in the country to permit electronic filing of protection orders. The system is Web-based and includes a high level of secure measures, and its implementation required modifications to legal and procedural rules. For example, the judicial branch passed special rules of court authorizing the electronic filing of protection orders and the use of digital signatures. Before electronic filing can be expanded statewide and to other locations (e.g., law enforcement agencies, prosecutors' and public defenders' offices), standardized protection order forms must be developed for use throughout the state.

Another technological development that is speeding forward is the application of XML (eXtensible Markup Language) to electronic filing, to data transfer systems such as protection order databases, and to integrated justice systems. For example, the Joint Committee of the Conference of State Court Administrators and the National Association of Court Management is collaborating with other judicial organizations to develop XML standards for court data (see National Center for State Courts, Court Technology Laboratory Web site).

XML, which is viewed as a universal translator between different computer languages (Emmons et al., 2001), uses document type definitions (DTDs; also called data tag definitions) to specify the allowable order, structure, and attributes of tags for a particular type of document. Tags mark and name the data elements in a document (Gibson, 2001). The use of DTDs allows translation even among different DTDs, which in turn allows a programmer to define fields easily in any program, from e-mail to SQL server. Once data tags are defined, data can be imported and exported to and from different systems and across platforms (e.g., from IBM to Macintosh). In other words, by setting clear categories for information, XML can allow any form of information to be transferred into any other XML-coded system.

These features of XML make it an excellent tool for overcoming barriers to data transfer and access. XML therefore has potential application to improve court processing of domestic violence cases when information related to the parties in the cases resides in different systems both within and outside the court (e.g., law enforcement agencies, prosecutors' offices, probation departments, social services, child support enforcement offices). It also has significant implications for removing the technology barriers to enforcing protection orders across jurisdictions.

A major issue for courts today is the tension between providing access to information for more effective delivery of justice and ensuring confidentiality of information to avoid causing harm to individuals (see Public Access to Court Records Web site). This tension is particularly significant for protection order databases, electronic filing of protection orders, and other systems designed to facilitate the transfer of information about domestic violence victims. Building comprehensive and user-friendly databases and systems that facilitate the entry of appropriate relief for domestic violence survivors and greater monitoring of batterers can conflict with other important goals of the justice system to protect survivors from further harm and to ensure their privacy (Emmons et al., 2001).

Protection order databases and other court records related to domestic violence cases differ significantly from other court data systems. Domestic violence cases always involve the potential for injury and death. Storing private information about the victim, such as where she lives or works, creates the risk the information will be disclosed, and the more widely accessible the information is, the more likely it is to become available to the batterer or someone who knows him.

Another issue related to confidentiality and privacy is the impact of the system's security on the victim's willingness to come forward to seek relief from the court, through either the protection order process or a cooperating witness in the prosecution of the batterer. Victims seeking a protection order are focused on achieving safety. To obtain an order, they must reveal in the petition and supporting documents the details of their abuse, which is inherently very personal information. They are not likely to know that they can refuse to give certain requested information or that they can provide an alternate phone number or address. Nor are they likely to know that the information they provide may be stored in local, state, and national databases. Similarly, survivors who consider using advocacy services provided by the prosecutor may be deterred by requirements to provide contact information. Although in many jurisdictions the court or community-based advocates can effectively advise victims of these issues and potential dangers, a better approach is to design protection order databases and other information systems that adequately protect privacy, confidentiality, and safety while allowing access for enforcement and provision of services (Emmons et al., 2001).

Although protection order databases, electronic filing systems, and other technology applications have many benefits, there are potential drawbacks for victim safety, including increased concerns about access to and release of private data. Data security and privacy issues must be addressed as the technology and mechanisms for access to the data are designed. Another important component is cross-agency communication and collaboration in the design and implementation of technology applications and monitoring how they are being used. This process may force communication among agencies that have not worked together in the past and produce significant secondary benefits.

PROFILES OF TWO TECHNOLOGY APPLICATIONS DESIGNED AND IMPLEMENTED TO PROMOTE VICTIM SAFETY

This section describes two applications of technology to improve how the justice system serves and protects domestic violence victims. The first is an application to support a domestic violence court, and the second is being implemented to store, track, and enforce protection orders. Both applications have the potential to be implemented in other jurisdictions.

The Domestic Violence Court Technology Application and Resource Link

This application is a product of a partnership between the New York State Unified Court System and the Center for Court Innovation in New York City. It was developed and implemented for use in the Brooklyn Domestic Violence Court and the Bronx Domestic Violence Court. The Center for Court Innovation is a public-private partnership of the New York State Unified Court System and the Fund for the City of New York. The center works closely with the New York State Unified Court System's Office of Court Administration to develop new ways of addressing community problems in the courts and to expand court innovations statewide. Some examples of these efforts are the Brooklyn and Bronx Domestic Violence Courts, the Midtown Community Court, and the Manhattan Family Treatment Court (Center for Court Innovation, forthcoming).

The Domestic Violence Court Technology Application and Resource Link is a comprehensive Web-based intranet system that runs on a court-based server housed in the State of New York Office of Court Administration in Albany. The Technology Application provides electronic links between the specialized domestic violence courts, district attorney's offices, probation departments, victim advocates, and treatment providers. Through these links, it facilitates the core functions and purposes of the domestic violence courts: efficient case processing; monitoring defendants' compliance with court-ordered batterer intervention programs, substance abuse treatment, and other terms of pretrial release and probation; reporting alleged violations of protection orders; and coordinating service delivery to victims. The Technology Application also allows the court to create orders of protection on-line. Soon, it will upload orders of protection automatically to New York State's Domestic Violence Registry.

The Technology Application includes important mechanisms to ensure the security of information maintained in the database and transmitted within and across the system partners. The first level of security is a proprietary program that prevents public access. Qualified users can gain access to the Technology Application only through dedicated phone lines or by logging in to a secure intranet address. When a user has connected to the Technology Application, the second level of security requires him or her to enter a personal log-in and password, which control access to the various components of the system. Clearly defined criteria govern the level and type of access a system user has, including the agency's identification and the user's position within the agency. In addition to these access controls, the Technology Application database logs all actions in the system, including data updates, deletions, and inquiries. The actions of individual users therefore are under constant surveillance.

An evaluation of the Domestic Violence Court Technology Application and Resource Link indicates that the system has improved practice within the court and among the partners in the specialized courts (Keilitz, Rubio, & Wentland, forthcoming). Judges are always aware of the status of defendants' compliance with court-ordered batterer intervention and other terms of orders of protection. Defendants are less able to use system gaps to evade accountability. Victim advocates report that the Technology Application has improved their ability to advise the court of defendant behavior that suggests heightened danger to the victim or the need for stronger controls on the defendant. These assessments indicate that this use of technology has the potential to significantly improve court responses to domestic violence.

The Protection From Abuse Database

Working in cooperation with the Pennsylvania Office of Court Administration, the Pennsylvania Coalition Against Domestic Violence (PCADV) has developed an automated civil protection order database known as the Protection From Abuse Database (PFAD). Pilot counties began entering live protection from abuse cases into PFAD in March 1999. To date, over two thirds of the 67 counties in Pennsylvania have voluntarily joined the PFAD project, providing Web access to protection from abuse orders to over 2,000 authorized users across the state (Emmons et al., 2001).

PFAD currently is the only full-text, Internet-based database in the country that provides access to advocates and private attorneys assisting plaintiffs to create the documents needed to obtain a protection from abuse order and archives the on-line records when those orders become inactive. The project has addressed privacy and public access issues in its implementation phase and provides an advocacy perspective on maintenance of PFAD records that must be immediately accessible to law enforcement agencies. PFAD has ensured that issues of the safety and privacy of the plaintiffs served by the system were incorporated in the design, implementation, and maintenance of the database.

Until the PFAD was developed, enforcement of protection from abuse orders (PFAs) in Pennsylvania was entirely dependent on paper copies of court orders. The Pennsylvania State Police required civil clerks of court (prothonotaries) to provide PFAs, modifications, continuances, extensions, and dismissals along with a data sheet to the local barracks. Prior to PFAD implementation in a county, proper completion of the data sheets required close scrutiny of each order filed along with complete knowledge of the types of relief afforded under Pennsylvania's Protection from Abuse Act. PFAD automates the protection order process, allowing each case to be completed on-line, along with the requisite data sheet. The data sheets completed on PFAD are legible, and the condition codes are error-free, which is critical to maintaining accurate records in the statewide registry.

In Pennsylvania, as in many states that are currently working on automation but have not yet automated statewide, there was no electronic data sharing among the clerks of court, nor was there a convenient method of researching past civil dockets statewide for defendants in PFA cases. Furthermore, the statewide PFA registry, maintained by the Pennsylvania State Police, houses only current orders and purges cases upon expiration of the order. PFAD provides these records for the courts and law enforcement to better assess cases presented to the court.

PFAD provides access to accurate and current records to counties enforcing out-of-county protection orders. In addition to providing information to local law enforcement to allow them to view the prothonotaries' records 24 hours a day, 7 days a week, these records can assist enforcement of Pennsylvania orders in other states, tribes, and territories as required by the VAWA. The technology can facilitate the verification process by providing current information from the clerks of courts even when the courts are not in session.

Lessons learned in developing and implementing the PFAD in Pennsylvania provide some guidance for those who are considering such an endeavor. These include clearly defining the goals of the database project and the expectations of the participants; planning for a long-term implementation process; gathering data as close to the source as possible (i.e., in the courtroom or during the filing and entering of the order); ensuring that victim advocates are meaningfully involved in development and implementation; building compliance with VAWA's full faith and credit provisions into the system (i.e., facilitate enforcement of your jurisdiction's orders as well enforcement of foreign orders); designing the system with the benefits of XML in mind (i.e., for information sharing even if the database does not use an Internet system initially); building in data security and safety planning (e.g., consider ways to avoid collecting phone numbers and other risky information); and planning security measures that assume some authorized users of the system will be defendants in protection order cases (Emmons et al., 2001).

CONCLUSION

Courts are the final arbiter of society's disputes and have the power to intervene directly in the lives of those who come before them. Through the broad reaches of court jurisdiction, judges and court staff can encounter domestic violence in nearly every type of case. In the movement to stop domestic violence, courts can exercise their power and authority to provide order where disorder reigns.

In the past decade, courts have begun to focus attention and resources on addressing domestic violence. A significant trend toward specialization of domestic case management is emerging (Keilitz et al., 2000). Now courts also are using technology not only to make case management more efficient but also to improve the ability of courts to protect domestic violence survivors and to convey to batterers that they no longer can manipulate the system to avoid accountability for their abusive and violent behavior. These processes and systems are far from perfect. Furthermore, they can pose dangers to survivors if they are not designed, implemented, and monitored with adequate attention to security and privacy concerns. Without these case management and technology innovations, however, domestic violence victims and their children would be deprived of one of the keys to their survival and well-being. Despite the potential for creating further harm to victims if court processes and technology applications are poorly designed or misused, courts should continue on the road to innovation in addressing domestic violence.

REFERENCES

Appel, A. E., & Holden, G. W. (1998). The co-occurrence of spouse and physical child abuse: A review and appraisal. *Journal of Family Psychology, 12,* 578–599.

Babb, B. (1998). Fashioning an interdisciplinary framework for court reform in family law: A blueprint to construct a unified family court. *Southern California Law Review, 71,* 469–545.

Bureau of Justice Statistics. (2000). *Intimate partner violence.* Washington, DC: U.S. Department of Justice.

Burt, M. R., Zweig, J. M., Schlichter, K., Kamya, S., Katz, B. L., Miller, N., Keilitz, S., & Harrell, A. V. (2000). *2001 Report: Evaluation of the STOP formula grants to combat violence against women.* Washington, DC: Urban Institute.

Buzawa, E., & Buzawa, C. (1996). *Domestic violence: The criminal justice response* (2nd ed.). Thousand Oaks, CA: Sage.

Cahn, N. R. (1992). Innovative approaches to the prosecution of domestic violence crimes: An overview. In E. S. Buzawa & C. G Buzawa (Eds.), *Domestic violence: The changing criminal justice response* (pp. 161–180). Westport, CT: Auburn House.

Carbon, S., Macdonald, P., & Zeya, S. (1999). Enforcing domestic violence protection orders throughout the country: New frontiers of protection for victims of domestic violence. *Juve-*

nile and Family Court Journal, 50, 39–54.

Center for Court Innovation. (Forthcoming). Domestic violence court technology application user manual. New York: Author.

Chandler, D. B. (1990). Violence, fear, and communication: The variable impact of domestic violence on mediation. Mediation Quarterly, 7(4), 331–346.

Conference of Chief Justices. (2000, August). Resolution in support of problem solving courts, adopted by the Task Force on Therapeutic Justice of the Conference of Chief Justices, in Rapid City, South Dakota.

Crenshaw, K. (1991). Mapping the margins: Intersectionality, identity politics, and violence against women of color. Stanford Law Review, 43, 1241.

Dakis, L. (1995, February). Dade County's domestic violence plan: An integrated approach. Trial, 44.

Dunford-Jackson, B., Frederick, L., Hart, B., & Hofford, M. (1998). Unified family courts: How will they serve victims of domestic violence? Family Law Quarterly, 32, 131–146.

Edleson, J. L. (1999a). Children's witnessing of adult domestic violence. Journal of Interpersonal Violence, 14, 839–870.

Edleson, J. L. (1999b). The overlap between child maltreatment and woman battering. Violence Against Women, 5, 134–154.

Emmons, S., Keilitz, S., Southworth, C., & Trukenbrod, S. (2001, August). Developing Web-based protection order databases for cross-jurisdictional enforcement. Paper presented at the Seventh National Court Technology Conference, Baltimore, MD.

Epstein, D. (1999a). Effective intervention in domestic violence cases: Rethinking the roles of prosecutors, judges, and the court system. Yale Journal of Law and Feminism, 11, 3–50.

Epstein, D. (1999b). Redefining the state's response to domestic violence: Past victories and future challenges. Georgetown Journal of Gender and the Law, 1, 127–143.

Field, J. K. (1996). Visiting danger: Keeping battered women and their children safe. Clearinghouse Review, 30(3), 295–307.

Fields, M. D. (1994). The impact of spouse abuse on children and its relevance in custody and visitation decisions. Cornell Journal of Law and Public Policy, 3, 221–252.

Flango, C. R., Flango, V. E., & Rubin, H. T. (1999). How are courts coordinating family cases? Williamsburg, VA: National Center for State Courts.

Fritzler, R. B., & Simon, L. M. J. (2000). Creating a domestic violence court: Combat in the trenches. Court Review, 37, 28–39.

Gibson, R. (2001, August). What is XML and why should I care? Paper presented at the Seventh National Court Technology Conference, Baltimore, MD.

Goelman, D. M., Lehrman, F. L., & Valente, R. L. (Eds.). (1996). The impact of domestic violence on your legal practice: A lawyer's handbook. Washington, DC: American Bar Association.

Goelman, D., & Valente, R. (1997). When will they ever learn? Educating to end domestic violence: A law school report. Washington, DC: American Bar Association.

Hanna, C. (1996). No right to choose: Mandated victim participation in domestic violence prosecutions. Harvard Law Review, 109, 1850–1910.

Hanna, C. (1998). The paradox of hope: The crime and punishment of domestic violence. William and Mary Law Review, 39, 1505–1584.

Harrell, A., & Smith, B. (1996). Effects of restraining orders on domestic violence victims. In E. Buzawa & C. Buzawa (Eds.), *Do arrests and retraining orders work? 214*. Thousand Oaks, CA: Sage.

Harrell, A., Smith, B., & Newmark, L. (1993). *Court processing the effects of restraining orders for victims of domestic violence*. Washington, DC: Urban Institute.

Hart, B. (1995, March) *Coordinated community approaches to domestic violence*. Paper presented at the Strategic Planning Workshop on Violence Against Women, Washington, DC.

Hart, B. J., & Hofford, M. (1996). Child custody. In Deborah M. Goelman, Fredrica L. Lehrman, and Roberta L. Valente (Eds.), *The impact of domestic violence on your legal practice: A lawyer's handbook* (pp. 1–6). Washington, DC: American Bar Association.

Healey, K., Smith, C., & O'Sullivan, C. (1998). *Batterer intervention: Program approaches and criminal justice strategies*. Washington, DC: National Institute of Justice.

Herrell, S. B., & Hofford, M. (1990). *Family violence: Improving court practice*. Reno, NV: Family Violence Project, National Council of Juvenile and Family Court Judges.

Hora, P. F., Schma, W. G., & Rosenthal, J. T. A. (1999). Therapeutic jurisprudence and the drug treatment court movement: Revolutionizing the criminal justice system's response to drug abuse crime in America. *Notre Dame Law Review, 74,* 439–537.

Jaffe, P. G. (1995). Children of domestic violence: Special challenges in custody and visitation dispute resolution. In N. Lemon, P. Jaffe, & A. Ganley, (Eds.), *Domestic violence and children: Resolving custody and visitation disputes* (pp. 19–30). San Francisco: Family Violence Prevention Fund.

Jaffe, P. G., Wolfe, D., & Wilson, S. (1990). *Children of battered women.* Newbury Park, CA: Sage.

Karan, A., Keilitz, S., & Denaro, S. (1999). Domestic violence courts: What are they and how should we manage them? *Juvenile and Family Court Journal, 50,* 75–86.

Keilitz, S., Davis, C. V., Flango, C. R., Garcia, V., Jones, A. M., Peterson, M., & Spinozza, D. M. (1997). *Domestic violence and child custody disputes: A resource handbook for judges and court managers*. Williamsburg, VA: National Center for State Courts.

Keilitz, S., Hannaford, P., & Efkeman, H. E. (1997). *Civil protection orders: The benefits and limitations for victims of domestic violence*. Williamsburg, VA: National Center for State Courts.

Keilitz, S., Guerrero, R., Jones, A., & Rubio, D. (2000). *Specialization of domestic violence case management in the courts: Findings from a national survey*. Williamsburg, VA: National Center for State Courts.

Keilitz, S., Rubio, D., & Wentland, P. (Forthcoming). *Manual for implementing data collection and communication projects*. Williamsburg, VA: National Center for State Courts.

Klein, A. (1996). Re-abuse in a population of court-restrained male batterers: Why restraining orders don't work. In E. Buzawa & C. Buzawa (Eds.), *Do arrests and restraining orders work?* (p. 192). Thousand Oaks, CA: Sage.

Klein, C. F., & Orloff, L. E. (1995). Representing a victim of domestic violence. *Family Advocate, 17,* 25.

Lemon, N., Jaffe, P., & Ganley, A. (1995). *Domestic violence and children: Resolving custody and visitation disputes*. San Francisco: Family Violence Prevention Fund.

Levey, L., Steketee, M., & Keilitz, S. (2001). *Lessons learned in imple-*

menting an integrated domestic violence court: The District of Columbia experience. Williamsburg, VA: National Center for State Courts.

Little, K., Malefyt, M. B., Walker, A., Tucker, D. D., & Buel, S. M. (1998). *Assessing justice system response to violence against women: A tool for law enforcement, prosecution and the courts to use in developing effective responses.* Washington, DC: U.S. Department of Justice.

McMillan, J., Walker, D., & Webster, L. (1998). *A guidebook for electronic court filing.* Williamsburg, VA: National Center for State Courts. Retrieved from National Center for State Courts Court Technology Laboratory Web site: http: www.ncsc.dni.us/NCSC/TIS/TIS99/electr99/Guidebook/HTML/EfileWest.htm.

Mahoney, M. R. (1994). Victimization or oppression? Women's lives, violence, and agency. In M. A. Fineman & R. Mykitiuk (Eds.), *The public nature of private violence: The discovery of domestic abuse* (pp. 59–92). New York: Routledge.

Menard, A., & Turetsky, V. (1999). Child support and domestic violence. *Juvenile and Family Court Journal, 50,* 27–38.

Merryman, M. (1995). *Specialized domestic violence courts: A new means to address an age-old problem.* Unpublished manuscript.

Miccio, G. K. (1999). A reasonable battered mother? Redefining, reconstructing, and recreating the battered mother in child protective proceedings. *Harvard Women's Law Journal, 22,* 89–122.

National Association of Drug Court Professionals and Drug Court Standards Committee. (1997). *Defining drug courts: The key components.* Washington, DC: U.S. Department of Justice.

National Center for State Courts, Court Technology Laboratory Web site. *XML information.* Retrieved at: http: ctl.ncsc.dni.us/xml_resources.htm.

National Council of Juvenile and Family Court Judges. (1994). *The model code on domestic and family violence.* Reno: Author.

National Council of Juvenile and Family Court Judges. (2001, March). *Federal Greenbook demonstration sites announced.* Retrieved from http: www.dvlawsearch.com/news/985852800.html.

Osofsky, J. D. (1999). The impact of violence on children. *The future of children: Domestic violence and children, 9,* 33–49.

Ostrom, B. J., & Kauder, N. B. (Eds.). (1999). *Examining the work of state courts, 1998: A national perspective from the Court Statistics Project.* Williamsburg, VA: National Center for State Courts.

Pagelow, M. D. (1990). Effects of domestic violence on children and their consequences for custody and visitation agreements. *Mediation Quarterly, 7,* 347–364.

Paternoster, R., Brame, R., Bachman, R., & Sherman, L. W. (1997). Do fair procedures matter? The effect of procedural justice on spouse assault. *Law and Society Review, 31,* 163–204.

Public Access to Court Records Web site: http: ctl.ncsc.dni.us/publicaccess.

Ptacek, J. (1999). *Battered women in the courtroom: The power of judicial responses.* Boston: Northeastern University Press.

Richie, B. (1996). *Compelled to crime: The gender entrapment of battered black women.* New York: Routledge.

Rottman, D., & Casey, P. (1999). Therapeutic jurisprudence and the emergence of the problem-solving courts. *National Institute of Justice Journal, 240,* 12–19.

Rottman, D., Efkeman, H. S., & Casey, P. (1998). *A guide to court and community collaboration.* Williamsburg, VA: National Center for State Courts.

San Diego Superior Court. (2000). *Evaluation report for the San Diego County domestic violence courts.* San Diego, CA: San Diego Superior Court.

Schechter, S. (1982). *Women and male violence.* Boston: South End Press.

Schechter, S., & Edleson, J. L. (1994, June). *In the best interests of women and children: A call for collaboration between child welfare and domestic violence constituencies.* Paper presented at the Domestic Violence and Child Welfare Conference, Racine, WI.

Schechter, S., & Edleson, J. L. (1999). *Effective intervention in domestic violence and child maltreatment cases: Guidelines for policy and practice.* Reno, NV: National Council for Juvenile and Family Court Judges.

Sewell, B. D. (1989). History of abuse: Societal, judicial and legislative responses to the problem of wife beating. *Suffolk Law Review, 23,* 983–1017.

Simon, L. M. J. (1995). A therapeutic jurisprudence approach to the legal processing of domestic violence cases. *Psychology, Public Policy, and Law, 1,* 43–79.

Sullivan, C. M., Tan, C., Basta, J., Rumptz, M., & Davidson, W. S. (1992). An advocacy intervention program for women with abusive partners: Initial evaluation. *American Journal of Community Psychology, 20,* 309–332.

Sviridoff, M., Rottman, D., Ostrom, B., Curtis, R. (1997). *Dispensing justice locally: The implementation and effects of the Midtown Community Court.* New York: Fund for the City of New York.

Tsai, B. (2000). The trend toward specialized domestic violence courts: Improvements on an effective innovation. *Fordham Law Review, 68,* 1285–1327.

Tyler, T. R. (1997). Procedural fairness and compliance with the law. *Swiss Journal of Economics and Statistics, 133,* 219.

Warren, R. K. (2000). Public trust and procedural justice. *Court Review, 37,* 12–16.

Wexler, D. B., & Winick, B. J. (1996). *Law in a therapeutic key: Developments in therapeutic jurisprudence.* Durham, NC: Carolina Academic Press.

Winick, B. Applying the law therapeutically in domestic violence cases. *UMKC Law Review, 69,* 1–63.

Zlotnick, D. M. (1995). Empowering the battered woman: The use of criminal contempt sanctions to enforce civil protection orders. *Ohio State Law Journal, 56,* 1153–1215.

Zorza, J. (1992). *Defending a battered woman accused of parental abduction.* New York: National Center on Women and Family Law.

9

Innovations in the Legal System's Response to Domestic Violence

Thinking Outside the Box for the Silent Majority of Battered Women

AMY P. BARASCH
VICTORIA L. LUTZ

The Story Behind the Story, by Victoria L. Lutz

My dad's heart attacks always seemed to occur between midnight and 5:00 A.M. And he had many. This was in the 1950s and 1960s, when doctors still made house calls. Dr. Lidle, our family physician, would arrive within minutes of my mother's emergency call. I would look out my bedroom window and see Dr. Lidle's old Chevy station wagon pull into our driveway and know that my dad would get the immediate help that he needed. I didn't expect Dr. Lidle to cure my dad permanently, but each time that Dad received the help he needed at the time he needed it, I knew he would be better.

During the 32 years since my father died, I have spent the majority of my legal career trying to help battered women. And I have frequently thought of Dr. Lidle and his station wagon. If Dr. Lidle had not driven to my home in the wee hours of the morning so often that he knew the route without asking directions, my dad would have died many years before he did. In a parallel vein, it has struck me that, if domestic violence crimes begin in the home, frequently at night and frequently seriatim, *domestic violence intervention must begin in the home, when it is needed and as often as it is needed.* It has also struck me that, in terms of domestic violence intervention, if *professional assistance* is needed at the home or at the courthouse—*wherever the victim*

accesses emergency relief—the best practice model is to provide that profes-
sional assistance where she needs it, when she needs it. The "mantra" must be:

- Immediate response
- By a trained professional
- Wherever the victim is

These proactive premises provide the theoretical foundation for four domestic violence intervention models pioneered by the Pace Women's Justice Center (PWJC, or the Center)[1] and discussed in this chapter: Project DETER,[2] the Family Court Legal Program (FCLP), the Center's Civil Legal Assistance Practicum (the Practicum), and the Center's Public Service Announcement (PSA) Agenda.[3] Three of these are legal programs that operate in New York State, and therefore under New York law, but all are easily adapted to any jurisdiction. None of these responses is theoretically complex. All four can be modified as long as the mantra is the same. Each works.

HOW THESE INTERVENTION MODELS SERVE THE "SILENT MAJORITY" OF BATTERED WOMEN

Project DETER, the FCLP, the Practicum, and the Center's PSA Agenda are initiatives that are designed specifically to assist the silent majority of battered women. These are the battered women whose specific needs are highlighted in the following program descriptions:

- Project DETER is designed to provide civil legal services 24 hours a day, 7 days a week, to victims of domestic violence who need civil redress at all hours of the day and night.
- The FCLP model is designed to provide an attorney to the many battered women whose court of choice is civil rather than criminal.
- The Practicum partners the legal and medical professions to provide holistic representation to the most marginalized of battered women, such as those with AIDS, severe posttraumatic stress disorder, and mental retardation.
- The PSAs are designed to provide legal information in the home via television to the three out of four battered women—3 million or so victims yearly—who not do report their injuries and/or do not see themselves as victims of domestic violence.[4]

These initiatives are designed as "front-end" service delivery or, to put it another way, "prehomicide" intervention. While the services provided by these programs vary, all four models have proved to be useful tools in the ongoing struggle against domestic violence; all are accepted by local police departments and community response network organizations; and thus all warrant consideration for adaptation in other communities.

WHY WERE THESE PROGRAMS CREATED?

One constant of the four programs is the emphasis on greater access to orders of protection. Thus, it is critical to acknowledge that these innovations are *not* designed to provide relief to the victim whose leg has been broken by her batterer or who is neither married to nor has a child in common with her abuser.[5] An order of protection may prove more dangerous than beneficial; if the victim believes the order will make matters worse, the system should heed her warning. It is undeniably true that orders of protection do not stop bullets. It is equally true that the vast majority of batterers do not use bullets.[6] We recognize the difficulties in dealing with potentially lethal batterers and of even recognizing who is a potentially lethal batterer. Risk assessment plays a ubiquitous role in everything we do at the PWJC.[7] This chapter, however, does not deal with the rare and tragic lethal domestic violence battery that makes the headlines; rather, it deals with the insidious epidemic of violation or misdemeanor-level intimate partner abuse suffered by the silent majority of millions of battered women, whose cries too often are muffled by apartment walls and systems that turn a deaf ear.[8]

Project DETER is an attempt to empower battered women when they call the police in an emergency. Many of these women need assistance with child support, housing, and other ancillary matters in order for the police response to be practicable. Yet police cannot provide legal representation. DETER attorneys train police and respond when the police respond, at the time when the victim needs the help most, that is, when her cheek is reddened with the mark of a hand. This immediate intervention has dramatically increased the numbers of orders of protection issued for those in need and, it is hoped, dispelled some women's fear of possible negative ramifications of involving the police.

The FCLP was created for two reasons: (1) so that women who need the personal and less public redress offered by civil courts, such as custody and child support, can obtain that critical relief with the assistance of an attorney; and (2) so that future generations of law students trained and working in this program will provide far better representation to victims of domestic violence than the majority of attorneys have in the past.[9] Because most orders of protection in the United States are civil, but most of our national intervention funding and initiatives over the past two decades have focused on criminal intervention, the FCLP is a direct response to the needs of the dramatically high number of victims who access aid in the civil arena.[10]

The Practicum provides holistic legal representation to the clients whom we affectionately call "the forgotten battered women" because most of them come to the Center after shelters have asked them to leave because of drug or parenting problems or after attorneys have refused to represent them because of their mental or physical limitations. Some of these clients have AIDS or severe posttraumatic stress disorder or are marginalized in other ways. Many are represented by the Practicum for a year or longer.

The goal of PSAs is to inform everyone who has a television (or who takes a subway or a bus and views billboards based on the PSA campaign) that orders of protection issued in any state, Indian tribal land, or U.S. territory should be enforced in every other state, Indian tribal land, or U.S. territory. It is hoped that these advertisements will inform victims, who may know absolutely nothing about domestic violence, that orders of protection are available to them and that these orders will be honored nationwide. For many of the millions who will see these advertisements, this may be the only domestic violence information available.

PROJECT DETER

[Project DETER] has helped us form a fabulous partnership in which we have been able to help women who I seriously believe would not have used the court system previously to take advantage of all that is available in family court. . . . The officers in particular feel fabulous about having another alternative to give to these women when they're out there speaking with them at that moment—to be able to call someone and to say, "tomorrow we'll meet, we'll get something done for you."

Captain Anne Fitzsimmons
White Plains Department of Public Safety, New York, October 1999

The Project DETER attorney's beeper began to go off late one chilly October evening. From her home, the attorney called the number displayed on the beeper, and, as always, a White Plains police officer answered the telephone. The officer explained that he had responded to a call from a woman named Katie,[11] who said that her boyfriend had been yelling and cursing at her all night; he had backed her up against the wall and, when she tried to get away, had kicked her in the thigh, causing her to fall down. She said that he had done this once before, in front of their daughter, but fortunately this time the girl had been asleep in another room. The officer was at Katie's home now and had just finished completing a domestic incident report.[12] The boyfriend had already fled the scene by the time the police arrived, but the officers had seen the bruise on the woman's leg and taken photographs of it. In many New York jurisdictions the police would not have believed they had the evidence to charge a misdemeanor, and, because the offense was not committed in their presence, they would not have initiated a criminal charge.[13] In White Plains, however, the police were willing to draft a criminal complaint charging the defendant with the misdemeanor of attempted assault, third degree. Katie indicated that she wanted to pursue her case in family court.

Then the officer put Katie on the telephone, and the attorney introduced herself as a Project DETER attorney and explained to Katie her legal options. Katie was told that she could file for a family court order of protection to get her boyfriend to stop hurting her; if that was what she chose to do, the attorney would meet and represent her the next morning.[14] The attorney also told her that she could file a separate complaint in criminal court and seek an order of protection there as well. The DETER attorney reiterated Katie's option to proceed in criminal court, in family court, or both. Katie said that she wanted an order of protection but did not want her boyfriend to face criminal charges. Katie's questions then came in a rush: What about her job (because her boyfriend usually called her there up to 10 times a day when he was angry, putting her job in jeopardy—and he was definitely angry that she had called the police) and child care for their 3-year-old daughter? Her boyfriend always told her that if she called the police, he would kidnap the girl and disappear. Could he do that? Would she lose her apartment because of an order of protection? What about taking time off from work to go to court? Could she get her boyfriend to stop drinking, which she considered part of the problem? The attorney answered her questions and told her that they could discuss these concerns further in the morning and that, as her lawyer, she would help Katie navigate the legal system.

The next morning, the attorney met Katie at the local public library, where they analyzed her situation.[15] From there they went to family court. Together they drafted a petition for an order of protection that outlined what had happened the night before, as well as a few prior incidents that came out as they talked. The attorney worked with Katie to request an order of protection carefully tailored to address her concerns. Katie and her boyfriend, Douglas, were not married, but they had a 3-year-old daughter, Jaquelyn, and he had signed an acknowledgment of paternity form at the hospital where Jaquelyn had been born. In New York State, that form meant that Douglas was recognized as the girl's father, so Katie and her attorney also filed a petition for custody of Jaquelyn, as well as a petition for child support. Later that day Katie appeared in front of the family court judge with her DETER attorney and was issued a temporary order of protection that instructed Douglas to stay away from her and their child until they came back to court in 2 weeks. It also required that Douglas neither call Katie at work nor visit their daughter's nursery school.

On the next court date, Douglas would be advised of his rights and obligations under the order, and the parties would address custody. The attorney explained to Katie how to have the police serve her boyfriend with the papers and what would happen when they came back to court. The attorney also gave Katie important information about the order of protection—that it did not go into effect until her boyfriend received a copy personally, and that it would help only if she was ready to call the police if he violated it. Katie agreed to meet with the DETER attorney in a week's time to prepare the case more fully.

Most victims of domestic violence do not have access to personal legal counsel when they dial 911 to seek emergency intervention or when they first find themselves in court.[16] During the past 2 years, the White Plains Department of Public Safety (WPDPS) and the PWJC have entered into a close and uniquely effective training and legal coordination partnership to rectify these crippling informational disconnects. During its first 6 months in operation, Project DETER represented over 44 clients like Katie.[17] Funded under Violence Against Women Act (VAWA) Grants to Encourage Arrest in 1999 and 2000, Project DETER links attorneys and police officers in an around-the-clock training and work collaboration. The success of DETER is based on two equally important components: (1) thorough, interactive, ongoing police training on domestic violence law and dynamics; and (2) attorney availability by beeper to the police 24 hours a day, 7 days a week, to provide immediate information and representation. The training component enhances police response and forges an invaluable collaboration between police and project advocate attorneys that is necessary to facilitate this "point of entry" service model.

Katie's example is typical of how Project DETER works. DETER attorneys wear beepers 24 hours a day for weekly shifts to respond to calls from the police.[18] Whenever the White Plains police are called to the scene of a domestic incident, and the case is one for Project DETER, the police beep an attorney and within minutes are able to put the victim on the phone with a lawyer who specializes in domestic violence representation in family court. This attorney then provides ongoing representation for the victim for the purposes of ex parte requests for orders of protection, support, and custody; hearings for permanent orders of protection; and the victim's other family court actions, including actions for violations of orders of protection.

In New York State, victims of domestic violence have a right to pursue a case against their abuser in family court, criminal court, or both courts. The difference between the two courts is that in criminal court, the case is brought by the district attorney, with the victim as a complaining witness, and the result when the prosecutor prevails may include some kind of punishment for the abuser—fine, probation, or incarceration. Criminal courts routinely issue orders of protection on behalf of victims of domestic crimes. Since victims are usually only peripherally involved in the criminal case, they are sometimes unaware of the status of their own order of protection. In addition, the victim almost never is in court to provide input into the drafting of the order of protection. The criminal courts generally issue a "full stay away"—an order that instructs the defendant to stay away from the victim, have no contact with the victim, and refrain from committing any crime against the victim.

By contrast, in family court the victim brings her own case, as in any civil litigation, and requests the specific provisions that she would like to have incorporated in the order of protection, which include the same provisions available in orders issued in criminal court and, frequently, more refined conditions relating to access to children. While she is there seeking protection, she may simultaneously petition the family court on issues of custody and child support. The goal of the family court is less to punish than to provide safety and security options for petitioners and their children by making provisions for custody and visitation, child support, probation, and counseling and domestic violence educational programs (e.g., batterers' intervention courses). For many victims, the level of their abuse may make their lives unsafe and untenable but still may not have risen legally to a level that the criminal court system can effectively control. In Katie's case, for example, the charge would probably have been harassment in the second degree, which is most often treated as only a violation-level offense. In fact, in New York, the vast majority of all domestic violence cases barely rise to the level of a misdemeanor.[19] For those cases, as for Katie's, there is a good chance that in criminal court the disposition would have been nothing more than a fine and a conditional discharge, with a nonrenewable 1-year order being the longest order of protection that a criminal court would give. In family court, due to the presence of "aggravating circumstances" Katie might be able to get a 3-year order of protection.[20] Minimally, she would be eligible for a 1-year order that might be renewed upon showing "special circumstances."[21] Moreover, the burden of proof for a final adjudication in family court is lower, a preponderance of the evidence, than in criminal court, where a conviction requires proof beyond a reasonable doubt.[22]

According to the New York State Office for the Prevention of Domestic Violence, roughly half of domestic violence victims in Westchester County have family court, as opposed to criminal court, orders of protection.[23] Fear of jail sentences (and the attendant loss of financial support) often impedes victim participation in the criminal prosecution of her batterer, reducing both conviction rates and numbers of orders of protection; for victims of color, immigrants, and other marginalized populations, these impediments increase exponentially. Based on Project history to date, clients served by DETER include a disproportionately high percentage of victims of color and immigrants (approximately 60% of clients served), almost all of whom want orders of protection but fear the power of the police.

In family court, Katie could obtain an order of protection to keep Douglas away from her; a visitation schedule that would provide for picking up and dropping off their daughter at a third location, such as her school; a mandated alcohol treatment program; and a batterers' education program supervised by the Department of Probation.[24] The solution could be carefully crafted to help Katie and her daughter with safety issues, to permit Katie to visit with both of her parents, and to ensure that Douglas receives assistance

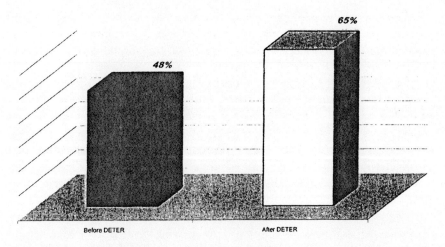

Figure 9.1. Percentage of women seeking temporary orders of protection before and after Project DETER.

to address his drinking and domestic violence problems and become a better father. Importantly for the victim of domestic abuse, the family court allows her to communicate directly with the judge from the inception of the case regarding her safety needs and concerns.

The implementation of Project DETER has dramatically increased the percentage of victims who obtain temporary and permanent orders of protection in family court. These increases are depicted in figure 9.1 and figure 9.2.

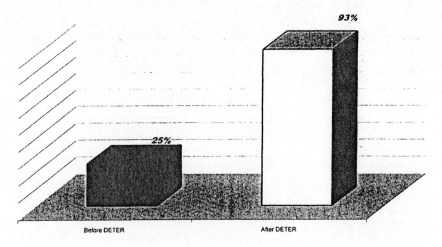

Figure 9.2. Percentage of women obtaining permanent orders of protection before and after Project DETER.

Victims who are given information and representation at the 911 call point of entry follow through to obtain a family court permanent order of protection between 90% and 97% of the time, as compared with 25% of the time for victims who do not benefit from these services.[25] Although it is understood in the community response network of service providers that many women do not follow through to obtain a permanent order of protection for valid reasons, DETER clients are empowered and given the advantage of knowledge and personal legal assistance starting from the moment they are most in need. This potency and vertical representation have resulted in statistics that defy preconceptions about battered women dropping cases and not going forward in court. It should also be noted that DETER attorneys work with advocates and prosecutors to ensure that safety issues remain paramount and prosecutions are facilitated whenever they are in the best interests of battered women.[26]

DETER seems to provide most battered women who use the service with the empowerment they seek to enable them to obtain not just temporary but "permanent" orders of protection.[27] For example, Rosa, Project DETER's first client, had been abused by her boyfriend for over a year and was concerned about immigration issues and about the effect of the abuse on her 4-year-old son. She had called the White Plains police five or six times but had never wanted them to file charges. With the assistance of the DETER attorney, Rosa obtained an order of protection and much-needed child support. After her court cases had concluded, Rosa said: "I was in a really bad situation. My boyfriend was abusing me. I would like to thank [my attorneys] for helping me out. . . . If it weren't for them I wouldn't feel safe about myself."

DETER is not a "luxury"; it is a necessity in a society in which many women fear police at the same time as they fear their batterers, and in which police admit that they consider domestic incident calls both some of the most difficult and the most potentially dangerous calls to which they are asked to respond.[28] Benefits to specific clients are the easiest to see. Equally if not more important are the systemic benefits inherent in DETER's training and legal coordination efforts to do the following:

- Increase law enforcement's understanding of state and federal domestic violence laws and policies
- Foster arrest and prosecution of batterers by empowering victims of domestic violence through the provision of immediate necessary resources
- Reduce the risk of false arrest and failure to protect allegations against law enforcement personnel because of the communion of civil attorneys and police at the earliest point in the domestic violence victim's interface with the criminal justice system
- Enhance the power of the police to make arrests, enforce and arrest for violations of orders of protection by exponentially increasing the number and duration of such orders

Many other local Westchester police departments have requested that Project DETER be expanded into their jurisdictions. The around-the-clock legal representation component of this project is one of the first of its kind in the country as far as the Center is aware and a potent way to ensure that victims of domestic violence receive immediate and reliable legal advice and representation. By putting a human face on what can be an intimidating and overwhelming legal system, and by coordinating with the criminal justice system but still representing the victim, DETER attorneys can assure battered women that they can enter the system without losing the control over their private lives that everyone deserves—and that their partners have tried to take away from them.

FAMILY COURT LEGAL PROGRAM

I feel that the family court externship not only gives students valuable and necessary tools to practice law in any field but also allows us to expand our ideas about domestic violence and its effects, and to perceive, firsthand, the courage and strength of the women forced to endure it.

Renée Fischer
Pace Law School, Class of 2001

Mondays were always crazy at the White Plains Family Court. In addition to the three judges' regularly scheduled cases, there were always a lot of "extras"—the cases that were filed that day requiring immediate access to the judge. Most of the extras were orders of protection cases, like Beverly's. Beverly arrived on the sixth floor of the courthouse looking startled and overwhelmed, dragging her two well-behaved boys along with her. Dressed in baggy jeans and sweatshirt, her hair falling over her face, she was asked by the volunteers at the family services desk what she needed. She told them about the most recent incident with her husband, Bob, who had been berating her for being fat and ugly, as usual, but this time had also grabbed her by the hair, thrown her down on the bed, and punched her. She thought her older son might have seen what happened. Beverly kept looking over her shoulder as though her husband might appear at any moment, even though as far as she knew he had gone to work this morning as usual.

The volunteer at the family services desk directed Beverly to the FCLP, where she met with a law student and an attorney.[29] After leaving her boys at the free day care center on the same floor of the courthouse, Beverly began to disclose to the student the almost constant abuse that she had been suffering for the past several years. The student drafted order of protection and custody petitions for Beverly, requesting that her husband be removed temporarily from the home and granting her temporary custody of the boys. Beverly then met with a representative from the Office of Child Support in the same office to draft a petition for child support. If she was going to be solely responsible for her sons, Beverly would have to give up working nights as a waitress in addition to her day job (she had taken the second job in response to Bob's request to bring in more money). When Beverly went into court, she was accompanied by the student and lawyer from the FCLP; she explained what had happened to the judge, and the student articulated the relief she needed. Beverly left the courthouse with a temporary order of protection, an immediately enforceable temporary order of child support, and an appointment with the attorney from Westchester/Putnam Legal Services, the Center's partner in this project, who would represent her throughout the rest of these proceedings.

About 3 months later, the attorney saw Beverly again but almost didn't recognize her. Dressed in a black outfit that flattered her slim figure, Beverly was holding her head high. She had obtained the permanent order of custody and was back with her lawyer to straighten out the visitation arrangement with her sons. Beverly told the attorney that she had recently been shown a photograph of herself with her husband and had not recognized the person in the picture. Today she felt she looked like herself.[30]

Once a month, in the White Plains courtroom of the Honorable Joan O. Cooney, supervising judge of the New York Family Court for the Ninth Judicial District, a group meets to discuss how Westchester County can improve its response to the crisis of domestic violence. Chaired by Camille F. Murphy, the director of the county's Office for Women, and created by County Executive Andrew Spano, the Domestic Violence Council boasts representatives from the county executive's office, the Office for Child Support, local police departments, the Office for the Aging, the district attorney's office, as well as the local shelters and advocacy groups.

In 1997, the Domestic Violence Council began to discuss ways in which it might improve the assistance that victims of domestic violence received in family court. Historically, when victims took their domestic violence problems to family court, they had petitioned without legal counsel. Judges, trying to decide what remedy would best fit the situation, likewise were left to their own devices. The PWJC had been hoping for some time to harness the energy of the student body to provide better legal services for victims of domestic violence entering family court. Although many financial resources are available for domestic violence projects that focus on the criminal courts and community advocacy programs designed to reinforce the understanding that domestic violence is a crime, less support has been given to the family court approach, although in many cases that is the court in which women would prefer to have their cases resolved. Statistics from the Department of Justice from 1995 indicate that only about half of women who suffer physical injury at the hands of their partners call the police, with an even lower number for those who suffer nonphysical abuse.[31] Many of these women will seek help instead by seeking civil orders of protection. Therefore, the council wanted an FCLP to assist these victims of domestic violence who number in the thousands each year in Westchester alone.[32]

Housed in a specially created office in the White Plains courthouse, the FCLP opened its doors in October 1999.[33] The FCLP offers immediate legal advice to battered women petitioning the family court. A student under the supervision of an on-site attorney interviews each woman who chooses to use the program's free services. The student drafts a petition for an order of protection, as well as for custody if necessary. An on-site Child Support Enforcement Unit representative is available to draft child support petitions. The client then files all three petitions and is represented by the student working under a student practice order (always accompanied by a Center attorney) in front of the judge on the order of protection.[34] Finally, if the order is issued, the client is advised regarding service of process and the next court appearance. The FCLP attorneys represent clients on their second court date if there is a good chance for settlement; all other cases are referred to Pace's partner, Westchester Putnam Legal Services, or one of the area shelters for ongoing legal representation.[35]

Since its launch, the FCLP has assisted over 600 women, filing over 800 cases,[36] keeping the women and their children safer by ensuring more carefully tailored orders of protection, referring to necessary services, and giving advice regarding the entire legal process so that the women know what to expect and how to proceed. To date, no woman represented by a student has failed to receive a temporary order of protection. The types of cases range from simple disorderly conduct to serious assault and stalking incidents. Some clients also choose to go forward in criminal court, so the program's attorneys often coordinate with the district attorney's office to provide appropriate and swift assistance.

Students from the Pace University School of Law work at the FCLP as part of an externship during the academic year and simultaneously take a seminar in domestic violence. During the summer, the program takes applications from law students around the country who are eager to participate in this innovative program. After the program had been in operation for a year, the county executive of Westchester decided to expand it into a second family court, the Yonkers Family Court, with the goal of making the program countywide as soon as possible.

The program is easily replicable, and the Center hopes that law schools across the country will eventually adapt it for their own local courts. There are manuals for both students and supervisors that are updated as needed. This program, like the Civil Legal Assistance Practicum described in the next section, combines efficient and responsible representation of underserved clients with unique training for young lawyers.

Women who are represented through the FCLP receive significant benefits that have long-term positive impact. One major advantage of the program is the reduced amount of time it takes women to receive child support. Many women feel trapped in abusive relationships because of financial constraints. Currently, without the assistance of the FCLP, women in Westchester

County who file for an order of protection and also want to get child support must make an independent appointment with the child support office, usually for no sooner than 2 weeks, and then must wait another 6 to 8 weeks for their first court appearance. At that appearance they receive an order of support, but it usually takes another 3 or 4 weeks before the applicant begins receiving checks. Through the FCLP, which works directly with a representative from the Office of Child Support, women can leave the courthouse that same day with an enforceable temporary order of child support in addition to a temporary order of protection. Often the court is then able to schedule all three of the client's court cases—orders of protection, child support, and custody for the same return date. This "one-stop-shopping" approach—possible only when community agencies work together to solve problems[37]—saves both the client and the courthouse valuable time.

In early 2001 the FCLP began a series of informal follow-up interviews with women who had been through the program to find out whether it was providing the right combination of resources, and to see if the women felt that they had benefited from its presence. Early results show that the FCLP is providing some much-needed information and reassurance on what is otherwise an overwhelming day. Said one woman after being assisted by FCLP staff to receive an order of protection, custody and support: "Everyone was very helpful when I felt desolate and alone. The process helps the abuser to respect the victim."[38]

CIVIL LEGAL PRACTICUM

Thank you all for everything. My nightmare is finally over. I was a victim of domestic violence and a survivor but no beating could ever hurt as much as a baby being taken away from its mother. Thanks to all of you, she's home.

Thank-you note to Center staff from Practicum client

Margaret was in court again. She had been there over two dozen times before for a myriad of problems: custody of her children, abuse by her husband, his accusations of abuse against her, and finally the forced removal of two of her four children. And now she was in court again, in front of the same judge, who seemed just as tired of seeing her as she was of being there. This time she was trying to get an order of protection against her husband for throwing her down the stairs, ripping a chain off her neck, and kicking her in the shins. It had taken all morning for the student extern at the FCLP to write her petition because Margaret was having trouble focusing today—we now know she has an IQ of 45—and was currently taking five different forms of medication. The stress of the recent incident had exacerbated her symptoms, as had the fact that her husband refused to purchase any food for her, insisting the 20-odd cans of tuna fish in the kitchen would simply have to do.

When Margaret appeared in front of the judge, he hauled out two huge files full of the record of Margaret's passage through the court system. Margaret used to be an executive secretary, but since she began to suffer from mental illness as well as abuse at the hands of her husband about 7 years ago, things had gone from bad to worse. Margaret had already lost one child to "the system" and had now been diagnosed as HIV-positive. Margaret's illegal drug use had been encouraged by her husband, who "worked off the books" and dealt drugs on the side. She had been regularly assigned attorneys when in court but had never been represented by the same lawyer twice.

After obtaining a temporary order of protection somewhat begrudgingly issued by the family court judge, the FCLP referred Margaret's case not to its regular legal services partner but to the Center's Civil Legal Assistance Practicum (the Practicum) for representation. An attorney from the Center spent long days reviewing with Margaret what her options were and what she could reasonably expect to obtain from the courts. Margaret's mental illness at times made her obstreperous and resistant to suggestion and had alienated the judge who had been assigned to her case. Because of her high health care costs and her inability to care for her children, she began working on a plan with her attorney to move into the extra apartment she and her husband owned, obtain one of the many family cars, and schedule regular visitation with her daughter. She had no access to money and had no idea how much money her husband had. Throughout the course of the representation, Margaret alternately thanked her lawyers for their dedication and berated them for suggesting that they could not obtain for her everything she deserved.[39]

Mentally impaired, physically impaired, and drug-abusing women confront a myriad of legal issues far more complex than those facing a "typical" domestic violence victim. Table 9.1 illustrates the cases handled by the Practicum for its first 11 clients. For these clients their own unique impairments compound the abuse they suffer and create a need for intensive legal representation. Table 9.2 illustrates the mental and physical challenges faced by the Practicum's first 11 clients.

This Practicum has been funded by a VAWA Civil Legal Assistance grant. It has permitted the Center, in partnership with John Jay Legal Services (a low-income legal assistance office housed in Pace University School of Law), Four Winds psychiatric facility, the Northern Westchester Shelter, and others to assist these particularly needy clients while simultaneously providing a unique opportunity for law students to interface with medical clinical partners in developing civil litigation strategies. The Practicum is offered as a four-credit legal-medical clinical internship in which students operating under a New York State practice order and under a supervising project attorney provide direct civil legal representation to these special-needs domestic violence victims. Referrals to this program come from a multitude of sources. Margaret learned of the program from the director of the FCLP. Other

Table 9.1.   CLA Case Distribution Chart (Pace Women's Justice Center)

Client Number*	1	2	3	4	5	6	7	8	9	10	11
Case type											
A. Name change	XX			XX							
B. Social Security number change	X										
C. Will	X	X	X	X				X		X	
D. Custody				X	X		X	X	X	X	X
E. Visitation		X	X	X	X			X	X	X	X
F. Divorce				X							
G. Support				XX		X		X			
H. Neglect				X			X		X		
I. Health care proxy				X							
J. Power of attorney				X							
K. Relocation					X			X			
L. Employment descrimination						X					
M. Support services				X				XX			
N. Bankruptcy				X							
O. Housing				X				X			
P. Orders of protection and violations				XX	X	X	X	X		X	X

All clients received ongoing domestic violence advocacy counseling, as desired, at shelters and through community support services. *All* clients were financially disadvantaged in the extreme.
    *Client numbers represent adults; 18 dependent children were also assisted in this project.

partners in the program, such as the Mental Health Association, Karla Digi-rolamo of Unity House in Troy, New York, and Four Winds, serve as both resources and referral sources for this project.

Few studies have examined the prevalence of domestic violence among women with disabilities, but the DisAbled Women's Network of Canada surveyed 245 women with disabilities and found that 40% had experienced abuse and 12% had been raped.[40] Perpetrators of the abuse were often

Table 9.2.   CLA Client Diagnostic Profile (Pace Women's Justice Center)

Client Number*	1	2	3	4	5	6	7	8	9	10	11
Diagnosis											
A. Posttraumatic stress disorder	X				X						
B. Bipolar disorder				X		X			X		
C. Schizophrenia			X								
D. Deafness								X		X	
E. AIDS			X								
F. Mental retardation							X				X
G. Substance abuse			X								
H. Clinical depression		X									

All clients received ongoing domestic violence advocacy counseling, as desired, at shelters and through community support services. *All* clients were financially disadvantaged in the extreme.
    *Client numbers represent adults; 18 dependent children were also assisted in this project.

spouses or ex-spouses (37%). Less than half these experiences were reported, due mostly to fear and dependency.[41]

Most private attorneys are not trained to represent battered women, especially those with psychiatric or substance abuse underlying their legal problems. Additionally, harried legal services advocates can rarely allocate as much time as is needed for the labor-intensive cases of psychiatrically impaired or substance-abusing victims, and they lack the help of forensic and clinical specialists, who are especially necessary for the effective representation of these clients. Law schools generally do not focus their legal training on ways to serve this population, and consequently there is an ever-increasing output of lawyers who are unprepared to represent these battered women.

The Practicum both addresses the unique needs of a traditionally underserved client population and trains new lawyers in skills that should be required of all practicing attorneys. Orders of protection, although important, by themselves do not provide the depth of legal support that victims, especially those who are physically and mentally marginalized, need to reestablish their lives. In its first year, the Practicum represented 11 special-needs clients. Eleven individuals may seem like a drop in the bucket, but those clients produced approximately 53 different cases, including name changes, social security number changes, wills, relocation, power of attorney, health care proxy, employment discrimination, bankruptcy, and housing, in addition to the "regular" orders of protection, custody, and visitation cases (see table 9.1). It is safe to say that without specialized attorneys in partnership with a range of local service providers, these clients would have been unable to take any real steps forward in the resolution of their lives. Moreover, working with law students provides a cost-efficient way to manage these overwhelming caseloads. Trained students can provide critical interviewing and counseling for clients, as well as serve papers, draft motions, and represent victims in court.

> Since that day in court over a year ago, Margaret has been living on her own, with a new car provided by her husband as part of the divorce settlement. She is participating in domestic violence counseling and therapy and is receiving full medication for what is now AIDS, with a manageably low co-payment. Margaret's divorce is still pending, but many of the larger battles have been won. Now, when Margaret goes to court, the judge listens to her, credits her account of the facts, and works with her attorneys to craft remedies that assist her and her children.

PUBLIC SERVICE ANNOUNCEMENTS

> "Hotel to Jail Tour" Full Faith and Credit Public Service Announcement (Fifteen seconds)
> Visual: Open on a hotel hallway. Muzak plays. Point of view of "guest" being led down hallway by bellhop. Bellhop smiles, turns, and nods, then

opens door to room. Close-up of doorknob turning. Cut to reveal dark jail cell with little window. Jail door slams shut.

Voice-over: "If you follow a woman who has an order of protection into another state, there are plenty of places that will put you up for the night. An order of protection is enforceable in every state, Indian tribal land, or U.S. territory.

Visual and voice-over: For more information about domestic violence or Orders of Protection, call 1-800-799-SAFE.

In 1995, Joan, a battered woman, sought the assistance of the PWJC in getting New York to recognize her New Jersey order of protection. Armed with a certified copy of a permanent order of protection, the woman had fled New Jersey and moved to New York to escape her batterer. She had good reason to fear this man, who had already violated the order five times, twice by violent behavior. Center attorneys explained that the VAWA had passed a few months earlier,[42] and that its mandates included the full faith and credit provision, which required that an out-of-state order of protection be "enforced as if it were the order of the enforcing state."[43] However, this guarantee of enforcement proved difficult to implement. After many telephone calls and much research, the Center finally was able to provide the assistance that Joan sought.

The Center's attorneys went on to conduct many trainings and to write about full faith and credit.[44] However, it became clear over time that, although the law enforcement community, the judiciary, prosecutors, and other members of the community response network received much information on full faith and credit and were eventually more and more comfortable with the legal principles involved, this information, like most legal information concerning orders of protection, never filtered down to battered women to any appreciable degree. In fact, Center clients currently come to us just as unaware that their orders are enforceable everywhere in the United States as our clients were in 1995. (Interestingly, they know they can get a speeding ticket in another state even though they have a New York driver's license, but they do not know that their orders of protection are equally enforceable in other jurisdictions.) This lack of knowledge may place the victim at serious risk if she is deterred from leaving her hometown because she believes her order of protection will not be valid elsewhere or if she travels out of state and does not believe that she can still call the police to help enforce her order.

This lack of basic domestic violence legal information led us at the Center to wonder if PSAs could help to spread the word about matters more important than athletic shoes and bathroom tissue.[45] The Center thus embarked on a mission to create PSAs, initially about full faith and credit for orders of protection, and eventually to encompass many legal information components (e.g., federal stalking and gun laws). The Violence Against Women Office, a division of the Department of Justice, Office of Justice Programs, has funded the Center to produce six versions of two full faith and credit commercials. The federal approval process for release of these PSAs is ongoing. The "Hotel to Jail" commercial that is outlined at the beginning of this section describes the first PSA that the Center produced, which helped convince the Violence Against Women's Office that the Center should produce more of these commercials.

What is set forth in the following is the history of the Center's pursuit of resources and partners to actually make the "Hotel to Jail" PSA. The creation of this commercial led the Violence Against Women's Office to authorize funding to produce more such advertisements. This process is presented in detail because, in many ways, parallel processes preceded the implementation of each of the four programs in this chapter.

Public Service Announcements: What We Did and What We Learned

I. What We Did
[1994]
   A. Got a bug in our bonnet!
- Identified an unmet educational need (i.e., telling domestic violence survivors that orders of protection are good throughout the United States).
- Tried, in vain, to find others who do this specialized, wide-scale education in order to "steal" their work.
- Determined someone had to get the word out, not just to police, prosecutors, judges, and so on, but also to battered women.

   B. Began to "think outside the box"
- Wrote a script and tag line for a PSA: "Your order of protection is good everywhere. Don't leave home without it."

[1995]
- Wrote to American Express for permission to adapt its "tag line" and were told to contact the company at a later time.
- Went ahead and filmed an in-house "trial" PSA:
  [Mother of small child is scrambling to fill her purse, grab the child, and leave her home. Camera pans to order of protection, which the mom had left on the coffee table.] Voice-over:
  > Visiting your mom in Minnesota?
  > Traveling to Texas for business?
  > Vacationing in Vermont?
  > . . . or are you escaping your abuser?
  > *Your order of protection is good everywhere.*
  > *Don't leave home without it.*

  [Screen shows national and local domestic violence hotlines]
- Recognized that as art directors, we made great lawyers.

[1996]
- C. Began to hawk our wares with ad agencies
  - Met with and educated art directors (including a sister of one of our attorneys), who agreed to do their pro bono work on our project.
  - "Courted" them . . . until they dropped us.
  - We got lucky! Other ad agents "picked up the threads" and began anew.

[1997]
- D. Conducted regular meetings with the new art directors, with deadlines, outlines, goals, and so forth, *and* lots of domestic violence education.
  - Provided lots of stroking and support to the artist (no money).
  - Gave the art directors their heads and reviewed scripts and storyboards.
  - Peddled the storyboards, (for example, with a nationally known women's clothing company (no money), the feds (no money), the state (no money).
- E. Engaged in creative fiscal management
  - Approached a foundation that gave us money for a different purpose and begged it to allow us to divert its money (also promised that its name would be on the PSA).

[1998]
- F. With $5,872.56, we paid "scale" to union workers to produce a 15-second PSA: "Hotel to Jail Tour."
  - Thirteen professionals took 9 hours to complete the filming.
  - Editing, adding music, getting clearance for use of phone numbers took another several months.
- G. Voilà: one finished PSA.

II. What We Learned
- A. Even attorneys can "think outside the box."
- B. Coordination and education are critical and are constant time drains.
- C. *Involvement of advocates is essential.*
- D. Stroking must be *great* when funding is *not* (we gave our art directors the Third Annual Domestic Violence Citizen Advocate of the Year Award in 1998 at a law school celebration).
- E. Be ready to be humble and experience rejection.
- F. Be ready to end up with a *super* PSA (which also is a great training piece)!

INNOVATIVE PROGRAMS FROM OTHER LAW SCHOOLS

While we at the PWJC are anxious to share our innovative work in the area of domestic violence, ours is not the only group trying to invent new solutions to this age-old problem. The American Bar Association (ABA) Commission on Domestic Violence publication *When Will They Ever Learn? Educating to End Domestic Violence—A Law School Report,* in which the commission described the need for law schools to incorporate domestic violence pedagogy in their curriculum, refers to some of the innovative approaches being taken across the country.[46] The report explained the many benefits of integrating domestic violence issues into core courses, upper-level courses, and clinical programs.[47] Educating law students about domestic violence enhances their ability to become better practitioners in many contexts, including criminal law, family law, ethics and professional responsibility, lawyering skills, case management, immigration work, and matrimonial practice, and even wills, bankruptcy, workplace discrimination, and on and on. Weaving domestic violence legal issues into the curriculum may also attract law school applicants, create a more diverse student body, lay the groundwork to encourage many public-private partnerships, and introduce new funding streams into the law school budgetary resource pool. Most important, addressing domestic violence systemically and throughout the law school curriculum sends a message of gender equality that can pervade and refresh the academic environment. At the same time, as the law school provides critical legal representation to hundreds of needy individuals in a community, it elevates the concept of "justice for all" to new heights.

As per the ABA report, the good news is that 57 law schools made the list of those institutions that offered domestic violence courses, clinics, or seminars or offered one course that was focused primarily on domestic violence. The bad news is that 57 schools are fewer than one-third of the 185 ABA accredited law schools. (There are also 40 unaccredited law schools in the United States.)[48] If domestic violence is of epidemic proportions, which is commonly acknowledged, and if domestic violence is a crime, which is universally accepted, how is it that two thirds of the law schools in the country give it no mention in their bulletins and lists of course offerings and clinics? Clearly, these schools can learn much from reading the commission's report.[49] The following highlights a few of the most interesting of the offerings available at the date of the report, many of which have approached issues as we have at the Center.

Student-Lawyer Advocates in Family Court

A few schools, such as Yale Law School[50] and Indiana University Law School,[51] have begun projects that assist women in obtaining orders of protection. A unique program in New York City harnesses the power of six local law schools to serve a large urban population. In 1997, the domestic violence advocacy group Sanctuary for Families, recognizing that most women entering the family court system in New York do so unrepresented and confused, initiated the Courtroom Advocates Project (CAP). In the last 4 years, CAP has trained over 600 law students and summer law firm associates as volunteer "advocates" who staff a "petitioners assistance table," under the supervision of an attorney. The CAP advocates accompany petitioners when they appear before family court judges at the first court appearance, as well as on their adjourn dates, and assist them with their cases as they move forward. By accessing such a broad base of volunteers, CAP is able to staff petitioner desks several days a week in four of the five New York City family courts.

Special Needs Populations

A number of law schools have targeted especially needy client populations in their immediate areas and developed projects to address those specific needs. The Family Violence Clinic of the University of Missouri Law School, under a VAWA grant, provides students with the opportunity to represent indigent battered women in 14 rural counties in protective custody and juvenile court cases.[52] The clinic receives referrals from police, shelters, and the courts and draws upon graduate students from relevant disciplines in case reviews. "Law students travel up to 100 miles to represent clients in protection order hearings."[53]

The Immigration and Human Rights Clinic at St. Mary's Law School in San Antonio, Texas, offers a 1-year clinic in which students assist immigrant battered women, a group that is among the most legally underserved and socially isolated of abuse victim populations.[54] Students are assigned several deportation cases and appear on a regular basis on the detained calendar of the immigration court to counsel detained immigrants and argue for undocumented women and children seeking legal residence pursuant to the VAWA. Each semester, clinical students travel to the border to provide immigration and naturalization services to residents of impoverished *colonias*. Students work individually and in teams on all aspects of their clients' cases.[55]

A special component of the University of Arizona Law School Domestic Violence Law Clinic offers free legal assistance to domestic violence survivors at the Pascua Yaqui Nation and the Tohono O'Odham Nation.[56] Students provide these especially isolated survivors with information about their legal rights in matters concerning child custody, divorce, child support, property retrieval, property division, and financial matters. The Indian Nations Program at the Domestic Violence Law Clinic provides free legal assistance to Arizona Indian Nations to formulate responses to domestic violence (drafting domestic violence codes and orders of protection, training tribal court judges, and providing research on successful domestic violence programs throughout Indian country).[57]

Community Response Approaches

Many law schools recognize the importance of partnering with nonlegal organizations to best address domestic violence issues. The Domestic Violence

Advocacy Project at George Washington University School of Law, in Washington, D.C., has created an interdisciplinary clinical domestic violence program, which is team taught by a psychologist and a clinical legal professor, and works in collaboration with the George Washington School of Medicine and Health Sciences' Department of Emergency Medicine—an approach that offers students training on the legal and psychosocial aspects of representing battered women.[58] Third-year, court-certified students represent clients seeking civil protection orders; prepare and try cases in court under faculty supervision; work on battered women's self-defense cases with local public defenders; and participate in reform projects seeking to improve the legal system's or community's response to domestic violence.

The Northeastern University School of Law houses the Domestic Violence Institute (DVI), which is underwritten by the Soros Foundation.[59] Students gain academic credit and experience representing battered women in family law cases handled in the probate courts through independent study and education placements at legal services offices, through legal projects at battered women's shelters and community agencies, and at the offices of private practitioners affiliated with the institute. First-year students with an interest in immediate training and volunteer opportunities may also apply to join BMC/DVI, a volunteer project in which law students staff the Boston Medical Center Emergency Department on nights and weekends, interviewing women and providing advocacy services where domestic violence issues are disclosed. In addition, the institute hosts an annual fall conference that introduces incoming students to legal advocacy for battered women in Massachusetts, and seminars and events are offered year-round to familiarize students with domestic violence issues, in general, and local abuse prevention initiatives, in particular.

Students at Widener University Law School have had a unique opportunity since the State of Delaware adopted its Protection from Abuse statute in 1994.[60] The Delaware Civil Clinic had been representing victims of domestic violence for some time, but the passage of the new law afforded Widener student attorneys an opportunity to be on the front lines as the Delaware courts went about the business of interpreting and applying the statute. Widener students in the Family Violence Outreach Clinic meet with victims of family violence in community centers in the city of Wilmington. They serve, among others, the city's underrepresented Latino population, providing guidance to clients who do not speak English.

There are many other equally excellent domestic violence programs at law schools throughout the country. These are merely a handful of examples of unusually creative approaches for unusually needy battered women.

CONCLUSION

This chapter has highlighted several diverse and somewhat unique approaches to domestic violence intervention. One obvious unifying programmatic factor is that attorneys have initiated each project. None of us has a degree in advertising; none thought that a law degree would make us around-the-clock service providers. And none of us was educated to teach. Yet these new job descriptions have become critical to our efforts to litigate domestic violence cases and to eradicate this societal epidemic. Why? Because the old answers have not worked for battered women, particularly for the silent majority of battered women. So we decided to "think outside the box," which for us meant thinking outside the normal scope of what lawyers do for a living to assist clients—both by expanding our own job descriptions and by partnering with other service providers. This vision beyond the walls of our respective job descriptions has made all the difference and has been the most unifying, important, and replicable component of these four programs. At the Center we have found what great domestic violence advocates have known all along, that is, if you have a fire in your belly, and you are not afraid to ask the tough questions (such as "What else can *I* do to help this victim?" and "How do we best enhance the safety of our clients?"), new and better solutions will emerge.

NOTES

1.   The Pace Women's Justice Center, an independently funded division of Pace University School of Law, is the first university-based center in the United States dedicated to eradicating domestic violence and furthering the legal rights of women through skillful and innovative use of the law. The Center's mission is to give those who support battered women, the elderly, women with low income, and victims of sexual assault the legal tools they need to stop violence against women, seek economic justice, protect families, and save lives. The Center is a training resource and a provider of legal services. The authors of this chapter are attorneys at the Center. Amy P. Barasch, is the director of externships, and Victoria L. Lutz is the executive director of the Center.

2.   A sampling of noteworthy programs from other law schools is set forth in a later section of this chapter.

3.   In 1994, husbands, former husbands, boyfriends, and ex-boyfriends committed more than 1 million violent acts against women; family members or other people they knew committed more than 2.7 million violent crimes against women (*Violence Against Women: Estimates from the Redesigned Survey*, by Ronet Bachman and Linda E. Salzman, August 1995, Bureau of Justice Special Report). A July 2000 research report by the U.S. Department of Justice Office of Justice Programs found that only about 26.7% of women who were physically assaulted by an intimate reported their victimization to the police. *Extent, Nature and Consequences of Intimate Partner Violence: Findings From the National Violence Against Women Survey*, by N. Tjaden and N. Thoennes (hereafter 2000 Survey).

4.   To access a New York State Family Court, a victim of domestic violence must be married to, divorced from, or have a child in common with her abuser to fulfill the "family relationship" requirements of the Family Court Act § 812(1) and New York Social Services Law § 459(a) (McKinneys 2000).

5. The Bureau of Justice Statistics (BJS) has reported that intimate-partner murder fell from 2,959 in 1976 to 1,809 in 1996. *Understanding Domestic Homicide,* by N. Websdale, 1999, Northeastern University Press, p. 5, citing the BJS 1998 report (Boston, MA). This number contrasts sharply with the millions of nonlethal domestic violence incidents that occur in the United States each year.

6. "Death by Intimacy: Risk Factors for Domestic Violence," by J. Johnson, V. Lutz, and N. Websdale, 2000, *Pace Law Review,* 20, p. 1101 (see footnote 89 and accompanying text for several lists of common and not so common lethality indices).

7. Criminal offenses in New York are organized in the penal law from more serious to less serious, as felonies, misdemeanors, or violations.

8. For a comprehensive discussion of the pedagogical goals of another law school domestic violence project, see "Case Study: A Battered Women's Rights Clinic: Designing a Clinical Program Which Encourages a Problem-Solving Vision of Lawyering That Empowers Clients and Community," by S. Bryant and M. Arias, 1992, *Journal of Urban and Contemporary Law,* 42.

9. "Gender Fairness Panel Still Finds Work to Do," by M. Halasa, *New York Law Journal,* north suburban edition, p. NS-4. This article stated that "there were 126,812 orders of protection issued in the state in 2000 for battered spouses." While family violence *is* criminal violence, many women do not want to access the criminal justice arena if they have a choice (see 2000 Survey, "Reasons for Not Reporting Victimization to the Police"). A woman may not want the father of her children "branded a criminal." She may fear immigration repercussions. She may not be able to "afford" having a father of four go to jail. She may fear retribution by her abuser's friends, or the abuser himself once he is released. Many women want to access a system before matters are completely out of control, and so they seek an order of protection at the earliest sign of abuse—a reaction our society should wish to encourage. In fact, women often know instinctively what statistical studies later prove. The 2000 Survey concluded that having a verbally abusive partner was the variable that most likely predicted a woman would be victimized by an intimate partner. Verbal abuse in New York is frequently categorized as disorderly conduct (N.Y. Penal Law § 240.20) or harassment in the second charge (N.Y. Penal Law § 240.26)—both violations rather than misdemeanors or felonies.

10. D = determine if referral indicated; E = educate victim regarding project services; T = telephone or beep project attorney; E = explain follow-up procedure; R = routinely advise victim of contact number.

11. The names of this victim and of all other people mentioned in the fact patterns described here have been changed, as have identifiable details about their cases.

12. Domestic incident reports are mandated by law in New York State (N.Y. Criminal Procedure Law § 140.10 (5)); other states have similar provisions.

13. In New York State, the penal law mandates arrest for all domestic violence felonies and most domestic violence misdemeanors: misdemeanor family offenses include harassment in the first degree, PL 240.25; aggravated harassment in the second degree, PL 240.30; menacing in the second and third degrees, PL 120.14 and PL 120.15; reckless endangerment in the second degree, PL 120.20; assault in the third degree, PL 120.00; and stalking in the fourth and third degrees, PL 120.45 and PL 120.50. The police are not required to arrest on a domestic violence misdemeanor if the victim asks them not to, but they are not permitted to ask the victim if she wishes an arrest. However, most domestic violence calls to the police and family offense petitions in family court are charged as harassment in the third degree or disorderly

conduct. These are classified as "violations" and do not trigger the mandatory arrest provisions.

14. Different states use the terms *order of protection, protection order, restraining order*, and *injunction*. All these orders that protect the safety of an individual by their conditions are enforceable in all 50 states, in the District of Columbia, on Indian tribal lands, and in United States territories. 18 U.S.C.A. § 2265 (1994 *et seq.*).

15. Project DETER attorneys have found that victims of domestic violence are far less hesitant to meet initially at a library or a local coffee shop; these nonthreatening locations increase the comfort level of the victim and the likelihood that she will choose to access the court system.

16. In New York State, for example, the family court is not mandated to provide legal representation until the hearing stage of the family offense proceeding, not as the battered woman walks into the courtroom with a black eye, traumatized by a recent act of violence, and seeking an ex parte immediate order of protection. Additionally, the most "savvy" and competent domestic violence prosecutor represents not the victim but rather "the people" and as such has obligations to societal interests that sometimes are not coextensive with those of the individual battered woman.

17. Project DETER's first and only attorney was Center staff attorney Rebecca Fialk, who, with the assistance of Karen Hogan, then a student and now a Center attorney, can be largely credited for the project's success.

18. A 1998 Department of Justice study indicates that nonlethal intimate violence is most likely to occur between 6:00 P.M. and midnight, and 30% of the reported incidents occur between 9:00 P.M. and midnight (*Violence by Intimates: Analysis of Data on Crimes by Current or Former Spouses, Boyfriends, and Girlfriends*, U.S. Department of Justice, March 1998).

19. Recent statistics collected by the Office for Court Administration of the State of New York indicate that of orders of protection filed in family court, 47% were harassment charges; 14%, menacing; 13%, disorderly conduct; 10%, assault in the third degree; 7%, reckless endangerment; 5%, attempted assault; and 4%, assault in the second degree. Of these, only reckless endangerment in the first degree and assault in the second degree are felonies; the rest are a mixture of violations and misdemeanors. It should also be noted that most order of protection petitions outside Westchester are drafted by petition clerks, who also select the relevant offense; petition clerks are not attorneys.

20. Aggravating circumstances include physical injury or serious physical injury to the petitioner, the use of a dangerous instrument against the petitioner by the respondent, a history of repeated violations of a prior order of protection by the respondent, prior convictions from crimes against the petitioner by the respondent or the exposure of any family or household member to physical injury by the respondent and like incidents. See, e.g., N.Y. Family Court Act. § 827.

21. See N.Y. Family Court Act § 842 (i). One such circumstance occurred when a battered woman's order was about to expire in 2 weeks and the respondent against whom it was issued purchased an apartment next to hers. The court saw this as a "special circumstance" and extended the order of protection for a second year (unreported case; details available at the Center).

22. Katie could have even gotten a family court order of protection the night she called the police. Under N.Y. Family Court Act § 821(4), local courts have the authority to issue family court orders of protection when the family court is not in session. These orders last only up to 4 days, within which time the petitioner must file in her family court. N.Y. Family Court Act §§ 154 (c) and (d).

23. As of September 19, 2000, there were 1,182 active family court and 1,470 active criminal court orders of protection. A greater preference for family court might be discerned from the number of "inactive" orders of protection: 15,967 for family court and 4,131 for Criminal Court (*Family Protection and Domestic Violence Intervention Act of 1994: Evaluation of the Mandatory Arrest Provisions, Final Report to the Governor and Legislature,* January 2001). While many variables may explain the numerical discrepancy, it is clear that family court is the court of choice for many.

24. Orders of protection must be personally tailored to individual circumstances to allow any hope of providing real safety. For instance, careful visitation provisions are vital: Visitation conflicts account for a substantial percentage of filed violations of orders of protection. See, e.g., *District of Columbia Courts: Final Report of the Task Force on Racial and Ethnic Bias and Task Force on Gender Bias in the Courts,* 1992, App. H at 21 (indicating that such provisions accounted for 31% of contempt motions in civil protection order cases involving custody).

25. Based on three years of statistical analysis, 1997–1999, the WPDPS, White Plains, NY.

26. During 2001, the Center hopes to analyze the impact that Project DETER has had on the prosecution of criminal cases, which impact members of the police department already believe to be positive in many respects, including enhanced training of all officers. The Center is also seeking funding to expand DETER to the health care arena to provide "point of access" legal representation from hospitals, via visiting nurses services, and so forth.

27. It should be noted that in New York, the longest order of protection commonly available (with extremely rare exception in cases involving child abuse or Supreme Court matrimonials) for a battered woman in a violation or misdemeanor family offense or criminal court proceeding is a 3-year order, which is called a "permanent" order.

28. This fact is expressed by local police in *City of Shelter: A Coordinated Community Response to Domestic Violence,* a series of training videos produced by Global Village Communications for the State of Ohio.

29. The Mental Health Association of Westchester has, for almost two decades, staffed this desk with trained volunteers.

30. With the advent of the combined courts, if she had a criminal court matter pending, Beverly could have addressed that issue with the same judge. Hawaii, California, New Hampshire, and the District of Columbia currently are experimenting with these special "combined courts." See also "Effective Intervention in Domestic Violence Cases: Rethinking the Roles of Prosecutors, Judges, and the Court System," by D. Epstein, 1999, *Yale Journal of Law and Feminism 11,* p. 3.

31. *Violence by Intimates;* 2000 Survey.

32. In the year 2000, a total of 3,030 family offense–related proceedings were handled by the Westchester family courts. Statistics were obtained from Nora Flynn, the chief clerk of the family court.

33. Coauthor Barasch is the founding director and implementer of this program; Center attorneys Karen Hogan and Tamara Mitchel now help her to ensure the FCLP's continued success. Locating office space for this program was as problematic in Westchester's already overcrowded courthouse as it would be for any other jurisdiction. In fact, the logistics in Westchester were probably more daunting than in most places because the Westchester County courthouse, proposed site of the FCLP, had just begun a multi-million-dollar, multiyear expansion project. The county exec-

utive, Andrew Spano, however, prioritized this need to the extent that a courtroom was gutted, and prisoners from the jail were brought in to turn this space into a suite for the FCLP. The authors cannot pass up this opportunity to applaud Mr. Spano's determination and note that, if the reader thinks that this program is impracticable in his or her own jurisdiction, Mr. Spano's groundbreaking efforts should encourage a contrary conclusion. A second FCLP site opened in October 2001 in the Yonkers Family Court.

34. A practice order must be obtained before a law student can argue as legal counsel to the court. Such an order was obtained by the Center from the New York Supreme Court Appellate Division Second Department in 1998 and was renewed in 2000 for a second 2-year period.

35. As far as we know, this project is unique in providing the combination of a student practice order, on-site offices for the drafting of petitions, and immediate access to the Office of Child Support.

36. The FCLP is different from a law school clinic, in which traditionally the clinic takes on a client, who is represented by students, often in pairs, for the duration of the court case. Due to the intensive nature of the representation, as well as the need for close attorney supervision, most clinics can represent only a handful of clients a year. The FCLP functions more on a "triage" basis, providing immediate legal assistance for a large number of people on day one and referring those cases that have continuing legal matters to other lawyers for that representation. Coauthor Victoria Lutz and the Center's director, Audrey Stone, actually began teaching "Domestic Violence: A Trial Advocacy Course" 2 years before the creation of the FCLP. Ms. Stone still teaches the two-credit classroom component of the FCLP. In addition, many law schools that do address domestic violence in a clinical setting do so through the criminal courts. At a 1999 conference of the American Bar Association Commission on Domestic Violence, some of the law schools that attended, and offer domestic violence clinics include American University, Washington College of Law, University of Baltimore, Brooklyn Law School, George Washington University Law School, Villanova University Law School West Virginia University College of Law, and Widener University Law School. Other local law schools that have domestic violence clinics in various forms include Columbia University School of Law, Fordham University School of Law, the City University of New York, Rutgers Camden Law School, and Albany Law School. For more information on law school domestic violence education and programs, see the discussion later in this chapter.

37. The Honorable Judith Kaye, chief judge of the State of New York, discusses the need for creative approaches to solving the problem of domestic violence in "Judicial Responses to Domestic Violence: The Case for a Problem Solving Approach," by J. S. Kaye and S. K. Knipps, 1999–2000, *Washington State University Law Review, 27,* p. 1.

38. See "Two-Thirds of Civil Protection Orders are Never Violated; Better Court and Community Services Increase Success Rates," by J. Joan Zorza and N. K. D. Lemon, April/May 1997, *Domestic Violence Report.*

39. Again, credit must be given to the untiring representation given to this client by Center attorneys Rebecca Fialk and Karen Hogan.

40. *Beating the "Odds": Violence and Women With Disabilities* (Position Paper 2), by J. Ridington, 1989, Vancouver: DisAbled Women's Network.

41. *Abuse and Women With Disabilities,* by Margaret Nosek and Carol Howland for VAWnet, 1998.

42. The Violence Against Women Act of 1994, Pub. L. No. 103–322, 108 Stat. 1796 (codified in scattered sections of 16 U.S.C., 18 U.S.C., 28 U.S.C., and 42 U.S.C.).

43. 18 U.S.C. § 2265 (1994).

44. "How New York Should Implement the Federal Full Faith and Credit Guarantee for Out-of-State Orders of Protection," by V. Lutz and C. Bonomolo, 1995, *Pace Law Review*, 16, pp. 9–32.

45. Advertising has produced positive results when ad campaigns are designed to increase awareness of illegal and socially unacceptable behavior. See, e.g., N. Fitzgerald, "U.S. Drug Policy Office Says 12-Market Test Is a Success," April 20, 1998, *ADWEEK*, p. 2 ("Phone calls to a major clearinghouse number from 12 major markets have increased 25 percent since the Office of National Drug Control Policy began a pilot anti-drug campaign . . . using ads supplied by various agencies through the Partnership for a Drug-Free America").

46. American Bar Association Commission on Domestic Violence, produced with the support of the Office for Victims of Crime, U.S. Department of Justice. The programs highlighted in this section are described in the commission's report. As of April 2001, the quoted document is the most up to date version published by the ABA. It should be noted that law school curricula and programs evolve and that the data from the report were already between 2 and 3 years old at the time the report was published, so that the programs described may have changed or even ceased to exist by the time the present book becomes available.

47. The authors of this chapter would note that, in the commission's report, the concept of a "center" as a law school vehicle for eradicating domestic violence through skillful and innovative use of the law was not segregated from the concept of the law school "clinic." However, these two constructs are somewhat different from each other. A "clinic," for example, the Pace Domestic Violence Prosecution Clinic under Professor Vanessa Merton, in which students prosecute domestic violence misdemeanor cases with the Manhattan District Attorney's Office, provides for intensive training, simulation experience, mentoring and feedback; it also has a specific and defined pedagogical mandate (e.g., the Prosecution Clinic would not handle a domestic violence family court case). A "center" is able to craft courses and programs that address a wide and changing spectrum of legal needs (e.g., a "clinic" most likely would neither produce public service announcements nor provide legal services 24 hours a day, 7 days a week).

48. Conversation with Pace Law School director of admissions, Cathy M. Alexander, April 13, 2001.

49. Available from the American Bar Association or on-line at www. abanet.org/abapubs/home.html.

50. Mildred Doody, TRO Project, 127 Wall Street, New Haven, CT 06520, (203) 946-4811.

51. Lauren Robel, Protective Order Project, 735 West New York Street, Indianapolis, IN 46202, (812) 274-2581.

52. Melody Daly, Family Violence Program, 203 Hulston Hall, Columbia, MO 65211, (573) 882-7244.

53. Lee Teran, Center for Legal and Social Justice, 2507 NW 36th Street, San Antonio, TX 78228, (210) 431-2596.

54. Ibid.

55. Center for Legal and Social Justice, 2507 NW 36th Street, San Antonio, Texas 78228, (210) 431-2596.

56. Zelda Harris, P.O. Box 210176, Tucson, AZ 85721, (520) 626-5232.

57. Ibid.

58. Domestic Violence Advocacy Project, 2000 G Street, NW, Suite 200, Washington, DC 20052, (202) 994-7463.

59. Claire Dalton and Lois Kanter, Domestic Violence Advocacy Project, 400 Huntington Avenue, Boston, MA 02115, (617) 373-8882.

60. Elizabeth Simcox, 3800 Vartan Way, Harrisburg, PA 17110, (717) 541-1992.

10

A National Study of the Integration of Domestic Violence Assessment Into State Child Welfare Practice

LINDA G. MILLS

CARRIE J. PETRUCCI

The link between domestic violence and child abuse is now well established in the literature (American Humane Association, 1994; Bowker, Arbitell, & McFerron, 1988; Edleson, 1999; Hart, 1992; Hotaling & Sugarman, 1986; Lyon, 1999; McKay, 1994; Mills, 1998a; O'Keefe, 1995; Stark & Flitcraft, 1988; Straus & Gelles, 1986; Straus, Gelles, & Steinmetz, 1980; Zorza, 1995). Despite the overlap of these two abuses, and the obvious practice implications posed when child protective services (CPS) workers detect domestic violence in a family with which they are working, little research has been done to explore the extent to which child protective agencies have integrated domestic violence into their actual assessment practices. Research generally focuses on efforts to train CPS workers to be sensitive to issues related to domestic violence (Aron & Olson, 1997a, 1997b; Fleck-Henderson & Krug, 1997; Magen, Conroy, Hess, Panciera, & Simon, 1995; Mills, 1998a; Mills et al., 2000).

Only one study to date has examined the extent to which domestic violence has been integrated into CPS assessment forms. In 1998, Mills (1998b) analyzed data from the 58 counties in California to determine the extent to which CPS risk assessment instruments have incorporated factors related to domestic violence. Mills found that many counties in California had not incorporated domestic violence into their assessment forms and that no counties had taken explicit steps to integrate the mother's needs into their assessment forms. This national study builds on that work and analyzes assessment forms gathered from every state in the United States to determine the extent to which domestic violence was integrated into the forms that public child welfare workers use to assess families.

Risk assessment instruments are the tools used by CPS workers to assess and determine appropriate interventions in a given case. They reflect agency policy insofar as the instrument itself represents the criteria any given agency wants workers to consider when dispatched to a family. Agency handbooks and training materials are also relevant to determining agency practice in relation to domestic violence. However, this study focuses exclusively on the forms workers complete when they assess family functioning. Although this analysis is narrower than a more comprehensive review of agency policies and practices, it nevertheless provides a glimpse into agency functioning in relation to domestic violence. Assessment forms—the papers workers fill in during their interviews with families—are specifically designed to focus the worker's attention on what is the most important information to collect in order to assess a family and intervene appropriately.

The child welfare assessment process is critical to the CPS agency's ability to determine the best interests of the child. A comprehensive assessment form, one that includes questions regarding child and spouse abuse, is most likely to reveal facts that will help determine the best outcome. A review of the assessment literature is provided as a backdrop to the practice question: Have CPS agencies incorporated domestic violence into their assessment instruments? The data gathered from all states reveal that most public child welfare agencies have not sufficiently incorporated domestic violence into their assessment forms. What is revealed is that assessments for domestic violence are integrated only to the extent that they may be affecting the child. Using a content analysis of the assessment forms, our data reveal that no states encourage workers to explicitly consider how intimate abuse may be affecting the victimized mother. It is possible that such policies are embodied in other documents, training, or policies but not included in the forms. We therefore call for more research to determine the extent to which these narrow criteria are used to assess families suffering from domestic violence.

RISK ASSESSMENT, CHILD WELFARE, AND DOMESTIC VIOLENCE PRACTICE

Risk assessment has been defined as "the systematic collection of information to determine the degree to which a child is likely to be abused or neglected at some future point in time" (Doueck, English, DePanfilis, & Moote, 1993, p. 442). Interest in formal risk assessment has been increasing over the last decade, in part, perhaps, due to the renewed emphasis on CPS agency accountability. The systematized collection of information also enables case workers to manage their increasing workloads (Doueck, English, et al., 1993).

The accuracy of risk assessments has never been confirmed (Doueck, English, et al., 1993; Doueck, Levine, & Bronson, 1993; Inkelas & Halfon, 1997; Milner, 1989; Murphy-Berman, 1994). For example, it is impossible to remove subjectivity from such concepts as "harm" and "temporality" (risk now vs. risk at some point in the future). Some authors have suggested that to help remove subjectivity or uncertainty, we should agree on "a set of basic harms from which the child should be protected" (Murphy-Berman, 1994, p. 194). Another concern is that risk assessments have always been inherently biased in favor of deeply rooted causes of behavior rather than external factors that focus on environmental or situational factors. In addition, sources of information differ, that is, some reports are based on first-hand information, others on secondhand information from such "witnesses" as neighbors or relatives. Finally, the danger of false positives (assessing for risk that does not materialize) adds great uncertainty to the process of assessment (Murphy-Berman, 1994).

Doueck, English, and colleagues (1993, p. 442) analyzed three common risk assessment instruments used in child welfare agencies. Three distinct differences were detected when current risk assessment instruments were compared with past methods of decision making: (1) a focus on future predictions versus past events, (2) a systematic and highly structured process with specific guidelines and criteria versus professional expertise, and (3) a link to empirical data and systematic development. However, in a "naturalistic" study of 50 Los Angeles emergency response workers, there was a discrepancy between the needs of workers in the field and the intent of the risk assessment instrument (Impellizzeri, 1995). Impellizzeri also found a tension between the factors workers identified as most critical prior to their investigation and the factors they actually considered while determining an appropriate intervention in a given case. The reliability of the risk assessment instrument was found to be low, which in turn implies that the instrument is poor at predicting future risk of violence.

In their study of recidivism of abused children in the public child welfare system, Inkelas and Halfon (1997) found a 50% rate of repeat violence in child abuse cases in California. They hypothesized that poor risk assessment might be one explanation for this alarming finding. Inkelas and Halfon (1997) call for studies of risk assessment methods to better ensure appropriate referrals and services to children.

Milner (1989) studied 307 administrators, researchers, and direct service providers to determine whether they understood the uses of the Child Abuse Potential (CAP) Inventory. Twenty-three percent of these professionals indicated that the CAP Inventory can be used to differentiate between abusive parents, neglectful parents, and parents of children who suffer from failure to thrive. This is not what the instrument was intended to do, however. This study, then, reveals that CPS personnel may think they understand the purpose of the instrument they use but actually be unaware of its shortcomings (Milner, 1989).

Risk assessment in child welfare is not without its advocates (DePanfilis, 1996; Doueck, English, et al., 1993). DePanfilis (1996) argues for the following ingredients:

> Risk assessment implementation will be more successful if the motivation for adopting risk assessment is based on realistic expectations, the model selected has credibility and the potential to improve practice, there is motivation to change based on these realistic expectations, and the process for implementation is well-planned. In addition to these driving forces, the process will be more successful if specific reasons for resistance are identified and addressed, rather than ignored. (p. 51)

In other words, effective implementation of risk assessment is a complex endeavor if it is to accomplish its intended goals. Perhaps most important, risk assessment can be fully effective only when people are thoroughly trained to use it. Doueck, English, and colleagues (1993) have also found that there are "many potential benefits" to the use of risk assessment instruments. More specifically, they conclude that such instruments enable workers to state specifically how they came to their assessment and intervention decisions.

THE INTEGRATION OF DOMESTIC VIOLENCE ASSESSMENT INTO CHILD WELFARE PRACTICE

Several authors believe in the efficacy of domestic violence risk assessment.[1] For example, Hansen and Warner (1992) argue that domestic violence assessment can be helpful "to validate occurrence of maltreatment for the judicial system" (p. 126). In addition, they found that it can "identify target areas for intervention and monitor progress throughout treatment" (p. 126).

Despite general support for the use of risk assessment in domestic violence cases, we are only just beginning to learn about the impact of domestic violence on children. Child witnessing of mother assault has only recently become a topic of serious study (Lehmann, 2000). More specifically, the results of studies suggest that children can suffer from internalizing and externalizing behaviors when they witness domestic violence (Jaffe, Wolfe, & Wilson, 1990). Some children may also be resilient in the face of violence between adults, or they may have delayed responses (Carlson, 1996). As is the problem generally with risk assessments, there remains a great deal of uncertainty about which harms children should avoid.

The integration of child welfare and domestic violence risk instruments poses unique problems. In a study conducted by Columbia University, a protocol was developed for workers employed by New York preventive services agencies that are charged with averting unnecessary placement of children into foster care. More than half of the workers felt such questions as "Has your companion forced you to have sex?" were too direct. In addition, some workers felt the protocol needed to be shortened and that the paperwork was "too time-consuming" or an unwelcome task. Further, a small number of workers felt that domestic violence should not be addressed at the first home visit. Workers believed the instrument should be tested cross-culturally. Overall, two thirds of the workers interviewed reported that the protocol should be state-mandated and that domestic violence assessment should be conducted in all child welfare cases. Despite this expression of support, a majority of workers felt that their mandate was the safety of the child; workers did not perceive themselves as advocates for battered women (Magen et al., 1995).

These empirical results confirm what many scholars have observed about the functioning of the child welfare system when domestic violence is at issue (Edleson, 1999; Mills, 1998a; Mills et al., 2000; Peled, 1996). The tension between the mandate to protect children and the need to assist and support battered mothers has been linked to agency demands and caseloads, differing philosophies, and the competition for support for what has been formulated as "competing causes" (Schechter & Edleson, 1994). Despite these tensions, clinicians and practitioners have stressed the importance of maintaining a positive bond between the battered mother and the child (Groves, 1999).

Methodology

CPS agencies in 49 states, excluding California,[2] were contacted via letter and telephone from July 1998 through August 1999 and were informed that a study was being conducted on the different types of risk assessment forms used by each state. After, in some cases, four attempts, all state CPS agencies except the Vermont agency complied with a request to provide a copy of the initial assessment form used by its children's social workers to assess the risk of abuse in children. Vermont does not use a standardized assessment form.

This study focuses on assessment forms because CPS workers use these forms to collect data on the families they investigate. Assessment forms help workers and supervisors make judgments about which families will have their children temporarily or permanently removed. Toward this end, the forms represent a statement about what the agency values in terms of information-gathering. Obtaining the forms proved difficult enough, and hence we decided not to ask for supporting materials such as policy and training manuals. The limitations of this data collection method are elaborated later.

Using a content analysis method, the risk assessment forms were examined to determine (1) whether domestic violence was included on the form and hence was considered a risk factor in cases being assessed for child abuse, and (2) the extent to which domestic violence was considered a risk factor. To determine extent, four categories were used to help group the findings: simple mention, brief description, general description, or explicit description, each of which is described in detail later. These categories were developed using the content analysis method (i.e., they emerged from the data as they were analyzed), and thus very few conflicts arose between raters. Once the categories were specified, each form was reviewed by at least two raters; conflicts between raters were resolved by rereading the forms together and analyzing them in light of the definitions set forth within each category.

A "simple mention" describes an assessment form that simply mentions domestic violence as a risk factor. For example, a "simple mention" would simply list domestic violence as one of several risk factors or ask if the interviewee "has a history of domestic violence as a victim or perpetrator."

An assessment form with a "brief description" is one that screens for domestic violence during more than one phase of the interview but asks only whether some form of violence exists, without defining the violence more precisely. A typical example of a brief description assessed whether the "caretaker's behavior is violent or out of control" in the safety assessment section and then assessed whether there are "problematic adult relationships in the household" in the child abuse and neglect section and/or risk section of the form. In the brief description forms there was no place for the CPS worker to describe the nature of the intimate violence because the form itself presented the only relevant description.

An assessment form with a "general description" defines the different levels of the risk of domestic violence, from no risk to high risk; however, it does not provide a space for the worker to describe the violence. For example, a general description assessment form may contain a matrix that ranks the severity of domestic violence risk. Examples of categories in the matrix include "no current or history of domestic violence," which constitutes no risk; "past but no current domestic violence," which constitutes a low risk; "very recent violent relationship, but perpetrator out of home or history of repeated violent relationships" as a moderate risk; and "current and frequent domestic violence" as evidence of high risk. In the general description assessment, no definition of domestic violence is given.

An assessment form that defines domestic violence and provides guidelines to workers for determining the severity of the violence falls under the "explicit description" label. For example, explicit description forms include matrices that consider "outburst of violence, resulting in physical injuries or serious threats of harm" as evidence of high risk. Explicit descriptions were distinguishable from the other categories because they defined the intimate violence specifically by "injury" and "harm" rather than by a broad label such as "violent relationship." The importance of this distinction must be underscored. CPS workers seem to have very different views about how to assess for domestic violence (Shepard & Raschick, 1999); explicit definitions help standardize how workers characterize what they are told during interviews. In other words, the explicit description category was distinguished by the requirement that the worker obtain specific information about the abuse (Was there a physical injury?) rather than be satisfied with simply stating the occurrence of abuse (Was there domestic violence?). In addition, detailed data are important for holding the perpetrator accountable for the abuse inflicted on the family. If the questions are too general, there is a propensity to blame both parents rather than the one abusing the family.

Findings

The current study reveals that only four states—Arkansas, Minnesota, New Jersey, and Wyoming—did not include domestic violence as a risk factor for child abuse (see table 10.1). Since Vermont does not use a standardized assessment form, no analysis could be performed. The remaining 44 states all list domestic violence as a risk factor, and the following percentages are based on this group.

Twelve states (27%) refer to domestic violence using the simple mention format—Alaska, Arizona, Florida, Idaho, Illinois, Louisiana, Mississippi, Montana, Nevada, Oklahoma, Rhode Island, and Texas. Fifteen states (34%) refer to domestic violence using the brief description model—Alabama, Delaware, Iowa, Kansas, Kentucky, Maine, Maryland, Nebraska, New Hampshire, New Mexico, New York, South Carolina, Virginia, West Virginia, and Wisconsin. Five states (11%) refer to domestic violence using the general description approach—Connecticut, Georgia, Indiana, Michigan, and Missouri. And 12 states (27%) refer to intimate abuse using the explicit description method—Colorado, Hawaii, Massachusetts, North Carolina, North Dakota, Ohio, Oregon, Pennsylvania, South Dakota, Tennessee, Utah, and Washington.

Ninety percent of all states, excluding California, have integrated domestic violence into their assessment formats in one way or another. At a minimum, most states (65%, or 32 out of 49) have included domestic violence as a criterion for assessing child abuse (simple mention, brief description, general description). A smaller percentage of states (24%, or 12 out of 49), using the explicit description model, have required workers to do more than just assess domestic violence as it relates to the abuse of a child. These states have taken deliberate steps to encourage workers to ask detailed questions about the kind of violence that is occurring.

For the 12 states using a simple mention format, workers gather data on domestic violence as one of several risk factors or otherwise as part of the

Table 10.1. Summary of State Departments of Children and Family Services Risk Assessment Forms

State	Deomestic Violence as Risk Factor?	Extent of Consideration	State	Deomestic Violence as Risk Factor?	Extent of Consideration
Alabama	Yes	Brief description	Nebraska	Yes	Brief description
Alaska	Yes	Simple mention	Nevada	Yes	Simple mention
Arizona	Yes	Simple mention	New Hampshire	Yes	Brief description
Arkansas	No		New Jersey	No	
California	See Mills (1998b)		New Mexico	Yes	Brief description
Colorado	Yes	Explicit description	New York	Yes	Brief description
Connecticut	Yes	General description	North Carolina	Yes	Explicit description
Delaware	Yes	Brief description	North Dakota	Yes	Explicit description
Florida	Yes	Simple mention	Ohio	Yes	Explicit description
Georgia	Yes	General description	Oklahoma	Yes	Simple mention
Hawaii	Yes	Explicit description	Oregon	Yes	Explicit description
Idaho	Yes	Simple mention	Pennsylvania	Yes	Explicit description
Illinois	Yes	Simple mention	Rhode Island	Yes	Simple mention
Indiana	Yes	General description	South Carolina	Yes	Brief description
Iowa	Yes	Brief description	South Dakota	Yes	Explicit description
Kansas	Yes	Brief description	Tennessee	Yes	Explicit description
Kentucky	Yes	Brief description	Texas	Yes	Simple mention
Louisiana	Yes	Simple mention	Utah	Yes	Explicit description
Maine	Yes	Brief description	Vermont	Does not use standardized risk assessment form	
Maryland	Yes	Brief description			
Massachusetts	Yes	Explicit description	Virginia	Yes	Brief description
Michigan	Yes	General description	Washington	Yes	Explicit description
Minnesota	No		West Virginia	Yes	Brief description
Mississippi	Yes	Simple mention	Wisconsin	Yes	Brief description
Missouri	Yes	General description	Wyoming	No	
Montana	Yes	Simple mention			

parent-interviewee's history (as victim or perpetrator). No additional information is gathered to determine the nature of the violence or its impact on the adult victim. Similarly, using the brief description model, 15 states require workers to define whether domestic violence is occurring. In these instances, intimate abuse is superficially defined as "problem adult relationships" or behavior that is "out of control." No reference is made to the impact of the violence on the victimized parent. Along these same lines, a very small number of states use the general description method in which the worker is directed to assess the domestic violence risk to the child (from no risk to high risk). No specific definition of intimate abuse is provided in these assessment forms, and hence no effort is made by the CPS worker to determine the nature or extent of the risk posed to the adult victim.

Only 12 states direct workers to do a detailed assessment of the domestic violence detected, using an explicit description approach. States using this format require workers to detail the extent of the domestic violence and its more general impact on the family and also to define, in specific detail, the kind of injury experienced by the child and the adult victim. Using this approach, workers are required to inquire into the injuries of other members of the household, in addition to the children. Although the explicit description format allows workers to define the intimate abuse in greater detail, it still fails to provide specific steps for assessing the adult victim's injury and corresponding trauma.

Limitations of the Study

There are several limitations to this study. Assessment forms are only one method used by CPS agencies to evaluate the extent to which the agency believes the worker should be concerned about domestic violence. Policy and training manuals, agency culture, and outside training on domestic violence clearly influence the extent to which CPS workers might be concerned about domestic violence. Obtaining the forms proved difficult enough. Despite this limitation, the forms provided a succinct and standardized method for evaluating the extent to which CPS agencies had integrated domestic violence into their assessment practices.

In addition, we did not investigate the policies of state agencies in terms of their referral practices. For example, we did not study whether any given CPS agency would open a case if the mother was being battered but the child had not witnessed the abuse. This information would be helpful for illuminating more explicitly the extent to which a CPS agency would take action in families experiencing domestic violence. Finally, an important limitation is that regional CPS offices were not contacted regarding their specific assessment formats, and therefore some variation may exist between state practices and local jurisdictions.

Implications for Domestic Violence Practice and Policy in CPS Agencies

A review of CPS assessment forms suggests that, on the surface, CPS agencies have truly begun to integrate domestic violence into their assessment formats. However, two important lessons can be drawn from these findings. First, most state forms only focus very generally on domestic violence and do not inquire about the specifics in the cases being investigated. Gathering only "general" information increases the possibility of gathering inadequate or inaccurate data. In addition, detailed questions are important for providing specific interventions that address domestic violence in the family. Magen, Conroy, and Del Tufo (2000) found that with direct and specific domestic violence screening, there was "an almost 300% increase in the number of women identified as having been battered" (p. 265). Shepard and Raschick (1999) found that even when CPS workers discussed safety issues with victimized mothers, they did not make referrals to domestic violence services.

These findings suggest the importance of developing specific protocols that encourage workers to engage the mother in the assessment and intervention process in a targeted and specified manner.

In addition, gathering specific information helps hold the abusive party accountable for the violence, rather than collapsing batterer and battered woman together and assuming both are equally culpable. Case examples from training efforts raise critical questions about how CPS workers understand domestic violence and its impact on children and adult victims. In a study of a domestic violence training effort in New York City, Magen and colleagues (1995) found that workers had made certain assumptions about adult victims, including that the victim was to blame for the abuse. Whitney and Davis (1999) found that CPS workers typically viewed the mother's behavior as negative rather than seeking to understand the domestic violence issues. In a study of four CPS-based domestic violence training programs, Mills et al. (2000) found that three recurring issues all too often influenced the responses of CPS workers to cases involving domestic violence. CPS workers held negative stereotypes about adult victims, were not necessarily prepared to empower battered women to protect their children, and were uncertain what action to take when a child witnessed domestic violence but was not directly abused.

Second, we learned from our review of assessment forms that of the 49 states included, domestic violence has now been integrated into 90% of CPS agency child abuse assessment forms. However, we also learned that the assessment considers only the effect of the violence on the child. In some cases, child welfare agencies have begun to recognize the usefulness of gathering data about the adult victims' experience of the violence and the impact of the intimate abuse on the family as a whole (see, e.g., Magen et al., 2000). No states use forms that consider the impact of the domestic violence on the adult victim and assess the capacity of the adult victim to be empowered to protect her children. It is possible that workers have been trained in these techniques and therefore do not need to rely on the forms to reflect their commitment to a practice that integrates mother and child into their interventions. Magen et al.'s (2000) study, however, suggests that if workers are not required, through the use of forms, to attend to issues related to domestic violence, they will be reluctant to collect specific information regarding such violence and its impact on the battered mother.

Additional data are necessary to understand more precisely how CPS workers interact with mothers and how they integrate policy and training into practice. The forms give us a glimpse into that practice and provide an important first step toward understanding how domestic violence has been integrated into child welfare practice. However, more research is necessary to fully understand how CPS workers may blame victims of domestic violence or otherwise be ill equipped to address the adult victims' injuries or corresponding trauma (Magen, 1999).

Important Next Steps

A number of scholars have underscored the importance of developing CPS models of intervention that do not revictimize the battered mother (Edleson, 1999; Mills, 1998a). Toward this end, it is important to develop an assessment process that integrates the battered mother and acknowledges the important role she could play in healing the victimized family.

Magen et al.'s (2000) Domestic Violence Screening Questionnaire provides specific descriptions of domestic violence and responds to many of the concerns raised by this study. We suggest that child welfare agencies incorporate this questionnaire into their risk assessment formats.

The screening questionnaire collects basic demographic information and details about conflicts, arguments, and abusive behavior. The questionnaire involves reading a very specific statement regarding domestic violence, including definitions of emotional, sexual, physical, and material abuse. Clients are asked about types of abuse, frequency of abuse, and current and past family history. Data are also collected regarding the woman's efforts to seek help. In addition, workers are asked to describe what actions they have taken to help battered mothers deal with the abuse. The form also includes a "consumer" satisfaction component to determine "how helpful it was to have been interviewed about domestic violence" (Magen et al., 2000, p. 256).

A more proactive adult victim–oriented approach should be integrated into the CPS assessment process to help address the battered woman's ongoing concerns. Training should correspond with the states' efforts to include domestic violence in their assessment formats. The goal of this training should be to help create partnerships between CPS workers and battered mothers. The screening questionnaire developed by Magen et al. (2000) could help focus child welfare workers on interviewing battered mothers in ways that allow them to assess the extent of the violence and also provide interventions that incorporate battered mothers without blaming them for the perpetrator's abuse.

Implications for Future Research

This study suggests that states have done a great deal to integrate domestic violence into their assessment forms. It also suggests the importance of thinking critically about current strategies that focus exclusively on the child and are therefore less likely to inquire specifically about the abuse the mother is enduring. Additional research is necessary to fully understand the importance of assessments that gather specific information and that highlight the individual role each parent plays in the abuse to which the child may be exposed. To do so provides opportunities for a more comprehensive and detailed assessment method and the possibility of holding the batterer accountable for the abuse. A more comprehensive assessment method could also focus child welfare workers on providing supportive services to battered mothers who are in need of such assistance. In turn, battered mothers can be helped to develop the internal and external resources they need to help their children.

NOTES

Special thanks to Phuong Hoang, who helped collect and analyze the data in this study.

1. A multitude of risk assessments are currently being developed at the research level; for batterers, see Kropp and Hart (1997) for the Spousal Assault Risk Assessment (SARA) Guide; Bersani et al. (1992) for the Taylor-Johnson Temperament Analysis; Rodenburg and Fantuzzo (1993) for the Measure of Wife Abuse; for women victims, see Saunders (1992); Marshall (1992) for Severity of Violence Against Women Scales; for batterers and the victim, see Shepard and Campbell (1992) for the Abusive Behavior Inventory; for children, see Grahamm-Bermann (1996) for the Family Worries Scale; for a comprehensive assessment, including family violence for batterers and victims, see Hudson and McMurtry (1997) for the Multi-Problem Screening Inventory (MPSI).

2. The study excluded California because an extensive study had already been conducted on that state's agency. See Mills (1998b) for the results of the California survey.

REFERENCES

American Humane Association. (1994, September). The link between child abuse and domestic violence. *Child Protection Leader*, 1–2.

Aron, L., & Olson, K. (1997a). Efforts by child welfare agencies to address domestic violence. *Public Welfare, 55*(3), 4–13.

Aron, L., & Olson, K. (1997b). *Efforts by child welfare agencies to address domestic violence: The experiences of five communities*. Washington, DC: Urban Institute.

Bersani, C. A., Chen, H. T., Pendleton, B. F., & Denton, R. (1992). Personality traits of convicted male batterers. *Journal of Family Violence, 7*, 123–134.

Bowker, L. H., Arbitell, M., & McFerron, J. R. (1988). On the relationship between wife beating and child abuse. In K.A. Yllö & M. Bograd (Eds.), *Feminist perspectives on wife*

abuse (pp. 158–174). Newbury Park, CA: Sage.

Carlson, B. (1996). Children of battered women: Research, programs, and services. In A. Roberts (Ed.), *Helping battered women: New perspectives and remedies* (pp. 172–187). New York: Oxford University Press.

DePanfilis, D. (1996). Implementing child maltreatment risk assessment systems: Lessons from theory. *Administration in Social Work, 20*(2), 41–59.

Doueck, H. J., English, D. J., DePanfilis, D., & Moote, G. T. (1993). Decision-making in child protective services: A comparison of selected risk-assessment systems. *Child Welfare, 72*, 441–452.

Doueck, H. J., Levine, M., & Bronson, D. E. (1993). Risk assessment in child protective services: An evaluation of the child at risk field system.

Journal of Interpersonal Violence, 8, 446–467.

Edleson, J. L. (1999). The overlap between child maltreatment and woman battering. *Violence Against Women, 5,* 134–154.

Fleck-Henderson, A., & Krug, S. (1997). Memorandum to Linda Mills and Colleen Friend.

Grahamm-Bermann, S. A. (1996). Family worries: Assessment of interpersonal anxiety in children from violent and nonviolent families. *Journal of Clinical Child Psychology, 25,* 280–287.

Groves, B. M. (1999). Mental health services for children who witness domestic violence. *Future of Children, 9,* 122–132.

Hansen, D. J., & Warner, J. E. (1992). Child physical abuse and neglect. In R. T. Ammerman & M. Hersen (Eds.), *Assessment of family violence: A clinical and legal sourcebook* (pp. 123–147). New York: Wiley.

Hart, B. (1992). Battered women and the duty to protect children. In State codes on domestic violence: Analysis, commentary, and recommendations. *Juvenile Family Court Journal, 43*(4), 79–80.

Hotaling, G., & Sugarman, D. (1986). An analysis of risk markers in husband to wife violence: The current state of knowledge. *Violence and Victims, 1,* 101–124.

Hudson, W. W., & McMurtry, S. L. (1997). Comprehensive assessment in social work practice: The Multi-Problem Screening Inventory. *Research on Social Work Practice, 7,* 79–98.

Impellizzeri, S. (1995). *Decision-making criteria of Los Angeles County social workers in assessment of child abuse.* Unpublished doctoral dissertation, University of California, Los Angeles.

Inkelas, M., & Halfon, N. (1997). Recidivism in child protective services.

Children and Youth Services Review, 19, 139–161.

Jaffe, P., Wolfe, D. A., & Wilson, S. (1990). *Children of battered women.* Newbury Park, CA: Sage.

Kropp, P. R., & Hart, S. D. (1997). Assessing risk of violence in wife assaulters: The Spousal Assault Risk Assessment Guide. In C. D. Webster & M. A. Jackson (Eds.), *Impulsivity: Theory, assessment, and treatment* (pp. 302–325). New York: Guilford.

Lehmann, P. (2000). Posttraumatic stress disorder (PTSD) and child witnesses to mother-assault: A summary and review. *Children and Youth Services Review, 22,* 275–306.

Lyon, T. D. (1999). Are battered women bad mothers? Rethinking the termination of abused women's parental rights for failure to protect. In H. Dubowitz (Ed.), *Neglected children: Research, practice, and policy* (pp. 237–260). Thousand Oaks, CA: Sage.

Magen, R. H. (1999). In the best interests of battered women: Reconceptualizing charges of failure to protect. *Child Maltreatment, 4,* 127–135.

Magen, R. H., Conroy, K., & Del Tufo, A. (2000). Domestic violence in child welfare preventative services: Results from an intake screening questionnaire. *Children and Youth Services Review, 22,* 251–274.

Magen, R. H., Conroy, K., Hess, P., Panciera, A., & Simon, B. (1995, July). *Evaluation of a protocol to identify battered women during investigations of child abuse and neglect.* Paper presented at the Fourth International Family Violence Research Conference, University of New Hampshire, Durham, NH.

Marshall, L. L. (1992). Development of the Severity of Violence Against Women Scales. *Journal of Family Violence, 7,* 103–121.

McKay, M. M. (1994). The link between domestic violence and child abuse: Assessment and treatment considerations. *Child Abuse, 73,* 29–39.

Mills, L. G. (1998a). *The heart of intimate abuse: New interventions in child welfare, criminal justice, and health settings.* New York: Springer.

Mills, L. G. (1998b). Integrating domestic violence assessment into child protective services intervention: Policy and practice implications. In A. R. Roberts (Ed.), *Battered women and their families: Intervention strategies and treatment programs* (pp. 129–158). New York: Springer.

Mills, L. G., Friend, C., Conroy, K., Fleck-Henderson, A., Krug, S., Magen, R., & Thomas, R. (2000). Child protection and domestic violence: Training, practice, and policy issues. *Children and Youth Services Review, 22,* 315–332.

Milner, J. S. (1989). Applications and limitations of the child abuse potential inventory. *Early Child Development and Care, 42,* 85–97.

Murphy-Berman, V. (1994). A conceptual framework for thinking about risk assessment and case management in child protective service. *Child Abuse and Neglect, 18,* 193–201.

O'Keefe, M. (1995). Predictors of child abuse in maritally violent families. *Journal of Interpersonal Violence, 10,* 3–25.

Peled, E. (1996). "Secondary" victims no more: Refocusing intervention with children. In J. L. Edleson & Z. C. Eisikovits (Eds.), *Future interventions with battered women and their families* (pp. 125–153). Thousand Oaks, CA: Sage.

Rodenburg, F.A., & Fantuzzo, J. W. (1993). The measure of wife abuse: Steps toward the development of a comprehensive assessment technique. *Journal of Family Violence, 8,* 203–228.

Saunders, D. G. (1992). Woman battering. In R. T. Ammerman & M. Her-

sen (Eds.), *Assessment of family violence: A clinical and legal sourcebook* (pp. 208–235). New York: Wiley.

Schechter, S., & Edleson, J. (1994, June). *In the best interests of women and children: A call for collaboration between child welfare and domestic violence constituencies.* Paper presented at the conference Domestic Violence and Child Welfare: Integrating Policy and Practice for Families, Racine, WI.

Shepard, M. F., & Campbell, J. A. (1992). The abusive behavior inventory: A measure of psychological and physical abuse. *Journal of Interpersonal Violence, 7,* 291–305.

Shepard, M. F., & Raschick, M. (1999). How child welfare workers assess and intervene around issues of domestic violence. *Child Maltreatment, 4,* 148–156.

Stark, E., & Flitcraft, A. (1988). Women and children at risk: A feminist perspective on child abuse. *International Journal of Health Services, 18,* 97–118.

Straus, M. A., & Gelles, R. J. (1986). Societal change and family violence from 1975 to 1985 as revealed by two national surveys. *Journal of Marriage and the Family, 48,* 465–479.

Straus, M. A., Gelles, R. J., & Steinmetz, S. K. (1980). *Behind closed doors: Violence in the American family.* Garden City, NY: Anchor Press, Doubleday.

Whitney, P., & Davis, L. (1999). Child abuse and domestic violence in Massachusetts: Can practice be integrated in a public child welfare setting? *Child Maltreatment, 4,* 158–166.

Zorza, J. (1995). How abused women can use the law to help protect their children. In E. Peled, P. Jaffe, & J. L. Edleson (Eds.), *Ending the cycle of violence: Community response to children of battered women* (pp. 147–169). Thousand Oaks, CA: Sage.

Preparing for Expert Testimony in Domestic Violence Cases

EVAN STARK

On a December evening, a distraught woman gave police in Torrington, Connecticut, a signed description of abuse by her husband, Anthony Borrelli. The statement read in part:

> ... about 3 am. We went to bed and he began to accuse me of cheating on him. He started cutting up my clothes, underwear and things with his knife ... cut up my license and social security card because they have my maiden name on them ... he said he was going to tie me up and I said not to. He took a pillow and put it over my face. I couldn't breathe. I gasped for air. He let me go and took a rope and tied my hands and feet together behind my back. It hurt. He kept putting the knife on my mouth and chest while he sat on my chest and put his knees on my arms. He said he was going to kill me. He cut the top of my lip and the bottom of my lip. . . . He kept saying he was going to kill me and my family, my two daughters and two sons. He got up, said it didn't matter if he went to jail—no matter how long he was in jail he would get out and kill us. He also put a lighter near my genital area ... he had a lit cigarette which he threw on the bed. It landed next to me. I thought the bed sheets would catch on fire. He then said "I missed you," picked up the cigarette and put it on my chest. (*State v. Borrelli*, 1993, pp. 88–89)

Mr. Borrelli was charged with kidnapping, assault, criminal mischief, unlawful restraint, and threatening. At the jury trial, Mrs. Borrelli surprised the prosecution by testifying that her husband had not committed the acts she had alleged in her statement. Instead, she claimed, it was actually she who had tied up and physically abused the defendant. She also testified that she made up her initial story because she wanted to get her husband into drug treatment.

Apart from sparse physical evidence, a previous domestic violence arrest, and the "excited utterances" of Mrs. Borrelli, the police provided no independent support for the prosecutor's case. The state's attorney asked me, an expert specializing in domestic violence, to explain to the jury what might motivate a woman in Mrs. Borrelli's situation to recant. In my testimony, I defined woman battering, provided general information about its incidence, demographic dimensions, and consequences, and reviewed common misconceptions about the dynamics in abusive relationships, including the myth that abuse was not really serious if a woman remained with the partner. I also described how the typical strategies batterers used to dominate their partners could create a hostagelike situation that caused their wives to deny, minimize, or blame themselves for the abuse. To link my testimony to Mr. Borrelli's crimes, the prosecutor described hypothetical situations based on the statement signed by Mrs. Borrelli and asked whether these were consistent with general knowledge in the field. Mr. Borrelli was convicted and sent to jail.

On appeal, Mr. Borrelli argued that the trial court erred in admitting my testimony. Traditionally, the admission of expert testimony was governed by a three-part test: (1) The subject matter had to be "beyond the ken of the average layman"; (2) the expert had to possess sufficient skill, knowledge, or experience in the field to aid the "trier of fact" in his search for truth; and (3) the state of the scientific knowledge involved had to be sufficiently developed to allow an expert opinion to be rendered (Strong, 1999). Borrelli's attorney insisted that neither I, as a sociologist, nor the domestic violence field, as a relatively new area of inquiry, met the "Frye test" for scientific and clinical rigor typically used to determine the reliability of expertise (criteria 2 and 3). In a precedent-setting decision, Connecticut's highest court disagreed. Rejecting the stringent test suggested by Frye (1923), it found that expert testimony was proper so long as the expert was qualified by his or her educational background, work experience, and/or research, the testimony focused on a subject not familiar to the average person, and it was helpful to the jury. The Connecticut ruling reinforced a Supreme Court decision made that same year which held that evidence (such as expert testimony) was admissible simply if its relevance outweighed its possible prejudicial effect (*Daubert v. Merrell*, 1993). Moreover, "relevance" can be established by showing that the evidence makes an element of culpability more or less likely or helps a judge or jury understand the evidence in a case or determine a fact that is at issue (Downs, 1996).[1]

Standards for expert testimony similar to those established in Connecticut make it possible for any advocate, social worker, or health or mental health professional with specialized knowledge of or experience with domestic violence to present testimony to help a judge or jury assess evidence or to correct misconceptions about woman battering and its effects.[2] Expert testimony in criminal cases involving domestic violence is by no means uncontroversial. Particularly since the Bobbitt and Menedez trials, there has been mounting sentiment that the use of what Alan Dershowitz (1994) glibly terms the "abuse excuse" in cases involving victims of domestic violence, wartime trauma, rape, kidnapping, child sexual or physical abuse, or compulsive gambling condones vigilantism and frees people who kill from personal responsibility (McCord, 1987; Westervelt, 1999). At the other end of the political spectrum, legal theorist Elizabeth Schneider (2000) argues that expert testimony can perpetuate stereotypes that are as demeaning of battered women as the myths it is designed to dispel, particularly when it focuses exclusively on a victim's psychology rather than the "reasonabieness" of her actions. Despite these sentiments, courts have generally concluded, as Sue Ostoff (1995), director of the National Clearinghouse for the Defense of Battered Women, insists, that "the introduction of expert testimony does not promote vigilantism; it promotes fair trials" (p. ii).

This chapter provides a broad overview of expert witnessing in criminal and civil cases involving woman battering. Drawing on case examples, the first section traces the milestones in the evolution of expert testimony on battering, the rationale and scope of domestic violence testimony, as well as the types of cases in which it is admitted and describes alternative conceptual approaches to representing the battering experience. The second section focuses on how to conduct a domestic violence evaluation in preparation for trial. The conclusion considers several dilemmas that confront the expert witness. There is a growing need for expert assessment of male perpetrators of domestic violence, as well as of children who have been co-victims of abuse. But this chapter is limited to the more common scenario, where a clinician, advocate, or researcher is asked to provide general information about woman battering and its effects in a criminal case, as in *Borrelli*, or to assess how battering has affected the perceptions and/or behavior of a specific woman.

THE EVOLUTION OF EXPERT TESTIMONY

Expert testimony on woman battering and its effects developed in response to ongoing dilemmas that arose in representing battered women who defended themselves against abuse. In the past, women who committed homicide or other crimes in the context of their battering rarely claimed self-defense or duress. Only three self-defense cases involving women reached the appellate courts in the United States before 1900 (Bochnak, 1981; Gellespi, 1989), and battered women made such claims even less often. Because a history of abuse could provide a motive for the alleged crime, battered women often concealed it. Another important reason for concealment was that a rigid standard of self-defense was applied to women modeled after what "the reasonable man" could be expected to do in a similar situation. This meant that their act would be excused only if they used a level of force equivalent to the immediate force they confronted. They could kill their assailant only if an armed assault was under way, opportunities to retreat or escape were closed, and the force used was no more than needed to prevent attack (Bochnak, 1981). Anything more and they went to jail, as many thousands of women did. Although the standard allows for variation in how individuals perceive danger, it typically made no provision for group differences such as those arising from gender inequality or, as significantly, for the fear and entrapment attendant on a history of being battered.

Battered women had few credible alternatives to self-defense. In *Women Who Kill*, Ann Jones (1980) provided a popular overview of the legal quandary women faced when they retaliated against abusive partners, even in the throes of an assault. Behind the norm of domesticity, the most obvious explanation when an otherwise respectable woman responded violently was that she was insane. Jones (1980) argued that it was easier for courts to acquit on the grounds of insanity than to acknowledge that the behavior widely viewed as part of the marriage contract could provoke a rational woman to violence. A variation on this theme was to appeal to the court's paternalism by portraying the abused woman as frail and helpless, promoting the stereotypical belief that women could be acted upon but not act reasonably on their own behalf. A third approach was to argue that the violence a particular victim suffered was far in excess of the norm. In short, the legal system acknowledged abuse only so long as the victim was framed as a passive, helpless, or ladylike victim driven mad by a moral deviate. These terms for protection were acceptable because they supported women's oppression as a class; legitimated the status of women as male property to be used, but not "abused"; denied women an affirmative capacity for aggression and rationality (which were presumably possessed only by men); sustained the distinction between "respectable" and "rough" women that excluded working-class, minority, and unconventional women from protection; and fostered the belief that moderate levels of violence against women were normal, hence not a topic for public concern.

The domestic violence revolution altered this situation dramatically. As community-based shelters were opened in dozens of communities in the late 1970s (Roberts, 1981), defense attorneys and feminist scholars sought to broaden the range of legal options available to battered women beyond insanity and incapacity. Women's "self-defense work" was designed to remedy the unequal treatment resulting from the application of male norms in the criminal justice system by assisting victimized women to get their voices heard in the courtroom (Schneider, 2000). Expert testimony was one way to do this.

In 1977, shortly after the first battered women's shelters opened in the United States, Michigan housewife Francine Hughes put her children safely in a car, then returned and set fire to the bed in which her husband was sleeping. Francine's attorney worried that a traditional self-defense plea would fail, largely because James was asleep when Francine set the fire and so did not face the imminent danger required by law. Instead, he won acquittal by arguing that she had been "temporarily insane." Although some feminists criticized this decision because it reinforced the belief that retaliating against abuse was "unreasonable" for a wife, a precedent was set when the years of abuse by James were documented for the court as the explanation for Francine's distorted perception (Jones, 1994; McNulty, 1980; Stark, 1995).

Three months before Hughes set fire to her house, feminist legal scholars Elizabeth Schneider and Nancy Stearns from the Center for Constitutional Law won an appeal from the Washington State Supreme Court that also helped set the stage for expert testimony on battering. Reversing the murder conviction of Yvonne Wanrow, the Washington court emphasized that a history of sex discrimination predisposed a "reasonable woman" to greater vulnerability than a man, hence to respond more readily (i.e., with less provocation) and with a higher level of violence than a man would have in an identical situation (Schneider, 2000). Wanrow also challenged the tendency for courts to exclude contextual evidence—such as a prior history of conflict between two parties—from self-defense cases involving battered women, opening the door for experts to argue that the experience of battered women had social validity and commonality, and so that their retaliatory acts might be "reasonable." The decision also implied that women act in self-defense under different circumstances and in different ways than men and that sex-based stereotypes interfere with how jurors interpret these acts.

Temporary insanity caused by abuse and the lower standard for retaliatory violence set by the so-called Wanrow instruction were the two lines of defense available to battered women when psychiatrist Elisa Benedek took the stand in the murder trial of Ruth Childers in Benton, Indiana, in 1978. Childers was charged with murdering her former husband, Clifford, who had battered her for 18 years. One day Clifford returned to their farm, intoxicated, and began throwing furniture and other possessions belonging to Ruth and her teenagers out of their rented moving van. After calling the sheriff, Ruth confronted Clifford with a shotgun and told him to leave. He lunged at her, the gun went off, and Clifford was killed. Expert testimony established that the gun had gone off accidentally, reducing the crime to involuntary manslaughter. But full acquittal required an explanation for why Ruth thought the shotgun was necessary in the first place, even though Clifford had neither threatened nor assaulted her that day.

To answer this question for the defense, Benedek relied on a psychological pattern known as *battered woman syndrome* (BWS) that had been described by Lenore Walker (1979, 1984, 1989). Benedek wove her narrative from two parallel themes, episodes of severe violence against Ruth Childers and the victim's deteriorating psychological state, depicting her incapacity to perceive alternatives to the shooting as an example of "learned helplessness," a form of depression brought on by abuse. Benedek explained why, based on the sense of futility and dependence imposed by the violence, battered women develop an exaggerated sense of their assailant's power and are convinced they are in greater danger than a third party might perceive. Despite Benedek's credentials, Ruth Childers was convicted and sentenced to 5 years in prison, the maximum allowed in Indiana for involuntary manslaughter.

Today, expert testimony on battering and its effects has been admitted, at least to some degree, in hundreds of cases and in each of the 50 states plus the District of Columbia (Downs, 1996; Schneider, 2000).[3] Of the 19 federal courts that have considered the issue, all but 3 have admitted the testimony in at least some cases.[4] Based largely on the new awareness of battering, governors in Massachusetts, Ohio, Illinois, New York, and 18 other states took the unprecedented step of pardoning battered women imprisoned for killing men who abused them.

The Rationale, Types of Cases, and Scope of Expert Testimony

The most common scenario in which expert testimony on battering and its effects has been accepted (90% of the states) involves traditional self-defense situations. More than half of the states have found the testimony relevant to assessing the reasonableness of the defendant's belief that she was in danger of imminent harm and/or of her actions in defense of herself or others. A significant number (37%) of the states have found the testimony relevant to the defendant's perception of the temporal proximity of the perceived danger to life or safety. Two states, Ohio and Missouri, limit the admissibility of expert testimony to self-defense cases by statute, and nearly 40% of the states require that the defendant raise a self-defense claim in order to introduce expert testimony (Parrish, 1995). Technically, there is no separate defense based on BWS or battering generally. Thus, expert testimony should only be used to support a woman's claim of self-defense, duress, or necessity, not to replace it (Schneider, 2000). But, particularly as a complement to a woman's testimony, the expert can help to dispel jurors' preconceptions about battered women, illuminate how battering shaped her understanding and response to perceived danger, bolster the defendant's credibility, show the existence of mitigating factors (e.g., at sentencing), and explain why her fears were "reasonable."[5]

Expert testimony has also been admitted by a substantial number of state courts in nontraditional self-defense situations, such as where a battered woman kills her batterer while he is sleeping (accepted by 29% of the states) or by hiring a third party to kill him (accepted by 20% of the states). In a case I have described at length elsewhere (Stark, 1995), I supported the self-defense claim of an Albanian woman, Donna B., who had been assaulted more than 300 times by her husband, though she had never called police and had visited her doctor only once, for a sprain caused when her finger was caught in a slammed car door. One night, before going to bed, Donna's husband beat her, dragged her across the room by the hair, and kicked her in the side. Donna climbed the stairs, took the gun her husband kept under his pillow, and shot him four times in the head at close range. She then went back downstairs, called the police, and returned to the bedroom to retrieve the weapon, fearful her husband would come after her.

In another case, I testified at the sentencing of a woman who put a knife in her sleeve, went into the street, and confronted a former boyfriend who had threatened to come to her apartment that night and "fuck her up really bad," something he had done in the past. Though she had had him arrested for previous assaults and had a court order restraining him from contacting her, he repeatedly returned to threaten and assault her. The woman had two daughters in her house, there was no phone, the electricity had been turned off, and the boyfriend had broken the lock on her front and back doors. As she walked up to the man, she told him, "If you're going to do me, do me now," expressing the unbearable anxiety of waiting until night to be assaulted. When he cursed her, repeated his threat, and pushed her away, she stabbed him.

Cases where battered women kill their partners in nonconfrontational situations like these challenge the expert to explain why the victim's sense of imminent danger is as reasonable as if she were confronted by a knife-wielding intruder. Nontraditional self-defense situations receive disproportionate publicity. In fact, in the vast majority (at least 75%) of the cases where they are charged with murder, battered women kill men in traditional self-defense situations, during an ongoing attack or where the imminent threat can be readily discerned (Maguigan, 1991).

A sizeable minority of states have admitted expert testimony in non-self-defense cases, such as where women are charged with crimes they claim to have committed out of duress or necessity caused by battering (16% of the states) or where a battered woman has been charged with a crime against someone other than the batterer (14% of the states). In U.S. v. Ezeiuaku (D.N.U. 1995), for example, a criminal court permitted the defendant, Mildred Akiagba, to introduce testimony from an expert on BWS and an expert on Nigerian custom. Ms. Akiagba pled guilty to conspiracy to distribute heroin but testified that her estranged husband had coerced her into this, that he had physically abused, controlled, and monitored her and threatened her with deportation because he was an American citizen and she was not. While expert testimony in this case was ultimately unsuccessful, the court recognized its general relevance in establishing fear of bodily injury for purposes of mitigating or downgrading a charge or sentencing level on the basis of duress or coercion. I have testified successfully in cases involving this line of defense where battering was the context in which a woman signed a fraudulent tax return, allowed narcotics to be stored in her house, sold or carried drugs for her partner, failed to protect or injured her children, or embezzled money on behalf of an abusive partner.

In 29% of the states, the prosecution has offered expert testimony to explain a battered woman complainant's recantation or prior inconsistent statements, as in Borrelli. In *Commonwealth v. Goetzendanner* (Mass., 1997), the Appeals Court of Massachusetts upheld the testimony of an expert witness concerning BWS to explain why a woman had a restraining order removed and recanted, though she had earlier presented evidence that the partner punched her in the face and body, beat her with a stick, held a knife to her throat, and raped her. Noting precedents from other state and federal courts, the court also defined the scope of such testimony. "Where relevant," the court held, evidence of (BWS) "may be admitted through a qualified expert to enlighten jurors about behavioral or emotional characteristics common to most victims of battering and to show that an individual victim or victim witness has exhibited similar characteristics." But the Massachusetts court limited the scope of such testimony "to a description of the general or expected characteristics shared by typical victims of a particular syndrome or condition." Thus, the testimony "may not relate directly to the symptoms exhibited by an individual victim." Twenty percent of the states have explicitly precluded experts from testifying that the defendant is in fact a battered woman or "suffering from 'battered woman syndrome' (quoted in Perry & Lemon, 1998, p. 35)."

Experts are also called frequently to rebut expert testimony that challenges the credibility of a woman's claim to be abused or discounts its importance. In one case, a young woman claimed to have been coerced by her boyfriend into embezzling over $300,000 from her employer. Shortly after her arrest and the boyfriend's death in an accident, she made a "suicidal gesture" and was diagnosed by psychiatrists as suffering from a "borderline personality disorder with histrionic and anti-social features." The woman's adherence to peculiar housework rituals also suggested an "obsessive compulsive personality disorder." The state's attorney believed she had woven an elaborate fantasy about abuse from things she had read or seen on television. His expert argued that borderline personality disorder (*DSM-IV* 301.83) included "a pervasive pattern of instability in interpersonal relationships" and "angry disruptions in close relationships" consistent with fights. In my testimony, I showed that the woman performed household rituals not because she had a psychiatric condition but because her boyfriend forced her to obey an elaborate set of "rules" he had devised. Fortunately, she had retained the original copy of "the rules." On the other hand, introducing expert testimony can trigger an adverse examination of the victim by an expert for the prosecution or opposing counsel, an issue to be carefully considered.[6]

Expert testimony on battering is also becoming increasingly common in civil cases, particularly those involving tort actions for damages, alimony, or custodial disputes.[7] The justice interests of battered women assume particular poignancy in divorce cases and custodial disputes. Here, too, in marked contrast to the past, most states now require courts to at least consider evidence of domestic violence, typically via expert testimony on battering and its effects. In *Burgos v. Burgos* (1997), I testified that Mr. Burgos had battered Mrs. Burgos, prevented her from securing education or employment outside the home, and caused her to suffer multiple injuries, hospitalization, chronic stress, and a loss of confidence. Although both parties had substantial and nearly equitable estates, the court recognized Mrs. Burgos's noneconomic contributions during the marriage and that her earning capacity was stunted by Mr. Burgos's conduct. It found that Mrs. Burgos required additional education, which was to be paid for by Mr. Burgos, supplemental income in the form of weekly alimony, and a share in Mr. Burgos's pension benefits.

Perhaps *the greatest need for expert witnesses in civil cases is to counter widespread ignorance about battering and its effects among mental health professionals* whose assessments have failed to take domestic violence into account, perpetuated common myths about abusive behavior, or mistakenly equated woman battering with other forms of marital discord for which both parties are equally responsible. Here are three examples.

The marriage in a 2001 case in New York City reached its nadir when the husband committed a near-fatal assault with a barbell after his wife announced she wanted a divorce. The husband pled guilty to the assault, but in his claim for an equal share of the considerable marital assets, he presented expert psychiatric testimony that a combination of medication and stress caused him to "crack," that his dependency and idealization of his wife were inconsistent with the profile typical of batterers, and that his previous threats and assaultive acts constituted what the psychiatrist termed "unfortunate, but normal dysfunction" typical of many "bad marriages."

In a custodial dispute, a 9-year-old-boy refused to go to court-ordered visitation with his father, whom he claimed to fear. The court-appointed psychologist concluded the boy suffered from "parental alienation syndrome" due to the mother's excessive criticism of her former husband and recommended the father get custody. The basis for the recommendation included the fact that the couple had been separated for over a year and that the mother refused to drop a restraining order. The judge ordered the boy taken to a juvenile shelter until he complied.

In *Knock v. Knock* (Conn., 1993), a 10-year-old girl—represented by legal services—asked to live with her father, whom the mother charged with abuse. The primary evidence of abuse was contained in a five-volume diary written in Chinese. Translation costs were prohibitive. A psychologist testified that, according to the Minnesota Multiphasic Personality Inventory (MMPI) and several other tests, the father had no propensity for violence. A record from a battered woman's shelter was inadmissible because an advocate had removed a page documenting an outburst when the girl told the mother, "I hope you die."

In rebutting the husband's psychiatrist in the dispute over marital assets, I summarized research showing that, in fact, an extremely dangerous subgroup of batterers present with dependent personalities, and so idealize their partners that the threat of separation evokes the feeling "If I can't have her, no one will" (Dutton & Kropp, 2000). In the custody case involving the boy, the psychologist naively assumed abuse ended with separation (when, in fact, separation is often the most dangerous period), falsely concluded that the mother's continued fears were exaggerated, and so never asked questions that could have uncovered the dramatic history of postseparation intimidation (Mahoney, 1991). Unaware that the husband was stalking the wife, sending her threatening letters, and making threatening calls, she urged the mother to drop the restraining order as a gesture of goodwill. In the second custody case, expert testimony was needed to show that standard psychological tests like the MMPI are not diagnostic in identifying abuse. When the mother testified that the husband frequently told the mother, "I hope you die" at the dinner table, the judge understood the origin of the girl's behavior at the shelter.

Absence of expert opinion in these types of cases may lead courts to hold victims accountable for actions over which they had little control or to approve arrangements for custody or visitation that inadvertently reinforce a perpetrator's power over the victim. However, the presentation of expert testimony is no guarantee of acquittal in a criminal case or victory in a civil dispute. Although cases involving domestic violence are reversed on appeal at a far higher rate than other types of cases, often because a court has failed to admit expert testimony, most convictions of battered women (about 60%) are affirmed. In 71 of the convictions that are affirmed, defendants used expert witnesses (Parrish, 1995).

Conceptual Models of Domestic Violence Testimony

Why a battered woman like Ruth Childers would finally retaliate after years of abuse may seem obvious. The injustice of awarding custody to the father whose criminal behavior is directly responsible for his wife's deficits may seem equally apparent (Stark, 1999, 2000). No matter. In the legal setting, few events elicit as much contention as when a woman who has suffered a long history of violence highlights her own victimization either to mitigate criminal acts or to justify her position in a civil case. The source of ambivalence is not hard to identify. Though justice is supposed to attend to "facts" and remain blind to character, courts weigh credibility and appeals for sympathy against the type of person the defendant is imagined to be, particularly if a serious crime is involved. Apart from the generic prejudice that attends women whose behavior contradicts sex stereotypes, battered women are especially vulnerable because their behavior, albeit exhibited under stress, often suggests character deficits that seem incompatible with victimization. Like Francine Hughes, Ruth Childers, or Donna B., they may endure dozens, even hundreds, of similar assaults seemingly without protest, return repeatedly to the abusive relationship, defend their partners against discovery or sanctions, alter their story, fail to report abuse, or, like Ms. Borrelli, misrepresent their situation in a court or other professional setting. When they suddenly retaliate, the court wants an answer to the question "Why now?" At the other extreme, a successful career or a history of independent and/or aggressive behavior can make jurors equally unsympathetic with a battered woman's plight. Because many battered women have denied abuse in the past, credibility is often an issue. The court wonders: Does this person tell the truth only when it benefits her? If no assault was in progress when the woman acted violently, or the assault was relatively minor, or she could have escaped or called for help, her claim to be terrified or entrapped may seem far-fetched. Even if she has obviously been victimized, comorbid psychiatric or substance use problems can lower her status in the court's eyes or appear to distort her perceptions or judgment.

In her 1979 book, *The Battered Woman*, and in numerous publications since, psychologist Lenore Walker (1984; 1989, 1991; Wilson, 1992) addressed many of these problems directly. Based on a volunteer sample of middle-class women, Walker (1979) differentiated battered women from women living in marriages that were simply unhappy or unfulfilling by three factors: the "continuous occurrence of life-threatening incidents of violence" (p. xiv); psychosocial factors that bound battered women to their batterers "just as strongly as 'miracle glue' binds inanimate substances" (p. xvi); and a "cycle of violence" through which they passed at least twice, involving stages of tension buildup, crisis, and reconciliation (pp. 55–70). The "miracle glue" in Walker's argument was "learned helplessness," a depressive sense of fatalism that was both created by and reinforced the two other facets of battering she identified, continuous, life-threatening violence and a cyclical pattern of men's responses that left women confused about the real dangers they faced. Women "stayed" with abusive men, Walker argued, because they were trapped by the cycle of violence, seduced by the hope of change, and felt alternately helpless or responsible. She dubbed this gestalt *battered woman syndrome.*

Arguments based on BWS offer the psychological substance lacking in the temporary insanity plea used in the Hughes case and shape it into a narrative of victimization that explains why women perceived danger where a "reasonable man" might not, thereby incorporating an advantage of *Wanrow* as well. The psychological condition traced to the violent behavior of the batterer explains why women "stay" if abuse is as bad as they claim. Moreover, because abuse follows the "cycle," it is predictable, explaining why a woman can anticipate (and respond protectively) to impending violence. Learned helplessness also addresses other behaviors that seem to defy common sense, such as why a battered woman might refrain from seeking help, keep her abuse a secret, or conclude that violence is her only option, even when she has seemed utterly passive and dependent. The expert on BWS describes abuse as a process with cumulative effects over time, shows that a victimized defendant shares the common characteristics described by the Walker model, and emphasizes how an acute sense of powerlessness distorted her perception of situations that an outsider might see as unthreatening.

Weighed by its acceptance in state courts, expert testimony on BWS is the most successful example of a new type of psychological evidence used to frame experiences of victimization. Today, however, the term *battered woman syndrome* is often used by courts or attorneys to refer to the generic issue of battering rather than to Walker's specific formulation.[8] Meanwhile, there is a growing consensus among experts in the field that the Walker model of BWS rests on a shaky empirical foundation and has limited forensic applicability. In the words of a focus group of judges, prosecutors, defense attorneys, expert witnesses, and advocates convened under the auspices of the U.S. Justice Department (Dutton, 1996), BWS "fails as a construct to incorporate the breadth of available knowledge about battering and its effects that may be relevant in these cases" (p. vii).[9] Courts that rely exclusively on the Walker model have discounted the credibility of victims who appear strategic or aggressive rather than "helpless" or dependent (e.g., *State v. Smith*, 1996), particularly if they are from income or ethnic groups stereotypically portrayed as aggressive. At the other extreme, courts have based punitive interventions (such as removing children) on the model's prediction that battered women do little to change their situation (see, e.g., *In re* Betty J. W., et al., W. Va., 1988).[10]

A closely linked psychological defense is based on symptoms of posttraumatic stress disorder (PTSD; *DSM-IV* 309.81), a psychiatric syndrome first described among Vietnam War veterans. Like BWS, the premise of the PTSD defense is that any normal person would respond in a similar way if confronted by identical circumstances (e.g., external threats and violence) that elicit "intense fear, helplessness, loss of control and threat of annihilation." Recognizing that the conventional formulation of PTSD fails to capture "the protean symptomatic manifestations of prolonged, repeated trauma," Herman (1992) identifies three symptom categories of what she terms "complex PTSD," hyperarousal (chronic alertness), intrusion (flashbacks, floods of emotion, hidden reenactments), and constriction, "a state of detached calm . . . when events continue to register in awareness but are disconnected from their ordinary meanings (p. 46)." The fear elicited by the traumatic event also intensifies the need for protective attachments and may lead women to unwittingly move from one abusive relationship to the next. Experts relying on this model assess (or test) the victim for symptoms of PTSD, link the substance of flashbacks to incidents of abuse, and explain how the "trauma" that overwhelmed the normal coping mechanisms of the self caused the victim to dissociate (e.g., not remember her own violence), become hypervigilant (e.g., to exaggerate the danger posed by a sleeping man), or use preemptive violence. Testimony based on BWS or PTSD can meet a number of critical challenges to legal narrative by reflexively documenting a new class of psychological harms caused by domestic violence, implicitly weighing these wrongs against the woman's own criminal act(s), and tracing her actions to her psychological state (and so, indirectly, to the domestic violence) rather than to her rational faculties or volition, thereby mitigating her guilt. At the same time, the images of helplessness and/or psychopathology on which these defenses rest can damage a woman's credibility by emphasizing her "distorted" or exaggerated perceptions (e.g., impugn her capacity as a parent because she is "sick") and discount the objective parameters or her subjugation (e.g., her responses may be "intratraumatic" rather than "post-traumatic"; Downs, 1996; Schneider, 2000). To compensate for the potentially stigmatizing effects of psychological defenses, experts have included a woman's futile efforts at resistance among the "learning" experiences that may lead her to conclude that survival requires retaliatory violence (Dutton, 1993); suggested a "psychological self-defense" based on an interactive model of identity (Ewing, 1987); and argued that living in a battering relationship gives victims a special and more astute (rather than distorted) perception of reality than the outsider. Experts are well-advised to remain eclectic, adapting a psychological approach that best suits the experiential evidence in a particular case.

An alternative to the psychological framework is suggested by increasing evidence that most battered women are relatively intact psychologically, resist abuse in numerous ways, and consider nonviolent forms of subjugation as salient as physical assault. The modal case in which experts are called may be described as "coercive control," an ongoing course of malevolent conduct consisting of strategies to hurt, coerce (e.g., through threats, isolation, and emotional abuse), and control a victim (Schecter, 1987; Schneider, 2000; Stark, 1995). While psychological and physical harms are included in an assessment of "coercive control," the model depicts a process of "entrapment" whereby objective constraints that deprive women of basic rights frustrate their efforts to seek help or to otherwise minimize, stop, resist, prevent, and/or escape from the battering. In contrast to testimony that emphasizes psychological traumatization, the expert who assesses for coercive control links structural inequality, the systematic nature of abuse, coercion and control in a particular relationship, and the harms associated with domination and resistance (Jones, 1994; Meier, 1993; Stark, 1995, 1999–2000). Since women's (frustrated) strategic prowess is a key facet of this assessment, the model can be used to support an affirmative defense strategy premised on the victim's independence, aggression, and credibility. Reconstructing the battering experience through the prism of coercive control resolves the central paradox of abusive relationships so far as courts are concerned without resorting to potentially demeaning psychological accounts, namely, why, in the context of abuse, an otherwise intelligent, mentally healthy woman appears to function in dependent, destructive, or self-destructive ways.

PREPARING THE CASE

Who Is an "Expert"?

Before the expert can testify, he or she must be qualified to provide the special knowledge being claimed in a process known as a voir dire. A résumé is presented, and opposing counsel and/or the judge review the expert's education, professional preparation and affiliations, credentials or licenses, employment, experience with victims and/or offenders, research, publications in the area, honors or awards, and any special training (including conferences attended) that bears on domestic violence. A clinician or advocate might be asked what proportion of his or her clientele are battered women, for instance. Qualification is expedited if the expert has been previously admitted to testify, but this is not a prerequisite.

Initial Consultation

During an initial consult with an attorney, prosecutor, or client, sufficient information is garnered to determine whether and what kinds of domestic violence expertise are relevant to the case; in addition, fees or related costs are described, the time frame is explored, and the access needed to relevant parties and documents is explained. Does the attorney want consultation, a preliminary assessment, a report, and/or generic or case-specific testimony, for instance? When is the case likely to be heard? I frankly discuss the strengths and limits of my involvement compared with potential witnesses with other skills. A common misconception is that only a licensed clinician can provide expert testimony because it involves a mental health assessment. In fact, woman battering is a condition of victimization, and a psychiatric diagnosis is usually not appropriate. If a clinical assessment is required by the court, however, I provide the names of experienced colleagues. I become involved in fewer than half of the cases in which I am consulted.

In civil cases, victims usually make the initial contact and pay the fee directly. Calls are often prompted by experience with attorneys whose knowledge of domestic violence is extremely limited. While it is important to validate a woman's need for support, successful testimony depends heavily on a positive working relationship with the attorney. The expert should be prepared to educate attorneys about abuse, provide them with relevant reading or citations, and work as a partner in developing questions, scheduling and interrogating witnesses, preparing clients for trial, and making recommendations for disposition (e.g., custodial arrangements). Consultation is a legitimate role for an expert, even if neither a report nor testimony is required.

The Role of Evaluation

Unless directed to special issues, the purpose of a pretrial evaluation is to answer three questions: (1) Is the client a battered woman? (2) If so, what were the dynamics of abuse? and (3) What are the consequences of abuse for the client and/or any children? If the battered woman is charged with violence or another alleged crime, an assessment may also consider (4) how the history of battering affected her perceptions and behavior related to the event. Documents and interviews with friends, family members, or witnesses may help answer these questions. But the critical information is almost always provided by the client interview.

Defining Woman Battering as Coercive Control

The assessment begins with a working definition that is based on experience and research rather than limited to the discrete acts of physical assault or threats typically covered by domestic violence statutes. I rely on the coercive control model, where battering is defined as a malevolent course of coercive conduct wherein one social partner dominates another through the use of violence (abuse), coercion (isolation, intimidation, and emotional abuse), and control.

Following the definition, the assessment explores whether and to what extent the partner employed violence, coercion, and control, the interplay of these strategies over the course of the relationship, how the woman responded, how she was harmed, and how these experiences shaped her perceptions and behavior.

The Framework for Examining Harms

An appropriate forensic framework should be selected based on the facts in a case and the victim's presentation. Many cases of what Johnson (1995) calls "common couple violence" involve allegations of injurious physical assault only. While emotional or psychological abuse can play a role in such cases, evaluation and testimony focus on the degree, frequency, and effects of violence on the safety of the woman and her children. Such an assessment may be relevant in a "duress" defense to a criminal charge (such as embezzlement, drug involvement, or signing a false tax return) or to custodial disputes where the court simply wants expert opinion about whether the client is or is not a "battered woman." In this instance, evidence of psychological harm is kept to a minimum because it can impugn a woman's credibility or parenting capacity.

Psychological models of victimization are relevant where clients charged with a serious crime evidence adaptations to severe physical abuse that include symptoms of BWS, PTSD, or a related complex that mitigate their criminal responsibility. Drawing on the vast trauma literature, the evaluator may administer formal psychological tests and/or clinically assess whether changes in feeling, perception, attitude, and behavior are the result of abuse. Here again, clinical assessment should be sensitive to its potential misuse to impugn the credibility of the victim as a witness to her abuse. A complete investigation of objective constraints in a battering relationship will often explain why fears and perceptions seem "exaggerated."

Evidence of PTSD or BWS may be relevant for explaining a victim's behavior in a specific situation. But the absence of traumatic reaction in no way negates the reasonableness of a battered woman's fear. To the contrary, battered women frequently remain relatively intact psychologically despite multiple episodes of physical abuse, deprivation, isolation, and control. In cases where the principal presentation of battering is a state of subjugation (or "duress") rather than severe physical injury or psychiatric disease, the working definition of battering as coercive control is most appropriate. Here the evaluator's attention is directed toward the existential condition of "entrapment" that compromises a woman's capacity to escape the battering, act independently, or protect herself or her children.

Documentation

Depending on whether the case is criminal or civil and whether it is relatively new or ongoing, prior to meeting the client, the evaluator reviews available records and evaluations from courts, corrections, criminal justice, medical, mental health, and behavioral health agencies; court-ordered evaluations of children; investigative reports of friends, witnesses, and family members; and records of related legal proceedings (depositions, trial transcripts, visitation orders, protection orders, judicial rulings, etc.). Although official documents rarely mention domestic violence explicitly, they may describe injuries, complaints, and other presentations suggestive of abuse (e.g., frequent "falls," "unwanted pregnancies," nonspecific complaints of pain, suicidality), as well as psychiatric and pseudopsychiatric diagnoses frequently misapplied to abused women such as "hysterical" or hypochondriac. In one case, when a client supported her supposed "delusions" with a daily record of abuse stretching back 7 years, her court-ordered treater changed her diagnosis to "obsessive." Conventional documentation of domestic violence is the exception rather than the rule, however, even where a victim has sought help aggressively.

A written chronology of abusive events prepared by the client is an important source of documentation that can help prompt memories prior to the interview, date episodes in relation to key life events, and help prepare the evaluator for the assessment and testimony. A Palestinian woman who had paralyzed her husband with a club was dubbed "of limited intelligence" by her attorney, primarily because she spoke little English. But the 50-page record of abuse she provided in Arabic proved key to acquittal. A chronology also saves the client time and money. With the client's written consent, the expert garners collateral information from witnesses, family members or friends, and treaters.

Unconventional sources often provide the most important supporting information. A common misconception is that the severity of domestic violence can be measured by injuries that come to the attention of doctors or the police. In fact, the high-risk condition of entrapment typically results from the cumulative effects of minor but frequent abusive episodes, in combination with isolation, intimidation, and control. Sources used to document these events may include date books, logbooks, telephone messages, diaries, letters (including threatening letters from partners), tapes, photographs, and other records. Unconventional documents may also help the court understand the pattern and degree of abuse. In one case, to establish how money became a focus of subjugation in the relationship, I matched dates of abusive episodes recorded in a woman's diary with the dates on which bills arrived for presents her husband gave her to make up for earlier abuse. In the case of Donna B., the key to acquittal was a logbook in which her husband had her record her daily activities (including any purchases, menus, thoughts of him, etc.). He would call her downstairs nightly to defend each entry, then beat her for not doing enough to advance their family. In another case, the wife of a prominent figure made notes in her calendar that her husband "lost it" or "went crazy" to document his abuse. The written list of "rules" in the embezzlement case covered everything from how the woman should dress or vacuum to whom she spoke with on the phone. Unconventional forms of documentation are not always admissible, but the expert can often refer to them as a basis by which an opinion was formed.

The Interview

Depending on the framework adapted, the interview is structured to determine the fact of abuse, as well as its dynamics, consequences, and significance. A preliminary discussion of the purpose of the interview and previous experience with battered women helps reduce a client's anxiety about revealing painful and potentially embarrassing details to a stranger. Victims are urged to share as much detail as they can, even if they do not consider the acts queried abusive. However, clients should also be informed that, in contrast to other clinical interviews, the information provided may be available to opposing counsel, to other experts, or even to partners via counsel.

Accurate recall can often be a serious problem in domestic violence evaluations. Battered women frequently adapt to coercion and control by repressing, denying, minimizing, or normalizing the danger they face, as well as by medicating the stress associated with abuse with substances that distort their memory. Conversely, victims may blame themselves for what happened or exaggerate their culpability, particularly if they feel guilty about their own violence. Donna B.'s husband sent her to Weight Watchers (which she liked because she got out of the house), then put her on a scale and beat her for not losing weight. Overeating is a common adaptation to abuse, but Donna blamed her "stupidity" and "forgetfulness" for the assaults, a conclusion the prosecutor tried to exploit. Ironically, self-blame can be protective because it helps clients maintain a sense of what I term "control in the context of no control." While evaluation is not counseling, it is appropriate to help clients understand their partner's culpability and weigh appropriate expressions of their own responsibility against defensive postures that could increase their vulnerability at trial. For example, prosecutors often exploit the propensity for battered women to recall abusive episodes they initially denied. In fact, as Herman (1992) suggests, the revision of a woman's story as memories surface is a sign of recovery from trauma and should be so reframed for the court.

To maximize accurate reporting, some practitioners recommend an intensive, all-day interview that follows events in a chronological order, moving gradually from neutral questions about family background, early dating experiences, and the like to more emotion-laden episodes (Thyfault, Browne, & Walker, 1987). This approach has the added benefit of simulating courtroom testimony. Walker and her colleagues also suggest structuring questions about violence—and testimony—around four different battering incidents: the first occurrence of violence in the relationship, the worst episode, the typical episode, and the most recent or fatal incident. Each of these narratives is followed by matching sets of detailed questions about the specific circumstances (e.g., time, place, duration), acts (e.g., slap, hit, knife), and outcomes of the incident (e.g., injury, help seeking, retaliation) before moving to the next episode. Obtaining consistent details about incidents provides a picture of violence that allows comparisons over time that can identify escalation or other changes in behavioral patterns.

I prefer shorter interviews spaced over several weeks and proceed from a semistructured narrative in the first meeting to a more structured assessment schedule that probes the occurrence of specific events. Repeat, shorter interviews exploit the fact that recall improves dramatically over time, particularly if the abuse has culminated in an event involving extreme violence, and have the added advantage of allowing the interviewer to fill gaps and clarify ambiguities. I also find that victims who discharge the anxiety surrounding an extreme episode of violence early in an interview can more readily explore less dramatic facets of the battering dispassionately and with greater accuracy.

The initial interview (or phase of the interview) captures the woman's "story" as she understands it, that is, in a rough chronological and narrative form. After reviewing the incident that precipitated the evaluation, the interview takes a standard psychosocial history that includes any familial history of violence, sexual abuse, or substance use; a history of earlier relationships, abusive or not; schooling; work history; and a history of major medical, mental health, or behavioral problems. The oft-claimed link between current victimization and violence in childhood is greatly exaggerated. Still, violence in the family of origin or in prior relationships contributes to a woman's understanding of the current relationship. An employment history can counter negative stereotypes of battered women or, conversely, illustrate how the abusive partner disrupted a woman's work life, caused her to lose a job (or workdays) or obstructed her career path. Information on prior pathology can also illuminate a woman's response pattern. However, the psychosocial history is also mined to provide baseline evidence of independence and resilience against which the effects of subsequent abusive experience can be weighed. Courts frequently want to know whether the victim's current state reflects abuse rather than long-standing personality problems.

The History of Battering

The next phase of the interview focuses on the current relationship and, depending on the framework of harms adapted, seeks to establish the existence and interplay of abusive strategies, the consequences of battering, and how the woman responded. The narrative account is guided by frequent prompts to sharpen recall, to direct attention to dimensions of experience not linked with abuse in the popular mind (such as isolation or control), and to keep the focus. This is followed by questions targeting specific dimensions of violence, coercion, and control, not covered in the narrative, that research or casework suggests are common and/or are associated with an elevated risk of fatality or entrapment.

Violence: The Adult Trauma History

With respect to the partner's *violence,* the evaluator seeks information on:

- The number, frequency, type, duration, and severity of assaults
- Injuries or chronic problems resulting from assault
- The typical assaultive incident

- The presence and/or use of weapons
- Sexual assault
- Assault during pregnancy
- Violence or other criminal conduct outside the relationship
- Violence in the presence of others, including children
- Violence while under the influence of alcohol or drugs
- Physical and/or sexual abuse of children

The narrative begins with the courtship and proceeds from the first episode of abuse ("What is the first abusive episode you remember?") to capture as many instances as possible of physical and sexual assault. In addition to asking about specific types of violence (choking, kicking, hitting with objects, etc.), I ask, "What did he do when he really wanted to hurt you?" and "What was the worst thing he ever did to you?" and/or "Has your partner ever hurt you so badly you needed a doctor?" and/or "Have you ever thought your partner might kill you?" Sexual coercion should be explored alongside sexual assault. I ask, for instance, "Has your partner made you do things sexually which hurt you?" and "Has your partner forced you to do things sexually which made you ashamed?" In cases involving punching, burning, or other forms of severe violence, incidents involving pushing, shoving, hair pulling, poking, and the like are often forgotten and can only be elicited through direct questions during the structured interview. A client who had stabbed her boyfriend recounted only three incidents of "violence," for instance. But the question "Did he ever put his hands on you when you didn't want him to?" elicited a detailed account of daily physical restraint. Although these events seemed trivial in isolation, involving pushing, grabbing, shoving, or "belly-bopping," their cumulative effect was the almost hostagelike state of feeling trapped that provoked her retaliatory assault. At the conclusion of the interviews, the expert should be able to summarize the range, frequency, duration, and severity of domestic violence. For example, in a case where a woman murdered her boyfriend, violence and intimidation were the primary tactics. Assessing whether the woman was battered, I wrote:

From the interviews and records reviewed, there can be no question that Dawn S. was battered by Felipe G., starting approximately a year before the stabbing incident, during the summer of 1992, and extending to head trauma inflicted on the night of the incident. Involving over 50 assaults, the violence included breaking into her apartment, stalking, choking, rape, knocking her down, punching her in the back, kicking her in the head and back, dragging her by the hair and slapping. In addition, he threatened to shoot her, held a gun to her head, and threatened her with a knife.

Estimates of the number of abusive episodes can help neutralize the misconception that only injurious, life-threatening violence constitutes abuse and dramatize the often "serial" nature of violence, where assaults occur once a week or more over many years. Donna B.'s husband first slapped her several days after they married, when she laughed on the phone while talking to her husband's uncle. A few nights later, she said she wasn't feeling well enough to make love, and he tied her hands behind her back with a belt and "had his way." She recalled a dozen similar incidents during the first year. Early in the second year of their marriage, the couple moved away from his family into their own apartment, and the husband implemented the nightly log ritual. From this point until she shot him 3 years later, Donna said, the beatings occurred "nightly," "constantly," and "all the time." Using specific questions about the frequency of assaults during limited time periods bounded by watershed events, I concluded there had been somewhere between 250 and 300 attacks in this relationship, an estimate experience tells me was probably conservative. The expert should be prepared to defend the estimate during cross-examination.

Coercion

Intimidation, threats, and emotional abuse are used to frighten the victim, induce compliance, and make her feel incompetent, stupid, or weak. An assumption underlying the assessment is that in inhibiting escape, coercion and control are as often the antecedents as the sequelae of ongoing assault and play a major role in eliciting stress-related behavioral and psychological problems. With respect to emotional abuse and intimidation, the evaluator should be particularly sensitive to the following factors:

- Chronic put-downs of woman, friends, or family members
- "Games" designed to make the woman feel "crazy" (called "Gaslight" games after the film by that name)
- Withdrawal from communication (e.g., the "silent treatment")
- Terrorizing or sadistic behaviors, particularly when the victim is sick or injured
- Paranoid, jealous, or homicidal fantasies
- Threats against the woman, family, friends, or pets, including threats to kill
- Monitoring or stalking
- Threats of suicide
- Use of children as "spies"

Compared with an assessment of violent acts, the range, meaning, and dimensions of coercive strategies are difficult to elicit and specify. Emotional abuse, threats, and overt acts of intimidation can be identified by asking questions like "When your partner wanted to insult you, what names were you called? How often did he do this?" or "Has your partner ever made you feel you can't do anything right?" "How does he do this?" or "What is the worst threat your partner ever made?" But intimidating behaviors are often devised to be invisible to outsiders. Indeed, their effect on the client is greatly magnified when the terror a woman feels contrasts with the outwardly benign appearance of her partner's acts. In one case, the partner of a star softball pitcher would walk onto the field when he became jealous and offer her a sweatshirt, an act that most observers interpreted as loving. Only she understood the message—that she would need to cover up her bruises that night—and went into a panic, which others attributed to "nerves." Although fear is an extremely sensitive indicator of actual risk in battering relationships, the ostensible normality of many situations that women describe as "crazy-making" leads them to distrust and even feel guilt about their instincts. One result is that women voluntarily change behaviors—quit school, reject a job offer, give up a night out with friends—because they sense their partners disapproval. Worse, inchoate fears may make them do things of which they are ashamed. To get at this situation, it is helpful to ask general questions about fear and humiliation: "Are there certain things you don't do or say anymore because you're afraid of how your partner will respond?" or "Do you ever feel you are walking on eggshells at home?" or even "What are the ways your partner scares you?" Where obsessive jealousy has been a factor, as it often is, intimidating tactics can be uniquely sadistic. In one case, a jealous ex-husband hid in a tree outside the house and jumped down when his former wife attempted to leave. Women are commonly expected to wear beepers so their partners can locate them at any moment. In the embezzlement case, the partner would beep in a number of a department store, for instance, and the client had to guess its significance (e.g., he wanted a new shirt). Despite the man's claim that the "beeper game" was a sign of love, when the woman's beeper went off during our interview, a rash formed on her arms and spread quickly to her neck (where her partner typically held and choked her when she failed the game or broke his rules). In other instances, batterers simply "lose it" to frighten their partners, driving at dangerous speeds, for example, or putting a fist through a car window. In one case, when a newlywed suggested a plan to redecorate the house, her partner picked up a sledgehammer and started smashing the walls.

Not all verbal attacks, insults, or demands that a partner behave in specific ways are examples of battering. Psychological abuse is effective in frightening or controlling an abused party because the past experience of assaultive violence conveys the implication that either the partner complies "or else. . . . "

Isolation from friends, family, helping professionals, and other sources of support removes the moorings from which a positive sense of self derives, increases the victim's dependence on her partner, increases her vulnerability to domestic violence, and keeps abuse secret. Since isolation is a relative state, the evaluator probes changes that have occurred during the target relationship or since the onset of abuse. A key question may be "Do you feel you can come and go as you please and talk to whom you like?" Key issues include the following:

- Restricted access to family members, friends, and coworkers
- Restricted access to medical care or other sources of help and protection
- Restricted access to common social arenas (church, school, work, etc.)
- Control over mobility and communication (car, phone, going out alone, etc.)
- Invasion of private spaces (e.g., diaries, answering machines, pocketbooks, drawers)

Isolation can be particularly important when a partner restricts a woman's access to an area of activity (work, the gym, going to church, having a relative sleep over) she has used as a "safety zone" to feel good about herself or contemplate alternatives to her situation. In the well-known "burning bed" case, for example, Francine Hughes set fire to the house immediately after her partner burned her schoolbooks, symbolically closing the one area in her life he did not control. To get at restrictions, I ask, "Were there things that you did or wanted to do that you have given up because your partner doesn't like them?" The case of Donna B. illustrated another common pattern: that violence and control escalate dramatically only after a pattern of isolation is established, often by a change in residence that removes the client from her support network. In one case, abuse became nearly fatal when the FBI had local police drop assault charges against a partner who had testified in a federal drug case, then relocated the family in another county. In some cases, isolation elicits a "Stockholm syndrome" of extreme dependency seen mainly among hostages and sexually abused children. In the embezzlement case, the woman's sense of identity became so closely linked to the approval she got for obeying the "rules" that she continued to perform the obsessive household rituals (and to embezzle tiny sums of money) after her boyfriend's death. Victims frequently increase their isolation voluntarily to placate the batterer. As a result, they may feel guilt or be unclear about the source of their isolation. In one case, a husband outwardly supported his wife's decision to return to work, but she felt compelled to quit after she found their children unfed or sleeping on the living room floor when she returned home. The possessiveness or jealousy that often motivates the batterer's attempts to isolate his partner sometimes feels like "love." One woman's partner told her it was unhealthy to take her children to a local diner where her mother and sister worked, a sign, she thought, that "he wanted to make us his family." Physical abuse began almost immediately after she lost daily contact with her family.

Control

That battering is motivated by "power and control" is almost a cliché in the domestic violence field. But we now appreciate how often control strategies are also the primary means by which partners exact material benefits from the victim, secure privileges, circumscribe her choices, and deny her access to the means required for safety or autonomy. Critical dimensions of control include the following:

- Control over money and other basic necessities (money, food, etc.)
- Control over coming and going
- Control over sexuality (when, where, how, with whom, etc.)
- Control over access to medical care or other helpers
- Control over interactions with friends, family, or children
- Violations of personal boundaries (reading diaries, listening to calls)
- Control over minute aspects of daily life (dress, domestic chores, etc.)
- Control over how the children are disciplined
- Control over how time is spent during the day

As with forms of coercion, control strategies extend to a range of micro-events (from what she says on the phone to who handles the TV changer) that are too broad to encompass with specific questions. Cases in which men control material necessities are common enough and can be usefully explored (and demonstrated in court) with the visual aid of the Power and Control Wheel developed in Duluth, Minnesota, by the Domestic Abuse Intervention Project (DAIP) and available from most local battered women's programs. Following the wheel, the expert can probe how money was handled in the household, then turn to sexuality, then access to family members, to how he exploited "male privilege," and so forth. Alternately, the evaluator can directly ask, "Who controlled the money in your household?" or "Were you forced to account for everything you spent?" or "Did you have to account for your time?" As with violence, however, dramatic acts of control are often less important in establishing entrapment—or in helping a court understand battering—than extracting the meaning and effects of forms of control that might appear minor, even trivial, to an outsider, but which were chosen for their special effect on the victim. In one family, for instance, a husband insisted that his wife answer the phone by the third ring; in another, the bed covers had to be so many inches from the floor. The very pointlessness of the rules exacerbated the degradation these women felt when they obeyed them. In these cases, I emphasized the exceptional intelligence and success of the victims—one was an Emmy Award–winning journalist, the other an honors graduate from Vassar—implicitly asking the court to imagine what it would take to make women of this caliber perform these humiliating acts. Control should not be confused with decision making, however. In the New York case involving marital assets, the wife was the sole source of income, hired the maids, and decided where the children went to school. The husband was content to design and build the new country estate, garden, and write his memoirs. The critical issue in identifying control is not who decides but "who decides who decides what."

Evaluating a woman's access to helpers is an important piece of assessing control. Batterers frequently prevent women from seeking help, regulate their interaction with helpers, punish them for seeking help, or force them to terminate care while they are still at risk. In one case, a physician who was ashamed to have his colleagues see his wife "sick" sprayed her with an insecticide to cure her cancer. Then, 24 hours after surgery, he insisted she return home, where she contracted an infection and almost died.

Strategies to Prevent Violence

Early discussions of domestic violence identified risk with women's ill-fated decision to "stay" with abusive men and the reluctance to seek help associated with psychological ambivalence, dependence, and a distorted perception of their situation. Current research reveals that most victims utilize a range of strategies to limit, minimize, resist, or escape the battering, including separation and seeking help from formal and informal sources. The evaluator catalogs these strategies and their efficacy: Whom did she tell? How, when, and with what consequence did she seek help? What did she do to avoid physical abuse? To minimize its consequences? Did violence stop when she called the police in the past, or did it escalate? Was the police response helpful or punitive (e.g., was she arrested along with her partner?) How did her partner respond when she refused sex or left the house? Did violence cease or escalate when she used force? How did she cope with threats or isolation? How did she resist control? I emphasize the arenas victims used as "safety zones" (see earlier discussion). The level of control determines whether actual social arenas are safety zones (like work, church, or school) or whether these merely symbolize independence (e.g., wearing certain clothes, keeping a diary, investing rituals with special meaning). Fatal confrontations (and final separations) are often precipitated when the abusive partner seeks to quash the victim's safety zone, as in the "burning bed" case. Since many clients internalize the image of themselves as "helpless," a catalog of their efforts at resistance, however ineffective or seemingly trivial, can be therapeutic, as well as informative for the court. If control is extensive, resistance may be forced "underground" and manifest itself in ways that appear self-deprecating or even self-destructive. Thus, when her husband sent her to the store to buy beer and cigarettes, Donna B. would "forget" to get beer, a failure she attributed to her "stupidity." Another client took a near-lethal dose of pills in front of her children when her husband was following her around the house with a video camera to show "how crazy I was." Both acts illustrate "control in the context of no control." By contrast with informal means of resistance, arrest, court orders, shelters, and convergent interventions are often ineffective in limiting the partner's access, a fact that explains why separation is so risky. The inappropriate, victim-blaming, or ineffective response of helpers is often an important part of a woman's entrapment. The special acuity Blackman (1986) identifies among battered women reflects both the routine (hence predictable) nature of much domestic violence (in contrast to other forms of assault), as well as the victim's need to concentrate on the details of her partner's behavior.

Consequences of Battering

Documenting the consequences of battering bears on the victim's credibility, helps support assessments that battering was serious or life-threatening, and supports a range of claims in civil cases, including access to mandated services, alimony, and financial liability. Again, however, the negative consequences of putting evidence of debilitating medical, psychological, or behavioral conditions into a public record should be weighed against its benefits. In an Alabama case in which I was consulted, the husband had beaten the wife so badly that she was hospitalized for head trauma. During the custody dispute, psychiatrists testified that the woman's IQ had suffered significantly (as a result of the attacks). Concluding that the intelligence loss impugned the woman's capacity to parent, the judge ruled that it was in the best interest of the child for the father to have custody.

Apart from injury, problems attributed to abuse should be credibly linked to the research literature and should occur in reasonable proximity to abuse experiences. As in the descriptive narrative, the primary means of identifying health problems will be through the "adult trauma history" of all known physical consequences of abuse, regardless of whether they prompted a medical visit or produced permanent physical changes (such as loss of teeth or hair), scars, or disability. In addition to the usual bruises, abrasions, and contusions, physical symptoms with a high risk of being linked to abuse include human bites, sexually transmitted diseases, or HIV disease; chronic pain syndromes; unwanted pregnancies, miscarriage, or multiple abortions; multiple or centrally located injuries, particularly to the face, breast, or abdomen; frequent headaches or nonspecific "pain all over"; and sleep disorders, anxiety, dysphagia, hyperventilation, or other physical problems associated with chronic stress.

There is no single profile of the psychological effects of battering, despite the widespread belief that battering is defined by a common core of symptoms. Battered women's reactions include emotional reactions (e.g., anxiety, sadness, anger); changes in beliefs and attitudes about self, others, and the world (e.g., self-deprecation, distrust, fear of the world); and symptoms of psychological distress or dysfunction (e.g., flashbacks, sleep problems, rapid weight loss or gain). Whether a particular battered woman meets criteria for a clinical diagnosis depends heavily on her resilience (based on family history and support systems), as well as on the types, intensity, and duration of violence, coercion, and control; the relative efficacy of adaptive and strategic responses; and the racial, social class, and cultural context. Battering is associated with a dramatically increased risk of alcoholism, drug abuse, attempted suicide, and mental illness, including psychosis, largely because victims self-medicate or attempt to "escape" from the chronic anxiety of living with coercive control. Even where clients have a previous history of these problems, their escalation—for example, from drug use to addiction—can be tracked in relation to the escalation of coercion and control. Functional assessments can often be key as well, particularly where no similar loss of function is evident prior to the onset of abuse or when the victim is out of the abusive relationship. There is no solid evidence that either battered woman syndrome or PTSD is more common among battered women than other populations, that it is more common than other psychological reactions, or that it has unique or greater relevance to understanding victimization than other clinical or legal issues. To the contrary, posttraumatic reactions leading to diagnoses other than PTSD (e.g., acute stress disorder, dissociative amnesia, major depressive disorder), as well as those that do not constitute classifiable psychiatric disease (e.g., shame, distrust, transient dissociative reactions) may be far more relevant than a limited assessment for PTSD.

Where liability or alimony is an issue, it may also be important to assess the socioeconomic consequences of battering. Psychologically, a victim's capacity to evaluate and respond to new relationships may be compromised by a history of abuse. She may suffer low self-esteem, believe she cannot succeed at her job or in school, and lose confidence in her parenting skills. As in *Burgos v. Burgos,* described earlier, the partner may be liable for the costs of treatment, job retraining or for personal support where abuse prevented a woman from advancing to the level normally reached by someone with her education and experience. Even where extraneous causes of debilitation are evident (such as abuse in childhood), the expert may estimate the proportion of the problem (and the associated costs) due to the current abuse, particularly if the partner knowingly exploited the woman's vulnerability.

In many cases, "liberty harms" are the most significant results of coercive control (i.e., the loss of freedoms taken for granted by most adult citizens). The "costs" of losing personal discretion over how one dresses, cooks, cleans, or spends one's earnings can be suffering. But courts are often more responsive to these constraints than to physical injury or psychological problems.

The Dynamics of Battering

Once the various elements of battering have been separately elucidated and juxtaposed to their consequences and the victim's strategies, a narrative can be constructed around the relative importance in this relationship of violence, coercion, and control, how the interaction of these strategies changed over time, and with what consequences. This narrative bridges the gap between the abstract legal concept of "battered woman" and how coercive control was manifest in a particular relationship. Dynamics may be framed as a staged experience involving watershed events or turning points associated with a change in the pattern, frequency, or severity of abuse. For example, in the case of Donna B., stage 1 was characterized by relatively minor and infrequent assaults and culminated when the couple moved to their own apartment and were isolated from the Albanian community because the husband had assaulted his mother. Without support or visibility, Donna B.'s vulnerability increased, leading to a sharp escalation in violence and control in stage 2. In the embezzlement case, the escalation of violence led to the woman's complete isolation from her family and the extended community of support she had garnered at work. In stage 2, the couple lived apart, but the fear and intimidation already established permitted the boyfriend to impose the "rules" with only occasional physical "discipline" if the woman was "bad." Alternately, dynamics may be described by summarizing each type of abuse in turn. The detailed history of a relationship is normally reserved for a report, but it can also be an extremely useful heuristic device in helping a judge or jury understand a woman's "story."

A Woman's Response to Impending Assault

The factors an evaluator considers to explain a woman's response to a particular abusive episode include her experiences of violence (past and present); the immediate signs of impending threat (e.g., risk factors such as the presence of weapons); "lessons learned" from previous attempts to avoid or limit harm; the objective constraints that constitute her degree of entrapment (e.g., her isolation, access to money or means of protection); and behavioral problems that might limit her capacity to accurately perceive or take advantage of credible sources of help or support.

The "lessons" a woman "learns" from previous attempts to modify abuse can be presented to show the rational basis for her calculated decision to retaliate in a certain way. For example, a woman fired at a man when he cut her off on the way to her car and put his hand in his pocket, as if to pull a gun. During the assessment, she explained that his previous assaults, as well as beatings by two former husbands, taught her "when men want to hurt you, they can hurt you bad." In the case of Elizabeth R., the client was charged with first-degree assault for stabbing her boyfriend in the downstairs hallway of their apartment house. As part of the defense, I described her attempts to prevent being seriously hurt: She had called the police many times, frequently screamed for help, called on neighbors, taken refuge at a neighbor's house, gone to the emergency room on four occasions, tried to defend herself with a bottle and a golf club, changed apartments, and locked her door; at the time of the stabbing, she was waiting for her brothers, whom she had called to remove Mr. E. from the house. By showing that these efforts had failed to prevent Mr. E's escalating attacks—the police had arrested her as well as Mr. E. when she called, and he had thrown her down a flight of stairs the previous evening—her own violent act was reframed as the culmination of a rational process of "learning" rather than as an act of vengeance.

Assessing Risk

Experts may be asked to assist in risk assessment at any phase of the judicial process, from pretrial assessment of offenders through correctional discharge and civil justice matters.[12] In the evaluation described here, I employ risk assessment to aid in custodial decision making and, more often, as part of a defense strategy, to demonstrate the level of risk a woman faced when she assaulted or killed an abusive partner.

A promising generic instrument available for predicting risk is the Spousal Assault Risk Assessment (SARA; Kropp, Hart, Webster, & Eaves, 1998), a set of guidelines composed of 20 items identified by the empirical literature and designed to enhance professional judgment about risk. Since the SARA is not a test (although it includes an analysis of psychological data), it can be used by the nonclinician. The procedure recommended resembles the evaluation discussed here in many respects and includes interviews with the partner and the victim, standardized measures of physical and emotional abuse and drug and alcohol abuse, and a review of collateral records.

As part of a defense strategy in a criminal case, risk assessment can be designed to answer the question: "Based on the prior history of battering in this relationship, what was the risk that the battered woman would be killed at the time she used violence against her partner?" Psychologist Angela Browne (1987) set the stage for this type of assessment when she reported that women who killed abusive partners could be distinguished from battered women who had not used violence by the level and frequency of physical and sexual violence to which they were subjected, the batterer's use of drugs and alcohol, the presence of weapons in the household, and the propensity for their partners to threaten or use violence against others, including their children. Drawing on Browne's work and subsequent research, Cambell (1995) developed the Danger Assessment (DA) Scale to predict spousal homicide around "women's perception of the danger of being killed by their partners." Although the DA Scale has been shown to predict short-term misdemeanor assault with some accuracy (Goodman, Dutton, & Bennett, 2000), its credibility in predicting homicide is still unknown. Nonetheless, research strongly suggests that the presence of these factors in any combination dramatically increases the chance that battering will culminate in a death. The scale is divided into two sections, one (part A) assessing the level of current violence and its dangerousness, the other (part B) providing an overview of the range of tactics employed by the batterer.

In assessing the probability of homicide in a battering relationship, I supplement the DA Scale with elements of coercion and control that experience suggests significantly elevate a woman's risk. In addition, I find it useful to consider the current situation separately from the contribution of past battering. With respect to *past violence,* the key risk factors considered are as follows:

- Presence and/or use of a weapon
- Sexual abuse
- Chronic drug and/or alcohol abuse
- Violence outside the home
- Threats to kill (or belief she will be killed)
- Control over all aspects of her life
- Restricted access to family members and friends
- Denial of food, money, clothes, or other necessities
- Paranoid, homicidal, or jealous fantasies
- Monitoring or stalking the victim
- Violence against children, other family members, or pets
- Serial abuse
- Terrorizing or sadistic behavior when the woman is sick or hurt

With respect to the *current situation,* the factors I assess as high-risk include:

The perpetrator is:
- Depressed or paranoid
- Obsessed with victim
- Threatening to commit suicide
- Stalking or monitoring the victim

The victim is:
- Separated from perpetrator or considering separation
- Seriously thinking about killing perpetrator
- Fearful she or the children will be seriously hurt or killed

Recent changes in the relationship indicating high-risk include:
- Sudden escalation (or change) in the pattern, severity, or frequency of assaults, isolation, intimidation, emotional abuse, or control
- A recent attack involving the threat of homicide
- The perpetrator has violated a restraining order
- The extension of abuse to children

Tabulating a score based on the number of risk factors presented allows comparison with other cases and a statement of "relative" risk that supports the client's perceptions or fears. In Donna's B.'s case, discussed earlier, the husband had routinely "had his way" with her sexually after an assault. But on the night she shot him, he went to bed without sex after dragging her across the floor by the hair and kicking her in the side, a change which she interpreted to mean that he now thought of her only as an object that could be disposed of.

Assessing Validity

Because the client interview is often the primary source of evidence that battering occurred, the court—as well as opposing counsel—naturally wants to know whether and why the expert finds the woman a credible source of information. In lieu of independent corroboration, the expert can only establish credibility with a reasonable scientific certainty based on the external and internal validity of her story. With respect to *external validity,* the paramount question for evaluation is whether the pattern of violence and control depicted is consistent with what is known about the dynamics in abusive situations, the personality and behavior of batterers, or the consequences of battering. In testimony, the evaluator may review basic knowledge about battering, then show why the material provided in the interview was consistent with this knowledge. Consistency between the narrative account and documents reporting specific episodes or witness accounts also helps to validate descriptions of other facets of abuse that are undocumented. But expert assessment never hinges on the occurrence of a single abusive episode. Even setting aside the defense mechanisms that lead victims to minimize or blame themselves for abuse, the complexity and duration of domestic violence often makes it impossible to reconstruct the actual sequence or nature of events. Instead, the major focus of evidence gathering is on the pattern or course of abusive conduct, on routine or typical incidents, and on strategies used to coerce and control victims, as well as to hurt them physically. Clients may mislead even a skilled interviewer about particular episodes. But they are extremely unlikely to credibly simulate a lengthy course of conduct that resembles coercive control.

I assess *internal validity* utilizing "criteria-based content analysis." This test, which was originally developed to assess truthfulness in cases of alleged sexual abuse, involves looking for repetition in word patterns and phrases (which indicates that a story is rehearsed), as well as repeating key questions. Additional factors that suggest internal validity include victims sharing responsibility for events, admitting their own acts of violence, and remembering extraneous details of traumatic events.[13]

CONCLUSION

Early work on women's self-defense stressed the positive role that expert testimony might play at trial in complementing the defendant's testimony and making her particular experience plausible to a jury. More recently, however, even sympathetic commentators have questioned whether its benefits in specific cases are worth the risk that expert testimony on battering and its effects will replace rather than support women's voices in the courtroom. One way this can happen is by substituting "a statistically derived average experience that women typically share for the detailed, potentially idiosyncratic experiences each of us has" (Scheppele, quoted in Schneider, 2000, p. 106). To the extent that the court relies on an expert to provide a window on common experiences, the authority and credibility of women as witnesses to their own experience may be reduced, a possibility reflected in the popular conceit that battering occurs "behind closed doors" (i.e., without a credible witness). The ambiguous political status of expert testimony is further reinforced by the dominant psychological models of abuse used in defense cases. Indeed, to the extent that the BWS and PTSD models lend the imprimatur of science to images of female dependence, pathology, and incapacity, they replicate the dilemmas that confronted battered women who killed abusers in the nineteenth century. Once again, defendants (as well as their advocates) must seek individual relief by appealing to stereotypes that alternately portray aggressive women as "bad" or "mad" and contrast the "helpless victim" with the "violent brute." This approach to woman battering accommodates an obvious social wrong—violence against women—without threatening, indeed by reproducing or even extending, the prevailing sexual hierarchy based on male dominance.[14]

Deciding how to best support a woman's voice in the legal setting is sometimes difficult, particularly when the state requests expert testimony to discount a victim's recantation or refusal to testify. Noninterference with a victim's choices is a basic tenet of the empowerment approach to women's self-defense work. Further, victims are assumed to be the best judge of their risks. Balanced against this individualized notion of empowerment is our civic obligation to protect vulnerable others from harm and uphold standards of community justice. After weighing these issues against the limited facts at my disposal, I chose to testify in *Borrelli*. But several years later, balancing similar concerns, I refused the state's request to testify in lieu of an immigrant woman who had been dragged from her workplace by the boyfriend on whom she depended for her residency permit and eventual citizenship. Some expert witnesses view themselves as "hired guns" in the courtroom or, conversely, as "forensic scientists" who provide facts (or diagnoses) on demand. Given the stakes involved, assuming these naive postures is a luxury the expert on woman battering cannot afford.

Another dilemma weighs the aim of expert testimony, to help judge and jury "walk in the shoes" of a woman, and the difficulty of doing this when the class or cultural underpinnings that frame a woman's decision making are foreign, perhaps even alien to our own. A week before Donna B. shot her husband, she packed her clothes and son into her car and prepared to leave. Then, realizing how complete her isolation would be from the Albanian community (as well as her family) if she left her husband, she returned to the house. Meanwhile, an Asian Indian client in a custody dispute believed she was obligated to provide unquestioned submission toward her husband and his male relatives, even to the point of serving a traditional dinner each evening to his paramour, who had taken up residence in their basement apartment. Obviously, psychological accounts of dependence are inappropriate in these cases, and the line between cultural integrity and coercive control is hard to draw.

To some, the hardest parts of expert testimony are the drama that attends a courtroom appearance, cross-examinations that seem mean-spirited, the need to simulate a level of certainty that is unfamiliar to researchers or, conversely, to provide an objective appraisal that differs markedly from frank advocacy. If helping a client you believe is legally innocent avoid painful jail time is gratifying, it can be personally devastating when a client you have come to know and care about is convicted, goes to jail, or loses custody of her children. And there are few more frustrating experiences than sitting in the witness chair without being able to fully answer questions or tell the "story" as you know it.

The battered women in whose cases experts become involved have suffered extensive, sometimes shocking, harms. In reporting these harms, the expert merely reflects their experience. But in asking the court to withhold the stereotypic imagery of victimhood and psychological dysfunction these experiences may evoke, the expert also does something more, asking judge and jury to step inside the world battered women inhabit to discover what they are struggling to defend, as well as to avoid or escape. Instead of wondering what sort of person would be drawn to this level of suffering, the expert must help the court envision the personhood needed to survive these incredible constraints. Through sheer will and raw courage, battered women propel themselves through a potentially paralyzing fear to find a hope that often has no objective confirmation in their immediate situation. If, despite the seeming totality of their oppression, battered women nonetheless experience a certain amount of control in the court context—or, at least, "control in the context of no control"—this is because, through the reconstruction and authentication of their story, they are put in touch with a larger social context in which their right to safety and independence is affirmed through what Judy Herman (1992) calls "an alliance of victim and witness."

NOTES

1. The first case to recognize that the subject matter of woman battering was beyond the ken of the average juror was a 1977 Washington, DC, case, *Ibn-Tamas v. United States* (D.C. 1979).

2. Still, according to a review (Parrish, 1995) of state policies, 25% of the states have required some evidence that "battered woman syndrome" is accepted in the scientific community in order to admit the testimony, while 33% of the states have explicitly required that the proffered expert must be properly qualified as such.

3. On the other hand, 18 states have also excluded expert testimony in some cases; of these, there is still doubt under case law about its admissibility only in Wyoming (Parrish, 1995).

4. A comprehensive search conducted in 1995 by the National Clearinghouse for the Defense of Battered Women for the Women Judges' Fund for Justice located over 350 cases (Parrish, 1995). The database included 238 state court (primarily appellate decisions, 31 federal court (mostly appellate) decisions, 30 trial court–level cases, 12 appellate decisions on pretrial motions, 13 civil actions, and 31 cases involving prosecution of batterers or male defendants charged with sexual assault where expert testimony on battering or sexual assault was discussed in court. The fact that the research largely excluded local court and civil cases suggests that the actual number of cases in which expert testimony has been an issue is probably in the thousands.

5. More than 25% of the states have found an expert can give an opinion on the "ultimate question" for the fact finder of reasonableness or whether the defendant acted in self-defense. But a larger group of states (37%) have held to the contrary.

6. Only Minnesota has found explicitly to the contrary.

7. Numerous possible third-party defendants may be liable in domestic violence cases, including hospitals, shopping centers, or employers (e.g., where security is impermissibly lax), psychiatrists who fail to report serious threats, police, and friends or relatives who assisted the abuser in carrying out his strategies. See Lehrman (1996, February–March).

8. Thus, it should not be assumed that states that have allowed testimony on "battered woman's syndrome" will only permit experts who use Walker's model. Indeed, testimony has been deemed relevant even where the primary dynamic was coercive control and little or no domestic violence occurred. See *People v. Daoust*, (Mich. Ct. App. 1998; see also *Knock v. Knock* (Conn. 1993).

9. For summaries of these views, see Schneider (2000); Downs (1996); Dutton (1996); and Stark (1995). Most battered women experience neither the "cycle of violence" nor "learned helplessness"; many experience a range of psychological and behavioral problems that fall outside the purview of BWS or, as often, function with minimal mental health problems; and the typical case involves frequent but low-level violence rather than the escalating and severe assaults described by Walker.

10. See, e.g., *State v. Kelly* (NJ 1984), which cites Walker's theory and identifies battering with demoralization and "sink(ing) into a . . . psychological paralysis."

11. Courts are increasingly turning to risk-assessment instruments to predict future violence by offenders in both civil and criminal proceedings. Although several promising instruments are currently being tested, however, a recent review concludes that "there is still relatively little published research on the reliability and validity of these tools" (Dutton & Kropp, 2000). Nor have the tools been tested in relation to the recurrence of specific types of abuse (e.g., coercion vs. violence; chronic, minor violence vs. spousal homicide). Risk prediction is facilitated because the high rateof repeated spousal physical assault (25% to 50%) significantly reduces the rate of falsely predicting that violence will occur (false positives). Unfortunately, however, the fact that most tests are designed to predict only violence (e.g., rather than coercive or controlling behaviors) increases the likelihood that they will falsely predict abuse will *not* recur (false negatives), an important limitation in custody cases. Even where a test is employed, the consensus is that its utility depends on the use of multiple methods and sources, such as those reviewed here.

12. In general, I prefer not to interview the abusive partner, even when he is made available, largely because long experience has convinced me that the quality of

information provided is corrupted by too many factors beyond my control. Nevertheless, as a check on the victim's credibility, I assume that, if interviewed, the partner would provide an account that is diametrically opposed to the victim's.

13. The coercive control model addresses these problems by identifying dependence with objective facets of domination rather than victim psychology and highlighting the victim's strategic prowess. But this framework can be interpreted undialectically, as yet further proof of a woman's incapacity, a reading that has led Ruth Jones (2000) to propose that court-appointed guardianship be used for women experiencing coercive control.

REFERENCES

Blackman, J. (1986). Potential uses for expert testimony: Ideas towards the representation of battered women who kill. *Women's Rights Law Reporter, 9,* 227, 237.

Bochnak, E. (Ed.). (1981). *Women's self-defense cases: Theory and practice.* Charlottesville, VA: Michie Co. Law Publishers.

Browne, A. (1987). *When battered women kill.* New York: Free Press.

Burgos v. Burgos (1997). WL 120300 (Conn. Superior Ct.).

Campbell, J. C. (1995). Prediction of homicide of and by battered women. In J. C. Cambell (Ed.), *Assessing dangerousness: Violence by sexual offenders, batterers and child abusers* (pp. 96–113). Thousand Oaks, CA: Sage.

Commonwealth v. Goetzendanner (Mass, 1997). App. CT. 679 N.E.2d 1362.

Daubert v. Merrell Dow Pharmaceuticals, Inc. (1993) 61 LW 4807-4808.

Dershowitz, A. M. (1994). *The abuse excuse and other cop-outs, sob stories and evasions of responsibility.* New York: Little, Brown.

Downs, D. (1996). *More than victims: Battered women, the syndrome society and the law.* Chicago: University of Chicago Press.

Dutton, D. G., & Kropp, P. R. (2000). A review of domestic violence risk instruments. *Trauma, Violence and Abuse, 1,* 171–181.

Dutton, M. A. (1993). Understanding women's response to domestic violence: A redefinition of battered women's syndrome. *Hofstra Law Review, 21,* 1191.

Dutton, M. A. (1996). *The validity and use of evidence concerning battering and its effects in criminal trials: A report to Congress under the Violence Against Women Act.* Washington, DC: U.S. Department of Justice, National Institute of Justice, and U.S. Department of Health and Human Services, National Institute of Mental Health.

Ewing, C. P. (1987). *Battered women who kill: Psychological self-defense as legal justification.* Lexington, MA: Lexington Books.

Frye v. U.S., 293 F. 1013 (D.C. Cir. 1923) at 1014.

Gillespie, C. (1989). *Justifiable homicide: Battered women, self-defense and the law.* Columbus: Ohio State University Press.

Goodman, L. A., Dutton, M. A., & Bennett, L. (2000). Predicting repeat abuse among arrested batterers. *Journal of Interpersonal Violence, 15,* 63–74.

Herman, J. L. (1992). *Trauma and recovery.* New York: Basic Books.

Ibn-Tamas vs. U.S. (D.C. 1979). 407 A.2d 626.

In the interest of Betty J. W. et al., (W. Va. 1988) cited Supreme Court of

Appeals, West Virginia, opinion filed July 1, 1988 No. 17482, reversal opinion written by Justice Miller, 371 S.E.2d 326, 327–328.

Johnson, M. (1995). Patriarchal terrorism and common couple violence: Two forms of violence against women. *Journal of Marriage and the Family, 57,* 283–294.

Jones, A. (1980). *Women who kill.* New York: Fawcett Columbine.

Jones, A. (1994). *Next time, she'll be dead: Battering and how to stop it.* Boston: Beacon Press.

Jones, R. (2000). Guardianship for coercively controlled battered women: Breaking the control of the abuser. *Georgetown Law Journal, 88,* 605–657.

Knock v. Knock (Conn. 1993). 224 Conn. 776, 783–786.

Kropp, P. R., Hart, S. D., Webster, C. W., & Eaves, D. (1998). *Spousal assault risk assessment: User's guide.* Toronto, Canada: Multi-Health Systems.

Lehrman, F. (1996). Elements of interpersonal domestic violence torts: Some nontraditional alternatives. *Domestic Violence Report 1*(3), 3.

Maguigan, H. (1991). Battered women and self-defense: Myths and misconceptions in current reform proposals. *University of Pennsylvania Law Review, 140,* 379–384.

Mahoney, M. (1991). Legal images of battered women: Redefining the issue of separation. *Michigan Law Review, 90*(1), 24–30.

McCord, D. (1987). Syndromes, profiles and other mental exotica: A new approach to the admissibility of nontraditional psychological evidence in criminal cases. *Oregon Law Review, 66*(19), 24–25.

McNulty, F. (1980). *The burning bed.* New York: Harcourt Brace Jovanovich.

Meier, J. S. (1993). Notes from the underground: Integrating psychological and legal perspectives on domestic violence in theory and practice. *Hofstra Law Review 21,* 1295–1366.

Ostoff, S. (1995). Introduction. In J. Parrish, *Trend analysis: Expert testimony on battering and its effects in criminal cases.* Philadelphia: National Clearing House for the Defense of Battered Women.

Parrish, J. (1995). *Trend analysis: Expert testimony on battering and its effects in criminal cases.* Philadelphia: National Clearing House for the Defense of Battered Women.

People v. Daoust (Mich. 1998). 577 N.W.2d 179 (CT. App.), 184–185.

Perry, A. L., & Lemon, N. K. D., (1998). State court decisions regarding the use of battered woman's syndrome testimony. *Domestic Violence Report, 3*(35), 42.

Roberts, A. R. (1981). *Sheltering battered women: A national study and service guide.* New York: Springer.

Schecter, S. (1987). Guidelines for Mental Health Practitioners in Domestic Violence Cases 4.

Schneider, E. M. (2000). *Battered women and feminist law making.* New Haven: Yale University Press.

Shepard, M., & Cambell, J. (1992). The Abusive Behavior Inventory: A measure of psychological and physical abuse. *Journal of Interpersonal Violence, 7,* 291–305.

Stark, E. (1995). Re-presenting woman battering: From battered woman syndrome to coercive control. *Albany Law Review, 58,* 101–156.

Stark, E. (1999–2000). A failure to protect: Unravelling "the battered mother's dilemma." *Western State University Law Review, 27,* 29–110.

State v. Borrelli (227 Conn. 1993). *Connecticut Law Journal, 153,* 85–89.

State v. Kelly (N.J. 1984) 478 A.2d 364, 372.

State v. Smith (W. Va. 1996) 481 S.E.2d 747.

Strong, V. W. (1999). *McCormick's book on evidence*. Eagon, MN: Westhorn Publishing Group.

Thyfault, R., Browne, A., & Walker, L. E. (1987). When battered women kill: Evaluation and expert witness testimony techniques. In D. J. Sonkin (Ed.), *Domestic violence on trial: Psychological and legal dimensions of family violence* (pp. 71–85). New York: Springer.

U.S. v. Ezeiruaka (D.N.J. 1995). WL263983.

Walker, L. (1979). *The battered woman*. New York: Harper and Row.

Walker, L. (1984). *The battered woman syndrome*. New York: Springer.

Walker, L. (1989). *Terrifying love: Why battered women kill and how society responds*. New York: HarperCollins.

Walker, L. (1991). Post-traumatic stress disorder in women: Diagnosis and treatment of battered woman syndrome. Special issue on psychotherapy with victims. *Psychotherapy*, 2821–2829.

Westervelt, S. A. (1999). *Shifting the blame: How victimization became a criminal defense*. Piscataway, NJ: Rutgers University Press.

Wilson, K., et al. (1992). Levels of learned helplessness in abused women. *Women and Therapy, 13*, 53–67.

Part III

HEALTH CARE, ADDICTIONS, AND MENTAL HEALTH TREATMENT

12

Helping Battered Women

A Health Care Perspective

MARY BOES

VIRGINIA McDERMOTT

There is no such thing as a single-issue struggle because we do not lead single-issue lives . . . Our struggles are particular but we are not alone.

—Audre Lorde

CASE HISTORY

In the midst of a winter ice storm, the wails of ambulance sirens signaled a new arrival to the overburdened emergency room staff every 5 minutes. The ER waiting area was already crowded. Within this onslaught of urgent accident cases and emergent needs of broken bones and flu, Julia Crouse was finally triaged. Aged 35, a white female, well-dressed, trembling, and speaking with a shaking voice, she said simply, "I fell." "While going to the mailbox," her husband, Jim, interrupted. "Where are you hurting, Julia?" asked the nurse. "It's her right arm," said Jim. "Do you hurt anywhere else, Julia?" "Like I said," Jim replied, "it's just her arm." "Excuse me," the nurse responded. "Julia's the patient, and I need to hear from her where she's having pain." Jim stood and moved closer to his wife, snarling, "You have a real attitude problem, nurse. Let us see a doctor now." "I'll take your wife back to an exam room now, Mr. Crouse," the nurse answered politely "where the doctor will see her." "Please go back to the waiting area, and we'll call you after the doctor has completed his exam."

Tammy, the registered nurse assigned to room 5, warmly greeted Julia and asked her to undress and put on a hospital gown. Vivid purple blotches covered her neck and chest. Small, circular brown scars on her abdomen appeared to be cigarette burns. Angry welts crisscrossed her back. Tammy asked the clerk for any old ER records, and five past visits over 2 years

255

revealed a history of Julia seeking help for stomachaches, migraines, and other vague psychosomatic complaints, but also two other falls resulting in a fractured left wrist and clavicle. Julia had denied abuse in the past. Dr. Almundson examined Julia. "Julia, your X rays show your arm wasn't broken, but I'm concerned about these scars and burns. Did your husband do this to you? Are you concerned about your safety at home?"

Julia sobbed and then spoke:

> I love my husband. He has a very stressful job and gets upset when he comes home and dinner isn't ready. I'm just not a good housewife. If I was more organized, he wouldn't be getting so upset. We just got a new puppy for our kids. Jim became angry, his meat was overcooked, and the puppy was pestering him under the table. He flung his plate across the room and picked up the puppy with both hands around his neck, choking him. The kids started hollering and raced over to try to stop him. He knew how crazy the kids and I were about Cinnamon. He strangled Cinnamon, then threw me across the table, and I hit my arm.
>
> I just can't take it anymore. He used to beat me, then apologize and tell me how much he loved me and bring me flowers the next day. Now, it seems every day he gets angrier and angrier. Now I'm afraid the kids are older, and they'll try to intervene and be hurt too. But where would we go, how would I support them? He makes me give him my entire paycheck every week, then just gives me $40 for the week's groceries. He goes out whenever he feels like it, but I can't see my family or else I have to call him every hour when I do go out. He said he'd kill me if I ever tried to leave him.

"Julia," Tammy said, "you don't have to live like this, and we're afraid for your safety if you would go home. We need to take some pictures now of your wounds, and then we have a private room where you can meet with our social worker. She will discuss all of your options with you."

INTRODUCTION

Behind closed doors, an epidemic of domestic violence lurks, and fear cloaks pain suffered in silence and isolation. Yet statistics reveal a wailing wall of sound etched in pain. Julia's domestic violence, recognized through the effective use of an ER screening protocol, could have been just another statistic lost in the bustle of the ER with an overworked staff. There are 4 million Julias each year. Not only in the ER but also in doctor's offices, clinics, and inpatient hospital rooms, women often remain unidentified as abuse victims and slide through the cracks in the health care system. But because of the chronicity of the abuse cycle, the victim will most likely return and may still be reached when appropriate screening protocols are in place.

DEFINING BATTERING

Battering is abusive behavior that is harmful physically, emotionally, and/or sexually and results in physical and psychological trauma and/or illness. The assault could be between family or household members who are residing together at the time of the abuse. It could be between separated spouses or persons divorced from each other and currently not residing together. It could be between persons who are parents of the same minor child, regardless of whether they have been married or have lived together at any time. Finally, the assault could also be between persons who have been family or household members residing together within the past year and are not resid ing together at the time of the assault; this includes partners in lesbian and gay relationships. The vortex in the cycle of violence is the desire of the perpetrator to maintain power and control. The abuser, who often is not violent to anyone else but his partner, uses "intimidation, emotional abuse, isolation, minimalizing, denying, blaming, children, male privilege, economic abuse, coercion, and threats to maintain dominance" (Dunphy, 1999, p. 497).

Two of the strongest associations noted for both lifetime and past-year abuse in recent studies were having ended a relationship within the past year and being in fear of a current or former lover. To our knowledge, these are the first studies in the literature that have reported a significant association between ending a relationship within the past year and physical abuse. In one study, 18% of the women reported being at the emergency room for acute trauma from abuse and also said they were living alone and did not have a significant relationship. This could reflect abuse inflicted by a former significant other, which represents an important and underinvestigated category of domestic violence (Bachman & Saltzman, 1995; Campbell, Kub, & Rose, 1996).

What proportion of women are battered, and where do they go for help when trapped in a battering situation? Research reports claim high rates of ER visits attributable to domestic violence: 22% to 35% for symptoms related to continuing abuse (Campbell, Pliska, Taylor, & Sheridan, 1994). Some women deny they have been abused, although objective evidence to the contrary may be overwhelming (Freund, Bak, & Blackhall, 1996; Keller, 1996).

Hospital staff should suspect domestic violence if a patient presents with physical trauma, especially central distribution of injuries (i.e., to the face, head, neck, throat, back, chest, breasts, abdomen, or genital areas) or bilateral distribution or injury to multiple areas. Unexplained bruises, whiplike injuries-consistent with shaking, areas of erythema consistent with slap injuries, lacerations, or burns may be further indications. Multiple injuries in various stages of healing or evidence of old injuries that may not have been treated could also alert staff to the presence of battering. An injury of an extent or type that is inconsistent with the patient's explanation; a patient who describes the alleged "accident" in a hesitant, embarrassed, or evasive manner; sexual assault; injuries during pregnancy; and substantial delay between onset of injury and presentation for treatment may also be indications of domestic violence.

These are not the only signs of battering, nor are instances of battering or domestic abuse limited to patients presenting in the ER. Suspected abuse or battering may appear in the course of taking the medical history. Some battered patients present with no signs of battering, and others may present with less obvious signs such as evidence of alcohol or drug abuse in patient or partner, vague or nonspecific complaints (e.g., headaches, migraines, musculoskeletal complaints, malaise/fatigue, insomnia, chest pain/palpitations, hyperventilation, gastrointestinal disorders, eating disorders, depression, or anxiety. These patients may be using the ER visit to seek protection and/or make a plea for help. Suicidal ideation or suicide attempts, as well as complaints of pain without evidence of injury or pathology, may be an indication of battering. Repeated use of ER services, many previous "accidents," and/or psychosomatic or emotional complaints may also alert health care professionals to the reality of a woman having been battered. An overly attentive or aggressive partner accompanying the patient, who may want to stay with the patient during the physical exam and answer questions, may be a strong indication of battering. No prenatal care, abused children, and a fear of going home may further alert the medical staff to the presence of domestic violence.

PATTERNS OF MALTREATMENT

Patterns of maltreatment in families can take many forms, including physical abuse, endangerment, sexual abuse, emotional abuse, neglect (physical, emotional, educational), or economic (Smith-DiJulio & Holzapfel, 1998). The batterer makes the victim feel responsible for inciting the abuse.

> Intimidating behaviors such as yelling, smashing objects, slamming doors, cause lingering fear and threaten the victim with the possibility of more violence. Such emotional abuse "can increase the batterer's control by making the victim feel that she deserves to be abused and that she has no other options." (Shepard, 1991, p. 89)

The battered wife syndrome has three major components: the cycle of violence, learned helplessness, and anticipatory fear (Blair, 1996). Victims of abuse are "brainwashed by terror." The victim of abuse often uses denial and rationalization when she remains in the battering relationship (Blair, 1986).

Battered women rarely report incidents to health care providers but instead seek assistance with psychosomatic conditions (chest pain, choking sensation, abdominal pain, fatigue, gastrointestinal disorders, and pelvic pain) or with injuries for which they offer inappropriate explanations (Greany, 1984).

PREVALENCE AND INCIDENCE FINDINGS

According to the Department of Justice figures:

- Approximately 95% of the victims of domestic violence are women.
- Every 9 seconds in the United States, a woman is assaulted and beaten.
- Each year, 4 million women are assaulted by their partners.
- An American woman is more likely to be assaulted, injured, raped, or killed by a male partner than by any other type of assailant.
- Every day, four women are murdered by boyfriends or husbands.
- 93% of women who killed their mates had been battered by them.
- 25% of all crime is wife assault.
- Domestic violence is the number one cause of emergency room visits by women.
- Women are most likely to be killed when attempting to leave the abuser. In fact, they are at a 75% higher risk than those who stay.
- The number one cause of women's injuries is abuse at home.
- Up to 37% of all women experience battering.
- 60% of all battered women are beaten while they are pregnant.
- 334% of female homicide victims over age 15 are killed by their partners.
- Abusive husbands and lovers harass 74% of employed battered women at work, either in person or over the telephone, causing 20% of the women to lose their jobs.
- Injuries that battered women receive are at least as serious as injuries suffered in 90% of violent felony crimes.
- In homes where domestic violence occurs, children are abused at a rate that is 1,500% higher than the national average.
- 50% of the homeless women and children in the United States are fleeing abuse.

INDICATORS OF ACTUAL OR POTENTIAL ABUSE

Included in the client's history will be her primary reason for contact, which may include vague information about the cause of the problem, discrepancies between physical findings and the description of the cause, attempts to minimize the injuries, inappropriate delay between time of injury and treatment, and inappropriate family reactions (e.g., lack of concern, overconcern, threatening demeanor). Information from a family genogram may reveal a history of family violence (child, spouse, elder), a history of violence outside of the home, incarcerations, violent deaths in the extended family, or alcoholism or drug abuse.

The health history may also give an indication of actual or potential abuse. The client may have a history of traumatic injuries, spontaneous abortions, psychiatric hospitalizations, or a history of depression or substance abuse. Sexual history may note prior sexual abuse, use of force in sexual activities, venereal disease, a child with sexual knowledge beyond that appropriate for his or her age, or promiscuity.

Actual or potential abuse indicators in the social history may include unwanted or unplanned pregnancy, adolescent pregnancy, social isolation (difficulty naming persons available for help in a crisis), lack of contact with extended family, unrealistic expectations of relationships or age-appropriate behavior, extreme jealousy by spouse or partner, rigid traditional sex-role beliefs, verbal aggression, belief in use of physical punishment, difficulties in school, truancy, or running away. The psychological history may indicate feelings of helplessness or hopelessness, feeling trapped, difficulty making plans for the future, tearfulness, chronic fatigue, apathy, or suicide attempts. Included in the financial history as indicators of actual or potential abuse may be poverty, finances that are rigidly controlled by one family member, unwillingness to spend money on health care or adequate nutrition, complaints about spending money on family members, unemployment, and use of elders' finances for other family members.

Family beliefs and values that may indicate actual or potential abuse include a belief in the importance of physical discipline, autocratic decision making, intolerance of differing views among members, or mistrust of outsiders. Finally, family relationships that show a lack of visible affection or nurturing between family members, suppression of autonomy, numerous arguments, temporary separations, dissatisfaction with family members, lack of enjoyable family activities, extramarital affairs, or role rigidity (inability of members to assume nontraditional roles) may also indicate actual or potential abuse.

HEALTH CARE SETTINGS AND PROBLEMS

Research has generated significant knowledge about the health consequences of abuse in numerous health settings. Studies have documented a significant prevalence of abused women in a variety of health care settings (emergency, primary care, prenatal), with a range of physical and mental health problems correlated with the abuse (e.g., chronic pain, depression) and a general lack of identification by health care professionals (Campbell & Parker, 1992). Noteworthy physical health problems found across studies (both population-based and clinical) are headaches, backaches, risk of sexually transmitted diseases (STDs), and sleeping problems (Ratner, 1995). Descriptive clinical studies have suggested important health-related effects, such as neurological problems, hypertension, and urinary tract infections. In the areas of mental health consequences, research findings include a link between abuse during pregnancy and substance abuse (McFarlane, Parker, & Soeken, 1996). Depression has also been substantiated as a significant mental health problem of battered women. Battered women, especially those who have been sexually abused, were also found to have low self-esteem. Forced sex in battering relationships was documented as having important physical and mental health ramifications, including low self-esteem and unintended pregnancy (Campbell, Pugh, Campbell, & Visscher, 1995).

RECOMMENDATIONS BASED ON RESEARCH

All women coming to a health care setting for any reason should be routinely screened for abuse. Findings from both studies on abuse during pregnancy and other health-related studies suggest that universal screening for all women (including adolescents) for intimate partner abuse at each health care system encounter needs to become routine practice. Research has indicated that 40% to 45% of physically abused women are also being forced into sex, with resulting physical (e.g., STDs, vaginal and anal tearing) and emotional (low self-esteem) consequences specific to the sexual assault (Eby, Campbell, Sullivan, & Davidson, 1995).

According to research findings (Eby et al., 1995), it is clear that battered women, especially those who are sexually abused, are at increased risk of contracting HIV/AIDS and other STDs. There are complex interactions related to this issue that need to be investigated further. Some data indicate that abusive men may be particularly reluctant to use condoms and/or that their sexual partners would be afraid to insist on condom use (Eby et al., 1995). Other abusers, already prone to jealousy, may interpret a request for safe sex practices as meaning that the woman has been sexually promiscuous. In actuality, the reverse is more likely to be accurate. To place the onus of responsibility on women for men to use condoms is naive and demonstrates a lack of understanding of the sexually coercive experiences of many women.

The basic development of vaginal HIV virus–killing agents is already completed, but the progress to clinical trials has been relatively slow. The National Institutes of Health should be urged to complete clinical trials on these agents if pharmaceutical companies are not progressing as swiftly as possible. Because of violence and sexual autonomy issues, this could be the most significant advance in the prevention of the spread of HIV/AIDS to women, short of a vaccine. A recent investigation of HIV/AIDS in Africa determined that one third of the women who had tested positive were beaten by their husbands after they informed them of the test results. The possibility of domestic violence in situations involving research on women's issues needs to be taken into account in institutional review board deliberations.

RECOMMENDATIONS OF MAJOR AUTHORITIES

The American College of Obstetricians and Gynecologists recommends that women aged 19 to 64 should be counseled on domestic violence as part of periodic evaluation visits, which should occur yearly as appropriate. Women aged 13 to 18 and over 65 should be counseled on abuse and neglect as part of periodic evaluation visits, which should occur yearly as appropriate.

The American Medical Association recommends that all female patients in emergency, surgical, primary care, pediatric, prenatal, and mental health settings should be screened for domestic violence. The American Nurses Association recommends that all women should receive routine assessment and documentation for physical abuse in any health care institution or community setting. Women at increased risk of abuse, such as pregnant women and women presenting in ERs, should receive targeted assessment.

The U.S. Preventive Services Task Force believed that there was insufficient evidence to recommend for or against the use of specific screening instruments for family violence, but including a few direct questions about abuse (physical violence or forced sexual activity) as part of the routine history in adult patients may be recommended on other grounds. These include the substantial prevalence of undetected abuse among adult female patients, the potential value of this information in the case of the patient, and the low cost and low risk of harm from such screening. All clinicians should be alert to physical and behavioral signs and symptoms associated with abuse and neglect. Any individual who presents with multiple injuries and an implausible explanation should be evaluated for possible abuse or neglect. Injured pregnant women and senior patients should receive special consideration for this problem. Suspected cases of abuse should receive proper documentation of the incident and physical findings (e.g., photographs, body maps); treatment of physical injuries; arrangements for counseling by a skilled mental health professional; and the telephone numbers of local crisis centers, shelters, and protective service agencies.

IDENTIFICATION, ASSESSMENT, AND INTERVENTION: FOUR STEPS TO SUCCESSFUL INTERVENTION WITH BATTERED WOMEN

These steps build on Roberts's (1996) seven-stage crisis intervention model. The first step, according to Roberts, is assessment of domestic violence severity, injuries, and lethality. In step 1, Schechter (1987, p. 9) focuses on identification.

Identification includes the use of clinical indicators: central injury pattern, patterned injuries (injuries look like the object that caused them), and injury or injuries inconsistent with the patient's or accompanying partner's explanation. The patient may claim to be "accident-prone" or "clumsy," or there may be multiple injuries in various stages of healing (pattern of injury); a history of trauma-related injuries; an unexplained delay between injury occurrence or severe symptom onset and seeking medical treatment; or a history of depression, tranquilizer and/or sedative use, eating disorders, substance abuse, or suicide attempts. The patient may have had multiple visits to the ER for symptoms of anxiety and/or depression (Boes, 1998), or she may be accompanied by an overly attentive or aggressive partner who insists on staying with her or refuses to leave her alone. The patient may display an inappropriate affect, appear fearful of partner, have a flat affect, avoid eye contact, and so forth. The final clinical indicator is that the accompanying partner has injuries to his hands, face, or arms.

To facilitate identification, the mental health professional can place posters, wallet-sized cards, or brochures on domestic violence in bathrooms, patient examination areas, or wherever other patient information is displayed. The patient must be interviewed alone and out of earshot and eyeshot of any accompanying partner. Using nonverbal communication when assessing the patient is also helpful. Ask the patient directly if she is being hurt or threatened by her partner. Show comfort in asking questions about domestic violence; practice with coworkers.

The second step to successfully intervene with a battered woman is to validate her experience. Believe what the battered woman tells you, and be prepared to hear information that may shock you or be painful to listen to. Empathize with the woman's experience and validate her feelings of fear, confusion, love, and hope; reassure her that her feelings are legitimate and normal. Offer positive messages to counter harmful past messages she may have received. The following messages are very simple and powerful: "You are not alone"; "This happens to many women"; "You are not to blame for the things your partner does"; "You are not crazy"; "You do not deserve to be abused"; "You do not deserve to be treated this way"; and "What happened to you is a crime."

Advocating for the woman's safety and expanding her options constitute the third step of successful intervention with battered women. The woman's safety must be the primary goal of all interventions. Ensure that your actions do not in any way compromise her safety, regardless of any other perceived benefits of those actions. Recognize that she is likely to be the best judge of what is safe for her. Offer information about the formal network of services that may be available. In particular, provide specific information about local domestic violence services or shelters. Explore informal resources and sources of support to which she may have access.

Provision of ongoing, unconditional support is the final step. Recognize that you, as a health care professional, may feel frustrated, angry, or helpless when dealing with battered women. Find support for yourself and avoid transferring your feelings of frustration onto the victim. Remember that it takes battered women an average of six to eight attempts before a final separation occurs, and that ending the relationship does not necessarily mean that the violence will end. Recognize that it is a "success" if the woman is talking about the violence and beginning to explore options. Tell yourself you have done a great job if you have utilized these four steps in your intervention.

ASSESSMENT

Assessment for all forms of violence should take place for all women entering the health care system, regardless of their point of entry. At each contact, clients should be assessed on the following points: physical safety; legal needs; support needs and options; economic status; feelings of blame, isolation, fear, and responsibility; resources available; community shelters; support groups and counseling; legal options; safety plan; and economic assistance.

Women can be categorized into three groups in terms of abuse: no risk, low risk, or moderate to high risk. Women with no signs of current or past abuse are considered at no risk. Women at low risk show no evidence of recent or current abuse. Assessment of moderate to high-risk status includes evaluation of a woman's fear of both psychological and physical abuse.

Lethality potential should be assessed (Campbell, 1986). Risk factors for homicide in abusive relationships include physical abuse that has increased in frequency and/or severity; the abuser has used a weapon (gun, knife, baseball bat) against her; the abuser has threatened to kill her; the abuser has choked or attempted to choke her; there is a gun in the home; the woman is forced into sex; children are abused; abuse has occurred during pregnancy; the abuser is violent outside of the home; the abuser uses crack, amphetamines, "ice," or a combination drugs; the abuser is drunk every day or almost every day or is a "binge" drinker; the abuser is violently and constantly jealous; the abuser makes statements such as "If I can't have you, no one can"; the abuser controls most or all of the woman's daily activities, money, and so on; and either partner has threatened or tried to commit suicide. The determined risk level should also be documented, and any past or present physical evidence of abuse from a prior or current assault should be either photographed or shown on a body map as well as described narratively. It is important that the assailant be identified in the record, which can be accomplished by the use of quotes from the woman or subjective information. These records can be very important for the woman in future assault and/or child custody cases, even if she is not ready to make a police report at the present time.

INTERVENTIONS

Immediate care for a woman in a potentially harmful or present abusive situation involves the development of a safety plan. Important questions include the following: "How can we help you be safe? Do you have a place to go?" A woman can be given assistance in looking at the options available to her. Shelter information and access to counseling and legal resources should be discussed. If a woman wants to return to her spouse or partner, she can be helped to develop plans that can be carried out if the abuse continues or becomes more serious.

When there are no obvious injuries, assessment for abuse is best included with the history about the patient's (both genders) primary intimate attachment relationship. Answers to general questions about the quality of that relationship should be assessed for feelings of being controlled or needing to control. A relationship characterized by excessive jealousy (toward possessions, children, jobs, friends, and other family members, as well as potential sexual partners) is more likely to be violent. The patient can be asked about how the couple solves conflict, for example, if one partner always needs to have the final say; frequent and forceful verbal aggression also can be considered a risk factor. Finally, the patient should be asked if arguments ever involve "pushing or shoving." Questions about minor violence within a couple's relationship help to establish the unfortunate normalcy of battering and to lessen the stigma of disclosure. If the patient hesitates, looks away, displays other uncomfortable nonverbal behavior, or reveals risk factors for abuse, she or he can be asked again later in the interview about physical violence.

If abuse is revealed, the professional's first response is critical. It is important that an abused woman realize that she is not alone; important affirmation can be given with a statement about the frequency of spouse/partner abuse.

RADAR: A DOMESTIC VIOLENCE INTERVENTION OF THE MASSACHUSETTS MEDICAL SOCIETY

RADAR action steps were developed by the Massachusetts Medical Society in 1992.

R = Routinely screen female patients. Although many women who are victims of domestic violence will not volunteer any information, they may discuss it if asked simple, direct questions in a nonjudgmental way and in a confidential setting. Interview the patient alone.

A = Ask direct questions. "Are you in a relationship in which you have been physically hurt or threatened?" If no, "Have you ever been?" "Have you ever been hit, kicked, or punched by your partner?" "Do you feel safe at home?" "I notice you have a number of bruises. Did someone do this to you?"

D = Document your findings. Use a body map to supplement the written record. Offer to photograph injuries. When a serious injury or sexual abuse is detected, preserve all physical evidence. Document an opinion if the injuries are inconsistent with the patient's explanation.

A = Assess patient safety. Before she leaves the medical setting, find out if she is afraid to go home. Has there been an increase in the frequency or severity of violence? Have there been threats to her children?

R = Review options and referrals. If the patient is in imminent danger, find out if there is someone with whom she can stay. Does she need immediate access to a shelter? Offer her the opportunity to use a private phone to make a call. If she does not need immediate assistance, offer information about hotlines and resources in the community. Remember that it may be dangerous for the woman to have this information in her possession. Do not insist that she take it, but make a follow-up appointment to see her.

If the patient answers yes to direct questions, encourage her to talk about her experiences. "Would you like to talk about what has happened to you?" "How do you feel about it?" "What would you like to do about this?" Listen nonjudgmentally. This serves both to begin the healing process for the woman and to give you an idea of what kind of referrals she may need. Supportively assure the client, "No one has to live with violence." "Help is available to you."

If the patient answers no or will not discuss the topic yet clinical signs are present which may indicate abuse, ask more specific questions. Make sure the woman is alone. "It looks as though someone may have hurt you. Can you tell me how it happened?" "Sometimes when people feel the way you do, it may be because they are being hurt at home. Is this happening to you?"

If the patient denies abuse, but you strongly suspect it, document your opinion and let her know there are resources available to her should she choose to pursue such options in the future. Make a follow-up appointment to see her.

IMPLICATIONS OF EARLY DETECTION

Screening is usually considered to be a secondary prevention strategy. The aim of secondary prevention is to detect a health risk as early as possible to reduce the prevalence of disease and disability. Early detection of an abusive relationship can help victims to escape before the violence escalates, the entrapment leads to further isolation, and chronic health problems limit the patient's options. At this secondary level of prevention, helping patients to understand that the abuse will only get worse and that it is having an impact on their health and their children will allow them to make more informed choices.

Screening for domestic abuse with patients who do not have a history of abuse is an opportunity for primary prevention. The aim of primary prevention is to preserve health by removing the precipitating causes of departures from good health. Screening informs patients that domestic violence is an important health care issue and lets them know that you are a safe person to talk to if they ever experience abuse or if someone close to them is being abused.

A patient's history of victimization should be taken into consideration during case management. Withholding prescriptions and limiting access to health care services are common tactics of abusers that must be taken into account when determining a treatment plán. Health care providers need to know about the current violence in a patient's life, as well as any past history. The following case study highlights the repetitive aspect of domestic violence and the cumulative effect of assault, which destroys the psyche as well as flesh and bone.

CASE HISTORY

Ms. Smith was a 30-year-old single female with a prior history of polysubstance abuse and domestic violence admitted to the hospital because of decreased self-care and strange behavior. Her family reported that she had lost 20 pounds during the past year and had been unable to maintain gainful employment. She had had six or seven jobs within a year and had been self-isolating, not talking to people or interacting with others.

Ms. Smith's mother, aged 53, was living and well. Her father also was alive and well. Her maternal grandmother and maternal grandfather both had depression. She had one sister, aged 32, who was well.

The parents described Ms. Smith as a normal child until age 14, when she was gang-raped by three neighbor boys and developed a lot of anger.

Since age 16 she has dated an abusive boyfriend who regularly beat her up and pounded her head on the floor. Recently he broke her nose and quit living with her, but then he moved back in within 6 months of the injury and has beaten her up regularly since that time. Unable to care for herself during the past year, she has not been showering or eating well; she has been unable to take care of her animals and always appears to have just woken up. Her sister had recently tried to pick her up from the house, and the patient came out of the house without a top on. Having not spoken for days, she has been crying all the time and has not had a menstrual period for 15 years. A neighbor reported that a 70-year-old neighbor man had been going into her trailer and molesting her. When confronted with this information, the patient stated, "There is nothing I can do about it—all men are like that." She felt that being beat on by men was a normal experience.

On admission to the hospital, the patient was variable in response to questions. She had a labile affect, from tearful to angry to blunted, and had difficulty with simple daily tasks such as showering.

Neuropsychiatric testing was limited due to lack of effort. Occupational testing recommended 24-hour supervision and help with activities of daily living. Ms. Smith received physical therapy for rehabilitation of long-standing gait disturbance. According to the speech pathologist she displayed no dysphasia.

During the course of her hospitalization, Ms. Smith was initially treated with electroshock and Ativan and Phenergan for headaches; Prozac was instituted for depression. Her affect, behavior, thought processing, and self-care continued to improve. These results were received spontaneously. Elopement, suicide, and safety precautions were discontinued. According to the patient's family, she had experienced severe physical abuse with repetitive and serious trauma to the head. A computed tumogram of the brain revealed residual changes in the frontal lobe. This was probably due to chronic brain damage from repeated assaults. She was eventually given the diagnosis of traumatic brain injury, and plans were made to allow cognitive and physical rehabilitation following discharge.

Despite her families subsequent interventions, Ms. Smith returned to live with her abuser. The end of this tumultuous relationship came only after multiple restraining orders filed by Ms. Smith, numerous apologies by her boyfriend, and brief reconciliations. While en route to the police station, fleeing the last attack, she was dragged from the car by her boyfriend who beat her head on the steps of the police department. Ms. Smith's final admission to the hospital required the insertion of a feeding tube as Ms. Smith could no longer eat or care for herself in any way.

The human cost of domestic violence is great in terms of injuries, chronic health problems, and quality of life, whereas the human cost of screening is minimal in terms of time, money, and opportunity.

NEED FOR PARTNER VIOLENCE PROTOCOLS

More than a decade ago, the surgeon general called for routine assessment · of abuse of pregnant women. *Healthy People 2000: Midcourse Review and 1995 Revisions* called for the training of health care professionals to address the needs of victims of violence (U.S. Department of Health and Human Services, 1995). Health officials recommend that standard protocols be implemented in health care settings in the belief that "early identification, supportive education, effective referral, and ongoing support and follow-ups for abused women at primary care sites could eventually reduce the prevalence of abusive injury by up to 75%" (Rosenberg & Fenley, 1991, p. 150).

The American College of Obstetricians and Gynecologists has emphasized the existence of partner violence and the need for routine assessment of all women (Chez & Jones, 1995). The American College of Nurse-Midwives promotes screening for all women presenting for midwifery care (Paluzzi & Houde-Quimbly, 1996). The position of the American Academy of Family Physicians is that family physicians must know how to recognize and treat family violence (American Academy of Family Physicians, Commission on Special Issues and Clinical Interests, 1994). The Council on Scientific Affairs of the American Medical Association lists four steps to increase detection of abuse among female patients, beginning with routine assessment documented in the medical record. Specific protocols for interviewing in cases of abuse during pregnancy and for identification, assessment, and intervention in health care settings have been published (Parker et al., 1993).

In contrast to official recommendations, studies show that abuse assessment is not routine (Hotch, Greenfeld, Mackay, & Pitch, 1996; McGrath et al., 1997), assessment protocols are not common in emergency departments (Issac & Sanchez, 1994), and documentation of abuse assessment in the maternity medical records of health clinics is low. A few studies have examined the extent to which abuse assessment has been incorporated routinely into primary care settings. One study found that 26% of female and 19% of male obstetricians and gynecologists screen for abuse (Parsons, Zaccaro, Wells, & Stovall, 1995). A survey of patients and physicians in a variety of primary care settings showed that most primary care physicians never inquired at a patient's initial or annual visit about physical or sexual abuse (Friedman, Samet, Roberts, Hudlin, & Hans, 1992). A survey of patients in one family practice found that only 6% of the women had been asked by their physician during a recent visit about abuse (Hamberger, Saunders, & Hovey, 1992).

Rodriguez, Bauer, McLoughlin, & Griembach (1999) studied physician interventions with partner abuse and found most physicians are missing opportunities in a variety of clinical situations to screen for domestic abuse. Their study points to the use of screening protocols incorporated into "self-administered history forms." Part of the problem is that physicians are not trained to view violence the way they do bacteria and viruses. Despite its vast medical consequences, domestic violence is included in only 53% of all U.S. medical school curricula, with only about 90 minutes devoted to the topic. It has taken 20 years of chiding by women's groups to produce even a flicker of medical attention to violence as a public health problem (Roberts, 1998). Physicians are also products of a social milieu in which women are devalued, and violence against them is not merely tolerated but is a form of entertainment (Roberts, 1998). In Brazil in 2001, the popular "Face Slap" song was an instant hit, making many women's groups furious. Dancing back and forth in unison, men pretend to slap their partners, and women sway as if reeling from fake blows, as the chorus insists, "I'll let you have it, Mama." Often the fake slap turns into real punches.

Some researchers have evaluated programs designed to increase abuse assessment. One study found that the detection rate for abuse remained unchanged after an education program for the physicians and nurses of an emergency department and that only 50% of the abuse reported on a screening questionnaire was included in the medical record (Roberts, Lawrence, O'Toole, & Raphael, 1997). Other research showed that identification of abuse increased to 11.6% when one question about assault by an intimate partner was added to a self-administered health history form in a primary care setting, in contrast to no identification when questioning was left to the discretion of health care providers (Freund et al., 1996). Few studies have been conducted to evaluate the effects of including assessment and referral protocols in health services. Researchers found that the use of a specific screen in prenatal clinics to assess for abuse during pregnancy resulted in a 9% higher detection rate than a routine social services interview (Norton, Peipert, Zierler, Lima, & Hume, 1995).

The following protocol is used to ensure continuity of social work coverage in one ER used in a previous study by one of the authors (Boes, 1997, pp. 179–185). Where locally available resources are provided, social workers would use the resources provided in their own communities. Telephone numbers were listed in the actual protocol, but they have been deleted here.

Protocol for Crisis Intervention in the Emergency Room

Protective/Abuse: Assessment
Visually assess the patient for the following suspicious injuries:

- Bruises of several colors (indicating they were sustained at different times).
- Bruises that have odd shapes, are clustered, or are located in unusual places for an accident to occur.
- Retinal damage (from being shaken).
- Orbital or facial fractures (if patient was not in a car accident, suspect domestic abuse).
- Rope burns or marks from restraints.
- Signs of hair pulling (bald spots, loose hair, or swollen scalp).
- "Fearful behavior" (the patient may speak very softly, look around when answering, question the confidentiality of the interview).

Verbal inquires:

- Conduct a patient interview without family present, then conduct an interview with the accompanying person to see if there is a conflict of information.
- What were the events that led to the patient's admission?
- Who constitutes the patient's household (obtain the ages and health of members)?
- Were any family members ever treated for mental health problems?
- What is the patient's past medical history? (You are looking for a pattern of "doctor-hopping" or similar injuries in the past.)
- How does the patient's caretaker express anger?

If spousal abuse is suspected:

- Encourage the victim to file a police report.
- Explain that for her safety, the victim could have the abuser arrested and held in custody and/or take out a protection against abuse order on a 24-hour basis for up to 1 year.
- Encourage the victim to call a hotline from the ER; accompany and assist her.
  - Women Against Abuse: _____
    (24-hour counseling, shelter for women and children, and legal counsel
  - WOMEN IN TRANSITION: _____
    (24-hour counseling)
- Be alert for abuse and neglect in the children.

VIOLENCE AGAINST WOMEN: A SOCIAL WORK PERSPECTIVE

Although battering has been around since the beginning of patriarchy, until recently it was a taboo topic. Even today, it is very difficult for both men and women to seek professional or emotional help. Domestic violence can occur in any home, and the perpetrators and victims come in many different forms.

In a social work situation, it is extremely important to not let the people and situations we are dealing with become too personal—it would be much too emotionally draining and detrimental to the goal of our work. However, a balance must be maintained because our clients cannot become a "statistic" or a depersonalized subject. We can talk about battering and violence against women without feeling strong emotions. These words do not conjure up the reality that these women are experiencing. Sometimes we begin to see these people as "social problems" and the problems as affecting not a living, feeling being but a "relationship" or "family." An important part of being a social worker is being able to see the client as someone who is experiencing a situation that is quite unique to her, and must be treated accordingly. When working with these women, we as social workers have come into their lives at a critical point. Everything that we do and say affects the outcome of their lives. We must know what is appropriate to say, the options we can present, and how to approach these women in a sensitive and nonjudgmental way.

Throughout this chapter, many generalizations have been made about women in battering situations. It is imperative to understand that they are just that—generalizations. Every woman's situation is different, and every woman will react differently when dealing with her issues. Our job as social workers is not to make a decision for her but to guide her in her options and provide a support system. This is a time in her life where she may feel a great loss of control because her partner has taken control away from her, making it all the more important to let her know that she has the power to decide what to do in her situation. Even though the woman's safety is our top priority, many women are not willing to leave a relationship when we first see them. Although our first instinct may be to get a woman out *fast*, forcing her before she is ready will help no one. This is an enormous step in her life, and she must remain in control of her circumstances. If a woman feels that we are encouraging her to do something she is not yet willing to do, we may push her away entirely, and then we can do nothing to help her.

As outsiders, we may be able to see clearly what needs to be done to remedy a situation. It may be difficult, but avoid citing all the data on the subject to convince a woman to leave. Also we should restrain from telling a woman that we know how she feels, because most likely we do not. We can offer support without being patronizing. Besides sounding pretentious and insincere, we may be contributing to the client's passivity. For example, if a client's partner hit her because the dishes were not done, she may say, "I know that it is wrong to not get the dishes done, especially when he works so hard all day, but I got home from work late and they just didn't get done." Our first thought may be to say, first of all, that she also worked hard all day and, second, that it is not only the woman's responsibility to do the dishes; partners should share the housework. However, if we take this approach, she may tell her partner, "My social worker says that we should share the housework." If we instead explore the situation with her and let her come to her own conclusions, she will feel empowered by the decision she has come to and will believe that she "owns" this feeling.

Power is an important issue to keep in mind when talking with domestic abuse clients. Many women may feel powerless in a situation because they do not know their options. Power can be seen as something huge, such as leaving an abusive relationship, but it can also be viewed in terms of small accomplishments. It is empowering just to have the knowledge that other options are available. Power can be as simple as carrying around the phone number to a local women's shelter.

There are many stereotypes about women who are abused, the most prevalent being that they are weak, passive, and powerless. As social workers, we need to understand that there is nothing powerless about surviving battering. Most battered women feel that they have few choices, so they choose the one that they believe has the most chance of success. For example, if a man hits a woman because dinner is not ready on time, she will strive to be more punctual with meals. We should not judge her reaction to the situation but instead present her with options and support. We must focus not just on the victimization but on empowerment.

Even the way we think has an enormous impact on how we deal with our clients. For example, we must not compare victims' experiences with those of nonvictims. A good example was presented by Stout and McPhail (1998, p. 223). Imagine a classroom full of students. Half of the students were seated with 80-pound bags situated over their heads. If these students said or did anything that the teacher did not like, the teacher had the power to drop these weights on to them. The other half of the class could move about freely and say whatever came to mind without fear of reprisal. Obviously, the two groups' actions and dialogues were very different. The same concept can be applied to women who fear the threat of violence from their partners. They may believe that a characteristic of battered women is their passivity and submissiveness when in fact these are not preset personality traits but reactions to the constant fear of violence. In addition, many people minimize the pain and emotional trauma that these women go through. They may think of an assault as "just a slap" and believe that there is much worse that could happen. However, if you really think about it, it becomes a different story. Think about the person you love the most in your life, a person you would trust with anything. Now imagine that same person being so emotional and angry that he or she slaps you across the face. If you think of this happening to yourself, you can at least begin to comprehend the mental anguish that battered women must face.

Battering is one of the most underreported crimes in our country. There are many reasons for why women do not turn in their perpetrators or just get up and leave. Safety is a confusing issue. Many women fear for their safety if they stay or if they leave—not only for themselves but also for their children. As social workers, we must let women know of safe options if they do decide to leave. Many communities have domestic abuse shelters at secret locations. We need to inform women of legal action they can take, such as restraining orders, and of preferred arrest policies, which are taken into consideration in many cities.

Many women are also concerned about how they will survive after being financially dependent on their partners. Since much abuse and violence is about power and control, a man may try to control a woman's money by either preventing her from working or only giving her an "allowance." We need to be familiar with the current welfare laws in order to let women know what resources are available. Although governmental assistance such as food stamps is stigmatized, it has been a lifesaver for many women. We must let them know that receiving such assistance is not something to be ashamed of, and that it is certainly preferable to staying in an abusive relationship.

Poor self-esteem is one of the main results of women being abused. Many women blame themselves for what their partners are doing to them. They feel that if only they had done something different, things might not have ended up this way. Many even appear to hate themselves and hate the fact that they tolerate their abuse. Most women do not go into a relationship expecting to be abused. In fact, they may have been the ones who most adamantly insisted that they would never let themselves get into such a situation. Consequently, severe depression is an emotion that can be expected. With this in mind, depression and self-esteem must be dealt with along with the abuse. Knowing that one is loved and it is worth surviving is crucial. We must build a sense of community, a support system for battered women. Most likely, if they do not have support, they will not leave.

Finally, as social workers it is helpful to have a few general principles to help guide us when working with abused women, because one wrong move on our part can seriously damage their lives. This list was taken from an excellent book about social work and women called *Confronting Sexism and Violence Against Women: A Challenge for Social Work* by Stout and McPhail (1998). The list is simply entitled "What Helps Battered Women?"

1. Draw on women's knowledge of what is right and wrong with their lives.
2. Give the women information about resources that can enable them.
3. Mobilize the resources of family and friends. . . . Contrary to the message that is given in many substance abuse programs, family members do not need to (and should not) use confrontational tactics with their loved one. What they should communicate is their belief in the woman's experience, their concern for the woman's welfare, and their willingness and ability to support her when she is ready to make a change in her life.
4. Listen without judging. . . . We need to move away from this need to understand, which often leads to blaming and labeling, and instead just validate the women's stories.
5. Provide suggestions while supporting the women's right to make their own choices.
6. Groups with other women who have had similar experiences are essential for battered women to move beyond their sense of self-blame and to nurture the hope that change is possible. (p. 231)

We would like to end this chapter with a call for action. It is important that we read about and study the subject of domestic violence, but that is not enough. Because we have chosen the professions of social work and health care, we are confronted with these issues every day. They cannot and will not be resolved until our society and our whole thought processes are changed. Domestic violence has its roots in patriarchy and the sexist attitude that women are objects to be controlled. We need to do whatever we can to change these attitudes. Do something outright, such as volunteering at a local battered women's shelter, or something more subtle, such as correcting a person who says or does something that promotes hatred of women. Our careers as social workers and health care professionals will be much more rewarding if we can really change someone's life.

Assessment and intervention protocols for domestic violence are available for use in hospitals and mental health settings (see Roberts, 2000). For a comprehensive examination of the emerging roles for the ER social worker and clinical nurse specialist with battered women, see Boes (1998, pp. 205–229).

REFERENCES

American Academy of Family Physicians, Commission on Special Issues and Clinical Interests. (1994). Family-violence: An AAFP white paper. *American Family Physician, 50,* 1636–1640.

Bachman, R., & Saltzman, L. E. (1995). *Violence against women: Estimates from the redesigned survey.* Document NCJ-154348. Washington, DC: Bureau of Justice Statistics, U.S. Department of Justice.

Blair, K. (1986). The battered woman: Is she a silent partner? *Nurse Practitioner, 11*(6), 38.

Boes, M. (1997). A typology for establishing social work staffing patterns within an emergency room. *Crisis Intervention, 3.*

Boes, M. (1998). Battered women in the emergency room. In A. Roberts (Ed.), *Battered women and their families* (2nd ed.). New York: Springer.

Campbell, J. C. (1986). Nursing assessment for risk of homicide with battered women. *Advances in Nursing Science, 8,* 36–51.

Campbell, J. C., Kub, J., & Rose, L. (1996). Depression in battered women. *Journal of the American Medical Women's Association, 51,* 106–110.

Campbell, J., & Parker, B. (1992). Review of nursing research on battered women and their children. In J. Fitzpatrick, R. Taunton, & A. Jacox (Eds.), *Annual review of nursing research* (Vol. 10, pp. 77–94). New York: Springer.

Campbell, J. C., Pliska, M. J., Taylor, W., & Sheridan, D. (1994). Battered women's experiences in the emergency department. *Journal of Emergency Nursing, 20,* 280–288.

Campbell, J. C., Pugh, L. C., Campbell, D., & Visscher, M. (1995). The influence of abuse on pregnancy intention. *Women's Health Issues, 5,* 214–223.

Chescheir, N. (1996). Violence against women: Response from clinicians. *Journal of Emergency Medicine, 27,* 766–768.

Chez, R. A., & Jones, R. F., III. (1995). The battered woman. *American Journal of Obstetrics and Gynecology, 173,* 677–679.

Department of Health and Human Services (1995). *Healthy people 2000: Midcourse review and 1995 revisions.* Washington, DC: Author.

Dunphy, L. M. (1999). *Management guidelines for adult nurse practitioners.* Philadelphia: Davis.

Eby, K., Campbell, J. C., Sullivan, C., & Davidson, W. (1995). Health effects of experiences of sexual violence for women with abusive partners. *Women's Health Care International, 14,* 563–576.

Emergency Nurses Association Nursing Practice Committee. (1992). *Triage: Meeting the challenge.* Chicago: Emergency Nurses Association.

Freund, K. M., Bak, S. M., & Blackhall, L. (1996). Identifying domestic violence in primary care practice. *Journal of General Internal Medicine, 11,* 44–46.

Friedman, L. S., Samet, J. H., Roberts, M. S., Hudlin, M., & Hans, P. (1992). Inquiry about victimization experiences: A survey of patient preferences and physician practices. *Archives of Internal Medicine, 152,* 1186–1190.

Greany, G. (1984). Is she a battered woman: A guide for emergency response. *American Journal of Nursing, 84,* 725–727.

Hamberger, L. K., Saunders, D. G., & Hovey, J. (1992). Prevalence of domestic violence in community practice and rate of physician inquiry. *Family Medicine, 24,* 283–287.

Hotch, D., Greenfeld, A., Mackay, K., & Pitch, L. (1996). Policy and procedures for domestic violence in Canadian emergency departments: A national survey. *Journal of Emergency Nursing, 22,* 278–282.

Isaac, N. E., & Sanchez, R. L. (1994). Emergency department response to battered women in Massachusetts. *Annals of Internal Medicine, 23,* 885–888.

Keller, L. E. (1996). Invisible victims: Battered women in psychiatric and medical emergency rooms. *Bulletin of Menninger Clinic, 60,* 1–21.

Lynch, V. A. (1995). Clinical forensic nursing: A new perspective in the management of crime victims from trauma to trial. *Critical Care Nursing Clinics of North America, 7,* 489–507.

McFarlane, J., Parker, B., & Soeken, K. (1996). Physical abuse and substance use during pregnancy: Prevalence, interrelationships, and effects on birth weight. *Journal of Obstetric Gynecological and Neonatal Nursing, 25,* 313–320.

McGrath, M. E., Bettacchi, A., Duffy, S. J., Peipert, J., Becker, B. M., & St. Angelo, L. (1997). Violence against women: Provider barriers to intervention in emergency departments. *Academy of Emergency Medicine, 4,* 297–300.

Norton, L. B., Peipert, J. F., Zierler, S., Lima, B., & Hume, L. (1995). Battering in pregnancy: An assessment of 2 screening methods. *Obstetrics and Gynecology, 85,* 321–325.

Novello, A. C., & Soto-Torres, L. E. (1992). Women and the hidden epidemics: HIV/AIDS and domestic violence. *The Female Patient, 17,* 17.

Padgett, D., & Brodsky, B. (1992). Psychosocial factors influencing nonurgent use of the emergency room: A review of the literature and recommendations for research and improved service and delivery. *Social Science and Medicine, 35,* 1189–1197.

Paluzzi, P. A., & Houde-Quimbly C. (1996). Domestic violence: Implications for the American College of Nurse-Midwives and its members. *Journal of Nurse Midwifery, 41,* 430–435.

Parker, B., McFarlane, J., Soeken, K., Torres, S., & Campbell, D. (May/June, 1993). Physical and emotional abuse in pregnancy: A comparison of adult and teenage women. *Nursing Research, 42(3),* 173–177.

Parsons, L. H., Zaccaro, D., Wells, B., & Stovall, T. G. (1995). Methods of and attitudes toward screening obstetrics and gynecology patients for domestic violence. *American Journal* of *Obstetrics and Gynecology, 173,* 381–387.

Ratner, P. A. (1995). Indicators of exposure and wife abuse. *Canadian Journal of Nursing Research, 27,* 31–46.

Roberts, A. R. (Ed.). (1996). *Crisis management and brief treatment.* Chicago: Nelson-Hall.

Roberts, A. R. (Ed.). (1998). *Battered women and their families* (2nd ed.). New York: Springer.

Roberts, A. R., & Schenkman Roberts, B. (2000). A Comprehensive Model for Crisis Intervention With Battered Women and Their Children. In A. R. Roberts (Ed.), *Crisis Intervention Handbook* (2nd ed., pp. 177–208). New York: Oxford University Press.

Roberts, G. L., Lawrence, J. M., O'Toole, B., & Raphael, B. (1997). Domestic violence in the emergency department, II: Detection by doctors and nurses. *General Hospital Psychiatry, 19,* 12–15.

Rodriguez, M., Bauer, H., McLoughlin, E., & Griembach, K. (1999). Screening and intervention for intimate partner abuse. *Journal of the American Medical Association, 282,* 468–474.

Rosenberg, M., & Fenley, M. A. (1991). *Violence in America: A public health approach.* New York: Oxford University Press.

Schechter, S. (1987). *Guidelines for mental health practitioners in domestic violence cases.* Washington, DC: National Coalition Against Domestic Violence.

Shepard, M. (1991). Feminist practice principles for social work intervention in wife abuse. *Affilia, 6.*

Smith-DiJulio, K., & Holzapfel, S. K. (1998). Families in crisis: Family violence. In E. M. Varcarolis (Ed.), *Foundations of psychiatric mental health nursing* (3rd ed.). Philadelphia: Saunders.

Stout, K. D., & McPhail, B. (1998). *Confronting sexism and violence against women: A challenge for social work.* New York: Longman.

U.S. Department of Justice (March, 1997). Violence by Intimates: Analysis of Data on Crimes by Current or Former Spouses, Boyfriends, and Girlfriends.

13

Mental Health Assessment Tools and Techniques for Working With Battered Women

THOMAS L. JACKSON
PATRICIA A. PETRETIC-JACKSON
TRICIA H. WITTE

This chapter provides mental health professionals with information regarding assessment strategies empirically demonstrated to be applicable to battered women. Although the tools and instruments presented are specific to battered women, many may be applicable to other trauma or victim populations. Additionally, since many battered women have experienced a variety of past and current life traumas and may show comorbid psychopathology, assessment concerns related to these compounding factors will be presented.

PHILOSOPHY

The philosophy underlying this chapter is threefold. First, we want to stress to the clinicians and researchers working with battered women that violence within the context of an intimate relationship cannot be viewed as simply another symptom of dysfunction. Second, we wish to state that, for essentially every case, violence is not caused by alcohol or substance abuse, and that treatment of the substance problem will not alleviate the violence. Dangerousness and the all-too-real risk of severe injury or death to a woman as a result of battering demand that violence be assessed directly and as an issue separate from that of the relationship. Third, from the outset it is necessary to clarify that many symptoms and, indeed, diagnosable disorders may be preexisting or, somewhat more likely, a reaction to the violence. The reactive conditions usually involve depressive, anxiety, and substance use disorders. The preexisting pathology may include PTSD from prior abuse, anxiety and mood disorders, as well as one or more of the personalty disorders, such as borderline personality disorder. This issue will be discussed further in the section on global assessment.

We also espouse the following principles:

1. *Assessment protocols should be developed that meet the identified needs of battered women. Additionally, clinicians should employ empirically supported methods and measures that permit the objective assessment of a client's unique presenting problems.* Given the specific symptoms that characterize a woman's response to battering, problem-specific assessments are of greatest utility. Within such a framework, battering is conceptualized as a form of trauma, and the woman's symptomatic response to the battering is viewed as a reaction to a situational event or trauma rather than as an indication of personality deficits that somehow caused the battering (Walker, 1984). Additionally, in planning assessment strategies, clinicians must be aware of the range of symptoms that may occur and be prepared for client diversity in the expression of problems related to the battering experience.

2. *A contextual and cultural perspective must guide assessment.* Clinicians must recognize and never underestimate the impact of cultural and lifestyle variables on the battered woman's response to battering and her recovery (Dutton, 1992b).

The National Violence Against Women Survey (Tjaden & Thoennes, 2000) found that rates of intimate partner violence varied significantly among women of diverse racial backgrounds. Asian and Pacific Islander women reported lower rates than women from other racial and ethnic minority groups, and African-American and Native American reported higher rates. However, differences were reduced when socioeconomic and other variables were controlled, suggesting the need for further research. The survey found little difference between Hispanic and non-Hispanic women's reports of physical violence. However, compared with national surveys, research using nonrepresentative samples (e.g., shelter residents) found no racial differences among African-American, Latino, and Anglo-American couples (Gondolf, Fisher, & McFerron, 1988).

Clinicians should be aware of the numerous cultural and institutional barriers that impede help-seeking behavior for cultural minorities (see West, 1998b). In terms of assessment, there are many factors to consider besides the victim's identified culture. These include age, social class, economic status, husband's occupational status, level of acculturation, prior exposure to violence, normative approval of violence, family structure, and cultural coping strategies (West, 1998b). Gondolf (1998) provides further information on the special needs of women from culturally diverse backgrounds that is of value in guiding clinical assessment of such women.

Small sample surveys of violence in same-sex relationships suggested partner violence in gay and lesbian couples was as prevalent as in heterosexual couples (Tjaden & Thoennes, 2000). However, in the National Violence Against Women Survey, opposite-sex cohabitating women reported victimization by a male partner at nearly twice the rate (20.3%) that same-sex cohabitating women reported victimization by a female partner (11.4%). Same-sex cohabitating women were three times more likely to be victimized by a prior male partner than by a female partner.

It is important to understand the similarities and differences between same-sex partner abuse and heterosexual partner abuse. Abuse among homosexual couples seems to take the same form (Morrow & Hawxhurst, 1989; Renzetti, 1989) and pattern (Renzetti, 1992) as abuse in heterosexual couples. Same-sex partner violence also shares some common correlates of violence found in heterosexual couples, such as abusers witnessing violence in the family of origin, substance abuse, dependency and autonomy conflicts, and power imbalances (West, 1998a). However, despite these similarities, some control tactics are unique to homosexual relationships. One common control tactic among lesbian couples is homophobic control, which includes such actions as threatening to tell one's partner's family, friends, or employer about her sexual orientation and stressing that she has limited options for assistance in the homophobic society (Hart, 1986). Another tactic among lesbian couples is the myth of mutual battering. Some lesbian batterers repeatedly tell their partners that violence in same-sex couples is perceived as an equal fight. This is an attempt to further control and victimize their partners by denying responsibility for their abusive behavior (Hart, 1986; Renzetti, 1997). Considerations for assessment of lesbian victims include the need to gather information about these unique forms of abuse (e.g., homophobic control), the role of each partner, and prior exposure to violence (West, 1998a). Clinicians should also be aware of barriers to treatment seeking for lesbian victims. For example, a lesbian victim may be concerned about revealing her sexual orientation to service providers (Farley, 1992). In addition, she may be highly sensitive to homophobic and discriminatory attitudes within community services (Lie & Gentlewarrier, 1991; Renzetti, 1992).

3. *Clinicians must engage in ongoing self-monitoring of their attitudes, feelings, and behaviors.* As stated in chapter 14, self-monitoring of both the client's and the clinician's values is essential. We want to reinforce the recommendation for clinicians to examine and continually monitor personal values concerning battering and adopt an objective global philosophy before beginning any assessment with battered women.

4. *Clinicians must develop and use a clear and parsimonious approach to battering that will guide their assessment process.* Several models have been developed to explain the nature of responses to traumatic events. Since battered women's symptoms are conceptualized as responses to trauma, these models have also been used to explain the psychological response of a battered woman (Dutton, 1992b; Walker, 2000). Accordingly, battered women

are thought to experience similar reactions and use similar coping mechanisms as do individuals experiencing other disastrous or traumatic events (Follingstad, Neckerman, & Vormbrock, 1988; McCann, Sakheim, & Abrahamson, 1988).

Using this trauma framework, a clinician can estimate the severity of a client's response to trauma by assessing four variables: (1) the specific nature of the traumatic experience, including the extent of physical injuries and the amount of perceived threat or danger; (2) the adjustment of the victim prior to her most recent traumatic episode; (3) the response of the victim's social support system; and (4) the victim's coping and response strategies and skills.

Many battered women have had several life-threatening experiences (Dutton, 1992a; Mechanic, Uhlmansiek, Weaver, & Resick, 2000). The clinician should be aware of the woman's likelihood of minimizing the risk of harm to herself, which may have profound effects on assessment and preassessment interventions.

Clinicians must recognize that assault by an intimate partner is a unique phenomenon. Clearly, the literature, clinical experience, and firsthand accounts point to several differences between such violence and assaults by a stranger (Stark & Flitcraft, 1988). This difference is also present in the literature on acquaintance rape versus stranger rape (Jackson, 1996).

Even though battering is typically an ongoing process as opposed to an isolated, discrete event, the current episode of battering, which most likely brought the victim in for treatment, needs to be addressed foremost. Accordingly, assuring the safety of the victim and her children is essential. The assessment process cannot be started in earnest until safety is ensured. Furthermore, the clinician must be aware that the choice to leave the relationship may place the battered woman in danger of being stalked, threatened, harassed, or actually harmed (Walker, 1987).

After assessing the current episode of abuse, the clinician must address the ongoing process of battering. There appears to be a developmental progression of battering that makes it a chronic problem rather than an isolated event (Dutton, 1999). In many cases, prior exposure to other forms of trauma may complicate the response to battering (Humphreys, Lee, Neylan, & Marmar, 1999), such as childhood abuse or prior adult sexual or physical assault (Foy, 1992). This aforementioned and complicating developmental progression of battering must be clarified as the assessment continues in order to ascertain the current overall psychological state and stage of the battering victim (Dutton, 1999).

Clinicians must be aware that the assault sequelae from an intimate relationship are different than those from assault by strangers or acquaintances. Unlike victims of assault from a nonintimate, the victim of intimate-partner assault often is (or feels) trapped in the home or situation in which the violence occurs. External factors such as cultural, financial, and child issues may inhibit her from leaving. In addition, the context of partner abuse typically is not limited to physical assaults but also includes emotionally abusive and controlling behaviors that further restrict the battered woman from removing herself from the battering relationship. In addition, when one is assaulted by a "partner," the meaning of the event is altered (Foa, Stetkee, & Rothbaum, 1989) on a cognitive level.

Clinicians must also be aware that an adult victim of intimate partner abuse may face a negative evaluation by her partner, family, friends, and society in general. Victim-blaming attitudes have been demonstrated elsewhere and are potentially rampant in battering situations. Finally, if the battered woman blames herself, she may suffer even more debilitating trauma symptoms (O'Neil & Kerig, 2000).

THEORETICAL CONSIDERATION OF SYMPTOMS AND SYNDROMES

A substantial body of literature has delineated the scope and constellation of symptoms of battered women. Walker (1984) identified a cluster of symptoms that characterize the response to battering and termed this response the *battered woman syndrome* (BWS), which she considers a subcategory of posttraumatic stress disorder (PTSD). Although some research has critiqued the scientific basis for BWS (McMahon, 1999), this or similar models using a PTSD symptom framework have gained general acceptance by clinicians and researchers.

There is considerable empirical support for the presence of PTSD symptoms in battered women, particularly women in shelter samples. Three clinical samples of women living in shelters or women attending communityself-help groups have indicated PTSD rates ranging from 45% to 84% (Astin, Lawrence, Pincus, & Foy, 1990; Houskamp & Foy, 1991; Kemp, Rawlings, & Green, 1991). Kemp et al. (1991) found that subjective distress regarding the battering was positively correlated with the presence and degree of PTSD, intrusion, depression, anxiety, and general psychopathology. The extent of abuse also was positively related to both the presence and the degree of PTSD, depression, anxiety, and overall symptom distress. Prevalence rates of PTSD in a community sample of battered women have not yet been reported. Additionally, cognitive aspects of coping in victim populations have become a focus of clinicians and researchers. Douglas and Strom (1988) identified three categories of cognitions, differentiating them as a function of their onset in relation to the battering relationship. Includedin the first group of cognitions are those held by the woman prior to the onset of abuse; as such, they may contribute to an increased vulnerability once the violence occurs. These cognitions could be associated with prior victimization experiences, rigid sex-role socialization, or exposure to other life experiences that affect self-esteem negatively. A second category of cognitions develop as a function of the battering experience itself. These cognitions include perceptions of severity of abuse, attributions about the cause of the violence, and attributions about the solution to the problem. Distorted beliefs related to the battering experience are associated with self-blame and contribute to depression, helplessness, and hopelessness. The third category of cognitions are associated with the negative psychological effects of the violence. This class of post-abuse cognitions include judgments of low self-worth and personal effectiveness.

The population of battered women is heterogeneous, characterized by a range of reactions and coping strategies (Follingstad et al., 1988). Despite this heterogeneity, there appear to be a number of frequently identified sequelae that should be screened for during assessment. Thus, a clinician must be knowledgeable about the range of symptoms while remembering that individuals differ substantially in their responses to trauma and in the severity of the symptoms expressed.

ASSESSING BATTERED WOMEN

In assessing the dimensions of any traumatic event or battering experience and obtaining a history of battering, the clinician can choose among several methods. We recommend a multimodal assessment of battering, using a combination of structured interview, open-ended interview, and standardized scale and questionnaire methods. It must be stressed here that we view assessment as an ongoing process—a videotape, if you will, rather than a single snapshot. The goal of assessment is to cast a nosological net around the battered woman to yield a comprehensive picture of her past, present, and likely future responses, symptoms, and situations, as well as her potential progress in treatment.

Throughout the remainder of the chapter, we present a variety of interviews and measures, highlighting those that we view as necessary, helpful, or relatively untested. This is not to say that any particular scale is of limited utility, merely that there is limited clinical experience or a paucity of literature to support its use, primarily because of the recent development of these scales.

Interviews

While we do not deem any particular method of interviewing as necessary for adequate assessment, we do view interviewing in general to be essential. Most clinicians begin with an open-ended interview, allowing the woman to "tell her story." This format helps build rapport and establishes the woman's prioritization of issues. A second option is to use a structured interview in lieu of an open-ended format; the structured interview allows for contextual issues to be assessed in more detail (see Lewis & Roberts, 2001). A third option, which we endorse, is to begin with an open-ended interview and follow up with a structured interview.

In terms of content, the clinician must obtain information regarding the last few battering incidents. Additionally, information on the initial incident and a representative incident should be obtained. This will help determine the pattern of the abusive cycle, as well as developmental progression and potential escalation over time. The clinician should obtain a clear understanding of the sequence of events, without phrasing questions in a way that appears to blame the victim.

One structured interview the clinician might wish to examine, primarily for use in forensic evaluations, is the Battered Woman Syndrome Questionnaire (BWSQ; Walker, 1984). Used in a major research study by Walker, this comprehensive interview requires 8 hours of face-to-face questioning by a trained interviewer. Although its length makes routine use impractical, clinicians may consider this measure as providing a model from which to derive their own clinical interview protocol. In the Appendix included to this chapter, we have included an interview guide that can be used with battered women.

Standardized Measures and Questionnaires

Prior to discussing the history and specific measures designed for battered women, we will present issues related to psychometric properties and more general psychopathology. Our strong reliance on empirically sound measures is mirrored by some of the requirements in Lewis and Roberts 2001. Essentially, we insist on reliability (both internal consistency and test-retest), some form of validity measure (hopefully construct), and high utility, meaning that the measure is both effective and efficient.

With regard to more general psychopathology, when working with battered women, the clinician should assess overall personality and psychopathology (Dutton & Gondolf, 2000). In doing so, he or she may find it difficult to differentiate battering-specific reactions that may meet diagnostic criteria from preexisting conditions. This differential assessment (premorbid conditions versus post-abuse trauma response) is crucial for accurate conceptualization of the presenting symptoms. This issue will be specifically addressed in the next section on global personality.

Assessing Global Personality Functioning

Given the varied emotional and behavioral sequelae associated with battering, serious consideration should be given to routine administration of a global measure of personality functioning.

The clinician is strongly encouraged to consider routine use of the Minnesota Multiphasic Personality Inventory–2 (MMPI-2; Butcher, Dahlstrom, Graham, Tellegen, & Kaemmer, 1989) with battered women, particularly those with a suspected or confirmed compounded rape reaction or a pre-assault history of psychiatric care. We view the MMPI-2 as absolutely essential to any assessment with battered women and other trauma victims. Its clinical utility makes it a worthwhile assessment tool, despite the lengthy administration time (1 to 1½ hours). The test is also particularly useful in detecting underlying anxiety and depression in women whose behavioral coping styles may mask such problems.

Variability in profiles may reflect differences in premorbid adjustment, time since assault, type of assault, and overall level of posttraumatic stress. Rosewater's (1982, 1985, 1987, 1988) studies of MMPI profiles of battered women have suggested that clinical scales on the MMPI are often highly elevated, indicative of high levels of distress. Profiles for women still in the battering relationship or those only recently removed from the battering situation differ from the profiles obtained from women who have been out of the battering relationship for a year. Analysis of the Harris-Lingoes subscales (Harris & Lingoes, 1968) is recommended to more accurately interpret clinical scale elevations. The MMPI-2 also has two PTSD subscales, subtle and obvious indicators of PTSD; both subscales need to be incorporated in a comprehensive assessment of symptoms.

Having considered all this, the issue of reactive versus preexisting psychopathology must now be addressed. It should be obvious that formerly nondepressed women are likely to become depressed when battering begins. Further, when an individual has a long-standing personality disorder that clearly predates any abusive relationships, that should be noted, as well as the effect of the abuse. It is for this reason and others that we view the MMPI-2 as an invaluable tool to be included in the comprehensive assessment of battered women.

Self-Report Measures

Originally, self-report questionnaires assessing battering experiences were designed to identify the nature of abusive incidents to which the battered woman was exposed in the course of a battering relationship. The earliest measures, such as the Conflict Tactics Scale (Straus, 1979), focused primarily on physically abusive acts with minimal attention to psychologically abusive acts and no inclusion of items assessing sexual abuse. The Revised Conflict Tactic Scale (CTS2; Straus, Hamby, Boney-McCoy, & Sugarman, 1996) includes additional types of partner abuse (sexual coercion) and a consequence factor (injury), along with additional and improved items to assess negotiation, psychological abuse, and physical abuse.

Subsequent questionnaires were developed that incorporated more information regarding forms of abuse other than physical. More recently, attention has shifted to more detailed assessment of psychological abuse within the context of the battering relationship (see O'Leary, 1999). The clinician has several measures from which to choose when assessing psychological abuse. The need for detailed analysis of psychological maltreatment will guide selection of the most appropriate questionnaire for a particular client. If a highly detailed measure of psychological abuse is desired, the Psychological Maltreatment of Women Inventory (PMWI; Tolman, 1989; see later discussion) or its abbreviated version (Tolman, 1999) is recommended. The 30-item Index of Spouse Abuse (ISA; Hudson & McIntosh, 1981) would also be an appropriate choice if general assessment of both physical and psychological abuse is desired in a single measure. The ISA has adequate psychometric properties and successfully discriminates between battered and non-battered women. Wording is designed for female victims; no version for male self-report is available. Another measure that could be used to assess psychological abuse is the Severity of (Physical) Violence Against Women Scales (Marshall, 1992), in which 46 events involving threats and actual violent acts are rated on seriousness, aggressiveness, and physical and emotional harm. Marshall suggests both clinical and research applications for the scale, and community and student norms are available. A recent scale developed by Murphy and Hoover (1999), the Multidimensional Measure of Emotional Abuse, emphasizes a multifactorial approach for measuring psychological abuse. Tolman (1992) also suggests that clinicians employ the Daily Checklist of Marital Activities (DCMA; Broderick, 1980) to supplement the information obtained on measures of psychological maltreatment. The DCMA is a 109-item checklist that includes behaviors in which the spouse may engage during the course of a day. Behaviors that occur are noted and are rated on a dimension of pleasantness or unpleasantness.

Thus, in order to assess the nature of abuse, a clinician may select from several measures. When making this choice, he or she should consider the measure's adequacy in providing specific information regarding the forms of abuse experienced by a particular client. The aforementioned scales, if not elaborated later in this chapter, are ones we consider helpful but not essential. For each scale listed below, we will indicate its level of utility for a comprehensive assessment.

Assessing Abuse

The Conflict Tactics Scale (CTS) and the Revised Conflicts Tactics Scale (CTS2) are widely used and, in our view, essential for the assessment of abuse. The CTS (Straus, 1979, 1990) measures the extent to which intimate partners engage in psychological and physical attacks on each other, as well as the extent to which they use negotiation and reasoning to deal with conflict. Straus (1990) reviews the psychometric properties of the CTS. The CTS2 (Straus et al., 1996) includes sexual coercion and physical injury from assaults in addition to the original subscales. This scale has 39 items that inquire about specific conflict tactics related to the various subscales. The respondent indicates how many times in a specified time period (usually 1 year) he or she has acted in that manner. This scale includes 78 items which ask how many times the respondent has committed each act, as well as how many times the respondent's partner has committed each act against him or her.

The Psychological Maltreatment of Women Inventory (PMWI; Tolman, 1989) is considered helpful, though not necessary, in assessing psychological abuse. The PMWI is a 58-item scale that samples a wide range of behaviors. Parallel forms for men and women assess the relative frequency of abusive behaviors. The PMWI yields two subscales, which measure dominance-isolation and verbal-emotional abuse. Preliminary validation research indicates that the scale successfully discriminates battered from nonbattered women based on the number of acts endorsed and the two-factor sum scores (Tolman, 1992). More recent work (Tolman, 1999) evaluated the validity of the PMWI and found that it adequately discriminated between physically abused women, women in distressed but nonabusive relationships, and women in satisfied and nonabusive relationships.

Assessing Danger

Because of the risk of harm for battered women, it is essential to use the Danger Assessment Scale (Campbell, 1986, 1995), which was derived for initial screening with battered women to assess their danger of homicide. The most recently revised version includes 15 yes-no items. Either the woman herself or a health or mental health professional can administer the scale. The total assessment takes approximately 10 minutes, while the follow-up with the woman to discuss her risk takes approximately 5 minutes. The scale is based on a match with demographic factors associated with increased risk of homicide, such as presence of firearms in the home, sexual abuse, use of drugs or alcohol on the part of the batterer, high level of control, violent jealousy, abuse during pregnancy, violence toward children, and attempts or threats of suicide by the woman.

Goodman, Dutton, and Bennett (2000) emphasized the need for empirically supported methods to assess the risk of danger for battered women. They found that the Danger Assessment Scale was able to predict short-term recurrence of abuse. It is strongly recommended for its short administration time, empirical underpinnings, and ability to provide the woman with a concrete measure of her risk of danger. Since informed decision making is an important goal in working with a battered woman, this quick measure will permit her to make a sound decision about her safety or risk of danger.

Assessing Prior Avoidance, Escape, or Protection Attempts

In the context of the clinical interview, most clinicians assess the battered woman's prior use of specific coping strategies in response to the abuse. However, consistent with her emphasis on this factor in her conceptual model, Dutton and colleagues have developed a written questionnaire to assess this dimension. The Response to Violence Inventory (Dutton, Hass, &

Hohnecker, 1989) assesses the nature and frequency of use of specific strate-gies in the past, perceived effectiveness in terms of protection from danger at the time, and rationale for not using nonemployed strategies. The measure is designed to be followed by an interview with the clinician to provide clari-fication and greater detail. A copy of this inventory can be found in Dutton (1992a). Dutton also stresses the importance of providing an opportunity for the battered woman to describe the means she has employed to protect herself and others in the past using an unstructured interview format. We consider this inventory a beneficial though not essential assessment measure.

Assessing PTSD Symptoms

Little literature exists that reports the use of psychometric measures to assess symptoms of intrusion, avoidance, and arousal in battered women (Dutton, 1992b). Administration of the Structured Clinical Interview (SCID) for the Diagnostic and Statistical Manual of Mental Disorders (DSM) is one option (Spitzer & Williams, 1986), but some level of training is required prior to administration. Another measure that assesses intrusion and avoidance symptoms is the Impact of Events Scale (IES; Horowitz, Wilner, & Alvarez, 1979). This 15-item scale has the advantage of having been used in several empirical studies of battered women. We suggest that routine administration of the IES is not necessary; if used, it should be supplemented by the adminis-tration of a measure that assesses arousal symptoms, such as the *Symptom Checklist* (SCL-90-R; Derogatis, 1977; see later discussion). Scores on the IES are correlated with the PTSD subscale of Keane, Malloy, and Fairbank (1984), which is derived from the MMPI, and the Crime-Related Post-Trau-matic Stress Disorder Scale (CR-PTSD; Saunders, Arata, & Kilpatrick, · 1990). The CR-PTSD is a modification of the SCL-90-R (Dutton, Perrin, Chrestman, & Halle, 1990).

The PTSD Symptom Scale (Foa, Riggs, Dancu, & Rothbaum, 1993) and the Posttraumatic Diagnostic Stress Scale (PDS; Foa, Cashman, Jaycox, & Perry, 1997) are other psychometrically sound measures linked to *DSM-IV* symptomatology. The 49-item PDS includes six components—PTSD diagno-sis, symptom severity scale, number of symptoms endorsed, specifiers related to onset and duration of symptoms, symptom severity rating, and level of impairment in functioning—and has been used in recent studies with severely battered women (Mechanic et al., 2000). The Distressing Event Questionnaire (DEQ; Kubany, Leisen, Kaplan, & Kelly, 2000) can also be used to assess PTSD symptomatology based on *DSM-IV* criteria. When administered to vari-ous samples of battered women, the DES exhibited adequate discriminant and convergent validity. Kubany recommends the concurrent use of the Traumatic Life Events Questionnaire (TLEQ; Kubany, Haynes, et al., 2000), which mea-sures trauma exposure across a variety of stressful events. Most of the aforementioned scales are helpful, but due to their recent development, they do not have solid enough literature bases for assessment purposes.

Additionally, assessing PTSD symptoms is complicated by the difficulty of differentiating between the posttraumatic responses to trauma and the traumatic responses by which the woman copes with battering. For example, if a woman is abusing substances in an attempt to cope with the stresses of battering, although substance use may be considered a form of avoidance, other intrusion and/or avoidance symptoms may not be evident in assessment. Therefore, any assessment of trauma symptoms must consider the moderating effects of both threats of abuse and substance abuse, both of which will mask signs of PTSD (Dutton, 1992b). As with the assessment of preexisting personality disorders, accurate assessment of PTSD symptoms may not be possible until the woman has been in a safe environment for a period of time (Horowitz, 1986).

Assessing Other Psychological Symptoms

Depression

The Beck Depression Inventory II (BDI-II; Beck, Steer, & Brown, 1996) is an excellent, face-valid measure of depression. It measures the severity of an individual's depressive symptoms using 21 self-report items corresponding to the symptoms found in the criteria from the Diagnostic and Statistical Manual of Mental Disorders-IV (American Psychiatric Association, 1994). The items are individually rated using a range of 0 to 3, with 3 being the most intense. Total scores on the BDI-II range from 0 to 63, with higher scores indicating greater depression. Levels of severity of depression are as follows: 0–13, minimal; 14–19, mild; 20–28, moderate; and 29–63, severe depression. Psychometric properties, including reliability and validity, are reported in the manual for the BDI-II and are excellent.

Trauma Symptoms

The Derogatis Symptom Checklist-90-Revised (SCL-90-R; Derogatis, 1992) can be a necessary tool for assessing a wide variety of symptomatology if this is required. It is a 90-item scale in which symptoms are rated for the severity of discomfort they have caused in the past week. The test yields separate scores for somatization, obsessive-compulsiveness, interpersonal sensitivity, depression, anxiety, hostility, phobic anxiety, paranoid ideation, and psychoticism. Advantages include the correspondence between item content and common trauma sequelae and the scale's utility as a screening device for more severe problems associated with compounded trauma response.

The Trauma Symptom Inventory (TSI; Briere, 1995) is an essential instrument for assessing trauma symptomatology. Particularly relevant for battered women who report a history of early childhood assault, it assesses current emotional, behavioral, and somatic symptoms associated with adult interpersonal victimization. The 117-item TSI includes nine clinical scales and three validity scales. The clinical scales include a range of symptom categories: anxious-arousal; depression; anger/irritability; intrusive experiences; defensive avoidance; dissociation; sexual concerns; dysfunctional sexual behavior; impaired self-reference; and tension-reduction behavior. The normative group includes battered women, and several published studies have reported use of this instrument with battered women in shelter samples.

More recently, Briere (2000) has developed the 40-item Cognitive Distortion Scales (CDS) to assess five types of cognitive distortions that are particularly relevant to battered women: self-criticism, self-blame, helplessness, hopelessness, and preoccupation with danger. The test has excellent psychometric properties, and early studies suggest that individuals with personal trauma (both child abuse and adult abuse experiences) are likely to score in the clinical range on the CDS scales. We find this scale helpful not only for initial assessment of dysfunctional cognitions common to battered women, but also for treatment planning.

Assessing Alcohol Abuse

Alcohol has consistently been one of the most commonly identified risk factors and correlates of violence. The instrument we recommend, other than the interview to assess alcohol use, is the Quantity-Frequency (QF) Questionnaire (Grant, Tonigan, & Miller, 1995). This straightforward measure assesses the individual's typical alcohol consumption over the last month, including typical number of drinks and the highest number of drinks. It can be an invaluable manipulation check against substance use inferences.

Assessing Attitudes

The Domestic Violence Blame Scale (DVBS) and Modified Domestic Violence Blame Scale (MDVBS) are extremely helpful for assessing blame, though not necessary for assessment. The DVBS (Sandberg, Petretic-Jackson, & Jackson, 1985) and the MDVBS (White & Petretic-Jackson, 1992), developed for administration to clinicians, are clinical research scales designed to assess multidimensional blame attribution concerning domestic violence in professional, public, and clinical groups. The DVBS provides four blame scores consisting of offender, societal, situational, and victim blame attribution. The MDVBS provides five blame scores, assessing victim, internal disposition (personality) of both victim and offender, societal, situational, and relationship blame. Norms are available for physicians, psychologists, lawyers, shelter workers, mental health professionals, college students, and shelter samples. The scale can be used to assess attitude change following educational programming or training. Clinician administration provides a means of clinician self-assessment.

Patterns of blame scores have been found to be related to theoretical orientation and recommendations for treatment. Preliminary clinical norms for battered women are available (Rogers, 1998). The scale can be used to identify salient attitudinal issues that would be a focus of treatment with battered women, such as degree of self-blame versus perpetrator blame. In clinical administration, the woman is asked to complete the scale twice, once as it applies to battered women in general and then specifically as it applies to her own situation.

As with the DVBS and MDVBS, we believe that the Inventory of Beliefs About Wife Beating (Saunders, Lynch, Grayson, & Linz, 1987) is helpful for assessing blame, although not essential for assessment. It has norm based responses of 675 students, 94 community respondents, 71 batterers, and 70 advocates for battered women. The measure yields five reliable subscales. Sympathetic attitudes toward battered women are correlated with liberal views about women's roles and sympathetic attitudes toward rape victims. Abusers and advocates are the most dissimilar in their attitudes, and male and female students obtain significantly different scores.

SUMMARY

This chapter has attempted to present a broad spectrum of interviews, assessment devices, and tools that assess the effects of battering on women. We argue that these approaches should be used within a contextual framework and in conjunction with each other to provide the most accurate overall picture of the client, leading to the most likely effective differential treatment recommendations. As with all assessments, there is no single tool or combination of devices and interviews that will be right for every battered woman. We would never advocate using a single battery but rather suggest that the reader view the material presented here as heuristically fertile and learn from each assessment.

APPENDIX: INTERVIEW GUIDE

Petretic-Jackson and Jackson (1996) provided an interview guide that was designed to identify a range of concerns relevant to battered women. We recommend that this material be assessed in interview:

1. The Nature and Circumstances of the Assault

a. Circumstances (who, what, when, where, how); also assess defensive violence on the part of the woman; determine her level of perceived threat of serious injury or death to herself or others

b. Attribution of blame (victim's perception of the "why" of assault; is blame placed on self or batterer?)
c. Assessment of other aspects of relationship with batterer aside from the abuse
d. Type and extent of coercion methods employed (verbal threats; use of intimidation; use of children; sexual assault)
e. Level and nature of violence (threats of death, use of a weapon, battering); assess last few battering incidents to determine potential escalation; use Campbell's measure or other information to assess risk of lethality from batterer

2. Postassault Interactions

a. Professional contacts (legal, medical, woman's shelter or center); assess adequacy of response to woman
b. Timeline between assault and help-seeking (self-care; who did she talk to? who determined that she would seek mental health services?)
c. Social support system (friends, family of origin, children)
   1. Partner
   2. Family of origin/children (style of family coping; allowance for victim control, dependency issues, levels of support and blame)
   3. Friends (levels of support and blame)

3. Victim's Initial Reaction

a. Self-perceptions (in your own words, describe your thoughts, your feelings)
b. Symptoms: refer to the categories of physical, cognitive, emotional, interpersonal, and relationship issues; assess fear and vulnerability due to association with severity of PTSD symptoms; evaluate congruence between self-reported problems or symptoms and other assessment data; assess changes in vegetative function—sleep, appetite, weight, menstruation, elimination associated with depression, and/or anxiety; assess suicidal ideation, plan; assess any sexual trauma
c. Initial changes in daily functioning (job performance; relationships; social life; change or maintenance of place and circumstances of residence; need to visit relatives, future plans, etc.)
d. Mental status changes: judgment, orientation to person, place, time, memory, affect, cognitive functions
e. Changes in personality or behavior reported by others if collateral reports are available; obtain woman's prior consent for this; examine congruence between reports of victim and significant others besides the batterer; evaluate anger risk of homicide to partner

4. Current Status

a. Evaluate mental status
b. Coping efforts and strategies: identify defenses; assess strategies to escape, avoid, and survive; cognitive/affective coping—assess intellectual insight with or without emotional working through

c. Symptom expressivity/issue of prolonged crisis: Is there more to come? What other personal or social factors can exacerbate stress symptoms?

d. Identify mediating variables: prior traumatic experiences; other current life stressors; level of social support; cognitive coping

e. Continue to chart current psychological response pattern
   1. Emotional: PTSD: fear, anxiety, and intrusion (day or night in terms of nightmares); depression and anxiety; hostility and anger
   2. Cognitive: blame, safety, trust, intimacy, guilt, and shame
   3. Biological: physiological hyperarousal; somatic disturbances
   4. Behavioral: aggressive behavior; suicidal behavior; substance abuse; impaired social functioning; personality disorders; interpersonal sexual problems; sexual acting out; sexual dysfunctions

f. Ability to evaluate self-perceived strengths and weaknesses

g. Changes in lifestyle, life events, social surroundings

h. Social and political context (current feminist perspective)

5. Course

a. Presence or absence of premorbid psychological history, prior psychiatric treatment, prior psychiatric hospitalization, psychotropic medications, depression, and suicide attempts

b. Social functioning related to partner, children, and/or friends: dating or relationship status; stay in/leave abusive relationship; personal revictimization/new relationship functioning; violence directed at children; trust; assertiveness

c. Educational, occupational, social, and familial adjustment

d. Symptom fluctuation (use a graph to chart the symptom course)

6. Attributions

a. Attribution of blame (self, situation, offender)

b. Self-efficacy rating: How well do you feel you are doing? Do you feel it is taking too long to get readjusted? What had you anticipated? Are you pleased or disappointed at where you are now in terms of gains?

c. Attributions to legal-medical-psychological community: Were law enforcement and medical professionals supportive? Accusing? What could have been done to facilitate your coping?

7. Future Orientation

a. Short-term plans and goals

b. Self-statements (ability to reinforce strategies used and gains made)

c. Realistic optimism regarding relationships and own recovery
   (I can recognize that sometimes I am responding to my current partner not for what he is doing but because I'm thinking about my ex. If I keep that in mind, I'll eventually be able to react to him given what I can judge from his behavior, not from my fears about what happened in the past.)

REFERENCES

American Psychiatric Association. (1994). *Diagnostic and statistical manual of mental disorders* (4th ed.). Washington, DC: Author.

Astin, M. C., Lawrence, K., Pincus, G., & Foy, D. (1990, October). *Moderator variables for PTSD among battered women.* Paper presented at the convention of the International Society for Traumatic Stress Studies, New Orleans, LA.

Beck, A. A., Steer, R. A., & Brown, G. K. (1996). *The manual for the Beck Depression Inventory-II.* San Antonio, TX: Psychological Corporation.

Briere, J. (1995). *The Trauma Symptom Inventory.* Odessa, FL: Psychological Assessment Resources, Inc.

Briere, J. (2000). *Cognitive Distortion Scales.* Odessa, FL: Psychological Assessment Resources, Inc.

Broderick, J. (1980). *Attitudinal and behavioral components of marital satisfaction.* Unpublished doctoral dissertation, State University of New York at Stony Brook.

Butcher, J. N., Dahlstrom, W. G., Graham, J. R., Tellegen, A. M., & Kaemmer, B. (1989). *MMPI-2: Manual for administration and scoring.* Minneapolis: University of Minnesota Press.

Campbell, J. (1986). Nursing assessment for risk of homicide with battered women. *Advances in Nursing Science, 8*(4), 36–51.

Campbell, J. (1995). Prediction of homicide of and by battered women. In J. Campbell (Ed.), *Assessing dangerousness: Violence by sexual offenders, batterers and child abusers* (pp. 96–113). Thousand Oaks, CA: Sage.

Derogatis, L. R. (1992). *SCL-90-R: Administration, scoring, and procedures manual-11.* Towson, MD: Clinical Psychometrics Research, Inc.

Douglas, M., & Strom, J. (1988). Cognitive therapy with battered women.

Special Issue: Cognitive-behavior therapy with women. *Journal of Rational Emotive and Cognitive Behavior Therapy, 6*(1–2), 33–49.

Dutton, M. A. (1992a). Assessment and treatment of post-traumatic stress disorder among battered women. In D. Foy (Ed.), *Treating PTSD: Cognitive-behavioral strategies* (pp. 69–98). New York: Guilford.

Dutton, M. A. (1992b). *Empowering and healing the battered woman.* New York: Springer.

Dutton, M. A. (1999). Commentary: Multidimensional assessment of women battering: Commentary on Smith, Smith, and Earp. *Psychology of Women Quarterly, 23,* 195–198.

Dutton, M. A., & Gondolf, E. W. (2000). Wife battering. In R. T. Ammerman & M. Hersen (Eds.), *Case studies in family violence* (2nd ed., pp. 323–348). New York: Kluwer Academic/Plenum Publishers.

Dutton, M. A., Hass, G., & Hohnecker, L. (1989). *Response to Violence Inventory.* Unpublished manuscript, Nova University, Ft. Lauderdale, FL.

Dutton, M. A., Perrin, S., Chrestman, K., & Halle, P. (1990, August). *MMPI trauma profiles for battered women.* Paper presented at the annual convention of the American Psychological Association, Boston.

Farley, N. (1992). Same-sex domestic violence. In S. H. Dworkin & F. J. Gutierez (Eds.), *Counseling gay men and lesbians: Journey to the end of the rainbow* (pp. 231–242). Alexandria, VA: American Association for Counseling and Development.

Foa, E. B., Cashman, L., Jaycox, L., and Perry, K. (1997). The validation of a self-report measure of posttraumatic stress disorder: The Posttraumatic Diagnostic Scale. *Psychological Assessment, 9,* 445–451.

Foa, E., Riggs, D. S., Dancu, C. V., & Rothbaum, B. O. (1993). Reliability and validity of a brief instrument for assessing posttraumatic stress disorder. *Journal of Traumatic Stress, 6,* 459–474.

Foa, E., Stetkee, G., & Rothbaum, B. (1989). Behavioral/cognitive conceptualization of post-traumatic stress disorder. *Behavior Therapy, 20,* 155–176.

Follingstad, D., Neckerman, A., & Vormbrock, J. (1988). Reactions to victimization and coping strategies of battered women: The ties that bind. *Clinical Psychology Review, 8,* 373–390.

Foy, D. W. (1992). Introduction and description of the disorder. In D. W. Foy (Ed.), *Treating PTSD: Cognitive-behavioral strategies* (pp. 1–12). New York: Guilford.

Gondolf, E. W. (1998). *Assessing woman battering in mental health services.* Thousand Oaks, CA: Sage.

Gondolf, E. W., Fisher, E. R., & McFerron, R. (1988). Racial differences among shelter residents. *Journal of Family Violence, 12,* 39–51.

Goodman, L. A., Dutton, M. A., & Bennett, L. (2000). Predicting repeat abuse among arrested batterers: Use of the Danger Assessment Scale in the criminal justice system. *Journal of Interpersonal Violence, 15,* 63–74.

Grant, K. A., Tonigan, J. S., & Miller, W. R. (1995). Comparison of three alcohol consumption measures: A concurrent validity study. *Journal of Studies on Alcohol, 56,* 168–172.

Harris, R. E., & Lingoes, J. D. (1968) *Subscales for the Minnesota Multiphasic Personality Inventory.* Mimeographed materials, Langley Porter Clinic.

Hart, B. (1986). Lesbian battering: An examination. In K. Lobel (Ed.), *Naming the violence: Speaking out about lesbian battering* (pp. 173–189). Seattle, WA: Seal.

Horowitz, M. (1986). *Stress response syndromes* (2nd ed.). Northvale, NJ: Jason Aronson.

Horowitz, M., Wilner, N., & Alvarez, W. (1979). Impact of Events Scale: A measure of subjective distress. *Psychosomatic Medicine, 41,* 209–218.

Houskamp, B. M., & Foy, D. W. (1991). The assessment of posttraumatic stress disorder in battered women. *Journal of Interpersonal Violence, 6,* 367–375.

Hudson, W., & McIntosh, S. (1981). The assessment of spouse abuse: Two quantifiable dimensions. *Journal of Marriage and the Family, 43,* 873–885.

Humphreys, J., Lee, K., Neylan, T., & Marmar, C. (1999). Trauma history of sheltered battered women. *Issues in Mental Health Nursing, 20,* 319–332.

Jackson, T. L. (1996). *Acquaintance rape: Assessment, treatment, and prevention.* Sarasota, FL: Professional Research Press.

Keane, T., Malloy, P., & Fairbank, J. (1984). Empirical development of an MMPI subscale for the assessment of combat-related post-traumatic stress disorder. *Journal of Consulting and Clinical Psychology, 52,* 888–891.

Kemp, A., Rawlings, E., & Green, B. (1991). Post-traumatic stress disorder (PTSD) in battered women: A shelter sample. *Journal of Traumatic Stress, 4,* 137–148.

Kubany, E. S., Haynes, S. N., Leisen, M. B., Ownes, J. A., Kaplan, A. S., Watson, S. B., & Burns, K. (2000). Development and preliminary validation of a brief broad-spectrum measure of trauma exposure: The Traumatic Life Events Questionnaire. *Psychological Assessment, 12,* 200–224.

Kubany, E. S., Leisen, M. B., Kaplan, A. S., & Kelly, M. P. (2000). Validation of a brief measure of posttraumatic stress disorder: The Distressing Event Questionnaire (DEQ). *Psychological Assessment, 12,* 197–209.

Lewis, S., & Roberts, A. R. (2001). Crisis assessment tools: The good, the bad, and the available. In *Brief treatment and crisis intervention, 1*(1), 17–28.

Lie, G. Y., & Gentlewarrier, S. (1991). Intimate violence in lesbian relationships: Discussion of survey findings and practice implications. *Journal of Social Service Research, 15,* 41–59.

Marshall, L. L. (1992). Development of the Severity of Violence Against Women Scales. *Journal of Family Violence, 7,* 103–120.

McCann, I. L., Sakheim, D., & Abrahamson, D. (1988). Trauma and victimization: A model of psychological adaptation. *Counseling Psychologist, 16,* 531–594.

McMahon, M. (1999). Battered women and bad science: The limited validity and utility of battered woman syndrome. *Psychiatry, Psychology, and Law, 6,* 23–49.

Mechanic, M. B., Uhlmansiek, M. H., Weaver, T., & Resick, P. A. (2000). The impact of severe stalking experienced by acutely battered women: An examination of violence, psychological symptoms, and strategic responding. *Violence and Victims, 15,* 443–458.

Morrow, S. L., & Hawxhurst, D. M. (1989). Lesbian partner abuse: Implications for therapists. *Journal of Counseling and Development, 68,* 58–62.

Murphy, C. M., & Hoover, S. A. (1999). Measuring emotional abuse in dating relationships as a multifactorial construct. *Violence and Victims, 14,* 39–53.

O'Leary, D. K. (1999). Psychological abuse: A variable deserving critical attention in domestic violence. *Violence and Victims, 14,* 3–23.

O'Neil, M. L., & Kerig, P. K. (2000). Attributions of self-blame and perceived control as moderators of adjustment in battered women. *Journal of Interpersonal Violence, 15,* 1036–1049.

Petretic-Jackson, P., & Jackson, T. (1996). Mental health interventions with battered women. In A. Roberts (Ed.), *Helping battered women* (pp. 188–221). New York: Oxford University Press.

Renzetti, C. (1989). Building a second closet: Third party responses to victims of lesbian partner abuse. *Family Relations, 38,* 157–163.

Renzetti, C. (1992). *Violent betrayal: Partner abuse in lesbian relationships.* Newbury Park, CA: Sage.

Renzetti, C. M. (1997). Violence and abuse among same-sex couples. In A. P. Cardarelli (Ed.), *Violence between intimate partners: Patterns, causes, and effects* (pp. 70–89). Boston: Allyn and Bacon.

Rogers, J. D. (1998). *Blame distribution and trauma-related symptoms with a domestic violence population.* Unpublished doctoral dissertation, University of Arkansas.

Rosewater, L. B. (1982). *The development of an MMPI profile for battered women.* Unpublished doctoral dissertation, the Union for Experimenting Colleges and Universities.

Rosewater, L. B. (1985). Schizophrenic, borderline or battered? In L. B. Rosewater & L. Walker (Eds.), *Handbook of feminist therapy: Women's issues in psychotherapy* (pp. 215–225). New York: Springer.

Rosewater, L. B. (1987). A critical analysis of the proposed self-defeating personality disorder. *Journal of Personality Disorders, 1,* 190–195.

Rosewater, L. B. (1988). Battered or schizophrenic? Psychologists can't tell. In K. Yllo & C. Bograh (Eds.), *Feminist perspectives on wife abuse* (pp. 200–216). Beverly Hills, CA: Sage.

Sandberg, G. G., Petretic-Jackson, P., & Jackson, T. L. (1985, May). *Definition and attribution of blame in domestic violence.* Paper presented at the Midwestern Psychological Association Convention, Chicago.

Saunders, B. E., Arata, C., & Kilpatrick, D. (1990). Development of a crime-related post-traumatic stress disorder scale for women within the Symptom Checklist-90-Revised. *Journal of Traumatic Stress, 3,* 439–448.

Saunders, D., Lynch, A., Grayson, M., & Linz, D. (1987). The Inventory of Beliefs about Wife Beating: The construction and initial validation of a measure of beliefs and attitudes. *Violence and Victims, 2,* 39–57.

Spitzer, R. L., & Williams, J. B. (1986). *Structured clinical interview for DSM III-R.* New York: New York State Psychiatric Institute.

Stark, E., & Flitcraft, A. (1988). Personal power and institutional victimization: Treating the dual trauma of woman battering. In F. M. Ochberg (Ed.), *Post-traumatic therapy and victims of violence* (pp. 115–151). Philadelphia, PA: Brunner/Mazel, Inc.

Straus, M. (1979). Measuring intrafamilial conflict and violence: The conflict tactics (CT) scales. *Journal of Marriage and the Family, 45,* 75–88.

Straus, M. A. (1990). New scoring methods for violence and new forms for the Conflict Tactics Scale. In M. A. Straus & R. J. Gelles (Eds.), *Physical violence in American families: Risk factors and adaptations to violence in 8,145 families* (pp. 535–559). New Brunswick, NJ: Transaction.

Straus, M. A., Hamby, S. L., Boney-McCoy, S., & Sugarman, D. B. (1996). The Revised Conflict Tactics Scale (CTS2): Development and preliminary psychometric data. *Journal of Family Issues, 17,* 283–316.

Tjaden, P., & Thoennes, N. (2000). *Extent, nature, and consequences of intimate partner violence: Findings from the National Violence Against Women Survey.* NCJ Report No. NCJ 181867. Washington, DC: U.S. Department of Justice.

Tolman, R. M. (1989). The development of a measure of psychological maltreatment of women by their male partners. *Violence and Victims, 4,* 159–177.

Tolman, R. M. (1992). Psychological abuse of women. In R. T. Ammerman & M. Hersen (Eds.), *Assessment of family violence: A clinical and legal sourcebook* (pp. 291–310). New York: Wiley.

Tolman, R. M. (1999). The validation of the Psychological Maltreatment of Woman Inventory. *Violence and Victims, 14,* 25–37.

Walker, L. (1984). *The battered woman syndrome.* New York: Springer.

Walker, L. (1987). Assessment and intervention with battered women. In L. Ritt & P. Keller (Eds.), *Innovations in clinical practice: A sourcebook* (vol. 6, pp. 131–142). Sarasota, FL: Professional Resource Exchange, Inc.

Walker, L. (2000). *Battered women and survivor therapy: A practical guide for the psychotherapist.* Washington, DC: American Psychological Association.

West, C. M. (1998a). Leaving a second closet: Outing partner violence in same-sex couples. In J. L. Jasinski & L. M. Williams (Eds.), *Partner violence: A comprehensive review of 20 years of research.* Thousand Oaks, CA: Sage.

West, C. M. (1998b). Lifting the political gag order: Breaking the silence around partner violence in ethnic minority families. In J. L. Jasinski & L. M. Williams (Eds.), *Partner violence: A comprehensive review of 20 years of research.* Thousand Oaks, CA: Sage.

White, P., & Petretic-Jackson, P. (1992, August). *Psychologists' patterns of blame attribution for wife abuse.* Paper presented at the meeting of the American Psychological Association, Washington, DC.

14

Battered Women

Treatment Goals and Treatment Planning

PATRICIA A. PETRETIC-JACKSON
TRICIA H. WITTE
THOMAS L. JACKSON

In a recent review of clinical practice with battered women, Lundy and Grossman (2001) note that practitioners working with battered women often use a combination of modalities and a range of models and theories to guide their interventions. At the same time, there is little empirical research on the effectiveness of therapeutic interventions with battered women. This limited knowledge may be attributed in part to the failure of mental health professionals to identify issues of domestic violence in treatment-seeking battered women. Battered women may not identify battering as their primary reason for seeking mental health services. Consequently, providers of medical, mental health, and substance abuse services need to be aware that domestic violence may be a significant contributing factor to a wide range of physical and mental health problems. Battered women have been found to be at increased risk for posttraumatic stress disorder (PTSD; Jones, Hughes, & Unterstaller, 2001), somatization, substance abuse (Elliott, 1994), suicidal ideation and risk (Thompson et al., 1999), panic disorder, and anxiety (Roberts & Burman, 1998). Additionally, although mental health professionals are becoming increasingly aware that PTSD is a common outcome of battering, a frequent criticism of clinicians who are unfamiliar with PTSD is that they often overlook trauma symptoms and limit treatment to a focus on depression (Jones et al., 2001). Finally, as Lundy and Grossman (2001) rightly point out, conducting psychotherapy process and outcome research is a difficult undertaking under any circumstances, but it may be further complicated when clients seek services on a sporadic basis because of poverty or safety issues.

Women who have been battered in their intimate relationships provide many unique treatment challenges for the clinician. Many battered women have experienced a variety of past and current life stressors in addition to discrete battering episodes. Prior trauma history often compounds their response to battering. For women who identify premorbid psychopathology, such as a history of depression or an anxiety disorder, symptoms may more accurately reflect their response to preexisting traumas. It is important for clinicians to recognize that symptoms such as intrusive thoughts, numbing of affect, substance misuse, dependency, and affective instability usually reflect a woman's posttraumatic response to her abusive environment. This conceptualization provides the focus for intervention, which most often deals with one or more of the following goals: increasing safety, enhancing problem-solving and choice-making skills, and ameliorating psychological effects of battering and related trauma. Recently, clinical researchers (Foa, Cascardi, Zoellner, & Feeny, 2000; Roberts & Roberts, 2000) have specified the additional focus of identifying a woman's personal resilience and other strengths so that she becomes the agent of her life change. While a comprehensive review of the literature on battered women is beyond the scope of this chapter, the reader is referred to several other sources for reviews of topics relevant to intervention. A further review of research on PTSD in battered women can be found in Jones et al. (2001), while a review of clinical theory, including recent integrated models, as well as outcome research can be found in the same volume (Lundy & Grossman, 2001). An overview of assessment of abuse and symptomatic distress in battered women can be found in Jackson, Petretic-Jackson, and Witte (2001). The current chapter provides a framework for intervention with women who are victims or survivors of violence in their primary intimate relationship and reviews intervention goals, planning, and specific strategies that address their needs.

PHILOSOPHY

We recommend that clinical interventions with battered women be guided by the following considerations:

1. *Intervention goals should be appropriate to an individual woman's needs and reflect her right to self-determination.* Therapy with battered women benefits from an integrated model that incorporates a feminist perspective (Lundy & Grossman, 2001). Both Dutton (1992a) and Walker (1993, 1994a, 1994b) employ a cognitive behavioral treatment and intrapersonal theory within a feminist framework. In this perspective the relationship between therapist and client is more egalitarian, and setting goals is a collaborative process. At the same time, the clinician must ensure that intervention

goals address several areas of concern: (1) increasing the woman's personal safety; (2) increasing her sense of empowerment, esteem, choice, and control; and (3) reducing psychological trauma resulting from the violence.

2. *Clinicians must develop and use a conceptual framework to guide the process of treatment.* Within the last two decades, several explanatory models have been developed that describe the nature of response to traumatic events. Clinicians and researchers have more recently used such models to explain the psychological response of a battered woman to her battering experience (Crowell & Burgess, 1996; Dutton, 1992a; Foa et al., 2000; Jones et al., 2001). A consistent finding across varied samples of battered women is that a substantial number of them (31% to 84%) exhibit PTSD symptoms (Golding, 1999). Such models conceptualize the battered woman's symptoms as a traumatic response to stress. Therefore, it is hypothesized that in the process of her postassault adjustment, a victim of battering will experience many of the same reactions and employ many of the same coping mechanisms used by individuals responding to other types of life crises (McCann, Sakheim, & Abrahamson, 1988).

However, assault by an intimate partner creates a specific set of circumstances that distinguish battering from other traumas (Stark & Flitcraft, 1988). Several issues are particularly salient with battering. First, the clinician must recognize that battering is a recent event for most women seeking clinical assistance. Thus, *ensuring the ongoing physical safety* of the battering victim must be considered paramount. A number of battered women experience life-threatening events with high frequency (Kubany, Haynes, et al., 2000; Kubany, Leisen, Kaplan, & Kelly, 2000; Mechanic, Uhlmansiek, Weaver, & Resick, 2000; Shackelford, Buss, & Peters, 2000). Although a battered woman may minimize the risk of harm to herself, she may be in danger of being stalked and subsequently injured or killed by her "partner," whether or not she remains in the relationship. Ironically, however, if she does choose to and is able to leave the relationship, she may be placing herself at a heightened risk for injury.

Second, battering is often a *chronic problem*, characterized by multiple incidents over a long period of time. In many instances, the *response to battering may also be compounded (e.g., complex PTSD) by prior exposure to other forms of trauma* (Humphreys, Lee, Neylan, & Marmar, 1999) such as childhood abuse or prior adult sexual and physical assaults. Multiple victimization experiences will also increase the likelihood of PTSD and other disorders (Jones et al., 2001). PTSD is often associated with greater suicide risk, so that clinicians should inquire about active suicidal ideation and intent with the presence of PTSD (Thompson et al., 1999).

Another consideration is that the consequences of an assault within an intimate relationship are different from those that occur when one is assaulted by a stranger (Jones et al., 2001). Because of marital commitments, financial ties, and child care, victims of intimate partner violence cannot as easily remove themselves from the situation as can victims of abuse by a nonintimate. Further, when abuse occurs within a "safe" intimate relationship, the meaning of the event is altered (Foa, Stetkee, & Rothbaum, 1989). The relationship between the victim and her offender is particularly important because it relates to the battered woman's ability to deal with her battering on a cognitive level. Battering is often accompanied by emotionally abusive and controlling behavior; as such, it often is part of a systematic pattern of dominance and control. The importance of such coercive behaviors on the part of the batterer must not be minimized, given that having a verbally abusive partner has been found to be the variable most likely to predict that a woman would be victimized by her intimate partner (Tjaden & Thoennes, 2000).

Finally, unlike child victims of familial violence, an adult woman who has been battered by a partner must deal with the element of social evaluation. She may be perceived as contributing to her victimization, more so than victims of other forms of violence. Such victim-blaming perceptions are commonly expressed directly to a battered woman by her abusive partner. However, similar perceptions may be shared by friends, family members, helping professionals, and the community at large, and ultimately they may be incorporated into the woman's cognitive schema. If a victim-blaming attitude is internalized, it can contribute to self-blame, a response to battering that has been found to be associated with more severe psychological maladjustment (O'Neil & Kerig, 2000).

3. *A contextual perspective must guide intervention.* Clinicians must recognize and not underestimate the impact of situational variables on the battered woman's response to battering and her recovery (Heise, 1998; Foa et al., 2000). Attitudes concerning domestic violence held by the woman, the community at large, the woman's support system, and the legal and health professionals she may encounter will influence her likelihood of seeking mental health services and will influence her decision to take action to leave an abusive relationship (Fleury, Sullivan, Bybee, & Davidson, 1998; LaViolette & Barnett, 2000; Simon et al., 2001; Ulrich, 1998; Wuest & Merritt-Gray, 1999).

More recently, clinicians have recognized that diversity in terms of race, ethnicity, or sexual orientation may provide further challenges for the battered woman. Although many aspects of the abuse may be similar, intervention with these women requires an awareness on the part of the clinician of the barriers to treatment seeking (e.g., family dynamics, culturally prescribed gender role, language, homophobia) faced by these women. At the same time, clinicians should be willing to openly examine their own values and address their lack of knowledge or biases regarding this diversity. While respecting the potential impact of diversity, it is important not to engage in stereotyping or overgeneralizing when working with a battered women of a different race, ethnic group, or sexual orientation. Each woman should be responded to as an individual, with unique experiences and needs. Clinicians must gain knowledge and experience, as well as seek supervision to better prepare them to deal with battered women from diverse cultures and/or those in same-sex relationships. The reader is referred to several sources for a more in-depth discussion of issues relevant to battered women representing such diversity: Lundy and Leventhal (1999) provide information relevant to interventions with lesbian and bisexual battered women; information on interventions with African-American, Native American, and Hispanic or Chicana battered women, respectively, may be found in Campbell and Gary (1998), Bohn (1998), and Torres (1998).

4. *Clinicians must engage in ongoing self-monitoring of their attitudes, feelings, and behaviors.* Self-monitoring relates to both client and clinician self-care. Ideally, a clinician should examine personal values concerning battering and adopt an objective treatment philosophy before beginning service provision to battered women. Furthermore, these values and feelings must be continually monitored over time. Of particular concern are the clinician's expectations for change or action by the woman. Often, clinicians will become quite frustrated when working with women who seek services and have not yet decided to terminate the battering relationship. If the clinician perceives that the woman does not share his or her own intervention goals, an ensuing sense of helplessness and/or a victim-blaming attitude may result. Strawderman, Rosen, and Coleman (1997) provide gender-specific guidelines for identifying and managing difficulties experienced by clinicians when working with battered women.

Additionally, working with battering victims may be highly stressful. Clinicians may experience psychological distress, commonly expressed as post-traumatic symptoms. The term *vicarious traumatization* has been used to describe such consequences of a clinician's exposure to the experiences of a trauma victim (McCann & Pearlman, 1990). We believe that ongoing attention to the issues of clinician assessment of personal risk, self-care (O'Halloran & Linton, 2000), exploration of the impact of any personal victimization history, and use of a supportive professional network is critical to reduce clinician burnout.

5. *The impact of clinical interventions must be evaluated.* Our empirically based understanding of treatment issues related to battered women is relatively meager compared with our knowledge regarding victims of other forms of trauma. Therefore, there is a need for continuing empirical research in this area, particularly with regard to program evaluation and treatment efficacy. Lundy and Grossman (2001) make specific suggestion for the foci of future treatment efficacy research. They stress the need for both large-scale research studies and detailed case studies. Handbooks providing details of empirically supported treatment protocols for the treatment of PTSD (Leahy & Holland, 2000; Smythe, 1999), as well as interventions for comorbid problems of depression and anxiety (Emery, 2000), facilitate clinician

assessment of client progress. Treatment packages provide descriptions of basic cognitive-behavioral techniques, therapist forms for assessment and record keeping, and client handouts and homework sheets. Such assessments can be supplemented by client feedback regarding the efficacy of specific symptom-focused interventions as well as the quality of the therapeutic alliance.

ISSUES COMPLICATING CLINICAL INTERVENTIONS WITH BATTERED WOMEN

The intervention process with battered women can be complicated by many factors. Issues on the part of the battered woman or the clinician can interfere with the therapeutic process. If these issues relate specifically to the client, they should be addressed in a direct and nonjudgmental manner. Clinician attitudes or behaviors that interfere with treatment should be attended to and modified.

Client Issues

Walker (1987) identified five problem areas that she believes should be addressed in work with battered women: manipulation, expression of anger, dissociation, denial and minimization of violence, and compliance. The issues of ambivalence, trust, emotional detachment, and self-blame can also be added to Walker's list. These behaviors reflect learned coping strategies that the battered woman has used to survive within the context of the abusive relationship. However, these strategies may become problematic when the battered woman uses them in other interpersonal relationships. It is not uncommon for such strategies to be used even when the woman is no longer in the battering relationship.

Manipulation

Working under the assumption that she can control her unstable world, a battered woman often develops a manipulative style (e.g., survival mode). She may be unwilling to believe that anyone else can protect her, and so she does not allow input from others. She may believe that she alone can control her environment to keep the batterer calm and herself safe.

Battered women develop unrealistic expectations of themselves; they expect perfection and are critical of their failure to control things. Because of impaired trust, they rely on no one. Clinicians should recognize the potential for power struggles to emerge in therapy and act to label and defuse them quickly. Open communication in therapy, shared treatment goals, and asking the client to identify potential problems with suggested treatment recommendations all serve to reduce manipulation.

Anger Expression

Novaco and Chemtob (1998) observed that anger has often been ignored as an outcome in many studies of domestic violence (Cascardi, O'Leary, Lawrence, & Schlee, 1995; Rodrigues, Ryan, Kemp, & Foy, 1997). However, Saunders (1994) found that 42.5% of domestic violence survivors seeking help from domestic violence programs and 32% of those seeking services at other types of programs reported irritability and outbursts of anger. It has also been suggested that the stress associated with the battering relationship leads to an increased risk of child abuse on the part of the woman (Jones et al., 2001).

When their battering experiences are validated in the therapeutic setting, battered women may begin to feel anger and, in some cases, rage. With battered women, anger may be expressed in an indirect manner, such as general hostility, gossip, sarcasm, and passive-aggressive behavior. When the battered woman begins to establish a sense of trust in the therapeutic relationship, anger may emerge in session. Expression of angry feelings is often disturbing to the woman and the clinician; however, anger is a common and legitimate response to perceived injustice or mistreatment. Rather than being fearful or critical of anger expression, the clinician needs to label these feelings as normal and identify the appropriate expression of such feelings both in and out of the therapeutic setting as a therapeutic goal. The message is that one can think and feel at the same time. Anger does not necessarily lead to unavoidable aggression. While the batterer may have used the excuse of being unable to control his actions because of overwhelming anger, a more constructive and realistic anger management approach is desirable. The distinction between the process involved in anger reduction and problem solving is critical and must be delineated.

Novaco and Chemtob (1998) delineate a cognitive behavioral approach to anger treatment that involves seven key components: client education; self-monitoring; constructing a personal anger provocation hierarchy; arousal reduction techniques of progressive muscle relaxation, guided imagery, and breathing-focused relaxation (see Bernstein, Borkovec, & Hazlett-Stevens, 2000, or Davis, Eshelman, & McKay, 2000, for detailed information on the use of these techniques); cognitive restructuring using self-instruction; assertiveness training as modeled by the therapist; and practicing cognitive, arousal, and behavioral coping skills while visualizing and role-playing progressively more intense anger-arousing scenes from the personal hierarchy.

Dissociation

Out-of-body dissociative experiences, frequently reported by child sexual abuse victims, may also be experienced by battered women. With severe battering the dissociative episodes may become more frequent and last for longer periods. Dissociative experiences make the battered woman wonder if she is "crazy."

Wagner and Linehan (1998) provide an excellent overview of this topic and detail how selected strategies of dialectical behavior therapy (DBT) may be applied to this problem. Dissociative experiences are conceptualized as functioning to avoid trauma-related cues, making the abuse episodes more tolerable. In the first stage of treatment, discussion of and processing of trauma events are avoided. Instead, the focus is on establishing stability and developing a therapeutic connection to the therapist. This does not negate assessment of such experience but instead calls for avoidance of prolonged discussions. Clients are then taught "crisis survival strategies," such as distracting techniques, engaging in self-soothing activities, and skills for improving the moment (e.g., relaxation). A second target is the regulation of negative affect, both in response to trauma cues and more generally. This is accomplished by teaching the client mindfulness skills (e.g., cultivating awareness of internal and external experiences) and emotional regulation skills. Throughout treatment, Linehan also uses techniques, such as exposure, borrowed from clinicians who have developed treatment programs that focus primarily on alleviating PTSD symptoms (Foa & Rothbaum, 1998; Resick & Schnicke, 1993) in other trauma populations. Wagner and Linehan also provide a useful discussion of common treatment obstacles and suggestions to overcome them.

Denial and Minimization

These cognitive strategies appear to develop over the history of abuse. They are used to establish some type of meaning for the victimization (Eisikovits & Enosh, 1997; Follingstad, Neckerman, & Vormbrock, 1988) and keep depression under control; unfortunately, the result is lowered self-esteem. Denial may be expressed by any of the rationalizations commonly used by battered women (Ferraro & Johnson, 1983):

- Denial of injury (failure to acknowledge being hurt)
  Example:
      He wasn't really abusive. He just shoved me.
      He didn't hurt me that bad. Just a few bruises.
- Denial of the victimizer (blame on external factors beyond the control of either partner)
  Example:
      His boss had been picking on him.
      His mother gets involved and criticizes the way the kids behave.
- Denial of options (both practical and emotional)
  Example:
      I couldn't make it on my own. I don't have the skills. No one else would want me.
- Denial of victimization (victim self-blame)
  Example:
      If I just wouldn't have picked on him. I knew better than to go out.

Related to such examples of denial and minimization are two other rationalizations identified by Follingstad et al. (1988). They include:

- Appeal to the salvation ethic (help him overcome his problem; endure
abuse until that is achieved)
Example
    I know he is basically a good man. I'm sure with a little time and
    understanding I can get him to . . .
- Appeal to higher loyalties (endure violence for "higher purpose," such
as religion or tradition)
Example:
    The children need to have two parents. I can't leave. Besides, I don't
    believe in divorce.

Since these rationalizations are considered to be more central to the woman's identity, their presence makes it much more difficult to leave the relationship. Therapeutically, it is advisable to ask the woman to keep a "paper
trail" to identify and challenge minimization related to injury. A woman
may be asked to keep a log of battering incident details or use photographs
to document bruises. Since telephone harassment is common, the woman
can use an answering machine to record the batterer's remarks to her. Logs,
journals, or diaries can be used to identify other cognitive distortions that
reflect other forms of denial. Such statements could then be challenged, replacing victim-blaming statements with those that place responsibility or
blame for the abuse on the batterer. Stalking behaviors need to be documented. The 25-item Stalking Behavior Checklist (SBC; Coleman, 1997),
which rates unwanted harassing and pursuit-oriented behaviors during a 6-
month period, can be used for this purpose.

Compliance and Willingness to Please

Compliance is demonstrated by the woman's willingness to engage in placat-
ing behavior with the batterer. Such behavior is similar to that identified in
other types of trauma victims (e.g., the Stockholm syndrome). In therapeutic
interactions, compliance may be evident in "yes, but" behavior; the woman
appears overly compliant with the therapist's suggestions for change in or
termination of the relationship, but then she fails to carry out these "seemingly agreed upon" suggestions. Although such behavior is often bewildering
to the clinician, continued contact with the batterer or returning to live with
him may be perceived as less threatening by the battered woman.

Ambivalence

One of the most formidable obstacles to successful intervention with battered
women is ensuring initial identification and contact with mental health service

providers. This problem can be only partially explained by victim ambivalence. Battered women only infrequently have sought the assistance of mental health professionals. Ambivalence is often expressed in treatment by apparently inconsistent behavior. For example, contact with the clinician may be urgently requested, but then the client may not attend a scheduled session. It is important for the clinician to understand the dynamics of such behavior. The inconsistencies must not be interpreted personally; it may be unwarranted to conclude that such client behaviors indicate a simple lack of motivation for therapy.

Trust Issues

Since trust is often related to "family" issues such as power, control, sexism, and intimacy, it is not surprising that it is an important issue in dealing with battered women. The clinician should note the following problems reported by the woman: expression of sex roles in a stereotyped manner; problems with setting boundaries in personal relationships; unassertiveness; failure to achieve emotional intimacy and sexual contact in subsequent relationships; and poor self-management skills due to expressed feelings of powerlessness and lack of control.

Rosenbloom and Williams (1999) have developed a self-help manual, based on McCann and Pearlman's (1990) constructivist self-development work, to address this area of cognitive functioning, which is often disrupted in response to trauma. Additionally, Rosenbloom and Williams (1999) include chapters that deal with four other areas of cognitive functioning: safety, control, esteem, and intimacy. A four-step process for belief identification and evaluation is presented for each area. The emphasis throughout the manual is facilitating women's use of coping strategies.

Emotional Detachment

Emotional expressiveness may be related to a woman's learned coping strategies in response to other forms of trauma, as well as her learned response to battering. For example, the child or adolescent victim of emotional, physical, or sexual assault may learn to detach herself from her feelings as a survival strategy. Such detachment strategies are difficult to overcome, but if the clinician can allow expressions of fear and anger within the therapeutic relationship, progress will usually be enhanced. Walker (2000) found that many of the battered women interviewed for her study experienced a sense of exhilaration at finally being able to speak about the abusive experience in such detail. Clinician permission facilitates the intervention goal of emotional catharsis.

Self-Blame and/or Guilt

The final client issues are self-blame and/or guilt. A number of researchers have identified self-blame as a common response to battering as women attempt to assign meaning to their abuse. Battered women may experience self-blame for causing the violence, self-blame for being unable to control its continuance, or self-blame for tolerance of the violence. Typically, there is a developmental progression, with battered women blaming themselves less as causal agents of the abuse but blaming themselves more for failing to leave over time.

Self-blame is expressed in the client's question "Why work with me?" Self-blame issues relate to the intervention goal of client self-management. Several strategies can be used successfully in working with a battered woman's self-defeating and self-blaming attitudes. These include a focus on her strengths, particularly as a survivor, and the use of cognitive techniques, such as identifying and replacing negative self-statements with positive ones. For example, a client may be encouraged to replace statements such as "What a stupid person I was to stay with him for so long" with statements such as "I did what I thought was best at the time. No one deserves to be hit. It was his problem. At least I survived. That's what's really important."

Kubany (1998) and his colleagues have studied guilt in battered women. One in four women reported guilt in the considerable to extreme range, and almost half reported moderate or greater guilt. The level of guilt experienced by a battered woman tends to be negatively correlated with the severity of violence that she experiences (Eisikovits & Enosh, 1997). Guilt is also positively correlated with psychopathology, particularly PTSD and depression, as well as negative self-esteem, shame, social anxiety and avoidance, and suicidal ideation (Kubany et al., 1996; Street & Arias, 2001).

In summary, by recognizing these common maladaptive coping strategies early, the clinician can "predict" thoughts, feelings, and behaviors on the part of the battered woman that may interfere with the process of therapy. Statements about identified client processes regarding self-blame, minimization of partner responsibility for the abusive incident, lack of trust in the clinician, and ambivalence toward therapy can be prefaced with comments such as "Frequently, women who have been battered by their partners say they experience a problem with taking responsibility for their abuse. You may or may not have similar feelings, but if you do, recognize that they are not unusual given the circumstances."

Clinician Issues

Gender

The issue of therapist gender has received considerable attention in the literature. It is our view that males are capable of being effective interventionists with battered women. However, work with battered women may pose certain challenges for the male clinician. Certainly, if a battered woman has strong negative reactions to working with a man or expresses a strong preference for a female clinician, that preference should be respected.

Male clinicians who experience anxiety about acceptance by battering victims may unknowingly engage in counterproductive therapist behaviors. The male clinician should be attuned to subtle alterations of his clinical style in response to dealing with issues common to battered women. Nonverbal behaviors and nuances of speech, such as the use of a softer tone and physical proximity, which are intended to convey a caring attitude, can also be interpreted as stereotypic, seductive, or threatening. Likewise, becoming more formal, using "technical" terminology, and being hypervigilant to body boundaries may distance the battered woman. A final caution for male clinicians (as well as inexperienced clinicians): Be particularly aware of the tendency to focus on "who did what to whom" in terms of physical actions and a concomitant failure to assess for any sexual aspects to the battering.

As with all victimization work, the values and attitudes that the clinician espouses regarding battered women and their victimization are of greater importance than gender. Certainly, our research suggests that gender may interact with values. Some male clinicians may find it difficult to validate the experiences of a battered woman if they identify with the male batterer. As a male clinical supervisor of one of the authors once grumbled while commenting on a statement made by a battered woman during a therapy session, "I can understand how he wanted to hit her when she made comments like that to him . . . just to get her to shut up." Likewise, female clinicians also have the potential to blame women for their victimization (e.g., "Why didn't she leave if it was that bad? I wouldn't have stayed if someone treated me like that"). Clinician gender alone will not predict success or failure in clinical interventions with battered women. A nonjudgmental, validating male clinician is highly preferable to a female clinician who holds victim-blaming attitudes toward battered women.

Clinician Values

Before beginning work with battered women, a clinician should have carefully examined his or her own biases and prejudices with respect to the myths and stereotypes associated with domestic violence. This self-awareness, termed *autodiagnosing* (Burgess & Holmstrom, 1979), ensures continual monitoring of feelings and possible prejudices concerning each particular client to avoid contributing to her revictimization. Such revictimization occurs when the clinician places himself or herself in the role of assessing whether a reported assault was "legitimate violence," or whether the battered woman "provoked" her assault, "overreacted," or "was masochistic." Prejudices may occur more often when there is a client history of substance abuse, multiple abuse perpetrators, a chronic abuse history with a partner, history of sexual infidelity, or child abuse. Frequently, inexperienced clinicians (or experienced ones who adhere to a victim precipitation model) look for explanations of violence within intimate relationships in psychopathology on the part of the victim or perpetrator. How else can we explain such "crazy" behavior in a "just world"? Victim labeling should alert the clinician to potentially victim-blaming attitudes.

Finally, self-examination of values and beliefs should also include a self-assessment of the clinician's own victimization history. If such a history exists, the clinician must be able to focus on client needs without interference from unresolved issues of his or her own personal victimization.

CLINICIAN ROLES AND SKILLS

The clinician should provide an environment that is a "safe place" for the client to express her emotions and thoughts (e.g., the concept of *containment*). The clinician should be alert to and avoid responses on his or her part that imply avoidance, attack, indifference, or overprotection. It is imperative that the clinician be knowledgeable concerning medical, police, and judicial procedures in his or her city, county, and state. Also, clinicians must be aware of attitudes held by the medical and law enforcement professionals within the community who are likely to be working with battered women. Educating a victim about what to anticipate in her interactions with professionals in these disciplines reduces anxiety and facilitates decision making.

Unfortunately, many family physicians and general practitioners report having little exposure to battered women and tend to greatly underestimate the prevalence of domestic violence. In addition, they may abrogate responsibility for the care of battered women when physical injuries are absent (Kahan, Rabin, & Tzur-Zilberman, 2000). For clinicians wishing to provide education or training for medical personnel, Naumann, Langford, and Torres (1999) describe ways battered women's experiences could be significantly improved if primary care providers properly assessed, intervened, and referred women whom they treat in their practice.

Although the topic of roles and skills of the clinician has been discussed in the context of philosophy and potential problems (e.g., values, biases, lack of objectivity), this section will provide suggestions to guide the clinician in the course of intervention with battered women. These suggestions are based on a listing of interventions designed to be used with victims of sexual assault (Petretic-Jackson & Jackson, 1990). The list also incorporates suggestions from the work of Courtois (1988), Dutton (1992a, 1992b), Walker (1994a, 1994b), and other clinicians working with trauma victims and survivors to provide a comprehensive set of guidelines for intervention.

Useful clinician attitudes, behaviors, and assumptions include the following:

1. Present a calm, professional, and supportive demeanor. It is important for the woman to know that the clinician is willing to be exposed to a recounting of her experiences and her reactions without rejecting her or recoiling from the details. The clinician should convey a sense

of professionalism and be aware of both verbal and nonverbal behaviors. The woman should feel that nothing is too horrible for her to tell to the clinician.

2. Develop a supportive relationship with the client. Through *empathic listening*, convey a sense of nonjudgmental acceptance and validation of the woman and her experience. *Advocacy* involves both letting the woman know that you are "on her side" and being willing to get involved within the community to address inequities in well-being. It indicates that you believe her story; you do not convey a sense of suspiciousness or doubt. Avoid carelessly worded statements such as "Why didn't you leave the house then?" or "Did it really happen that way?" which would imply victim blaming.

3. Provide *validation* for the victim's feelings, thoughts, and behaviors. Let her know that her responses are not abnormal and that she is not "crazy," given her battering experience. Identifying her symptoms as coping responses used by many other women who have undergone similar trauma serves to reduce her sense of isolation. Stress that action and self-disclosure facilitate the recovery process.

4. Respond to the victim's unique immediate concerns and needs. Attend to both verbal and nonverbal cues. Answer her questions. Do not offer false reassurances. Avoid statements such as "He won't really hurt you."

5. Let the victim set the tone and pace of the intervention. Resist the impulse to "push" her to discuss topics. Allow her to retain a sense of control in the interaction.

6. Anticipate a variety of physical and emotional responses on the part of the victim. Remember that a woman's response is a function of her personal style interacting with the circumstances of her battering experience. Attend to the client's unique symptom constellation. While individuals vary, identification of symptoms within the behavioral, emotional, cognitive, physical, and interpersonal domains provides an organizational framework for directing intervention strategies. Remember that self-medication (e.g., drug and alcohol abuse) or numbing is common among battered women. Assess and address such factors. Work collaboratively on establishing a list of alternative, healthy coping strategies. Ruzek, Polusny, and Abueg (1998) have written an excellent chapter on assessment and treatment of concurrent PTSD and substance abuse.

7. Focus on immediate affective experiences. Use *reflection* of the woman's emotional responses. Losses associated with battering and other forms of victimization often cannot be compensated; they can be grieved.

8. Convey an understanding of the woman's situation by the use of techniques such as *clarification*, *labeling*, and *generalizations*. Statements can be prefaced with comments such as "Some women who have been battered by their partners are concerned about what their friends may think or whether or not they are 'wrong' to stay. Is that something that is a concern for you?"

9. Encourage client decision making and planning to allow her to regain a sense of control. Education is therapeutic. Be an advocate for safety and skill-building options. Use the techniques of *clarification* and *selective interpretation* to evaluate alternatives in decision making. Avoid a controlling style; don't make decisions for the victim or attempt to "rescue" her. Let her know you will support her decisions; such victim self-determination leads to empowerment.

10. Facilitate self-care on the part of the woman. *Guided imagery* exercises, *hypnosis*, and *relaxation* techniques may be used to deal with dissociative issues. *Body awareness* techniques, *physical exercise*, or *self-care* actions as simple as taking a bubble bath or applying body lotion facilitate a better sense of bodily control, as well as self-care and nurturance.

11. Set the stage for the development of a "survivor" mentality. Begin to set the stage for self-recovery in the initial interview by sharing coping strategies used by other women who have successfully coped with battering. These coping skills demonstrate that the woman possesses many strengths. Emphasize what she did "right," while *reframing* her maladaptive coping strategies (e.g., substance use) as attempts to cope, not pathology. Her survival skills will allow her to reach recovery goals of autonomy and control. Transformation may be a lifelong process. Facilitate the acquisition of coping and mastery skills through the techniques of *rehearsal* and *anticipatory guidance*.

12. Offer hope and realistic reassurance. Suggest that the woman will feel in greater control of her life as time progresses and she acquires skills to ensure her safety and improve her decision-making ability. Use the concept of life crisis or trauma to explain her thoughts, feelings, and attitudes. It is useful to remind her that, although she has undergone a severe trauma, her experience does not preclude her ability to return to normal functioning.

KEY CONCEPTS IN TREATMENT

Crisis Intervention

Crisis intervention is an important clinical service for battered women, although crisis intervention with women who have not yet decided to end their abusive relationships often proves to be frustrating to the clinician involved. With crisis intervention, the battered woman is typically seen soon after a battering episode. In many communities, women's shelters may provide crisis counseling in addition to shelter as a part of advocacy following an acute episode of violence. In addition, shelters often provide crisis services or women's groups to women not residing at the shelter. See chapter 17 for a comprehensive discussion of the elements of crisis intervention by police, social workers, hospital emergency room staff, hotlines, and shelters. The creader is referred to Roberts and Roberts (2000) and Roberts and Burman (1998) for an excellent discussion of such interventions.

The clinician should develop a written protocol to assist in devising a safety plan for a woman. First, the clinician should gather information about the most recent battering incidents. The woman should be asked to provide nas much detail as she can recall. Can she identify cues from the batterer's behavior that may signal an impending battering episode? These cues are frequently recognized by the battered woman, although she may not readily be able to verbalize what they are unless prompted to recognition by careful clinician questioning.

Thus, the first goal related to safety is to identify a pattern in the batterer's nonverbal behavior, thinking, and speech that serves as a cue to an impending battering episode. When a pattern is identified, the woman can recognize the early signs and maximize the likelihood of leaving the situation without harm. The second goal is to identify all basic needs that must be met to allow the woman to escape successfully in the event of a dangerous battering incident. She should make a checklist of necessary items to take with her: extra keys, money, clothes for her and the children, and copies of important papers, such as children's birth certificates. Having all these things together in a single location that is easily accessible to her in an emergency is vital. Other concerns relate to care of pets and objects of sentimental value. The third goal is to identify the step-by-step procedure to be followed in the escape plan. Specifically, delineate the sequence of behaviors she must follow to actually get out of the house. In terms of the actual escape plan, is a telephone available? If not, or if it cannot be used, can a signal be arranged with a neighbor to call the police? The woman needs to determine the best route to take from whatever room she may be in. Also, how can she best get the children out?

Short-Term Therapy

Short-term therapy using either an individual or a group format may be beneficial to the battered woman. Several books and chapters describe treatment for battered women in considerable detail (Dutton, 1992a; Foa et al., 2000; Monnier, Briggs, Davis, & Ezzell, 2001; Roberts & Burman, 1998; Roberts & Roberts, 2000; Walker, 1994b), although no manualized treatment protocols are currently available.[1]

The emphasis in treatment for battered women has followed the direction taken with other victim populations, with a focus on addressing cognitive aspects of functioning. Topics in decision making include financial, legal, relationship, and educational issues. Many therapists have emphasized the value of a feminist orientation, which places the abuse in a social context and emphasizes empowerment of the woman. Dutton (1992a) refers to the focus of these clinical interventions as *choice making*. A woman may benefit from problem-solving training (D'Zurilla & Nezu, 1999) to facilitate choice making. With the problem-solving model the client is empowered, since she retains the locus of control for decision making.

The focus of intervention in short-term therapy for a woman who has ended the battering relationship should still address evaluation of continuing concerns for safety, as well as decision- or choice-making skills and symptom relief strategies. There is also an emphasis on assisting the woman in regaining a sense of autonomy and control over her life, and on the woman developing or identifying a personal social support network for herself.

Therapeutic tasks that have been identified in the clinical literature (Courtois, 1988; Dutton, 1992a, 1992b; Foa et al., 2000; Walker, 1993, 1994a, 1994b) as being important when treating PTSD symptoms in various trauma groups (termed posttraumatic therapy by Dutton when used with battered women) include the following:

1. Integration of the traumatic experience by reexperiencing the traumatic event
2. Management of subsequent stress
3. Facilitation of affective expression
4. Determination of a meaning from victimization (e.g., "trauma themes," "cognitive schemata," "self-blame," or "errors of logic")
5. Identification of resilience and other strengths
6. Focus on the woman as the active agent of change

For the battered woman the therapeutic task of reexperiencing the traumatic event must be approached with caution and sensitivity. A problem may occur if the clinician inadvertently creates a retraumatization experience, as opposed to a therapeutic experience, by asking the woman to reexperience the battering event. Before beginning this task, it is necessary to create a therapeutic environment that is safe for the woman. The task of reexperiencing the trauma is best achieved through a woman telling her story. While flooding and other techniques have been employed with victims of other forms of trauma to facilitate a reexperiencing of the traumatic event, they are not recommended for battered women. If avoidance is the primary presenting problem, the clinician may have to facilitate the storytelling process through the use of experiential techniques and documents, photographs, police reports, and so forth. Exposure has gained acceptance as an efficacious technique for reducing PTSD by allowing the victim to reexperience the trauma under carefully controlled conditions.

Stress management techniques are used to regulate responses when reexperiencing trauma leads to excessive arousal or spontaneous intrusions, such as thoughts, nightmares, and flashbacks. Techniques to manage stress include: refocusing attention on external reality; using relaxation techniques; employing dosing (a technique in which attention is systematically shifted toward and away from the traumatic experience); time management skills; personal self-care in terms of nutrition, rest, and reduced activity; developing a support system; and discrimination or problem-solving skills by which prior and current situations can be evaluated.

SUMMARY

This chapter has attempted to present many sensitive, complex issues that arise when treating women who have experienced violence in their intimate relationships. Providing services to victims and survivors of battering can be both rewarding and challenging for the clinician. We strongly believe that only through an appreciation of, and sensitivity to, the issues presented in this chapter can a clinician make an informed decision regarding whether or not to work with this population. We hope that the material included in this chapter will facilitate increased knowledge, consciousness-raising, and clinical competence when working with victims and survivors of intimate violence so that the basic goals of assisting women to achieve violence-free living and reempowering them to become survivors rather than victims can be achieved.

NOTE

1. For clinicians interested in viewing a videotape that illustrates clinical interventions with battered women, Walker (1994a) has developed one that comes with an accompanying viewer's manual. The tape consists of reenacted segments that illustrate a variety of therapeutic issues and interventions from Walker's survivor therapy (see also Walker, 1994b), a feminist-oriented therapy approach tailored to battered women. The tape highlights how to conduct an abuse history and labeling of the abuse, negotiation of boundary issues, dealing with an acute medical crisis, cognitive restructuring, safety plan review, and exploration of future options. The manual includes basic information on battered women (e.g., forms of abuse, abuse dynamics, why battered women stay in the relationship); specifics of survivor therapy (e.g., basic goals, stages of treatment, special challenges); an overview of the case presented in the video; and appendixes that provide annotated references for professionals and annotated self-help titles for clients.

REFERENCES

Barnett, O. W. (2001). Why battered women do not leave, part 2: External inhibiting factors—Social support and internal inhibiting factors. *Trauma Violence and Abuse, 2,* 3–35.

Beck, A., Rush, A., Shaw, B., & Emery, G. (1979). *Cognitive therapy of depression.* New York: Guilford.

Belknap, J., & Hartman, J. L. (2000). Police responses to woman battering: Victim advocates' reports. *International Review of Victimology, 7,* 159–177.

Bernstein, D. A., Borkovec, T. D., & Hazlett-Stevens, H. (2000). *New directions in progressive relaxation training: A guidebook for helping professionals.* Westport, CT: Praeger.

Bohn, D. K. (1998). Clinical interventions with Native American battered women. In J. C. Campbell (Ed.), *Empowering survivors of abuse: Health care for battered women and their children* (pp. 241–258). Thousand Oaks, CA: Sage.

Burgess, A., & Holmstrom, L. (1979). Sexual disruption and recovery.

American Journal of Orthopsychiatry, 49, 648–657.

Campbell, D. W., & Gary, F. A. (1998). Providing effective interventions for African American battered women: Afrocentric perspectives. In J. C. Campbell (Ed.), *Empowering survivors of abuse: Health care for battered women and their children.* Thousand Oaks, CA: Sage.

Cascardi, M., O'Leary, K. D., Lawrence, E. E., & Schlee, K.A. (1995). Characteristics of women physically abused by their spouses and who seek treatment regarding marital conflict. *Journal of Consulting and Clinical Psychology, 63,* 616–623.

Coleman, F. (1997). Stalking behavior and the cycle of domestic violence, *Journal of Interpersonal Violence, 12,* 420–432.

Courtois, C. A. (1988). *Healing the incest wound: Adult survivors in therapy.* New York: Norton.

Crowell, N., & Burgess, S. (Eds.). (1996). *Understanding violence against women,* Washington, DC: National Academy Press.

Davies, J. M., Lyon, E., & Monti-Catania, D. (1998). *Safety planning with battered women: Complex lives/difficult choices.* Thousand Oaks, CA: Sage.

Davis, M., Eshelman, E. R., & McKay, M. (2000). *The relaxation and stress reduction workbook* (5th ed.) Oakland, CA: New Harbinger.

Dutton, M. (1992a). *Empowering and healing the battered woman.* New York: Springer.

Dutton, M. (1992b). Assessment and treatment of post-traumatic stress disorder among battered women. In D. Foy (Ed.), *Treating PTSD: Cognitive-behavioral strategies* (pp. 69–98). New York: Guilford.

Dutton, M. (1998). Forensic evaluation and testimony related to domestic violence. In L. VandeCreek, S. Knapp, & T. Jackson (Eds.), *Innovation in clinical practice: A sourcebook* (Vol. 16, pp. 293–311). Sarasota, FL: Professional Resource Press.

Dutton, M. (1999). Commentary: Multidimensional assessment of women battering: Commentary on Smith, Smith, and Earp. *Psychology of Women Quarterly, 23,* 195–198.

D'Zurilla, T., & Neza, A. (1999). *Problem-solving therapy: A social competence approach to clinical intervention* (2nd ed.). New York: Springer.

Eisikovits, Z., & Enosh, G. (1997). Awareness of guilt and shame in intimate violence. *Violence and Victims, 12,* 307–322.

Elliott, D. (1994). Assessing adult victims of interpersonal violence. In J. Briere (Ed.), *Assessing and treating victims of violence* (pp. 5–16). San Francisco: Josey-Bass.

Emery, G. (2000). *Overcoming depression: A cognitive-behavioral protocol for the treatment of depression.* Oakland, CA: New Harbinger.

Ferraro, K., & Johnson, J. (1983). How women experience battering: The process of victimization. *Social Problems, 30,* 325–339.

Fleck-Henderson, A. (2000). Choice and empowerment for battered women who stay. *Social Work, 45,* 472–473.

Fleury, R. E., Sullivan, C. M., Bybee, D. I., & Davidson, W. S. (1998). "Why don't they just call the cops?" Reasons for differential contact among women with abusive partners. *Violence and Victims, 13,* 333–346.

Foa, E. B., Cascardi, M., Zoellner, L. A., & Feeny, N. C. (2000). Psychological and environmental factors associated with partner violence. *Trauma, Violence, and Abuse, 1,* 67–71.

Foa, E. B., & Rothbaum, B. O. (1998). *Treating the trauma of rape: Cognitive behavioral therapy for PTSD.* New York: Guilford.

Foa, E., Stetkee, G., & Rothbaum, B. O. (1989). Behavioral/cognitive conceptualization of post-traumatic stress disorder. *Behavior Therapy, 20,* 155–176.

Follingstad, D., Neckerman, A., & Vormbrock, J. (1988). Reactions to victimization and coping strategies of battered women: The ties that bind. *Clinical Psychology Review, 8,* 373–390.

Golding, J. M. (1999). Intimate partner violence as a risk factor for mental disorders: A meta-analysis. *Journal of Family Violence, 14,* 99–133.

Heise, L. L. (1998). Violence against women: An integrated ecological framework. *Violence Against Women, 4,* 262–290.

Humphreys, J., Lee, K., Neylan, T., & Marmar, C. (1999). Trauma history of sheltered battered women. *Issues in Mental Health Nursing, 20,* 319–332.

Jackson, T., Petretic-Jackson, P. & Witte, P. (2002). Mental health assessment tools and techniques for working with battered women. In A. Roberts (Ed.), *Handbook of domestic violence intervention strategies: Policies, programs and legal remedies.* New York: Oxford University Press.

Jones, L., Hughes, M., & Unterstaller, U. (2001). Post-traumatic stress disorder (PTSD) in victims of domestic violence: A review of the research. *Trauma, Violence and Abuse, 2,* 99–119.

Kahan, E., Rabin, S., & Tzur-Zilberman, H. (2000). Knowledge and attitudes of primary care physicians regarding battered women: Comparison between specialists in family medicine and GPs. *Family Practice, 17,* 5–9.

Kilpatrick, D., Veronen, L., & Resick, P. A. (1980, November). Brief behavioral intervention procedure: A new treatment for recent rape victims. Pa-

per presented at the annual meeting of the Association for Advancement of Behavior Therapy, New York.

Kubany, E. S. (1998). Cognitive therapy for trauma-related guilt. In V. M. Follette, J. I. Ruzek, & F. R. Abueg, (Eds.), *Cognitive behavioral therapies for trauma* (pp. 124–161). New York: Guilford.

Kubany, E. S., Haynes, S. N., Abueg, F. R., Manke, F. P., Brennan, J. M., & Stahura, C. (1996). Development and validation of the Trauma-Related Guilt Inventory (TRGI). *Psychological Assessment, 8,* 428–444.

Kubany, E. S., Haynes, S. N., Leisen, M. B., Ownes, J. A., Kaplan, A. S., Watson, S. B., & Burns, K. (2000). Development and preliminary validation of a brief broad-spectrum measure of trauma exposure: The Traumatic Life Events Questionnaire. *Psychological Assessment, 12,* 200–224.

Kubany, E. S., Leisen, M. B., Kaplan, A. S., & Kelly, M. P. (2000). Validation of a brief measure of posttraumatic stress disorder: The Distressing Event Questionnaire (DEQ). *Psychological Assessment, 12,* 197–209.

LaViolette, A., & Barnett, O. W. (2000). *It could happen to anyone: Why battered women stay* (2nd ed.). Thousand Oaks, CA: Sage.

Leahy, R. L., & Holland, S. J. (2000). *Treatment plans and interventions for depression and anxiety disorders* (with CD-ROM). New York: Guilford.

Lerner, C. F., & Kennedy, L. T. (2000). Stay-leave decision making in battered women: Trauma, coping, and self-efficacy. *Cognitive Therapy and Research, 24,* 215–232.

Lundy, M., & Grossman, S. (2001). Clinical research and practice with battered women: What we know, what we need to know. *Trauma, Violence, and Abuse, 2,* 120–141.

Lundy, S., & Leventhal, B. (1999). *Same-sex domestic violence: Strategies for change.* Thousand Oaks, CA: Sage.

Martin, A. J., Berenson, K. R., Griffing, S., Sage, R. E., Madry, L., Bingham, L. E., & Primm, B. J. (2000). The process of leaving an abusive relationship: The role of risk assessments and decision-certainty. *Journal of Family Violence, 15,* 109–122.

McCann, L., & Pearlman, L. A. (1990). Constructivist self-development theory as a framework for assessing and treating victims of family violence. In S. M. Stith & M. B. Williams (Eds.), *Violence hits home: Comprehensive treatment approaches to domestic violence* (Vol. 19, pp. 305–329). New York: Springer.

McCann, L., Sakheim, D., & Abrahamson, D. (1988). Trauma and victimization: A model of psychological adaptation. *Counseling Psychologist, 16,* 531–594.

Mechanic, M. B., Uhlmansiek, M. H., Weaver, T. & Resick, P. A. (2000). The impact of severe stalking experienced by acutely battered women: An examination of violence, psychological symptoms, and strategic responding. *Violence and Victims, 15,* 443–458.

Meichenbaum, D. (1977). *Cognitive-behavior modification.* New York: Plenum.

Monnier, J., Briggs, E. C., Davis, J., & Ezzell, C. E. (2001). Group treatment for domestic violence victims with posttraumatic stress disorder and depression. In L. VandeCreek & T. Jackson (Eds.), *Innovations in clinical practice: A sourcebook* (Vol. 19, pp. 113–128). Sarasota, FL: Professional Resource Press.

Najavits, L. M., Weiss, R. D., & Liese, B. S. (1996). Group cognitive behavioral therapy for women with PTSD and substance use disorder. *Journal of Substance Abuse Treatment, 13,* 13–22.

Najavits, L. M., Weiss, R. D., Shaw, S. R., & Nuenz, I. R. (1998). "Seeking safety"; Outcome of a new cognitive-behavioral psychotherapy for women with posttraumatic stress disorder and substance dependence. *Journal of Traumatic Stress, 11,* 437–456.

Naumann, P., Langford, D., & Torres, S. (1999). Women battering in primary care practice. *Family Practice, 16,* 343–352.

Novaco, R. W., & Chemtob, C. M. (1998). Anger and trauma: Conceptualization, assessment and treatment. In V. M. Follette, J. I. Ruzek, & F. R. Abueg (Eds.), *Cognitive behavioral therapies for trauma* (pp. 162–190). New York: Guilford.

O'Halloran, T. M., & Linton, J. M. (2000). Stress on the job: Self-care resources for counselors. *Journal of Mental Health Counseling, 22,* 354–364.

O'Neil, M. L., & Kerig, P. K. (2000). Attributions of self-blame and perceived control as moderators of adjustment in battered women. *Journal of Interpersonal Violence, 15,* 1036–1049.

Pape, K. T., & Arias, I. (2000). The role of perceptions and attributions in battered women's intentions to permanently end their violent relationships. *Cognitive Therapy and Research, 24,* 201–214.

Peled, E., Eisikovits, Z., Enosh, G., & Winstok, Z. (2000). Choice and empowerment for battered women who stay: Toward a constructivist model. *Social Work, 45,* 9–24.

Petretic-Jackson, P., & Jackson, T. L. (1990). Crisis intervention with sexual assault victims. In A. R. Roberts (Ed.), *Crisis intervention: Techniques and issues* (pp. 124–152). Pacific Grove, CA: Wadsworth.

Resick, P. A., & Schnicke, M. K. (1993). *Cognitive processing therapy* for rape victims: A treatment manual. Thousand Oaks, CA: Sage.

Rhodes, N. R., & McKenzie, E. B. (1998). Why do battered women stay? Three decades of research. Aggression and Violent Behavior, 3, 391–406.

Roberts, A. R., & Burman, S. (1998). Crisis intervention and cognitive problem-solving therapy with battered women: A national survey and practice model. In A. R. Roberts (Ed.), Battered women and their families: Intervention strategies and treatment programs (2nd ed., pp. 3–28). New York: Springer.

Roberts, A., & Roberts, B. (2001). A comprehensive model for crisis intervention with battered women and their children. In A. Roberts (Ed.), Crisis intervention handbook: Assessment, treatment and research (2nd ed., pp. 177–208). New York: Oxford University Press.

Rodrigues, N., Ryan, S. W., Kemp, H. V., & Foy, D. W. (1997). Posttraumatic stress disorder in adult female survivors of childhood sexual abuse: A comparison study. Journal of Consulting and Clinical Psychology, 65, 53–59.

Rosenbloom, D., & Williams, M. B. (1999). Life after trauma: A workbook for healing. New York: Guilford.

Ruzek, J. I., Polusny, M. A., & Abueg, F. R. (1998). Assessment and treatment of concurrent posttraumatic stress disorder and substance abuse. In V. M. Follette, J. I. Ruzek, & F. R. Abueg (Eds.), Cognitive behavioral therapies for trauma (pp. 226–255). New York: Guilford.

Saunders, D. G. (1994). Posttraumatic stress symptoms profiles of battered women: A comparison of survivors in two settings. Violence and Victims, 9, 31–44.

Shackelford, T. K., Buss, D. M., & Peters, J. (2000). Wife killing: Risk to

women as a function of age. Violence and Victims, 15, 273–282.

Simon, T. R., Anderson, M., Thompson, M. P., Sacks, J. J., Crosby, A. E., & Shelley, G. (2001). Attitudinal acceptance of intimate partner violence among U.S. adults. Violence and Victims, 16, 115–126.

Smith, A. (2001). Domestic violence laws: The voices of battered women. Violence and Victims, 16, 91–111.

Smythe, L. (1999). Overcoming posttraumatic stress disorder: A cognitive behavioral exposure-based protocol for the treatment of PTSD and the other anxiety disorders. Oakland, CA: New Harbinger.

Stark, E., & Flitcraft, A. (1988). Personal power and institutional victimization: Treating the dual trauma of woman battering. In F. M. Ochberg (Ed.), Post-traumatic therapy and victims of violence (pp. 115–151). New York: Brunner/Mazel.

Strawderman, E., Rosen, K. H., & Coleman, J. (1997). Therapist heal thyself: Countertransference and the treatment of battered women. Journal of Family Psychotherapy, 8, 35–50.

Street, A. F., & Arias, I. (2001). Psychological abuse and posttraumatic stress disorder in battered women: Examining the role of shame and guilt. Violence and Victims, 16, 65–78.

Thompson, M. P., Kaslow, N., Kingree, N., Puett, R., Thompson, N., & Meadows, L. (1999). Partner abuse and posttraumatic stress disorder as risk factors for suicide attempt in a sample of low-income, inner-city women. Journal of Traumatic Stress, 12, 59–72.

Tjaden, P., & Thoennes, N. (2000). Extent, nature and consequences of intimate partner violence. NCJ Report No. NCJ 181867. Washington, DC: U.S. Department of Justice.

Torres, S. (1998). Intervening with battered Hispanic pregnant women. In J. C. Campbell (Ed.), *Empowering survivors of abuse: Health care for battered women and their children* (pp. 259–270). Thousand Oaks, CA: Sage.

Ulrich, Y. C. (1998). What helped most in leaving spouse abuse: Implications for interventions. In J. C. Campbell (Ed.), *Empowering survivors of abuse: Health care for battered women and their children* (pp. 70–78). Thousand Oaks, CA: Sage.

Veronen, L., & Kilpatrick, D. (1983). Stress management for rape victims. In D. Meichenbaum & M. Jaremko (Eds.), *Stress reduction and prevention* (pp. 341–374). New York: Plenum.

Wagner, A. W., & Linehan, M. M. (1998). Dissociative behavior. In V. M. Follette, J. I. Ruzek, & F. R. Abueg (Eds.), *Cognitive behavioral therapies for trauma* (pp. 191–225). New York: Guilford.

Walker, L. (1987). Assessment and intervention with battered women. In L. Ritt & P. Keller (Eds.), *Innovations in clinical practice: A sourcebook* (Vol. 6, pp. 131–142). Sarasota, FL: Professional Resource Exchange.

Walker, L. (1993). *Survivor therapy clinical assessment and intervention workbook*. Denver, CO: Endolar Communications.

Walker, L. (1994a). *The abused woman: A survivor therapy approach*. New York: Newbridge Communications.

Walker, L. (1994b). *Battered women and survivor therapy: A practical guide for the psychotherapist*. Washington, DC: American Psychological Association.

Walker, L. (2000). *The battered woman syndrome* (2nd ed.). New York: Springer.

Wan, A. M. (2000). Battered women in the restraining order process: Observations on a court advocacy program. *Violence Against Women, 6,* 606–632.

Webb, W. (1992). Treatment issues and cognitive behavior techniques with battered women. *Journal of Family Violence, 7,* 205–217.

Wuest, J., & Merritt-Gray, M. (1999). Not going back: Sustaining the separation in the process of leaving abusive relationships. *Violence Against Women, 5,* 110–133.

15

Promising Directions for Helping Chemically Involved Battered Women Get Safe and Sober

THERESA M. ZUBRETSKY

Chemically involved battered women often find themselves in the ultimate Catch-22: Substance use may begin or escalate as a response to the trauma of victimization, and efforts to stop using substances may precipitate abusive partners' use of increased violence. A battered woman's words about her own recovery capture the essence of the dilemma. She said, "As an alcoholic, AA and treatment saved my life; as a battered woman, it nearly killed me." Yet, despite significant correlations between domestic violence and chemical dependency and intimate links between safety and sobriety, domestic violence advocacy programs and substance abuse treatment programs are frequently ill prepared to provide the range and depth of services needed for chemically involved battered women to get *both* safe and sober. In addition, the system is no better prepared to respond to the safety-related needs of battered women whose partners are involved with substances and who seek services in substance abuse treatment programs.

The common roots shared by the domestic violence and substance abuse service systems provide a strong foundation for cooperative relationships. Long before there was a formalized movement, women were helping other women, sheltering them in their homes, in churches, and in other places of refuge. One of the strengths of the battered women's movement has been its reliance on empowerment through peer support. When women connect with other women, isolation breaks down, self-blame is challenged, fears are normalized as reasonable and proportionate, and women become empowered with information, hope, and support.

Similarly, when Bill W. started Alcoholics Anonymous (AA), it was with the idea that there were no better people to help alcoholics recover from addiction than alcoholics themselves. The core of the fellowship is simple and personal: Recovery begins when one alcoholic talks with another alcoholic, sharing experience, strength, and hope.

However, one of the primary limitations of the recovery movement was that it originated as a response to addiction *in men's lives*. It wasn't until the 1980s, a full 50 years after AA was founded, that the role of substances and the limitations of traditional treatment in women's lives would be recognized. Out of this recognition grew a model for treating women's addiction based on connection, a model in which a woman's substance abuse is addressed in the context of her health and her relationship with her children, family, community, and society.

The emergence of the domestic violence and substance abuse service systems subsequent to these peer support movements expanded the breadth of available assistance and created mechanisms for community education and prevention. But the trend toward professionalism in both fields has also prompted a gradual shift away from peer support to a hierarchy of power between "professional" and "client," a shift from *strength-based* to *deficit-based* approaches. This chapter will explore the unmistakable connections between substance abuse and violence in women's lives; the strength-based models within each of the service systems that best support the goals of safety and sobriety (specifically, *woman-defined advocacy* [Davies, 1998], the *relational* model [Finkelstein, 1996; Surrey, 1985] and *harm reduction* [Harm Reduction Coalition, 2001]); and the resulting opportunities for enhanced coordination and collaboration between the two systems.

THE LINK BETWEEN DOMESTIC VIOLENCE AND SUBSTANCE ABUSE

Etiology

Women who have been victims of violence have a higher risk of alcohol and other drug problems (Kilpatrick, Resnick, Saunders, & Best, 1998) and frequently respond to the trauma of victimization by using alcohol or other drugs (Paone, Chavkin, Willets, Friedman, & Des Jarlais, 1992; Russell & Wilsnack, 1991). Battered women often report that, in addition to medicating the emotional and physical pain of trauma, their chemical use helped to reduce or eliminate their feelings of fear and therefore became part of their day-to-day safety-related strategies (Jones & Schechter, 1992). It is therefore no surprise that battered women are disproportionately represented in chemical dependency treatment populations (Bergman, Larsson, Brismar, & Klang, 1989; Covington & Kohen, 1984; Miller, 1998).

There are a number of other ways in which victimization and chemical use are often related. Many victims' initial or escalated use of substances is coerced or manipulated by their abusive partners, from the extreme of women being tied down and forcibly injected with drugs to the more subtle pressure abusers place on victims to use certain drugs in social contexts to avoid personal embarrassment or to enhance sexual satisfaction.

Battered women are at increased risk of abusing legal drugs (U.S. Department of Health and Human Services, 1991), which are frequently prescribed in response to common health complaints, including chronic headaches, abdominal pains, sexual dysfunction, joint pains, muscle aches, and sleep disorders (Randall, 1990). This medication not only may alleviate the presenting symptoms but also may provide relief from the emotional and physical pain of the abuse. In fact, many chemically dependent battered women are addicted to drugs that were prescribed by the health care providers from whom they sought help (Flitcraft & Stark, 1988). Further, when prescription drugs are used in combination with alcohol (a common use pattern for women), the health-related consequences can be particularly devastating and potentially lethal (Galbraith, 1991).

Increased Vulnerability to Violence and Coercion

Whatever the etiology, a battered woman's use of substances provides the abuser with yet another weapon of coercion. He may use her substance use as the excuse for his violence; he may threaten to expose her substance use to friends, family, or authorities; he may be the primary or sole supplier of the drugs, increasing her dependence on him by exploiting her dependence on drugs (Finkelstein, 1996). Chemically involved battered women may be particularly vulnerable to sexual exploitation, either being forced into sexual activity in exchange for drugs or being prostituted by their partners as a source of income for drugs (Hart & Jans, 1997). If they are HIV-positive and/or with partners who are HIV-positive, victims may be threatened with infection, denied access to medication or medical attention, or threatened with having their HIV status revealed (Hart & Jans, 1997).

Barriers to Help

Chemically involved battered women also face additional barriers to help by virtue of their substance use. They are less likely to be believed or taken seriously by others; they are more likely to be blamed for the violence (Aramburu & Leigh, 1991); they face an enormous gap in emergency shelter services that systematically deny admission to chemically involved women; their chemical use may increase their risk of HIV, exposing them to even further discrimination in their help-seeking efforts; if mothers, they risk losing custody of their children to a system that deems them "unfit"; if pregnant, they face criminalization rather than services designed to support their recovery (Paltrow, 1998). Substance use can also compromise cognitive functioning and motor coordination, making victims less able to develop and implement safety-related strategies.

LIMITATIONS OF CURRENT RESPONSES

Despite the enormous obstacles that chemically involved battered women face, they remain active help seekers and surface in a wide variety of systems, including the domestic violence and substance abuse treatment systems. Unfortunately, these two service systems are often unprepared and ill equipped to respond to women's dual needs for safety and sobriety.

Limitations of Traditional Substance Abuse Treatment

Perhaps as few as 10% of substance abuse counselors include an assessment for adult domestic violence as part of the intake process to substance abuse treatment (Bennett & Lawson, 1994). Even when domestic violence is identified, it is often assumed that treatment for the substance abuse must occur before the victimization can be addressed.

One of the concerns with the "sobriety first" approach is that it does not consider the increased risk of violence that a woman's recovery may precipitate. Batterers often are resistant to their partners' attempts to seek help of any kind, including substance abuse treatment. In response, they may sabotage the recovery process by preventing victims from attending meetings or keeping appointments, by stocking the refrigerator with beer, or by restricting access to the resources victims need to comply with their treatment plans (transportation, child care, and health insurance). Abusers may also intensify their use of violence in order to reestablish control.

Many chemically dependent battered women leave treatment in response to the increased danger or are not able to comply with treatment demands because of the obstacles created by their partners' sabotage efforts. Others are terminated from treatment for "noncompliance" or "resistance" to treatment. Even when a battered woman *is* able to complete a treatment program, being revictimized is a strong predictor of relapse (Haver, 1987). The consequences of battered women's inability to successfully complete treatment are further exacerbated when treatment is leveraged or mandated by the criminal justice or child welfare system, and can include incarceration or loss of custodial rights.

An additional concern with the "sobriety first" approach is that it fails to address the fact that battered women often rely on substances as part of their safety-related strategies. Substance-using battered women often report that the substances helped them cope with their fear and manage the daily activities of their lives in the face of ongoing abuse and danger (Minnesota Coalition for Battered Women, 1992). These are women who may be particularly resistant to engaging in a recovery process until they are confident that they can achieve genuine safety from the violence. For these women, an intervention framework that requires "sobriety first" may be destined to fail.

Limitations of Domestic Violence Program Responses

The current rhetoric about chronology of care for chemically involved battered women suggests a shift from "sobriety first" to "safety first." The irony of such a shift is that the domestic violence service system has historically failed to meet the safety-related needs of this population of battered women.

Chemically dependent battered women often have very limited or no access to safe shelter through the emergency domestic violence shelter network because of their addiction (Collins, Kroutil, Roland, & Moore-Guerra, 1997). While admission and discharge policies must consider the safety needs of all shelter residents, policies that prohibit access by chemically dependent battered women are commonplace and cut off many women from a vital resource. In trainings conducted with domestic violence program staff from several states, a few recurring themes surface and provide insight into the persistence of nonadmission policies of domestic violence programs. These include limited resources to address the complexity and demands of chemically involved battered women (an obstacle also identified by Collins et al., 1997); adherence to the traditional substance abuse treatment view that woman-defined responses to addiction are "enabling"; and harmful and inaccurate attitudes and beliefs about addicted women—for example, that the chemically involved are dangers to themselves and others, that they will be unable to comply with shelter rules, that they will be dishonest, and that they will neglect their children—attitudes frequently rooted in negative personal experiences with friends or family members who have alcohol or other drug problems (Roth, 1991).

Whether or not these beliefs about the chemically involved are statistically founded, domestic violence programs typically determine eligibility for shelter services by assessing on the basis of an individual's presentation at the time of intake. Intake counselors ask questions to determine whether any particular individual poses a safety risk to herself or others, what her abilities are with regard to being able to participate in communal living, and so forth. The categorical exclusion of chemically involved battered women from emergency shelter services is no more justifiable than the categorical exclusion of *any* group of women for whom there is a demonstrated—or perceived—statistical risk for undesirable or problematic behavior.

Even when domestic violence programs have admission criteria that allow chemically dependent battered women into a shelter, they often do not conduct appropriate screening for substance abuse and fail even to minimally evaluate the addiction treatment needs of sheltered battered women (Bennett & Lawson, 1994). The end effect is a "don't ask, don't tell" policy. Shelter staff don't ask, and consequently they miss an opportunity to interrupt the deadly progression of women's alcohol or other drug addictions, problems that may significantly impair battered women's efforts to get safe; and battered women don't tell because they fear that to do so might jeopardize their shelter stay.

In instances in which the domestic violence program does ask and women do tell, the programs typically require a substance abuse evaluation and compliance with any subsequent treatment plan that might be recommended. The implicit expectation is often that women will proceed in linear fashion to the end goal—abstinence and recovery—an expectation that is no more realistic than to expect a battered woman to leave her abusive partner the first time she reaches out for help. Recovery is a process, not an event, and domestic violence responses that view relapse in a broader context—as an opportunity for intervention rather than a basis for shelter discharge—would better support chemically involved battered women's difficult journeys toward safety and sobriety.

Lack of Connection Between the Fields

Despite the unmistakable connections between victimization and substance use, there is a notable lack of connection between the domestic violence and substance abuse treatment systems (Collins et al., 1997). Meeting the needs of substance-using battered women, however, demands an effective working relationship between the two service systems—a relationship consistently identified as important by workers in both fields, but an undertaking fraught with multiple obstacles to cooperation (Bennett & Lawson, 1994; Levy & Brekke, 1990; Rogan, 1985; Wright, 1985). The battered women's movement is a grassroots social change movement based on a sociopolitical analysis of domestic violence, while the alcoholism field works from a medical model and provides treatment from a perspective that understands chemical dependency as a disease. Traditional substance abuse treatment is male-centered, depoliticized, and confrontational, whereas domestic violence advocacy is typically woman-defined and political and considers the victim as the expert regarding her situation. The subsequent conflicts that emerge in attempts to coordinate services to individuals affected by both problems are understandable and predictable (Collins et al., 1997).

Domestic violence programs do refer women to chemical dependency treatment agencies more frequently than the reverse occurs, which may suggest that domestic violence programs have a greater desire to forge cooperative relationships with providers of substance abuse treatment (Bennett & Lawson, 1994). There is, however, a less charitable explanation that may account for the high referral rates by domestic violence programs. The lack of information and training on chemical dependency among domestic violence program staff and/or the existence of harmful attitudes and beliefs about chemically dependent women may deter domestic violence advocates from directly providing services to this population. The subsequent referrals may then become a way to shift primary responsibility for difficult cases to another agency or to someone else's caseload. In fact, Collins et al. (1997) note that once victims are referred by domestic violence programs to substance abuse treatment, it is rare for those referred to receive domestic violence services simultaneously.

MODELS FOR IMPROVED RESPONSES TO CHEMICALLY INVOLVED BATTERED WOMEN

Coordination Models

To the extent that domestic violence and substance abuse treatment programs are working together, the predominant model for cooperation is based on the goal of achieving cross-screening and cross-referral through cross-training. A common feature of this model is to develop screening tools and provide subsequent training on their appropriate use. The increased identification that results from routine screening, combined with the existing linkages between the respective service systems, enhances chemically involved women's access to both safety-related and recovery services. In many instances, these models include the sharing of staff resources (e.g., assessments conducted by a domestic violence advocate on-site in a substance abuse treatment program, or the reverse), cofacilitated women's educational or support groups, or ongoing coordinated case management.

These coordination initiatives have been successful to varying degrees, depending largely on the abilities of the domestic violence and substance abuse staff to develop and sustain a supportive and respectful relationship. The more deeply intertwined the service provision of the two fields becomes, however, the more visible the differences, and the greater the potential for friction between staff. Even when the involved staff are prepared for the inevitable conflicts and committed to working them through, conflicts between woman-defined advocacy and traditional treatment often become insurmountable. When this occurs, the relationships may simply collapse. Often, the best that can be hoped for is that staff develop a tolerance of each other, resulting in the provision of parallel services that fail to integrate important elements of the other and ultimately limit the effectiveness of the assistance offered.

Coordination Initiatives and the Relational Model

When the substance abuse treatment program is one that provides treatment grounded in a *relational* or *self-in-relation* model (Surrey, 1985)—a model that is highly compatible with woman-defined advocacy—coordination between the two systems is often more integrated and more effective. Relationships between the domestic violence and substance abuse program staff are more likely to flourish, enhancing trust and commitment and ultimately facilitating women's safety and sobriety.

Just as the domestic violence field recognizes that there are myriad motivators and barriers to a woman's decision to seek help or leave a violent partner, relational models take into account the myriad motivators and barriers to a woman's successful recovery and embrace the need for comprehensive and individualized treatment planning. The relational model expands the focus of treatment to one in which the interrelationships between a woman and the treatment program, her children, other family members, and her community become central, rather than incidental, to the treatment.

Relational models of treatment are strength-based and more likely to foster an empowering framework through which to provide assistance to women. They typically incorporate important support services into the treatment program such as women-only groups and mechanisms to promote and strengthen maternal relationships; they respond to the effects of violence and trauma as integral to women's recovery; they affirm nontraditional relationships in identifying family and friend support networks rather than relying on traditional family systems interventions that are often dangerous for battered women; and they actively promote the development of meaningful support systems (Finkelstein, 1996).

Additionally, by acknowledging the important role of sociopolitical influences on women's lives, including sexism, racism, and poverty, relational models of intervention reject pathologizing frameworks for understanding women's victimization and addiction. Viewed through a relational model lens, domestic violence is understood as a common "disconnection" in women's lives; battered women's efforts to try to stop the violence and salvage the relationship are understood not as pathology but as an active strategy to maintain connection with their intimate partners. Although use of a relational model does not guarantee attention to safety-related needs, the integration of safety planning into treatment planning is a more natural process within a relational model than it is within traditional treatment settings.

Limitations of Coordination Model

There is little question that cross-training models of coordination between the domestic violence and substance abuse fields have brought about meaningful improvements in the response to chemically involved battered women. The availability of expert help for developing a safety plan is a tremendous assist to a woman struggling to comply with a treatment plan that her abusive partner is intent on sabotaging; the availability of recovery services is a similarly huge assist to women whose chemical use is interfering with their ability to get and stay safe. There is further evidence that coordination models are more effective when services are provided through complementary frameworks rather than simply relying on cross-referrals to adequately address the needs of chemically involved battered women.

However, while many coordinating agencies develop written memoranda of agreement outlining their respective responsibilities and expectations for working together, it is relatively rare for coordination efforts to be additionally supported by explicit policy development and implementation within the respective coordinating agencies. The absence of policies and procedures that institutionalize appropriate responses and the subsequent absence of accountability standards can contribute to inconsistent staff responses, which, in turn, undermine the existing agreements. Further, without supporting policies, the life of these agreements is often completely dependent on the interest of committed individuals within the respective systems. If these key staff members leave their positions, the agreements often leave with them.

Another limitation of these coordination initiatives is that the substance abuse treatment programs, even when operating from within a relational context, usually provide treatment from an abstinence model framework. The pathway to recovery may be more flexible in meeting the individual needs of women, but the ultimate goal still requires abstinence. A similar limitation can exist in the provision of domestic violence services. Even when advocates support battered women in whatever choices they make and respect their rights to make those choices, they often hold on to "leaving" as the ultimate goal. For some women, however, abstinence and/or leaving may be either very distant outcomes or outcomes never realized.

Harm Reduction

Because batterers' violence and coercion often directly interfere with a battered woman's ability to achieve and sustain abstinence, *harm reduction* is another approach to substance abuse treatment that holds promise for working with chemically involved battered women. Although relational models may incorporate many of the principles of harm reduction, harm reduction holds as its central goal *to reduce harm;* whether or not abstinence ever 1bnbecomes a goal of the harm reduction process is completely contingent on the individual. Consider a standard description of harm reduction:

> Harm reduction accepts, for better and for worse, that licit and illicit drug use is a part of our world and chooses to work to minimize its harmful

effects rather than simply ignore or condemn them. . . . Understands drug use as a complex, multi-faceted phenomenon . . . and acknowledges that some ways of using drugs are clearly safer than others. . . . Establishes quality of individual and community life and well-being—not necessarily cessation of all drug use—as the criteria for successful intervention and policies. . . . Calls for non-judgmental, non-coercive provision of services and resources to people who use drugs and the communities in which they live in order to assist them in reducing attendant harm. . . . Affirms drug users themselves as the primary agents of reducing the harms of their drug use, and seeks to empower users to share information and support each other in strategies that meet their actual conditions of use. . . . Recognizes that the realities of poverty, class, racism, social isolation, past trauma, sex-based discrimination and other social inequalities affect people's vulnerability to and capacity for effectively dealing with drug-related harm. . . . Does not attempt to minimize or ignore the real and tragic harm and danger associated with licit and illicit drug use. (Harm Reduction Coalition, 2001)

Notice how this parallels a description of woman-defined advocacy:

The response to domestic violence must be built on the premise that women will have the opportunity to make decisions—that she is the decision maker, the one who knows best, the one with the power. . . . [This] does not ensure that a battered woman or her children will be safe—rather, it seeks to craft the alternatives that will enhance women's safety, given the realities facing each battered woman. It is not the goal of woman-defined advocacy that women should stay in violent relationships, but when staying provides the best possible alternative, woman-defined advocacy supports a woman's decision and works with her to keep her and her children as safe as possible. Until all systems respond sympathetically and effectively for all battered women, and until batterers stop battering, the response to battered women must acknowledge these limitations and the realities of women's lives. Woman-defined advocacy is advocacy for the real—not the ideal—world and for women with real, not stereotypic, lives. . . . Systemic advocacy to improve local agency and policy responses to domestic violence is an integral part of woman-defined advocacy. (Davies, 1998)

The compatibility of harm reduction and woman-defined advocacy is striking and renders the tension between "sobriety first" and "safety first" moot, since both models are rooted in meeting the individual where she's at, and beginning wherever she is willing and able to begin. Like woman-defined advocacy, the harm reduction model acknowledges the limitations of any intervention in light of the personal and systemic obstacles to the ideal goal (safety or abstinence). Both models recognize that there are risks attached to every decision an individual might make and that the individual's set of priorities and evaluation of risks may differ from that of the service provider. Both models actively engage the client in identifying and evaluating risks and benefits of different options and identifying ways to reduce risk, recognizing that the individual's perspective is, ultimately, the only one that counts. Some battered women report that they needed to get safe before they could even consider giving up their use of substances; for others, getting sober was the prerequisite to implementing safety-related strategies. Making an offer of help conditional upon an expectation that the client will follow a predetermined chronology of care or a particular path to safety or sobriety is both unrealistic and futile.

Persistent Obstacles

Harm reduction and the relational model are compatible not only with woman-defined advocacy but also with each other; together, they hold great promise for responding to the needs of chemically involved battered women. Comprehensive and relational models of substance abuse treatment, however, are not readily available in most communities across the country; and harm reduction, which rubs against the grain of the more traditional abstinence models, has not yet gained the legitimacy within the substance abuse field that it deserves. Further, the availability of these substance abuse treatment approaches does not solve the problem of domestic violence programs' reluctance to expand their provision of services, especially emergency shelter, to chemically involved battered women.

The task for domestic violence service providers in improving responses to chemically involved battered women is, in the abstract at least, less difficult than that for the substance abuse treatment system. Domestic violence advocates need to make neither a philosophical nor a practical shift from their long-standing practice of woman-defined advocacy and safety planning; they need only extend their emergency shelter services to this population of battered women using the same kinds of woman-centered approaches that are effective for non–chemically involved battered women. And there is increasing urgency for them to do so.

National welfare reform law requires screening for substance abuse as part of the process for receiving assistance, and many states have passed laws to also require screening for domestic violence, resulting in an increase in identification and referral of chemically involved battered women to local domestic violence services and substance abuse treatment. Further, anecdotal reports nationwide suggest that shelter populations are changing from those largely composed of battered women in need of safety to women with multiple distressors in addition to their need for safety, including chemical use, mental health problems, HIV, and serious mental illness.

If these anecdotal reports are accurate, the changing population may well be a result of improved systems' responses to battered women, which create more and better options for safety and preclude many women's need for shelter but still fall short of meeting the needs of previously underserved women for whom solutions to safety are more complex. Another possibility is that the actual number of chemically involved women in shelter populations is the same, but the rate of identification is increasing. Either way, domestic violence programs have an increased awareness of the prevalence of chemical dependency in the lives of battered women in shelter and an increased motivation to better meet their needs.

If one of the obstacles to domestic violence programs proactively serving the emergency shelter needs of chemically involved women is their own set of inaccurate beliefs and negative attitudes about this population of women, then the gains to be had through training are significant. In addition, just as the substance abuse field needs the active involvement of domestic violence service providers to ensure appropriate responses, domestic violence programs need the active support of the substance abuse community. When this support is consistent with the domestic violence program philosophy and practice, the ability of domestic violence programs to respond effectively will be strengthened.

Integrated Models

There is growing support for more fully integrated models of responding to the needs of chemically involved battered women, including top-down reform requiring substantial structural and administrative changes in funding streams and mechanisms for delivering services on a continuum of care (Center for Substance Abuse Treatment, 1997). Less ambitious integration calls for all needed domestic violence and substance abuse services (with the notable exception of emergency shelter) to be provided under one roof ("one-stop shopping").

Any model that seeks to minimize the burden on the person in need of services by offering her access to comprehensive assistance—whether through a continuum of care or a single port of entry—deserves serious consideration and pursuit. However, the existing service system currently lacks the necessary infrastructure to support these approaches.

The missing link in "one-stop shopping" models is that the staff members who implement them often have expertise in *either* domestic violence or substance abuse but not in *both*. Even when domestic violence or substance abuse program staff are trained by experts in the relevant field, training alone does not adequately prepare them to deliver individualized, comprehensive services that meet the diverse and complex needs of chemically involved battered women. Often, the result is a program that does not fully integrate the best practices of both systems but rather delivers services through its own primary framework of understanding, compromising either safety or sobriety in the process. Responsible and meaningful service provision demands the requisite knowledge, skills, and experience—qualifications that, at present, are more readily found *within* the respective service systems.

While in an ideal world there might be comprehensive assistance for a person in need to address the multiple distressors in his or her life, the truth is that our service systems are highly compartmentalized and are likely to stay that way for some time to come. Although it is important to view solutions to the lack of connection between the substance abuse and domestic violence service systems from a more global perspective and to advocate for needed systemic reform, it is equally important to search for solutions in the here and now. Coordination initiatives may be the most effective and the most feasible options available within the parameters of the existing service systems in their efforts to support the needs of chemically involved battered women. Further, based on the significant accomplishments of many coordination initiatives across the country, it *is not* necessarily a compromise to advocate for the effective expansion of coordination models rather than giving priority to the promotion of fully integrated models.

Coordination Initiative Project Outcomes

The potential outcomes of coordination initiatives extend far beyond cross-identification and cross-referral and greatly increase chemically involved battered women's access to complementary assistance for both problems. Substance abuse treatment programs and domestic violence programs should consider the impact of *all* program components, policies, and procedures on chemically involved battered women, including screening and intake; the development of treatment plans (in substance abuse programs); crisis intervention, counseling, case management, and client education; report and record keeping; referrals; client confidentiality; on-site safety and security; community prevention and education; and employee assistance. Evaluating and modifying existing polices and procedures to better support the needs of chemically involved battered women not only maximizes the effectiveness of the services provided but also institutionalizes the response.

For example, many substance abuse treatment programs routinely contact partners of clients as "collateral contacts" (a mechanism by which to gather accurate information about the client's drinking and drug use). Whether a victim is being asked to provide information about her abuser's substance use or the abuser is being solicited to provide information on the victim's drug use, the potential for unintentionally colluding with the abuser and endangering the victim is great. If the program has clearly defined policies and procedures that require all staff to conduct effective and ongoing screening for domestic violence and subsequently exclude victims and abusers from serving as collateral contacts, safety for battered women can be increased.

Upon admission to domestic violence shelters, residents often must agree to certain rules, such as adherence to curfews or participation in particular shelter activities, that may conflict with a recovering woman's established

AA meeting schedule. Some shelter programs, in the interests of "fairness," enforce these rules with residents without exception; in this case, they might encourage the woman to find a meeting that does not conflict with shelter requirements, justifying that it is only a short-term inconvenience and failing to recognize the important role a "home" meeting can play in a person's recovery support system. Without interest in and a mechanism for waiving program requirements to better support women's recovery efforts, women may be forced to choose between emergency shelter and sobriety support.

Domestic violence and substance abuse treatment programs can also modify existing program components to increase the identification of chemically involved battered women and their motivation to access help and support. For example, by integrating alcohol and other drug education into battered women's support groups—to discuss the use of alcohol or other drugs as a response to trauma; the dangers of frequent and continued use; the ways in which chemical use can interfere with battered women's abilities to implement safety strategies; the difficult challenges for women in recovery; and the benefits of recovery in women's lives—domestic violence programs can communicate a nonjudgmental invitation to women who may be struggling with chemical use in private to reach out for help. (Of course, proactive efforts to identify chemical users among a population of battered women residing in shelter are recommended only in those programs that welcome chemically involved battered women into their shelter and are prepared to respond supportively rather than punitively.) This integration of education on alcohol and other drugs can also sensitize nonusing women to the difficulties faced by chemical-using women, thereby directly addressing a concern frequently voiced by domestic violence programs that more flexible admission and discharge policies for chemical-using battered women can have a negative impact on other shelter residents, particularly those who may be struggling with their own recovery and/or who have chemically involved partners. Similarly, substance abuse treatment programs can integrate domestic violence education into family program groups, women's groups, and other counseling settings to sensitize, inform, and potentially link unidentified victims with safety-related assistance.

In addition to the program improvements that can be achieved through coordination initiatives, these approaches may also provide the greatest opportunity for substance abuse professionals and domestic violence advocates to develop the requisite expertise in the "other" problem, which may, in turn, more fully support the successful development and implementation of integrated models. Coordination efforts pair substance abuse professionals and domestic violence advocates *as equal partners,* operating from a premise of respect and deference to the other's expertise in a partnership that can minimize turf battles and maximize learning. It is highly unlikely that either system holds the answer independent of the other regarding what will best help chemically involved battered women. As coordination initiatives multiply, there will likely be a process of joint discovery that will best inform the development of future responses.

SAFETY IMPLICATIONS FOR BATTERED WOMEN WITH CHEMICALLY INVOLVED PARTNERS

The safety implications for battered women in the substance abuse treatment system are relevant not only for those who are themselves chemically involved but also for women whose abusive partners are chemically involved. Batterers are regularly engaged in substance abuse treatment, and victims are regularly engaged in services designed for family members of chemically involved persons, without counselors' knowledge of or attention to the potential consequences for victim safety.

Chemically Involved Batterers

The belief that alcoholism causes domestic violence is widely held both within and outside of the substance abuse field, despite a lack of information to support it. Although research indicates that among men who drink heavily, there is a higher rate of perpetrating assaults resulting in serious physical injury than exists among other men, the majority of abusive men are not high-level drinkers, and the majority of men classified as high-level drinkers do not abuse their partners (Straus & Gelles, 1990).

Even for batterers who do drink, there is little evidence to suggest a clear pattern that relates the drinking to the abusive behavior. The vast majority (76%) of physical assaults committed by batterers who use alcohol occur in the absence of alcohol use (Kantor & Straus, 1987), and there is no evidence to suggest that alcohol use or dependence is linked to the other forms of coercive behaviors that are part of the pattern of domestic violence. Economic control, sexual violence, and intimidation, for example, are often part of a batterer's ongoing pattern of abuse, with little or no identifiable connection to his use of or dependence on alcohol.

In addition to the evidence that alcohol is neither a necessary factor nor a sufficient explanation for men's intimate violence, there is evidence that treatment for the chemical dependency does *not* stop the violence. Battered women with drug-dependent partners consistently report that during recovery the abuse not only continues but often escalates, creating greater levels of danger than existed prior to their partners' abstinence. In the cases in which battered women report that the level of physical abuse decreases, they often report a corresponding increase in other forms of coercive control and abuse—the threats, manipulation, and isolation intensify (Minnesota Coalition for Battered Women, 1992). In response to the increased danger, battered women may attempt to sabotage their partners' recovery efforts as a safety-related strategy. These attempts, however, are likely to be perceived by the substance abuse counselor as evidence of the need for codependency treatment rather than the need for safety-related assistance.

Impact of Codependency Treatment on Battered Women

Most often, the partners of batterers in chemical dependency treatment are directed into self-help programs such as Al-Anon or codependency groups. Like other traditional treatment responses, however, these resources were not designed to meet the needs of victims of domestic violence and often inadvertently cause harm to battered women.

The goals of Al-Anon and codependency treatment typically include helping family members of alcoholics to get "self-focused," practice emotional detachment from the substance abusers, and identify and stop their enabling or "codependent" behaviors. Group members are encouraged to define their personal boundaries, set limits on their partners' behaviors, and stop protecting their partners from the harmful consequences of the addiction. While these strategies and goals may be useful for women whose partners are not batterers, for battered women, such changes will likely result in an escalation of abuse, including physical violence.

Battered women are often very attuned to their partners' moods as a way to assess their level of danger. They focus on their partners' needs and "cover up" for them as part of their survival strategy. Battered women's behaviors are not symptomatic of some underlying "dysfunction" but are necessary lifesaving skills that protect them and their children from further harm. When battered women are encouraged to stop these behaviors through self-focusing and detachment, they are, in essence, being asked to stop doing the things that may be keeping them and their children most safe.

The particular danger of codependency treatment for battered women, however, is grounded in a more general problem with the overall codependency framework. Both the feminist and relational model views hold that most of the characteristics ascribed to codependency (nurturing, responsibility for family, caretaking, defining self in terms of one's relationships) are aspects of the traditional female gender role that itself is a by-product of the subordination of women in a racist and sexist culture (Babcock & McKay, 1995; Collins, 1993). Codependency ignores the cultural context that gives rise to patterns of female behavior and, in so doing, transforms a socially constructed phenomenon into an individual pathology.

Codependent behaviors are explained in terms of the "dysfunctional" family and are viewed through a disease framework, labeling affected individuals as "sick" and "addicted to relationships." Codependency treatment encourages individuals to accept personal responsibility to become "healthy," which is further defined as becoming an "autonomous, individuated, separate self" (Collins, 1993). Codependency draws attention away from the effects of women's oppression in a racist and sexist world, renames the effects of that oppression as a "condition" of the oppressed, and makes women responsible for it (Hagan, 1989). To make matters worse, women are held to a standard of health that is decidedly male, ignoring the relational context in which most women are socialized to view themselves.

Need for Effective Coordination

Linkages between substance abuse and domestic violence services can facilitate the provision of accurate and complete information about available resources to battered women whose partners are chemically dependent so that they can make informed choices and set realistic expectations about the potential benefits of these different sources of help. It is critical that women understand the purposes of Al-Anon and codependency groups and the limitations of these forums as sources of accurate information regarding safety-related concerns. They should also be given access to safety-planning assistance through the local domestic violence program. Empowering women with accurate information will help them make decisions that best meet their individual needs.

Furthermore, when substance abuse programs operate from within a relational model in providing assistance to women whose partners are chemically dependent, many of the potential conflicts between the domestic violence and substance abuse service systems can be successfully avoided. Woman-defined advocacy and the relational model are feminist approaches to providing empowering assistance to women that recognize the resourcefulness, resilience, and courage that women bring to the process and that build on these strengths. When operating in tandem to respond to the needs of battered women affected by their own or their partners' substance abuse, the respective goals of the domestic violence and substance abuse service systems become mutually supportive, rather than competing, goals.

SUMMARY

Even limited connections based on cross-referrals between the domestic violence and substance abuse treatment systems increase women's opportunities to get their safety and recovery needs met. With the emergence of new models of substance abuse treatment that are more compatible with woman-defined advocacy come even richer opportunities for the systems to work together. In fact, coordination models between the systems may be more likely to be developed and sustained when the respective systems are working from a unified philosophical and practical framework, a unification made possible through the increased availability of relational and harm reduction models of substance abuse treatment.

Multiple obstacles to cooperation between the domestic violence and substance abuse service systems have been explored in this chapter, but there are others that further complicate the landscape and impede the integration of services, including the limitations of highly compartmentalized programming and staffing, limitations imposed by managed care, and funding restrictions (CSAT, 1997). Whatever the existing obstacles, both systems have a mutual responsibility to ensure that their respective responses promote victim safety and recovery from addiction. As long as there remains a disconnection between the domestic violence and substance abuse fields, battered women whose lives are affected by their own or their partners' chemical use will continue to pay the heaviest price.

NOTE

Sections two and four adapt from and build upon "The False Connection Between Adult Domestic Violence and Alcohol," by T. M. Zubretsky and K. M. Digirolamo, 1996, in A. R. Roberts (Ed.), *Helping Battered Women*, New York: Oxford University Press.

REFERENCES

Aramburu, B., & Leigh, B. (1991). For better or worse: Attributions about drunken aggression toward male and female victims. *Violence and Victims, 6*, 31–42.

Babcock, M., & McKay, C. (1995). *Challenging codependency: Feminist critiques.* Toronto: University of Toronto Press.

Bennett, L., & Lawson, M. (1994). Barriers to cooperation between domestic-violence and substance-abuse programs. *Families in Society: The Journal of Contemporary Human Services, 75*, 277–286.

Bergman, G., Larsson, G., Brismar, B., Klang, M. (1989). Battered wives and female alcoholics: A comparative social and psychiatric study. *Journal of Advanced Nursing, 14*, 727–734.

Center for Substance Abuse Treatment. (1997). *Substance abuse treatment and domestic violence.* DHHS Publication No. (SMA) 97-3163. Rockville, MD: U.S. Department of Health and Human Services.

Collins, B. G. (1993). Reconstruing codependency using self-in-relation theory: A feminist perspective. *Social Work, 38*, 470–476.

Collins, J. J., Kroutil, L. A., Roland, E. J., & Moore-Gurrera, M. (1997). Issues in the linkage of alcohol and domestic violence services. In M. Galanter (Ed.), *Recent developments in alcoholism, Volume 13: Alcoholism and violence.* New York: Plenum.

Covington, S. S., & Kohen, J. (1984). Women, alcohol and sexuality. *Advances in Alcohol and Substance Abuse, 4*, 41–56.

Davies, J. (1998). *Safety planning with battered women.* Thousand Oaks, CA: Sage.

Finkelstein, N. (1996). Using the relational model as a context for treating pregnant and parenting chemically dependent women. In B. L. Underhill & D. Finnegan (Eds.), *Chemical dependency: Women at risk* (pp. 23–44). Binghamton, NY: Haworth.

Flitcraft, A., & Stark, E. (1988). Violence among intimates: An epidemiological review. In V. D. Van Hasselt, R. L. Morrison, A. S. Bellack, & M. Hersen (Eds.), *Handbook of family violence* (pp. 159–199). New York: Plenum.

Galbraith, S. (1991). Women and legal drugs. In P. Roth (Ed.), *Alcohol and drugs are women's issues* (Vol. 1, pp. 150–154). Metuchen, NJ: Scarecrow.

Hagan, K. (1989). *Codependency and the myth of recovery*. Atlanta: Escapadia Press.

Harm Reduction Coalition. (2001). *Principles of harm reduction*. Available on-line: www.harmreduction. org/prince.html.

Hart, B. J., & Jans, F. (1997). *Drugs, alcohol and addiction*. Harrisburg: Pennsylvania Coalition Against Domestic Violence.

Haver, B. (1987). Female alcoholics: IV. The relationship between family violence and outcome 3–10 years after treatment. *Acta Psychiatric Scandanavia, 57*, 449–456.

Jones, A., & Schechter, S. (1992). *When love goes wrong*. New York: HarperCollins.

Kantor, G. K., & Straus, M. A. (1987). The "drunken bum" theory of wife beating. *Social Problems, 34*, 213–230.

Kilpatrick, D. G., Resnick, H., Saunders, B., & Best, C. (1998). Victimization, posttraumatic stress disorder and substance use and abuse among women. In Cora Lee Wetherington & Adele B. Roman (Eds.), *Drug addiction research and the health of women* (pp. 285–307). Rockville, MD: U.S. Department of Health and

Human Services, National Institutes of Health, National Institute on Drug Abuse.

Levy, A. J., & Brekke, J. S. (1990). Spouse battering and chemical dependency: Dynamics, treatment, and services delivery. In D. Finnegan (Ed.), *Aggression, family violence and chemical dependency* (pp. 81–97). Binghamton, NY: Haworth.

Miller, B. A. (1998). Partner violence experiences and women's drug use: Exploring the connections. In Cora Lee Wetherington & Adele B. Roman (Eds.). *Drug addiction research and the health of women* (pp. 407–416). Rockville, MD: U.S. Department of Health and Human Services, National Institutes of Health, National Institute on Drug Abuse.

Minnesota Coalition for Battered Women. (1992). *Safety first: Battered women surviving violence when alcohol and drugs are involved*. Minneapolis: Author.

National Institute on Drug Abuse. (1989). *National Household Survey on Drug Abuse: Population estimates 1988*. DHHS Publication No. (ADM) 89-1636. Washington, DC: U.S. Goverment Printing Office.

Paltrow, L. M. (1998). Punishing women for their behavior during pregnancy: An approach that undermines the health of women and children. In Cora Lee Wetherington & Adele B. Roman (Eds.), *Drug addiction research and the health of women* (pp. 467–501). Rockville, MD: U.S. Department of Health and Human Services, National Institutes of Health, National Institute on Drug Abuse.

Paone, D., Chavkin, W., Willets, I., Friedman, P., & Des Jarlais, D. (1992). The impact of sexual abuse: Implications for drug treatment. *Journal of Women's Health, 1*, 149–153.

Randall, T. (1990). Domestic violence begets other problems of which physicians must be aware to be effective. *Journal of the American Medical Association, 264,* 943–944.

Rogan, A. (1985). Domestic violence and alcohol: Barriers to cooperation. *Alcohol Health and Research World,* Winter 85/86, 22–27.

Roth, P. (Ed.). (1991). *Alcohol and drugs are women's issues: Vol. 2. The model program guide.* Metuchen, NJ: Scarecrow.

Russell, S. A., & Wilsnack, S. (1991). Adult survivors of childhood sexual abuse: Substance abuse and other consequences. In P. Roth (Ed.), *Alcohol and drugs are women's issues* (Vol. 1, pp. 61–70). Metuchen, NJ: Scarecrow.

Straus, M. A., & Gelles, R. J. (1990). *Physical violence in American families.* New Brunswick, NJ: Transaction.

Surrey, J. (1985). *The "self-in-relation": A theory of women's development.* Stone Center for Developmental Services and Studies, Wellesley College. Wellesley, MA.

U.S. Department of Health and Human Services. (1991). *Healthy People 2000: National health promotion and disease prevention objectives.* DHHS Publication No. PHS 91-50212. Washington, DC: U.S. Government Printing Office.

Wright, J. (1985). Domestic violence and substance abuse: A cooperative approach toward working with dually affected families. In E. M. Freeman (Ed.), *Social work practice with clients who have alcohol problems* (pp. 26–39). Springfield, IL: Thomas.

Part IV

CRISIS INTERVENTION, ADVOCACY,
AND SPECIALIZED PROGRAMS

16

Children Exposed to Domestic Violence

The Role of Impact, Assessment, and Treatment

PETER LEHMANN
STEPHANIE RABENSTEIN

The purpose of this chapter is to provide social workers with a broad, practice-based overview of the literature documenting children exposed to domestic violence. Exposure can occur in many different ways (Edleson, 1999); however, in this chapter, exposure is generally defined as seeing and/or hearing and/or intervening in an attempt to stop the violence. Although children exposed to the repeated physical, sexual, and psychological assaults of their mothers by male caretakers or father figures have been considered forgotten (Elbow, 1982) and invisible (Fantuzzo, Boruch, Beriama, Atkins, & Marcus, 1997), within the last 15 years the mental health field has made many contributions toward understanding the short- and long-term impact on its youngest survivors. For example, a large body of books and edited volumes have detailed the negative impact on children exposed to domestic violence (e.g., Barnett, Miller-Perrin, & Perrin, 1997; Edleson & Eisikovits, 1996; Geffner, Jaffe, & Sudermann, 2000; Holden, Geffner, & Jouriles, 1998; Jaffe, Wolfe, & Wilson, 1990; David and Lucile Packard Foundation, 1999; Peled, 1997; Roberts, 1998). Additionally, at least 100 empirical and clinical descriptive papers have been published that document the experiences of children.

The profession of social work has a significant role to play in understanding how to best assess and intervene with exposed children. In the course of a professional day, it is likely that direct practice social workers will observe the immediate and long-term indicators of violence on children and families.

343

Consequently, most professionals employed in schools, hospitals, shelters for battered women, and children's mental health settings, to name a few, will need to make informed decisions about their practice when confronted with exposed children. This chapter, therefore, will be divided into three main sections. First, a discussion on the estimates of exposure to violence will highlight the seriousness of this issue. This summary provides a basis for understanding the impact of such experiences and ultimately intervening. Second, a cursory review of the literature will be presented, including a focus on a number of impact, moderating or mediating, and resilience factors. This discussion will also include a summary of the more recent focus on the traumatic and posttraumatic indicators some children exhibit. Third, we present a summary of assessment and treatment protocols. Finally, a case illustration highlights the various assessment and treatment issues.

ESTIMATES OF CHILD EXPOSURE TO DOMESTIC VIOLENCE

Reliable estimates of child exposure to domestic violence are critical to the social work profession for a number of reasons. Primarily, the recognition of child exposure is relatively new. In the last 15 years, child exposure has been redefined so that it is no longer a "social condition" or a difficulty that has always existed but a "social problem" or a malady that has serious mental health implications for children (Barnett, Miller-Perrin, & Perrin, 1997, p. 5). Growing societal concern in this area has allowed interested researchers and clinicians to consider how widespread exposure to violence has become. An additional reason that reliable estimates are important is associated with intervention. Correct appraisals of child exposure allow practitioners to design interventions that will target the specific needs of children; included here is a sensitivity toward cultural and racial differences (Canino & Spurlock, 2000; Paniagua, 1998). Finally, as professionals look to the future, reliable estimates will drive public health models as a preventive measure for children across the life span (see Fantuzzo, Moore, & Noone, 2000; Fantuzzo & Mohr, 1999; Wolfe & Jaffe, 1999, for examples).

Although the precise numbers of children exposed to domestic violence will likely never be known, some estimates have been commonly accepted in the field by researchers and policy makers alike. Such estimates have ranged from 3.3 million children (based on 2.2 children per family; Carlson, 1984, 1996) to 10 million children in the United States (Straus, 1991) and 500,000 children in Canada (McLeod, 1987).

More recently, Fantuzzo and Mohr (1999) have outlined a number of sources for estimating more exact numbers of children exposed to domestic violence. While these sources have some limitations, they nevertheless offer both social workers and professionals examples of databases on which to base decisions. One central source of information is national crime reports. A new system, the National Incident Based Reporting System (NIBRS), has been designed to collect national data on 57 types of crimes, categorizing 5 related to domestic violence (assault offenses; forcible, nonforcible rape; disorderly conduct; and nonviolent family offenses). Although the NIBRS provides prevalence data on domestic violence, Fantuzzo and Mohr suggest that this database does not yield information about children's exposure to domestic violence.

Other sources of information are population-based surveys (Fantuzzo & Mohr, 1999), which generally make national telephone surveys of homes to gain information on domestic violence. The National Family Violence Survey (NFVS) and the National Crime Victimization Survey (NCVS) are two examples. Again, these sources do not generally detail the nature of the child's exposure, but they do provide percentage estimates of families per 1,000 households that have children of certain ages. For example, the NCVS reported that 9.3 women per 1,000 households were physically attacked by their partners in 1993 and that children under 12 years of age lived in more than half of those homes (Greenfield, Rand, & Craven, 1998).

A final and even more promising procedure for estimating rates of exposure is the Spousal Assault Replication Program (SARP; Fantuzzo & Mohr, 1999), which selected misdemeanor domestic violence cases and developed a database investigating several areas specifically asking about exposure rates. The findings made a number of important discoveries about estimates, including the high rates at which children were directly exposed (e.g., 81% of sample exposed); the early ages at which children were exposed to multiple incidents of violence (e.g., in North Carolina, 42% of children aged 5 and younger were exposed to multiple abuses); and the relationship between ages and exposure to substance abuse and violence (e.g., in Omaha, Nebraska, 14% of children aged 5 and younger experienced both).

HOW CHILDREN EXPOSED TO DOMESTIC VIOLENCE ARE IMPACTED

The difficulties of predicting estimates of exposure to domestic violence have not prevented the practice field from identifying how large numbers of children have been impacted. One consistent approach has been the "case study" design, using clinical and anecdotal information about this population. A second approach has been the development of a classification system aimed at summarizing the empirical literature. The following section provides a summary of the empirical contributions toward understanding impact. The summary is divided into two main groupings: The behavioral and emotional impact factors and the traumatic impact factors. Each grouping is divided into impact, moderating or mediating, and protective factors. In summarizing these findings, we acknowledge that there is considerable over-lap between the two groupings. At the same time, we agree with Famularo, Kinscherff, and Fenton (1992) that exposed children can exhibit behavioral disorders without exhibiting posttraumatic stress disorder (PTSD), whereas some children may exhibit PTSD without displaying other disorders.

Behavioral and Emotional Factors

Impact Factors

Table 16.1 represents a summary of behavioral and emotional responses typically observed in children exposed to domestic violence. Here, most stud-ies have relied on measurements that focus on child and parent reports of impact behaviors. Within these reports, one main instrument, the Child Be-havior Checklist (CBCL; Achenbach & Edelbrock, 1983), has become a con-stant or standard upon which many assessments of impact have been made. The CBCL is a 120-item instrument completed by mothers that measures child behavior via three broad features. Overall, there is a great deal of con-sistency in the findings that children are at risk for exhibiting a host of internalizing (e.g., anxiety, depression, withdrawal, confusion, self-blame); externalizing (e.g., aggression, delinquency-related behaviors); and social competency (e.g., difficulty making and keeping friends, poor problem-solv-ing skills, problems at school) problems.

The subcategories of cognitive and physical functioning, while being part of the social competency and internalizing terminology, may also be consid-ered as separate impact factors. A review of the cognitive functioning litera-ture suggests that exposure to violence acts as a form of modeling for present and future behavior. Likewise, there appears to be a close relationship be-tween exposure to violence and physical well-being. Children who are ex-posed to domestic violence have more physical or health-related problems (e.g., headaches, stomachaches, general pains, developmental delays).

Long-term functioning is also important in understanding the impact of child exposure to domestic violence. Of critical significance is the notion that violence is a learned behavior that affects individuals at every level of the family. Social workers, therefore, must be concerned about the extent to which violence within families may be passed to future generations.

Mediating or Moderating and Protective Factors

Based on a summary of the impact factors in table 16.1, many children are affected in some way as a result of being exposed to domestic violence. At the same time, no two children are likely to be impacted in the same manner. Therefore, the literature has begun to focus on what might differentiate each child. Following are three subcategories to inform social workers regarding this process, including child, secondary, and family variables. To help further

Table 16.1   Behavioral and Emotional Factors Affecting Exposed Children

Impact Factors	Mediating/Moderating Factors	Protective Factors
Behavioral/Emotional Responses	*Child Factors*	*Child Factors*
	Age	Intelligence
Internalizing, externalizing, and social competency problems	Type of exposure	Interpersonal skills
	Singular vs. multiple exposure	Emotion and problem-focused
	Child exposure to maltreatment	skills
Cognitive Functioning	Child exposure to community violence	Temperament
Academic difficulties	Child exposure to media violence (e.g., television, videos)	Child's appraisal of events
Approval of violence		Child's knowledge of safety
Poor thinking-through skills associated with problem solving	Time since last violent event	
	Child temperament (e.g., shy, fearful)	*Family Factors*
Physical Functioning		Strong and positive parental or family support
	Family Factors	No history of multiple victimization
Somatic and physical complaints		
Developmental delays	Intensity and chronicity of maternal exposure to violence/ maternal impairment	Emotional availability of mother
	Co-occurrence of substance or drug abuse	Role of extended family
Long-Term Behavioral and Emotional Functioning	Single-parent household	*Community Factors*
Adult depression and reduced self-esteem	Poverty	Availability of community safe homes or shelters
Poor interpersonal skills	The importance of a cultural context	Response of community providers
Intergenerational repetition of violence		School intervention projects
Adult criminal behavior	*Secondary/Associated Factors*	
	Legal difficulties	
	Multiple moves (homes and schools)	
	Inappropriate law enforcement	
	Already existing school and/or community-related problems	

This table represents summary findings from a number of sequential comprehensive reviews, including those of Jaffee, Wolfe, & Wilson (1990); Fantuzzo & Lindquist (1989); Wolfe & Jaffe (1991); Kolbo, Blakely, & Engleman (1996); Barnett, Miller-Perrin, & Perrin (1997); Margolin (1998); Osofsky (1999); Edleson (1999); Rossman, Hughes, & Rosenberg (2000); and Mohr, Noone Lutz, Fantuzzo, & Perry (2000).

delineate differences, Rossman (2000) has focused on mediating or moderating and protective factors. *Mediating factors* refer to variables that come between the event (e.g., exposure violence) and the outcome (behavioral or emotional factors), whereas *moderating factors* refer to conditions that exist prior to exposure. For example, table 16.1 shows that child maltreatment (prior or ongoing physical and/or sexual abuse) could be a mediating factor, whereas age or poverty could moderate the outcome.

Protective factors are variables that may lessen children's vulnerability to overall negative adjustment. These may be thought of as either internal or external resources that reduce impact. In this case, the findings generally point to three main explanations, namely, child, family, and community supports. These variables rarely stand on their own but should always be considered as part of a systemic interaction within the child's life (Osofsky, 1999). For example, a child's ability to cope positively with exposure to domestic violence may in part be determined by the quality and quantity of family or parental supports.

Traumatic Factors

The second group of behaviors used to explain how children exposed to domestic violence are impacted may be found in the understanding of PTSD. Traditionally, PTSD falls under the nomenclature of the *Diagnostic and Statistical Manual of Mental Disorders* used to diagnose mental disorders. The diagnosis of PTSD is based on six major criteria (A through F). The *DSM-IV* provides the following definition of trauma: "(1) the person experienced, witnessed, or was confronted with an event or events that involved actual or threatened death or serious injury, or a threat to the physical integrity of self or others; (2) the person's response involved intense fear, helplessness or horror" (American Psychiatric Association, 1994, p. 428). While the type of childhood trauma can vary, symptoms are quite similar. Criteria 2 through 4 are grouped into three main types of trauma-related behaviors, including those of reexperiencing, avoidance, and arousal. Criteria 5 and 6 represent the duration of symptoms and the disturbance of symptoms.

Impact Factors

Table 16.2 represents a summary of posttraumatic symptoms children are likely to exhibit. As may be seen, trauma symptoms are divided into four criteria, each having a constellation of symptoms. Criterion A, or the traumatic event, represents two initial signs of distress or symptoms that suggest a response to living with violence; that is, the child will exhibit fear, helplessness, or a sense of terror. In addition, the child will have been exposed to events that are considered potentially harmful to him- or herself.

Criterion B refers to reexperiencing symptoms or those behaviors in which the child resees or relives moments of the violence in his or her "mind's eye." Typically, this occurs in a waking state, such as when a child has vivid memories or begins to act or feel as if the violence is recurring. One important component of the reexperiencing criterion is the type of cues that act as potential triggers. These can be infinite, including smells; television or video violence; facial or bodily features that remind the child of a violent parent; or certain words or phrases. Reliving also occurs in the form of dreams or nightmares that often take the form of disrupted sleep patterns or night terrors. Most traumatized children experience physiological re-

Table 16.2 Traumatic Factors Affecting Exposed Children

Impact Factors	Mediating/Moderating Factors	Protective Factors
A. *Exposure to Traumatic Events*	*Child Factors*	*Child Factors*
	Age or developmental level	Age or developmental level of
Threat to physical integrity	Proximity to violent event	child
Intense fear, terror	Multiple maltreatment experi-	Coping ability of child
	ences	Temperament
B. *Reexperiencing*		
	Family Factors	*Family Factors*
Intrusive recollections	Nature of the trauma (Type I	Social support
Dreams/nightmares	vs. Type II)	Positive cohesion or stability
Acting or feeling like event re-	Relationship with perpetrator	within family
curring	Coping and mental health of	
Distress to exposure cues	maternal caretaker	*Community Factors*
Physiological reactions to cues	Quality of parent-child relation-	
Posttraumatic play	ship	Positive school environment
	Parent underestimation of	that emphasizes conflict man-
C. *Avoidance*	symptoms	agement or trauma manage-
		ment
Avoids thoughts or feelings of		Support groups for parents
event	*Secondary/Associated Factors*	
Avoids activities or places		
linked to event	Greater traumatic response vul-	
Cannot recall aspects of event	nerability for females	
Decreased interest in activities	Dissociation	
Feeling estranged	Nervous system dysfunction	
Restricted range of affect	Disrupted social relationships	
Sense of foreshortened future	Increased anger	

D. *Arousal*

Trouble sleeping
Trouble concentrating
Anger outbursts
Hypervigilance
Exaggerated startle response

E and F. *Duration and Disturbance*

More than 1 month
Impairment in social or other
important areas of child functioning

Long-Term Behavioral, or Emotional Functioning

Depression
Low self-esteem
Guilt or feeling responsible
Separation anxiety
Substance-abuse problems
Long-term academic problems

This table represents summary findings of sequential comprehensive reviews found in Pynoos & Eth (1984, 1986); Rossman (1994); Arroyo & Eth (1995); Lehmann (1997); Shahinfar & Fox (1997); Rossman (1998); Lehmann & Carlson (1998); Rossman, Hughes, & Rosenberg (2000); Geffner, Jaffe, & Sudermann (2000); Kerig, Fedorowicz, Brown, & Warren (2000); Lehmann (2000); and Halligan & Yehuda (2000).

sponses in the form of heart palpitations, nervousness, or feeling sweaty, generally co-occurring with the remaining responses.

As children reexperience, they also may express criterion C, or avoidance symptoms. Essentially, children will exhibit distress in the form of trying to avoid thoughts, feelings, people, or places associated with the violent event. A typical behavior may be gradual or rapid withdrawal from those persons, friends, or family members the child had been close to. Connected to avoidance is the feeling or sense of an uncertain future. One secondary or associated feature closely linked to avoidance symptoms is a numbing or dissociative response; Kerig, Fedorowicz, Brown, and Warren (2000) point out that behaviors such as "spacing out," "tuning out," and/or "confusion" may suggest a dissociative strategy intended to cope with chronic traumatic situations.

Criterion D, or arousal, captures some of the physiological consequences of a child's exposure to traumatic events. Ongoing symptoms may include difficulty sleeping or concentrating in addition to irritability and anger-related responses. Two hallmark symptoms of this criterion are startle responses and hypervigilance. In both cases, symptoms represent a combination of internal physiological and emotional responses to the actual event or to the perceived event (e.g., responding to cues that remind the child of the violence).

Criteria E and F represent duration and disturbance of symptoms. Here, duration of symptoms is divided into acute or chronic, while disturbance assesses social and other areas of functioning.

Finally, the secondary or associated responses found in table 16.2 may at first seem separate from PTSD. However, these responses should be considered comorbid because traumatized children frequently exhibit behavioral disorders other than PTSD (March, 1999). Although the literature on childhood exposure to violence with respect to these responses is broad and varied, awareness of their presence with PTSD provides the social worker with a context for assessing and treating traumatized children.

Mediating, Moderating, and Protective Factors

Similar to table 16.1, the definitions encompassing mediating, moderating, and protective factors are also applicable to the posttraumatic responses of exposed children. Like the behavioral and emotional factors affecting children, the traumatic factors can be moderated by many variables such as age and development.

Age and developmental differences in large part determine the extent to which children exhibit PTSD symptoms. For example, Kerig et al. (2000) and Lehmann and Carlson (1998) have outlined the developmental differences in traumatized children according to infancy, childhood, and adolescence. What is significant here is that some symptom variation will be present according to stage of development and maturation. Traumatic responses are also related to proximity; that is, distress is greater the closer to the event (e.g., physical and psychological closeness) the child may be.

As outlined in table 16.2, the nature of the typology, that is, differentiating between Type I and Type II trauma (Terr, 1991), is important for social workers' assessment and intervention skills. In the case of domestic violence, Type II trauma is seen as exposure to violence that is long-lasting, chronic, and often perpetrated by someone the child knows or with whom the child and maternal figure have a relationship. Although typical symptoms include PTSD, Terr added a number of abnormal coping behaviors, including denial, depression, dissociation, and rage. Type II trauma is contrasted with Type I trauma, which is usually a onetime event in which the stressor originates outside of the family (e.g., tornado, car accident). Consequently, the impact of Type II trauma may be moderated (e.g., by a preexisting relationship with the perpetrator) or mediated (e.g., intensity of the violence) by the responses of significant others.

The protective factors, again, interact with internal and external variables associated with the child, decreasing the possibility of extreme or chronic traumatic responding. While child factors may be similar to those found in table 16.1, Shahinfar and Fox (1997) and Rossman, Hughes, and Rosenberg (2000) note the importance of social support within and outside of the immediate family. Parental warmth and well-being of the non-abusing parent, parent-to-child guidance and structure, in addition to the availability of community services, should be seen as some of the influences that protect the child from traumatic responses.

THE IMPORTANCE OF ASSESSMENT AND TREATMENT

The previous discussion supports the view that violence against women is a serious social problem that affects the mental, emotional, and physical health of large numbers of children. Further, the empirical literature continues to illustrate a broad range of nontraumatic (table 16.1) and traumatic (table 16.2) symptoms exhibited in these children. Consequently, within the last decade, social workers and other mental health clinicians have begun to use a number of assessment and treatment protocols for shelter and nonshelter groups of children. Without question, this development has expanded the field, making it possible for clinicians to intervene quickly and efficiently. At the same time, we argue that assessment and intervention must be driven by the major consideration of safety. We believe it is critically important for social workers to constantly monitor lethality and risk of danger (Goodman, Dutton, & Bennett; 2000; Hastings & Hamberger, 1997; Kropp, Hart, Webster, & Eaves, 1995; Lehmann, 1998; Rossman, 1994) and suggest *no* clinical decision can be made without considering the safety of all family members. In this vein, safety includes the possibility of perpetrator violence against mothers, as well as perpetrator or mother maltreatment of children. A summary of assessment and intervention protocols is provided in the following. The protocols may be useful to populations of children in shelters for battered women and/or in mental health settings.

Assessment

Some families come to treatment clearly requesting help with issues resulting from their experiences of violence in the home. The connection between the child's symptoms and incidences of physical and/or verbal assaults is often disclosed in the initial session. In clinical settings other than shelters, families may request treatment for the child's behavior without having made the connection between the identified behavior and the violence. On other occasions, even when families are questioned directly and specifically, members deny that violence has occurred. We have found that in these homes, fear colludes with the power and control utilized by the abuser, along with a myriad of other factors, to shroud the family and its interactions in secrecy.

Social workers must be able to assess children and families thoughtfully and methodically so that as much physical and emotional safety as possible is provided for all family members. When an intact family with a biological father or stepfather comes for treatment and violence is disclosed, we *strongly* advocate for an assessment process that separates the adult partners and ideally the children from the abusive parent for individual mini-interviews. It is better to take more time, erring on the side of caution, than to inadvertently create an environment that is potentially dangerous or one in which a child or caretaker makes a disclosure in the presence of the abuser.

Social workers who assess children exposed to domestic violence will find it helpful to see the assessment process as multidimensional, with a focus on integrating multiple domains of functioning. Here, we find the ideas of Pepler, Catallo, and Moore (2000) useful because the authors concentrate on a number of systemic factors that affect children. Assessing the mother-father, child-mother, child-father, sibling, peer, school, and community relationships through the use of paper-and-pencil tests and/or clinical interviews can shed some light on the systemic context. In addition, information the child discloses about him- or herself by any of these methods will add to the information needed to provide treatment. For example, assessing child depression may occur through the use of a pencil-and-paper instrument or through art therapy techniques (Malchiodi, 1990), while a clinical interview that asks about disrupted relations with the mother and/or father may provide a much broader perspective from which to make treatment decisions. The witness to violence interview (Arroyo & Eth, 1995; Pynoos & Eth, 1986), a clinical interview process that is useful in many settings, elicits the child's experiences of and coping with violence in a face-to-face format. In either case, an assessment may warrant more than one type of intervention, thus allowing multiple approaches based on the needs of the child and family.

Treatment

Immediate Intervention

Immediate intervention refers to crisis intervention, which seems to be most useful with children immediately following their exposure to violence and/ or when a family initially enters a shelter. The focus of this approach is an immediate intervention in which the child can be made to feel safe, can have her or his feelings validated, and can begin problem solving along with the social worker or child advocate. Problem solving includes an education component in which a child's affect is normalized and she or he learns how to anticipate and deal with uncomfortable emotions. Safety planning with the child is another very important component of this intervention. A crisis approach with children is usually short and calls for the clinician to take an active and direct role. The active involvement of mothers is also important in helping children with their particular crises. This particular approach may be useful with children who exhibit symptoms of PTSD (e.g., Arroyo & Eth, 1995; Lehmann & Carlson, 1998; Nader, 1999), as well as those who exhibit other behavioral symptoms (e.g., Lehmann & Matthews, 1998).

Group Therapy

Group therapy for children exposed to domestic violence includes therapy for children and/or the non-abusing parent, parent training, as well as school-based prevention approaches. All of these approaches are therapeutic and process oriented, with education- and information-based components.

Groups for children evolved out of shelter programming, which initially attempted to provide support for a child's experiences. For the most part, groups appear to have similar purposes and designs, that is, to provide education, information, and coping skills to exposed children who may be experiencing moderate difficulty. In 8 to 12 weeks, children's groups cover topics such as safety planning, anger, responsibility for the violence, problem solving, and self-esteem, to name a few.

Mothers' and children's groups are an important and more recent development in intervening with exposed children. Generally, this approach has grown as a result of the belief that child rearing is affected by the multiple parent stressors (e.g., poverty, sole parenting, isolation, emotional distress of parent, and custody or access issues) associated with domestic violence (Holden, Geffner, & Jouriles, 1998; Levendosky & Graham-Bermann, 2000; Rabenstein & Lehmann, 2000). Often, parent and/or child groups provide necessary emotional support in addition to coping and skill building that enhance parent-child relations.

To date, the role of school-based prevention represents the most far-reaching attempt to influence youth attitudes about relationships and violence. Wolfe and Jaffe (1999) have conceptualized some primary and secondary prevention efforts, that is, targeting children and adolescents before domestic violence occurs and also during the early signs of its occurrence. We have proposed a developmental model encompassing school-based awareness or public education programs that teach about violence awareness, dating violence, and conflict resolution skills, among others. We also advocate a secondary prevention approach using community-based interventions whenever early signs of violence are disclosed.

Ongoing Therapy

Finally, knowledge of how exposure to domestic violence impacts children has prompted the development of a variety of clinical interventions that may be considered ongoing. Although not all children require treatment as listed in table 16.3, some do present serious behavior problems and emotional responses that require intervention. Ongoing therapy, therefore, may be divided into home-based interventions, family therapy, and individual therapy having a PTSD focus. A recognition of PTSD and an emphasis on controlling and coping with such responses are critical for exposed children, since there is significant evidence that failure to resolve traumatic events can have long-term consequences (Wilson & Raphael, 1993). Consequently, we believe there are some critical therapeutic goals for the social worker to consider in his or her ongoing work with children and families. Here we adapt the ideas of Nader and Mello (2001) to include (1) hearing everything from the child and family, including the worst and the most minute details; (2) recognizing the omissions, distortions, and/or distractions the child and family may have, and what emotional meaning this may have for them all; (3) recognizing many of the intense impressions and perceptions of the event; (4) correcting the minimization or possible exaggeration of elements of the particular event; (5) identifying the fantasies of family members, particularly revenge fantasies; (6) helping the child and family to identify and deal with emotions associated with the violence; and (7) providing a sense of personal and family resolution that promotes a normal childhood and a nonviolent future.

Home or family visitations and family therapy approaches acknowledge the impact of domestic violence on parent-child relationships. In effect, these interventions attempt to help families cope with the aftereffects of violence, particularly as they attempt to manage any number of life and family changes (Lehmann, Rabenstein, Duff, & Van Meyel, 1994; Rosenberg, Giberson, Rossman, & Acker, 2000). Collectively, these interventions include (1) de-escalating the crisis atmosphere in the home, (2) making safety from

Table 16.3   Assessment and Treatment Protocols

Assessment	Immediate Intervention	Group Therapy	Ongoing Therapy
Paper-and-Pencil Instruments	*Crisis Intervention*	*Education and Support*	*Trauma-Based Therapy*
(Achenbach & Edlebrock, 1983; Barnett et al., 1997; Kerig et al., 2000; Nader, 1997)	(Arroyo & Eth, 1995; Feindler & Owens, 1997; Lehmann & Carlson, 1998; Lehmann & Matthews 1999; Nader, 1999; Rosenberg & Rossman, 1990)	(Foote, 1998; Loosley, 1997; Montgomery, 1991; Peled & Davis, 1995)	(Kerig et al., 2000; Nader & Mello, 2000; Silvern et al., 1995)
Clinical Interviews		*Mothers'/Childrens' Group*	*Individual/Play Therapy*
(Ganley & Schecter, 1996; Lehmann et al., 1994; Malchiodi, 1990; Pynoos & Eth, 1986)		(Peled & Edleson, 1995; Rossman, 1999, in Rossman et al., 2000; Rabenstein & Lehmann, 2000)	(Kot et al., 1998; Nader, 1999; Silvern et al., 1995 Van Fleet et al., 1999)
		School-Based Prevention	*Family Therapy*
		(Gamache & Snapp, 1995; Sudermann et al., 1996; Wolfe et al., 1997)	(Lehmann et al., 1994; Scheeringa, 1999)
			Home-Based Visitation Programs
			(Jouriles et al., 1998; Barnett et al., 1997 Rosenberg et al., 2000)

violence a primary task, (3) dealing with discipline and child management, (4) improving the quality of parent-child involvement, (5) supporting the enhanced role of mothers, (6) helping children understand custody and/or access issues, and (7) creating a nonviolent home environment.

Case Illustration

The case illustration that follows provides a summary of 10 therapy sessions with a child and his mother. Furthermore, the case previews a sampling of some of the impact, assessment, and treatment issues social workers are likely to address with children and their families. Family names have been changed.

Vincent is 10½ years old. His apparent sadness and lack of emotional expressiveness belie a wry sense of humor. He loves books, soccer, and cross-country running and can be found in the waiting room of the children's mental health center where he was referred, reading and wearing one of his many favorite team jerseys. His mother, Joy, is concerned about his high anxiety, which can result in stomach cramps and vomiting. Vincent also gets pains in his legs when he is upset about something, has nightmares, and occasionally wets the bed or soils himself during the day. Bedtimes are particularly difficult. He finds ways to postpone his nighttime routines and prowls around the house checking and rechecking the doors and windows. He persistently asks if he can sleep on the couch on the main level of his home. Joy has noticed that Vincent is losing interest in his friendships. Until recently, he enjoyed playing with friends at school and in the neighborhood; now he comes straight home from school and does not ask to play outside.

Vincent has been exposed to serious and chronic violence for 9 of his 10 years. Joy's relationship with Vincent's father, Wayne, was physically, emotionally, and sexually abusive. As a 3-year-old, Vincent saw his father hold a knife to Joy's neck. Wayne was verbally aggressive with Vincent, berating the boy so intensely that he would curl up in a fetal position at Wayne's feet. On other occasions, Wayne expected 4-year-old Vincent to keep up on 5-mile bike trips across the busy streets of the city where they lived. When Vincent was 5, Joy noticed times when he "stared off into space." A pediatrician said Vincent was having seizures and prescribed valproic acid. Vincent became extremely violent, the medication was discontinued, and the aggression stopped. Joy was admitted into the hospital for depression, and Vincent's "episodes" were not followed up. Joy and Wayne separated when Vincent was 6. Although Joy has sole custody, Vincent sees his father every Wednesday and every other weekend.

Joy met Walter when Vincent was 8 years old. Initially, Walter was kind, loving, and attentive to both Joy and Vincent. Virtually overnight, however, he became moody and controlling. He forbade Joy from using birth control. She became pregnant, miscarried, and conceived again. Walter's moodiness erupted without warning into fits of violent rage, and Walter would slap, punch, and push Joy after Vincent was in bed. Shortly after Brian, Vincent's half brother, was born, Walter shook the crying infant. Joy managed to flee with the children to a women's shelter pursued by Walter's threat that he would find and kill her. After a 3-week stay, and afforded with a restraining order, Joy left the shelter and rented a house, and the family began to reconstruct their lives. Nine months later, Joy and Vincent came to a children's mental health agency at a local hospital for treatment.

The Assessment

Vincent, his mother, and his little brother were initially interviewed by the social worker. In the beginning, Vincent said he did not know exactly why he had been brought to this meeting; however, Joy responded that she wanted Vincent to "talk about his feelings to someone else." Further, Joy stated he "has a lot of feelings" about the physical and emotional abuse perpetrated by his father and stepfather against her. Although Vincent spoke easily about his interests in sports, reading, and academics, he was much less forthcoming about his thoughts, feelings, and sensations and the abusive incidents he had witnessed.

The social worker asked Vincent about the three clusters of symptoms that constitute traumatic stress responses. (Vincent also completed PTSD and depression instruments.) As Joy listened to Vincent, her eyes widened at his understated reports about his stomachaches, vomiting, and anxiety about bedtime. Vincent's accounts about the abuse he saw that was perpetrated by his father were vague, although his memories of the abuse perpetrated by his stepfather, Walter, were clearer and more detailed. Quietly, Joy described her perspectives on Vincent's symptoms as more severe and pervasive than what he originally identified. Given this discrepancy, the social worker scheduled a second appointment for Joy alone. This meeting provided an uninterrupted opportunity to get a full account of Joy's views on Vincent. It also meant that the social worker could construct a more complete picture of the family's 11-year abuse history without distressing Vincent unnecessarily and without Joy having to censor the story. Joy completed a number of assessment instruments that supported Vincent's difficulties as well as the stress the family was experiencing.

Clinical Formulation and Treatment Planning

The social worker consulted with her colleagues about a treatment plan before meeting a third time. After reviewing the circumstances of the family, it seemed that one useful approach could be to assist Vincent with a focus that was immediate and crisis centered. Vincent was not displaying any aggressive behavior at home or at school, which was somewhat atypical given his past exposure. At the same time, Vincent was doing well at school and maintaining his grades. His difficulties with peers appeared to be related to a lack of interest in friends and restricted affect rather than bullying or difficulties making and keeping friends. The profile that emerged was of a child with many strengths who was internalizing rather than externalizing his personal pain. Vincent and Joy disclosed some anxiety-based behaviors, including restlessness at bedtime and various physical complaints. Although Joy, the social worker, and the consultants suspected that the stomach and joint pains, as well as the nighttime enuresis (bed-wetting) and encopresis (soiling), were related to the stress and trauma, the team supported a referral to a pediatrician with a query about the nature of these concerns.

The social worker's impression was that Vincent was in need of symptom relief. The team suggested that Vincent should be seen individually. The goal of this intervention was to identify the signs of his anxiety, link the anxiety to the awful things he had seen and heard, and then provide him with cognitive and behavioral strategies for dealing with his worry. After three or four sessions, the social worker would see the family again to assess whether the interventions were easing some of Vincent's difficulties.

This plan was presented to Vincent and Joy in a third meeting. Vincent, though less than enthusiastic, agreed that he would like to "not feel so sick" in his stomach and not have so many aches. Joy wholeheartedly supported the plan and made an appointment to the pediatrician.

Vincent was seen alone for the fourth session. This work focused on teaching him about traumatic stress and anxiety as a frequent outcome of witnessing violence in his home. When Joy brought Vincent in for the fifth session, the social worker noticed that Joy was visibly shaking and very tearful—a major change from her previous presentations. The worker set aside that day's treatment plan to meet with Joy and Vincent. On their way to the appointment, Joy had seen Walter, her ex-partner and Brian's father, on the street. Although they did not speak, Joy had seen Walter pointing and laughing at her as he stood with a group of people. Vincent had not seen this happen, but he listened, still and vigilant, as his mother related the incident and her fears for their safety. When questioned, Vincent said he was not afraid or worried, but his quieter than usual demeanor suggested otherwise. The remainder of the session was spent talking about reactivating a family safety plan. The social worker also talked with Joy about who might help her process this experience. Joy identified a psychologist she was seeing and a battered woman's help line she had accessed in the past.

The social worker met with Vincent and his mother for the sixth session to talk about how the week had gone after their alarming encounter with Walter. Joy said that Vincent was more anxious than usual but agreed that given the incident from the week before, some heightened anxiety was understandable. The following week, at the seventh session, Joy reported that there were no noticeable repercussions from the past experience and that both she and Vincent were feeling better. The social worker saw Vincent alone for the second half of this session to reestablish the contract for work on his anxiety. This work was completed in sessions eight and nine.

Table 16.4 (adapted from Lehmann & Rabenstein, in press) outlines the assessment and treatment plan up to the 10th session with Vincent and Joy. The worker invited Joy and Vincent for a 10th family session. The pediatrician had confirmed that there were no indications that Vincent's physical problems were medical and strongly endorsed his involvement in therapy. Both Vincent and his mother reported that bedtime anxieties and nighttime accidents had lessened, and, aside from a brief bout with the stomach flu, the vomiting had stopped. Vincent said that he had not experienced any joint pain recently and that he was going to be competing in the regional cross-country finals. Joy, Vincent, and the social worker agreed that, given their efforts in treatment, a break was in order. Here the worker suggested that a more intense approach to trauma work with Vincent was contraindi-

Table 16.4   The Assessment and Treatment Plan with Vincent

Assessment Model	Screening Tools	Short-Term Goals	Treatment Plan
Medical		Referral to pediatrician for soiling/bed wetting	No medical intervention required
Psychological	1. Direct inquiry of symptoms as well as administration of PTSD and depression questionnaire 2. Administration of behavior/coping questionnaire 3. Family functioning questionnaire 4. Art therapy, draw-a-person test	1. Identify PTSD in four domains 2. Alleviate overall symptom distress 3. Assess self-esteem and personal distress 4. Assess for social support	1. Psychoeducation about traumatic stress 2. Develop appropriate cognitive and behavioral responses to Vincent's worry and anxiety 3. Work on coping strategies to help Vincent with biological father visits
Family Systems Interview	1. Inquire about immediate (relations with bio: father/stepfather and larger social context (school, friends)	1. Support family coping	1. Work at strengthening mother/child relations 2. Develop family safety plan
Crisis Assessment	1. Assesss level of crisis for Joy and Vincent	1. Assess risk factors 2. Support affected 3. Develop problem solving capacity	1. Refer Joy back to her individual therapist

cated given his constant contact with his father, Wayne. Instead, the worker commented, "Vincent needs the coping strategies he has developed in order to manage these regular visits with his dad." Joy and Vincent nodded in agreement and decided that the worker should call the family in 4 weeks.

CONCLUSION

The social work profession recognizes that children's exposure to domestic violence represents a very real social problem that is often dangerous or even life-threatening. The issues surrounding children and/or their families and the immediate and long-term impact of experiencing violence are multidimensional, requiring professionals to have an intelligent and informed understanding of all the dynamics involved. Therefore, this chapter has proposed a classification system highlighting a number of behavioral or emotional and traumatic indicators that social workers are likely to observe. Furthermore, some assessment and treatment protocols have been suggested for practice. Finally, a case example demonstrating crisis-focused work with a child has illustrated some of the substantive issues social workers will encounter in the course of their work with families.

REFERENCES

Achenbach, T. M., & Edelbrock, C. S. (1983). *Manual for the child behavior checklist and revised child behavior profile*. Burlington: Department of Psychiatry, University of Vermont.

American Psychiatric Association. (1994). *Diagnostic and statistical manual of mental disorders* (4th ed.). Washington, DC: Author.

Arroyo, W., & Eth, S. (1995). Assessment following violence-witnessing trauma. In E. Peled, P. G. Jaffe, & J. L. Edleson (Eds.), *Ending the cycle of violence: Community responses to children of battered women* (pp. 27–42). Thousand Oaks, CA: Sage.

Barnett, O. W., Miller-Perrin, C. L., & Perrin, C. D. (1997). *Family violence across the lifespan: An introduction*. Thousand Oaks, CA: Sage.

Canino, I. A., & Spurlock, J. (2000). *Culturally diverse children and adolescents: Assessment, diagnosis, and treatment* (2nd ed.). New York: Guilford.

Carlson, B. E. (1984). Children's observations of interparental violence. In A. R. Roberts (Ed.), *Battered women and their families* (pp. 147–167). New York: Springer.

Carlson, B. E. (1996). Children of battered women: Research, programs, and services. In A. R. Roberts (Ed.), *Helping battered women: New perspectives and remedies* (pp. 172–187). New York: Oxford University Press.

David and Lucile Packard Foundation. (1999). *The future of children: Domestic violence and children*. Los Altos, CA: Author.

Edleson, J. L. (1999). Children's witnessing of adult domestic violence. *Journal of Interpersonal Violence, 14,* 839–870.

Edleson, J. L., & Eisikovits, Z. C. (Eds.). (1996). *Future interventions with battered women and their families*. Thousand Oaks, CA: Sage.

Elbow, M. (1982). Children of violent marriages: The forgotten victims. *Social Casework, 63,* 465–471.

Famularo, R., Kinscherff, R., & Fenton, T. (1992). Psychiatric diagnoses of maltreated children. *Journal of the American Academy of Child and Adolescent Psychiatry, 31,* 863–867.

Fantuzzo, J., Boruch, R., Beriama, A., Atkins, M., & Marcus, S. (1997). Domestic violence and children: Prevalence and risk in five major U.S. cities. *Journal of the American Academy of Child and Adolescent Psychiatry, 36,* 116–122.

Fantuzzo, J. W., & Lindquist, C. U. (1989). The effects of observing conjugal violence on children: A review of empirical literature. *Journal of Family Violence, 4,* 77–94.

Fantuzzo, J. W., & Mohr, W. K. (1999). Prevalence and effects of child exposure to domestic violence. In *The future of children: Domestic violence and children* (pp. 21–32). Los Altos, CA: The David and Lucile Packard Foundation.

Fantuzzo, J. W., Mohr, W. K., & Noone, M. J. (2000). Making the invisible victims of violence against women visible through university/community partnerships. In R. A. Geffner, P. G. Jaffe, & M. Sudermann (Eds.), *Children exposed to domestic violence: Current issues in research, intervention, prevention, and policy development* (pp. 9–24). New York: Haworth.

Feindler, E. L., & Ovens, R. E. (1997, June). *Crisis intervention for child witnesses of domestic violence: A model for psychological consultation.* Paper presented at the Second International Conference for Children Exposed to Domestic Violence, London, Ontario.

Foote, K. (Ed.). (1998). *No violence = good health: A group program manual to be used with preschool-aged children who have witnessed family violence.* London, Ontario: Merrymount Children's Centre.

Gamache, D., & Snapp, D. (1995). Teach your children well: Elementary schools and violence prevention. In E. Peled, P. G. Jaffe, & J. L. Edleson (Eds.), *Ending the cycle of violence: Community response to children of battered women* (pp. 209–231). Newbury Park, CA: Sage.

Ganley, A. L., & Schecter, S. (1996). *Domestic violence: A national curriculum for children's protective services.* San Francisco: Family Violence Prevention Fund.

Geffner, R. A., Jaffe, P. G., & Sudermann, M. (Eds.). (2000). *Children exposed to domestic violence: Current issues in research, intervention, prevention, and policy development.* New York: Haworth.

Goodman, L. A., Dutton, M. A., & Bennett, L. (2000). Predicting repeat abuse among arrested batterers: Use of a danger assessment scale in the criminal justice system. *Journal of Interpersonal Violence, 15,* 63–74.

Greenfield, L., Rand, M., & Craven, D. (1998). *Violence by intimates: Analysis of data on crime by current and former spouses, boyfriends, and girlfriends.* Washington, DC: U.S. Department of Justice.

Halligan, S. L., & Yehuda, R. (2000). Risk factors for PTSD. *PTSD Research Quarterly, 11,* 1–8.

Hastings, J. E., & Hamberger, K. (1997). Sociodemographic predictors of violence. *Anger, Aggression, and Violence, 10,* 323–335.

Holden, G. W., Geffner, R. A., & Jouriles, E. N. (Eds.). (1998). *Children exposed to marital violence: Theory, research, and applied issues.* Washington, DC: American Psychological Association.

Holden, G. W., Stein, J. D., Ritchie, K. L., Harris, S. D., & Jouriles, E. N. (1998). Parenting behaviors and beliefs of battered women. In G. W. Holden, R. A. Geffner, & E. N. Jouriles (Eds.), *Children exposed to marital violence: Theory, research, and applied issues* (pp. 289–336). Washington, DC: American Psychological Association.

Jaffe, P. G., Wolfe, D. A., & Wilson, S. (1990). *Children of battered women.* Newbury Park, CA: Sage.

Jouriles, E. N., McDonald, R., Stephens, N., Norwood, W., Spiller, L. C., & Ware, H. S. (1998). Breaking the cycle of violence: Helping families departing from battered women's shelters. In G. W. Holden, R. A. Geffner, & E. N. Jouriles (Eds.), *Children exposed to marital violence: Theory, research, and applied issues* (pp. 337–370). Washington, DC: American Psychological Association.

Kerig, P. K., Fedorowicz, A. E., Brown, C. A., & Warren, M. (2000). Assessment and intervention for PTSD in children exposed to violence. In R. A. Geffner, P. G. Jaffe, & M. Sudermann (Eds.), *Children exposed to domestic violence: Current issues in research, intervention, prevention, and social development* (pp. 161–184). New York: Haworth.

Kolbo, J. R., Blakely, E. H., & Engleman, D. (1996). Children who witness domestic violence: A review and empirical literature. *Journal of Interpersonal Violence, 11,* 281–293.

Kot, S., Landreth, G. L., & Giordano, M. (1998). Intensive child-centered play therapy with child witnesses of domestic violence. *International Journal of Play Therapy, 7,* 17–36.

Kropp, P. R., Hart, S. D., Webster, C. D., & Eaves, D. (1995). *Manual for the spousal assault risk assessment guide* (2nd ed.). Vancouver, BC: British Columbia Institute Against Family Violence.

Lehmann, P. (1997). Child witnesses to mother assault and PTSD in shelters for battered women. *Journal of Family Violence, 12,* 241–257.

Lehmann, P. (1998). *Severity of violence matrix.* Unpublished instrument. University of Texas at Arlington, Arlington, TX: Author.

Lehmann, P. (2000). Posttraumatic stress disorder (PTSD) and child witnesses to mother assault: A summary and review. *Child and Youth Services Review, 22,* 275–306.

Lehmann, P., & Carlson, B. E. (1998). Crisis intervention with traumatized child witnesses in shelters for battered women. In A. R. Roberts (Ed.), *Battered women and their families: Intervention strategies and treatment programs,* 2nd edition (pp. 99–128). New York: Springer.

Lehmann, P., & Matthews, R. (1998). Crisis intervention with families in shelters for battered women. *Journal of Family Psychotherapy, 10,* 71–75.

Lehmann, P., & Rabenstein, S. (2002). Children exposed to domestic violence: Some practice-based impact, assessment, and treatment issues. In A. R. Roberts & G. Greene (Eds.), *Social workers' desk reference.* New York: Oxford University Press.

Lehmann, P., Rabenstein, S., Duff, J., & Van Meyel, R. (1994). A multidimensional model for treating families that have survived mother assault. *Contemporary Family Therapy, 16,* 7–25.

Levendosky, A. A., & Graham-Bermann, S. A. (2000). Trauma and parenting in battered women: An addi-

tion to an ecological model of parenting. In R. A. Geffner, P. G. Jaffe, & M. Sudermann (Eds.), *Children exposed to domestic violence: Current issues in research, intervention, prevention, and social development* (pp. 25–35). New York: Haworth.

Loosley, S. (Ed.). (1997). *Children who witness woman abuse: Treatment considerations.* London, Ontario: Ministry of Social and Community Services.

Malchiodi, C. (1990). *Breaking the silence: Art therapy with children from violent homes.* New York: Brunner/Mazel.

March, J. S. (1999). Assessment of pediatric posttraumatic stress disorder. In P. A. Saigh & J. D. Bremner (Eds.), *Posttraumatic stress disorder: A comprehensive text* (pp. 199–218). Boston: Allyn and Bacon.

Margolin, G. (1998). Effects of domestic violence on children. In P. K. Trickett & C. J. Shellenbach (Eds.), *Violence against children in the family and the community* (pp. 57–101). Washington, DC: American Psychological Association.

McLeod, L. (1987). *Battered but not beaten: Preventing wife abuse in Canada.* Ottawa, Ontario: Canadian Advisory Council on the status of Women.

Mohr, W. K., Noone Lutz, M. J., Fantuzzo, J. W., & Perry, M. A. (2000). Children exposed to family violence: A review of empirical research from a developmental-ecological perspective. *Trauma, Violence, and Abuse, 1,* 264–283.

Montgomery, M. (1991). *Children's domestic abuse program: Group manual.* Mount Dora, FL: Kidsrights.

Nader, K. (1997). Assessing traumatic experiences in children. In J. P. Wilson & T. M. Keane (Eds.), *Assessing psychological trauma and PTSD* (pp. 291–348). New York: Guilford.

Nader, K. (1999). *Psychological first aid for trauma, grief, and traumatic grief* (3rd ed.). Austin, TX: Author.

Nader, K., & Mello, C. (2001). Interactive trauma/grief-focused therapy with children. In P. Lehmann & N. Coady (Eds.), *Theoretical perspective in direct social work practice: A generalist-eclectic approach* (pp. 382–401). New York: Springer.

Osofsky, J. D. (1999). The impact of violence on children. In *The future of children: Domestic violence and children* (pp. 33–49). Los Altos, CA: David and Lucile Packard Foundation.

Paniagua, F. A. (1998). *Assessing and treating culturally diverse clients* (2nd ed.). Thousand Oaks, CA: Sage.

Peled, E. (1997). Intervention with children of battered women: A review of current literature. *Children and Youth Services Review, 19,* 277–299.

Peled, E., & Davis, D. (1995). *Group work with child witnesses of domestic violence: A practitioner's manual.* Thousand Oaks, CA: Sage.

Peled, E., & Edleson, J. L. (1995). Process and outcome in small groups for children of battered women. In E. Peled, P. G. Jaffe, & J. L. Edleson (Eds.), *Ending the cycle of violence: Community responses to children of battered women* (pp. 77–96). Newbury Park, CA: Sage.

Pepler, D. J., Catallo, R., & Moore, T. E. (2000). Consider the children: Research informing interventions for children exposed to domestic violence. In R. A. Geffner, P. G. Jaffe, & M. Sudermann (Eds.), *Children exposed to domestic violence: Current issues in research, intervention, prevention, and social development* (pp. 37–57). New York: Haworth.

Pynoos, R. S., & Eth, S. (1984). The child as witness to homicide. *Journal of Social Issues, 40,* 87–108.

Pynoos, R. S., & Eth, S. (1986). Witness to violence: The child interview. *Journal of the American Academy of Child Psychiatry, 25,* 306–319.

Rabenstein, S., & Lehmann, P. (2000). Mothers and children together: A family group treatment approach. In R. A. Geffner, P. G. Jaffe, & M. Sudermann (Eds.), *Children exposed to domestic violence: Current issues in research, intervention, prevention, and social development* (pp. 185–206). New York: Haworth.

Roberts, A. R. (Ed.). (1998). *Battered women and their families: Intervention strategies and treatment programs* (2nd ed.). New York: Springer.

Rosenberg, M. S., Giberson, R. S., Rossman R., B. B., & Acker, M. (2000). The child witness of family violence. In R. T. Ammerman & M. Hersen (Eds.), *Case studies in family violence* (2nd ed., pp. 259–291). New York: Plenum.

Rosenberg, M. S., & Rossman, B. B. R. (1990). The child witness to family violence. In R. T. Ammerman & M. Hersen (Eds.), *Treatment of family violence* (pp. 183–210). New York: Wiley.

Rossman, B. B. R. (1994). Children in violent families: Current diagnostic and treatment considerations. *Family Violence and Sexual Assault Bulletin, 10,* 29–33.

Rossman, B. B. R. (1998). Decartes's error and posttraumatic stress disorder: Cognition and emotion in children who are exposed to parental violence. In G. W. Holden, R. A. Geffner, & E. N. Jouriles (Eds.), *Children exposed to marital violence: Theory, research, and applied issues* (pp. 223–256). Washington, DC: American Psychological Association.

Rossman, B. B. R. (1999). *Frost Foundation final report.* Unpublished manuscript, University of Denver.

Rossman, B. B. R. (2000). Posttraumatic response and children exposed to domestic violence. In R. A. Geffner, P. G. Jaffe, & M. Sudermann (Eds.), Children exposed to domestic violence: Current issues in research, intervention, prevention, and social development (pp. 85–101). New York: Haworth.

Rossman, B. B. R., Hughes, H. M., & Rosenberg, M. S. (2000). Children and interparental violence: The impact of exposure. Philadelphia: Taylor and Francis.

Scheeringa, M. (1999). Treatment for posttraumatic stress disorder in infants and children. Journal of Systemic Therapies, 18, 20–31.

Shahinfar, A., & Fox, N. A. (1997). The effects of trauma on children: Conceptual and methodological issues. In D. Cicchetti & S. L. Toth (Eds.), Developmental perspectives on trauma: Theory, research, and intervention (pp. 115–140). Rochester, NY: University of Rochester Press.

Silvern, L., Karyl, J., & Landis, T. Y. (1995). Individual psychotherapy for the traumatized children of abused women. In E. Peled, P. G. Jaffe, & J. L. Edelson (Eds.), Ending the cycle of violence: Community responses to children of battered women (pp. 43–76). Thousand Oaks, CA: Sage.

Straus, M. (1991, September). Children as witness to marital violence: A risk factor for lifelong problems among a nationally representative sample of American men and women. Paper presented at the Ross Round Table on Children and Violence, Washington, DC.

Sudermann, M., Jaffe, P. G., Schieck, E., Watson, L., Lehmann, P., & Greer, G. (1996). A.S.A.P.: A school-based anti violence program (Rev. ed.). London, ON: London Family Court Clinic.

Terr, L. (1991). Childhood traumas: An outline and overview. American Journal of Psychiatry, 140, 10–20.

Van Fleet, R., Lilly, J. P., & Kaduson, H. (1999). Play therapy for children exposed to violence: Individual, family, and community interventions. International Journal of Play Therapy, 8, 27–42.

Wilson, J., & Raphael, B. (Eds.). (1993). International handbook of traumatic stress syndromes. New York: Plenum.

Wolfe, D. A., & Jaffe, P. (1991). Child abuse and family violence as determinants of child psychopathology. Canadian Journal of Behavioral Science, 23, 282–299.

Wolfe, D. A., & Jaffe, P.G. (1999). Emerging strategies in the prevention of domestic violence. In The future of children: Domestic violence and children (pp. 133–144). Los Altos, CA: The David and Lucile Packard Foundation.

Wolfe, D. A., Jaffe, P. G., Wilson, S. K., & Zak, L. (1985). Children of battered women: The relation of child behavior to family violence and maternal stress. Journal of Consulting and Clinical Psychology, 53, 657–665.

Wolfe, D. A., Werkele, C., & Scott, K. (1997). Alternatives to violence: Empowering youth to develop healthy relationships. Thousand Oaks, CA: Sage.

17

A Comprehensive Model for Crisis Intervention With Battered Women and Their Children

ALBERT R. ROBERTS
BEVERLY SCHENKMAN ROBERTS

Case Scenarios

Do you know what some women get for their birthdays? A black eye, a punch in the ribs, or a few teeth knocked out. It's so frightening because it doesn't just happen on their birthday. It may be every month, every week, or even every day. It's so frightening because sometimes he abuses the kids, too. Or maybe she's pregnant and he kicks her in the stomach in the same spot where, just a few minutes ago, she felt the baby moving. It's so frightening because the woman doesn't know what to do. She feels so helpless. He's in control. She prays he'll come to his senses and stop. He never does. She prays he won't hurt their kids. He threatens to. She prays he won't kill her. He promises he will. (Haag, undated)

We were married 13 years. It was okay until the past 5 years and he started to hit me to hurt me. He was doing drugs. He was usually high or when he couldn't get drugs, he'd hit me cause he couldn't have it. We'd get in an argument because he'd want money and I'd say no and that's how it would start. He punched and kicked me. Usually I had a black eye and black and blue marks on my legs. He used to steal my money—he stole my Christmas money and my food stamps. He tried to say someone broke into the house, but I knew he had it.

My ex-husband drank every day, especially in the summer. He is very violent. I fear for my life that one day he will get me alone and kill me. He hated my

365

little dog because I spoiled him. He would tell me that he was going to drop kick him (he only weighed 4 pounds). I had to give my dog away because I didn't want him to hurt it. I had to give up my family and friends for the same reason. He broke my nose without even thinking twice. He also tried to strangle me a couple of times and he didn't let go until I faked passing out. I've had to fake a blackout, and that is the only reason I am alive. For all he knew, I could have been dead when he left me lying there on the floor.

The descriptions of the fear, anguish, and physical injuries to which battered women are repeatedly subjected comes from Al Roberts's research files. Case illustrations are included in this chapter to acquaint crisis intervenors, social workers, nurses, psychologists, and counselors with the painful history of the women they will be counseling and assisting. Increasingly, battered women are turning to emergency shelters, telephone crisis intervention services, mental health centers, and support groups for help. Recognition of the need for and actual establishment of crisis intervention services for victims of the battering syndrome have increased dramatically since the 1970s.

The most promising short-term interventions with battered women include 24-hour crisis hotlines, crisis-oriented support groups, shelters for battered women, and/or therapy. Although only a small number of research studies have been conducted on the effectiveness of different types of crisis services for battered women, one research article analyzing 12 outcome studies demonstrated positive outcomes. Tutty, Bidgood, and Rothery (1993) studied outcomes of 76 formerly battered women in Canada after completion of a 10- to 12-session support group. They found significant improvements in self-esteem and locus of control and decreases in stress and physical abuse 6 months after treatment (Tutty et al., 1993). Gordon (1996) examined 12 outcome studies on the effectiveness of intervention by community social services, crisis hotlines, women's groups, police, clergy, physicians, psychotherapists, and lawyers. In summary, it seems that battered women consistently found crisis hotlines, women's groups, social workers, and psychotherapists to be very helpful. In sharp contrast, the battered women respondents reported that usually police, clergy, and lawyers are *not* helpful to different types of abused women (Gordon, 1996).

This chapter will examine the alarming prevalence of woman battering, risk factors and vulnerabilities, precursors to crisis episodes, and resilience and protective factors. In addition, the following types of crisis intervention programs will be discussed: early intervention by police-based crisis teams and victim assistance units; assessment and detection in the hospital emergency room; electronic technology to protect battered women in imminent danger; specific intervention techniques used by crisis hotlines and battered women's shelters; and short-term treatment for the victim's children. The chapter will also discuss the importance of referrals.

SCOPE OF THE PROBLEM

Woman battering is one of the most life-threatening, traumatic, and harmful public health and social problems in American society. Recent estimates indicate that each year approximately 8.7 million women have been victims of some form of assault by their partners (Roberts, 1998; Straus & Gelles, 1991; Tjaden & Thoennes, 1998). Partner violence continues to be the single greatest health threat to American women under the age of 50. On an annual basis, more women sustain injuries as a result of domestic violence than from the combined total of muggings and accidents (Nurius, Hilfrink, & Rafino, 1996).

Women who suffer the most severe injuries require treatment in hospital emergency rooms and hospital trauma centers. It is estimated that 35% of emergency room visits are made by women who need emergency medical care as a result of domestic violence–related injuries (Valentine, Roberts, & Burgess, 1998).

A study published in the *Journal of the American Medical Association* found that up to one in five pregnant women are abused by their partners during pregnancy, with prevalence rates ranging from 0.9% to 20.1% (Gazmararian et al., 1996). Battering during pregnancy endangers both the woman and the fetus, with some of the risks being "miscarriage, preterm labor, chorioamnionitis, low birth weight, fetomaternal hemorrhage, abruptio placentae, and in some cases fetal death or neonatal death" (Carlson & McNutt, 1998, p. 237).

The frequency and duration of violence range from women who are hit once or twice (and make a decision to end the relationship immediately) to women who remain in the relationship and are beaten with increasing frequency for an extended period, which may last for many years (Roberts & Burman, 1998). Petretic-Jackson and Jackson (1996) and Walker (1985) found a strong correlation between women who had suffered chronic abuse and the onset of bipolar disorder, anxiety disorder, posttraumatic stress disorder (PTSD), panic disorder, and/or depression with suicide ideation.

A telephone survey of 16,000 persons from across the nation (8,000 women and 8,000 men) provided research findings on the prevalence, incidence, and consequences of violence against women, including rape and physical assault (Tjaden & Thoennes, 1998). The researchers found that physical battering is widespread among American women of all racial and ethnic groups. The following are Tjaden and Thoennes's major findings:

52% of surveyed women said they were physically assaulted as a child by an adult caretaker and/or as an adult by any type of perpetrator.

1.9% of surveyed women said they were physically assaulted in the previous 12 months.

18% of women surveyed said they experienced a completed or attempted rape at some time in their life, and 0.3% said they experienced a completed or attempted rape in the previous 12 months.

Although there were only 7 emergency shelters for battered women in 1974 (Roberts, 1981), by 1998 there were more than 2,000 shelters and crisis intervention programs coast-to-coast for battered women and their children (Roberts, 1998). Through crisis intervention, many women are able to regain control of their lives by identifying current options and goals and by working to attain those goals. The children of battered women may also be in crisis, but their plight has sometimes been overlooked as the domestic violence programs focused their efforts on emergency intervention for the women. The progressive programs now incorporate crisis intervention for children (as well as for the mothers) in the treatment plan.

Battered women are usually subjected to a prolonged pattern of abuse coupled with a recent severe attack; by the time the victim makes contact with a shelter, she is generally in need of both individual crisis intervention and a crisis-oriented support group. Abused women are subjected to an extended period of stress and trauma that results in a continual loss of energy. The woman is in a vulnerable position, and when a particularly severe beating takes place or when other factors occur (e.g., the abuser starting to hurt the children), the woman may be thrust into a state of crisis (Young, 1995).

Effective treatment for battered women and their children in crisis requires an understanding of crisis theory and the techniques of crisis intervention. According to Caplan (1964), Janosik (1984), and Roberts (1996b), a crisis state can occur rapidly when the following four things happen:

1. The victim experiences a precipitating or hazardous incident.
2. The incident is perceived by the woman as threatening to her or her children's safety, and as a result tension and distress intensify.
3. The battered woman attempts to resolve the situation by using customary coping methods and fails.
4. The emotional discomfort and turmoil worsen, and the victim feels that the pain or anguish is unbearable.

At this point of maximum discomfort, when the woman perceives the pain and torment as unbearable, she is in an active crisis state. During this time there is an opportunity for change and growth, and some women are mobilized to seek help from a 24-hour telephone crisis intervention service, the police, the hospital emergency room, or a shelter for battered women.

The emphasis in crisis assessment is on identifying the nature of the precipitating event and the woman's cognitive and affective reaction to it. The five most common precipitating events that lead battered women in crisis to seek the help of a domestic violence program are (a) an acute battering incident resulting in serious physical injury; (b) a major escalation in the degree of violence, for example, from shoving and slapping to attempted strangulation or stab wounds; (c) an impairment in the woman's hearing, sight, or thought process as a direct result of severe batterment; (d) a high-profile story in the news media about a woman who was brutally murdered by her partner after suffering in silence for many years; and (e) a serious abusive injury inflicted on the woman's child. Often the precipitating event is perceived by the woman in crisis as being the final incident, or "last straw," in a long history of violence (Edington, 1987; Podhorin, 1987; Roberts, 1998; Schiller-Ramirez, 1995).

Crisis intervention with battered women needs to be done in an orderly, structured, safe, and humanistic manner. The process is the same for victims of other violent crimes, but it is particularly important to respond quickly to abused women because they may continue to be in danger as long as they remain in a place where the batterer can locate them. Crisis intervention activities can result in the woman either returning to her precrisis state or growing from the crisis intervention so that she learns new coping skills to use in the future (Roberts, 1998).

BATTERED WOMEN AT HIGH RISK OF CRISIS EPISODES

For some women, the effects of partner abuse can be short-term, with a quick recovery, while for others the result is chronic dysfunction and mental health disorders. Domestic violence researchers have found that among women who are battered for many years, those who receive the most severe forms of injury seem to have the highest risk for the following difficulties: nightmares and other sleep disturbances, reenactment of trauma, major depression, posttraumatic stress symptoms, substance abuse, self-destructive behavior, psychosexual dysfunction, and/or generalized anxiety disorder. Research studies indicate that, in general, these women's mental health problems were not present early in the relationship but developed as a result of the repeated acts of violence (Gleason, 1993; Woods & Campbell, 1993).

Posttraumatic stress disorder (PTSD) may occur when an individual perceives an event as life-threatening to herself or significant others. Characteristic features of PTSD identified in the clinical literature are as follows:

1. Integration of the traumatic experience by reexperiencing the traumatic event (through recurrent and/or intrusive thoughts, flashbacks, nightmares, or other intense reactions)
2. Management of subsequent stress (increased arousal and hypervigilance)
3. Facilitation of affective expression

4. Determination of the meaning of victimization (Petretic-Jackson & Jackson, 1996, p. 210)

As a result of one or more severe battering incidents, some battered women have had their cognitive schemas or mental maps altered. According to Valentine, under extreme duress, the battered woman's schema is imprinted strongly with a survival message that guides the victim even after the crisis has passed. Victims are then left with the chore of either assimilating that event into their previously existing schemas or altering their schemas to incorporate this terrifying event. She states that "PTSD symptoms consist of intrusive thoughts [nightmares], hypervigilance [i.e., startle responses], and avoidance [i.e., blunted affect to avert all reminders of the incident]" (see chapter 11, Valentine, 2000).

Crisis intervention and time-limited treatment with battered women must be approached with empathy, sensitivity, and caution. When an abused woman is suffering from PTSD, if the crisis intervenor asks the woman to "reexperience" the violent event, the counselor may inadvertently precipitate a retraumatization rather than the intended therapeutic opportunity (Petretic-Jackson & Jackson, 1996). Before crisis intervention is initiated, it is critically important to create a safe, highly flexible, empowering environment where symptom relief strategies are emphasized. If avoidance, startle overreactions, and nightmares are the primary presenting problems, the crisis intervenor may well facilitate the narrative and storytelling process by utilizing experiential techniques, art therapy, poetry, photographs, and/or police reports.

Stress management techniques can build on the battered woman's inner strengths and potential for positive growth. Examples of these techniques are progressive relaxation, guided imagery, refocusing one's attention on external reality, good nutrition, developing a support system, and using "dosing"—"a technique in which attention is alternately shifted toward and away from the traumatic experience" (Petretic-Jackson & Jackson, 1996, p. 210). Many battered women seem to have developed very limited affective expression as a result of suppressing their emotions. In addition, because battered women generally suppress feelings of anger, they may suddenly express rage a year or two after leaving the batterer.

Many battered women who experienced three or more traumatic and severe battering incidents often take a long time to gain a sense of control of their environment. Their self-esteem, trust in men, and cognitive assumptions are often shattered. The survivor's low self-esteem, weak decision-making skills, intrusive thoughts, and flashbacks often result in a series of acute crisis episodes. The crisis intervenor or counselor needs to help the woman build trust while bolstering her self-esteem. This is done through modeling, reframing, stress inoculation, relaxation techniques, exercise, thought stopping, encouraging journal entries, solution-based therapy, and cognitive restructuring.

TRAUMATIC BATTERING EVENTS, LEGAL ACTION, MEDICAL INJURIES, AND SLEEP DISTURBANCES AS PRECURSORS TO CRISIS EPISODES

Several types of traumatic, life-threatening mental health and legal events or situations often can precipitate a crisis. These include:

- A battered woman sustaining a life-threatening injury (e.g., a concussion, multiple stab wounds, a miscarriage, or strangulation).
- A child being severely physically or psychologically harmed by the batterer.
- The victim obtains a restraining order or files for divorce, and her taking legal action enrages the batterer, resulting in stalking, terroristic threats, and/or a rapid escalation of the battering incidents.
- A battered woman encounters explicit kidnapping or terroristic death threats against herself, her children, and/or her elderly parents.
- The batterer has already made explicit death threats against the formerly battered woman, and he is soon to be released from prison or a residential drug treatment program.

In Robert's (1996a) study of 210 battered women, the majority of the participants interviewed had experienced one or more severe beatings. The outcomes of these beatings were manifested in anxiety, depression, sleep disturbances, panic attacks, and intrusive thoughts. The following are illustrations of sleep disturbances:

Somebody chases me or is trying to kill me. I can't remember the last pleasant dream I had.

I have nightmares about him burning up the house. I keep dreaming that the kids and I were trapped in the house with flames all around us and we couldn't get out. I would see his face in the flames, point at us and laughing while we are crying and in pain.

I have the same nightmare a few times a week. I see this guy who looks like my former boyfriend (drug dealer who was shot 3 years ago by the Newark police). He is raising up out of the casket, and he said he loved me and is coming back to stab me to death so I can join him in hell. I wake up screaming, shaking, and sweating. A lot of times I can't fall asleep even though I'm mentally and physically exhausted. The next day at work I'm very jumpy and afraid to talk to any of the men in the office. When my supervisor asks me something, I get this flashback and am reminded of my nightmare and I start crying. I go into the ladies room sometimes for an hour and cry and cry, and then leave work early. I go home and try to calm down by smoking cigarettes and talking with my daughter.

In crisis intervention work with battered women, clinicians must be prepared to understand a range of potential precipitants and precursors. Crisis clinicians need to be aware of the aftermath of traumatic events, common triggering incidents, and precursors to crisis episodes in order to provide battered women with the most appropriate interventions.

RESILIENCE AND PROTECTIVE FACTORS

The previous section examined high-risk groups and trauma, sleep disturbances, and other precursors to crisis episodes. Those groups of individuals with preexisting risk factors and trauma histories have difficulty recovering. In sharp contrast, some abused women have significant inner strengths, also known as *resilience* and *protective factors,* that have been found to mediate and lessen the impact of stress related to battering. The most common protective factors include high self-esteem, a social support network, and cognitive coping skills. One of the most important components of maximizing a battered woman's recovery is accomplished through believing in the client and helping her to realize her strengths. Many battered women feel trapped, socially isolated, and overwhelmed by the physical and emotional pain they have endured. Crisis intervenors and counselors can help the woman to recognize alternative coping strategies.

During the past decade, a growing number of crisis intervenors, counselors, social workers, and psychologists have recognized that a strengths perspective that builds on the resilience of individuals is much more fruitful to helping clients grow and change in positive directions than the previous 50 years of emphasis on pathologizing the client (Saleebey, 1997). The strengths perspective of crisis intervention utilizes empowerment, resilience, healing and wholeness, collaboration, and suspension of disbelief. *Empowerment strategies* create opportunities for individuals and communities (Roberts & Burman, 1998). *Resilience* focuses on accelerating growth and identifying inner capabilities, knowledge, and personal insights. *Healing* refers to the ability of the body and mind to resist disease and chaos. The resilience literature incorporates a strong belief that individuals have self-righting tendencies and a spontaneous inclination toward healing and survival (Saleebey, 1997; Weil, 1995). *Collaboration* refers to clients, counselors, crisis intervenors, and family members all working together to help strengthen the client. *Suspension of disbelief* refers to the ending of pessimism and cynicism and the affirmation of belief, learned optimism, self-protective strategies, a sense of humor, and commitment to change.

An integrated approach to crisis intervention combines Roberts's (1996b) seven-step crisis intervention practice model with solution-based therapy. See Greene et al. in the *Crisis Intervention Handbook* (Roberts, 2000) for a discussion and several case applications of an integrated model of solution-based therapy. This practice model emphasizes building on and bolstering one's inner strengths, protective factors, latent coping skills, and positive attributes. It systematically reinforces the importance of realistic goal setting, identifying and explicating the positive exceptions in situations or behavior patterns, and the importance of the dream and miracle questions. We firmly believe that crisis intervention based on enhancing positive coping skills, rediscovering the exceptions and positive alternatives to crisis situations, building on and optimizing the client's bright spots and inner strengths, and seeking partial and full solutions will become common practice during the 21st century.

Tedeschi and Calhoun (1995) interviewed over 600 college students who had recently experienced significant stressful life events, including a parent's death, being the victim of a crime, or receiving an accidental injury. The goal of their research was to determine which personality factors might lead to personal growth when an individual is confronted with a crisis situation. The researchers identified the characteristics of extroversion, openness, agreeableness, conscientiousness, and having an "internal locus of control" as benefiting persons in crisis by allowing them to find some positive outcome connected to what might otherwise be viewed as a devastating circumstance. For instance, those who indicated growth from the traumatic experience were more likely to report that they had experienced positive change (i.e., developing a new area of interest, forming a new relationship, or enhancing one's spiritual beliefs).

Some battered women develop positive coping strategies, whereas others develop negative and potentially self-destructive coping strategies. Examples of positive coping strategies include using formal and informal social support networks, seeking informational support, and requesting help from a shelter for battered women. Examples of negative coping mechanisms are dependence on alcohol or drugs or suicide attempts.

Positive coping strategies help women to facilitate their own survival and expedited recovery. The core focus of Lazarus and Folkman's (1984) conceptualization and application of the coping process is based on how an individual makes an appraisal of the stressful event. Appraisal takes place when an individual experiences an event and determines that it is "excessive relative to resources." There are two levels of appraisal related to coping responses.

1. Primary appraisal is viewed as the first level, wherein a person evaluates whether the event has the potential to cause harm (i.e., physical injury), to instill fear, or to interfere with a goal. More specifically, the individual decides whether a particular situation is at risk. The outcome reflects the individual's assessment of the stressful life event and the significance of the event for that individual's well-being.
2. When the event is perceived as harmful or threatening, the individual enters into secondary appraisal, wherein the available resources for coping are examined. When a person is confronted with a circumstance

that is perceived as threatening or harmful, the person "enters into secondary appraisal" when she makes efforts to cope with the event (e.g.,
leaving the violent home immediately and living with a relative or at a
shelter). (Lazarus & Folkman, 1984)

Battered women in crisis who are contemplating leaving the violent relationship are confronted by both internal and external barriers. Recent legislation, policy reforms, and federal funding initiatives have resulted in increased funding for transitional housing, job training, and concrete services
for battered women. These societal and community-wide changes have empowered and improved the economic status of some battered women who
were trapped by poverty, limited welfare checks and food vouchers, no employment skills, a lack of affordable housing, and no affordable child care.
However, these policy changes and reforms are not enough.

As noted by Carlson (1997), the following four internal barriers often
keep the battered woman trapped in a recurring pattern of acute crisis episodes: "low self-esteem; shame and self-blame for the abuse; poor coping
skills; and passivity, depression, and learned helplessness" (p. 292). Carlson
(1997) proposed an intervention model grounded in both an ecological perspective and Lazarus and Folkman's (1984) stress and coping paradigm. This
practice model should be used by licensed mental health clinicians who are
also trained in domestic violence (Carlson, 1997). The intervention is summarized as follows:

- Practice orientation: nonjudgmental acceptance, confidentiality, and a
  belief in self-determination of the client
- Engagement and developing a collaborative relationship
- Assessment (based on Petretic-Jackson and Jackson [1996], as discussed
  earlier in this chapter)
- Intervention: development of a safety plan, increasing information, enhancement of coping, enhancement of problem-solving and decision-
  making skills, and reducing isolation by increasing social support.

Unfortunately, although it is important to study the correlation between
coping methods in facilitating crisis resolution among battered women, there
is a dearth of research in this area. A thorough review of the research related
to crime victimization and the connection between cognitive appraisal, attributions, and coping mechanisms indicates no conclusive findings (Frazier &
Burnett, 1994; Frieze & Bookwala, 1996; Johnson, 1997; Wyatt, Notgrass, & Newcomb, 1990). Examples of specific strengths are high self-
esteem, having a devoted mother, conscientious performance at work or a
job training program, or having a social support network.

Much of the professional literature on this topic focuses on the cognitive
resources individuals employ when coping with unexpected, stressful life
events (Folkman & Lazarus, 1985; Lazarus & Folkman, 1984). Coping has

been defined by Folkman (1984) as "cognitive and behavioral efforts to master, reduce, or tolerate the internal and/or external demands that are created by the stressful transaction" (p. 843). These demands include perceptions of potential loss and/or harm, at which time the individual evaluates choices for coping via problem-focused and emotion-focused strategies. Problem-focused strategies are based on the use of problem-solving and action plans, whereas emotion-focused strategies utilize the control of negative or distressing emotions.

CRISIS INTERVENTION BY POLICE-BASED CRISIS TEAMS AND VICTIM ASSISTANCE UNITS

Surveys of police departments around the United States indicate that approximately 80% to 90% of the police officers' time is spent on service calls, also known as order maintenance activities, for such incidents as assaults among family members, neighbor disputes, bar fights, traffic accidents, and individuals who are drunk and disorderly. The police may have the skills to intervene and resolve a dispute among neighbors, a bar fight, or a traffic accident, but they are rarely skilled in providing crisis intervention and follow-up counseling with victims of domestic violence (Roberts, 1996a, 1990).

In recognition of the large amount of time police spend responding to repeat family violence calls and their lack of clinical skills, a growing number of police departments have developed crisis intervention teams staffed by professional crisis clinicians and/or trained volunteers.

Victims often turn to their local city, county, or township police department when confronted with the unpredictable injuries or life-threatening danger posed by domestic violence. As a result of the *Thurman* case (in which a battered woman was awarded $2.3 million in her lawsuit against the Torrington, Connecticut, police department for its failure to protect her from her violent husband), more police departments have been responsive to calls from domestic violence victims. Police can respond quickly to domestic violence calls and can transport the victim to the local hospital emergency room or the battered women's shelter. In some cities, police receive backup from the crisis team, which arrives at the home or police department shortly after the police transport the victim to police headquarters. The first such crisis team began in 1975 at the Pima Country District Attorney's Office in Tucson, Arizona. The acceptance of and growing reliance on this program by the Tucson Police Department is revealed by the significantly increased number of police referrals to the crisis team—there were a total of 840 police referrals in 1977, compared with 4,734 referrals in 1984. It should be noted that these figures reflect referrals for all types of crime victims, but most referrals are for domestic violence cases. Since violence in the home constitutes a considerable percentage of police calls, abused women are frequent beneficiaries of this innovative system.

The following description of the program in Tucson will illustrate the intervention procedures utilized by victim assistance programs:

> The Pima County Victim Witness Program has received national recognition for providing immediate crisis intervention to battered women and other crime victims. It also has served as a model for similar programs in other cities. The program was initiated in 1975 with a grant from the Law Enforcement Assistance Administration (LEAA). The grant-funded program was so successful that, when the grant expired, city and county officials agreed to pay for its continuation. The crisis intervention staff uses two police vehicles (unmarked and radio equipped) to travel to the crime scene. The mobile crisis teams are on patrol every night between 6:00 P.M. and 3:00 A.M.. At all other times they are contacted via a beeper system. (Roberts, 1990)
>
> Domestic violence cases are potentially the most dangerous for the crisis counselors. The staff members work in pairs, generally in a team of a male and a female. They are given an intensive training program in which they are taught self-defense, escape driving, and how to use a police radio, as well as crisis-intervention techniques.

During the mid-1980s through the 1990s, a small but growing number of police departments developed a program to provide immediate crisis counseling to victims of domestic violence, as well as victims of other violent crimes such as rape. The crisis intervention team provides the following services: crisis counseling, advocacy, transportation to and from medical centers and shelters, and referrals to social service agencies. The majority of clients, over the years, have been battered women.

The crisis intervention team staff are civilian employees, trained volunteers from the community, or clinical social workers (e.g., New York City collaborative programs between Victim Services and NYPD; Austin, Dallas, and Houston Police Departments; Plainfield, New Jersey, Police Department). A crisis team (always working in groups of two) is notified of a crisis situation via the police radio, and the crisis counselors usually meet the police at the crime scene. The police, after determining that the counselors will not be in danger, may leave the home. The clinicians utilize a basic crisis intervention model of assessing the situation, discussing the options, forming a plan of action, and aiding the victim in implementing the plan. The New York and Texas programs have between 3 and 18 full-time staff members and 2 to 4 graduate student interns each semester, as well as trained volunteer workers.

The programs are funded by city or state criminal justice grants, city or county general revenue grants, and federal violence against women grants. Initially, all of the budgets came from a combination of state and city grants.

In its first year of operation, the Houston crisis intervention program was budgeted at $159,000. The amount had increased to $351,000 by the program's third year of operation.

As of 1998, similar programs had been developed under the auspices of the police departments in many cities, including South Phoenix, Arizona; Santa Ana, San Diego, and Stockton, California; Indianapolis, Indiana; Detroit, Michigan; Omaha, Nebraska; Las Vegas, Nevada; East Windsor, Plainsboro, South Brunswick, and South River, New Jersey; Rochester, New York; Memphis, Tennessee; and Salt Lake City, Utah. However, there are still many communities that have not initiated this type of program. It is hoped that the success of these 24-hour crisis intervention programs will encourage other localities to establish a similar type of service.

VOCATIONAL TRAINING FOR BATTERED WOMEN

Thousands of battered women in large urban areas are trapped in an intergenerational cycle of poverty, violence, and a dearth of marketable job skills. As part of President Clinton's welfare-to-work initiative, battered women's programs in some cities developed job training programs specifically for women who were previously abused by their partners. For example, Victim Services in New York City initiated two innovative employment skills training programs. Victim Services' first welfare-to-work training program, Project RISE, began in New York City in late 1997 to help victims of domestic violence who have been recipients of welfare enter the workforce with good paying jobs. Project RISE provides six-month training programs to teach formerly battered women computer skills (specifically, Microsoft Word and Excel). The second innovative program, Project Superwomen, assists domestic violence survivors to obtain nontraditional employment in blue-collar positions (which traditionally were held solely by men) that offer a stable income and benefits but do not require advanced training. The women receive three months of training to prepare them to work in building maintenance positions, which have the advantage of flexible hours and, often, rent-free housing. The women learn such skills as replacing broken locks; handling light plumbing repairs; and spackling, sanding, and painting apartment walls.

ASSESSMENT AND INTERVENTION IN THE EMERGENCY ROOM

A visit to the emergency room may provide the initial opportunity for some victims to recognize the life-threatening nature of the violent relationship and to begin making important plans to change their situations. At a growing number of large hospitals in urban areas, crisis assessment and intervention are being provided to battered women by emergency room staff.

A recommended way for emergency rooms to handle detection and assessment of batterment is through an adult abuse protocol. Two of the pioneers in the development of these protocols are Karil Klingbeil and Vicky Boyd of Seattle, who in 1976 initiated plans for emergency room intervention with abused women. The social work department of the Harborview Medical Center in Seattle developed an adult abuse protocol that provides specific information on the assessment to be made by the involved staff—the triage nurse, the physician, and the crisis clinician. Using a protocol serves two purposes. First, it alerts the involved hospital staff to provide the appropriate clinical care; second, it documents the violent incident so that if the woman decides to file a legal complaint, "reliable, court-admissible evidence" (including photographs) is available (Klingbeil & Boyd, 1984).

Although this protocol was developed for use by emergency room crisis clinicians, it can easily be adapted for use by other health care personnel. The following case example describes how the adult abuse protocol has been successfully used.

Case Example

Mrs. J was admitted to the emergency room accompanied by her sister. This was the second visit within the month for Mrs. J and the emergency room triage nurse and social worker realized that her physical injuries were much more severe on this second visit. Mrs. J was crying, appeared frightened, and in spite of the pain, she constantly glanced over her shoulder. She indicated that her husband would follow her to the emergency room and that she feared for her life. The social worker immediately notified Security.

Mrs. J indicated that she just wanted to rest briefly and then leave through another entrance. She was 4 months pregnant and concerned about her unborn child. She reported that this had been the first time Mr. J had struck her in the abdomen. The social worker spent considerable time calming Mrs. J in order to obtain a history of the assaultive event. Consent for photography was obtained and Mrs. J indicated that she *would* press charges. "The attack on my child" seemed to be a turning point in her perception of the gravity of her situation, even though Mr. J had beaten her at least a dozen times over the previous two years.

While the social worker assisted in the history taking, a physician provided emergency medical care: several sutures over the right eye.

With Mrs. J's permission, an interview was conducted with her sister who agreed to let Mrs. J stay with her and also agreed to participate in the police reporting. When Mrs. J felt able, the social worker and sister helped her complete necessary forms for the police who had been called to the emergency room.

Although the physician had carefully explained the procedures and rationale to Mrs. J, the social worker repeated this information and also informed her of the lethality of the battering, tracing from her chart her last three emergency room visits. Mrs. J was quick to minimize the assaults but when the social worker showed her photographs from those visits, documenting bruises around her face and neck, she shook her head and said, "No more, not any more." Her sister provided excellent support and additional family members were on their way to the emergency room to be with Mrs. J. When the police arrived Mrs. J was able to give an accurate report of the day's events. . . . She realized there would be difficult decisions to make and readily accepted a follow-up counseling appointment for a Battered Women's group. (Klingbeil & Boyd, 1984, pp. 16–24)

It should be noted that all cases are not handled as easily as this one. The two aspects of Mrs. J's situation that led to a positive resolution were (a) the immediate involvement of emergency room staff and their discussion with the patient of her history and injuries, and (b) the availability of supportive relatives.

Before the woman leaves the emergency room, the crisis clinician should talk with her about whether to return home or to seek refuge with friends, with family, or at a shelter for abused women. The emergency room staff should be able to provide names and phone numbers of referral sources. It is helpful if the pertinent information is printed on a small business-size card (which is easy to tuck away in a pocket or purse) and given to all abuse victims, as well as to suspected victims (Klingbeil & Boyd, 1984). Even if a woman refuses to acknowledge that her current bruises are the result of batterment, she may decide to keep the card for future use.

Merely having an adult abuse protocol does not ensure that it will be used. A study conducted by Flaherty (1985) at four Philadelphia hospitals found that the protocol was used selectively, mainly for victims who volunteered that they had been battered. The medical staff thus ignored the opportunity to help batterment victims who were not able to volunteer the information. The researchers cited the following reasons for underutilization of the protocol:

1. Some physicians and nurses did not regard battering as a medical problem.
2. Some of the emergency room staff believed that it would be an invasion of privacy to ask a woman questions about how she was injured.
3. Many viewed completing the protocol as an additional burden when they were already overworked.

Of those medical personnel who did recognize batterment as a legitimate problem, the most frequently used intervention technique was the tear-off list of referral sources, which was printed at the bottom of the protocol.

There is a crucial difference between Flaherty et al.'s Philadelphia study and the procedures described previously by Klingbeil and Boyd (1984) in Seattle. The Philadelphia study requested the cooperation of nurses and physicians but did not involve medical crisis clinicians. In contrast, the Harborview Medical Center protocol was created and implemented by the hospital's social work department. It emphasized a multidisciplinary team approach, with the social workers taking the lead role in conducting screening and assessment, often talking to the victim while the physician provided medical treatment.

The information just presented would indicate that the involvement of medical social workers is advisable and perhaps necessary in successfully implementing a crisis assessment and intervention system with battered women in the hospital emergency room.

INTERVENTION TECHNIQUES USED BY TELEPHONE HOTLINES AND BATTERED WOMEN'S SHELTERS

Battered women in crisis may reach out for help in any of a number of ways. The initial contact is generally by telephone, making the phone a lifeline for many women. Violence often occurs late in the evening, on weekends, or on holidays, and shelter staff are usually available 24 hours a day to respond to a crisis call. But a woman in crisis who has just been brutally beaten probably does not know the name or phone number of the local shelter. A frequent scenario is that of a woman and her children hastily escaping from home late in the evening and fleeing to a neighbor's home to make an emergency call for help. Not having the number of the local shelter, these women generally contact the police, a toll-free statewide domestic violence hotline, or the city- or community-wide crisis hotline (which aids people in all types of crisis). If the woman contacts the community-wide hotline, there is generally a brief delay while the worker gathers some basic information and then gives the caller the phone number of the closest shelter. An alternative is for the crisis intervenor to take the caller's phone number and have the shelter worker call her back.

When a battered woman in crisis calls a hotline, it is essential that she be able to talk immediately to a trained crisis clinician—not be put on hold or confronted with an answering machine or voice mail. If she is not able to talk to a caring and knowledgeable crisis intervenor, she may just give up, and a valuable opportunity for intervening in the cycle of violence will have been lost. In these situations time is of the essence; if the violent male is still on the rampage, he is likely to search for her, thereby endangering not only his mate but the neighbor as well.

Hotline workers distinguish between a *crisis call*—one in which the woman is in imminent danger or has just been beaten—and other types of calls in which the individual is not in immediate danger but is anxious or distressed and is seeking information or someone to talk to. The overriding goal of crisis intervention is ensuring the safety of the woman and her children. To determine whether the call is a crisis call, the worker asks such questions as:

- Are you or your children in danger now?
- Is the abuser there now?
- Do you want me to call the police?
- Do you want to leave, and can you do so safely?
- Do you need medical attention?

Progams have different policies regarding transporting women who need refuge but have no way to get there. Although some shelters will send staff to pick up the woman at her home, it is more common for shelter policy to prohibit staff from doing so because of the possibility of the staff member being attacked by the abuser. In cities that have a crisis intervention team affiliated with the police department (e.g., New York City, or Plainsboro and East Windsor, New Jersey), the shelter staff can contact the police, who investigate the situation and radio for the victim advocate or crisis counselor to transport the victim and her children to the shelter. Many times the police themselves are prevailed upon to provide the transportation. Another alternative is for the victim advocate from the shelter to meet the battered woman at the local hospital emergency room.

Once the urgent issues pertaining to the woman's physical safety have been resolved, the crisis intervenor can begin to help the victim talk about her situation and discuss possible courses of action. Throughout this process it is important for the crisis intervenor to remember that he or she can present different alternatives, but the client must make her own final decisions in order to be empowered.

The following is a step-by-step guide to intervention with battered women (originally developed by Jones, 1968), which is included in the training manual prepared by the Abuse Counseling and Treatment (ACT) program in Fort Myers, Florida. It is referred to as the A-B-C process of crisis management—the A referring to "achieving contact," the B to "boiling down the problem," and the C to "coping with the problem."

  A. Achieving contact
    1. Introduce yourself: name, role, and purpose.
    2. If a phone call, ask the client if she is safe and protected now.
    3. Ask the client how she would like to be addressed: first name, surname, or nickname; this helps the client regain control.
    4. Collect client data; this breaks the ice and allows the client and clinician to get to know each other and develop trust.
    5. Ask the client if she has a clinician or if she is taking any medication.
    6. Identify the client's feelings and ask for a perception check.

B. Boiling down the problem
  1. Ask the client to describe briefly what has just happened.
  2. Encourage the client to talk about the here and now.
  3. Ask the client what is the most pressing problem.
  4. Ask the client if it were not for said problems, would she feel better right now.
  5. Ask client if she has been confronted with a similar type of problem before, and if so, how she handled it then. What worked and what didn't?
  6. Review with the client what you heard as the primary problem.
C. Coping with the problem
  1. What does the client want to happen?
  2. What is the most important need—the bottom line?
  3. Explore what the client feels is the best solution.
  4. Find out what the client is willing to do to meet her needs.
  5. Help the client formulate a plan of action: resources, activities, time.
  6. Arrange follow-up contact with the client.

Careful recruitment and thorough training of crisis intervention staff is essential to a program's success. It is also necessary for an experienced clinician to be on call at all times for consultation in difficult cases. In addition to knowing what to say, clinicians need to learn about the tone of voice and attitude to be used while handling crisis calls. Crisis clinicians are advised to speak in a steady, calm voice, to ask open-ended questions, and to refrain from being judgmental.

A shelter's policies and procedures manual should include guidelines for crisis staff. For example, the ACT program in Fort Myers, Florida, has developed a 45-page training manual, which includes sections on shelter policies and procedures, referral procedures, and background information on domestic violence that discusses both the victims and the abusers. The ACT manual explains the wide variation in the emotional reactions of the women who call for help. The client's speaking style may be "fast, slow, hesitant, loud, barely audible, rambling, loss of words, [or] normal." Her emotional reaction may be "angry, highly upset, hysterical, withdrawn, laughing, calm, icy, guilty, or a combination of these" (Houston, 1987, p. 5). No matter what characteristics the caller exhibits, the crisis clinician's task is to try to help the victim cope with the immediate situation. However, the guidelines also advise crisis clinicians to avoid the pitfall of believing they need to provide the caller with immediate, expert solutions to her problems. Crisis clinicians should not subject themselves to feelings of guilt if they cannot help an abused woman resolve her situation. If the clinician suspects child abuse or neglect, he or she is required to notify the supervisor and then report the suspected abuse to the appropriate agency (Houston, 1987).

Shelter staff are confronted with a dilemma when the caller is an abused woman who is under the influence of drugs or alcohol or who has psychiatric symptoms. Although such women are victims of batterment, they also have a significant problem which the staff are not trained to treat. Shelter policy generally requires crisis intervenors to screen out battered women who are under the influence of alcohol or drugs, but there are exceptions. At Womanspace (in central New Jersey), women with drug or alcohol problems are accepted provided they are simultaneously enrolled in a drug or alcohol treatment program (Hart, 1999). Likewise, it is the crisis clinician's responsibility to determine whether a woman's behavior is excessively irrational or bizarre or whether she is likely to be a danger to herself or others. If a woman is suspected of having psychiatric problems, she is generally referred to the psychiatric screening unit of a local hospital or to a mental health center for an evaluation.

TELEPHONE LOG

Battered women's shelters usually maintain a written record of all phone calls, whether or not they are crisis calls. In addition to seeking such routine information as name, address, phone number, marital status, and ages of children, the form may include the following: (a) the questions "Are you in immediate danger?" "Do you want me to call the police?" and "How did you get our number?"; (b) action taken by the crisis clinician; and (c) follow-up action (Hart, 1999). Shelters, which are often overcrowded, may also have a section of the form on which the counselor can indicate whether the family is able to be housed immediately, is to be referred to another shelter or safe home, or needs to be put on a waiting list.

Womanspace developed a one-page telephone log form, which on the front asks many of the questions just listed, and on the reverse side contains further screening questions and an explanation of their shelter's policies. An example is the following printed statement, which explains the program's policy on weapons (Hart, 1999):

We do not allow weapons in the shelter.

We ask that you not bring a weapon or anything that may be used as a weapon with you.

Do you own a weapon?

If yes, do you agree to let us keep it in a safe place for you?

The advantage of printing this and other procedural statements on every telephone form is to ensure that all crisis workers impart the same basic information. At the bottom of each form is a list of nine of the most frequently used telephone numbers, including those of three area police departments. The advantage of having these numbers on every form is that during a crisis, they are always readily available, and valuable time is not lost searching for them.

ART THERAPY

Art therapy has been used effectively with women as well as children who have been subjected to domestic violence. As part of a comprehensive treatment approach in shelters for battered women and their children, art therapy can help victims (including young children) communicate their painful experiences in a nonverbal manner that is less threatening than traditional talk therapy. The goal of art therapy is to deal with the violence that took place, while also empowering the mother and enhancing her parenting skills. It is helpful in initiating the healing process for the mother and her children to have the opportunity to communicate what has occurred through their drawings (Riley, 1994).

Art therapy is also helpful when working with young children who have limited verbal ability. The following illustration shows how art therapy was used in a family session with a battered 23-year-old mother and her 4-year-old son:

> Although this child was not able to draw complete figures and fully describe the reason that brought him to the shelter, he was able to tell a story about the images he created. He said that the figure on the upper right was sneaking up on the smaller round circle directly to the left of it, which he identified as a "rock star." He said that the first figure bit the rock star in the leg. This very young boy was able to articulate the same story theme that his mother expressed in more detail. His mother explained through her picture that the 4-year-old had bitten the abuser's leg when the abuser last attacked the mother. (McGloughlin, 1999, p. 53)

INDIVIDUALIZED TREATMENT FOR CHILDREN

Battered women who seek temporary shelter to escape from the violence at home generally have children who come to the shelter with them. The children often feel confused, afraid, and angry. They miss their father and do not know if or when they will see him again. It is not uncommon for children to be misinformed or uninformed about the reason they were suddenly uprooted from their home, leaving their personal possessions, friends, and school to stay at a crowded shelter. Similarly, the children may not realize that all of the other children have come to the shelter for the same reason.

Moreover, large numbers of these children have at one time or another also been victims of physical abuse. The 1986 Annual Report from the Family Violence Center in Green Bay, Wisconsin, provided data on child abuse committed by the batterer. The center found that close to half (73) of the 148 abusers of the women had on one or more occasions also beaten their children (Prelipp, 1987).

The following is a true story written by Lisa, a 10-year-old girl who came to a shelter after her father's violent attack on her mother.

My Life, by Lisa

One day around two months ago my mom and dad got into a fight. First, my mom and I come home from the mall. We had a really nice time there. But, when we came home our nice time got to be terrible. I knew they were going to get into a fight so I went into my bedroom and did my homework. I knew he was going to talk to her about something, but I didn't know what. Then I heard my mom start screaming and I went to the door and asked what was wrong. My dad said, "Oh, nothing is wrong. Go do your homework." But I knew something was wrong so I went and prayed to God. My dad was really mean that night. I hated him so bad. My mom did not deserve to get hurt. I love her more than anything else in the entire world. Then I heard my mom scream something but I didn't understand what she said because my dad covered her mouth with his hand. Afterward she told me she said call the cops. Anyway, I went back to the door by the bedroom and told my mom I needed help on my homework, but I didn't. I just wanted my mom to come out of the bedroom because I was afraid. Then they both came out. And I hugged my mom and went to bed. Then my dad started to strangle my mom. So I went out and told my dad to stop. He told me to go back to the bedroom and go to sleep. So, I did. But I was so stupid. Then I heard my mom screaming. So I went back into the living room and he was kicking my mom. He wouldn't stop, he kept kicking her in her arm and legs. I told him to stop. He told me to go back to bed but I said, No! Then he took his guitar and was gonna hit her over the head. But I went on top of my mother. He told me to get off. But I said, No. So he put down the guitar, then he got her ice for her arm. Then I went to sleep crying. The next morning I didn't go to school and she didn't go to work. Then he called up the house and talked to her for a while. He threatened to kill her. So we left to go to the shelter. And here I am *now*. (Arbour Disabuse, 1986)

This girl was fortunate in that her mother brought her to the Jersey Battered Women's Service in northern New Jersey, which has a carefully developed counseling program for battered mothers and their children. Sadly, however, there are still a number of shelters that offer only basic child care services; they do not provide the art therapy and crisis counseling needed to help children deal with the turmoil of recent events (Alessi & Hearn, 1998).

Nevertheless, innovative techniques for helping children have been incorporated into the programs of the more progressive shelters. St. Martha's Hall, a shelter in St. Louis, Missouri, provides counseling for the children, and also requires mothers to participate in parenting classes and to meet with the coordinator of the children's program about establishing family goals and meeting the child's individual needs. The program also provides opportunities for mother and child to participate jointly in relaxing recreational activities (Schiller-Ramirez, 1995).

Two other types of intervention—coloring books and groups for children—are used at some shelters.

Coloring Books as Part of an Individualized Treatment Approach

Some shelters utilize specially designed coloring books that discuss domestic violence in terms children can understand. Laura Prato of the Jersey Battered Women's Service in Morristown, New Jersey, has created two coloring books (Prato, undated), one for children aged 3 to 5 entitled *What Is a Shelter?* and another for 6- to 11-year-olds called *Let's Talk It Over*. In addition to the children's books, Prato has written two manuals for shelter workers that serve as a discussion guide for counselors. The books contain realistic, sensitive illustrations that depict the confused, sad, and angry emotions the children are feeling. They are illustrated in black and white so that the children can color the pictures if they wish. Funding for preparation and printing of the books and manuals came from the New Jersey Division of Youth and Family Services. The purpose of the coloring books and the way in which they are to be used are explained in the introduction to the counselor's manuals. The manuals state that the books are used as part of the intake and orientation process for all children who stay at the shelter. The stated objectives of the books are as follows:

- To provide assurances of the child's continued care and safety
- To encourage children to identify and express their feelings
- To provide information needed for children to understand what is happening in their families
- To provide information that will improve each child's ability to adapt to the shelter setting
- To begin to assess the individual child's needs and concerns

The clinicians' manuals stress the importance of how the book is presented to the child, as shown in the following passage:

> The process surrounding the use of the orientation books is extremely important. It is likely to be the initial contact between the counselor and the newly arrived family and one that will set the tone for future interactions.

Consistent with the JBWS Children's Program philosophy, this initial meeting communicates respect for mother and child and acceptance of their feelings. (Prato, undated)

Before meeting with the child, the clinician meets privately with the mother to show her the book, explain its purpose, and ask for her permission to read the book to her child. The clinicians are advised to read any available intake information prior to meeting with the child so that they are better able to "anticipate the individual child's special concerns and place the child's responses in a meaningful context" (Prato, undated). The books have been prepared in a way that encourages the child's active participation. Throughout both books there are several places where the child can write his or her thoughts on the page. For example, one of the pages in *Let's Talk It Over* focuses on a child staying at a shelter who misses her father. The caption under the picture states:

> Many children at the shelter think a lot about their fathers, and that's okay. You may not see your father for a while until everyone in your family has a chance to think about things carefully. The little girl in the picture is wondering about her father. . . . What questions do you think she is asking?

There is a place on that page for the child's response to the question. The response could be written by the child or dictated to the counselor, who would write it in the book. On the next page is a large blank space and a caption that reads, "You may use this page to draw a picture of your father." Books such as those developed by the Jersey Battered Women's Service are very appropriate in helping children cope with the crisis that has led to their staying at the shelter.

GROUP TREATMENT FOR CHILDREN

Another way to help children cope is through therapeutic groups such as the approach developed at Haven House, a shelter for battered women and their children in Buffalo, New York. Alessi and Hearn (1998) initiated the group approach when they observed the maladaptive ways in which the children at the shelter reacted to the crisis they were experiencing. The children tended to be aggressive and attempted to resolve problems through hitting. They had considerable anxiety, "biting their fingernails, pulling their hair, and somaticizing feelings as manifested by complaints of headaches and 'tight' stomachs" (Alessi & Hearn, 1998, p. 163). They had ambivalent feelings toward their fathers, loving them as well as hating them.

The two group leaders established a six-session treatment program for children ages 8 to 16 focusing on the following topics: "(1) the identification and expression of feelings; (2) violence; (3) unhealthy ways to solve problems; (4) healthy ways to solve problems; (5) sex, love, and sexuality; and (6) termination and saying goodbye" (Alessi & Hearn, 1998, p. 167). To provide an indication of the scope of the group sessions, the following summarizes the content of the session on violence.

The purpose of the session on violence is to give children an opportunity to explore and express feelings about the violence in their families and how it has affected them. This helps children break down their denial and minimization of the problem. It also gives them a chance to learn that other families have similar problems and that many families do not. The following questions are presented to each of the children for reflection and discussion:

1. Why did you come to Haven House?
2. Do you think it's right for a man to hit a woman or a woman to hit a man, and why?
3. Do you think it's right for a parent to hit a child, and why?
4. How do you think you've been affected by the violence in your family?
5. Do you think you'll grow up to be violent or accept violence in intimate relationships?

The children are always given homework to keep the session alive between meetings. For example, after the discussion on violence, they are asked to develop a minidrama on family violence to be presented the next week. Following the session on healthy problem solving, they are asked to prepare a list of healthy ways of coping with their problems (Alessi & Hearn, 1998).

TECHNOLOGY TO PROTECT BATTERED WOMEN

During the 1990s, some battered women in imminent danger seem to have benefited from different types of technology, including alarm/security systems; panic alarms in conjunction with electronic bracelets; cell phones preprogrammed to 911 for an emergency police response; and instant cameras that provide an immediate photographic record documenting the assault and battery.

A few corporations, notably B.I., Inc., T.L.P. Technologies, Inc., ADT Security, and Transcience, have developed electronic monitors to protect women from domestic abuse. T.L.P. Technologies created an alarm system that is fully operational "even when the phone lines are down and when there is no electrical power" (Roberts, 1996c, p. 93). Law enforcement officers install the system in the abused woman's residence. The system includes a radio transmitter with a battery backup, a remote panic or motion-detector device, and an antenna. When the woman is in danger, she transmits an alarm directly to the police radio channel, unlike with other systems, in which a private security company serves as an intermediary (Roberts, 1996c).

ADT established the AWARE Program, which stands for Abused Women's Active Response Emergency Program, in 1992; by 1997 the program was operational in 150 cities across the United States. The women who participate in this program are selected by prosecutors, law enforcement officials, and shelter directors, and they receive an electronic emergency pendant, worn around the neck, denoted by ADT. If the batterer is endangering the woman at her home, she activates the pendant, sending a silent alarm to ADT, which notifies the police to respond to the emergency alarm. Each city police department, in collaboration with the prosecutor's office, establishes its own criteria for participation in the AWARE Program, but typically all women who receive the pendant must "(1) be in imminent danger, (2) have a restraining order against the abuser, and (3) be willing to prosecute the abuser and testify against him in a court of law, if he is apprehended as a result of the use of the ADT security system" (ADT, 1999, p. 2). Through the AWARE Program, ADT installs a security system at the woman's residence, and each woman receives a pendant that is operational within a radius of 100 feet from her home system. (Whenever the woman is more than 100 feet from her home, the pendant does not work; therefore, this system offers excellent protection in the home but not at work or other community locations.)

In addition to the ADT pendant system, a number of prosecutors' offices and battered women's shelters have made arrangements with mobile phone companies to provide abused women with preprogrammed cell phones, so that they can press one button to be automatically connected to 911 police emergency system. This offers women protection when they are away from home. Although no system is foolproof, these electronic devices provide battered women with increased security.

It is the high cost of electronic devices that has prevented *all* battered women who are in danger from having access to enhanced protection through the latest technology. Because of funding limitations (and the fact that the women are generally not financially able to purchase expensive equipment on their own), criminal justice agencies and battered women's shelters are forced to allocate these scarce resources to women whom they determine are at the highest risk for a life-threatening assault. Usually, these devices are reserved for women who are living apart from the batterer and who have obtained a restraining order (also known as an order of protection) from the court. Local battered women's shelters in cooperation with law enforcement agencies, may be able to contact manufacturers directly and discuss the possibility of donations of some equipment, or a reduced cost if bulk purchases are made. Statewide and community-wide domestic violence coalitions may also target their fund-raising activities toward the acquisition of these electronic devices.

It is vitally important that battered women receive both short-term emergency assistance and long-term security services. Electronic pendants and other electronic technology should be initiated widely to protect the safety of thousands of women who have been severely battered, who have left a violent relationship, and who are still fearful that an abuser will return to harm them again. Funding for these devices should be provided by government agencies and corporate sponsors. Research studies should be conducted to learn which emergency electronic devices provide the most protection for women who have been battered, as well as the drawbacks to particular devices (Roberts, 1996c).

High-intensity Polaroid cameras are being used by police departments and hospital emergency rooms to document the injuries perpetrated by the batterer. Photos that carefully document the woman's injuries are extremely valuable when the case goes to court and may serve to prevent future, more lethal, assaults either because the batterer will be sent to prison on the basis of the indisputable evidence documented in the photographs or because the judge will issue a harsh warning of a prison sentence if he ever assaults the woman again.

Some police officers carry the Spectra instant point-and-shoot camera with them on domestic violence calls, to make a photographic record of the injuries as well as the overall scene at the home (e.g., a knife or gun on the table; children disheveled and crying; damage to doors, walls, or furniture due to the batterer's rampage; a phone cord ripped out of the wall). The advantage of using an instant camera is that the officers can be certain they have accurately photographed the injuries and the disarray at home before leaving the scene.

Similarly, emergency room staff are using these cameras when examining women who admit to being abused or are suspected of being a victim of abuse. Physicians, nurses, or social workers employed in the emergency room are often the first to see the woman following a severe assault. Some abused women with severe injuries go straight to the emergency room without contacting the police. The significant role of medical personnel in identifying victims of domestic violence cannot be overemphasized. Dr. Elaine Alpert, of the Boston University School of Medicine, has stated the importance of hospital personnel taking instant photos of the battered woman's injuries:

> Often, the image, taken on-the-spot, may serve as the only visible evidence that violence has taken place. Cigarette burns, scratches, welts, bite marks, bruises and cuts heal and disappear. But the photo reveals, conclusively, that abuse did take place—and can serve as a crucial piece of incriminating evidence in civil or criminal proceedings against the batterer. (Poremba, 1997, p. 7)

REFERRAL

Knowledge of referral sources is essential when intervening on behalf of abused women in crisis situations. It is just as important for the police, hospitals, and human service agencies to know about and refer to programs helping battered women and their children as it is for staff at domestic violence treatment programs to refer clients to appropriate community resources.

It is frequently determined that the battered woman needs a variety of services, such as job training and placement, low-cost transitional housing, day care, and ongoing counseling; therefore, referral should be made to the appropriate service providers. In its 1995 year-end report, St. Martha's Hall in St. Louis itemized the agencies to which its clients had been referred (Schiller-Ramirez, 1995). Most women were referred to three or more agencies, and several clients were given nine or more referrals, depending on their individual needs. The most frequently used referral sources were as follows:

Legal services

Medical care

Careers for Homemakers

Job bank

Day care programs

Women in Need (WIN), long-term housing for single women

Alcoholics Anonymous

Women's Self-Help Center, providing counseling and support groups

St. Pat's, a Catholic social service agency that finds low-cost housing and provides classes in budgeting money and other life skills

Examples of other, less frequently used, referral sources were

A shelter in another state	Dental care
Alateen	GED program
Al Anon	Crisis nursery
Literacy Council	Victim services
Big Brothers	Red Cross

There are two ways in which programs providing crisis intervention services can facilitate the referral process: (a) by publicizing their services to the population at large and to other service providers, and (b) by becoming knowledgeable about community services needed by their clients and in some instances accompanying them to the appropriate agencies.

Publicize the program through the following methods:

1. Print brochures that describe the program's services and have business cards that provide the program's name and phone number. These materials should be made available in large quantity to police officers, emergency room staff, and other potential sources of referral to the program.

2. Participate in interdisciplinary workshops and seminars on family violence so that the program can become widely known. In addition, this enables the staff to learn about appropriate programs to which their clients can be referred.
3. Attend in-service training programs for police officers, countrywide hotline staff, emergency room staff, and others to discuss referral of abused women and to resolve any problems in the referral process which may have occurred.
4. Alert the public through newspaper articles and public service announcements on radio and television, with the program's phone number prominently mentioned.

Become familiar with community resources: Information for crisis clinicians on appropriate referral sources should be available in several ways:

1. The phone number of the most urgently needed agencies—such as the police, victim assistance program, drug/alcohol treatment programs, and psychiatric screening unit—should be readily available, preferably printed on each intake sheet or telephone log form.
2. The program's training manual should contain a section on the most frequently used referral sources. For example, the manual of the ACT program in Fort Myers, Florida, contains eight pages of often-used referral sources, which list the address, phone number, office hours, and services provided for each source.
3. Most major metropolitan areas have a comprehensive resource guide (published by the local United Way or an affiliate such as Call for Action) that provides a comprehensive listing of all of the community services in that area. All programs serving abused women and their children should have a copy of and be familiar with their community's resources handbook.

The way in which referrals are made is extremely important, since it may affect the outcome. All too often, victims in crisis do not follow through in making the initial contact with the referral agency. Clinicians and advocates at St. Martha's Hall and other shelters provide support by accompanying the client to the agency in order to demonstrate how to obtain services. This is viewed as a positive alternative to the often intimidating and frustrating experience encountered by women who are given a referral but are expected to fend for themselves.

SUMMARY AND CONCLUSION

A number of important issues and techniques relating to crisis intervention with battered women and their children have been examined in this chapter. Specific methods for crisis intervention in different settings have also been discussed. As increased numbers of women in acute crisis seek help, crisis clinicians and victim advocates must be prepared to respond without delay. Crisis intervention for battered women and their children may do much to alleviate the emotional distress and anguish experienced by those exposed to the trauma of domestic violence. Because of their experience and specialized training, crisis clinicians and medical social workers can play a vital role in assisting women and children in crisis.

Law enforcement officers, victim advocates, hospital emergency room staff, and clinicians at citywide crisis lines and battered women's shelters often come in contact with abused women who are experiencing a crisis. Effective crisis intervention requires an understanding by these service providers of the value and methods of crisis intervention, as well as the community resources to which referrals should be made. Battered women are often motivated to change their lifestyle only during the crisis or postcrisis period. Therefore, it is important for service providers at community agencies to offer immediate assistance to battered women in crisis. With an estimated 8 million couples involved in battering episodes annually, policy makers and program developers should give priority to expanding urgently needed crisis-oriented and follow-up services for battered women and their children.

NOTE

Reprinted from A. R. Roberts (Ed.) (2000). *Crisis intervention handbook: Assessment, treatment, and research* (pp. 177–208). New York: Oxford University Press. Reprinted by permission of the publisher.

REFERENCES

ADT. (1999). Aware program brochure. Washington, DC: Author.

Alessi, J. J., & Hearn, K. (1998). Group treatment of children in shelters. In A. R. Roberts (Ed.), *Battered women and their families* (2nd ed., pp. 159–173). New York: Springer.

Arbour, D. (1986, December). *Disabuse Newsletter*, p. 4. Morristown, NJ: Jersey Battered Women's Service.

Arbour, D. (1987, February 12). Director, Jersey Battered Women's Shelter, Morristown, NJ. Personal communication.

Caplan, G. (1964). *Principles of preventive psychiatry.* New York: Basic Books.

Carlson, B. E. (1997). A stress and cop-ing approach to intervention with abused women. *Family Relations, 46,* 291–298.

Carlson, B. E., & McNutt, L. (1998). Intimate partner violence: Intervention in primary health care settings. In A. R. Roberts (Ed.), *Battered women and their families* (2nd ed., pp. 230–270). New York: Springer.

Edington, L. (1987, February 19). Executive Director, Sojourner, Indianapolis, IN. Personal communication.

Flaherty, E. W. (1985, February). *Identification and intervention with battered women in the hospital emergency department: Final report.* Philadelphia: Philadelphia Health Management Corp.

Folkman, S. (1984). Personal control, and stress and coping processes: A theoretical analysis. *Journal of Personality and Social Psychology, 46,* 839–852.

Folkman, S., & Lazarus, R. S. (1985). If it changes it must be a process: Study of emotion and coping during three stages of college examination. *Journal of Personality and Social Psychology, 48,* 150–170.

Frazier, P. A., & Burnett, J. W. (1994). Immediate coping strategies among rape victims. *Journal of Counseling and Development, 72,* 633–639.

Frieze, I., & Bookwala, J. (1996). Coping with unusual stressors: Criminal victimization. In M. Zeidner et al. (Eds.), *Handbook of coping: Theory, research and applications* (pp. 303–321). New York: Wiley.

Gazmararian, J. A., Laxorick, S., Spitz, A. M., Ballard, T. J., Saltzman, L. E., & Marks, J. S. (1996). Prevalence of violence against pregnant women. *Journal of American Medical Association, 275,* 1915–1920.

Gleason, W. J. (1993). Mental disorders in battered women: An empirical study. *Violence and Victims, 8,* 53–68.

Gordon, J. (1996). Community services available to abused women in crisis: A review of perceived usefulness and efficacy. *Journal of Family Violence, 11*(4), 315–329.

Greene, G. J., & Lee, M. (1996). Client strengths and crisis intervention: A solution focused approach. *Crisis Intervention and Time-Limited Treatment, 3*(1), 43–63.

Haag, R. (Undated). The birthday letter. In S. A. Prelipp (Ed.), *Family Violence Center, Inc. training manual.* Green Bay, WI: mimeographed.

Hart, P. (1999, June). Executive Director, Womanspace, Lawrenceville, NJ. Personal communication.

Houston, S. (1987). *Abuse Counseling and Treatment, Inc. (ACT) manual.* Fort Myers, FL: ACT.

Janosik, E. H. (1984). *Crisis counseling.* Belmont, CA: Wadsworth.

Johnson, K. (1997). Professional help and crime victims. *Social Service Review, 71,* 89–109.

Jones, W. A. (1968). The A-B-C method of crisis management. *Mental Hygiene, 52,* 87–89.

Klingbeil, K. S., & Boyd, V. D. (1984). Emergency room intervention: Detection, assessment and treatment. In A. R. Roberts (Ed.), *Battered women and their families: Intervention strategies and treatment programs* (pp. 7–32). New York: Springer.

Lazarus, R. S., & Folkman, S. (1984). *Stress, appraisal and coping.* New York: Springer.

McGloughlin, M. (May, 1999). *Art therapy with battered women and their children.* M.A. thesis, Eastern Virginia Medical School, Norfolk, Virginia.

Nurius, P., Hilfrink, M., & Rafino, R. (1996). The single greatest health threat to women: Their partners. In P. Raffoul & C. A. McNeece (Eds.), *Future issues in social work practice* (pp. 159–171). Boston: Allyn and Bacon.

Petretic-Jackson, P., & Jackson, T. (1996). Mental health interventions with battered women. In A. R. Roberts (Ed.), *Helping battered women: New perspectives and remedies* (pp. 188–221). New York: Oxford University Press.

Podhorin, R. (1987, February 12). Director, Womanspace, Lawrenceville, NJ. Personal communication.

Poremba, B. (Ed.). (Spring 1997). Instant evidence: Break the cycle of family violence. Cambridge, MA: Polaroid Corporation.

Prato, L. (Undated). What is a shelter? Let's talk it over; What is a shelter? A shelter worker's manual; Let's talk it over: A shelter worker's manual. Morristown, NJ: Jersey Battered Women's Service.

Prelipp, S. (1987, February 13). Director, Family Violence Center, Green Bay, WI. Personal communication.

Riley, S. (1994). *Integrative approaches to family art therapy.* Chicago: Magnolia Street Publishers.

Roberts, A. R. (1981). *Sheltering battered women.* New York: Springer.

Roberts, A. R. (1988). Crisis intervention: A practical guide to immediate help for victim families. In A. Horton & J. Williamson (Eds.), *Abuse and religion* (pp. 60–66). Lexington, MA: D. C. Health.

Roberts, A. R. (1990). *Helping crime victims.* Thousand Oaks, CA: Sage.

Roberts, A. R. (1996a). A comparative analysis of incarcerated battered women and a community sample of battered women. In A. R. Roberts (Ed.), *Helping battered women: New perspective and remedies* (pp. 31–43). New York: Oxford University Press.

Roberts, A. R. (1996b). Epidemiology and definitions of acute crisis in American society. In A. R. Roberts (Ed.), *Crisis management and brief treatment: Theory, technique and applications* (pp. 16–33). Chicago: Nelson-Hall.

Roberts, A. R. (1996c). Police responses to battered women. In A. R. Roberts (Ed.), *Helping battered women* (pp. 85–95). New York: Oxford University Press.

Roberts, A. R. (Ed.). (1998). *Battered women and their families* (2nd ed.). New York: Springer.

Roberts, A. R., & Burman, S. (1998). Crisis intervention and cognitive problem-solving therapy with battered women: A national survey and practice model. In A. R. Roberts (Ed.), *Battered women and their families: Intervention strategies and treatment programs* (2nd ed., pp. 3–28). New York: Springer.

Saleebey, D. (1997). *The strengths perspective in social work practice* (2nd ed.). White Plains, NY: Longman.

Schiller-Ramirez, M. (1995). *St. Martha's Hall year end report 1994.* St. Louis, MO: St. Martha's Hall.

Straus, M., & Gelles, R. (1991). *Physical violence in American families.* New Brunswick, NJ: Transaction.

Tedeschi, R. G., & Calhoun, L. G. (1995). *Trauma and transformation growing in the aftermath of suffering.* Thousand Oaks, CA: Sage.

Tjaden, P., & Thoennes, N. (1998). Battering in America: Findings from the National Violence Against Women Survey. *Research in Brief* (60–66). Washington, DC: National Institute of Justice, U.S. Department of Justice.

Tutty, L., Bidgood, B., & Rothery, M. (1993). Support groups for battered women: Research on their efficacy. *Journal of Family Violence, 8,* 325–343.

Valentine, P. V., Roberts, A. R., & Burgess, A. W. (1998). The stress-crisis continuum: Its application to domestic violence. In A. R. Roberts (Ed.), *Battered women and their families* (2nd ed., pp. 29–57). New York: Springer.

Walker, L. E. (1985). Psychological impact of the criminalization of domestic violence on victims. *Victimology: An International Journal, 10,* 281–300.

Weil, A. (1995). *Spontaneous healing.* New York: Knopf.

Woods, S. J., & Campbell, J. C. (1993). Posttraumatic stress in battered women: Does the diagnosis fit? *Issues in Mental Health Nursing, 14,* 173–186.

Wyatt, G. E., Notgrass, C. M., & Newcomb, M. (1990). Internal and external mediators of women's rape experience. *Psychology of Women Quarterly, 14,* 153–176.

Young, M. A. (1995). Crisis response teams in the aftermath of disasters. In A. R. Roberts (Ed.), *Crisis intervention and time-limited cognitive treatment* (pp. 151–187). Thousand Oaks, CA: Sage.

18

Beyond Shelters

Support Groups and Community-Based Advocacy for Abused Women

LESLIE M. TUTTY

MICHAEL ROTHERY

During the past 20 years, as society has finally acknowledged the extent and serious nature of the abuse that many women endure from their intimate partners, shelters for battered women have become fixtures in communities across North America. The safety and support offered to residents and their children have been essential in assisting many to leave abusive relationships and start a new life (Dziegielewski, Resnick, & Krause, 1996; Tutty, in press; Tutty, Weaver, & Rothery, 1999). However, given that serious abuse in intimate couple relationships is widespread, shelters cannot serve all who come to their doors, often sending away as many as they take in.

Furthermore, not all women leaving abusive relationships seek shelter services (Gondolf & Fisher, 1988). The Canadian Violence Against Women Survey from 1993 reported that only 13% of women leaving abusive spouses went to transition houses (Rodgers, 1994). Most women stayed with friends or relatives (77%); others moved into a new residence (13%) or stayed at a hotel (5%). The reasons women gave for not using shelters included not needing such help (40%), seeing their abuse as too minor (25%), being unaware of shelter services (16%), or having no services available in their community (14%).

Why do a relatively small percentage of abused women utilize shelters? According to Weisz, Taggart, Mockler, and Streich (1994), many women choose not to use the shelter system because they have the resources to access preferred alternatives. Thus, transition homes are serving those who need them most, providing, as Weisz and colleagues term it, "options for women who have few options" (p. 7).

Shelters offer stays of from 3 to 6 weeks, a short period in which to make complicated and fundamentally important decisions. If a woman does decide to leave her partner, she then faces a myriad of other decisions about supporting herself and her children, finding accommodations, and coping with pressure to return to the abusive relationship. Once she leaves the shelter, she may well be vulnerable to further abuse; therefore, many women remain at considerable risk and in a state of anxiety long after they have left the security of a transition home.

What services are available to the vast majority of abused women who leave their spouse without using an emergency shelter, whose short shelter stay is behind them, or who remain with a partner hoping that he will change? This chapter describes services for such women, services that are not based in shelters or that extend shelter services into the community. These include support groups and shelter outreach and follow-up advocacy programs. Each type of service will be described, including research findings about their impacts and, when available, the voices of women who have participated in them.

SUPPORT GROUPS FOR ABUSED WOMEN

Group intervention with abused women began in shelters, where, since women were already living communally, it made sense to provide information about partner abuse in a group format. The value of the information was enhanced when residents had the opportunity to share their own experiences and provide feedback to others. Of all the benefits of group intervention, the sense of commonality, or the "all being in the same boat phenomenon," relieved the guilt that many of the women felt about their choices (Yalom, 1995).

The group format was adopted by community agencies serving women who wanted to learn about abuse, who were considering leaving an abusive partner, or who had left but still felt the need for support. The groups were primarily presented as being supportive, implying that although the results might be therapeutic, the women were not necessarily perceived as "needing therapy" (Pagelow, 1992). While abused women do report such common problems as low self-esteem (Aguilar & Nightingale, 1994; Trimpey, 1989), anxiety (Trimpey, 1989), depression (Cascardi & O'Leary, 1992), learned helplessness (Wilson, Vercella, Brems, Benning, & Renfro, 1992), and social isolation (Pressman, 1989), these are best seen as the result of being in an assaultive relationship rather than as factors predisposing them to enter into such partnerships.

More recent research (Astin, Ogland-Hand, Coleman, & Foy, 1995; Dutton & Painter, 1993; Kemp, Green, Hovanitz, & Rawlings, 1995; Tutty, 1998) suggests that symptoms such as anxiety and depression reflect post-traumatic stress disorder, conceptualized as a normal response to traumatic events. This supports the argument that women assaulted by their partners do not necessarily require therapy, since they are responding quite normally to painful and confusing difficulties. However, even after women leave abusive relationships, they may struggle with troubling aftereffects (Tutty, 1993), as well as with the economic and emotional problems associated with a marital separation. Given this, supportive services will often be appropriate.

Several writers have described individual approaches to working with assaulted women (Mancoske, Standifer, & Cauley, 1994) or a combination of group and individual approaches (Webb, 1992). Interestingly, Rinfret-Raynor and Cantin (1997) found that using a feminist perspective is more important than whether the counseling is in a group or individual format. Still, most authors propose using support groups (Campbell, 1986; Holiman & Schilit, 1991; NiCarthy, Merriam, & Coffman, 1984; Seskin, 1988; Trimpey, 1989; Tutty, Bidgood, & Rothery, 1993).

The benefits of offering support in groups include the fact that groups reduce social isolation, one of the significant effects of being in an abusive relationship. Members of support groups provide encouragement to each other, allowing women to see that their reactions to the abuse are not unique. Group members are often at different stages in their acknowledgment of having been abused and their willingness to decide what to do about it. Some may come to the group suspecting that something is not right but not fully recognizing the seriousness of their situation. Others may have left their partners or may be in the process of deciding whether to do so. The opportunity to learn from others' experiences is clearly present and is seen as a prime benefit of the group process.

Most groups for abused women are time limited and are offered in weekly 2-hour sessions over 10 to 16 weeks. Group leaders are either professionals or peers—women who have themselves suffered abuse—and one or two facilitators may lead the groups.

Most authors recommend that those who work with battered women adopt a feminist belief system that condemns violence, avoids assigning responsibility for the violence to victims, recognizes how social institutions perpetuate violence, and focuses on violence rather than the couples' interactions (Pressman, 1984; Hartman, 1983).

In 1984, Pressman listed guidelines for intervention that remain common themes in abused women's support groups. First, the safety of the woman is critical, and, if she has not already made one, the group should assist her in developing a safety plan in case of further outbreaks of violence. Denial or minimization about the abuse may need to be identified and confronted in a supportive way or through education about the dynamics of couple violence. The women may need to explore their reasons for having stayed in abusive relationships in an effort to reduce their sense of self-blame. Assisting them to identify ways that they have resisted the abuse or acted to protect themselves and their children can help with this goal—and may have a positive impact on women's self-esteem and sense of efficacy.

Many groups discuss not only traditional male and female roles but also how such beliefs legitimize the abuse of women by allowing them to be seen as men's rightful property. Further, women may need to be allowed to feel angry about having been victimized, as well as to grieve the loss of their relationship and the hopes they had invested in it. Finally, isolation is reduced if women develop strong bonds that may evolve into support networks that operate beyond the boundaries of a group's formal meetings.

Types of Group Intervention for Abused Women

According to Schopler and Galinsky (1993), support groups fall midway on a continuum between self-help groups and therapy groups. Support groups differ from therapy groups in that, while professionals may lead the group, an essential component is that group members support and teach their peers. Whereas self-help groups are normally led by people who have experienced the problem that is the focus for the group, this is not necessarily so in support groups.

Most of the support groups described in the literature can also be considered psychoeducational, since they offer information about intimate partner violence in addition to providing opportunities for women to interact with each other (Abel, 2000).

Group approaches for assaulted women that are not as easily categorized as support groups tend to be more structured and take a skill-training focus, such as making vocational plans (Ibrahim & Herr, 1987) or learning to be assertive (Cox & Stoltenberg, 1991; Hartman, 1983). Another exception to the support group model is the "You're Not Alone" groups described by Babins-Wagner, Tutty, and Rothery (in preparation) that utilize a narrative and feminist approach with abused women and are seen as therapeutic rather than psychoeducational. The women are provided with little standardized information, and the emphasis is on group interaction and process. Nevertheless, across settings the most commonly utilized group format is support groups.

Research on Groups for Abused Women

In contrast to the considerable literature on the efficacy of groups for male perpetrators, there has been little outcome research conducted on group programs for assaulted women. Of five published studies on groups for women, four (Cox & Stoltenberg, 1991; Holiman & Schilit, 1991; Rinfret-Raynor & Cantin, 1997; Tutty et al., 1993) found statistically significant pretest-posttest improvements in areas such as self-esteem, anger levels, attitudes toward marriage and the family, and depression. With a sample of 38 women attending a more process-oriented group, Babins-Wagner et al. (in preparation) reported statistically significant pretest-posttest improvements on physical and nonphysical abuse, self-esteem, clinical stress, family relations, depression, and sex roles. However, marital satisfaction worsened to a significant extent, a probable consequence of women acknowledging the severity of violence and emotional abuse in their relationships.

Rinfret-Raynor and Cantin (1997) compared feminist group treatment, feminist individual treatment, and nonfeminist individual treatment for abused women. The variables were abuse, as measured by the Conflict Tactics Scales, self-esteem, assertiveness, social adjustment, marital assertion, and dyadic adjustment. The authors found no significant differences between the approaches; women changed, on average, in all three. In another comparison, Cox and Stoltenberg (1991) reported improvements in one skill-training group but not the other. In contrast to the primarily significant improvements noted in the aforementioned quantitative studies, the results of Rubin's (1991) single-case design with six group participants showed inconsistent responses to the group from the participants, with some women improving and others who did not.

This body of research displays methodological problems that are typical in exploratory research in a developing field, such as small sample sizes (Cox & Stoltenberg, 1991; Holiman & Schilit, 1991; Rubin, 1991), a lack of random assignment to conditions, and no control groups (the exception being Cox and Stoltenberg, 1991). Despite these deficits, the results can be interpreted as providing initial evidence of the efficacy of group intervention with assaulted women.

A secondary analysis of the Tutty et al. (1993) data is the only research we have seen that examines the contribution of group process elements to outcomes (Tutty, Bidgood, & Rothery, 1996). This reanalysis found no consistently superior program outcomes that could be attributed to group characteristics, although the data, while based on small sample sizes, suggest some advantages of two-leader groups over time. Efforts to determine whether particular client groups received greater benefits from the program revealed no consistently superior outcomes at posttest for select subpopulations: clients with previous support group experience versus "first-timers," cohabiting clients versus those living with no adult partner, or younger versus older clients. The limited number of follow-up cases revealed that gains might be less sustainable for older clients and those with repeated group involvements, suggesting their need for different kinds of postprogram support.

Characteristics of Support Group Members

What do we know of the characteristics of women who attend support groups? Do they differ from shelter residents? Tutty, Rothery, Cox, and Richardson (1995) conducted qualitative interviews with 32 women who had elected to attend a support group in a community agency. The support group members had a number of characteristics that differentiated them from another 54 women who had sought emergency shelter from the same agency: They were significantly more likely to be legally married, were more educated, and reported higher family income levels. With respect to family violence characteristics, they experienced less severe levels of both physical and nonphysical abuse from their partners and had significantly fewer previous shelter admissions (most, 72%, had never resided in a shelter). Although the physical and nonphysical abuse was less severe than that reported by shelter residents, all but 6 women described their partners as using some physically violent acts, and the reported levels of emotional abuse were substantial.

The authors conducted second interviews with 19 of the 32 women after they had completed the support group. The remainder of this section focuses on these interviews. As with members of most support groups for abused women, there was a mix of those still living with their assaultive partner and those who had left. At the time of initial interviews, 5 of the 19 were no longer residing with their partners. Four to 6 months later, at follow-up, an additional 4 women had left their abusive relationships. Understandably, the needs and issues of the women who had left their partners were different from those of the women who had not left.

Reasons for Attending the Group

In the initial interviews, several women who were still with their partners commented that their reason for seeking help was fear due to escalating violence:

> It was a particularly bad fight. He was sort of sitting on me on the couch and saying, "Shut up and listen to me." He was not letting me leave the room—it was starting to get a little more physical than it had been. I can see if this continues it is going to get into hitting. It's already shoving, it's already screaming at me: "I'm not mad, just shut up and listen to me." So that's what it was, a particularly bad fight.

Another group member commented that her partner's violence had escalated to a point that she could no longer tolerate:

> My whole being is consumed by the abuse. There isn't a minute that goes by, unless I really try, that I don't think about it. And you're always tap-

dancing on eggshells. Inside my body feels sick all the time, and I just want to get out of it.

Three women were concerned about the effects of the violence on their children:

The bottom line is that, in future, the two women who marry my sons will not have to live with violence. I'm frightened the whole pattern is going to repeat in them and that scares me terribly.

Another respondent who was in the process of deciding whether or not to leave her partner commented:

When I first decided to come here (to the support group), I thought, "This will help me decide whether to leave or stay with my husband." But now I'm not so much in the area of leaving or staying, I want to learn how to deal with the situation and how to break the cycle. If I have to leave, maybe this will give me more courage.

In summarizing her decision to seek help, another woman stated:

I think it was either die or try. You know, try to get help or just end it.
    Interviewer: End the relationship?
    Not only that—life itself. It's either reach out and try to pick yourself up or just lie down and die.

Two women who had already left their partners before the start of the group stated diverse reasons for seeking help. One had simply recognized a general need to initiate change:

I went there because I had to do something. I knew he wasn't going to.

The other respondent acted on having come to perceive her husband's behavior as abusive. Previously, she says:

I thought we just fought all the time and were in a big power struggle, but I didn't see it as abuse.

Comments Regarding the Utility of the Group

In evaluating their experiences in the support group, there were no important differences between women who remained with their partners compared with those who had already left. Both sets of clients commented on the competence of the group leaders (in these 10-week groups, most of the leaders were social workers), the utility of the support that they received from fellow group members, and the value of information provided.

Several women shared their initial hesitation about going to a support group, fearing that it would simply be a place where people griped:

> I was scared that it would be nothing but a complaining session . . . like everybody comes and complains about their ex.

The same women noted that what they found, instead, was a supportive environment where group facilitators and members were easy to talk to. Many remarked that the group was an excellent experience, with four women stating that they appreciated the way in which the group was structured:

> The group made me realize that I'm not the only one and that I'm not going crazy. I really felt that I was losing touch with reality and the group has put me in touch. "No, I'm not crazy and, yes, I will survive. It is not the end of the world." It really put things into better perspective, and it's given me a whole new network.

Nine women commented on the expertise of the facilitators:

> The thing that was good was the facilitator's capacity to keep the focus of the group where it needed to be without shutting anybody up, and I think that's a remarkable talent.

Other group members reiterated this, noting that they appreciated the fact that the leaders kept the sessions focused and ensured that each participant was given the opportunity to contribute.

> I really felt comfortable with her. She acted as a very good group facilitator. She'd stop people from going on too long and saying really negative things to another person.

Developing trust and safety was an important trait of the group leader for other group members:

> She said what she was doing, what she wasn't going to do, and then did it. So my trust level around her went way up.

> She was really caring and understanding and made it a safe place to share.

Many of the respondents found that the other group members provided significant support:

> I don't think there's anywhere else I could have gone to get that kind of support . . . the girls were sweet and we got all the names and want to contact each other.

I met a couple of girls who I'll keep in touch with. It's helpful to have somebody who's been in the same situation.

The group has given me back myself. If things get really bad again, I can phone someone, and for that I'm truly thankful.

For several participants, listening to the stories of other women was helpful:

Not only to be aware that you are not alone, but to be aware of how other people handle things and how they worked or haven't worked. That way, you can learn from the other people's experiences as opposed to just struggling on your own.

Hearing various perspectives from several women led to valuable insights. What seemed critical was that the women felt understood by both the counselors and the group members and, as a result, felt less isolated:

I don't feel so alone. I know for a fact that if I needed to reach out, there would be somebody there for me now.

Women also expressed satisfaction with the information provided in the group, especially on the cycle of violence and abuse in general:

It was learning the cycles involved, how abuse happens and what is usually going through his head, what is going through her head . . . the mechanics of it. Once I was able to see how that happens, I saw how it related to my own life. Also to know that there's ways of changing it.

One person mentioned the importance of realizing that her experience had been described and studied in work with other women:

It was liberating to know that it was actually written in a book, and it wasn't in my mind. The most important part was where she showed the cycle. Like you have the actual blowup, and then he's sorry, and then you're mounting up to the next blowup. Wow! That's what it's like.

Others indicated that the group helped them clarify values and confront their choices:

I put up with it (the abuse), and I guess that's 50% of the problem because I let him do it. So I just decided that I should change myself.

It helped me to realize that this isn't what I need in my life, learning what abuse is, and starting to really like myself.

The group really helped me to identify what abuse was, to make sure that

I wasn't taking responsibility for my husband's abuse, to make sure that I was clear that I wasn't deserving of it in any way.

People deserve to be treated well. . . . I'm treated like royalty [in the group].

Developing a safety plan and recognizing danger were identified as important forms of help:

The group taught me the escape plan, having a plan in your head of what you're going to do in a situation that becomes uncontrollable.

I have become so aware of the danger that I've become more guarded . . . but I also feel I'm being smarter.

I do feel I know how to be safe. I am putting a stop to it, as soon as it happens, I say, "Stop, I don't need this."

Several women who had separated from their partners reflected on the changes they had made as a result of attending the support groups:

The emotional stuff is noticeably changing. The anger level is way down, and I don't feel sad/mad all the time. I still get mad, and I still get sad, but it's not all the time like it was.

The whole awareness of what I've been through has made me stop and look at what we were when we were together. I used to really question myself. Now, I have no questions about that, I know I did nothing wrong in that relationship. I was trying to function on a healthy level, and he wasn't, and I was reacting out of fear because I didn't know what to expect. Even that realization made me realize that I'm not the sick person here. I'm a person who had a lot to deal with all at the same time.

I feel more self-confident now; my self-esteem is higher, and my understanding of life has changed. I no longer see things in relationships as black and white. The same rules don't apply in unhealthy relationships.

The reported changes for women who remained with their partners were remarkably similar to those of the women who had left:

Not that my self-esteem is in the sewer, but living with this for so long, I don't really know what the norm is. I've been second-guessing myself for 10 years, but I feel that I'm more in control now than I have been for a long time.

When your self-esteem is so low, it's like, this is what I deserve. When you elevate your self-esteem, you get to a point where you're not going to put up with that crap anymore. I am an adult. I am fully capable of making it on my own. I know I have options. I know that I have choices.

It is notable that the improvements highlighted in the qualitative interviews are consistent with findings from quantitative research described earlier (Cox & Stoltenberg, 1991; Holiman & Schilit, 1991; Rinfret-Raynor & Cantin, 1997; Tutty et al., 1993).

The Process of Support Groups

Moldon (in press) conducted a qualitative study of support groups, interviewing eight women who attended a support group called the Safe Journey program. From these women's comments, Moldon developed a framework to describe how the group provides an environment in which abused women move from the "lost self" to the "reclaimed self." She entitled the process "Reclaiming Stories" and views it as a spiral that incorporates both the content and the process of attending a support group. As she describes it:

> The framework itself has three distinct stages: the lost self, sharing in sisterhood, and reclaiming the self. Two tools facilitate the process of moving from stage to stage: establishing safety and knowledge building. The main focus of the themes is connecting to self and others to begin re-writing stories. In other words, re-writing stories describes a process of psychological and relational healing and change that is generated through the group connections. (Moldon, in press)

The group members develop a sense of safety both from building trust with the other members and the leaders and from being willing to disclose some details of the abuse in their intimate partner relationships. They begin to realize how much of themselves they have forsaken to cope with the relationship and begin to develop bonds with each other as they identify common experiences that result from being in an abusive partnership. The group members utilize information about the cycle of violence and the common experiences of women in abusive partner relationships to consider reclaiming their lives and making new decisions about how they will behave differently in their current relationships or whether they will separate and start anew. This succinctly described process model provides a useful overview for conceptualizing the interaction of group content and process and is congruent with other descriptions of the benefits of groups for abused women (Hartman, 1983; NiCarthy et al., 1984; Pressman, 1989; Seskin, 1988).

OUTREACH AND FOLLOW-UP
ADVOCACY PROGRAMS

Although shelters have become established as the primary organizations to assist abused women, they are often overwhelmed and offer only time-limited assistance; in addition, "Services for nonsheltered women in both rural and urban communities are . . . inadequate" (Davis, Hagen, & Early, 1994, p. 702). New alternative interventions, outreach, and follow-up advocacy programs were developed in the 1990s and have become important supplements to shelter services. Outreach programs offer counseling to abused women who may never have sought shelter residence or could not be accommodated in a transition house because of a lack of space. Follow-up programs are offered primarily to previous shelter residents who have decided to establish a life independent of their assaultive partners, although some will also counsel women who have returned.

Gondolf (1998) reports a rare research study on one outreach model. This program was developed especially to serve women who had been to court because their partners were involved with the justice system. A total of 1,895 women from an initial sample were contacted by program staff within several weeks of their court contact and offered three services, the first two of which were shelter-based: group sessions, individual sessions, and telephone counseling. Almost half of the women could not be reached, and another third refused services. The majority of refusals (60%) were because the women saw no need for such assistance.

Interestingly, only one fifth of the women contacted accepted any of the three options. A small number (21) attended the shelter-based groups or individual counseling (7); however, only 5 group members completed more than four sessions of the 12-week group. The 43 women who took advantage of the telephone counseling reported problems such as recurring abuse from their partners and needing help for their children. Most were available for only one phone counseling session and either could not be reached for a second interview (48%) or were no longer interested (22%). Gondolf concluded that the outreach efforts were "minimally successful" and suggested that we need to learn more about the needs of different client groups of abused women in order to more effectively provide assistance.

Follow-up programs have been more extensively described. The programs are typically small, employing one or two staff members (Tutty, 1993, 1996) or utilizing volunteer community advocates (Sullivan & Bybee, 1999). Most follow-up programs offer services for a limited time, from three months to one year. Some maintain offices in the shelter, enabling workers to meet their prospective clients while still in residence, while others have offices in the community. Follow-up programs have been developed for both emergency and second-stage shelters.

Follow-up workers or community advocates fulfill many roles depending on the expressed concerns of the battered woman program participant. They often assist women to access community resources such as housing, employment, vocational upgrading, or financial assistance. They may be educators, providing information on woman abuse. They may act as advocates with legal representatives, child welfare, or social assistance personnel. During often-weekly visits, they provide supportive counseling on such issues as self-esteem and how women can cope with threats or pressure to reunite with ex-partners or with their children's reactions to the separation. In many ways, the follow-up worker may function as a case manager in that she may be, in all probability, the one community worker who is knowledgeable about the range of services with which each woman is involved or from which she might benefit in the future. In addition to providing individual counseling and advocacy, follow-up workers may offer support groups on such topics as self-esteem, grief, and coping with childhood abuse.

Little research has followed women through the shelter experience or identified what happens to them after they leave the shelter and what they need to facilitate developing a life free of violence. Exceptions include Gondolf and Fisher (1988), Holiman and Schilit (1991), and several studies on follow-up and advocacy services (Sullivan, 1991; Sullivan & Bybee, 1999; Sullivan & Davidson, 1991; Sullivan, Tan, Basta, Rumptz, & Davidson, 1992; Sullivan, Campbell, Angelique, Eby, & Davidson, 1994; Tutty, 1993, 1996), each of which found support for extending services to abused women beyond a shelter stay. Additional research conducted by Sullivan and Rumptz (1994) looked at the efficacy of advocacy services for African-American women, concluding that despite the serious nature and complexity of obstacles, the program was beneficial.

Issues for Follow-Up Program Clients

We turn now to findings from qualitative research with women clients of three follow-up programs (Tutty, 1993, 1996; Tutty et al., 1995). All the women had resided in emergency shelters, and so they had, on average, experienced more serious levels of violence and abuse than the previously described support group members. Tutty and colleagues (1995) interviewed 35 women, both while they resided in the shelter and again 4 to 6 months later. They then compared the concerns of the 21 women who connected with the shelter follow-up program with those of the 14 women who had not. While some of the issues about which women were concerned as they prepared to leave the shelter had been resolved (such as housing and finances), others continued to be of concern, particularly those related to safety, continued contact with the ex-partner, and dealing with various aspects of the legal system, especially those related to custody and access to children. Four to 6 months after having left the shelter, the most important and frequently mentioned issues were those pertaining to career and jobs, finances, legal aspects of family conflict, children's reactions, self-esteem, emotional support, safety, housing, new relationships, and childhood abuse. Nine of 21 follow-up clients and 6 of the non-follow-up group continued to feel threatened by their partners.

Although the problems outlined by the two groups of women were similar, the women in the follow-up program described using the support of the worker to assist them in dealing with ongoing abusive incidents. In general, the women involved with the follow-up program seemed more connected with resources in the community than they had been during the initial interview, much more so than the women who were not involved. By the time of the follow-up interviews, only 4 of the 21 follow-up clients still lacked emotional support in their lives. Notably, in 3 of these cases, the only support the women received was that offered by the follow-up worker, and this was clearly vital.

Ten women who were no longer living with their partners and were involved with the follow-up program experienced considerable improvement in their self-esteem. They described feeling stronger emotionally, more assertive, more confident in themselves, more energetic, less hopeless, and less lonely than they had been when they were living with their partners. Notably, no members of the non-follow-up group reported improvements in their self-esteem since leaving the shelter. Of interest also was the fact that considerably more follow-up clients were involved in school or job training activities than were members of the nonprogram group.

The next section documents the concerns of follow-up program clientele. They are drawn from interviews with 42 women from three different follow-up programs, all with similar formats.

The Characteristics of Follow-Up Program Clients

As mentioned previously, there were some important differences between the shelter clientele who then received the services of the follow-up program and members of the support groups. The shelter clients were, on average, younger, less educated, more likely to live in common-law relationships, and more likely to have lower incomes. They reported significantly higher levels of both physical and nonphysical abuse and were more likely to have previously sought shelter help; the police were involved in more of the incidents that led to their shelter admission, and the clients were more likely to have witnessed family violence as children.

The following quotations describe incidents that led several follow-up clients to seek the safety of a shelter:

> This is a 12-year relationship, and I'd just had enough of it. I was getting older, I've lost jobs because of him, I went bankrupt because of him. I didn't want my boys going through that much longer. So, that was it, I just left. We were doing fine until August, and he found out where we lived and he started coming around. He assaulted me, and I went to stay with my sister. He found out I was there, and he assaulted me there. I charged him with the police.

> Should I have laid charges against him before? Yes, most definitely. He's not going to get help. It's much more than him just assaulting me physically. I can't turn around and charge him with rape, but I should be able

to. But basically, it is rape. It makes you angry because they have a right to get away with it.

The stories of these women are not unusual among those who seek shelter. They illustrate the risks that women face after they leave the security of transition homes to once again live in the community. More generally, we can summarize the main issues that follow-up program clients discussed with their workers.

Relationship with Ex-Partner

The most serious concern for the majority of the follow-up clients was the ongoing relationship with their ex-partners. This conclusion parallels the findings of another study of women who lived in a second-stage shelter (Russell, Forcier, & Charles, 1987). It is well accepted that women are at increased risk of being severely beaten or murdered by their spouses after they have separated (Pagelow, 1984). Ellis's research (1992) suggests two peak times after a woman has left her assaultive partner when she is at increased risk of further violence. The first period is in the initial several months after the separation. While safe housing is an effective deterrent to most men, after a woman leaves the emergency shelter, she is at increased risk once again. The follow-up worker provides emotional support to women starting at this point in time, as well as assisting them to make safety plans and seek legal assistance.

The second high-risk period is 18 to 24 months later, when, according to Ellis (1992), signs that a woman is establishing herself successfully on her own may provoke further violence. Since many follow-up programs do not extend beyond a year, it is not known whether this period is truly a hazardous phase and most clients will again need support, or whether providing social support throughout the early stages of the separation will help women to more successfully disengage from their partners so that continuing violence is less of an issue.

In the study by Tutty et al. (1995), the relationship with an ex-partner was not an issue for a small number of women who had fled the relationship and had no further contact, or those whose reason for staying at the shelter was not an abusive intimate partner relationship. However, women who were obliged to stay in contact with their ex-partners often found the interaction conflictual. In some cases, the abuse and controlling behavior continued although the couple were not living together; in others the relationship became stressful because of pressure to reunite. Some men threatened or attempted to intimidate their partners, many in respect to access to the children or applying for full custody, a common occurrence according to Beaudry (1985). Comments from the follow-up clientele give a sense of the nature of the threats to personal safety:

He came over here 2 weeks ago, had me up against the wall by the throat. He more or less told us he was buying us one-way tickets to [another

country]. He doesn't want to pay for them [support for the children]. . . .
He says, "You can go willingly, or problems can be taken care of." I said,
"Oh, we're back to that again?" and I brushed it off.

Interviewer: So, he's still threatening your life?

Oh, he does like you wouldn't believe! He hasn't threatened to take
(2-year-old son) since last year, so . . . that's nice.

Interviewer: It's not a problem that he knows where you are?

No. . . . Well in some sense there is. 'Cause we fight when we're together. When he comes over, we still fight a lot.

As with any relationship separation, women may feel ambivalent about
having left. Simply because a relationship has been abusive does not mean
that women do not grieve its loss. Difficulty in coming to terms with the
death of a relationship can leave a woman especially vulnerable to de-
clarations from her partner that he has changed and will never be abusive
again:

He keeps bugging me that he's changed and quit drinking. But about once
a month he tends to mess that up. My daughter keeps saying, "He has quit
drinking but please don't get back together." I said, "I don't plan on it."
I guess he still tells them that we're going to get back together.

Interviewer: Was he putting more pressure on you in the early days
after you left?

Oh yes. My mom and dad sent down an answering machine because I
was getting 8 or 10 calls a day.

Pressure to reunite can change to threats if a woman rebuffs the pleas for
a reconciliation:

He threw a steak knife into my arm after I took my stuff. He was threatening, but he was doing that when I was there, too. He tried to get me back,
and then he followed me out here. I really didn't want to go back because
I knew what he was like, but I was feeling insecure about being here . . .
and he started giving me money.

Interviewer: Did you have any trouble with him after he came out of
jail?

Yes. Constantly phoning and saying he loves me and wants to be with
me and in the next breath I'm an [expletive] because I wouldn't let him
see me. He said that if anything happens to the car or if he goes to jail,
that those people will come and shoot me dead.

Emotional Support

The importance of emergency shelters as a refuge from assaultive partners
and as a place that provides the opportunity for women to make decisions
about their own future without the interference of their partner is well documented. However, given the time restrictions on women's stays in transition

houses (three weeks in most houses), if women decide to live independently, they not only need to plan how to ensure their continued safety beyond the shelter but also are faced with a number of new issues, many of which are concerned with basic human needs. They must find and furnish new housing (often accomplished in the shelter and aided by shelter staff). Finances are an issue for most women. They may need to register their children in new schools and help them cope with the aftermath of the many changes they have undergone in a short time. Overriding each of these concerns is how to cope with their ex-partners. Thus, emotional support can be seen as a comprehensive category that both incorporates and transcends the other issues.

Many of the interviewees commented about the loneliness and anxiety of living on their own, some for the first time in their lives. Feeling inadequate and having low self-esteem were commonly mentioned. Such feelings have the potential to interfere with a woman's ability to make decisions or to present herself in the best light when dealing with agency representatives or employers. Low self-esteem and living in depressing circumstances can lead some women to contemplate suicide. These factors may also lead to marital reconciliation, despite this not being the desired alternative.

A number of the women commented on self-esteem issues and the importance of the support that they received from the follow-up counselor:

> I don't know where I would have been today if it wasn't for her [the follow-up worker]. Many times I wanted to take a bottle of sleeping pills and just check out.

Low self-esteem, social isolation, and depression make it more difficult to deal effectively with all the other issues described in this chapter. The emotional support that the women experienced in their meetings with follow-up workers should thus be considered a core element of the program.

Legal Issues

A number of women were dealing with divorce or custody issues or were pressing charges against their partners, and interacting with the legal system and going to court was anxiety-provoking. We have noted earlier that the most common reason women return home is to give their partners another chance, but the second most frequent reason is lack of support or follow-through by the legal system (Johnson, Crowley, & Sigler, 1992). To assist a woman in coping with such difficulties, the follow-up worker might, for example, accompany her to the lawyer's office or to court, or describe court procedures so that she will know what to expect when her own case is heard. Without such support, women are more likely to drop charges against their partners:

> The follow-up worker came to the lawyers with me a few times. . . . She went to court with me, and I won my assault charges against him.

Interviewer: Was it helpful having the worker with you?

Oh, definitely! I would have never been able to do it with him . . . 'cause I was just shaking and vibrating. The follow-up worker helped me with the peace bond . . . and we wrote up a statement about what happened that day that I had the police come over. I had trouble seeing him at court. On court day he'd come and be this wonderful dad.

Interviewer: Did he fight you for custody?

Yes, that was one thing that the follow-up worker helped me through. I probably would have given him everything and walked away just so I could get away. That's why I finally decided to leave him because I was at the point where I was ready to give him everything . . . so I was surprised that I was even able to have the house and keep the kids.

Coping With Children

Two types of issues with children stood out as difficult for a number of the follow-up clients: coping as a single parent with children's behavior and dealing with visitation by the ex-partner. The strength of children's reaction to the separation of their parents can be a factor that leads to reconciliation in some families. A number of comments alluded to concerns about children's behavior and feelings:

Working through my emotional problems and trying to deal with the children's emotional upsets [was hard]. Wondering if it would all level out. The fear of taking on the responsibility of raising children properly without a partner, knowing it is a long-term commitment.

I could have handled him, but I couldn't handle the kids. I couldn't handle him going through the kids and the kids putting the same amount of pressure on me. I gave him free visitation rights, I didn't stop him from at any time. . . . I could have, but then I would have paid for it through the boys. Because "Well, mom won't let dad come see me now." That was the type of ammunition he used.

Even when women are emotionally resigned to having left their partners, if they have children, they are likely to continue experiencing problems during access visits. This second major concern about coping with custody disputes and visitation is reflected in several comments:

He wants to get back together. He's pretty hard to deal with, I find, at the best of times. I've been trying to avoid him as much as I can, but it's hard because he sees the boys every other weekend, that's his visitation rights.

It's hard. He has the right to see them anytime he wants to, and I can't stop him. If I want him to see them every weekend, he won't and says he's busy this week and next week. Then all of a sudden he'll want to see them, and I'll have to let him. First he was seeing them every week, and then he couldn't come one week. I said, "That's fine," and he wouldn't see them for 2 or 3 weeks. The kids would start wondering why he wasn't coming anymore. Sometimes it was months, and I'm the one who has to see the kids hurting. Then all of a sudden after 4 or 5 months he'd want to see them that day. I'd tell my lawyer I didn't want him to see them now, they've adjusted to not seeing him anymore, and she'd say I have to let them go.

Finally, problems with finances and finding adequate housing were raised by a number of follow-up program clients. Finding a place to live and settling into a new residence are obviously top priorities for women who wish to establish independent lives. DeKeseredy and Hinch (1991) found that women who were unable to find accommodations were likely to return to their previous relationships out of desperation. In other instances, leaving a battering relationship can be one step to becoming homeless. Studies of homeless women (Breton & Bunston, 1992) have found that many had previously left abusive partners and lived in emergency shelters, but were unable to secure long-term accommodations.

Women who were previously married are at a high risk of living in poverty especially if they have children; often even if a husband provides support to children, the wife's standard of living goes down while his stays about the same (Lein, 1986). Commonly, women either receive no child support or receive it only sporadically, and with a husband who is controlling and abusive, it is even less likely that such support will be forthcoming.

Of the follow-up clients who disclosed their income, a large proportion relied on social assistance. While almost two thirds of the women discussed finances with their follow-up worker, none described it as their most important issue. Since most of the women were already on social assistance when they moved out of the shelter, financial concerns may have been less pressing, although several commented on how difficult it was to live on the income provided. Others commented about the stigma of being on welfare:

I don't want to be on Social Services. I hate being classed as a single mom on welfare. I don't tell many people I'm on welfare. If you're around that office and see the people that come out of there, it would depress you. I don't want to be there.

SUMMARY AND CONCLUSIONS

The shelter-based follow-up program studied clearly met one of its goals, which was lessening the need for previous shelter residents to reenter the shelter for support. With the initiation of the program two years earlier, the shelter reported substantially fewer readmissions, with those women who did return doing so for appropriate safety reasons. An important further question is whether follow-up programs adequately assist women who wish to live separately from an abusive partner.

Several women commented that having the support of the follow-up program prevented them from returning to their abusive partners. These quotations provide a fitting conclusion to the discussion of the efficacy of follow-up programs:

> I never could have left without the follow-up worker and the shelter. The worker really helped me.

> I've fallen back quite a few times, made some pretty bad decisions. One day, I had my bags packed ready to go back to my partner, and I was going to quit this course.
> Interviewer: What helped you get through that?
> The follow-up counselor, the support group.

> If you're not going to have a follow-up program, you shouldn't have a shelter. All you're doing is giving temporary assistance for her to go back to what she just came from. He's going to kill her, or she's going to become so codependent that there's nothing else that she can be. So if [you're] serious, go the extra step.

Generally, this review of nonshelter programs and programs that extend shelter into the community suggests the importance of seeing the provision of shelter beds as only an initial step in addressing the needs of abused women and their children. Shelters are necessary but not sufficient. They do an excellent job of protecting the safety of many women and helping them in the first step of a transition to a violence-free life. However, a majority of abused women do not use shelters, and those that do have needs for support that continue well after they are back in the community (Bowker & Maurer, 1985; Gondolf & Fischer, 1988). Support groups, shelter outreach, and follow-up services are essential complements to residential shelter services, and the women themselves tell us that they provide essential knowledge, resources, and social support at a time when an escape from violence seems impossibly difficult.

REFERENCES

Abel, E. (2000). Psychosocial treatment for battered women: A review of empirical research. *Research on Social Work Practice, 10,* 55–77.

Aguilar, R., & Nightingale, N. N. (1994). The impact of specific battering experiences on the self-esteem of abused women. *Journal of Family Violence, 9,* 35–45.

Astin, M. C., Ogland-Hand, S. M., Coleman, E. M., & Foy, D. (1995). Posttraumatic stress disorder and childhood abuse in battered women: Comparisons with maritally distressed women. *Journal of Consulting and Clinical Psychology, 63,* 308–312.

Babins-Wagner, R., Tutty, L., & Rothery, M. (in preparation). *You're not alone: An evaluation of a group for abused women.* Unpublished manuscript.

Beaudry, M. (1985). *Battered women.* Montreal, QU: Black Rose Books.

Bowker, L., & Maurer, L. (1985). The importance of sheltering in the lives of battered women. *Response to the Victimization of Women and Children, 8,* 2–8.

Breton, M., & Bunston, T. (1992). Physical and sexual violence in the lives of homeless women. *Canadian Journal of Community Mental Health, 11,* 29–43.

Campbell, J. (1986). A survivor group for battered women. *Advances in Nursing Science, 8*(2), 13–20.

Cascardi, M., & O'Leary, D. (1992). Depressive symptomatology, self-esteem and self-blame in battered women. *Journal of Family Violence, 7,* 249–259.

Charles, N. (1994). The housing needs of women and children escaping domestic violence. *Journal of Social Policy, 23,* 465–487.

Cox, J. W., & Stoltenberg, C. (1991). Evaluation of a treatment program for battered wives. *Journal of Family Violence, 6,* 395–413.

Davis, L., Hagen, J. L., & Early, T. J. (1994). Social services for battered women: Are they adequate, accessible and appropriate? *Social Work, 39,* 69511–704.

DeKeseredy, W. S., & Hinch, R. (1991). *Woman abuse: Sociological perspectives.* Toronto, ON: Thompson.

Dutton, D., & Painter, S. (1993). The battered woman syndrome: Effects of severity and intermittency of abuse. *American Journal of Orthopsychiatry, 63,* 614–622.

Dziegielewski, S. F., Resnick, C., & Krause, N. B. (1996). Shelter-based crisis intervention with battered women. In A. R. Roberts (Ed.), *Helping battered women: New perspectives and remedies* (pp. 159–171). New York: Oxford University Press.

Ellis, D. (1992). Woman abuse among separated and divorced women: The relevance of social support. In E. C. Viano (Ed.), *Intimate violence: Interdisciplinary perspectives* (pp. 177–189). Washington, DC: Hemisphere.

Gondolf, E. W. (1998). Service contact and delivery of a shelter outreach project. *Journal of Family Violence, 13,* 131–145.

Gondolf, E., & Fisher, E. (1988). *Battered women as survivors: An alternative to treating learned helplessness.* Lexington, MA: Lexington Books.

Hartman, S. (1983). A self-help group for women in abusive relationships. *Social Work With Groups, 6,* 133–134.

Holiman, M., & Schilit, R. (1991). Aftercare for battered women: How to encourage the maintenance of change. *Psychotherapy, 28,* 345–353.

Ibrahim, F., & Herr, E. (1987). Battered women: A developmental life-career counselling perspective. *Journal of Counseling and Development, 65,* 244–248.

Johnson, I., Crowley, J., & Sigler, R. (1992). Agency response to domestic violence: Services provided to battered women. In E. Viano (Ed.), *Intimate violence: Interdisciplinary perspectives* (pp. 191–202). Washington, DC: Hemisphere.

Kemp, A., Green, B., Hovanitz, C., & Rawlings, E. (1995). Incidence and correlates of posttraumatic stress disorder in battered women. *Journal of Interpersonal Violence, 10,* 43–55.

Kurz, D. (1996). Separation, divorce, and woman abuse. *Violence Against Women, 2,* 68–81.

Lein, L. (1986). The changing role of the family. In M. Lystad (Ed.), *Violence in the home: Interdisciplinary perspectives* (pp. 32–50). New York: Brunner/Mazel.

Mancoske, R., Standifer, D., & Cauley, C. (1994). The effectiveness of brief counselling services for battered women. *Research on Social Work Practice, 4*, 53–63.

Moldon, J. (in press). Rewriting stories: Women's responses to the Safe Journey group. In. L. Tutty & C. Goard (Eds.), *Reclaiming self: Issues and resources for women abused by intimate partners.* Halifax, NS: Fernwood Books.

NiCarthy, G., Merriam, K., & Coffman, S. (1984). *Talking it out: A guide to groups for abused women.* Seattle, WA: Seal Press.

Pagelow, M. (1992). Adult victims of domestic violence: Battered women. *Journal of Interpersonal Violence, 7*, 87–120.

Pressman, B. (1984). *Family violence: Origins and treatment.* Guelph, Ontario: University of Guelph Office for Educational Practice.

Pressman, B. (1989). Treatment of wife-abuse: The case for feminist therapy. In B. Pressman, G. Cameron, & M. Rothery (Eds.), *Intervening with assaulted women: Current theory, research and practice* (pp. 21–45). Hillsdale, NJ: Erlbaum.

Rinfret-Raynor, M., & Cantin, S. (1997). Feminist therapy for battered women: An assessment. In G. Kaufman Kantor, & J. L. Jasinski (Eds.), *Out of the darkness: Contemporary perspectives on family violence* (pp. 219–234). Thousand Oaks, CA: Sage.

Rodgers, K. (1994). Wife assault: The findings of a national survey. *Juristat Service Bulletin: Canadian Centre for Justice Statistics, 14*(9), 1–21.

Rubin, A. (1991). The effectiveness of outreach counselling and support groups for battered women: A preliminary evaluation. *Research on Social Work Practice, 1*, 332–357.

Russell, M., Forcier, C., & Charles, M. (1987). *Safe Choice: Client satisfaction survey.* Report prepared for Act II, Vancouver, British Columbia.

Schopler, J., & Galinsky, M. (1993). Support groups as open systems: A model for practice and research. *Health and Social Work, 18*, 195–207.

Seskin, J. (1988). Sounds of practice II: Group work with battered women. *Social Work With Groups, 11*, 101–108.

Sullivan, C. (1991). The provision of advocacy services to women leaving abusive partners: An exploratory study. *Journal of Interpersonal Violence, 6*, 41–54.

Sullivan, C., & Bybee, D. I. (1999). Reducing violence using community-based advocacy for women with abusive partners. *Journal of Consulting and Clinical Psychology, 67*, 43–53.

Sullivan, C., Campbell, R., Angelique, H., Eby, K., & Davidson, W., II, (1994). An advocacy program for women with abusive partners: Six-month follow-up. *American Journal of Community Psychology, 22*, 101–122.

Sullivan, C., & Davidson, W. (1991). The provision of advocacy services to women leaving abusive partners: An examination of short-term effects. *American Journal of Community Psychology, 19*, 953–960.

Sullivan, C., & Rumptz, M. (1994). Adjustment and needs of African-American women who utilized a domestic violence shelter. *Violence and Victims, 9*, 275–286.

Sullivan, C., Tan, C., Basta, J., Rumptz, M., & Davidson, W. (1992). An advocacy intervention program for women with abusive partners: Initial evaluation. *American Journal of Community Psychology, 20*, 309–332.

Trimpey, M. (1989). Self-esteem and anxiety: Key issues in an abused women's support group. *Issues in Mental Health Nursing, 10,* 297–308.

Tutty, L. (1993). After the shelter: Critical issues for women who leave assaultive relationships. *Canadian Social Work Review, 10,* 183–201.

Tutty, L. (1996). Post-shelter services: The efficacy of follow-up programs for abused women. *Research on Social Work Practice, 6,* 425–441.

Tutty, L. (1998). Mental health issues of abused women: The perceptions of shelter workers. *Canadian Journal of Community Mental Health, 17,* 79–102.

Tutty, L. (in press). *Shelters for abused women in Canada: A celebration of the past, challenges for the future.* Ottawa, ON: Family Violence Prevention, Health Canada.

Tutty, L., Bidgood, B., & Rothery, M. (1993). Support groups for battered women: Research on their efficacy. *Journal of Family Violence, 8,* 325–343.

Tutty, L., Bidgood, B., & Rothery, M. (1996). The impact of group process and client variables in support groups for battered women. *Research on Social Work Practice, 6,* 308–324.

Tutty, L., Rothery, M., Cox, G., & Richardson, C. (1995). *An evaluation of the Calgary YWCA family violence programs: Assisting battered women and their children.* Final Report to the Family Violence Prevention Division, Health Canada.

Tutty, L. M., Weaver, G., & Rothery, M. A. (1999). Residents' views of the efficacy of shelter services for abused women. *Violence Against Women, 5,* 869–925.

Webb, W. (1992). Treatment issues and cognitive behavior techniques with battered women. *Journal of Family Violence, 7,* 205–217.

Weisz, G., Taggart, J., Mockler, S., & Streich, P. (1994). *The role of housing in dealing with family violence in Canada.* Ottawa, ON: Canada Mortgage and Housing Corporation.

Wilson, K., Vercella, R., Brems, C., Benning, D., & Renfro, N. (1992). Levels of learned helplessness in abused women. *Women and Therapy, 13*(4), 53–67.

Yalom, I. (1995). *The theory and practice of group psychotherapy* (4th ed.). New York: Basic Books.

19

Interventions for Batterers
Program Approaches, Program Tensions

BEA HANSON

In the field of domestic violence, programs that work with the abuser or batterer are often looked upon with suspicion by advocates and service providers who work with victims of domestic violence. What are the goals of these programs? Do they work? Do they address the needs of battered women? Do they stop domestic violence? Aren't they just taking away from funding that could be used for battered women? Most of those who ask such questions are looking for simple answers to a complex social problem.

Even within the field of batterer intervention, the debate over the purpose and effectiveness of programs is not more advanced than that between advocates for victims of domestic violence. Batterer intervention programs argue over goals: Are they meant to provide education to abusers or change their abusive behavior? They argue over intervention techniques: Are lectures with controlled discussions or therapeutic groups more appropriate? They argue over identification of the forces that enable battering to happen: Is it patriarchal culture, poor family communication patterns, history of abuse as a child, or a psychological disorder?

In the early 1970s the battered women's movement began as a demand for recognition of and an end to violence against women in the home and instigated a proliferation of services and reforms to address domestic violence. These groups were by no means monolithic in terms of theory and practice but held varied beliefs, political assumptions, and programmatic goals to help battered women (Schechter, 1982). This rapid development of domestic violence services and policies emanating from groups grounded in different approaches and theories plays itself out again in work with batterers. In the same way that services for victims of domestic violence emerged from such disparate philosophies as those held by the battered women's movement, mental health agencies, crime victim assistance programs, private psychotherapists, and family systems practitioners, these same theories emerged and continue to compete for primacy in theory and practice development in work with batterers. From service providers helping victims to become survivors to practitioners working with abusers, to researchers, feminists, advocacy agencies, and funders for abuser and victim programs, there is profound disagreement about how or even whether to intervene with batterers. Some researchers find that batterer intervention programs are an important part of preventing further domestic violence (Edleson, 1996), and others find that such programs do not deter future violence (Harrell, 1991). Some advocates maintain that programs for men who batter may be dangerous and hold out false hopes for women (Hart, 1988); others do not want funds that could be used for victims reallocated to "help" batterers (Schechter, 1982). Given the wide range of professionals involved in the field of domestic violence, this lack of common ground has created tensions between programs and general confusion in the field.

Tension between theories is common in social science research and practice, especially in the development of new areas of knowledge, such as domestic violence and batterer intervention. Merton (1968) calls this tension *polarization*, wherein controversies in social science are polarized, with each "side" attacking and counterattacking the other, creating progressive alienation between the parties to the conflict. Soon the battle becomes more focused on status than on a search for truth, and each group begins responding largely to stereotyped versions of what the other is saying. As a result, dialogue ends, perspectives become entrenched, and growth and development in the field become stymied. This creates a form of goal displacement wherein practice theory perspectives are valued over finding the most effective intervention for the client.

For social work practitioners, this polarization creates confusion both in developing programs and in working with individual clients. For social work administrators, in determining if batterer intervention programs fit into the purview of the agency: Are substance abuse agencies, mediation programs, mental health agencies, or battered women's advocates appropriate venues for batterer intervention programs? For social work managers, in determining the best program approaches for working with batterers: Should batterer work be in the context of the individual, family, or cohort group? For social work practitioners, in determining their role vis-à-vis the batterer: Are social workers trying to educate, punish, support, or change the batterer? According to Robbins, Chatterjee, and Canda (1998, 1999), with this lack of clear theoretical direction, social workers usually use one or a combination of three approaches: (1) rejecting the use of theory and instead focusing on specific practice and interventions; (2) theoretical dogmatism, accepting a specific theory as universally true and applying it to all clients and client situations; and/or (3) undisciplined eclecticism, mixing and matching bits and pieces of different theoretical approaches. While these approaches may seem effective to the individual practitioner, they do not truly incorporate social work theory, nor do they advance the study and theoretical development of social work (Robbins, Chatterjee, & Canda, 1999; Witkin & Gottschalk, 1988). Therefore, the real practice of social work involves a synergistic relationship between theory and practice, with practice influencing theory development and vice versa.

The purpose of this chapter is to identify and begin to unravel the myriad approaches and complex tensions that exist in the field of batterer intervention. I will examine the history of batterer intervention programs, including the impact of feminism and the battered women's movement, social work, and the criminal justice system; deconstruct the debate over the purpose of these programs; identify the range of models used in batterer intervention, based on the literature; review the literature on the effectiveness of programs; determine important elements for batterer intervention programs based on existing data; and outline areas for further study.

DEFINITION OF TERMS

In any discussion, we need to establish a common ground regarding language and terminology. The terms *domestic violence* and *battering* are used throughout this chapter and warrant particular attention.

Domestic Violence

In this chapter, *domestic violence* refers to the pattern of behavior used to maintain power and control over another person in an intimate relationship, including physical and sexual assault, verbal abuse, and emotional abuse. While other terms, such as *family violence, spouse abuse*, and *battered women* are often used to refer to this pattern, *domestic violence* is frequently viewed as the more neutral and encompassing definition.

Sometimes these terms are used synonymously. For example, Fields (1996), writing a foreword in Roberts's (1996) book, *Helping Battered Women*, in the first page, uses terms interchangeably, referring to "woman-battering," "family violence," "wife beating," and "domestic violence" to identify the same concept. More commonly, however, these terms are used quite deliberately to indicate a specific political and/or theoretical perspective on the issue (Roche & Sadoski, 1996; Herzberger, 1996; Weitzman & Dreen, 1982). *Family violence* and *spouse abuse* connote a belief in domestic violence as the result of a family communication or relational problem within the family system; *wife abuse* and *battered women* attribute domestic violence to a systematic result of patriarchal relationships, often excluding relationships in which the partners are not married and same-sex relationships. The term *domestic violence*, while problematic in that it is sometimes charged with minimizing the criminal aspects by separating crimes in the home from other kinds of crime, and with contextualizing the problem as domestic when much "domestic" abuse happens in public and at the workplace (e.g., stalking, abuse in public), in this discussion of a wide range of programs and program philosophies, it is often considered the most neutral term.

Battering

While the term *domestic violence* is often used to imply a more encompassing, less value-laden view of the problem, there are different definitions of *battering* or abusive behavior that lead to different practice implications. Most policy makers, as expressed in the laws they pass, consider only the most severe forms of abuse as battering, including various forms of physical attack, some threatening behaviors, and sometimes harassment, such as stalking (Edleson, 1996). These definitions place battering in the realm of criminal behavior—physical assaults, attempted assaults, and threatening and menacing behavior, which fall under the category of crime in most states (Schechter & Edleson, 2000). Other definitions concentrate on physical violence and include emotional and sexual abuse only in accompaniment with physical violence (Herzberger, 1996). Still others conceptualize battering as a logical outcome of relationships of dominance and inequality, focusing on a pattern of behavior rather than specific incidents, and include a range of behaviors from emotional and verbal abuse to threats and physical and sexual violence (Pence & Paymar, 1985; Shepard, 1991). In order to encompass the widest range of behaviors associated with battering and domestic violence, in this chapter, the term will encompass both criminal and noncriminal behavior unless otherwise noted.

USE OF TERMINOLOGY TO DIFFERENTIATE PERSPECTIVES

The field of social work is replete with debates about and arguments over what is the best policy, practice approach, or model for a particular social problem (e.g., Karger & Midgley, 1994; Point/Counterpoint, Journal of Social Work Education). Social work researchers examine different practice approaches, evaluate their effectiveness, and compare them with other approaches. These examinations are often viewed from particular perspectives: intrapsychic, behavioral, family systems, feminist, and so on. Researchers are often cast into specific "boxes" that "describe" their perspectives—he is a behaviorist, or she has a family systems perspective—categories readers and other researchers often use to support or discredit the author's theories, sometimes without even reading the work (Merton, 1968).

Practice and research on batterer intervention programs are no exception—programs are evaluated and research projects are often constructed from specific theoretical perspectives. Each perspective uses language to differentiate its theories and practices from others (Healey, Smith, & O'Sullivan, 1998). For example, the term *domestic violence* has a gender-neutral connotation, whereas *wife abuse* or *woman abuse* links with other violence against women and notes the injuries inflicted on women by male partners, and *marital violence* or *family violence* connects violence to problems of communication or dynamics within the "family system." Literature based on feminist theories of battering is often described as "profeminist," indicating support of feminist goals, and refers to the overarching paradigms of "sexism," "patriarchy," or "misogyny" as enabling woman abuse to exist. Mental health professionals talk about "counselors" or "therapists" providing "treatment" to "clients," while profeminist "facilitators" or "instructors" provide "interventions" or "education" to "batterers" using a didactic format described as "classes," and family systems "counselors" work on the "communication skill deficits" of the "family system" in "couples therapy" and "support groups."

Examining titles of books and articles often indicates the theoretical perspective of the author: (1) *Violence Against Wives: A Case Study Against the Patriarchy* (Dobash & Dobash, 1979) refers to the "patriarchy," which clearly places the article within a profeminist framework, while "violence against wives" implies the sanctions that marriage places on men's abuse of women; (2) "Social Skill Deficits in Maritally Violent Men" (Holtzworth-Munroe, 1992) attributes the problem to a "social skills" deficit, indicating a behavioral approach to the problem and implying violence as a dynamic in a marriage; (3) "Marital Violence: Characteristics of Abusive Couples" (Rosenbaum & O'Leary, 1981) stems from a family systems approach, attributing the violence to the dynamics between the members of the couple; (4) "Personality Characteristics of Male Spouse Abusers" (Beasley & Stoltenberg, 1992) implies possible intrapsychic influences on abusive men; (5) "The Case for Bottling Up Rage" (Berkowitz, 1973) implies a behavioral problem for violence; and (6) "The Origin and Structure of the Abusive Personality" (Dutton, 1994) attributes the problem to personality disorders.

HISTORY OF BATTERER INTERVENTION PROGRAMS: EMERGING FROM THE BATTERED WOMEN'S MOVEMENT

The traditional response to domestic violence has been to pretend it does not exist, accept it, or attribute it to various physiological or psychological explanations (Thorne-Finch, 1992). Before the women's movement in the early 1970s, the problem of male violence against women was viewed as insignificant and attributable mainly to individual—and frequently female—pathology (Thorne-Finch, 1992). In the early 1970s, the women's and battered women's movements identified "wife beating" as a social problem in the United States and vocalized the need for an expanded public role in identifying and responding to domestic violence (Martin, 1976). The movement began a nationwide mindshift by reframing what some men called "discipline" or "obedience" as abuse and violence. Only in the latter part of the 1970s did social services begin to cater specifically to the needs of battered women. Prior to that time, services were uncoordinated, requiring women to locate disparate services—accepting emergency funds from the Salvation Army to flee an abuser, for example, or finding themselves in a shelter for the homeless with no security from abusers or specialized services for victims of domestic violence. Some services were inappropriate: Police officers responding to a domestic incident would walk the husband around the block to "cool off" instead of making an arrest, leaving the woman with no criminal recourse; mental health clinics would provide only couples counseling in cases of domestic abuse; welfare offices had no process for emergency assistance in cases of women fleeing abusive partners. Service providers in a wide range of settings began to express the need for a range of public services such as shelters, counseling centers, and support groups for victims of domestic violence, including batterers' intervention programs to address the behavior of abusers.

With the expansion of public awareness about domestic violence as a result of the battered women's movement, an increased urgency to provide effective legal, educational, and therapeutic interventions for batterers emerged (Bennett & Piet, 1999). Batterers' programs began as voluntary men's responses to the message of the battered women's movement and an attempt at confronting, among men, the feminist notion that patriarchy enables men to batter and abuse their female partners. Founded in 1977, EMERGE was developed at the request of women working in Boston area shelters and is often identified as the first batterer intervention program in the country (Schechter, 1982). Similar programs began to crop up elsewhere, with the philosophy that male dominance and misogyny were the root of violence against women, and that abusive men were willful and responsible and should be held accountable for their behavior.

The profeminist batterer intervention programs were to resocialize men to work toward equality for women and to take responsibility for their behavior. Stopping physical violence was not the only purpose. These programs were also designed to help batterers end the ongoing pattern of coercive control. They developed group counseling models to educate men and help them change their behavior. The programs focused on reframing violent acts as examples of controlling behaviors rather than impulsive or random eruptions of violence. A feminist framework for intervention was used to challenge sexist, abusive behavior and to allow men to test honest, nonabusive ones.

ROLE OF SOCIAL WORK AND OTHER MENTAL HEALTH PROFESSIONALS IN DOMESTIC VIOLENCE SERVICES

The profeminist program philosophies of early batterer intervention programs such as EMERGE and RAVEN (Rape And Violence End Now), a program in St. Louis, clearly contrasted with those of the established mental health professions, which focused on keeping the family intact and often viewed domestic violence as a relational problem (Mederos, 1999). During this time, the field of social work, in its quest for professional status, increasingly emphasized psychoanalytic and psychodynamic theory, which led to a narrow individual and intrapsychic view of people and sharp contrast with the profeminist policies of the early domestic violence movement (Thorne-Finch, 1992). Social work's involvement in domestic violence and batterers' intervention began as a face-off with feminists. Instead of the feminist focus on putting the woman first and providing concrete services for women (e.g., physically helping to move a battered woman out of the home and into a safe shelter), early social work emphasized mutual support of both men and women, often from an individualistic psychotherapeutic perspective, advocating consciousness-raising groups for men in an effort to change male attitudes and behavior toward women (U.S. Commission on Civil Rights, 1978).

In early government hearings in response to the growing battered women's movement, testimony was given from a "social work perspective," emphasizing the importance of the "orientation" of the "therapist" and the involvement of men in the "therapeutic process." Feminists testified against this approach, denouncing the "male-dominated therapeutic establishment" as sexist and reflective of the second-class citizenship of women (U.S. Commission on Civil Rights, 1978). These early encounters between feminists and social workers created a framework in which the two groups were diametrically opposed.

Although social work's professional theory base has expanded to include systems theory and an ecological perspective, psychological perspectives on the life span continue to dominate much of the field's knowledge about human behavior (Robbins, Chatterjee, & Canda, 1999). Even systems-based theories have largely retained a micro- and meso-level focus for direct practice rather than a broader focus for social action (Robbins, Chatterjee, & Canda, 1998). However, the push for social action and advocacy of a feminist perspective within social work practice has been growing in the field of domestic violence (e.g., see Ahrens, 1980; Davis & Hagen, 1988, 1992; Roche & Sadoski, 1996; Tierney, 1982; Valentich, 1996).

CRIMINAL JUSTICE SYSTEM RESPONDS UNDER PRESSURE OF BATTERED WOMEN'S ADVOCATES

As the domestic violence movement expanded, increasing attention was given to the role of the criminal justice system in responding to domestic violence. Until the 1980s, domestic violence was largely ignored as a criminal problem by the criminal justice system. Responding police officers talked to the abuser but rarely made an arrest, leaving the man at home and the woman vulnerable to additional violence because she dared to call for help (Schechter, 1982). Court diversion and mediation programs were considered innovative criminal justice responses to "family disputes"; they involved stopping formal criminal proceedings against the person who had violated the law in favor of processing through noncriminal disposition (Laszlo, 1978). Diversion and mediation programs included both misdemeanor and felony assaults; felonies were reduced to misdemeanors to allow jurisdiction of the lower court. By definition, mediation considered the problem mutual and involved the disputants arriving at a written agreement that was not legally binding. As a result, if the mediation did not work and the domestic abuse continued (as it often does), the person who was being battered needed to wait until another assault happened before returning to court.

In an early study of mediation cases in Massachusetts, involving crimes ranging from threats to assault with a dangerous weapon to attempted homicide, 75% were determined "successful" because an agreement was reached and no further criminal complaints were issued within the two-year span of the study (Laszlo, 1978). However, advocates found that mediation and diversion programs were actually placing women in more danger. Women now risked additional violence because they had no orders of protection or other legal recourse and found themselves needing to file additional charges after subsequent incidents of violence, since the mediation agreement was not legally binding. As a result, the criminal justice system was often viewed as a hindrance, not a help, for battered women.

As public awareness of domestic violence increased and in response to pressure from battered women's advocates, the criminal justice system began to set up more rigid and systemic responses to domestic violence. By 1988, every state had passed acts that created civil and criminal remedies for victims of domestic violence, and by 1992, protective orders were available to abused women in all 50 states (Roberts, 1996). Crime victim advocates, battered women's advocates, and mental health agencies developed batterer intervention programs in many areas across the country.

In the early 1980s, the Domestic Abuse Intervention Project (DAIP), located in Duluth, Minnesota, gained national recognition as the first community-based reform project to successfully negotiate a community coordinated response to domestic violence (Pence, 1983). This response encompassed the police, criminal and civil court systems, advocates, and battered women working together to address domestic violence. Since the development of the community coordinated response model, many municipalities throughout the United States and elsewhere have attempted to replicate or adapt the model (Balzer, 1999; Holder 1999).

One significant aspect of this coordinated response involves the court system, which has become a primary referral source for many batterer intervention programs. Physically abusive men were arrested, tried, and given the option of serving their sentences or being placed on probation with strict conditions of refraining from further violence while attending a mandatory batterer intervention program (Mederos, 1999).

WHAT IS THE PURPOSE OF BATTERER INTERVENTION PROGRAMS?

The historical tension between the focus on societal change within the battered women's movement, the individual and family focus of social workers and other mental health providers, and the focus on crime in the criminal justice system has created a struggle of purpose within the movement and among service providers regarding the role of batterer intervention programs. A wide variety of interventions and expectations exist for batterer intervention programs: to punish abusers who are caught by the criminal justice system; to hold men accountable for their abusive behavior; to educate men about sexism, the patriarchy, and the role that domestic violence plays in maintaining a patriarchal system; to change behavior by providing tools to control and manage anger, and thus create healthy, loving relationships; and to change intrapsychic patterning by identifying and resolving childhood and other impacting trauma that leads to battering as an adult.

Despite the lack of clarity regarding the purpose of batterer intervention programs, recent years have witnessed a marked increase in referrals to and proliferation of such programs. The increased referrals are part of the criminal justice system's growing response to domestic violence since the beginning of the battered women's movement. Referrals to programs have grown primarily through the courts as more and more states recognize domestic violence as a crime and develop specific programs to address the problem.

MODELS OF BATTERER INTERVENTION PROGRAMS

Different theories of domestic violence offer divergent explanations of the root causes of battering and emphasize specific focal points for intervention and change (e.g., Adams, 1988; Brandl, 1990; Healey et. al., 1998). While the techniques used to address battering may overlap between models, the key differences are the primary focus or area of intervention on the individual, family, or social/cultural level (Healey, Smith, & O'Sullivan, 1998). For a more detailed review of domestic violence theories, see chapter 2.

Individual Models

Individually focused models identify the root cause of violence as grounded in the psychology and history of the individual batterer. Psychological approaches emphasize that personality disorders or early experiences of trauma predispose some individuals to violence. Some proponents of this model believe that without identifying and addressing the abuser's deep-rooted and unconscious motive for aggression, they cannot end violence but only suppress it temporarily. Others believe that batterers have mental health and personality disorders that must be treated in order to stop violent behavior.

Most of the literature in this area emphasizes the characteristics and clinical assessment of individual batterers. Batterers are seen as fragile individuals with problems such as poor impulse control, aggression, low self-esteem, fear of intimacy, emotional dependence, fear of abandonment, and impaired ego functioning (Adams, 1988; Green, 1984; Kane, Staiger, & Ricciardelli, 2000; Ragg, 1999; Rosenbaum, Goldstein, & O'Leary, 1980). Primary diagnoses for these individuals include a range of mental illnesses and personality disorders, such as obsessive-compulsive, paranoid, borderline personality, passive-aggressive, pathological, depression, narcissistic, and antisocial (e.g., Beasley & Stoltenberg, 1992; Dutton, 1994, 1995a; Hart, Dutton, & Newlove, 1993; Hastings & Hamberger, 1988; Hotaling & Sugarman, 1986; Steinmetz, 1980; White & Gondolf, 2000). Some of the literature examines correlations between battering and other social problems, such as alcohol and substance use and abuse (e.g., Hamilton & Collins, 1981; Kantor & Straus, 1987), other criminal behavior (e.g., Hotaling, Straus, & Lincoln, 1989), and witnessing and/or experiencing abuse and neglect as a child (e.g., Dutton, 1995b; Simoneti, Scott, & Murphy, 2000; Straus, Gelles, & Steinmetz, 1980).

Researchers and practitioners have developed a number of typologies and overarching characteristics of men who batter (e.g., Adams, 1990; Gondolf, 1987d; Saunders, 1992). In a review of the literature on typologies of male batterers, Holtzworth-Munroe and Stuart (1994) suggested three descriptive dimensions: (1) *family-only batterers*, who are generally reported to engage in the least severe types of violence, exhibit little psychopathology, and tend to be less likely to have violence-related legal problems; (2) *dysphoric/borderline batterers*, who are often found to perpetrate moderate to extreme battering, including sexual abuse, and are more likely to evidence borderline and schizoid personality characteristics, and have drug and/or alcohol problems; and (3) *generally violent/antisocial batterers,* who not only engage in moderate to severe violence against their partners but also have the most extensive history of general criminal behavior and are more likely to have substance abuse problems and antisocial personality disorders. A further study identified a fourth group, *low-level antisocial batterers,* who exhibit antisocial behavior and moderate levels of domestic and general violence (Holtzworth-Munroe, Meehan, Herron, & Stuart, 1999).

Most recently, the literature in this area has broadened its focus to examine the development and use of risk assessment tools to predict and assess repeat abusers (e.g., Gondolf & White, 2001; Goodman, Dutton, & Bennett, 2000; Hilton, Harris, & Rice, 2001). Dutton and Kropp (2000) review the history of risk assessment lists and recent efforts to empirically validate the proliferation of risk assessment scales; they conclude by supporting the need for more published research on the reliability and validity of these tools. If properly applied, risk assessment scales could assist in serving as the basis for determining the treatment or program for individual batterers and safety assessment for victims (Dutton & Kropp, 2000).

Family Models

The family systems approach views domestic violence from an interactive perspective (e.g., Lloyd, 1999; Margolin, 1979; Neidig & Friedman, 1984; Weitzman & Dreen, 1982). Using this approach, violent behavior is seen as a relationship issue and part of a chain of escalating retributive strategies used alternately by each member of the couple. Family systems theory leads to treatment that involves improving communication and conflict resolution skills between couples and among family members. Both members of the couple, as well as others in the family unit, can develop communication and conflict resolution skills through "solution-focused brief therapy" that locates the problem in the interaction rather than in the pathology of one individual; that focuses on solving the problem rather than looking for causes; and that accentuates the positive—for example, examining occasions when the couple avoided violence.

However, conceptualizing domestic violence solely in transactional terms and using conjoint counseling in relationships have been roundly criticized as ignoring or minimizing the violent behavior and the gendered nature of violence (Avis, 1999; Bograd, 1984; Edleson & Tolman, 1992; Erickson, 1992; Golden & Frank, 1994; Kaufman, 1992; Lloyd, 1999; Margolin & Burman, 1993; Meth, 1992; Shamai, 1999). In response, some family therapists whose work has been characterized by sensitivity to issues of abuse, gender inequality, trauma, and analyses of power have developed therapeutic models, assessment frameworks, criteria for initiating couples work, and guiding principles toward the goal of stopping violence while ensuring the safety of the victim (Bograd & Mederos, 1999; Shamai, 1999).

Social and Cultural Models

Central to social and cultural models of batterer intervention programs is the attribution of domestic violence to the social structure and to cultural norms and values, with the primary factor being men's subordination of women (e.g., Edleson & Tolman, 1992; Kurz, 1993; Mederos, 1999; Pence & Paymar, 1993). The overarching focus develops from a feminist perspective and a gender analysis of power. In intimate (heterosexual) relationships where domestic violence is occurring, the primary aggressors are typically men, and the victims are women. Social and cultural models directly link violence in the family to the status of individual members of the family and to socialization—men are socialized to be dominant and women to be subordinate. The focus of profeminist batterer intervention programs is to stop not only physical and sexual violence but also the equally, if not more, pervasive patterns of verbal and psychological abuse, such as humiliation, constant criticism, jealous accusations, monitoring activity, controlling involvement with family and friends, and inability to tolerate disagreement. A batterer often rationalizes his violence on the grounds that it was necessitated by his partner's action: She provoked or caused it, and he simply reacted as would any "normal" man.

Feminist-based batterer intervention programs developed group counseling and education models focusing on male resocialization toward equality and attempting to raise consciousness about sex role conditioning and how it constrains men's emotions and behavior. Programs with a feminist philosophy present a model of egalitarian relationships along with the benefits of nonviolence and of building relationships based on trust instead of fear; they support confronting men over their use of power and control tactics in relationships with women.

Social and cultural models of batterer intervention have historically used a "one-size-fits-all" model. Increasingly, researchers and practitioners have identified the need to address a variety of community- and group-specific issues, such as the impact of class, race, and ethnicity on the dynamic of domestic violence, including the development of culturally and racially specific models of batterer intervention programs, as well as concomitant problems such as alcohol and drug use and underlying mental health problems (e.g., Edleson, 1996; Edleson & Tolman, 1992; Gondolf, 1997; Mederos, 1999). In addition, addressing issues of battering in same-sex relationships is often "beyond the scope" of the social and cultural theoretical models of batterer intervention programs (Pence & Paymar, 1993). The need to reconcile the existence of domestic violence in relationships between two women or two men with the feminist philosophy that sexism and patriarchy enable domestic violence is key.

BATTERER INTERVENTION AND TREATMENT TECHNIQUES

One of the most highly debated areas of literature regarding batterer intervention is in discussions of treatment perspectives and specific interventions in working with abusers. Until the battered women's movement in the early 1970s, male violence against women, when it was considered a problem, was attributed to some aspect of the individual man (Schechter, 1982), primarily as a physiological problem or function of an intrapsychic disorder (Thorne-Finch, 1992). Feminists in the 1970s helped to shift understanding of and treatment for male violence away from the various physiological and intrapsychic perspectives and moved toward the incorporation of the social context of violence, namely, the impact of sexism and the violence of men against women (e.g., Schechter, 1982; Thorne-Finch, 1992). In response to the feminist movement's critique of the physiological and intrapsychic approaches, most of the literature on batterer treatment shifted to either working with the couple from a family systems approach or working with the batterer in a group with other batterers with an emphasis on psychoeducational and cognitive-behavioral techniques (Dutton, 1995a; Edleson & Tolman, 1992; Thorne-Finch, 1992). Considerable controversy developed and continues among and between the family systems and group treatment approaches regarding the appropriateness and effectiveness of these interventions.

Beginning in the late 1970s, treatment models utilizing a group modality for batterer intervention grew out of the battered women's movement. Public pressure on the criminal justice system to respond more effectively to batterers and reaction to the existing physiological, intrapsychic, and family systems approaches led to the creation of batterer intervention programs (Dutton, 1995a; Thorne-Finch, 1992). The first treatment groups to specifically work with male batterers were voluntary groups that used a social learning orientation focused on improving conflict resolution skills (Dutton, 1995a; Ganley, 1981; Ganley & Harris, 1978).

In the early 1980s, batterer intervention groups for men who were mandated by the courts were developed in Duluth, Minnesota, by the Duluth Abuse Intervention Project (DAIP), a grassroots monitoring and coordinating organization for local agencies that intervene in domestic violence as part of a community coordinated response (Pence, 1983; Pence & Paymar, 1993). Based on the work of Paulo Freire (1970), DAIP developed a "cultural offensive" against domestic violence, confronting the belief system that legitimizes men's abusive behavior (Mederos, 1999). DAIP incorporated direct work with batterers into a systemic approach involving the police, courts, battered women's advocates, social service agencies, and other community institutions working together to combat domestic violence (Mederos,

1999; Pence & Paymar, 1993; Pence & Shepard, 1999;). The groups incorporated a profeminist, psychoeducational model, focusing on challenging the belief systems that legitimize and obscure the abusive behavior of men.

As a result of the expansion of proarrest policies, which view domestic violence as criminal behavior rather than the result of faulty communication between couples or mental illness, referrals to group batterer intervention programs have increased. Research on batterer interventions has followed this trend in that the overwhelming majority of research on battering interventions has been conducted with batterers who have been court mandated, primarily to group batterer intervention programs, while very little evaluative research has been conducted on the effectiveness of couples treatment (Brown & O'Leary, 1997).

Most current group treatment programs are psychoeducational, focused on teaching behavior and attitude change, with many having an underlying profeminist orientation (Edleson & Tolman, 1992). The programs vary in length, but most are short-term, ranging from 6 to 32 weeks (Edleson & Syers, 1990; Eisikovits & Edleson, 1989). Programs include a range of cognitive behavioral intervention techniques, such as anger management, problem-solving skill training, and communication training (Eddy & Myers, 1984; Sonkin, Martin, & Walker, 1985); development of social skills, such as communication, assertiveness, and stress-reduction (Edleson, 1984; Holtzworth-Munroe, 1992; Sonkin et al., 1985); and self-observation (Edleson, 1984).

ROLE OF IDEOLOGY IN EVALUATING BATTERER INTERVENTION PROGRAMS

Theoretical models of batterer intervention programs are an important part of the knowledge base because they provide a framework to help organize observations for understanding, as well as being used scientifically for the purposes of explanation and prediction. When we use theoretical models to examine social problems, we often interpret them as established, "fact-based," objective ontological perspectives devoid of ideology. However, values and ideological positions are inherent in all theory and knowledge (Berger & Luckmann, 1966; Kramer, 1975; Robbins et al., 1999). Mannheim (1952) coined the term *relationism* to denote the epistemological perspective of sociology of knowledge as a recognition that knowledge must always be known from a certain position.

Sargent (1972) defines an *ideology* as an integrated "value or belief system that is accepted as fact or truth by some group. It is composed of sets of attitudes toward the various institutions and processes of society. It provides the believer with a picture of the world both as it is and as it should be, and, in so doing, it organizes the tremendous complexity of the world into something fairly simple and understandable" (p. 1). Alternative ideologies may view the same set of facts and arrive at different interpretations (Kramer, 1975). Sometimes the underlying assumptions of any given theory can be associated with different political positions, and often they are used to support or oppose specific interventions and policies that affect clients (Robbins et al., 1999).

The ideological position of the proponents of various theories is an important consideration in evaluating batterer intervention programs. For example, a person who strongly believes that early childhood experiences are at the root of domestic violence in adulthood may tend to look for previously undiscovered traumatic childhood experiences, such as witnessing or experiencing abuse as a child. This approach will likely intensify, create, or bring to the surface unpleasant memories that might have been less pronounced if the source of the problem was identified as present-day stressors. Recalling these memories probably will be easier in the confines of an individual session than in a large group; additional time or specific techniques may be needed to elicit early memories. Advocates for this perspective may themselves be interested in maintaining an individualized caseload, perhaps on a long-term basis. Politically they may be motivated by governmental funding cuts to long-term therapeutic treatment and the increase in managed care forms of treatment.

A person, however, who strongly believes that society's patriarchal structure is the root cause of domestic violence may tend to attribute the problem to men in general or a sexist society. In this case, interventions would need to be systemic rather than individualized, emanating from a push to change the laws, working with criminal justice and social systems, with an emphasis on accountability of offending males. Proponents of this perspective are interested in systemic social change that advocates for the rights of, and possible reparations to, women. They may prioritize shelter and other services that enable women to escape from abusers over services to batterers.

A person who strongly believes that inappropriate family dynamics are the root causes of domestic violence may tend to attribute the problem to communication breakdowns between family members. Interventions could involve the entire family and emphasize behavior, such as appropriate communication techniques and patterns. Advocates of this perspective may be politically motivated by the need for long-term, intensive work with families, and perhaps support politics that emphasize keeping the family together.

The preceding descriptions are generalizations, but the primary point is that it is important to identify and examine the underlying ideologies of the various interventions and programs—what are their underlying political beliefs and how do these beliefs translate into their work with batterers.

EFFECTIVENESS OF BATTERER
INTERVENTION PROGRAMS

Given the ideological struggles in the field of batterer intervention and domestic violence, it is no surprise that an underlying tension for batterer intervention programs is caused by the lack of agreement among major stake-
holders about how to define an effective program. The answer hinges to a
great degree on what changes we expect in an abuser's behavior in order to
deem a program successful (Edleson, 1996). The literature is full of published program evaluations that use quite different success criteria. At one
end of the continuum, some researchers have used typically significant positive change or statistically significant changes in a desired direction among
participants to claim success (Neidig, 1986; Neidig, Friedman, & Collins,
1985), such as reducing the number of violent incidents or lowering the
lethality of violence. At the other end of the continuum, advocates have
pressed for nothing short of a transformation of program participants "until
men are prepared to take social action against the woman-battering culture"
(Gondolf, 1987a, p. 347) and become "accountable" men (Hart, 1988).
These positions illustrate the ends of the continuum along which there are
many positions concerning what signals a program that "works" (Edleson,
1996).

Over the past two decades there have been at least 35 published single-
site evaluations of batterer intervention programs, and these evaluations
have been extensively reviewed (Crowell & Burgess, 1996; Davis & Taylor,
1999; Dobash, Dobash, Cavanagh, & Lewis, 1996; Dutton 1987, 1995a;
Edleson & Tolman, 1992; Eisikovits & Edleson, 1989; Hamberger & Hastings, 1993; Rosenbaum & O'Leary, 1986; Saunders & Azar, 1989; Tolman & Bennett, 1990; Tolman & Edleson, 1995).

Davis, Taylor, and Maxwell (2000) identify three generations of studies
of batterer intervention programs. Initial studies, and still the largest proportion of the literature, are primarily descriptive, examining batterers assigned
to treatment programs without any comparison group (e.g., DeMaris
& Jackson, 1987; Deschner & McNeill, 1986; Dutton, 1987; Edleson &
Grusznski, 1988; Edleson, Miller, Stone, & Chapman, 1985; Feazell, Mayers, & Deschner, 1984, 1990; Johnson & Kanzler, 1993; Neidig et al., 1985;
Purdy & Nickle, 1981; Rosenbaum, 1986; Shupe, Stacey, & Hazelwood,
1986; Tolman, Beeman, & Mendoza, 1987; Tolman & Bhosley, 1991;
Waldo, 1986). Later, quasi-experimental designs of varying quality appeared
in the literature, comparing outcomes between batterers who completed
treatment and those who were assigned to treatment, but failed to complete
it (e.g., Douglas & Perrin, 1987; Edleson & Grusznski, 1988), as well as
batterers who were mandated to treatment by the courts to batterers who
received other interventions (Chen, Bersani, Myers, & Denton, 1989; Do-

bash et al., 1996; Dutton, 1987; Harrell, 1991). Most recently, more pure experimental investigations have appeared in the literature, including randomly assigned batterers to treatment conditions and no-treatment control groups (Davis et al., 2000; Dunford, 2000; Feder & Forde, 2000; Palmer, Brown, & Barrera, 1992; Taylor, Davis, & Maxwell, 2001).

However, instead of reaching any agreement regarding the purpose and effectiveness of batterer intervention programs, most of the literature seems to point more toward the increased emphasis on sophistication of research studies in the field. Many of the early descriptive and quasi-experimental studies have been criticized for methodological shortcomings (Davis et al., 2000; Edleson, 1996; Gondolf, 1987b). Criticism has included the validity of basing recidivism rates on self-reports by the batterer instead of obtaining confirmation by the victim and/or the criminal justice system; generalizability of small sample sizes; validity in the length of follow-up after program completion in determining the cessation of violence (e.g., six months, one year, three years, or more); and the determination of an acceptable program attrition rate. For example, in early studies, recidivism rates varied from 7% to 47%, making interpretations of the results difficult.

Nearly all of the published evaluations of batterer intervention programs are quantitative. The one recent exception is Scott and Wolfe's (2000) qualitative analysis of interviews with nine "reformed" batterers. Furthermore, the emphasis on using control groups and improving quantitative experimental designs to evaluate and develop programs indicates a belief that experimental inquiry will determine the appropriateness and effectiveness of batterer intervention programs (Davis et al., 2000; Gondolf, 1985, 1987b). However, so far, program evaluations have not supported expansion or discontinuation of specific batterer intervention programs based on research results.

Some research has shown programs to have effectiveness in stopping or reducing abusive behavior. One review of evaluation studies found that in different programs, using varying methods of intervention, 53% to 85% of men stop their physically abusive behavior subsequent to involvement in batterer intervention programs (Edleson, 1996). One study found that men who participated in longer-term programs (26 weeks) showed significantly lower recidivism rates at 6 and 12 months after sentencing than those who either participated in shorter-term programs (8 weeks) or received unrelated sentencing such as community service, fines, or probation (Davis et al., 2000). Another study found that two out of three men randomly assigned to receive either structured educational programs or those combining education with group processing were reported to have stopped violent behavior by their women partners during 6- and 18-month follow-up periods and achieved more stable outcomes than did those randomly assigned to a less structured self-help program (Edleson & Syers, 1990, 1991). One national survey suggested that about 90% of the batterers do not physically abuse their wives while attending the program, and two-thirds to three-fourths of those who complete the prescribed program report no violence after one year (Feazell et al., 1984).

However, other research has found batterer intervention programs to be largely ineffective. One study found that court-ordered programs were ineffective in reducing violence, and, in fact, batterers receiving no treatment had fewer subsequent police reports than batterers who received intervention (Harrell, 1991). Another study, of primarily voluntary participants, found that only 1% actually completed the program (Gondolf & Foster, 1991). A study of programs across the country found immense program diversity and concluded that national standards for batterer intervention programs were needed (Gondolf, 1990).

Two recent experimental evaluations attempted more rigorous science by examining the program effect of conventional batterer education programs compared with a control group (Davis et al., 2000; Feder & Forde, 2000). In evaluating probation-mandated referrals, Feder and Forde (2000) randomly assigned men convicted of misdemeanor domestic violence into experimental or control conditions. Men in the control group were sentenced to 1 year probation, while men in the experimental group were sentenced to 1 year probation and 26 weeks of group sessions from a local batterer intervention program. The research found no clear effects of the program on the offenders' attitudes, beliefs, and behaviors. In fact, the men assigned to the batterer program were more likely to be rearrested than those in the control group unless they attended all of the court-mandated sessions. However, even those who attended all sessions were only slightly less likely to be rearrested than those in the control group who were not mandated to group sessions.

In evaluating judicially mandated referrals, Davis et al. (2000) randomly assigned men convicted of misdemeanor domestic violence, in cases where the prosecution, judge, and defense agreed to treatment, to either 39 hours of a batterer intervention group (some were assigned to complete the treatment in 26 weeks, and others in 8 weeks) or a community service program irrelevant to domestic violence. The purpose of the experiment was to assess the impact of treatment on men presumed to be motivated, since it is often argued that an intervention cannot be expected to work for individuals against their will. The results showed that treatment completion rates were higher for the 8-week group than for the 26-week group. However, only defendants assigned to the 26-week group showed significantly lower recidivism 6 and 12 months after sentencing compared with defendants in the control group, indicating that longer programs appear to be more effective than shorter programs. Nonetheless, victim reports of new incidents did not differ statistically across the experimental and control groups.

EVALUATING PROGRAM EFFECTIVENESS

Based on the inconclusive research and practice experience, the debate continues regarding whether any type of batterer intervention program works or works very well. Gondolf (2001) posits several possible interpretations of the results of experimental studies: (1) Batterer programs are either ineffective or add very little to arrest, court adjudication, and probation; (2) batterer programs are in their infancy and need improvement, such as screening for compounding problems such as alcohol and drug abuse and mental health issues; and/or (3) batterer programs are not themselves a cure but a reinforcing component of a coordinated community response to domestic violence, wherein a program's success reflects only the effectiveness of the overall system in addressing domestic violence.

Edleson (1996) outlines this debate in a discussion of how various constituencies have different criteria for whether or not a program "works." According to Edleson (1996), the degree to which one goes beyond acts of physical violence and threats to define the meaning of success is the most controversial aspect of evaluations of batterer intervention programs. Some of the harshest critics claim that a program does not "work" until the societal structures that allow men to abuse women are abolished, whereas some advocates in the criminal justice system claim that a program "works" if the abuser stops the physical abuse, even if the emotional and psychological abuse continues or even escalates. Some battered women believe that a program "works" if the batterer stops the abuse, in the way in which the woman defines abuse.

Berger and Luckmann (1966) clarify these differences in definition of whether or not a program "works" from a social constructionist view, examining programs from their own perspective: "One does certain things not because they *work*, but because they are *right*—right, that is, in terms of the ultimate definitions of reality promulgated by the . . . experts" (p. 118). In the world of domestic violence and batterer intervention programs, who is considered an "expert" depends on one's perspective. An "expert" may be identified as a researcher who has studied domestic violence interventions; a practitioner who has direct experience working with battered women and other victims of domestic abuse; any woman who knows the impact of sexism, a form of abuse, on her life; or a battered woman who has experienced domestic violence firsthand.

While a person working from a positivist perspective might say that rival theories should be able to be resolved through objective experimental testing, what is convincing to one researcher, practitioner, or policy maker may not be convincing to another. Samples may be too small or not generalizable; the reliability and validity of the tool may be in question; and experimentation is not always the way in which theories are supported. According to Berger and Luckmann (1966), power in society includes the power to validate a theory rather than empirical support, and varied definitions of reality are decided upon in the sphere of rival social interests, which are then translated into theoretical terms. In other words, the decision about which program "works" and which "expert" will be heralded as "*the* expert" is political and will be determined *in advance* of the theory that supports the specific intervention.

What this would mean for batterer intervention programs is that it is not necessarily the result of studies that will indicate the supported theoretical perspective and intervention program for batterers but the connection to power in society by each of the programs. Evaluations of batterer intervention programs must include an examination of each program's connection to power, such as funding and funders, legitimators (i.e., government agencies, regulators, legislators), the domestic violence movement, advocacy organizations, professional agencies and associations, and researchers.

RECOMMENDATIONS

Even as research debates the effectiveness of batterer intervention programs, these programs continue to proliferate as proarrest policies bring increasing numbers of batterers to court for offenses related to domestic violence. In fact, by the late 1990s, nearly every state used batterer intervention programs; administrators estimated that nearly 80% of their clients were referred by the courts (Healey et al., 1998).

Since studies indicate that 31% of women will be physically or sexually assaulted by an intimate partner in their lifetimes (Collins, Schoen, Joseph, Duchon, Simantor, & Yellowitz, 1999), an intervention that also reduces the likelihood of future domestic violence will benefit women. In addition, because many women stay with their partners even after their arrest and conviction, it is essential to identify and use effective programs that can change abusive behavior rather than simply delaying it during a period of incarceration (Taylor et al., 2001).

The following recommendations are designed to help practitioners and policy makers navigate as the field develops:

1. Develop coordinated community responses to domestic violence. Emerging research seems to indicate that batterer intervention programs are only as effective as the overall system, including establishment of consistent police and court action for domestic violence, accountability of batterer intervention programs to the criminal justice system, swift and decisive sanctions for batterers who drop out of programs or reoffend, and providing appropriate ongoing outreach, support, and services to victims. Research also seems to indicate that batterer programs without clear internal and external accountability measures may be more harmful than no batterer program at all.

2. Develop standards for batterer intervention programs. In the wake of replication of the community coordinated response model, batterer intervention programs began to spring up in municipalities across the country as a resource for court-referred batterers. While some states have developed standards for batterer intervention programs, including program length, philosophy and model of intervention, and rules of participation, other states have not developed standards. New York State, for example, has no approved state-sanctioned standards for batterer intervention programs. In New York City, batterer programs for mandated participants can vary in length from as few as 4 to as many as 52 sessions, interventions can range from lecturing to psychodynamic "therapy," and rules and regulations can be strict (e.g., participants must be on time with minimal absences) or lenient. As batterer intervention programs with divergent philosophies, practices, and requirements continue to operate and grow, and to receive funding and court-mandated referrals without an overall framework or agreed set of principles to guide the process, many researchers are identifying a need for overarching standards and guidelines for programs (Gondolf, 1990; Healey et al., 1998).

3. Develop innovative programs beyond shelter for women and weekly batterer intervention programs for men. Clearly, researchers, practitioners, and policy makers have not found "the answer" to intervening with batterers or providing safety for women. New innovative programs are being developed and should be evaluated and replicated.

4. Provide alternatives to shelter programs. Instead of requiring battered women and their children to leave home, school, and friends and escape to a shelter, provide home and personal security devices to keep the home safe. Alternatives to shelter programs can provide women who have exclusionary orders of protection with a home alarm system, window gates and secure doors, a cell phone with immediate 911 access, and a spot in the local police precinct's most dangerous location list. While not appropriate for all battered women, enhanced security may enable some women to remain at home without totally disrupting their lives and the lives of their children. Another alternative includes requiring batterers to wear location detectors that send an alarm to the precinct if the batterer is in the vicinity of the battered woman's home.

5. Residential programs for batterers can be developed instead of removing battered women and children from their homes and forcing them to seek shelter in new communities. A pilot program that has tested this alternative is Beit Noam, a 4-month residential program in Ra'anana, Israel, for male batterers who are in criminal proceedings because of serious domestic violence, including felonies, and who have been referred for treatment (Rosenberg & Keynan, 1999). The program engages the men in a process designed to change their abusive behavior. The men are required to be employed during the day, to pay for their stay at Beit Noam, and to continue financial support of their families. The program has a rigid schedule, and men are responsible for the daily

upkeep and running of the house, including buying food, cooking meals, and doing the laundry. Every night, after dinner, the men participate in individual and group therapy and art therapy sessions to address topics such as parenting, sexuality, self-control, relationships, and cognitive self-control. Since Beit Noam opened its doors in 1997, more than 500 men have applied to and 120 men have completed the program. All the men receive support and follow-up treatment and telephone counseling services, and they are referred to social services in their own communities. While Beit Noam encourages the wives or partners of batterers to seek help in their communities, the women are not required to participate in any program unless they are interested.

Preliminary research, conducted by Israel's National Insurance Institute, involving interviews with Beit Noam staff, probation officers, and the partners of 19 men who had completed the program at least 6 months earlier, found that only one man who completed the program had reoffended. While these preliminary results are encouraging, claims of overwhelming success at this point should be viewed with caution (Gondolf, 2001). Additional rigorous research is needed, including a larger sample size and a longer span of time following release. However, reframing the intervention for domestic violence as removing the man from the home is an innovation that warrants greater attention.

6. Develop models that directly address race, class, and sexual orientation to address the needs of batterers in these communities. Since emerging research seems to indicate that batterer programs need clear internal and external accountability measures, programs that specifically address the needs of men of color, as well as gay men and lesbians, must be developed in coordination with the criminal justice system. One way to develop these programs is through collaboration between established accountability-based batterer intervention programs and community-based programs for people of color as well as for gay and lesbian communities.

CONCLUSIONS

Battering and domestic violence are complex social problems. No one model will "fix" the batterer, just as no one intervention will provide the full range of services needed by battered women and their children. While researchers have made progress in the sophistication of studies of batterer intervention programs, more work needs to be done to identify elements of effective programs, as well as the impact of coordination and accountability between programs and the criminal justice system.

Meanwhile, the number of batterer intervention programs continues to multiply, and the courts, probation, and social service agencies are increasingly referring batterers to these programs as a result of proarrest laws in cases of domestic violence. The study of batterer intervention programs and the criminal justice system alone will not answer the question of what "works."

The "industry" of batterer intervention as a whole needs to be examined, including the role and perspective of the courts, other referral agencies and programs, funders, policy makers, regulators, battered women's advocates, and the batterer intervention programs themselves. These key players have the potential to guide society's response to domestic violence and batterer intervention programs regardless of research results.

It has taken us centuries to begin to view battered women as a population in need of a societal response. In the last 30 years, services for battered women have grown exponentially. However, battering continues. Now is it time to determine how we intervene with the batterer? To decide how and when we, as a society, should impose punishment and/or try to change abusive behavior? The truth is, unless these men change their behavior, the cycle of domestic violence will continue uninterrupted.

REFERENCES

Adams, D. (1988). *Treatment models of men who batter: A profeminist analysis.* In K. Yllo & M. Bograd (Ed.), *Feminist perspectives on wife abuse* (pp. 176–199). Newbury Park, CA: Sage.

Adams, D. (1990). Identifying the assaultive husband in court: You be the judge. *Response to the Victimization of Women and Children, 13,* 13–16.

Ahrens, L. (1980, summer). Battered women's refuges: Feminist institutions vs. social service institutions. *Aegis,* 41–46.

Avis, J. M. (1992). Where are all the family therapists: Abuse and violence within families and family therapy's response. *Journal of Marital and Family Therapy, 18,* 225–232.

Balzer, R. (1999). Hamilton Abuse Intervention Project: The Aotearoa experience. In M. F. Shepard & E. L. Pence (Eds.), *Coordinating community responses to domestic violence: Lessons from Duluth and beyond* (pp. 239–254). Thousand Oaks, CA: Sage.

Beasley, R., & Stoltenberg, C. D. (1992). Personality characteristics of male spouse abusers. *Professional Psychology: Research and Practice, 23,* 310–317.

Bennett, L., & Piet, M. (1999). Standards for batterer intervention programs: In whose interest? *Violence Against Women, 5,* 6–24.

Berger, P. L., & Luckmann, T. (1966). *The social construction of reality: A treatise in the sociology of knowledge.* New York: Doubleday.

Berkowitz, L. (1973, July). The case for bottling up rage. *Psychology Today,* 24–31.

Bograd, M. (1984). Family systems approaches to wife battering: A feminist critique. *American Journal of Orthopsychiatry, 54,* 558–568.

Bograd, M., & Mederos, F. (1999). Battering and couples therapy: Universal screening and selection of treatment modality. *Journal of Marital and Family Therapy, 25,* 291–312.

Brandl, B. (1990, August). *Programs for batterers: A discussion paper.* Department of Health and Social Services, Division of Community Services, Bureau for Children, Youth and Families, Madison, WI.

Brown, P. D., & O'Leary, K. D. (1997). Wife abuse in intact couples: A review of couples treatment programs.

In G. K. Kantor & J. L. Jasinski
(Eds.), *Out of the darkness: Contemporary perspectives on family violence* (pp. 194–207). Thousand
Oaks, CA: Sage.

Chen, H., Bersani, C., Myers, S., &
Denton, R. (1989). Evaluating the
effectiveness of a court-sponsored
treatment program. *Journal of Family Violence, 4,* 309–322.

Collins, K. S., Schoen, C., Joseph, S., Duchon, L., Simantor, E., & Yellowitz,
M. (1999, May). *Health concerns
across a woman's lifespan: The Commonwealth Fund 1998 survey of
women's health*. New York: The
Commonwealth Fund.

Crowell, N., & Burgess, A. W. (1996).
*Understanding violence against
women*. Washington, DC: National
Academy.

Davis, L. V., & Hagen, J. L. (1988, December). Services for battered
women: The public policy response.
Social Service Review, 649–667.

Davis, L. V., & Hagen, J. L. (1992).
The problem of wife abuse: The interrelationship of social policy and social work practice. *Social Work, 37,*
15–20.

Davis, R. C., & Taylor, B. G. (1999).
Does batterer treatment reduce violence? A synthesis of the literature.
Women and Criminal Justice, 10,
63–93.

Davis, R. C., Taylor, B. G., & Maxwell, C. D. (2000, January). *Does
batterer treatment reduce violence?
A randomized experiment in Brooklyn*. New York: Victim Services.

DeMaris, A., & Jackson, J. K. (1987).
Batterers reports of recidivism after
counseling. *Social Casework, 68,*
458–465.

Deschner, J., & McNeill, J. (1986). Results of anger control training for battering couples. *Journal of Family Violence, 1,* 111–120.

Dobash, E. R., & Dobash, R. (1979).
Violence against wives: A case study

against the patriarchy. New York:
Free Press.

Dobash, R., Dobash, R. E., Cavanagh,
K., & Lewis, R. (1996). Re-education programmes for violent men: An
evaluation. *Research Findings, 46,*
1–4.

Douglas, M. A., & Perrin (1987, July).
Recidivism and accuracy of self-reported violence and arrest. Paper
presented at the Third National
Family Violence Research Conference, Durham, NH.

Dunford, F. (2000). The San Diego
Navy Experiment: An assessment of
interventions for men who assault
their wives. *Journal of Consulting
and Clinical Psychology, 68,* 468–
476.

Dutton, D. G. (1987). The outcome of
court-mandated treatment for wife
assault: A quasi-experimental evaluation. *Violence and Victims, 1,* 163–
175.

Dutton, D. G. (1994). The origin and
structure of the abusive personality.
Journal of Personality Disorders, 8,
181–191.

Dutton, D. G. (1995a). *The domestic assault of women: Psychological and
criminal justice perspectives*. Vancouver: University of British Columbia.

Dutton, D. G. (1995b). Trauma symptoms and PTSD-like profiles in perpetrators of intimate abuse. *Journal of
Traumatic Stress, 8,* 299–316.

Dutton, D. G., & Kropp, P. R. (2000,
April). A review of domestic violence
risk instruments. *Trauma, Violence
and Abuse, 1,* 171–181.

Eddy, M. J., & Myers, T. (1984). *Helping men who batter: A profile of programs in the U.S.* Texas Department
of Human Resources, Austin, TX.

Edleson, J. L. (1984, May–June). Working with men who batter. *Social
Work, 29,* 237–242.

Edleson, J. L. (1996). Controversy and
change in batterers' programs. In
J. L. Edleson & Z. C. Eisikovits

(Eds.), *Future interventions with battered women and their families* (pp. 154–169). Thousand Oaks, CA: Sage.

Edleson, J. L., & Grusznski, R. J. (1988). Treating men who batter: Four years of outcome data from the Domestic Abuse Project. *Journal of Social Service Research, 12,* 3–22.

Edleson, J. L., Miller, D. M., Stone, G. W., & Chapman, D. G. (1985). Group treatment for men who batter. *Social Work Research and Abstracts, 21,* 18–21.

Edleson, J. L., & Syers, M. (1990, June). The relative effectiveness of group treatments for men who batter. *Social Work Research and Abstracts, 26,* 10–17.

Edleson, J. L., & Syers, M. (1991). The effects of group treatment for men who batter: An 18-month follow-up study. *Research in Social Work Practice, 1,* 227–243.

Edleson, J. L., & Tolman, R. M. (1992). *Intervention for men who batter: An ecological approach.* Newbury Park, CA: Sage.

Eisikovits, Z. C., & Edleson, J. L. (1989). Intervening with men who batter: A critical review of the literature. *Social Service Review, 63,* 384–414.

Erickson, B. M. (1992). Feminist fundamentalism: Reactions to Avnis, Kaufman, and Bograd. *Journal of Marital and Family Therapy, 18,* 263–267.

Feazell, C. S., Mayers, R. S., & Deschner, J. (1984). Services for men who batter: Implications for programs and policies. *Family Relations, 33,* 217–223.

Feder, L., & Forde, D. R. (2000, June). *A test of the efficacy of court-mandated counseling for domestic violence offenders: The Broward Experiment.* Executive summary of final report. Washington, DC: National Institute of Justice.

Fields, Marjory, D. (1996). Foreword. In A. R. Roberts (Ed.), *Helping battered women: New perspectives and remedies* (pp. xi–xiii). New York: Oxford University Press.

Findlay, P. C. (1978). Critical theory and social work practice. *Catalyst, 3,* 53–68.

Freire, P. (1970). *Pedagogy of the oppressed.* New York: Herder and Herder.

Ganley, A. (1981). *Participant's manual: Court-mandated therapy for men who batter—A three-day workshop for professionals.* Washington, DC: Center for Women's Policy Studies.

Ganley, A., & Harris, L. (1978). *Domestic violence: Issues in designing and implementing programs for male batterers.* Paper presented at the 86th annual convention of the American Psychological Association, Toronto.

Golden, G. K., & Frank, P. B. (1994). When 50–50 isn't fair: The case against couple counseling in domestic abuse. *Social Work, 39,* 695–696.

Gondolf, E. W. (1985). Anger and oppression in men who batter: Empiricist and feminist perspectives and their implications for research. *Victimology: An International Journal, 10,* 311–324.

Gondolf, E. W. (1987a). Changing men who batter: A developmental model for integrated interventions. *Journal of Family Violence, 2,* 335–349.

Gondolf, E. W. (1987b). Evaluating programs for men who batter: Problems and prospects. *Journal of Family Violence, 2,* 95–108.

Gondolf, E. W. (1987c). Seeing through smoke and mirrors: A guide to batterer program evaluation. *Response to the Victimization of Women and Children, 10*(3), 16–19.

Gondolf, E. W. (1987d, July). *Who are those guys? A typology of batterers based on shelter interviews.* Paper presented at the Third National Family Violence Research Conference, Durham, NH.

Gondolf, E. W. (1990). An exploratory survey of court-mandated batterer programs. *Response, 13,* 7–11.

Gondolf, E. W. (1997). Batterer programs: What we know and need to know. *Journal of Interpersonal Violence, 12,* 83–93.

Gondolf, E. W., & Foster, R. A. (1991). Pre-program attrition in batterers programs. *Journal of Family Violence, 6,* 337–349.

Gondolf, E. W., & Russell, D. (1986). The case against anger control treatment programs for batterers. *Response, 9,* 2–5.

Gondolf, E. W., & White, R. J. (2001, April). Batterer program participants who repeatedly reassault: Psychopathic tendencies and other disorders. *Journal of Interpersonal Violence, 16,* 361–380.

Goodman, L. A., Dutton, M. A., & Bennett, L. (2000, January). Predicting repeat abuse among arrested batterers: Use of the Danger Assessment Scale in the criminal justice system. *Journal of Interpersonal Violence, 15,* 63–74.

Green, H. W. (1984). *Turning fear to hope.* Nashville, TN: Thomas Nelson.

Hamberger, L. K., & Hastings, J. E. (1993). Court-mandated treatment of men who assault their partners: Issues, controversies, and outcomes. In N. Z. Hilton (Ed.), *Legal responses to wife assault: Current trends and evaluation* (pp. 188–229). Newbury Park, CA: Sage.

Hamilton, C. J., & Collins, J. J. (1981). The role of alcohol in wife beating and child abuse: A review of the literature. In J. J. Collins (Ed.), *Drinking and crime: Perspectives on the relationship between alcohol consumption and criminal behavior* (pp. 253–287). New York: Guilford.

Harrell, A. (1991, October). *Evaluation of court-ordered treatment for domestic violence offenders.* Washington, DC: Urban Justice Institute.

Hart, B. (1988). *Safety for women: Monitoring batterers' programs.* Harrisburg: Pennsylvania Coalition Against Domestic Violence.

Hart, S. D., Dutton, D. G., & Newlove, T. (1993). The prevalence of personality disorder amongst wife assaulters. *Journal of Personality Disorders, 4,* 328–340.

Hastings, J. E., & Hamberger, L. K. (1988). Personality characteristics of spouse abusers: A controlled comparison. *Violence and Victims, 3,* 5–30.

Healey, K., Smith, C., & O'Sullivan, C. (1998, February). *Batterer intervention: Program approaches and criminal justice strategies.* Report of ABT Associates to the National Institute of Justice, Washington, DC.

Herzberger, S. D. (1996). *Violence within the family: Social psychological perspectives.* Boulder, CO: Westview.

Hilton, N. Z., Harris, G. T., & Rice, M. E. (2001). Predicting violence by serious wife assaulters. *Journal of Interpersonal Violence, 16,* 408–423.

Holder, R. (1999). Pick 'n mix or replication: The politics and process of adaptation. In M. F. Shepard & E. L. Pence (Eds.), *Coordinating community responses to domestic violence: Lessons from Duluth and beyond* (pp. 255–271). Thousand Oaks, CA: Sage.

Holtzworth-Munroe, A. (1992). Social skill deficits in maritally violent men: Interpreting the data using a social information processing model. *Clinical Psychology Review, 12,* 605–617.

Holtzworth-Munroe, A., Meehan, J. C., Herron, K., & Stuart, G. L. (1999). A typology of male batterers: An initial examination. In X. B. Arriagapa & S. Oskamp (Eds.), *Violence in intimate relationships* (pp. 45–72). Thousand Oaks, CA: Sage.

Holtzworth-Munroe, A., & Stuart, G. L. (1994). Typologies of male batterers: Three subtypes and the differences among them. *Psychological Bulletin, 116,* 476–497.

Hotaling, G. T., Straus, M. A., & Lincoln, A. (1989). Intrafamily violence and crime and violence outside the family. In L. Ohlin & M. Tonry (Eds.), *Family violence* (pp. 315–376). Chicago: University of Chicago Press.

Hotaling, G. T., & Sugarman, D. B. (1986). An analysis of risk markers in husband to wife violence: The current state of knowledge. *Violence and Victims, 1,* 101–124.

Johnson, J., & Kanzler, D. (1993). Treating domestic violence: Evaluating the effectiveness of a domestic violence diversion program. *Studies in Symbolic Interaction, 15,* 271–289.

Kane, T. A., Staiger, P. K., & Ricciardelli, L. A. (2000). Male domestic aggression: Attitudes, aggression, and interpersonal dependency. *Journal of Interpersonal Violence, 15,* 16–29.

Kantor, G. K., & Straus, M. A. (1987). The "drunken bum" theory of wife beating. *Social Problems, 34,* 213–230.

Karger, H. J., & Midgley, J. (1994). *Controversial issues in social policy.* Needham Heights, MA: Allyn and Bacon.

Kaufman, G. (1992). The mysterious disappearance of battered women in family therapists' offices: Male privilege colluding with male violence. *Journal of Marital and Family Therapy, 18,* 233–243.

Knudsen, D., & Miller, J. (Eds.). (1991). *Abused and battered: Social and legal responses to family violence.* New York: De Gruyter.

Kramer, F. A. (1975, September/October). Policy analysis as ideology. *Public Administration Review,* pp. 509–517.

Kurz, D. (1993). Social science perspectives on wife abuse: Current debates and future directions. In P. B. Bart & E. G. Moran (Eds.), *Violence against women: The bloody footprints* (pp. 252–269). Newbury Park, CA: Sage.

Laszlo, A. (1978, January 30–31). Presentation on "Court diversion: An alternative to spousal abuse cases." *Battered women: Issues of public policy.* Washington, DC: United States Commission on Civil Rights.

Lloyd, S. A. (1999). The interpersonal and communication dynamics of wife battering." In X. B. Arriagapa & S. Oskamp (Eds.), *Violence in intimate relationships* (pp. 91–111). Thousand Oaks, CA: Sage.

Mannheim, K. (1952). *Essays on the sociology of knowledge.* New York: Oxford University Press.

Marcus, I. (1994). Reframing "domestic violence": Terrorism in the home. In M. A. Fineman & R. Mykitiuk (Eds.), *The public nature of private violence: The discovery of domestic abuse* (pp. 11–35). New York: Routledge.

Margolin, G. (1979). Conjoint marital therapy to enhance anger management and reduce spouse abuse. *American Journal of Family Therapy, 7,* 13–23.

Margolin, G., & Burman, B. (1993). Wife abuse versus marital violence: Different terminologies, explanations and solutions. *Clinical Psychology Review, 13,* 59–73.

Martin, D. (1976). *Battered wives.* New York: Pocket Books.

Mederos, F. (1999). Batterer intervention programs: The past and future prospects. In M. F. Shepard & E. L. Pence (Eds.), *Coordinating community responses to domestic violence: Lessons from Duluth and beyond* (pp. 127–150). Thousand Oaks, CA: Sage.

Merton, R. K. (1968). *Social theory and social structure.* New York: Free Press.

Meth, R. L. (1992). Marriage and family therapists working with family violence: Strained bedfellows or compatible partners? A commentary on Avis, Kaufman and Bograd. *Journal of Marital and Family Therapy, 18,* 257–261.

Neidig, P. H. (1986). The development and evaluation of a spouse abuse treatment program in a military setting. *Evaluation and Program Planning, 9,* 275–280.

Neidig, P. H., & Friedman, D. H. (1984). *Spouse abuse: A treatment program for couples.* Champaign, IL: Research Press.

Neidig, P. H., Friedman, D. H., & Collins, B. S. (1985). Domestic conflict containment: A spouse abuse treatment program. *Social Casework, 66,* 195–204.

Office for the Prevention of Domestic Violence. (1998, January). *Model domestic violence policy for counties.* State of New York, Albany.

Palmer, S., Brown, R., & Barrera, M. (1992). Group treatment program for abusive husbands: Long-term evaluation. *American Journal of Orthopsychiatry, 62,* 276–283.

Pence, E. L. (1983). The Duluth Domestic Abuse Intervention Project: Toward a coordinated community response to domestic abuse. *Hamline Law Review, 6,* 247–280.

Pence, E. L., & Paymar, M. (1985). *Power and control: Tactics of men who batter.* Duluth, MN: Duluth Abuse Intervention Project.

Pence, E., & Paymar, M. (1993). *Education groups for men who batter: The Duluth model.* New York: Springer.

Pence, E. L., & Shepard, M. F. (1999). An introduction: Developing a coordinated community response. In

M. F. Shepard & E. L. Pence (Eds.), *Coordinating community responses to domestic violence: Lessons from Duluth and beyond* (pp. 3–23). Thousand Oaks, CA: Sage.

Pirog-Good, M., & Stets-Kealey, J. (1985). Male batterers and battering prevention programs: A national survey. *Response, 8,* 8–12.

Purdy, F., & Nickle, N. (1981). Practice principles for working with groups of men who batter. *Social Work With Groups, 4,* 111–122.

Ragg, D. M. (1999). Dimensions of self-concept as predictors of men who assault their female partners. *Journal of Family Violence, 14,* 315–329.

Robbins, S. P., Chatterjee, P., & Canda, E. R. (1998). *Contemporary human behavior theory: A critical perspective for social work.* Boston: Allyn and Bacon.

Robbins, S. P., Chatterjee, P., & Canda, E. R. (1999). Ideology, scientific theory, and social work practice. *Families in Society: The Journal of Contemporary Human Services, 80,* 374–384.

Roberts, A. R. (1996a). Court responses to battered women. In A. R. Roberts (Ed.), *Helping battered women: New perspectives and remedies* (pp. 96–101). New York: Oxford University Press.

Roberts, A. R. (1996b). Police responses to battered women: Past, present, and future. In A. R. Roberts (Ed.), *Helping battered women: New perspectives and remedies* (pp. 85–95). New York: Oxford University Press.

Roche, S. E., & Sadoski, P. J. (1996). Social action for battered women. In A. R. Roberts (Ed.), *Helping battered women: New perspectives and remedies* (pp. 13–30). New York: Oxford University Press.

Rosenbaum, A. (1986). Of men, macho, and marital violence. *Journal of Family Violence, 1,* 121–130.

Rosenbaum, A., Goldstein, D., & O'Leary, K. D. (1980). *An evaluation of the self-esteem of spouse abusive men.* Paper presented at the annual convention of the American Psychological Association, Montreal, Canada.

Rosenbaum, A., & O'Leary, K. D. (1981). Marital violence: Characteristics of abusive couples. *Journal of Consulting and Clinical Psychology, 49,* 63–71.

Rosenbaum, A., & O'Leary, K. D. (1986). The treatment of marital violence. In N. S. Jacobsen & A. S. Gurman (Eds.), *Clinical handbook of marital therapy* (pp. 385–405). New York: Guilford.

Rosenberg, H., & Keynan, O. (1999). *Beit Noam: A new direction for men who batter.* Ra'anana, Israel: Beit Noam.

Sargent, L. T. (1972). *Contemporary political ideologies.* Homewood, IL: Dorsey.

Saunders, D. G. (1992). A typology of men who batter: Three types derived from cluster analysis. *American Journal of Orthopsychiatry, 62,* 264–275.

Saunders, D. G., & Azar, S. T. (1989). Treatment programs for family violence. In L. Ohlin & M. Tonry (Eds.), *Crime and justice, A review of the research: Vol. 11. Family violence* (pp. 481–546). Chicago: University of Chicago Press.

Schechter, S. (1982). *Women and male violence: The vision and struggles of the battered women's movement.* Boston: South End Press.

Schechter, S., & Edleson, J. L. (2000). *Domestic violence and children: Creating a public response.* New York: Center on Crime, Communities and Culture for the Open Society Institute.

Schneider, E. M. (1994). The violence of privacy. In M. A. Fineman & R. Mykitiuk (Eds.), *The public nature of private violence: The discovery of domestic abuse* (pp. 36–58). New York: Routledge,

Scott, K. A., & Wolfe, D. A. (2000). Change among batterers: Examining men's success stories. *Journal of Interpersonal Violence, 15,* 827–842.

Shamai, M. (1999). Couple therapy with battered women and abusive men: Does it have a future? In J. L. Edleson & Z. C. Eisikovits (Eds.), *Future interventions with battered women and their families* (pp. 201–215). Thousand Oaks, CA: Sage.

Shepard, M. (1991). Feminist practice principles for social work intervention in wife abuse. *AFFILIA, 6(2),* 87–93.

Shupe, A., Stacey W. A., & Hazelwood, L. R. (1986). *Violent men, violent couples.* Lexington, MA: Lexington Books.

Simoneti, S., Scott, E. C., & Murphy, C. M. (2000). Dissociative experiences in partner-assaultive men. *Journal of Interpersonal Violence, 15,* pp. 1262–1283.

Sonkin, D. J., Martin, D., & Walker, L. (1985). *The male batterer: A treatment approach.* New York: Springer.

Steinman, M. (1990). Lowering recidivism among men who batter women. *Journal of Police Science and Administration, 17,* 124–132.

Steinman, M. (1991). *Woman battering: Policy responses.* Cincinnati, OH: Anderson.

Steinmetz, S. K. (1980). Violence-prone families. *Annals of the New York Academy of Sciences, 347,* 351–365.

Straus, M. A., Gelles, R. J., & Steinmetz, S. (1980). *Behind closed doors: Violence in the American family.* Garden City, NY: Anchor/Doubleday.

Syers, M., & Edleson, J. L. (1992). The combined effects of coordinated criminal justice intervention in women abuse. *Journal of Interpersonal Violence, 7,* 490–502.

Taylor, B. G., Davis, R. C., & Maxwell, C. D. (2001). The effects of a group batterer treatment program: A randomized experiment in Brooklyn. *Justice Quarterly, 18,* 171–201.

Thorne-Finch, R. (1992). *Ending the silence: The origins and treatment of male violence against women.* Toronto: University of Toronto Press.

Tierney, K. J. (1982). The battered women movement and the creation of the wife beating problem. *Social Problems, 29,* 207–219.

Tolman, R. M., Beeman, S., & Mendoza, C. (1987, July). *The effectiveness of a shelter-based structured group treatment for men who batter.* Paper presented at the Third National Family Violence Research Conference, Durham, NH.

Tolman, R. M., & Bennett, L. W. (1990). A review of quantitative research on men who batter. *Journal of Interpersonal Violence, 5,* 87–118.

Tolman, R. M., & Bhosley, G. (1991). The outcome of participation in shelter-sponsored program for men who batter. In D. Knudsen & J. Miller (Eds.), *Abused and battered: Social and legal responses to family violence* (pp. 113–122). Hawthorne, NY: Aldine de Gruyter.

Tolman, R. M., & Edleson, J. (1995). Intervention for men who batter: A review of research. In S. R. Stith & M. A. Straus (Eds.), *Understanding partner violence: Prevalence, causes, consequences, and solutions* (pp. 262–273). Minneapolis, MN: National Council on Family Relations.

Trattner, W. L. (1974). *From poor law to welfare state: A history of social welfare in America.* New York: Free Press.

U.S. Commission on Civil Rights (1978, January). *Battered women: Issues of public policy.* Consultation sponsored by the U.S. Commission on Civil Rights, Washington, DC.

Valentich, M. (1996). Feminist theory and social work practice. In F. J. Turner (Ed.), *Social work treatment* (4th ed., pp. 282–318). New York: Free Press.

Waldo, M. (1986). Group counseling for military personnel who battered their wives. *Journal for Specialists in Group Work, 11,* 132–138.

Weitzman, J., & Dreen, K. (1982, May). Wife beating: A view of the marital dyad. *Social Casework,* 259–265.

White, R. J., & Gondolf, E. W. (2000). Implications of personality profiles for batterer treatment. *Journal of Interpersonal Violence, 15,* 467–487.

Witkin, S. L., & Gottschalk, S. (1988, June). Alternative criteria for theory evaluation. *Social Service Review,* 211–224.

Part V

VULNERABLE AT-RISK GROUPS
AND MULTICULTURAL ISSUES

20

Domestic Violence Among Lesbian Couples

JANICE L. RICKS
CAROL (JAN) VAUGHAN
SOPHIA F. DZIEGIELEWSKI

NEGATIVE STEREOTYPING
OF LESBIAN WOMEN

Throughout history, lesbian women have been affected in every aspect of their lives by traditional male-centered beliefs and societal norms that provide the basis for heterosexual standards. These heterosexual norms and standards have given rise to myths about lesbian women, creating misrepresentations that are deceptive and destructive. Furthermore, these misperceptions can contribute to present-day expectations that lead to heterosexism and homophobia. According to Richards (1990), in the late 1800s a woman was suspected of being a lesbian if she had any of the following traits. Personality traits included being viewed as cold and unemotional or talking loudly and using slang. Physical traits consisted of having "square shoulders" and a "solid build," small breasts, or an enlarged clitoris. Social traits included showing a capacity for or competence in athletics and a lack of interest in or incapacity for domestic occupations. Dress and outward appearance traits included not wearing a corset and wearing "bobbed" or "short" hair. Since lesbianism was perceived as a problem, the alleged causes of it were of great interest: These included masturbation, the fear of pregnancy, or the overdevelopment of female friendships. In addition, women's colleges that encouraged athletics and the masculinization of the female mind were targeted for contributing to homosexual behavior in women (Richards, 1990).

To purge society of lesbianism, which was perceived as an immoral and corrupt condition, anomalous cures were developed. These included bromides, baths, and douches, as well as fallacious surgical procedures such as oophorectomy (removal of the ovaries) and clitoridectomy (removal of the clitoris). Surgery on the adrenal gland was also practiced as a remedy for lesbianism (Richards, 1990). More recent history shows that it was not until 1981 that the *Diagnostic and Statistical Manual of Mental Disorders (DSM-III)* finally removed lesbianism and homosexuality from its list of mental disorders. Unfortunately, negative and destructive attitudes toward lesbians persist into the present day and are reflected in many aspects of society. Many lesbians are affected by negative attitudes within their families of origin. They are often rejected by family members and rarely find confirmation; if they do, it is often rooted in feelings of tolerance, not open acceptance. The misgivings and misrepresentations to which lesbian women have been subjected have inspired them to establish their own culture and value system in an attempt to create an environment that is nurturing and safe. Unfortunately for lesbians who suffer in relationships in which battering or other abuse occurs, the perceived safety of the lesbian couple within the lesbian community has become a destructive myth.

DOMESTIC VIOLENCE IN THE LESBIAN COMMUNITY

At the onset of the modern women's movement of the 1970s, women began to reject traditional male values and definitions of women's roles and to redefine themselves in terms of women's experiences and women's perspectives. Lesbians, being an integral part of the women's movement, also began to identify themselves in terms that were diametrically opposed to, or a rejection of, traits that were seen as male. Since violence was relegated to the spectrum of male behaviors, lesbians rejected it as a possible characteristic in themselves. According to Renzetti (1992), lesbian relationships were idealized as egalitarian, noncompetitive, and free of the power struggles that plagued heterosexual relationships. Lesbian communities have been viewed as a safe and protective haven from the prejudice of the world, and they are often the only source that provides a sense of familiarity and kinship for some lesbians (*Domestic Violence in Lesbian Relationships* [DVLR], 2000). The lesbian subculture traditionally has not recognized the concept of domestic violence within the confines of its own community. The idea that violence within a relationship might be part of a larger dynamic of power and control is only beginning to be recognized in lesbian communities (Leventhal, 1999). This is not surprising given that, for many years, the existence of domestic violence went unrecognized in both gay and straight communities (Heer, Grogan, Clark, & Carson, 1998). This provided a foundation for the creation of a concept of denial that has endangered battered lesbians and allowed them to remain invisible within both heterosexual and homosexual communities. Furthermore, lesbians who believed that domestic violence did not exist within their community created a fictional sense of safety, thereby setting a dangerous precedent that negated the need for the development of helping resources. Consequently, in the past, lesbians have lacked the knowledge and support necessary to enable them to respond effectively to battered women who lived in their communities (Van Wormer, 2001).

MYTHS ABOUT LESBIAN BATTERING

Besides the false concept that women are not violent, other myths diminish the significance of lesbian domestic violence. These myths contribute to damaging beliefs that are held by both victims and outside lesbian support systems, including helping professionals and law enforcement. Generally same-sex domestic violence has been perceived as mutual and did not reflect the same power and control dynamic as heterosexual battering. The myth that same-sex domestic violence is "mutual battering" or a "fair fight" is damaging on several fronts. Renzetti (1992) and Farley (1992) point out that lesbian victims are more likely to defend themselves than are heterosexual women, and the lesbian community, which encourages self-defense against abuse, sees this kind of self-defense as mutually abusive. The victim will accept the label of mutual batterer even if she has defended herself only once. Renzetti (1992) also believes that the batterer would use this description to avoid accepting responsibility for her behaviors. This is problematic because shelter workers and counselors, as well as family and friends, would all too readily apply the label of mutual batterer to lesbians, whereas they would not impart this same interpretation to heterosexual women who defend themselves.

Other myths contribute to a justification for the lack of adequate or appropriate response from law enforcement, helping professionals such as the battered women's shelter system, and the victim herself (Heer et al., 1998). One myth is that children are not involved in lesbian domestic violence. In fact, lesbians do have children who witness the violence in the home. A victim may remain in a battering relationship for fear of losing custody of her own children or for fear of leaving the abuser's children alone with the abuser. The myth that domestic violence is endemic among the poor or people of color both dismisses the cultural and economic immensity of domestic violence by reducing it to a "blue-collar brawl" and negates the fact that domestic violence crosses all social strata and is totally nondiscriminating. The myth that the batterer is larger or more butch and the victim is smaller or more femme has resulted in the police either making no arrest, arresting the wrong partner, or arresting both partners when responding to a domestic violence call involving two women. Judges will often issue no restraining order or will issue mutual orders. The myth that women batterers do not inflict as much damage as men causes shelter workers, counselors, family, and friends to downplay the extent of damage done to the victim (L.A. Gay & Lesbian Center, 2001; Leventhal & Lundy, 1999; McClennen & Gunther, 1999; Shomer, 1997).

DYNAMICS OF SAME-SEX RELATIONSHIPS

It is important to recognize that same-sex relationships experience many of the same dynamics as heterosexual relationships. While one might assume that two women in a relationship would be exempt from inequality and the abuses it produces, lesbians have been raised in a heterosexual culture, and some couples imitate and repeat the patterns of inequality, dominance, and submission that are endemic among heterosexual couples (Laird, 1998). When domestic violence is acknowledged in lesbian relationships, it is defined differently than heterosexual domestic violence primarily because of the unequal power base that men and women possess. Men are expected to be dominant and are considered to be the primary partners in relationships. Their gender determines their status, creating dominance dictated by sex at birth and continuing throughout life (Leventhal & Lundy, 1999). In contrast, women have historically been seen as caregivers, the nurturers of life and love. It has long been believed that females represented the softer and kinder sex, weaker and less aggressive than their male counterpart. This doctrine provided the basis for the opinion that domestic violence is a male act that originated in the imbalance between men and women in heterosexual relationships (Leventhal & Lundy, 1999). According to McClennen and Gunther (1999), one major misconception about same-sex domestic violence is the "assumption that there has to be gender-role conflict in order for abuse to occur. Within homosexual relationships there is no gender-role conflict; therefore, abuse in such relationships does not exist. . . . domestic violence is not about male and female. Domestic violence is about fear and control" (p. 95). Domestic violence within gay communities can be directly associated with the heterosexual doctrine of power and control without gender role conflict.

Because a relationship model in which one person holds greater power and control has been applied to homosexuals as well as heterosexuals, it is important to be aware of the parallels between heterosexual battering and homosexual battering. Both are driven by the need for power and control, and both are driven by the abuser's need to dominate and disempower the victim (DVLR, 2000). Power and control and the need to dominate motivate the battering lesbian as much as they do the male who batters. Another similarity is the frequency and severity of lesbian battering that follows the same "cycle of violence" identified in heterosexual abuse. A period of tension precipitates the violence, a violent explosion occurs, and then a honeymoon phase follows in which the abuser apologizes, minimizes the behavior, and promises never to do it again (McClennen & Gunther, 1999). There is also the dynamic in which lesbian victims, like their heterosexual counterparts, display the same behaviors of recanting, minimizing, and taking responsibility for the abuse, while the abuser maintains control and remains overly possessive and isolating (Shomer, 1997).

UNIQUENESS AND DISCRIMINATION

Concurrent with similarities to heterosexual domestic violence are a number of important differences in lesbian partner abuse. Homophobia is seen as the primary problem for women who are abused by other women (Griffin, 2000). The lesbian batterer's tactics often focus on issues that are used as weapons of discrimination in the heterosexual world and thus that are major stressors to any lesbian even under the best of circumstances. Potential loss of family, friends, jobs, and children may be primary reasons that women do not come out as lesbians. The batterer will use these concerns to intimidate and control her partner. She may threaten to expose the victim to her employer, causing her to lose financial stability. The potential threats represent real losses that would be significant in the battered woman's life, and the fear of this happening keeps the victim isolated and afraid (DVLR, 2000). Abused and battered lesbians are victims not only of same-sex domestic violence but also of homophobia and heterosexism. Same-sex batterers can use the conditions created by homophobia and heterosexism to wield highly effective weapons against their partners (Leventhal, 1999).

Lesbians often have trouble finding help from mainstream agencies, which may not be equipped to offer services to same-sex couples and whose service providers may be homophobic and misinformed (Griffin, 2000). Although lesbians can go to battered women's shelters, they often do not feel welcome or understood because the literature and the available help are heterosexually oriented (Davidson, 1997). More frightening is the reality that, as a woman, the batterer can check herself into the same shelter where her victim has escaped merely by claiming that she was abused (Friess, 1997). Even the commonly used feminist term *wife abuse* or *spouse abuse* is unintentionally heterosexist (Van Wormer, 1999).

Lesbian victims and perpetrators may be afraid to seek help for fear of rejection and stigmatization from the heterosexual community. Lesbians will often feel pressured to keep silent about the abuse, not wanting to create a negative impression of same-sex relationships that could give heterosexual society more ammunition against the lesbian and gay community (Shomer, 1997). According to Griffin (2000), gays and lesbians are striving for the same rights and acceptance that heterosexuals enjoy. Lesbians may be reluctant to expose the presence of domestic violence in their relationships, fearing that doing so will add to the negativity that heterosexuals already employ regarding homosexuals.

As one may well imagine, poor resources, homophobia, and invisibility make it difficult for battered lesbians to get help. Because battering has been defined primarily as a heterosexual problem, many lesbians may not recognize that domestic violence is happening to them. If they should choose to leave the relationship and seek help, it is likely that there is nowhere for them to go (National Coalition of Anti-Violence Programs [NCAVP], 1998). In many ways, gays and lesbians do not have the same responses, protections, and services as heterosexuals (Ocamb, 2000).

Embracing the notion of violence between women seems contradictory when one considers the essence of lesbian identity and pride. Once domestic violence takes place in a relationship, it becomes impossible to separate the experience of being a lesbian from the experience of being battered. The battered lesbian is incapable of developing a sense of self or a sense of pride to combat the homophobic discrimination she encounters. When she is battered by her own partner and finds no refuge in the community she is a part of, this can lead to long-lasting questions about her lesbian pride and identity as a lesbian (Leventhal, 1999).

ROLE OF SUBSTANCE ABUSE

Confounding the problems experienced in lesbian domestic violence is the abuse of alcohol within gay communities. Reports show that gays and lesbians are three times more likely than the heterosexual population to develop alcoholism (Niolon, 2000). This increased risk is the result of several factors. First, in gay communities, socialization has traditionally centered around gay bars (DiNitto & McNeece, 1990; Israelstam & Lambert, 1986; Kelly, 1990; Nichols, 1989). Additionally, the use of alcohol or other substances is a way to deal with feelings of alienation and isolation generated by homophobia and oppression. Women's bodies metabolize alcohol in such a way that they are more impaired by it than are men (McClennen & Gunther, 1999). Substance abuse plays a facilitative, not a causal, role in lesbian domestic violence by disinhibiting certain behaviors in the abuser. There is evidence that substance abuse facilitates intimate violence in that it becomes the basis on which the abuser's behaviors are excused. Victims, abusers, and friends "explain away" the battering because of the partner's substance abuse (Renzetti, 1992).

POWER RELATIONS

While substance abuse is highly correlated with lesbian domestic violence, other factors also lead to violence in lesbian relationships. These include power imbalance, dependency, jealousy, and witnessing intergenerational violence. Many victims of lesbian abuse have witnessed aggression in their families of origin. Batterers often will use past experiences as an excuse to batter, and sometimes victims will not leave abusive relationships because, having grown up with abuse, they view it as "normal" (Shomer, 1997).

Relative power has been defined in terms of decision making, division of labor, and resource status. Often batterers are believed to be the primary decision makers in abusing relationships. These individuals are also less yielding, being perceived as the takers, not the givers. Couples in which abuse occurs also have unequal differences in divisions of labor, intelligence, and social class, and the greater the differences, the greater the abuse. The partner's satisfaction with the relationship is lower in relationships marked by power imbalance than in more egalitarian relationships. Equality of power and role sharing are vital to both satisfaction and durability of lesbian relationships (McClennen & Gunther, 1999).

Lesbians often are caught between their gender socialization to be caretakers, constantly striving to attune themselves to the needs of others, and the feminist ideal, which encourages independence, personal autonomy, and self-actualization. Gender socialization can result in a lesbian woman becoming enmeshed (physically, emotionally, and socially) within her relationship. In this type of relationship, a lesbian abuser is able to isolate her partner as a principal tactic of coercion and control (McClennen & Gunther, 1999). In battering relationships, the abuser tends to be most dependent, and violence occurs when the victim wants more autonomy. The greater the victim's desire for independence, coupled with greater dependence on the part of the abuser, the greater the frequency and types of abuse (Renzetti, 1992).

Abuse in relationships occurs when one partner wants more autonomy and/or the abuser becomes overly jealous and possessive. Jealousy, therefore, is also associated with abuse. Overdependency of the abuser frequently manifests itself in jealous tirades, and battering is often the end result. Abusers display jealousy in the form of extreme possessiveness by interrogating, haranguing, and putting restrictions on their partners' behaviors. This may take the form of accusing them of infidelity, requiring that they account for every minute they are apart, and restricting dress and contact with other people. The jealousy and overdependency of the batterer may also manifest themselves through substance abuse. Under the influence, a batterer may feel stronger, more independent, and more aggressive and may act out her aggression by becoming violent toward her partner. As mentioned earlier, along with the belief that alcohol or other substances make her feel power-ful, she may also believe that she is not responsible for her actions while under the influence, thus facilitating battering.

PREVALENCE

Young lesbians have few, if any, role models. There are no dating norms for lesbian adolescents, and until recently there have been no available models of gay and lesbian relationships (Niolon, 2000). A study by Martin and Hatrick (1988) found that the third most frequent problem for gay and les-bian adolescents is violence (cited in Niolon, 2000). Over 40% had suffered violence because of their sexual orientation, and 49% of the violence oc-curred within their family from parents or siblings. In order to create a coor-dinated response to violence against gay communities, the National Coali-tion of Anti-Violence Programs (NCAVP) was formed in 1984. In 1995 this coalition, in conjunction with the National Gay and Lesbian Task Force, was formed to respond to violence against gay communities. The first report was released in 1996 and reflected 2,352 cases of documented same-sex do-mestic violence (NCAVP, 1998). In October 1997 the second annual domes-tic violence report was released in conjunction with National Domestic Vio-lence Awareness month. According to this report, 3,327 cases of same-sex domestic violence had been reported, and 1,582 (48%) were by women; this represented a 41% increase over the total number of cases reported in 1996. The report released by the NCAVP in 1999 documented 2,574 cases of same-sex domestic violence. This lower number (down from 3,327) reflected loss of funding and staff in agencies that had previously contributed to this prevalence report. Reasons for the underreporting of domestic violence, be-sides inadequate staffing and the fear of coming out, include the fact that reporting same-sex abuse is directly related to the victim's perception of available help. If the victim does not perceive that help is available, the abuse will go unreported. This factor may account for the low number of reports that have been received in the past. The fact that most lesbian and gay rela-tionships are not recognized within heterosexual society has allowed the truth about same-sex domestic violence to be distorted. Actual cases of same-sex domestic violence were reported as "one roommate killed another" or "a dispute between friends," thus diminishing the truth (Ocamb, 2000). An extrapolation from prevalence calculations in 1991 revealed that a mini-mum of 330,000 lesbians are victims of partner abuse each year (McClen-nen & Gunther, 1999). Research attempts to determine the prevalence of same-sex domestic violence have found rates to be between 25% and 33%, which is comparable to the findings on heterosexual couples (NCAVP, 1999). This means that one in every four lesbians who are in a relationship are in one where abuse occurs. Combine that with the lack of support, agencies, shelters, and counselors that address lesbian battering, and the crisis that results can be appalling, dangerous, and life-threatening.

IMPLICATIONS FOR COUNSELING

If the victim, the batterer, or the couple decides to seek help, they are more likely to go to a mental health professional than to shelters or other agencies. Given the high probability that any female client has experienced intimate violence, it is imperative that the therapist receive proper training to effectively help these clients; the client must not be "revictimized" by being treated insensitively by the helping professional. Mental health professionals also need to be aware of the traumatizing nature of other referral sources such as legal and medical systems and how these external systems can contribute to the victim's internal sense of low self-esteem (Campbell & Raja, 1999; Heer et al., 1998). For this reason, programs that include the services of a battered lesbian hotline can provide immediate referrals and information to the survivor of domestic violence (Heer et al., 1998).

In a study by Renzetti (1992), victims identified specific responses that they wanted from therapists. A key desire was that the focus in therapy be on the counselor's helping the client to regain self-esteem while recognizing that low self-esteem is the result of the battering, not vice versa. Counselors need to identify the victim's experience with battering; they must not minimize the abuse because the batterer was a woman; and they must not lay blame for the abuse on the victim. Specific attention needs to be given toward empowering the woman in order to build client strengths (Van Wormer, 2001). The counselors who were rated as most helpful by victims were those who helped the victim "name the violence" by connecting the words *battered* and *lesbian*. Accepting that one is being battered is the first step in overcoming denial that one woman could abuse another. Conversely, those victims who rated counselors as unhelpful cited the counselors' denial of the battering as the main source of dissatisfaction (Renzetti, 1992). Heer et al. (1998) remind all practitioners of the need to first sensitize professionals working in the area of domestic violence regarding the issues involved in lesbian battering. When this is not done, a problem may result in learning how to help community members become more comfortable with the issue.

There are conflicting opinions about the benefits of using couples counseling in cases of lesbian domestic violence. Warnings against couples counseling stem from (1) fear for the victim's safety; (2) the view that the batterer is using therapy only as a means to keep the victim from leaving; and (3) concern that the system's theoretical base of couples counseling maintains the idea of dual responsibility, which can be victim blaming and can absolve the abuser of responsibility. Some models hold that in couples counseling the victim will not feel safe enough to disclose what actually happens at home; the counseling then ends up colluding in ongoing violence (McClennen & Gunther, 1999). Others believe that trying to preserve the relationship makes the victim vulnerable to more abuse. Couples usually do not benefit from couples counseling because the cycle of violence is nearly impossible to stop (Renzetti, 1992). Another argument against couples counseling is that it does not help the batterer to stop battering (the batterer needs help from programs specifically designed for batterers in order to change) and that it can actually be dangerous for the victim (Network for Battered Lesbian and Bisexual Women [NBLBW], 2001).

Batterers may go to couples counseling as a sign of remorse, but often this is just an attempt to keep the victim from leaving (NBLBW, 2001). Batterers often are described as charming, articulate, and above all manipulative. Once in couples counseling, it is possible that the tables will be turned so that the therapist and the batterer end up working on what is "wrong" with the victim. This leaves the abuser unaccountable for her actions and disregards the victim's physical and emotional well-being.

Couples counseling is often based on the family systems or codependency model, which proposes that both individuals share responsibility for the abusive nature of the relationship. This is inherently victim blaming and can be especially damaging if the victim has defended herself. As already mentioned, many counselors are too willing to call this mutual abuse, thus reinforcing the victim's low self-esteem and self-blame. Under the aegis of this model, a therapist may interpret the victim's desire to stay with the batterer as evidence of codependency. The therapist may see the victim's alcohol or drug problem as the cause rather than the result of the abuse. Ultimately these suppositions turn the focus of therapy toward changing the victim while the behavior of the abuser goes unchallenged.

These arguments are valid and compelling. The therapist needs to be mindful of and guard against them should couples counseling with such a couple be undertaken. Some circumstances may warrant couples counseling for couples in battering relationships. Couples may seek such counseling in order to stay together and improve their relationship; they may see the counseling as the only way to accomplish this. Separating them into individual and group therapy may seem contrary to why they sought help in the first place. The two women in the couple may not have enough ego strength to go to separate therapies, and so they may not follow through on referrals. Under these circumstances, counseling involving the couple is a way to keep these women in treatment so as to provide them with an alternative to isolation and continued violence. Couples counseling also can be a prelude to other therapies. A couple may be more willing and motivated to use other treatment modalities after establishing an alliance with a couple's counselor (McClennen & Gunther, 1999).

Taking these warnings into account, McClennen and Gunther (1999) insist upon signed contracts between the couple and therapist if the couple is going to receive counseling while remaining in the relationship. The couple must sign a contract stating that the batterer takes responsibility for her actions and outlines alternate ways to deal with her feelings of frustration and anger. The victim has in place a plan to leave the relationship should the violence increase. If possible, separate therapists do individual counseling, and both therapists attend couples counseling sessions. Children who are old enough should attend occasional cocounseling sessions and be provided with play therapy to help deal with their feelings about what goes on at home. Furthermore, ground rules can be put in place for the couple in therapy. The safety of the victim is the foremost priority. Both partners must agree that the violence must stop and any recurrence must be reported to the therapist. No violence or threats will be tolerated in therapy, but anger and conflicts will be welcome. Both must agree that the batterer is solely responsible for her violent behavior, and the therapist teaches them the difference between feelings/impulses and actions/behaviors (McClennen & Gunther, 1999).

Finally, counselors must listen to what their clients say they want. Although some therapists may help a victim by naming the violence, these same therapists may also try to preserve the relationship, initiating couples counseling despite the victim's reluctance (Renzetti, 1992). On the other hand, when a couple seeks to save its relationship through couples counseling and the therapist responds by referring members of the couple to separate treatments, it provides a dangerous precedent by which the couple may not get any help at all, allowing the abuse to continue. The measure of success in couples counseling does not necessarily mean that the individuals stay together. For some couples it may mean separating from each other in order to break the cycle of violence. If a practitioner insists on maintaining either polarized view (i.e., that couples counseling is never viable and couples should break up, or that the practitioner must use counseling to save the relationship), he or she may be prevented from joining with the clients. This separation can prevent the establishment of the kind of therapeutic alliance necessary for effective treatment. Furthermore, if this path is followed, clients do not get the help they need to stop the violence.

In conclusion, it is clear that domestic violence is not a problem only within heterosexual relationships. It is also not a gender issue, focusing on men abusing and battering women. Because women who batter women are not a part of the feminist ideal to which most lesbians subscribe, violence between women may seem abstract and incomprehensible. Since domestic violence between women has not been recognized in the past, the truth about violence between women has remained hidden behind a shroud of denial. The lesbian community, the heterosexual community, and the professional community have had difficulty grasping the concept of violence between women (Heer et al., 1998), and this denial allows victims of domestic violence to remain invisible. Homophobia has kept lesbians trapped in abusive relationships and has prevented existing agencies from properly addressing the problem of same-sex abuse. In order to help effectively, professionals must become educated about and sensitive to the issues surrounding lesbian domestic violence. They must gain understanding and knowledge regarding the needs of battered lesbians so that they can provide effective assistance and stop the cycle of violence.

REFERENCES

Campbell, R., & Raja, S. (1999). Training mental health professionals on violence against women. *Journal of Interpersonal Violence, 14,* 1003.

Davidson, R. (1997). *The gay community's dirty secret—domestic violence—is finally coming out of the closet.* Available on-line: www.salon.com/feb97/news/news2970227.html.

DiNitto, D. M., & McNeece, C. A. (1990). *Social work: Issues and opportunities in a challenging profession.* Englewood Cliffs, NJ: Prentice-Hall.

Domestic violence in lesbian relationships. (2000). Available on-line: www.en.com/user/allison/l_dv.html 1–3.

Farley, N. (1992). Same-sex domestic violence. In S. H. Dworkin & F. J. Guiterrez (Eds.), *Counseling gay men and lesbians of the rainbow* (pp. 231–241). Alexandria, VA: American Association for Counseling Development.

Friess, S. (1997, December 9). Behind closed doors: Domestic violence (gay domestic violence). *The Advocate,* 48.

Griffin, R. M. (2000). *Breaking the silence: Sociologist studies woman-to-woman sexual violence.* Available on-line: www.gayhealth.com.

Heer, C., Grogan, E., Clark, S., & Carson, L. M. (1998). Developing services for lesbians in abusive relationships: A macro and micro approach. In A. R. Roberts (Ed.), *Battered women and their families*

(2nd ed., pp. 365–384). New York: Springer.

Hyde, J. (1990). *Understanding human sexuality.* New York: McGraw-Hill.

Israelstam, S., & Lambert, S. (1986). Homosexuality and alcohol: Observations and research after the psychoanalytic era. *International Journal of Addictions, 21,* 509–537.

Kelly, G. (1990). *Sexuality today: The human perspective.* Guilford, NY: Duskin.

L.A. Gay & Lesbian Center. (2001). *Partner abuse/domestic violence.* Available on-line: www.gay-lesbian-center.org.

Laird, J. (1998). *Lesbians and lesbian families: Reflections on theory and practice.* New York: Columbia University Press.

Leventhal, B., L., & Lundy, S. E. (1999). *Same-sex domestic violence: Strategies for change.* Thousand Oaks, CA: Sage.

McClennen, J. C., & Gunther, J. (1999). *A professional guide to understanding gay and lesbian domestic violence.* Lewiston, NY: Edwin Mellen Press.

National Coalition of Anti-Violence Programs. (1998). *Annual report on lesbian, gay, bisexual, transgender domestic violence.* Available on-line: www.vaw.umn.edu.

National Coalition of Anti-Violence Programs. (1999). *Annual report on lesbian, gay, bisexual, transgender domestic violence.* Available on-line: www.avp.org.

Network for Battered Lesbian and Bisexual Women. (2001). *Is your girlfriend abusive? You are not alone.* Available on-line: www. nblbw.org.

Nichols, M. (1989). Sex therapy with lesbians, gay men, and bisexuals. In S. Lieblum & R. Rosen (Eds.), *Principles and practice of sex therapy* (pp. 269–296). New York: Guilford.

Niolon, R. (2000). *Domestic violence in gay and lesbian couples.* Available on-line: www.Psychpage.com.

Ocamb, K. (2000). The crisis of same-sex domestic violence. *Lesbian News, 25*(6), 45.

Renzetti, C. M. (1992). *Violent betrayal: Partner abuse in lesbian relationships.* Newbury Park, CA., Sage.

Richards, D. (1990). *Lesbian lists: A look at lesbian culture, history, and personalities.* Boston: Alyson Publications.

Shomer, A. (1997). Lesbian domestic violence: Our tragic little secret. *Lesbian News, 22*(8), 24.

Van Wormer, K. S. (1999). *Social work with lesbians, gays and bisexuals: A strength's erspective.* Boston: Allyn and Bacon.

Van Wormer, K. S. (2001). *Counseling female offenders and victims: A strengths-restorative approach.* New York: Springer.

21

Latina Battered Women

Barriers to Service Delivery and
Cultural Considerations

GLORIA BONILLA SANTIAGO

This chapter provides an overview of the recent cultural barriers and social
service and legal needs of Latina battered women. It also includes an analysis
of the socioeconomic, cultural, and ethnic factors that contribute to domestic
violence. Latina women have parents, grandparents, or great grandparents
from Latin America—Puerto Rico, Cuba, Mexico, the Dominican Republic,
or Central or South America. The Latino population in the United States
experienced a 60% growth rate during the 1990s, positioning it at virtual
parity with the African-American population (U.S. Bureau of the Census,
2001).

The 2000 U.S. Census shows that while Latino subgroups vary considerably
in their levels of poverty and education, the gap between Latinos and the general U.S. population is significant. Latino men continue to have the highest
labor force participation rates of any group in the country, and Latina women
have once again increased their workforce presence as well. In spite of this
high level of labor participation, Latinos are still three times likelier than whites
to be poor. Latino children, in particular, are significantly affected by poverty.
Latino single-mother families are still more likely to be poor than comparable
black and white families (U.S. Bureau of the Census, 2001).

In light of the growth of the Latino population in the United States and
the substantial economic, social, and cultural diversity among Latino ethnic
groups, a serious discussion about domestic violence is timely. As the prevalence of family violence has been recognized, and shelter services, police pro-

arrest laws, and orders of protection have become more readily available, the oppression and brutal assaults against Latina battered women are finally being acknowledged as well (Kaufman Kantor, Jasinski, & Aldarondo, 1998; Keefe, 1982). However, because of cultural and religious beliefs, Latina battered women continue to use existing community agencies to escape a violent home.

In a recent review of Latina battered women who are incarcerated or receiving services from shelters or Hispanic women's centers, I found that because of language and cultural barriers, most of these women had received no assistance or protection from police, legal aid, welfare, family counseling agencies, or community mental health centers. This chapter concludes with policy and practice recommendations for legislators, community leaders, social work administrators, and battered women advocates for improving the correctional response to Latina battered women. I recognize that there is an urgent need for pro bono legal services and client advocacy for the women in this study, and that traditional law enforcement and judicial agencies should provide culturally sensitive, bilingual services to this oppressed group.

BACKGROUND

Domestic violence against women occurs in families from all cultural and ethnic groups (Gondolf, Fisher, & McFerron, 1991; O'Keefe, 1994; Straus & Gelles, 1990; Straus & Smith, 1990), and intervention policies and practices in treating battered women should accommodate their diverse cultural backgrounds. Nevertheless, research or information on the cultural aspects of domestic violence against women and how they differ among ethnic groups is very limited. Few studies document the prevalence of domestic violence against Latinas. Most research on the abuse of women has focused on the Anglo-America population, and most of the literature has ignored cross-cultural differences or acknowledges that cross-cultural differences in abuse of women have been minimally explored (Straus & Smith, 1990). Ethnic and sociocultural factors are key determinants of the behavior of Latina women in abusive domestic relationships (Bauer, Rodriguez, Szkupinski-Quiroga, & Flores-Ortiz, 2000).

Ethnic heritage is a manifestation of values, attitudes, personality, and behavior. Different ethnic groups receive different societal opportunities and rewards, and they share certain attitudes and goals. Given the prevalence of spouse and partner abuse across ethnic groups and social classes, it is critical to consider the impact of social and cultural factors on the behaviors of abused Latina women. These factors are important in determining the kind of interventions, both legal and social, that are necessary to effectively address the needs of battered women (Bauer et al., 2000). Although the United

States is composed of many ethnic groups, the emphasis of social services have has been on assimilation—that is, conformity with Anglo-American values. Services offered to various ethnic groups are judged and categorized in accordance with their adherence to the dominant culture. Nonetheless, ethnic and cultural diversity constitutes the fabric of American society (Cafferty & Chestang, 1976), and cultural factors are relevant to all aspects of helping battered women. Ethnicity is a key factor in determining gender roles, norms, and values that can significantly shape women's responses to abuse (Bauer et al., 2000).

Studies and statistics have established that the situation of Latina women is different from that of white and black women. Latinas face sociopolitical barriers of gender, national origin, race, social isolation, poverty, and language that can influence how they deal with a battered condition. While women across ethnic and social groups face domestic abuse, for Latina women, the abuse is exacerbated by high poverty levels, lack of resources, and the combination of underemployment, undereducation, and cultural isolation (West, Kaufman, & Jasinski, 1998). Feelings of vulnerability and helplessness because of a lack of resources, the dearth of bilingual or bicultural services from social service organizations, hospitals, and shelters, as well as the cultural isolation experienced by Latinas who do not speak English or whose cultural norms differ from those prevailing in the United States converge and set certain boundaries on battered Latina women. The impact of these differences on Latinas' lives has led researchers to conclude that these women need support services that are targeted to their specific issues to a greater extent than do other battered women (Gondolf et al., 1988; O'Keefe, 1994; West et al., 1998).

These cultural factors are exacerbated for undocumented battered Latina women. There is compelling evidence that America's new undocumented migrants are increasingly likely to be women and children. Many researchers have also indicated that more women will be migrating to the United States without their spouses because women are more likely to find jobs in the "hidden" service economy. However, while more immigrant women are coming to the United States seeking a better quality of life for themselves and their families, the barriers they face are tremendous. Fearing deportation and/or the loss of her children, a Latina immigrant battered woman may be intimidated by her partner's threat to report her to the U.S. Immigration and Naturalization Service. She may not realize that domestic violence is against the law, that she has legal options to stop the battering, and that agencies and community resources are available to support her.

There may also be inhibitions based on cultural issues and ambiguities about domestic violence. Different countries and cultures may have their own values and attitudes toward a "woman's place," family, marriage, sex roles, and divorce. Cultural factors such as machismo (male dominance), *marianismo* (female submission), and traditional family structures with strictly defined sex roles and a strong Catholic tradition are key determinants of the responses of Latina women to domestic abuse (Maciack, Guzman, Santiago, Villalobos, & Israel, 1999). In addition, a major cause of domestic violence is rooted in society's tradition of the unequal power of men and women.

These numerous factors combine to make Latina women feel isolated and powerless to escape the cycle of violence. Criminal justice practitioners, social service providers, and immigrant assistance agencies can play a critical role in identifying domestic violence and giving immigrant battered women information about the help that is available in their communities. In addition, these practitioners can be advocates and change agents for new services to bridge the gap between agencies and battered Latina women.

People from Latin America often share a regional heritage that includes abuse from governmental officials, the military, and local law enforcement officials. Indeed, recent immigrants often are escaping police and military force, and so they bring with them memories of and suspicions about the assistance available from enforcement agencies. A battered Latina woman may be wary of the police, who may have acted in a violent, repressive manner toward the community at large, and also must decide whether to seek help from an outsider who does not share her language or any of her cultural values. She is therefore often left to fend for herself at a time of extreme danger and urgency.

Human service providers thus should incorporate cultural factors into their care and intervention and their legislative policy. Law enforcement officials' education strategies must be coordinated with community-based organizations and Latino advocates. Otherwise, the education programs will reflect ingrained stereotypes and merely intensify the problems that the education efforts seek to remedy.

DESCRIPTIVE SURVEY

This comparative study obtained information on the cross-cultural aspects of abuse of both Latina and Anglo-American battered women. Interviews were conducted with 25 Latina women and 25 white women residing at the Edna Mahan women's correctional facility in Clinton, New Jersey; two resource centers for Latina women in Camden and Newark, New Jersey; and several women's shelters in New Jersey. The study focused on women's attitudes toward wife abuse and their perception of what constitutes abuse and examined cross-cultural issues and aspects of abused Latina women and the implications for treatment and intervention.

FINDINGS

These women had been given long sentences because of (1) the possession of drugs (the most common reason for the rise of undocumented Latina inmates), (2) the distribution of drugs, (3) robbery and property crimes, and (4) murder as a result of domestic violence. The Latina women incarcerated at Clinton were mostly from poor urban areas and were poorly educated, with a fourth-grade reading level and even poorer occupational skills. The youngest woman we interviewed was 18, and the oldest was 58.

Many of the Latina women who participated in our focus group came from Central America, the Dominican Republic or the Caribbean. Others came from poor urban areas and considered themselves "mainland Latina" (born and raised in the United States). The majority were undocumented immigrants. Many of the women stated that they felt isolated in this country because they did not understand the language, culture, legal system, or social systems; consequently, they often suffered the triple burden of discrimination based on sex, race, and their undocumented status.

The lack of education of this group of respondents is noticeably poorer compared with that of other females. Because of the high rate of pregnancy among adolescent Latinas, these women are also less likely than other females to finish high school or to complete an education or job-training program.

Although domestic violence cuts across ethnic, religious, and economic lines, these undocumented Latina women face serious difficulties because of both their abuse and their undocumented status. The focus groups revealed that many immigrant Latina women were isolated and trapped in violent homes, afraid to turn to anyone for help. The results of the survey of Latina women revealed that 34% had experienced some form of domestic violence by their partners, in both their country of origin and the United States.

There were some significant differences between the Latinas and the Anglo-American battered women we studied. The Latina women were more tolerant of wife abuse, and their perceptions of what constituted wife abuse differed from those of our Anglo-American subjects. For example, such acts as hitting or verbal abuse had to occur more frequently to be considered abuse by Latina women. Some acts perceived as abusive by the Anglo-American women were not considered as abusive by the Latina women, including verbal abuse and the failure to provide adequate food and shelter. Latina women were much more likely to consider an act as "physical abuse" because of their society's more frequent use of weapons such as knives and guns, which was seen as a threat to their life. The following quotations reflect the feelings of anger, fear, and isolation of two Latinas:

The first time I went to the hospital [he] had broken my nose and cut my head open. He hit me on the head with metal, and I got 17 stitches over my ear. I can't hear well on that side since that happened. The other time, I was pregnant with my third child. . . . [he] hit me and kicked me with a weapon so that I almost miscarried in my 6th month. You know, [my son] has always been a slow learner, and I think it's because of the beating before he was born. (Interview with shelter participant, August 20, 1992)

One time the neighbors called the police. They heard screaming and yelling. He had been hitting me and throwing knives and threatening me around the house. A police officer came to the door and asked if everything was all right. You know, he stood right behind me, and I had to say that everything was fine. I was afraid he'd do something if I did. (Interview with shelter participant, August 10, 1992)

The economic existence of battered Latinas is often based on "underground" employment sources and markets. Many of these battered women are not native speakers of English and have limited English-language comprehension. Thus they are unemployable due to their lack of skills and competencies at higher rates than white or black women. The choices available to Latina women in response to being abused and leaving home were few in comparison to those available to white women. White women felt that they could go to a shelter or police and feel temporarily protected. Latinas have a sense of futility in seeking police assistance:

I never called the police here because [he] told me that they will deport us if I do. I've thought about learning some English, but between work and the kids there is hardly any time. So I've never really asked anybody for help. Anyway sometimes the police did come and never pay attention to my story, since he was there and always got to tell that it was a family misunderstanding. (Interview with inmate participant, Edna Mahan correctional facility, July 1992)

In this study with the Latina focus group, the women faced the precarious, often untenable, situation of the "double-blind" empowerment through the disempowerment of a male member of the community. The internal conflict and external pressure to cast police officials as outsiders, hostile to the community, frustrate the development of empowerment. There is evidence that officers have reacted to such arrest policies by arresting both the man and the woman, in a so-called dual arrest. This occurred with Latinas in our study. Empowerment is unlikely when women are treated as if they have acted illegally, are as culpable as the batterer, or cannot be believed.

RECOMMENDATIONS

New methods and strategies to respond to cultural and racial differences must be central in dealing with the domestic violence movement. The issues, problems, and experiences of battered Latinas have not been taken into consideration in the human services and social work community or by direct social service providers in state government. The governmental infrastructure charged with enforcing the laws that protect women has failed to adopt legal procedures that are effective in addressing cultural and behavioral patterns that differ from that of the dominant culture (Weller, Martin, & Lechland, 2001). The justice and correctional systems need to adopt new approaches for dealing with the Latino family that incorporate a better understanding of the culture and the ways in which Latinos interact with the courts and other governmental institutions.

Extensive cultural diversity education efforts must be linked to mandatory arrest policies to inform the community of the policies and duties of the police. As documented by Wiist and McFarlene (1998), social service workers need to inform abused women that retaliatory abuse is a common response when reporting abuse to the police. Fears of deportation must be addressed through extensive education efforts and by the good-faith conduct of the appropriate agencies.

A great deal of work with domestic violence has centered on establishing and maintaining shelters and increased traditional social services. These are recognized as critical provisions for battered women. However, Latinas have not received sufficient resources and services to address their multiple needs within these shelters. Alternative, culturally appropriate services need to be available for those Latinas who may seek assistance, but all would not consider leaving their homes for cultural, financial immigration issues. Similarly, mainstream organizations need to hire competent bicultural staff and develop bicultural training methods and programs. Governmental and law enforcement agencies need to find effective ways to inform the Latino community of the process, as well as providing bilingual services and literature. An effective approach would be to develop partnerships with community-based organizations, hospitals, and churches as a vehicle to reach out to women who would not otherwise contact the legal system.

Latino and community-based organizations must be retrained to provide new services to Latina battered women. These organizations also need to be provided with the financial and political flexibility to develop and implement domestic violence shelters and services. The Latino community leadership must prioritize domestic violence initiatives with the legislature and government officials in order to address this serious and growing problem.

REFERENCES

Bauer, H. M., Rodriguez, M. A., Szkupinski-Quiroga, S., & Flores-Ortiz, bY. G. (2000). Barriers to health care for abused Latina and Asian immigrant women. *Journal of Health Care for the Poor and Underserved,* 11(1), 33–44.

Cafferty, P. S. J. & Chestang, L. (Eds.).

(1976). *The diverse society: Implications for social policy.* Washington, DC: NASW Press.

Gondolf, E. W., Fisher, E., & McFerron, R. (1991). Racial differences among shelter residents: A comparison of Anglo, Black and Hispanic battered women. In R. I. Hampton

(Ed.), *Black family violence: Current research and theory* (pp. 103–113). Lexington, MA: Lexington Books.

Keefe, S. E. (1982). Help-seeking behavior among foreign-born and native-born Mexican Americans. *Social Science and Medicine, 16,* 1467–1472.

Maciack, B., Guzman R., Santiago, A., Villalobos, G., & Israel, B. (1999). Establishing LA VIDA: A community-based partnership to prevent intimate violence against Latina women. *Health Education and Behavior, 26,* 821–840.

O'Keefe, M. (1994). Racial/ethnic differences among battered women and their children. *Journal of Child and Family Studies, 3,* 283–305.

Straus, M. A., & Gelles, R. J. (1990). How violent are American families? Estimates from the national family violence resurvey and other studies. In M. A. Straus & R. J. Gelles (Eds.), *Physical violence in American families* (Appendix B, pp. 95–112). New Brunswick, NJ: Transaction.

Straus, M., & Smith, C. (1990). Violence in Hispanic families in the United States: Incidence rates and structural interpretations. In M. A. Straus & R. J. Gelles (Eds.), *Physical violence in American families: Risk factors and adaptations to violence in 8,145 families* (pp. 341–368). New Brunswick, NJ: Transaction.

U.S. Bureau of the Census. (1998). *Poverty in the United States: Hispanic.* Washington, DC: Department of Commerce.

U.S. Bureau of the Census. (1997). *Population of the United States: Current population survey—March 1997, detailed tables.* Washington, DC: Department of Commerce.

U.S. Bureau of the Census. (2001). *Overview of Hispanic population: Census brief.* Washington, DC: Department of Commerce.

Weller S., Martin, J. A., & Lederach, J. P. (2001). Fostering culturally responsive courts: The case of family dispute resolution for Latinos. *Family Review Court, 39,* 185–202.

West, C. M., Kaufman, G., & Jasinski, J. L. (1998). Sociodemographic predictors and cultural barriers to help-seeking behavior in Latina and Anglo American battered women. *Violence and Victims, 13,* 361.

Wiist, W. H., & McFarlane, J. (1998). Utilization of police by abused pregnant Hispanic women. *Violence Against Women, 4,* 677–693.

22

Asian Battered Women

Assessment and Treatment

MO YEE LEE

As a result of the work of feminist activists, scholars, and practitioners who have been the force behind the battered women's movement, the issue of spouse abuse has gained increased prominence in American society. The Violence Against Women Act of 1994 signifies a fundamental change in the criminal justice system and reflects the recognition that violence against women is a crime with far-reaching, harmful consequences for families, children, and society (U.S. Department of Justice, 1996). Despite the proliferation of collective knowledge and understanding of domestic violence against women and its treatment, the experience of Asian battered women has been understudied (Lee & Au, 1998; Lum, 1998). Asian-Americans are a fast-growing group in the United States, constituting 3.5% of the overall population in 1997 (U.S. Department of Commerce, 1998). It has been projected that by the year 2050, Asian Pacific Islanders will constitute 8.2% of total population. To better understand domestic violence and provide effective interventions to stop violence in intimate relationships, it is important to produce additional images of domestic violence that capture the experiences of a broader range of men, women, and children. This chapter reviews the experiences of Asian battered women and provides suggestions for culturally sensitive and competent assessment and treatment for them. The discussion is also informed by interviews conducted with prominent Asian professionals and activists working with Asian battered women.

PREVALENCE OF DOMESTIC VIOLENCE
AGAINST ASIAN WOMEN

Defining the prevalence of domestic violence for Asians is an extremely difficult task. The existing prevalence studies of domestic violence against women
make few references to race or ethnicity (Kanuha, 1994). Official statistics
in both the United States and Canada do not include Asians as a separate
category in their analyses. In addition, only a few population-based studies
have examined the prevalence of domestic violence in Asian communities.
Because of a lack of systematic data, perception of domestic violence against
women in Asian communities is clouded by myths and biases. One myth
holds that domestic violence is not a problem for Asian women because they
rarely utilize services provided by shelters or other social services agencies.
Findings from the National Violence against Women Survey (NVAW) indicated that Asian and Pacific Islander women were significantly less likely to
report physical and sexual victimization than the general U.S. population
(lifetime prevalence rate of 51.9% vs. 55%), especially sexual violence (6.8%
vs. 18.2%); 76% of these acts were intimate violence (Tjaden & Thoennes,
1998). Findings of studies focusing on domestic violence against women,
however, have suggested that it might be an important but silent problem in
Asian communities (e.g., Dasgupta & Warrier, 1996; Ho, 1990; Huisman,
1996; Song, 1996; Yoshihama, 1999). Song (1996) studied 150 immigrant
Korean women in Chicago; 60% of the women reported being battered, and
22% experienced some form of sexual violence by their partners. Using a
population-based sample of Japanese women in Los Angeles, Yoshihama
(1999) reported a lifetime rate of physical and/or sexual violence by intimate
partners of 61%. Professionals and activists working with Asian battered
women in North America have unanimously described domestic violence
against women as an ignored, invisible, but significant problem in Asian
communities across all socioeconomic strata (Lee & Au, 1998; Lum, 1998).
There are, however, problems of underreporting as well as underutilization
of women's shelters and other social services because of cultural and/or language barriers.

CULTURAL AND CONTEXTUAL
INFLUENCES AND HELP-SEEKING
RESPONSES TO DOMESTIC VIOLENCE

Asians consist of diverse groups from different parts of Asia who come to
North America for various reasons and at different times. They consist of
but are not limited to Chinese, Filipino, Korean, Indonesian, Japanese, Ma-
laysian, Singaporean, Southeast Asian (Cambodian, Laotian, Vietnamese),
South Asian, and Thai people.

The help-seeking responses of Asians to problems of living are likely to be culturally embedded and influenced by their worldviews, interpersonal ecology, sociohistorical background, acculturation, and social learning (Yamashiro & Matsuoka, 1997). Traditional Asian culture is mostly dominated by a patriarchal ideology (Lum, 1998). Because of the higher status of men and the value placed on harmony in interpersonal relationships, Asian women are generally less likely than other women to openly challenge male behaviors. Studies regarding responses of Asian women to domestic violence have repeatedly cited "tolerance," "endurance," and "being silent" as the most common coping mechanisms by victims and survivors (Chan, 1989; Mills & Granoff, 1992; Song, 1996). Such a pattern of help-seeking responses may also be related to a general sense of fatalism derived from the Eastern philosophy of accepting the natural course of life events (e.g., the idea of Karma or the Buddhist doctrine that "all life is subject to suffering"; Yamashiro & Matsuoka, 1997).

Because of the importance of collective existence and family lineage in traditional Asian cultures, many Asians may avoid utilizing formal services for fear of shaming the family name and/or losing face (Lum, 1998). The passivity of many Asian women in response to domestic violence has to be understood within a cultural context. For Asian women influenced by traditional values, disclosing domestic violence is not just a demonstration of self-assertiveness or "saying no" to the violence. Such an act may also mean exposing weakness to outsiders, shaming the family name, violating the virtues of perseverance and endurance, challenging male supremacy, and bringing disruption to the family. So, instead of developing a "survivor mentality" (e.g., "I am a victim of domestic violence, but it is not my fault, and I deserve to be helped") as commonly understood from a feminist perspective, the woman might instead develop an "instigator mentality" (e.g., "I am the bad person who brings shame to myself or the family"; Lee & Au, 1998).

For Asian women who choose not to be silent about the abuse, their attempts to utilize professional services may be thwarted by cultural and/or language barriers, as well as a lack of knowledge about appropriate sources of help (Lum, 1998; Yoshihama, 1999). A lack of linguistic and/or cultural sensitivity on the part of mainstream service providers may also create barriers to help seeking, especially for Asian women who are newcomers or who have limited English proficiency (U.S. Commission on Civil Rights, 1992). Understanding the dilemmas encountered by Asian battered women has significant implications for developing culturally sensitive and competent services for this population.

TREATING ASIAN BATTERED WOMEN

Asian battered women in North America face tremendous pressure and many obstacles in confronting and escaping abuse; many of these obstacles are pervasive and deeply rooted in cultural values and contextual barriers. The following treatment programs and interventions have been established to assist Asian battered women to combat violence in intimate relationships.

Asian Women's Shelters

The establishment of Asian women's shelters involves the efforts of concerned Asian grassroots activists and professionals to provide culturally and linguistically sensitive services for those who cannot effectively utilize mainstream services because of cultural and language barriers. The Center for the Pacific-Asian Family at Los Angeles, founded in 1981, was the first Asian women's shelter established in the United States (CPAF, 1997). Currently, other Asian women's shelters have been established in major U.S. cities that have sizable Asian populations. These shelters provide crisis intervention, hotline services, residential services, legal services, referral services, counseling, support groups, advocacy, accompaniment services, and community education to domestic violence victims and their families. Their distinctive aspect, however, is their attempt to provide culturally and linguistically sensitive services to their clients. For instance, many of these shelters provide 24-hour Asian multilingual hotline services to assist Asian battered women who may have language barriers (e.g., AWS, 1997; CPAF, 1997; New York Asian Women's Center, 1992). Further, most shelters provide a language match between the shelter staff and battered women. In order to provide a culturally sensitive environment, some Asian women's shelters allow women to prepare ethnic food for themselves and their children. Such a minor modification assists many Asian women and their children to better adjust to their life at shelters (AACI, 1997). Besides Asian women's shelters that specifically serve Asian women, some mainstream shelters attempt to provide culturally sensitive services by hiring Asian staff (SNBW, 1997). Such a situation is more prevalent in Canada because there are no ethno-specific women's shelters. Culturally and linguistically sensitive services are provided mainly through Asian-speaking staff and interpreters.

Counseling Asian Battered Women

Similar to working with any battered woman, it is important to assure safety and stabilize clients, explore and validate feelings, listen actively and reflectively, examine coping skills, assist clients to acknowledge the abuse without blaming themselves, empower clients by exploring options and building on strengths, and help clients to develop a viable plan for the future (Roberts & Burman, 1998; Walker, 1994). If the situation is perceived to be lethal, it is important to develop a safety plan with the woman and provide the necessary assistance accordingly. Helping professionals, however, may need to attend to certain specific clinical issues and challenges when working with Asian battered women.

Assessment

Presence of spouse abuse. Asian battered women might not directly seek help for violence-related problems but instead have other complaints that are perceived as more socially and psychologically acceptable. Common complaints are somatic problems such as insomnia and headaches (Chan & Leong, 1994; Kleinman, 1982) or behavioral problems of children (Lee, 1996). Norton and Manson (1992) noted that among Southeast Asian battered women seeking help at a mental health clinic, *none* presented family violence as an issue in their initial disclosure of problems. It is important for helping professionals to consider the possibility of violence in working with Asian women even when the initial presenting problem is not spouse abuse. Some signals that warrant further exploration include clients' difficulty in identifying causes of somatic complaints or depressed feelings and clients' ambivalence in talking about couple relationships despite hints of dissatisfaction.

The intensity of the problems. As a result of the tendency to endure and tolerate abuse, the precipitating event to seeking professional help is likely to be a serious crisis for many Asian battered women. The delayed help-seeking behaviors also mean that the problem may tend to be more severe by the time it comes to the attention of helping professionals (Lee, 1996). Because of the fear of shame and losing face, and the cultural norms of self-reliance and inhibition of emotions, Asian battered women may outwardly appear to be less distressed and more reserved than to other battered women in similar situations (Lum, 1998). The discrepancy between the expressed emotionality of the victims and the severity of the abuse is an important factor to consider when working with an Asian battered woman.

Specific cultural beliefs or practices regarding problem perception and solution finding. Because cultural values influence a person's problem perception, perceived solution, and help-seeking behaviors (Green, 1995; Lee, 1996), it is important to be sensitive to culturally based dynamics in understanding the client's perception of her situation. Some useful areas to explore include the following: (1) What is the nature of the perceived problem? (2) What are the cultural values that may engender such a perception or contribute to the problem of abuse? (3) What and who are involved in the solution? Who is perceived as the expert in resolving the abuse and the related problems? (4) Is the client's perceived solution in conflict with the legal norms of society? (5) What are the client's perceived strengths and weaknesses in terms of resources, including cultural and situational barriers and resources? (6) Are there values in the client's culture that can be used as a leverage point for the client and therapist to coconstruct useful alternative solutions? For example, Asian culture places great importance on children carrying on the family lineage. Many Asian battered women sought help only after they realized the detrimental effect of spouse abuse on their children, or when the abusers started hurting their children (AWS, 1997; DCH, 1997).

Immigration-related issues. It is important to make culturally sensitive assessments when working with Asian battered women who are also immigrants. The following issues should be explored in assessment: reasons for immigration, length of stay in North America, legal or nondocumented immigration status, language abilities, contact with cultural and mainstream institutions, social life, values concerning family, relationships, and work (Congress, 1997). Such information will help the therapist to develop a contextualized understanding of the client's situation. It also provides information regarding the client's resources and strengths that can be utilized, or barriers and obstacles that need to be overcome, in the helping process.

Joining and Engagement

Because of cultural values of harmony, male superiority, collectivism, and obligation, disclosing battering problems to an "outside" helping professional is almost equivalent to shaming the family name or losing face. In addition, many Asian women have no prior experience with therapy. As such, it is of utmost importance to successfully join with the client to prevent early dropout and to establish a trustful, therapeutic relationship.

Joining with the client's dilemmas of seeking help. It is important to explicitly recognize the client's dilemmas in seeking help and normalize the emotion of shame or guilt (Sue & Sue, 1990). Opening the door for an Asian battered woman to talk about her dilemmas serves to validate her feeling of ambivalence and educate the therapist about the client's culturally embedded perception of her problems. Because of the strong fear of shaming the family name and losing face, issues of confidentiality should be communicated clearly and unambiguously to Asian clients early on in therapy.

Strengthening motivation. To reaffirm and strengthen a client's motivation, it is important to (1) discover what makes the client decide to not tolerate the situation and make an effort to seek help, (2) compliment her ability to seek help despite various obstacles, and (3) reframe her help-seeking behavior as an act congruent with cultural values. For instance, building on the traditional value of family well-being and harmony, seeking cessation of abuse can be reframed as an *other-oriented* effort to benefit the well-being of the whole family, including the children and/or the abuser (Lum, 1998).

Joining with the client's culturally embedded mode of communication. Because people from different sociocultural backgrounds will have developed diverse "comfort zones" regarding modes of social interaction and communication, helping professionals working with Asian battered women should observe and respect characteristics of both verbal and nonverbal communication styles in their clients. Because Asians tend to be more reserved and inhibited about emotions, clients should be given time and space to open up at their own pace and in a way that is comfortable for them. Lack of direct eye contact should not be misinterpreted as a symptom of avoidance or anxiety; it may be a sign of respect (Chung, 1992). Being silent or reserved does not necessarily mean resistance or unwillingness to seek help; it may be just a matter of needing more time to open up.

Imparting the structure of help. Many Asian battered women may not have prior experience with a women's shelter, therapy, or other forms of treatment. It is important for helping professionals to clearly explain to them the structure of help treatment to lessen their anxiety regarding seeking professional help. This is especially important in a women's shelter environment. In addition, it is important to educate clients about the purpose and process of therapy or treatment, services available for battered women, and their rights and responsibilities. Helping professionals should take the initiative to find out whether Asian battered women have any questions about information that has not been covered.

Tangible assistance. Asian people tend to be pragmatic and instrumental. Concrete actions, including case management services, financial support, residential services, legal services, support groups, tutoring services for children in shelters, and so forth, may be crucial in establishing a positive relationship between the client and the helping professional (Sue & Sue, 1990). Providing tangible assistance is a way to demonstrate the professional's willingness to help and his or her competence (Huang, 1991). Also, it is imperative for treatment to focus on the present and future and to be goal-oriented, with clear indicators of progress, in order to maintain the client's positive motivation (Paniagua, 1994).

Empowering Asian Battered Women

Empowering battered women to become survivors rather than victims represents a major treatment goal (Walker, 1994). Because isolation is a widely used strategy by Asian male batterers in controlling their spouses, and many Asian women also lack language skills to access useful information, educating women about their rights and the services available to them becomes an important part of the empowering process. Not replicating the dynamics of abuse, in which women are told what to do or what is best for them, it is important for helping professionals to recognize the cultural dilemma for Asian women in leaving an abusive relationship and fully respect their decisions regarding their marriages and at the same time provide them with the required assistance (AACI, 1997; CPAF, 1997). Such a process may take longer and be manifested in the women's repeated struggles of leaving and returning to the abusers. However, Asian battered women will need to rediscover and reconnect with their needs and resources in their own way and at their own pace in order to experience an empowering process that fosters an internal locus of control and a positive sense of self. Consequently, there is a greater likelihood for them to develop solutions that are appropriate to their needs and viable in their unique cultural milieu.

Couple and Family Therapy

Because of the issue of power imbalance in relationships, most feminist therapists have cautioned against using couple therapy (Walker, 1994). However, strongly influenced by the ideals of "marriage for life" and family togetherness despite adversity, couple therapy might be an appropriate form of treatment for Asians; often it was requested by both Asian men and women (CFLSMT, 1997; CSC, 1997). Couple therapy can be a viable choice of treatment when it is provided under the following conditions: (1) The woman requests couple treatment; (2) there is a cessation of violence in the relationship; and (3) the man is willing to take responsibility for the abuse (CFLSMT, 1997; UCCESS, 1997). Likewise, because traditional Asian culture is a high-context culture in which people pay great attention to the surrounding context of an event to define the appropriateness of one's behaviors (Hall, 1983), intervention at the family system level can sometimes lead to effective solutions in ending violence in intimate relationships. Kibria (1993), in studying the family life of Vietnamese Americans, suggested that social support for battered women and social pressure and stigma placed on the abusers could be effective in stopping marital violence.

As a rule of thumb, helping professionals need to consider *face-saving techniques* when involving the broader family system. Saving face is an important cultural factor in social interaction among Asian people. Face-saving techniques allow people to make beneficial changes in their habitual behaviors that may have contributed to or maintained the abuse without having to go through the negative emotional experiences associated with losing face, which can lead to defensive behaviors and massive denial of the problem. Face-saving techniques assist the couple in identifying what they can do to contribute to a violence-free relationship and what other family members can do to facilitate the desired change. The focus of face-saving techniques is on identifying, eliciting, reinforcing, expanding, and consolidating the desired change in the couple relationship. It is also important to compliment everyone's motivation and efforts in realizing the solution.

Community Education

With the high-context Asian culture, condemnation of domestic violence against women by the community will be effective in preventing violence in intimate relationships because of the social pressure created by the community against such behaviors. Educating Asian communities about the detrimental consequences of domestic violence for individuals and their children, including the legal consequences, will, in the long run, reduce its occurrence and increase community pressure on batterers to stop their abusive behaviors. In addition, Asian battered women often do not seek help because they are unaware of available services. Effective dissemination of information about domestic violence and available services constitutes helpful outreach efforts to this population. Many Asian women's shelters and ethno-specific community organizations have made community education a priority in their efforts to combat domestic violence against Asian women (e.g., AACS, 2000; AWS, 1997; CFLSMT, 1999; DCH, 1997).

CONCLUSION

Because of both cultural and contextual factors, domestic violence against women in Asian communities is largely an ignored, invisible, but important problem. Domestic violence against women is a multifaceted problem that has significance at both the individual or family and the community level. Besides providing culturally sensitive and competent counseling and support services to Asian battered women and their families, community education regarding services for victims and legal consequences of domestic violence for offenders serves an important preventive function. More important, combating domestic violence involves coordinated efforts from a multitude of service providers, including professionals at women's shelters, mental health centers, social service agencies, and police departments and in the legal/justice arena. Despite having good intentions to assist Asian battered women, these professionals may find it difficult to reach out to them because of cultural and/or language barriers, as well as a lack of knowledge about Asian communities. Some effective ways that have been used by ethno-specific service organizations to build bridges and improve networking and coordination are providing consultations and cultural competence training to mainstream organizations, providing interpreter services for clients who have language difficulties, conducting studies on Asian battered women, and organizing conferences around issues of Asian battered women to raise awareness. There is no quick and easy solution to stop violence in intimate relationships. The ultimate well-being of Asian battered women and their children, however, depends on how well the legal, criminal, mainstream, and ethno-specific service systems coordinate with each other to serve in their best interests.

REFERENCES

AACI. (1997, May 9). Personal communication, Asian Americans for Community Involvement.

AACS. (2000, April 16). Personal communication, Asian American Community Services.

AWS. (1997, May 12). Personal communication, Asian Women's Shelter.

CFLSMT. (1997, May 20). Personal communication, Chinese Family Life Services of Metropolitan Toronto.

Chan, S. L. L. (1989). *Wife assault: The Chinese Family Life Services experience.* Toronto, ON: Chinese Family Life Services of Metropolitan Toronto.

Chan, S., & Leong, C. W. (1994). Chinese families in transition: Cultural conflicts and adjustment problems. *Journal of Social Distress and the Homeless, 3,* 263–281.

Chung, D. K. (1992). Asian cultural commonalities: A comparison with mainstream American culture. In S. M. Furuto, R. Biswas, D. K. Chung, K. Murase, & F. Ross-Sheiff (Eds.), *Social work practice with Asian Americans.* Newbury Park, CA: Sage.

Congress, E. (1997). The use of culturagrams to assess and empower culturally diverse families. *Families in Society: The Journal of Contemporary Human Services, 75,* 531–540.

CPAF. (1997, June 11). Personal communication, Center for the Pacific-Asian Family.

CSC. (1997, May 22). Personal communication, Chinatown Service Center.

Dasgupta, S. D., & Warrier, S. (1996). In the footsteps of "Arundhati": Asian Indian women's experience of domestic violence in the United States. *Violence Against Women, 2,* 238–259.

DCH (1997, May 14, 21). Personal communication, Donaldina Cameron House.

Green, J. W. (1995). *Cultural awareness in the human services: A multi-ethnic approach.* Needham Heights, MA: Allyn and Bacon.

Hall, E. T. (1983). *The dance of life.* Garden City, NY: Doubleday.

Ho, C. K. (1990). An analysis of domestic violence in Asian American communities: A multicultural approach to counseling. In L. Brown & M. P. P. Roots (Eds.), *Diversity and complexity in feminist therapy* (pp. 129–150). New York: Haworth.

Huang, K. (1991). Chinese Americans. In N. Mokuau (Ed.), *Handbook of social services for Asian Americans and Pacific Islanders.* New York: Greenwood Press.

Huisman, K. A. (1996). Wife battering in Asian American communities. *Violence Against Women, 2,* 260–283.

Kanuha, V. (1994). Women of color in battering relationship. In L. Comas-Diaz & B. Greene (Eds.), *Women of color* (pp. 428–454). New York: Guilford.

Kibria, N. (1993). *Family tightrope: The changing lives of Vietnamese Americans.* Princeton, NJ: Princeton University Press.

Kleinman, A. (1982). Neurasthenia and depression: A study of somatization and culture in China. *Culture, Medicine and Psychiatry, 6,* 117–190.

Lee, E. (Ed.). (1997). *Working with Asian Americans: A guide for clinicians.* New York: Guilford.

Lee, L. C., & Zane, N. W. S. (Eds.). (1998). *Handbook of Asian American psychology.* Thousand Oaks, CA: Sage.

Lee, M. Y. (1996). A constructivist approach to the help-seeking process of clients: A response to cultural diversity. *Clinical Social Work Journal, 24,* 187–202

Lee, M. Y., & Au, P. (1998). Chinese women in North America: Their experiences and treatment. In A. R. Roberts (Ed.), *Battered women and their families* (pp. 448–482). New York: Springer.

Lum, J. (1998). Family violence. In L. C. Lee & N. W. S. Zane (Eds.), *Handbook of Asian American psychology* (pp. 505–525). Thousand Oaks, CA: Sage.

Marsella, A. J., DeVos, G., & Hsu, F. L. K. (Eds.). (1985). *Culture and self: Asian and Western perspectives.* New York: Tavistock.

Mills, C. S., & Granoff, B. J. (1992). Date and acquaintance rape among a sample of college students. *Social Work, 37,* 504–509.

Mokuau, N. (Ed.). *Handbook of social services for Asian Americans and Pa-*

cific Islanders. New York: Green-wood.

New York Asian Women's Center. (1992). *New York Asian Women's Center: Tenth anniversary report 1982–1992.* New York: Author.

Norton, I. M., & Manson, S. M. (1992). An association between domestic violence and depression among Southeast Asian refugee women. *Journal of Nervous and Mental Disease, 180,* 729–730.

Paniagua, F. A. (1994). *Assessing and treating culturally diverse clients: A practical guide.* Thousand Oaks, CA: Sage.

Roberts, A. R. (Ed.). (1998). *Battered women and their families.* New York: Springer.

Roberts, A. R., & Burman, S. (1998). Crisis intervention and cognitive problem-solving therapy with battered women: A national survey and practice model. In A. R. Roberts (Ed.), *Battered women and their families* (pp. 3–28). New York: Springer.

SNBW. (1997, May 9). Personal communication, Support Network for Battered Women.

Song, Y. I. (1996). *Battered women in Korean immigrant families.* New York: Garland.

Sue, D. W., & Sue, D. (1990). *Counseling the culturally different: Theory and practice.* New York: Wiley.

Tjaden, P., & Thoennes, N. (1998, November). *Prevalence, incidence, and consequences of violence against women: Findings from the National Violence Against Women Survey.* National Institute of Justice, Research in Brief. Washington, DC: U.S. Department of Justice.

UCCESS. (1997, May 13). Personal communication. Vancouver, BC: United Chinese Community Enrichment Services Society.

U.S. Commission on Civil Rights. (1992, February). The plight of battered Asian American women. In *Civil rights issues facing Asian Americans in the 1990s* (pp. 174–180). Washington, DC: Author.

U.S. Department of Commerce. (1998). *Statistical abstract of the United States, 1998: The national data book* (118th ed.). Springfield, VA: National Technical Information Services.

U.S. Department of Justice. (1996, April). *Criminal victimization 1994: National Crime Victimization Survey.* NCJ-158022. Washington, DC: Author.

Walker, L. (1994). *Abused women and survivor therapy: A practical guide for the psychotherapist.* Washington, DC: American Psychological Association.

Yamashiro, G., & Matsuoka, J. K. (1997). Help-seeking among Asian and Pacific Americans: A multiperspective analysis. *Social Work, 42,* 176–186.

Yoshihama, M. (1999). Domestic violence against women of Japanese descent in Los Angeles: Two methods of estimating prevalence. *Violence Against Women, 5,* 896–897.

23

Elder Abuse and Gerontological Social Work

PATRICIA BROWNELL

Case Scenarios

Spouse

Mr. and Mrs. M. are both 90 years old. Mr. M., now retired, was a manual laborer and is in excellent health. Mrs. M. has a heart condition and is physically frail and emotionally depressed. Both refuse home care beyond the 28 hours a week of home health care funded by Medicare, in spite of the around-the-clock care needs of Mrs. M., which Mr. M. provides. One afternoon Mr. M. gets drunk and beats up Mrs. M. in the front yard, where the neighbors can witness it. An ambulance is called, and Mrs. M. is hospitalized. She claims not to remember the abuse incident and refuses to prosecute her husband.

Adult Child

John P., age 35, threatens his father, Mr. P., in order to obtain his signature on a check for $5,000, which the son uses to buy drugs. On prior occasions, John has stolen money and possessions from his parents, who provide him with board and room and care for him when he returns from prison or drug rehabilitation. Mr. and Mrs. P. are encouraged to sustain this relationship by John's substance abuse counselors, who view them as a resource for John in the community.

Caregiver

Maddy, a private home attendant, moves in with her client, Mrs. G., a widow who has Alzheimer's disease. Maddy is accompanied by her adult daughter. They obtain Mrs. G.'s bankcard and take her jewelry. Mrs. G. states that she gave them the bank card and valuables voluntarily.

Adult Daughter and Son-in-Law

Samantha and her husband, Peter B., do not insist that Samantha's elderly parents, Mr. and Mrs. T., get in-home assistance even though they can afford it. The older Mr. and Mrs. T. have both been showing signs of dementia, and the manager of their condominium has expressed concerns about their safety. The adult children claim to be trying to respect the wishes and autonomy of their parents.

PURPOSE OF CHAPTER

The purpose of this chapter is to provide an overview of elder abuse and neglect, including the scope of this social problem; definitions, profiles, and causative theories of abuse; assessment, detection, and intervention strategies; mistreatment involving special populations; and current and future issues of concern. The role of the professional social worker will be emphasized throughout.

SCOPE OF PROBLEM AND THE ROLE OF THE GERONTOLOGICAL SOCIAL WORKER

According to demographic projections by the U.S. Census Bureau, as many as 60.8 million Americans will be 65 years of age or older by the year 2025 (Koff & Park, 1999). The good news is that this increase is generated by the aging of the baby boomers, the large post–WWII cohort born between 1946 and 1964, acknowledged to be among the most educated, affluent, and health-conscious cohort of elders the world has ever seen. Gerontological social workers will enjoy unprecedented opportunities to engage older adults in enhancing the quality of their postretirement lives through innovative senior center programs, stimulating educational activities, and exciting senior volunteering opportunities.

However, the increasing longevity of Americans results in vulnerabilities as well. The Census Bureau projects that by 2025 there will be 25.1 million Americans at least 75 years of age and more than 6 million who will be 85 years or older (Koff & Park, 1999). Minority elders are projected to constitute a growing proportion of the older population. The old-old (age 85 years and older) are known to be especially vulnerable to elder abuse and neglect due to increased frailty and care needs, and little research has been done on the risks faced by older members of minority groups. In addition, there has been growing recognition of the problem of elder abuse during the past 20 years, according to Dr. Rosalie Wolf, president of the National Committee for the Prevention of Elder Abuse and Neglect and a leading expert on elder abuse (personal communication, May 1988; November 2000). Studies to date have demonstrated a 3 to 12 per 1,000 prevalence rate of elder abuse among adults 60 years of age and older (Pillemer & Finkelhor, 1988; U.S. House of Representatives, 1990). A recent national study on elder abuse in the United States found an incidence rate of 1.2% (Thomas, 2000). Given the hidden nature of domestic violence, this is thought to be greatly under stated. With the projected increase of older adults in the United States, the number of elder abuse situations can be expected to increase as well.

Because of the complex nature of elder abuse, the emotional dynamics linking victim and abuser, and the multiple service systems that must be engaged to ensure a successful service plan, social workers are the professionals who are best equipped to address this social problem. This is because professional social workers have expertise in practice with families and individuals, experience in working as part of interdisciplinary teams, knowledge of service systems and how to engage them on behalf of clients, and skill in identifying service needs and advocating for new policies and programs. Social workers are also employed in many different agency and institutional settings, where they may come into contact with elder abuse and neglect (Brownell, 2000).

With increasing numbers of older adults enjoying extended longevity, gerontological social work is coming into its own as an important field of practice. Understanding policy and practice pertaining to elder abuse is essential for all social workers engaged in working with older adults and their families.

DEFINITIONS OF ELDER ABUSE AND NEGLECT

The most commonly used definitions of elder abuse and neglect include physical, psychological, financial, and active (or intentional) and passive (or unintentional) neglect (Wolf & Pillemer, 1984). Elder abuse and neglect are categorized according to the behaviors of the abuser, the intent of the abuser, and the perceptions and to some extent the decisional capacity and health status of the victim. According to Wolf and Pillemer, these include the following:

- Physical abuse: the infliction of physical pain or injury; physical coercion (confinement against one's will). Behaviors associated with physical abuse include slaps, bruising, sexual molestation, cuts, burns, and physical restraints.

- Psychological abuse: the infliction of mental anguish. Behaviors associated with psychological abuse include name-calling, infantilizing, frightening, humiliating, intimidating, threatening, and isolating.
- Financial abuse: the illegal or improper exploitation and/or use of funds or other resources. Examples include stealing possessions or money, embezzling stocks, and manipulating or intimidating the victim to give up possessions or money.
- Active neglect: refusal or failure to fulfill a caretaking obligation, including a conscious and intentional attempt to inflict physical or emotional distress on the elderly victim. Behaviors associated with this form of abuse include deliberately abandoning a care-dependent older adult or deliberately withholding food or health-related services.
- Passive neglect: refusal or failure to fulfill a caregiving obligation excluding a conscious and intentional attempt to inflict physical or emotional distress on the elder. Behaviors associated with this form of elder abuse are consistent with behaviors associated with active neglect, but they are perpetrated by abusers who lack the knowledge, ability, or capacity to fulfill caregiving responsibilities.

PROFILES OF ELDER ABUSE AND NEGLECT

Elder abuse as a form of domestic violence by definition includes victims and perpetrators (unless the definition is expanded to include self-neglect). Understanding all possible relationships between the victim and the abuser, as well as the emotional dynamics involved, is essential to the detection, assessment, and intervention process. Profiles of abuse can include spouse or partner abuse, adult children, dependent grandchildren, and formal and informal caregivers, as well as strangers who prey on the loneliness and vulnerability of the elderly. Elder abuse and mistreatment as a form of domestic violence suggest the involvement of at least one family member or significant other. Abuse and neglect can be perpetrated against older adults by formal caregivers in community and institutional settings.

A number of theoretical explanations for elder abuse and neglect have been proposed. The following is a partial listing:

- Aging-out spouse abuse: Abusive behavior by one spouse or partner toward the other may have been a long-term constant in the relationship, and now the victim and possibly the abuser have passed their 60th birthdays (Brandl, 2000).
- Victim impairment: The victim may self-neglect or abuse, refuse all needed services because of lack of insight into need or capacity to care for self, or become vulnerable to abuse through choice of companions or lack of self-protection (Dick-Muehlke, Yang, Yu, & Paul, 1996).

- Caregiver stress: Abuse may be perpetrated by an overwhelmed or unprepared caregiver. The caregiver may be a spouse, an adult child or other relative, or a formal caregiver such as a nurse or home health aide (Anetzberger, 2000).
- Abuser impairment: The abuser is physically and/or mentally impaired. Mental illness, dementia, developmental disability, and/or substance abuse may be a factor (Brownell, Berman, & Salamone, 1999; Ramsey-Klawsnik, 2000).
- Abuser criminality: Abusive behavior may be perpetrated by a stranger or criminal with the intent to defraud the victim or gain from the victim's distress (Brownell, 1998; Heisler, 2000).

For the helping professional, an awareness of the older person's lifestyle, care needs, decisional capacity, and immediate and extended family situation is important in assessing the degree of risk for abuse or neglect to which the older person may be subject.

CATEGORIES OF ELDER ABUSE

With the exception of self-abuse and neglect, elder abuse and mistreatment always include a victim (who must be at least 60 years of age) and an abuser. Elder abuse and mistreatment can be further explained by breaking them down into several categories.

Domestic Violence (Family Maltreatment)

Elder abuse as a form of domestic violence involves a victim and an abuser who have an informal or intimate relationship. Examples include spouses or partners; parents or grandparents and adult children or grandchildren; siblings; aunt/uncle and nieces/nephews; or friends/significant others. The victim may be care-dependent or may be the caregiver of the abuser. Behaviors of family members and significant others that are defined as elder abuse or mistreatment may or may not constitute a crime. For example, adult children are not legally responsible for parents in many states. Failure to provide needed services to a care-dependent adult parent, as long as this does not involve misappropriation of the parent's funds, is not a crime, unless codified in state law and regulation. Neither is psychological abuse such as yelling, infantilizing, or threatening a care-dependent older adult with placement in a nursing home. On the other hand, subjecting or threatening to subject an older adult to bodily harm, stealing, and sexual abuse are examples of forms of elder abuse that are defined as crimes by most state penal codes and can subject the perpetrator to arrest and prosecution.

Institutional Abuse

Elder abuse as a form of institutional abuse involves a care-dependent victim and an abusive formal caregiver (e.g., nurse's aide, nurse, home health aide). Institutional abuse can occur in a nursing home, hospital, or the victim's home, with the abuser part of a formal care system. Depending on the severity of the neglect or mistreatment of a care-dependent older adult by a formal caregiver, the abuse or neglect may constitute a criminal offense. Most state laws mandate reporting of any suspected or actual abuse or neglect of a formal caregiver against a care-dependent older adult to the state department of health. Perpetrators may be subject to criminal investigation, prosecution, fines, and loss of license to practice.

Stranger Crime

Elder abuse can also occur in the form of a crime committed against an adult aged 60 or older by someone not related or even known to the victim. Examples are mail fraud and other scams, robberies and burglaries, and extortion. While any crime against an older adult may result in arrest and prosecution of the perpetrator, some offenses are extremely difficult to prosecute. For example, in mortgage scams, a contractor may convince an older adult to sign a second mortgage to cover home repairs; if the other adult subsequently becomes unable to cover the monthly payments, he or she may lose the home. If the older adult was mentally competent when he or she signed the mortgage agreement, this may not be a prosecutable offense.

ASSESSMENT, DETECTION, AND INTERVENTION STRATEGIES

The helping professional should be alert to the possibility and risk of elder abuse and neglect when serving older adults in social service or health care settings. In addition, they should be knowledgeable about assessment criteria and techniques. According to Breckman and Abelman (1988), a good assessment requires the professional to gather six categories of information from the client or patient. These include safety, access, cognitive status, emotional status, health and functional status, and social and financial resources. Additional categories are patterns of abuse and cultural beliefs, traditions, and immigration history.

Detection: What Are Signs and Symptoms of Elder Abuse and Neglect?

As noted earlier, elder abuse is often defined as physical, psychological or emotional, financial abuse, and intentional or unintentional. Elder abuse is further defined in accordance with behaviors or acts on the part of the perpetrator. In conducting a preliminary assessment of whether an older adult may be the victim of elder abuse, a social worker should be alert to signs and symptoms that may suggest a problem.

Physical

- Bruises, welts, scratches, burns, fractures, lacerations, or punctures
- Bleeding under the scalp or missing patches of hair
- Signs of excessive or insufficient medication (agitation or decreased alertness)
- Missing eyeglasses, dentures, hearing aids
- Dehydration
- Decubitus ulcers (pressure sores); signs of restraints like rope burns
- Soiled clothing or poor hygiene
- Unexplained genital infections or venereal disease (sexual abuse)

Psychological

- Sleep disturbances
- Change in eating patterns
- Unexplained weight changes
- Depression and crying
- Paranoid references
- Low self-esteem
- Extreme fearfulness
- Confusion and disorientation
- Apathy or agitation

Financial

- Complaints of hunger or lack of food
- Unexplained inability to pay bills
- Overinvolvement of family member in client's financial affairs
- Refusal of client or caregiver to pay for needed assistance, even though finances appear to be adequate
- Unexplained withdrawals from bank account.

Caution should be taken in interpreting any of these signs and symptoms of abuse, however. Particularly in older patients with Alzheimer's disease, dementia, or clinical depression, many of these indicators of abuse or neglect resemble symptoms of other problems. A thorough psychosocial assessment is necessary to determine whether abuse or neglect is involved and, if so, whether it is intentional or unintentional on the part of the abuser or caregiver. Even if the client is not experiencing active abuse or neglect, the presence of any of these signs and symptoms of abuse can suggest a vulnerability to abuse or exploitation, and preventive services should be considered.

Assessment: Is Elder Abuse a Factor, and What Is the Level of Risk to the Victim?

An assessment of elder abuse and neglect should take into consideration a number of factors. Does the cognitive capacity of the client suggest an empowerment or protective strategy? Is the client at imminent risk of harm? How can the client's autonomy and self-determination be taken into consideration? How best can the needs and capacity of the client be balanced against the needs and capacity of the family or formal caregiving system? A good assessment should include the following components.

Safety

A safety assessment is essential in any situation in which elder abuse or neglect is suspected. Questions that should be asked include: Is the person in immediate danger? Does the person understand the risks and consequences of decisions concerning safety? What steps can be taken to increase safety?

- Is the client in immediate danger?
- Who has access to the client's household?
- Are there family members or friends who can serve in a protective capacity?
- What about the potential for abusive behavior?

Access

Helping professionals should ensure that they or others have access to the person who may be at risk of elder abuse or neglect. Questions to ask include: Are there barriers preventing access to the victim in case of danger? Can a trusted family member or friend assist if necessary? Is the victim or suspected victim a candidate for adult protective services or legal advocacy services?

- Is client or a family member seeking to prevent an investigation or assessment of the client's safety?

Cognitive Status

Assessment of the cognitive status of a victim or suspected victim is critical because adults (including older adults) have the right to self-determination unless they are suspected or found to be sufficiently cognitively impaired to preclude their ability to protect themselves from harm. Questions that should be asked include: Does the victim or suspected victim show evidence of dementia or other impairment? If cognitive impairment is present, is it the result of a reversible health or mental health condition, or is it related to organic causes and irreversible? Is it severe enough to impair decision-making capacity?

- To what extent does the client's impairment render him or her unable to understand the possible risks or consequences of his or her situation?
- To what extent does the client's impairment render him or her unable to reliably report on his or her circumstances?

Emotional Status

Helping professionals assessing the risk of elder abuse and neglect should evaluate the emotional status of the actual or suspected victim. First, cognitive impairment should be ruled out if evidence of emotional distress is identified. Second, the presence of emotional distress should be assessed and explored. Questions that should be asked include: Does the older adult appear to be depressed, ashamed, guilty, fearful, and/or angry? Is he or she reluctant to discuss the possibility of abuse or neglect, in spite of evidence that this may be occurring? Does he or she rationalize or dismiss family tension or conflict?

- Does the client manifest depression, paranoia, fear, or anxiety? To what extent can this be explained by the disease stage?
- Does the client show evidence of denial? To what extent is this related to the disease stage?

Health and Functional Capacity

The presence of medical problems should be explored, and a determination made as to whether mistreatment could have caused or exacerbated them. Related issues to be explored include the extent to which the older person requires assistance with activities of daily living, and, if so, who provides it. It is important to note whether a caregiver has the ability (emotional, cognitive, intellectual, and financial) to provide this care in a responsible way. A good assessment by a helping professional should also explore any physical or cognitive limitations that may limit potential victims' ability to protect themselves.

- Could mistreatment cause or exacerbate existing medical conditions?
- Is the client capable of self-protecting?

Social and Financial Resources

Assessing social and financial resources for the older person is one of the most important and difficult tasks of a helping professional. In instances of possible family maltreatment, the perpetrator is by definition part of the victim's social network. Often both the victim and the perpetrator share a strong incentive to conceal the abuse. Financial resources may be insufficient to buffer the victim against maltreatment. Rather, they may provide an incentive for financial abuse by an unscrupulous or needy abuser. Some older people may become unnecessarily frugal—due to cognitive impairments or because of an exaggerated fear of impoverishment—and family members may feel constrained from insisting that the older person spend down his or her assets unwillingly. Helping professionals should take care not to jump to the conclusion that these family members are intentionally withholding needed services from the older person, although this in fact may be the case. It is especially important to assess family members and significant others living with the older person or having access to the household. Impaired family members and significant others represent a high risk even for an unimpaired older person, and their presence and any social or health problems they may have should be noted.

- Does the client have family members, friends, or formal supports who provide reliable care?
- Does the client have sufficient financial resources?
- Do family members interact with the client in a manner that is consistent with their cultural values?
- Are there any family members or others with access to the client's home who are mentally ill, substance abusers, or have a history of criminal behavior?
- Are the designated caregivers for the client capable of providing and willing to provide the level of care necessary for the client's well-being?

Client Attributes

While studies of elder abuse and mistreatment have reported mixed findings about the characteristics of elder abuse victims that predict abuse or mistreatment by others, some client attributes have been found to pose a risk or vulnerability for abuse or exploitation (Baxter & Schroeder, 1996; Hamel et al., 1990).

- Is the client abusive or violent?
- Does the client exhibit behaviors such as repeated questioning, extreme clinging, incessant talking, extreme passivity, or constant moving and wandering?
- Does the client have a history of being abused or mistreated?
- Does the client have friends or companions apart from family members?
- Is the client a substance abuser?
- Is the client a caregiver for an impaired or dependent family member?

Pattern of Abuse

Any assessment of elder abuse, neglect, or maltreatment should include an evaluation of the frequency and intensity of the abuse, as well as the intent of the abuser. It is also important to note whether the abuse has increased in frequency and severity over time. Some studies on younger spouse abuse and child abuse suggest that abuse can escalate over time; however, elder abuse may be more chronic and persistent and still have a negative effect on the health and quality of life of the older victim. The intent of the abuser is important to note because this information can help to determine the appropriate intervention. For example, abuse perpetrated by a spouse in the secondary stage of Alzheimer's disease would suggest a different intervention strategy than abuse perpetrated by a substance-abusing grandchild.

- Has abuse intensified or become more frequent over time?
- Is the perpetrator aware that the behavior in question can be categorized as abusive?

Cultural Beliefs, Traditions, and Immigration History

An emergent area of concern is that of the impact of culture and ethnicity on domestic violence. Congress (1994, 2001) presents a model form, the *culturagram*, which can be used by helping professionals to assess a client's cultural beliefs, traditions, and immigration history. This form can be used to assess the risk and impact of elder abuse and maltreatment on a family, based on the family's cultural background and degree of acculturation (Brownell, 1997). For example, an older parent who is a recent immigrant sponsored by an adult son or daughter may be expected to serve family members by cooking, cleaning, caring for grandchildren, and generally behaving like a servant. This may be viewed by the adult children as justified repayment for board and room but be experienced by the elder parent as exploitation, humiliation, and abuse. For a broader discussion and additional examples, see Brownell (1997).

- Is the abusive behavior considered normative in the victim's culture of origin?
- Is the behavior of the perpetrator considered normative by the victim but aberrant by others?
- Is the behavior considered aberrant in the victim's country of origin but normative in the United States?

Intervention Strategies: What Are the Most Effective Strategies for Ensuring the Safety and Well-Being of Older Adults at Risk of or Experiencing Abuse or Neglect?

Planning and implementing effective intervention strategies for elder abuse and neglect requires multifaceted assessments that incorporate the dimensions outlined earlier. Three main categories of interventions are social services, health and mental health services, and use of the legal and criminal justice system. While these categories are not mutually exclusive, decisions about which option to use depend on a number of factors, including the mental and physical characteristics of both the victim and the abuser, the preference of the victim and the intent of the abuser, and whether the abusive act or acts meet the standard of a crime as defined by the New York State penal code. It is essential that all phases of this process include environmental as well as client assessments. Categories of intervention include the following:

- Prevention
- Protection: adult protective services; case management
- Counseling and treatment
- Respite and assistance
- Empowerment: education and training
- Law enforcement and courts
- Living arrangements

Is the Client at Risk of Abuse or Neglect but Not Currently Experiencing This Problem?

Older adults can protect themselves from abuse, maltreatment, and exploitation. Learning to avoid falling victim to scams is important. Refusing to provide housing or resources for substance-abusing or dangerously mentally ill relatives is another. Ensuring that sufficient in-home assistance is available to avoid overstressing available caregivers or ensuring the care of potentially abusive dependent relatives is also important. In New York City, the Elderly Crime Victims Resource Center of the Department for the Aging is a good resource for information on protection from elder abuse, as is the state attorney general's office.

Assessing the cognitive capacity of an older adult at risk of abuse or exploitation is essential. Like adults of any age, older adults have the right to make decisions about their lives that may seem to reflect poor judgment, unless they are suspected of lacking the capacity to make an informed decision or being unable to understand the consequences of their decisions. Assessments by adult protective services that reveal the need for involuntary intervention are important. However, the unimpaired older adult who refuses services may need to be called or monitored until he or she is ready to make changes to ensure better protection from harm.

Are Adult Protective Services Appropriate?

- Is the client willing to accept services voluntarily, and does he or she still have sufficient cognitive capacity for informed consent? Arrange for appropriate services.

- Is the client unwilling to accept services voluntarily, and does he or she still have sufficient cognitive capacity for informed consent? Educate and seek negotiated consent.
- Does the client lack capacity? Consider financial management, guardianship, special court proceedings with adult protective services or a relative who can be trusted and engaged in this process.

Is There a Need for Caregiver Support?

- Is the caregiver amenable to joining a support group, receiving meals on wheels, or accepting formal supports?
- Is the caregiver willing to consider therapy?
- Is the caregiver willing to consider respite services?

Does the Caregiver Have Impairment?

- Is the caregiver willing to obtain counseling or substance abuse or mental health treatment or to participate in a batterers' group?
- Is the caregiver willing to limit contact with the client?
- Is the caregiver willing to apply for financial support?
- Is the behavior of the caregiver toward the client such that involvement with the criminal justice system is warranted?

Social Service Interventions

One important intervention strategy for older adults who may have risk factors such as impaired cognition, inadequate social supports, and a history of abuse or exploitation, but are not currently being victimized, is prevention.

Examples of social services that are available for victims of elder abuse include the following:

- Adult protective services for victims (and/or perpetrators) who are cognitively or physically impaired and are unable to protect themselves from harm, lack capacity to understand the consequences of decisions can put them at risk of harm, and are a danger to themselves or others.
- Community-based services for people aged 60 and older, funded through the Older Americans Act and supplementary funding, and provided by not-for-profit or area aging agencies
- Victim services that provide counseling for crime victims, either in the community or in the courts, and batterers' programs for perpetrators of abuse; social services can include concrete services such as changing broken locks and providing emergency funds for food and rent

Health and Mental Health Interventions

- Medical and mental health (including substance abuse) services for older victims of abuse who require treatment for medical or mental health conditions that precede or result from abuse

- Medical and mental health (including substance abuse) services for impaired perpetrators of abuse
- Home health and nursing care for victims of abuse who choose to stay in their homes but remain at risk of abuse or exploitation

Legal and Criminal Justice Interventions

- Guardianships and power of attorney for victims who are at risk of exploitation and lack capacity to manage their finances or protect themselves from harm
- Orders of protection to enable law enforcement personnel to arrest abusers if they threaten victims
- Police, district attorneys, and services of the state attorney general for older people who fall victim to scams and other nonfamilial forms of exploitation; types of crimes committed by family members, significant others, and strangers that can be prosecuted in New York State include assaults, menacing, burglary, trespassing, robbery, rape, and larceny

ASSISTING THE BATTERER

Domestic violence advocates often resist the option of providing services to the batterer, on the grounds that finite resources should be targeted to the victim. In cases of elder abuse and neglect, however, it often is necessary to assist the abuser to ensure that the victim will accept services. Particularly in the case of an impaired abuser, studies have demonstrated that an older victim is often very protective of his or her abuser if that person is an impaired adult child, grandchild, or spouse or partner (Brownell & Berman, 2000).

CONCLUSION

All forms of domestic violence are difficult to address. Elder abuse is an exceptionally complex social problem because of the diversity of older adults, in terms of financial, health, and mental health status, family and partner relations, cultural traditions, and living arrangements. While mandatory reporting laws in most states are based on a perceived parallel between child and elder abuse, legal distinctions between the status of children and adults in society call into question the application of a mandatory reporting system based solely on the age of the adult.

At the same time, the Older Americans Act mandates state and area aging agencies to offer services to adults aged 60 and older who may be experiencing abuse or mistreatment by a family member or significant other. State social service and mental hygiene laws mandate county-based adult protective service (APS) agencies to provide assessment and case management services to adults aged 18 and older, living in the community, who appear to be at imminent risk of harm from which they are unable to protect themselves due to mental or physical impairments. APS agencies can intervene in these situations on an involuntary basis if necessary. For frail older adults living in nursing homes and receiving formal caregiving services, state laws mandate reporting of suspected elder abuse and neglect to state departments of health. The criminal justice system provides intervention opportunities for elder abuse situations that rise to the level of a crime as defined by state penal codes.

Elder abuse is usually categorized as financial or material abuse or exploitation, emotional or psychological mistreatment, physical abuse, or intentional or unintentional neglect. Perpetrators of elder abuse can include spouses or partners, adult children, grandchildren and other relatives, and neighbors and friends, as well as formal caregivers. While the stereotype of the typical elder abuse situation involves a frail, dependent elderly victim and an opportunistic or unfeeling caregiver, social workers experienced in working with elder abuse victims and their families know that the picture can be much more complicated. Often, elder victims are caregivers for impaired and dependent abusers, such as elderly spouses or partners who are alcoholics or suffer from dementia, or adult children with substance abuse or mental health problems. Impaired elderly victims can also be dependent on their abusers for valued services that enable them to remain in their own homes. Even unimpaired elder abuse victims can be deeply attached to abusers who are family members and loved ones, making interventions that seek to separate victims and abusers difficult to carry out.

Elder abuse is a complex phenomenon, and any actual or suspected case of elder abuse must be assessed before an intervention strategy is formulated and initiated. By remaining alert to the possibility of abuse, social workers can improve the safety and well-being of the older clients they serve.

REFERENCES

Anetzberger, G. J. (2000). Caregiving: Primary cause of elder abuse? *Generations,* Summer, 46–51.

Baladerian, N. J. (1998). Recognizing abuse and neglect in people with severe cognitive and/or communication disorders. In *Understanding and combating elder abuse in minority communities* (pp. 214–218). Irvine, CA: Archstone Foundation.

Baxter, E. C., & Schroeder, J. E. (1996). Persons with dementia: At-risk and vulnerable. In *Silent suffering: Elder abuse in America* (pp. 124–128). Irvine, CA: Archstone Foundation.

Bitondo, C., & Goins, A. M. (2000). The role of the interdisciplinary geriatric assessment in addressing self-neglect of the elderly. *Generations,* 24 (11), 23–27.

Brandl, B. (2000). Power and control: understanding domestic violence in later life. *Generations, 24,* 11, 39–45.

Breckman, R., & Adelman, R. (1988). *Strategies for helping victims of elder mistreatment.* Newbury Park, CA: Sage.

Brownell, P. (1997). The application of the culturagram in cross-cultural practice with elder abuse victims. *Journal of Elder Abuse and Neglect, 9*(2), 19–33.

Brownell, P. (1998). *Family crimes against the elderly: Elder abuse and the criminal justice system.* New York: Garland.

Brownell, P. (2000). *Elder abuse: A challenge for gerontological social work in the new millennium.* Update: Newsletter of the New York State Chapter of the National Association of Social Work, Special Issue on Aging and Social Work, New York: NASW.

Brownell, P., & Berman, J. (2000). The risks of caregiving: Abuse within the relationship. In C. Cox (Ed.), *To grandmother's house we go and stay* (pp. 91–101). New York: Springer.

Brownell, P., Berman, J., & Salamone, A. (1999). Mental health and criminal justice issues among perpetrators of elder abuse. *Journal of Elder Abuse and Neglect, 11*(4), 81–94.

Buttell, F. P. (1999). The relationship between spouse abuse and maltreatment of dementia sufferers by their caregivers. *American Society of Alzheimer's Disease, 14*(4), 230–232.

Congress, E. P. (1994). The used culturagrams to access and empower culturally diverse families. *Families in Society, 75*(9), 531–540.

Congress, E. P. (2001). Ethical issues in work with culturally diverse children and their families. In Webb, N. B. (Ed.), *Culturally diverse parent-child and family relationships* (pp. 29–53).

New York: Columbia University Press.

Dick-Muehlke, C., Yang, J. A., Yu, D., & Paul, D. M. (1996). Abuse of cognitively impaired elders: Recognition and intervention. In *Silent suffering: Elder abuse in America* (pp. 129–139). Irvine, CA: Archstone Foundation.

Fulmer, T., & O'Malley, T. A. (1987). *Inadequate care of the elderly: A health care perspective on abuse and neglect.* New York: Springer.

Fulmer, T., Ramirez, M., Fairchild, S., Holmes, D., Koren, M. J., & Teresi, J. (1999). Prevalence of elder mistreatment as reported by social workers in a probability sample of adult day health care clients. *Journal of Elder Abuse and Neglect, 11*(3), 25–36.

Hamel, M., Gold, D. P., Andres, D., Reis, M., Dastoor, D., Grauer, H., & Bergman, H. (1990). Predictions and consequences of aggressive behavior by community-based dementia patients. *Gerontologist, 30*(2), 206–211.

Hasselkus, B. R. (1997). Everyday ethics in dementia day care: Narratives of crossing the line. *Gerontologist, 37*(5), 640–649.

Heisler, C. J. (2000). Elder abuse and the criminal justice system: New awareness, new responses. *Generations, 24*(11), 52–58.

Johnson, T. F. (2000). Ethics in addressing mistreatment of elders: Do we have ethics for all? *Generations, 24*(11), 81–92.

Koff, T. H., & Park, R. W. (1999). *Aging public policy: Bonding the generations.* Amityville, NY: Baywood.

Lyman, K. A. (1989). Day care for persons with dementia: The impact of the physical environment on staff stress and quality of care. *Gerontologist, 29,* 557–560.

Moon, A. (2000). Perceptions of elder abuse among various cultural groups: Similarities and differences. *Generations, 24*(11), 75–80.

Ott, J. M. (2000). The role of adult protective services in addressing abuse. *Generations, 24*(11), 33–38.

Paveza, G. J., Cohen, D., Eisendorfer, C., Freels, S., Semla, T., Ashford, J. W., Gorelick, P., Hirschman, R., Luchins, D., & Levy, P. (1992). Severe family violence and Alzheimer's disease: Prevalence and risk factors. *Gerontologist, 32,* 493–497.

Pearlin, L. I., Mullan, J. T., Semple, S. J., & Skaff, M. M. (1990). Caregiving and the stress process: Overview of concepts and their measures. *Gerontologist, 30*(5), 583–594.

Pillemer, K., & Finkelhor, D. (1988). The prevalence of elder abuse: A random sample survey. *Gerontologist, 28*(1), 51–57.

Quinn, M. J., & Tomita, S. K. (1997). *Elder abuse and neglect: Causes, diagnosis, and intervention strategies* (2nd ed.). New York: Springer.

Ramsey-Klawsnik, H. (2000). Elder-abuse offenders: A typology. *Generations, 24*(11), 17–22.

Reis, M. (2000). The abuse-alert measure that dispels myths. *Generations, 24*(11), 13–16.

Reis, M., & Nahmiash, D. (1998). Validation of the indicators of abuse (IOA) screen. *Gerontologist, 38,* 471–480.

Teresi, J. A., Holmes, D., Dichter, E., Koren, M. J., Ramirez, M., & Fairchild, S. (1997). Prevalence of behavior disorder and disturbance to family and staff in a sample of adult day health care clients. *Gerontologist, 37,* 629–639.

Thomas, C. (2000). The first national study of elder abuse and neglect: Contrast with results from other studies. *Journal of Elder Abuse and Neglect, 12*(1), 2000, 1–14.

U.S. House of Representatives. (1990). *Elder abuse: A decade of shame and inaction.* Washington, D.C.: U.S. Government Printing Office, No. 101–752.

Wolf, R. S., & Pillemer, K. (1984). *Definitions of elder abuse and neglect.* New York: New York City Elder Abuse Coalition.

Name Index

Subject Index

hostage syndrome. *See* Stockholm syndrome
host homes, 17, 18
hotlines, victim, 38, 93, 366, 380–84
for Asian battered women, 475
for battered lesbians, 459
early history of, 17, 18
House of Ruth (Baltimore, Md.), 40
House Select Committee on Aging), 16
housing issues, 16, 18, 259, 374, 414
Houston (Tex.) Police Department, 376, 377
Hull House Domestic Violence Court Advocacy Project (Chicago), 136
hypertension, 261
hypnosis, as battering treatment, 312

Ibn-Tamas v. United States, 248n.1
Idaho, 208
identification (crisis intervention step), 263, 270
ideology, batterer intervention evaluation and, 432–33
IES. *See* Impact of Events Scale
Illinois, 136, 208, 221
immigrants, 466, 468, 477, 493
Violence Against Women Act and, 193
Immigration and Human Rights Clinic (St. Mary's Law School), 193
Impact of Domestic Violence on the Children, The (ABA report), 15
Impact of Events Scale, 288
impulse control, 26, 428
Index of Spouse Abuse, 286
Indiana, 133, 208, 377
Indiana University Law School, 192
injuries. *See* head injury; medical injuries and problems
insanity pleas, 219, 220
insomnia. *See* sleep problems
instigator mentality, Asian battered women and, 474
institutional abuse, 488
insurance discrimination statutes, 129
intake units, judicial, 155, 159–60
integrated treatment models, 332–33, 334
intermittent reinforcement, abusive relationship tolerance and, 14, 29, 34

International Association of Chiefs of Police, 82, 107, 123–24
International Women's Year conference (1977), 86
Internet. *See* World Wide Web
interventions/treatment programs (battered women), 18, 38–41, 78, 127, 262–66, 270–71, 298–315
Asian women's issues and, 474–80
clinician roles and skills, 310–12
community-wide, 118–23, 426–27, 431–32, 438
complicating issues, 303–10
key concepts, 312–14
legal system innovative projects, 173–95
See also crisis intervention
interventions/treatment programs (batterers), 11–13, 19, 41–42, 419–41
effectiveness of, 434–38
history of, 423–27
ideology's role in evaluation of, 432–33
judicial system and, 127, 130, 139–41, 427, 431, 432, 436, 438–39
purpose of, 427
recommendations for, 438–40
techniques utilized, 431–32
theoretical models, 427–30
interventions/treatment programs (children), 344, 351, 353–55, 368
lesbian couples and, 461
myths and realities concerning, 14–15
shelter-based, 19, 352, 353, 384–88
interventions/treatment programs (elder abuse), 493–96, 497
interviews (assessment tool), 283–84, 352–53
intimacy problems, 428
intrusive thoughts, 371
Inventory of Beliefs About Wife Beating, 291
Iowa, 8, 94, 208
ISA. *See* Index of Spouse Abuse
isolation. *See* social isolation

jealousy, 52, 58–59, 238, 260, 264, 265, 457
Jersey Battered Women's Service (N.J.), 385, 386–87